The Random House Collector's Encyclopedia
Victoriana to Art Deco

Editors	Ian Cameron
	Elizabeth Kingsley-Rowe
	Halina Tunikowska
	Christopher Fagg
	Bettina Tayleur
Designer	Tom Carter
Picture researcher	Philippa Lewis
Researchers	Elisabeth Cameron
	Tessa Clark
	Hamish Johnson
	Patricia Newnham
	Margaret Wiener
	Serena Penman
	Peter Vidal
	Arthur Butterfield
	Jean Richardson
	Corinne Molesworth
Photographer	Angelo Hornak
Editorial Consultants	Hugo Morley-Fletcher
	Elisabeth Aslin
	Malcolm Haslam
	Beresford Hutchinson
	Gabriella Gros-Galliner
	Charlotte Gere
	Dennis Sharp
	James Ayres
	John Culme
	William Tilley
	Philippe Garner
	Ian Venture
	Jeremy Cooper
	Jack Franses

In compiling this book, the editors have drawn on the knowledge and experience of specialists, who are listed here as editorial consultants. A book of this sort has to work to the most rigorous editorial scheme in order to achieve the necessary consistency of treatment. The final content of the book, and any errors which may have crept into it, can therefore be attributed only to the editorial team.

The Random House
Collector's
Encyclopedia
Victoriana to Art Deco

Introduction by ROY STRONG

Director of the Victoria & Albert Museum

Random House New York

A Carter Nash Cameron book

First Printing
Copyright © 1974 by William Collins Sons & Co. Ltd.
All rights reserved under International and Pan-American Copyright Conventions. Published in the United States by Random House, Inc., New York, and simultaneously in Canada by Random House of Canada Limited, Toronto. Originally published in Great Britain as *The Collector's Encyclopedia* by William Collins Sons & Co. Ltd., London and Glasgow.

Library of Congress Cataloging in Publication Data
Main entry under title:
The Random House collector's encyclopedia, Victoriana to Art Deco.
1. Art objects – Dictionaries.
1. Title: Collector's encyclopedia.
NK28.R36   745.1   74-5380
ISBN 0-394-49450-4

Manufactured in Spain
First American edition

Frontispiece: a Victorian interior. A room in 18 Stafford Terrace, Kensington. The house belonged to the Punch cartoonist Linley Sambourne, from 1871 to 1910. Photograph by A. F. Kersting.

INTRODUCTION

It would be impossible to think of any century other than our own which could codify its artefacts so soon after their production into eras of 'style'. Art Nouveau and Art Deco, which are within the lifetime of a considerable proportion of the population, can already be examined as seemingly distant eras of the past. The emergence of the history of art as an evolution of style in this manner seriously began in the nineteenth century with the definition of successive forms of Gothic architecture into Norman, Early English, Decorated, and Perpendicular. With the rise of professional art historians and critics in the late nineteenth century and their apotheosis in the twentieth, this form of codification spread to embrace such terms as mannerism, baroque, rococo or neo-classical, the exact meanings of which are now fiercely fought over in a way which would have amazed the people who actually lived during the periods when these styles were formed.

Such classification of the visual styles of the past was matched simultaneously by the labelling of the movements of the present into cubism or surrealism, Op or Pop. We live in an age when visual historical awareness has become so acute that we can begin to define the immediate past almost as soon as we have left it. The conception of Art Nouveau and Art Deco as eras of the dead art of the past would be equivalent to the age of Charles I viewing the reigns of Elizabeth I and James I as serious areas for careful research and documentation instead of regarding them, in the way they were to be looked upon until the Romantic revival of the nineteenth century, as little more than ages of an archaic rudeness.

This attitude epitomizes a great revolution, representing as it does an enormous acceleration in the apparatus of revivalism. In the early to mid 'seventies, the young wish to dress, however inaccurately, in the manner of their parents living in the 'thirties and 'forties. In clothes and theatre we can even detect a serious flicker of interest in the 'fifties, in clothes evoking the New Look and in the leather and back-combed hair of the Rock and Roll era. We have yet to define and start seriously collecting its products but we shortly will.

Of the two great decorative styles which emerged in the period covered by this volume, Art Nouveau is the most extensively researched and defined. The 'sixties were the age of the Art Nouveau revival, which was prompted by a passionate interest in the art of Aubrey Beardsley whose brilliant and corrupting images entered popular mythology for the first time in paperbacks and poster pin-ups. Earlier, though, we had all been entranced by the visions of Paris of the *belle époque* as evoked by the decor of *Gigi*, by the settings of successive revivals of the plays of Oscar Wilde and of the musical version of George Bernard Shaw's *Pygmalion*, *My Fair Lady*. During

the 'sixties, William Morris wallpapers and fabrics, seminal for Art Nouveau, were reprinted (mostly in the wrong colours) and became clichés of interior decoration. Liberty reproduced its turn-of-the-century fabrics, and the work of Charles Rennie Mackintosh and the Glasgow School was the subject of a major exhibition in Edinburgh and London. Copies of Mackintosh chairs even appeared on the market. All this disseminated Art Nouveau to a mass audience as an historical phenomenon.

Art Deco, more than Art Nouveau, captures us because of its heady nostalgia. It was a style which was still alive throughout World War II ('Utility' was one of its last expressions), and in Britain its death knell was finally struck by three major events, the exhibition *Britain Can Make It*, the Festival of Britain, and the Coronation. By 1953 a definite new style in interior decoration existed. We enter the era of flush doors, different coloured walls, Regency stripes, G-Plan, and Scandinavian import. For any of us who grew up in the 'fifties and reached maturity in the 'sixties (an era of yet more styles, such as Op and Pop), the 'twenties and 'thirties seemed as remote as the eighteenth century. Although the cult of the 'twenties might be traced back to a seminal theatrical production, Sandy Wilson's *The Boy Friend*, persistent nostalgia for the 'twenties and 'thirties must have been reinforced by the potent influence of television. As few recent films were ever shown on television, the generation which grew up in the post-war years, the first to be subjected to this medium, was visually nurtured on the products of Hollywood between the wars. The heroes of style were star idols, Marlene Dietrich or Clark Gable, Bette Davis or Fred Astaire. Film decor at its best, as for instance in the movies of Ernst Lubitsch, are the supreme statements of Art Deco style, as brilliant and fantastic as any creation for a *fete champetre* in the eighteenth century. The sets in a musical such as *Evergreen* are an index of Art Deco at its purest, and Jessie Matthews, its star, moves and dances to recall the poses of a hundred figurines of the period in which a willowy flat-chested woman adores the sun's rays, inclines towards a dog, or leaps in exultant physical fitness, a role for women which was again new in the 'twenties and 'thirties.

Art Deco as a style is still too close for us to disentangle what is good and significant as against what is undoubtedly debased mass-produced trash. Nostalgia has glorified this period, but the role of the collector of its artefacts is to seek out the best of its creations. More than Art Nouveau, Art Deco, the most recent style covered here, still remains a voyage of discovery.

ROY STRONG

ABOUT THIS BOOK

Although *The Collector's Encyclopedia: Victoriana to Art Deco* is designed to be a completely self-contained volume, the ideas behind its compilation are developed from those which shaped its predecessor, the Encyclopedia of Antiques. Above all, the two books share the guiding principle that the usefulness of any work of reference depends on the clarity with which its editors have defined its aims and its working limits at the outset. This process of definition is largely a negative one of deciding what shall be excluded in order to concentrate the coverage usefully on a more or less manageable area.

The first volume dealt with post-Renaissance antiques, ending at 1875, thus dealing only with antiques in the strict sense of items over a hundred years old. This had the advantage of avoiding the desultory coverage that most general books on antiques offer on the late nineteenth and early twentieth centuries. It also left the way open for a volume that would be the first reasonably comprehensive factual reference work on the decorative arts of this period, on items which are collected in the same way as antiques.

Because a degree of temporal overlap with the previous book seemed essential to cover developments that began before 1875, the starting point for this book is 1851, the year of the Great Exhibition, an event which summarized technological achievements in the applied arts. Even if the stimulus which it provided was the negative one of an awful vision of enterprise devouring the traditional values of craftsmanship, of fitness in form and decoration, it was enough of a landmark to make a convenient starting point. We have gone back beyond 1851 only where it is necessary for the reader's comprehension of later developments. The one exception here is the coverage of Japan which became an important influence during the late nineteenth century: we have provided rather more background material here as it seemed essential to the appreciation of developments after 1851.

The end date we have chosen is 1939, the start of World War II, which spelled the end of some of the European enterprises which are covered here. After the war, the styles of the 'thirities returned to some extent and were not superseded until the 'fifties. The significance of 1939 for this book is that it is perhaps the most recent end date that would not have been entirely arbitrary.

The subject limitations have been continued and slightly extended to remove musical instruments which became less decorative than functional. Painters are included only where they have worked as designers or craftsmen or where their work is reproduced on, say, ceramics or tapestries. Architects are more widely represented, but only for their influence on design, particularly of furniture. Sculptors have entries only where their work has appeared as small bronzes or ceramic figures. We have not attempted to deal with anything involving paper and print: maps and prints, books, bindings and printed ephemera are therefore all omitted. Other specific exclusions are coins and medals, dolls and children's playthings, needlework, militaria and ethnographica. The general criterion for inclusion has again been that an object or class of objects must have been intended to have some aesthetic appeal – there is thus little about old domestic equipment. Key examples from museums are covered, but otherwise the choice of entries has been slanted towards the collectable.

We have tried to compress the maximum amount of information into the available space, employing a highly condensed style to avoid relying on abbreviations. As users of an encyclopedia will be looking for facts, we have removed any expressions of personal tastes and opinions which would only dilute the factual content. Except for biographical entries, which are listed under surnames, all article headings are given in the usual word order, i.e. 'antimagnetic watch' not 'watch, antimagnetic' and 'Australian silver' not 'silver, Australian'.

Cross references are indicated by asterisks, which are used in most articles only where following the reference through will provide the reader with further information that is specifically about the subject he has initially looked up. In addition, asterisks are used to mark all mentions of people who have entries in the book. In the most general articles, such as national or stylistic entries, cross-reference asterisks are used more liberally to give an indication of the range of more detailed related entries. In captions, asterisks are used to show entries elsewhere in the book that are represented in the illustrations.

The effort of giving a very compact summary of the available information in each entry has meant shearing away a mass of subtleties and qualifications and trying to concentrate on the more typical examples. Therefore generalizations should not be read as categorical: a statement that an object was made of silver or glass should not be taken as a statement that it was not also made in ceramics.

A book of this sort cannot be to any large extent a work of original research but has to rely instead on collating the widest possible range of existing material. Where the problem of the Encyclopedia of Antiques was often one of selecting

a tiny proportion from a plethora of facts, the period 1851–1939 has in many respects been less well documented than the thoroughly researched eighteenth and early nineteenth centuries. It is inevitable that the deficiencies in the available facts should be evident in many entries here. As the applied arts of the twentieth century, in particular, are more thoroughly researched, many gaps should be filled. At the moment, though, there are massive lacunae in our knowledge of the period, and the warning given in the previous paragraph thus applies more strongly to this volume than it did to the last.

We have departed from the methods of the previous volume in a number of ways. Instead of defining every technical term, we have avoided excessive repetition by not dealing again with the most basic terms. Where developments have occurred during our period, we have provided modified definitions. We have also repeated the definitions of some less commonplace but nevertheless important terms. As a limited number of styles and movements were crucial in shaping the applied arts from 1851 to 1939, long articles have been devoted to these rather than to national entries which have less relevance in a period of improved communications and increasingly inter-national styles. Entries on objects which do not specify a country of origin should be taken as indicating more or less general currency throughout Britain, Europe and North America.

The end matter of the book includes a section on marks and a bibliography. Again we have to repeat the point which was made about these in the Encyclopedia of Antiques: no brief appendix can give an adequately detailed selection of silver and ceramic marks. Rather than make a pretence of balanced coverage, we have chosen to limit ourselves to the date letter systems of the three surviving English assay offices and to the ceramic marks which require illustration to supplement the descriptions in the text. The bibliography is arranged under alphabetical headings in the same way as the main text but with the addition of a few more general headings. Only books in English are mentioned – many of the books listed have bibliographies giving the main works in other languages. Books which are still useful have been included even if they are long out of print, as they will be obtainable through libraries.

A to Z ENCYCLOPEDIA

Aalto, Hugo Alvar Henrik (b 1898). Finnish architect and furniture designer. First important design (c1930), sofa-bed with thick, upholstered seat and back on tubular steel frame, adjustable back. Use of bent, laminated birchwood during 1930s influenced international design, e.g. armchair (adaptation of cantilevered chair) with U-shaped loops of laminated birchwood supporting continuous, scrolled, plywood panel forming seat and back. Also designed chairs, three-legged stools, and tables with solid wooden legs separating at knee into several pieces of laminated wood then curving in to support top. Founded Artek in Helsinki (1931), to manufacture and market designs for furniture, light fittings, and fabrics.

Aarne, Johann Victor (b 1863). Finnish-born goldsmith, silversmith, and enameller working in St Petersburg. From 1891, workmaster for St Petersburg branch of *Fabergé. Work distinguished by meticulous technique and fine colour enamels. Favourite motifs: delicately carved gold or silver swags, and garlands of flowers and leaves. From c1917, directed most prominent silver and jewellery firm in Vyborg, Finland. Marks: BA or JVA.

Abbotsford style. Term used from c1880 in Britain to describe imitation Gothic furniture made during 1820s and 1830s for Abbotsford, Scottish home of writer, Sir Walter Scott.

Abraham, Robert Frederick (1827–95). English porcelain painter. Studied art in Paris and Antwerp; historical scenes and portraits hung at Royal Academy and British Institution, 1846–53. Painted in style of William Etty. Decorator at Coalport Porcelain Works (Shropshire), c1860–65; work includes painted panels on vases in Sèvres style, shown at International Exhibition, 1862. Art director at Hill Pottery, Burslem, Staffordshire, in 1860s. Succeeded G. *Eyre at factory of W. T. Copeland in 1865; art director there until death.

Abraham, Robert John (1850–1925). English pottery painter; son of R. F. *Abraham. From c1875, designed and painted tiles for factory of W. T. *Copeland, including portraits, and narrative series of sporting ages, Health, Strength, Courage, and Fortitude. Worked for independent decorators in Stoke-on-Trent, Staffordshire, in 1880s.

acacia wood. Yellow-brown or golden-brown hardwood sometimes used by Arts & Crafts Movement designers for chairs and small cabinets. Wood of false acacia (Robinia pseudacacia).

acid engraving or **etching.** Technique of glass decoration revived in late 19th century Europe and America; became common decorative feature on table and decorative ware. Glass objects first coated with wax or other acid-resistant substance (e.g. gum or varnish), then incised with fine steel point; exposed surface then subjected to acid, either pure hydrofluoric, or mixed with sulphuric or ammonia. Incised design emerges in wide variety of textures, from rough stippling to white, satiny finish. Depth of line controlled by length of acid application. See also satin glass.

acid gilding. In ceramics, production of gilded designs with matt and brilliantly polished sur-

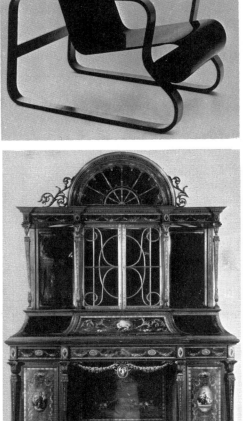

Top
Alvar Aalto. Chair designed for sanitorium at Paimo, Finland (1929–33). Laminated birchwood frame, bent plywood seat.

Above
Adam Style. Painted mahogany display cabinet with glazed centre and mirror sides. Width 5ft7in.

Right
George William Adams. Silver-gilt *christening mug, made by Chawner and Co., London 1868. Height 4¾in.

faces. Acid applied to portions of design intended to remain matt leaves rest of surface slightly raised, so that when whole is gilded and burnished, etched areas are unpolished. Process used at Minton factory from 1863, later by other firms.

acorn motif. Traditional finial decoration in shape of acorn; revived in America during 1850s and 1860s.

Adamesk pottery. English art pottery made (1904–14) by Adamsez Ltd, Scotswood-on-Tyne,

Northumberland. Decorative ware for indoor and garden use includes vases, plant pots, bird baths, monumental urns, fonts, and inkstands; covered with feldspathic glaze, coloured with metallic oxides. Work usually marked with monogram of MJA, or ADAMESK impressed.

Adam, Francis (1878–1961). Silversmith and metalworker; originally wrought-iron craftsman in Hungary; continued in London in partnership, then started own workshop c1920. Made staircase for Tate Gallery, London; also gold plate for Truro Cathedral, Cornwall. Taught at Central School of Arts and Crafts, London, 1906–58.

Adam style. Neo-classical style derived from designs of architect Robert Adam (1728–92) and his brother James. Reproduction furniture popular in Britain from c1870: chairs (often painted) have shield-shaped backs and straight, tapering, square-section legs; gilt caryatids with rams' heads on cabinet bases; manufacturers include *White & Mansfield. In silver, style revived in 1860s, fashionable c1870–c1900: mainly based on Graeco-Roman vases, featuring acanthus leaves, oak and acorn motifs, laurel sprays, drapery swags, festoons, etc.

Adams, George William (fl mid 19th century). English silversmith, made knives, forks, spoons, for Chawner & Co.; supplied *Garrard's and *Hunt & Roskell; exhibited at Great Exhibition, London (1851). Mark: GA (from c1840).

Adams, John (1882–1953). English potter and ceramic designer. Trained at Hanley, Staffordshire, and in London. Worked as decorator for B. *Moore in Stoke-on-Trent, Staffordshire. Head of Durban School of Art, South Africa. Among partners, with wife Truda (1921), of *Carter, Stabler & Adams, at Poole Pottery; managing director (1921–49). Mark: monogram of JA.

Adams, William, & Sons (Potters) Ltd. Staffordshire firm operating from late 18th century in Stoke-on-Trent and at Greenfield Works, Tun-

stall (opened 1834). Made earthenware and iron-stone table services, toilet sets, etc. for overseas market. Noted for brightness and variety of painted and printed decoration; sponged stencils and relief patterns occur. Black basalt, jasper ware, and porcelain also made. Parian groups and figures produced at Stoke-on-Trent factory, widely exported. Marks normally incorporate name ADAMS, or initials, WA & S, and sometimes name of design. Name underwent several minor changes, and versions include W. & T. Adams (1865-1899). From 1891, ENGLAND added to mark. Date claimed for foundation of firm (1657) appears in some versions. Production continues.

Adams Vase. Made by Tiffany & Co.; design by P. *Farnham, 1893-95. For presentation to Edward Dean Adams, chairman of American Cotton Oil Co. Solid gold studded with pearls and semi-precious stones; decorated with classical figures and enamel. Lid rock-crystal carved with floral motifs. In Metropolitan Museum, New York.

Adelphi Silver Plate Co. American manufacturers of gold, sterling and plated silver hollow-ware; specialized in sterling silver mounts for cut glass. Founded c1890; out of business 1904-15. Mark: beehive with ADELPHI SILVER PLATE CO., N.Y.

adjustable chair. Chair with adjustable back, e.g. *Morris chair. Also American *patent furniture, e.g. upholstered chair based on deck chair, 1869; in upright position, back upholstery extends below seat level; when legs extended to widest angle, back joins seat, forming lounge chair. Mechanized model with iron framework, 1871, usable as easy chair with foot rest, lounge, bed, etc.

ADT. See Rubelles.

Aerial Blue. See Rookwood Pottery.

aerography. In ceramics, application of colour by means of airbrush or atomizer. Colour sprayed on surface of tiles through stencilled design, e.g. by Minton, Hollins & Co. in mid 19th century, results in grainy appearance of colour and slight unevenness in edges of motif. Technique introduced (1883) by L. A. *Fry at Rookwood pottery to achieve smooth transition between shades of ground colour on Rookwood Standard ware.

Aesthetic or **Art movement.** Informal artistic movement in England from 1860s to late 1880s. Reaction against feeling that art must serve other purpose – moral, social, etc. – and, in part, against contemporary taste as shown in Great Exhibition (1851). Blurred distinction between graphic arts and painting; helped to raise status of design to level of painting, sculpture, and architecture. Sources include Pre-Raphaelite painting of William Holman Hunt (1827-1910), John Everett Millais (1829-96), and D. G. *Rossetti in 1850s; medieval principles of design and craftsmanship revived in Arts and Crafts movement led by W. *Morris. In firm, Morris, Marshall, Faulkner & Co. (formed 1861), Morris, E. *Burne-Jones, and P. *Webb, as main designers, aimed to improve design standards in tapestries, wall papers, furniture, stained glass, domestic utensils, and small amount of pottery,

*Aesthetic movement. Ebonized side chair with cane seat, designed by E. W. *Godwin. c1875.*

mainly tiles. American painter, James McNeill Whistler (1834-1903), worked in Paris from mid 1850s and settled in London by 1863. Influenced in work by contemporary French painters and by Japanese art, important inspiration of movement, without accepting socialist principles behind Morris's attitude to design. Ideal of art for art's sake expressed in Ten O'clock Lecture (1885) and The Gentle Art of Making Enemies (1890). Whistler's home in London designed by architect E. W. *Godwin, collector of Japanese art (included in International Exhibition [1862] and available in London by 1870s), who designed furniture in *Anglo-Japanese style from 1860s, often using satinwood or ebonized wood. Furniture with painted decoration became fashionable in 1870s. Designs by Godwin and, later, Whistler anticipated Art Nouveau and Glasgow style of 1890s. T. *Jeckyll also made furniture, often in ebonized wood, with oriental inspired decoration; for Norwich firm of *Barnard, Bishop & Barnard, designed wrought iron ware and cast brass, often using sunflower motif which became popular symbol of movement. Designs for extension of 1, Holland Park, London house of financier and Greek Consul General, Alexander Ionides, include bedroom suite (1875) combining light and ebonized woods, with lacquer decoration. Other designers involved include W. *De Morgan (tiled porch), W. *Crane (overmantel, ceiling decoration, and frieze), Morris, Burne-Jones, and Webb (furniture, tapestries, and textiles). Metalwork of Webb, in medieval idiom, echoes his architecture. Architect, N. *Shaw, associated with revival of 18th century Queen Anne style in London, mid 1870s. Ceramics of period demonstrate attitudes of movement, emphasizing fine design, and individually made pieces of high quality. Wide variety of styles include *japonisme* apparent in work of factories, e.g. *Mintons Ltd, J. *Wedgwood & Sons, and *Worcester. Medieval influences on slipware pottery made in West of England at works of C.H. *Brannam and *Watcombe Pottery also seen in work of artist potters, e.g. E. *Elton. In Midlands and North of England, group of potteries established under influence of C. *Dresser. *Linthorpe Pottery perhaps first in Europe to be influenced by Pre-Columbian pottery. Work of W. *Ault, *Burmantofts, and *Bretby Art Pottery in turn gave rise e.g. to *Salopian Art Pottery in Shropshire. Movement contributed to development of fashion for decorative tiles and fast growth of industry from 1860s. Wall tiles in general use from early 1870s frequently feature symbols of movement, e.g. lily, peacock, sunflower; also Japanese subjects. Firm of W. B. *Simpson & Sons used work of many artists. Tiles of *Maw & Co. designed notably by W. *Crane and L. F. *Day. Decorative tiles made in America by J. G. *Low. Silversmiths, *Elkington & Co. among first in England to adopt Japanese style in enamel work in 1860s introduced silver ware in same style soon afterwards; inspired by work of *Tiffany & Co., winners of gold medal at Paris exhibition of 1878, for textured silver with decoration in copper and other base metals in fashion of much Japanese ware.

Attitude of movement adopted by poet and playwright Oscar Wilde (1854-1900) in 1870s, and derided in 1880s by humorous magazine, Punch. Wilde, although satirized in comic opera Patience, by W. S. Gilbert and A. Sullivan, contributed to spread of movement in America with series of lectures coinciding with performance of Patience in New York.

Movement largely dissipated in late 1880s, but influenced work of A. H. *Mackmurdo and Century Guild, and attempt by S. *Image to re-define place of art in society. Influenced work of C. F. A. *Voysey in Art Nouveau.

Afghan carpets. Major 20th century types marketed as Quarquin (cheapest), Davlatobad,

Afghan carpet. Kazan, late 19th century. 10ft3in. × 8ft3in.

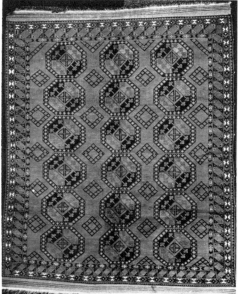

Agata glass. Bowl made by *New England Glass Company, 1887–89. Height 5¼in.

Agra carpet. Late 19th century. 7ft × 4ft.

Alabaster glass. Made by *Stevens & Williams, c1920. Height of stoppered bottle 7¼in.

and Pendiq. In coarse to medium-fine weave, with long pile, often of goat or camel hair. Typically patterned with unjoined octagons in range of reds and browns. From 1920s, in response to European fashion, also in golds and yellows obtained by chemically rinsing red rugs (process generally detrimental, as tended to weaken fibres). Traditional Turkestan types also made, including Mouri (*see* West Turkestan), and Beluchi: predominantly black and purple rug with camel or white patches.

Agata glass. American blown art glass; mottled, shading white to rose, Developed by J. *Locke and patented 1887 by *New England Glass Co. Variant of *Peachblow.

agate. Variegated type of chalcedony. In natural state, e.g. greyish-white, greenish, blue, orange or brown, usually banded white. Various colours used for cameos, intaglios, signet rings, and brooches; some produced artificially by staining or by steeping in honey or hot oil. Much of this work carried out in Idar-Oberstein, Germany, where brilliant colours obtained by dyeing. Milky variety with green or rust-coloured inclusions known as moss-agate. Occurrence, worldwide.

agate glass. Streaked opaque or semi-opaque glass imitating natural hardstone. Dates from antiquity, but many new versions in 19th century, when became one of most popular *stone glasses for decorative ware. In L.C. *Tiffany's Agate ware, coloured glass metals are run together and then polished. Bohemian versions (e.g. by F. *Egermann) add basalt, lava, or slag to glass mixture, which is then cooled irregularly, producing turbidity in glass body and creating effects of agate. British version made by *Sowerby's Ellison Glass Works.

Agra (Uttar Pradesh). Indian carpet making centre from c1600. Jail industry established mid 19th century; with first factory, founded in late 19th century by German firm, Otto Weylandt & Co., produced Agra's finest quality carpets. All workers Muslim. Weylandt expelled at outbreak of 1st World War and factory taken over by *East India Carpet Co. Indian firm, Kailas Carpets, organized cottage industry c1918, capturing American market. Industry badly affected by 1930s Depression.

Ahrenfelt, Charles (1807–93). Porcelain manufacturer, born in Germany, worked in France. Established decorating workshop at Limoges

(Haute-Vienne) in 1880s. Hard-paste porcelain produced from 1894. Also from 1890s, made porcelain at Altrohlau, Bohemia. Succeeded in business by son, Charles J. Ahrenfelt (b 1856).

aide-mémoire or **souvenir.** Lavishly ornamented slim, fitted case (c3½ × 2¼ × ¼in.) for note-taking; fitted with lead pencil and ivory or paper leaves. Fine examples in gold, ivory, tortoiseshell, enamel with inlaid or encrusted jewels, etc. Two main forms: 18th century *tablette and 19th century *carnet de bal. Both often inscribed with *souvenir* or *souvenir d'amitié* on cover.

Airy, Sir George Biddell (1801–92). Distinguished English horologist; Astronomer Royal, 1835–81. With E. B. *Denison, responsible for laying down specifications for *Westminster Palace Clock. Designed sidereal clock for Greenwich Observatory, 1873. Many articles published.

ai-same. *See* same-nuri.

aji (Japanese, 'taste' or 'relish'). Patina of Japanese lacquer.

Akahada. Japanese kiln at Koriyama in Nara prefecture, established in Momoyama (1573-1615) or subsequent early Edo period. Production of pottery, thought to resemble Hagi wares, lapsed from late 17th to mid or late 18th century. Raku ware and pottery with thick, light-coloured glazes, sometimes with enamel decoration, made after revival. Noted in 19th century for work of *Mokuhaku.

alabaster glass. Late 19th century American semi-matt art glass, obtained by treating glass surface with hydrofluoric acid. One of speciali-

ties of *Mount Washington Glass Works. Term also applied to early 19th century European (especially French) opaque glass with matt surface.

albany couch. *See* reading seat.

Albers, Josef (b 1888). German painter, designer, and stained glass artist; born in Bottrop, Westphalia, studied art at Berlin, Essen, and Munich. Student at Bauhaus from 1920; one of pioneers of Functionalist style; director of Bauhaus glass workshop and teacher in furniture design from 1923. Master of furniture workshop, lettering, and wallpaper design from after 1928. Furniture characterized by linear, structural design, often rectilinear with contrasting wood tones, e.g. light and dark oak, in single piece. Emigrated to America in early 1930s; taught at Black Mountain College, North Carolina, and Harvard University, Cambridge, Massachusetts, 1933-49; moved to Yale University as professor in 1950.

albert. Fine gold watch chain with bar at one end and spring hook to hold watch at other. Usually worn by men, but ladies' alberts with bar and tassels in gold chain patterns also found. Fashionable in late 19th century Britain. Name derives from gift of watchchain, seal, and key to Prince *Albert by jewellers of Birmingham (1845).

Albert of Saxe-Coburg-Gotha (1819–61). Consort of Queen Victoria (married 1840). Chief instigator of Great Exhibition, London, 1851. Designed settings for some of British crown jewels; also wreath of orange blossom and fruit, with matching brooches and earrings, in porcelain, enamel, and frosted gold for Queen Victoria. Also designed brooch (made up by *Garrard & Co.) given to Florence Nightingale to commemorate work in Crimea, collar and badge of Order of Star of India, Life Guards' helmets, and possibly Albert Medal (a civil award for life saving).

Albertine glass. Late 19th century American art glass; forerunner of *Crown Milano glass; similar technique and appearance. Made chiefly by *Mount Washington Glass Works.

Alcock, Samuel (b c1846). English porcelain painter. Worked at factory of W. T. *Copeland from 1880s. Painted figures in classical or contemporary costume in soft, delicate style, within elaborate gilt or jewelled borders. Work includes dessert services and large vases decorated with allegorical figures.

ale and spirit measures. Vessels, made from Middle Ages to 19th century, to hold stated quantity of alcohol. Occasionally made in sets with capacities from 1 gallon to ½-gill; capacity sometimes stamped on side. Baluster shape most common English style, with wide variety of thumb-pieces on lidded examples; made throughout 19th century in pewter, copper, and bronze. Distinctive Scottish *thistle measure dates from 19th century. Other notable Scottish form is tappit-hen, manufactured until c1860: tall, cylindrical, lidded tankard with concave mid-section, and domed lid with finial.

ale warmer. Copper or brass vessel for heating beer, in shape e.g. of boot, or cone (called ass's ear), with tin-plated interior. Has long, wooden handle for pushing warmer into open fire. 18th century examples rare, but widely produced during 19th century. Numerous modern reproductions.

*Thomas Allen. *Minton vase decorated by Thomas Allen. One of a pair c1875.*

Alexandra Porcelain Works. *See* Wahliss, Ernst.

alexandrite. Gemstone, variety of chrysoberyl first found in Ural Mountains, 1830; named after Alexander II of Russia, because discovered on his birthday. Green or greenish-brown colour changes to red or reddish-brown with transmitted light. Used mainly in rings, brooches, and bracelets.

Alexandrite glass. Parti-coloured transparent art glass, shading citron yellow to rose then blue. Patented c1902 by T. *Webb & Sons. Colour variations produced by uneven heating of glass body. Made later by *Stevens & Williams, but glass body of transparent yellow was overlaid with rose and blue glass, these casings then cut through to reveal yellow base.

Allen, Thomas (1831-1915). English pottery and porcelain painter. Work for Mintons in Staffordshire includes figures painted on vases in Sèvres style, shown at International Exhibition, 1862. Studied at Stoke-on-Trent School of Art while working at Mintons, and won scholarship to South Kensington School, London, 1852-53. Again at Mintons, 1854-75. Normally painted figure subjects, occasionally flowers. From 1876 until retirement (c1900), decorated earthenware and bone porcelain at Wedgwood factory.

Aller Vale Art Potteries. English pottery established 1865 near Newton Abbot, Devon, making earthenware for domestic and, later, architectural use; traded as Aller Pottery. After damage by fire in 1881, reopened as Aller Vale Art Potteries. Dark red body decorated with plant forms in brown and dark green slip under yellowish glaze, used to make vases, mugs, teapots, etc., some pieces also inscribed with mottoes. Vases in variety of shapes decorated with autumn crocus plant in shades of cream and green against dark blue ground. After amalgamation with *Watcombe Pottery (c1901), traded as Royal Aller Vale & Watcombe Art Potteries.

Alloa Glass Works. Scottish glasshouse founded 1750 in Alloa, Clackmannanshire. Made glass bottles at first; later also decorative *Nailsea glassware, often with band and loop decoration in opaque enamels.

almandine. *See* garnet.

Aller Vale. Cup and saucer and inkwell. Mark Aller Vale. c1895.

Alma-Tadema, Sir Lawrence (1836-1912). Dutch-born painter, settling in London, 1870. Designed furniture for American millionaire, 1884, e.g. ebony, ivory, and bronze for framework, carved and inlaid with metal, wood, and precious stones; onyx slabs for table tops (made by *Johnstone & Jeanes, London).

Alpine pink. Coloured porcelain paste introduced at Wedgwood factory in 1936 for use in tableware, etc. Porcelain also tinted grey.

Alpujarra rugs. Traditionally, made by peasants in Las Alpujarras, Spanish Pyrenees; used locally as bed covers and altar cloths rather than floor coverings. Also made in 19th and 20th centuries by Fabrica Nacional de Alfombras, Madrid. Loops of coloured wool or silk pulled through heavy hand-made linen backing to make rough pile. Strips, usually 27in. wide, made on handlooms with iron rods to wind loops; large rugs made up of several strips sewn together. Fringe woven separately and sewn on. Loops sometimes omitted from certain sections to form embossed design with looped areas against flat woven background. Colours simple: often only two, sometimes up to ten. Designs traditional, with Turkish, Persian, and Caucasian elements. Typical motifs include tree of life, vase of flowers (often with supporting birds), stars, geometrical figures, lions rampant, and other beasts. Exported to America from c1925.

Altdeutsches Glas. 19th century glass made in imitation of old German glass, e.g. gilded and richly enamelled *Humpen,* drinking glasses with classical decoration, or versions of old green *Waldglas.* Chiefly Bohemian, forming large part of output of F. *Heckert glasshouse from c1870; also produced by *Rheinische Glashütten. *See also* Cyprus glasses.

Altrohlauer Porzellanfabriken A.G. Creamware factory established in 1811 at Altrohlau, Bohemia, under direction of M. *Zdekauer (1844-1909), and *Hutschenreuther family from 1909; now trades as Altrohlauer Porzellanfabriken. Porcelain produced from late 19th century; much exported.

Altwasser (Silesia). Hard-paste porcelain tableware, made in Altwasser by firm Tielsch & Co., shown at Great Exhibition in London (1851). Later, much exported to America. Factory sold to *Hutschenreuther family in 1918. Mark: eagle with outstretched wings and initials C.T.

*Amateur ceramic painters. Dish, painted c1880 on *Minton blank.*

Aluminia Faience Manufactory. Danish pottery established (1863) in Copenhagen. Bought *Royal Copenhagen Porcelain Factory in 1882, and moved it into own premises (1884), with P. *Schou as director. Until c1900, output mainly restricted to moderately priced earthenware for everyday use. Under direction of F. *Dalgas from 1902, artistic value increasingly sought in design; C. *Joachim among painters. Bowls, vases, etc., with underglaze decoration in shades of brown, yellow, blue, green, and purple shown in America at St Louis World's Fair, 1904. Marks: ALUMINIA in oval (from 1863), A with device of three waves replacing crossbar (from 1903); ironstone china marked with waves across centre of circle (from 1929).

aluminium. Light, silver-coloured metal discovered 1827, but not used industrially until 1850s. Then small amount of experimental jewellery (e.g. bracelets and demi-parure in aluminium and gold) made; regarded as curiosities.

amateur ceramic painting. Decoration of pottery and porcelain by amateur painters fashionable in England in 1870s and 1880s. At *Minton's Art-Pottery Studio, classes taught by employees of Minton factory. *Howell & James held annual exhibitions of work by amateurs from 1876. Similar exhibitions followed in other parts of England, and books were published giving information on patterns and technique. Undecorated ceramics, issued e.g. by Mintons, usually bear factory mark. Painters normally signed and dated work. In America, *Rookwood Pottery sold blanks for decoration, notably by *Womens' Pottery Club in early 1880s. Newcomb College Pottery arose from activity of similar group of decorators in New Orleans in 1890s.

amber. Resin from prehistoric pine tree, mainly found on Baltic coast. Colour from pale yellow to brown; reddish-orange amber from Sicily popular during 19th century. Used for necklaces, bracelets, pendants, and rings. Vogue for plain strings of amber beads, sometimes faceted, during 1880s under influence of Arts & Crafts movement. Pieces of amber, polished but otherwise left in natural rough shape, popular for pendants. Amber containing trapped fly much prized, worn as lucky pendant.

Amber Onyx glass. American art glass; version of *Onyx glass range (patented 1889). Outer casing, containing uranium oxide and traces of iron oxide, fused onto opal glass lining; vessels then subjected to heat and gas fumes to produce swirls in shades of transparent amber.

Amberina glass. American art glass, shading rich ruby to pale yellowish amber; produced by reheating amber glass and gold base at furnace mouth. Developed by J. *Locke and patented 1883 by *New England Glass Co. Later also made by *Libbey Glass Co. and *Mount Washington Glass Works (*see* Rose Amber). Popular for wide range of decorative and table ware. *See also* Plated Amberina.

amboyna or **amboina.** Hard, durable wood with decorative grain (curly or sometimes bird's eye), from Amboyna and Ceram islands in Indonesia; light, reddish-brown shades used for veneers and inlays, e.g. in American French style furniture.

American Colonial style. 19th century furniture style based on antique forms; started c1865, accelerated by furniture shown at Centennial Exhibition in Philadelphia, 1876. Originally applied to accurate reproductions of 18th century designs, e.g. bannister-back and slat-back chairs, high-backed upholstered armchairs, gate-leg tables with straight, turned legs, Windsor chairs. Elements used by C. A. *Coolidge and H. H. *Richardson. Term applied later to Eclectic furniture combining elements of Colonial and other American styles. Manufacturers include L. and J. G. *Stickley. Still made. cf Old World style.

American Encaustic Tiling Company. Ohio tile manufacturer established 1875 at Zanesville.

*Amboyna wood. English Art Deco *cocktail cabinet c1932. Height 5ft5in.*

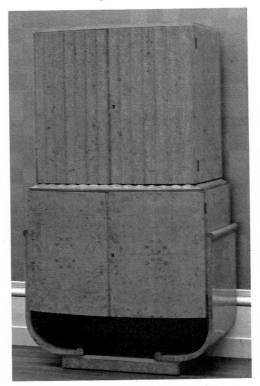

Produced large quantity of glazed wall tiles and encaustic floor tiles. Relief plaques made in terracotta, e.g. by H. *Mueller; K. *Langenbeck also employed. Tiled panels depict draped female figures, naked children, etc. Opening of new factory (1892) celebrated by issue of commemorative tiles. L. V. *Solon designed hand-painted plaques and series of animal cartoons. Glazed plaque (c1905), Frogs Dancing, bears circular relief mark, AMERICAN ENCAUSTIC/TILING Cº. LIMITED, surrounding NEW YORK/WORKS/ZANESVILLE, O. Other marks include A.E.T.Cº.

American flatware. Numerous eating utensils, designed for specific purposes, e.g. fish knives and forks, marrowbone scoops, pie, salad, and fruit forks, produced in silver and electro-plate in large quantities in America after c1850, e.g. by *Gorham Manufacturing Company, Reed & Barton, Rogers & Co. Production reflected changing European table manners in early 19th century. Number of courses served at dinner greatly increased, each course consisting of one kind of food, e.g. fish, soup, meat. Much controversy as to correct order and method of eating; over 100 manuals on table etiquette appeared c1830–c1860, e.g. 'Etiquette for Americans', 'The Young Lady's Friend'. Uncertainty about conventions produced compromises, e.g. three-pronged pie fork, with inside prong flattened into cutting blade; also melon knife, cutting blade terminating in threefold tines. Continuing interest in European manners, especially Court fashions, allied with fierce competition between manufacturers inspired proliferation of new inventions and designs, e.g. macaroni and spaghetti servers, bread, cheese, and cake knives, butter pick, mango fork; thus by c1880, complete set of American cutlery included 57 different utensils in wide variety of decoratively engraved designs (compared with 18th century maximum total of 72 pieces). Educational cutlery produced for children, designed to make child hold implement in approved fashion, e.g. baby spoons with barrier on 'wrong' side of spoon, training forks with finger shield to indicate correct grip. All designs profusely illustrated in contemporary manufacturers' catalogues.

American glass. Some fine cut and engraved glass throughout 19th century, but pressed glass manufacture increased, becoming three-quarters of total American output from mid century; used for plates, dishes, jugs, vases, lamps, candle-holders, etc; also, many novelties and large quantity of commemorative ware, e.g. *historical flasks. 1875–90, emphasis on development of *art glass, e.g. *Burmese, *Agata, *Crown Milano; also, vogue for opal-decorated ware (e.g. by C. F. *Monroe Co.), especially on *Smith Brothers vases. Principal glasshouses of period: *Mount Washington Glass Works, *Boston & Sandwich Glass Co., *New England Glass Co., *Hobbs, Brockunier & Co., and *Libby Glass Co.

American hardware industry. Cast brass, iron, bronze articles, domestic fixtures and fittings, mass-produced c1860–c1915 by numerous manufacturers. Include bottle openers, boxes, *bird cage hooks, *brackets, coal vases, clothes hooks, doorbells, *door knockers, *door furniture, desk blotters, inkwells, kitchen hardware. Articles often ornately decorated with eclectic

American glass. Locke Art vase by Joseph Locke. Needle-etched decoration. Pittsburgh, Pennsylvania. c1925. Height 5¼in.

repertoire of floral, foliate, and naturalistic motifs; advertised to retailers throughout country by manufacturers', or wholesalers', catalogues, e.g. by *Belknap Hardware & Manufacturing Co., Louisville, Kentucky; Benjamin Allen & Co., Chicago, Illinois; M. S. Benedict Mfg. Co., East Syracuse, New York; Sargent & Co., New Haven, Connecticut.

American horological industry. Wall and shelf clocks produced in Connecticut factories from 1807 by Eli Terry, S. *Thomas, etc; 30-hour or 8-day weight-driven movements in wood or brass. Clock movements used for barter before Connecticut currency crisis caused industry to crash in 1837. Thereafter, all movements of machine-rolled brass. Shelf and wall clocks exported from 1842, e.g. by C. *Jerome, include 30-hour clock with OG frame. Trade improved; numerous firms operating, e.g. *Ansonia Clock Co., Newhaven Clock Co. Clocks typically incorporate count wheel striking mechanism and pendulum mounted forward of movement, with dial cut away to show *escapement, or stamped brass disc for setting alarm. Spring-driven movements (from 1845) allowed variations of rectangular case, e.g. steeple clock (Elias Ingraham), beehive clock. By 1850, New England industry dominated European markets previously controlled by *Black Forest clock industry. Marine movement with balance wheel made from 1850 by Charles Kirke, Silas B. Terry, Bainbridge etc. Tall (long-case) clock craft industry continued in Pennsylvania until 1860; typical clock has plain wooden case, 6–7ft high, metal dial plate 10½–c12 in. square, weight-driven brass movement; 30-hour version had endless rope winding mechanism, 8-day has two weights. Grandmother clock, 4ft high version of tall clock, also made. From 1842, E. *Howard made *regulator clock with plain banjo case, wooden bezel, simple 8-day movement; other clocks made for home market include lyre clock, with lyre-shaped case made by A. Willard Jr, Lemuel Curtis; girandole clocks (very rare) signed by Lemuel Curtis. Machine-made watch industry revived (1854) by E. *Howard and A. *Dennison. Many companies founded c1850–80, but few successful, e.g. Elgin National Watch

Left
American Horological Industry. Movement of 'One Day Rose Cottage Time Piece' by Jerome & Co., New Haven, Connecticut. Escape wheel at front of movement; pallets formed from bent steel strip. Disc at centre for setting alarm. Frame height 3in.

Below
American Horological Industry. Alarm clock with pin-pallet lever escapement and printed paper dial, diameter 6in.

Bottom left
American horological industry. Beehive clock by Brewster, c1860. Decorated with view of White House.
Bottom right
American horological industry. Steeple clock. Case decorated with print of desert scene. Made by Jerome & Co. Late 19th century.

Co., Illinois, 1864, Auburndale (Massachusetts) Watch Co., 1875. Aaron Buck patented *Waterbury Watch 1878, sold for $4; Ingersoll brothers made *dollar watch from 1892; Hamilton Watch Co. founded 1892. Apart from cheap watches, many fine *precision watches also made, but American trade suffered increasing competition from higher quality Swiss factory-made models. Domestic clock industry, concentrated in fewer hands after 1875, flourished into 20th century; *OG clock made up to 1914. Metal-cased lever alarm clock introduced 1875, *synchronous mains clock perfected by Henry Warren in 1914. These, with subsequent developments, formed basis of 20th century American clock industry.

American Union thermoplastic daguerreotype case. American Civil War period daguerreotype case modelled on pressed wood or horn styles and cast in relief pattern out of 'composition' materials.

American Victorian furniture. Furniture made in America c1840–c1900. Characterized by increasing use of mechanization from c1840 and proliferation of mass-produced furniture, e.g. *Grand Rapids furniture. *See:* American Colonial, Architectural style, Art furniture, Chippendale style, cottage furniture, Craftsman furniture, Eastlake style, Eclectic furniture, Egyptian revival style, Elizabethan style, French style, horn furniture, Japanese style, Louis XVI, Mission style, Old World style, Prairie School furniture, Renaissance revival style, reproduction furniture, rococo style, Romanesque style, Roycroft Shops, Shaker furniture, spool-turned furniture, Turkish style. *See also* patent furniture, convertible furniture.

American Woman's League. Business established in University City, near St Louis, Missouri, for education and general advancement of women, largely through correspondence courses, e.g. in business, journalism, languages,

Left
American Victorian furniture. Shaving stand. Walnut. c1880.

Below left
American Victorian furniture. Carved and gilded ottoman by Gottlieb Vollmar. c1865.

Below
Amphora. Porzellanfabrik. Earthenware vase.

or photography. Over 300 students learned overglaze painting on porcelain through correspondence course; about 30 more in University City. Ceramics department, *University City Pottery, consisted of about 40 students in all. League foundered in 1911.

amethyst. Pale mauve to deep purple crystalline quartz gemstone. When heated turns golden yellow; in this form sometimes sold as topaz. Found e.g. in Russia, Brazil, Uruguay, and Ceylon. Usually cabochon mixed cut; large stones step cut. Much used in ecclesiastical rings; also for brooches, earrings, necklaces, etc.

Amphora Porzellanfabrik. Bohemian pottery established at Turn-Teplitz (Trnovany, near Teplice) for manufacture of earthenware and porcelain. Many porcelain figures exported. Mark: three stars contained in burst of rays over RS K (proprietors: Reissner & Kessel).

Amritsar (Punjab). Indian carpet making centre from c1610, when East India Co. introduced weaving. Industry expanded c1840, with influx of Kashmiri and Punjabi refugees, among them shawl and carpet weavers. First factory founded 1860 by Indian company, Devi Sahai Chamba Mal (later Arora Carpet Co.); by 1900, biggest Amritsar firm, with 300 looms. Sizable factory industry developed 1870–1900, employing c5,000 workers. Largely controlled by wealthy Hindus, under European supervision, with Muslim labour force on contract basis. Export handled partly by American firms, who demanded pastel colours imitating antique carpets, to go with reproduction French furniture. Designs at first taken from Native States and Central Asia, with Mouri type (*see* West Turkestan) predominant. By c1900, designs mostly Persian, or supplied by overseas buyers, e.g. Flemish and Aubusson types. Cotton warp and weft used; knots in dry wool yarn. By early 20th century, several European companies established, e.g. *Mitchell & Co. (English), Mullar (Austrian, established 1910, amalgamated with Greek, G. P. *Stavrides in 1920); all bought in 1922, with other small companies, by *East India Carpet Co. Amritsar and Kashmir only carpet centres to use talim (shorthand) method for transcribing traditional designs, with exception of East India Carpet Co.'s factories.

Amstelhoek. Dutch pottery, furniture, and silver workshops in Amsterdam, in late 19th century. Earthenware decorated with inlaid designs in green, white, and blue clay on ochre or brick-red ground. Decoration includes wave patterns, geometrical motifs, and stylized animals or birds; forms inspired by Greek pottery. Pottery merged with Haga (1907) and then De Distel (1912). Mark: monogram of AH in circle or oval, sometimes with AMSTELHOEK/AMSTERDAM HOLLAND.

Andersen, David. Norwegian retail and manufacturing silversmiths and enamellers; founded 1876 in Oslo by David Andersen. c1900, produced Art Nouveau silver lamps, vases, etc., designed by J. *Tostrup and G. *Gaudernack, who made e.g. elaborate *plique-à-jour* bowl with dragonfly handles, 1907. Firm also noted for intricate *plique-à-jour* enamel spoons, and clock cases etc. decorated with enamel and semiprecious stones.

*Andirons. Polished steel, designed by E. W.
Gimson and made by Alfred Bucknell. c1910.

andirons or **fire-dogs.** Supports for burning logs,
used in open fireplace; made in pairs; commonly
have three feet: two in front, and long back foot
extending to rear of hearth. Usually have upright
guard, or standard, to prevent logs rolling out of
hearth, terminating in decorative finial. Made in
wrought or cast iron, also brass, steel, and, rarely,
gilded or silver-mounted bronze. With 19th
century development of grate, became purely
ornamental: used e.g. as rest for long-handled
fire irons.

aneroid (Greek, 'liquid-free') **barometer.** Uses
effect of pressure variation on evacuated chamber; mooted by Leibnitz and others c1700, but
practical difficulties prevented construction
until c1840. Comprehensive patent taken out
(1844) in France by Lucien Vidie. First models,
produced to his specifications by clock and
watch makers: shallow metal box covered by
flexible metal diaphragm; screw thread converted inward and outward movement of diaphragm to rotation of pointer on dial. Vidie's
instruments poorly received in France, but
approved by G. B. *Airy in England, and sold
widely from c1850, many through firm of E.
*Dent & Son. Alternative type, adapted from
pressure gauge, uses deflection of curved,
flattened metal tube; introduced c1850 by E.
Bourdon, despite Vidie's patent. Both awarded
medals at Great Exhibition of 1851. Improved
types based on Vidie system, with linkage of
levers to move pointer, developed after patent
expired (1859); simple domestic version
standardized by c1865. Made in large numbers in
France e.g. by Naudet, Hulot & Cie., and in
England by Negretti & Zambra, who also
produced pocket type from 1861. Later improvements include replacement of vacuum chamber
by metal bellows, c1900; temperature compensation by bi-metallic link in mechanism, or small
amount of gas in chamber or bellows; use of
temperature-constant nickel or beryllium alloys,
c1930. Aneroid barometers often found in
combination mounts, e.g. with clock, or in
banjo-shaped wooden case with mercury
thermometer in neck. *See* barometer, barograph.

Angell, Joseph III (c1816–c1891). English silversmith; became head of family firm, Joseph
Angell & Sons, London, in 1849. Claimed to
have pioneered use of enamel on domestic
articles shown at 1851 Great Exhibition, Lon-

*Joseph Angell. Milk pitcher from tea service
decorated in silver gilt with scenes from Aesop's
fables. Decoration is free-standing and can be
removed. 1851.*

don. Favoured formal styles with bulbous and
angular shapes, roccco scrolls and Elizabethan
strapwork. Produced claret jugs, usually
straight-necked with frosted leaf and vine
decoration, centre-pieces, and many tea and
coffee sets, including parcel-gilt set exhibited
1851, decorated with frosted high relief illustrations from Aesop's Fables. Silver gilt casket
with chased medallions depicting Anthony and
Cleopatra now in Victoria & Albert Museum,
London. Mark (entered 1849): J.A in oval.

Anglo-French style. *See* Quaint style.

Anglo-Japanese style. British furniture style inspired by Japanese exhibits at International Exhibition in London, 1862, and by C. *Dresser.
Typified by light, elegant supports and asymmetrical construction. Best-known exponent:
E. W. *Godwin; also H. *Batley and T. *Jeckyll.
Trade pieces characterized by Japanese motifs
grafted onto European forms, e.g. asymmetrical
fretwork panels, imitation bamboo legs, and lacquered or painted panels. Manufacturers include
B. *North & Sons, W. *Watt, *Jackson &
Graham. *See also japonisme.*

Anglo-Turkey loom. *See* machine-knotting.

Ängman, Jacob (1876–1942). Swedish silversmith; studied at Stockholm Technical School,
working part-time in bronze foundry; studied
metal sculpture in Berlin, and jewellery in
Weimar under H. *van de Velde; 1904–07,
managed engraving, casting, and metalwork
departments for Elmquist of Stockholm; in 1907,
joined *G.A.B. Exhibited frequently and toured
in Europe and America.. *Rosenholm pattern
(1935) typical of his simple, restrained designs
for tableware.

aniline or **coal tar dyes.** Earliest *synthetic dyes;
derived from coal tar; in general use in carpet
production by 1869. Aniline isolated in 1834;
first used for dyestuffs in 1856, when aniline
mauve and magenta (fuchsin) discovered. Fuch-

*Jacob Angman. Fruit bowl with hooped handle
from which hang ornaments symbolizing the
Scandinavian Guilds. Width 9¼in.*

sin first manufactured commercially in 1858 in
France by Renard Frères of Nonancourt (near
Lyon), then in England in 1860 by Simpson,
Maule & Nicholson. Aniline yellow produced in
1863, followed by Manchester brown (important
to carpet trade because of affinity for wool).
Aniline black synthesized in 1865; alizarin crim-
son in 1869. Orange widely used in Middle
Eastern carpets, 1860–70.

Use spread rapidly (e.g. to Turkestan and
China); superseded vegetable dyes in carpet
industry, because of quick, cheap production,
but lower standards resulted. Initially, harsh
aniline colours unstable, fading when exposed to
light or damp. In oriental carpets, often used in-
congruously beside subtler vegetable dyes;
method of softening colours by washing wool in
chlorine solution – evolved c1900 in New York –
weakened fibres and produced deceptive patina.
In Persia, use banned in carpet industry c1900;
re-introduced, 1910. From c1925, anilines
generally superseded by other more reliable and
stable synthetic dyes.

animal furniture. Made in Britain c1860, e.g.
armchairs covered in tiger skin, with head and
paws arranged as if animal were about to spring,
and chairs with giraffe, rhino, or zebra legs. *cf*
horn furniture.

Animaliers, Les. 19th century school of French
sculpture which grew up around work of A-L.
*Barye and P-J. *Mène, as part of reaction
against academic and neo-classical styles. Group
specialized in closely-observed naturalistic portrayals of wild and domestic animals, usually
edited in bronze either by *cire-perdue* or sand-
casting processes. Term, *animalier*, originally
applied to Barye as criticism of 'undignified'
concern with animal, rather than human subjects; but rapidly adopted as convenient,
effective description of any sculptor producing
small animal bronzes.

animal jewellery. First popular as *sporting
jewellery in 1870s. In 1920s and 1930s, brooches
made as slightly facetious representations of cats,

Animal jewellery. Victorian tortoise brooch with engraved mother-of-pearl back. Set with border of green garnets, gold-mounted.

poodles, and birds; very expensive materials, e.g. diamonds with ruby eyes. Many examples made by *Cartier. Copied cheaply in base metals and paste. *See also* insect jewellery.

Ansonia Clock Company. American company founded 1851 in Ansonia, Connecticut; moved to New York, 1879. Made e.g. wall and shelf clocks in Connecticut style, including *OG clocks; version of French four-glass regulator (from c1860); from c1870, 12in. drop-*dial clock with visible pendulum; *ticket clocks (1904-06). Factory closed c1930. Mark: A in a diamond, within a circle.

antimagnetic watch. Watch with balance, balance spring, and *escapement of non-magnetic (i.e. non-ferrous) materials. Gold used for non-magnetic balance springs in chronometers from late 18th century; palladium from c1880; later, palladium alloys and nickel steel. *See also* elinvar.

aogai (Japanese, 'blue-green shell'). Oriental embedded or encrusted lacquer decoration of flaked, chipped, or powdered iridescent, blue-green, mother-of-pearl aogai or abalone shell *(Haliotis)*. First used in China (yün-mu-k'o or *lac burgautée*), late Ming period (1368-1644); introduced into Japan c1620. In Japanese variety (aogai or aogai-zaiku), largish flakes used for limited sections of background or main design, or to enhance details. From mid 18th century, *Somada school specialized in and gave name to type of aogai work using paper-thin slivers in detailed, mosaic-style patterns covering most of surface area. Style increasingly popular during 19th century, widely copied, and found on large range of lacquer objects. Also used interchangeably with *raden as generic term for any mother-of-pearl lacquer decoration.

appointments clock. Clock-operated aide-mémoire devised 1891. Drum with slots marked in hours driven by clock movement; appointments written on ivory tablets, fed into slots; at appointed time, alarm rings and tablet is ejected.

aquamarine. Blue to green gemstone of beryl family: blue colouring may be obtained by heat treatment. Best stones clear sky-blue; greenish variety popular in 19th century. Usually step-cut; large stones needed for good colour. Found in e.g. Brazil, Russia, Madagascar, United States, and South-West Africa.

Arabia. Finnish ceramics factory, established (1874) as subsidiary of Swedish factory, Rörstrand. Early work conservative in style, though influenced by romantic, nationalistic atmosphere in which Finnish design developed. Mass-produced vases printed or hand-painted, e.g. with leaves or geometrical motifs. Success at home and in export enabled factory to become independent of Rörstrand in 1916. 1920s and 1930s, period of fast development. Products include sanitary, technical, and household ware in earthenware or porcelain and, notably, individual work by artist potters, provided with facilities, materials, and salaries, for completion of own designs. F. *Kjellberg employed from mid 1920s, T. *Muona, A. *Siimes, and M.

*Schilkin from 1930s. Under direction of K. *Ekholm (1931-48), ceramics museum established (1943) and new studios built for artists in Helsinki (1948). K. *Franck head of design projects from 1945, active in production of new lines. Factory, largest ceramic producer in Finland, now part of Wärtsilä combine (established 1769).

Arak. *See* Sultanabad.

archaeological jewellery. 19th century jewellery design greatly influenced by archaeological finds. Excavations following Napoleon's Egyptian campaign (1799) led to Egyptian style: lotus, scarabs, and hieroglyphs popular motifs until 1880s. Designs kept closely to original colours of finds, e.g. brown, bright blue, dull green, rust-red; lapis lazuli veneer, sard, and carnelian used, but most decoration in enamelled gold. Discovery of Tutankhamun's tomb (1922) revived vogue; many pieces purported to contain actual archaeological finds.

Sir Austen Layard's excavations at Nineveh and book, 'Nineveh and its Remains' (published 1848) inspired Assyrian jewellery in England. Examples made by, e.g. *Garrard & Co., *Hunt & Roskell, and R. *Phillips. Motifs taken from friezes and sculpture found at Nineveh executed in gold chased in shallow relief, often featuring ram's head.

Celtic style jewellery inspired by goldwork found in excavations in Britain and Ireland during early 19th century. Most pieces made by Scottish and Irish jewellers (*see* Scottish jewellery, Scotch pebbles) using local materials, e.g. granite, agate, cairngorm, amethyst, river pearl, bog oak, yellow-green Connemara marble; often set in locally-mined gold and silver, particularly in Ireland. Motifs include ring brooch or shield-shaped brooch made in gold decorated with *entrelac. Tara brooch among finds frequently copied. Inspired

Left
Arabia. Earthenware jug from Fennia series. 1902.

Below
Arabia. Soup tureen from dinner service exhibited at Paris Exhibition, 1900. Decorated with Finnish views.

Liberty's *Cymric range. Celtic and Assyrian styles only found in British and Irish jewellery.

Most influential archaeological jeweller, Fortunato Pio Castellani, worked in Etruscan style, based on Etruscan jewellery excavated from 1836 in Italy. Son, A. *Castellani, showed Etruscan style pieces at International Exhibition, London (1862); work imitated by R. *Phillips, C. *Doria, C. *Giuliano, and J. Brogden. In France, Etruscan jewellery made notably by L. *Fontenay. Popular motifs include acanthus, anthemion, amphora, acorns, corn ears, Greek key pattern; executed in gold worked in manner close to original Etruscan technique to give delicate, granulated effect; *filigree used in decoration.

Architectural Pottery Company. English pottery established (1854) at Poole, Dorset. Produced variety of tiles, tin-glazed earthenware and terra-cotta for architectural use. Marked work with name in full or Ap.Co/Poole/Patent. Supplied biscuit ware for decoration by W. *De Morgan. Taken over by *Carter & Co. in 1895.

Architectural style. Furniture style developed in America during 1880s by H. H. *Richardson and Prairie School architects; in Belgium by Art Nouveau style designers V. *Horta, H. *van de Velde, and G. *Serrurier-Bovy c1900. Furniture designed as integral part of total building, in styles that blend with architectural surroundings. Chief exponents were architects, hence name. Strongly influenced 20th century design.

Ardebil rugs. From Caucasian-Persian border region. 20th century types Turkish-knotted, with Caucasian designs. *See* Persian carpets.

Arekawa, Toyozo (fl 20th century). Japanese potter working near Tajimi in Gifu prefecture. Specialized in production of bowls in Shino style for tea ceremony; coarse-textured white pottery decorated under glaze with abstract or plant motifs.

Gabriel Argy-Rousseau. Pâte-de-verre vase. c1925.

argentan or **argentine.** Early trade name for *German silver, containing less copper than later alloys, more brittle. Patented 1836, used as base for fused plating and electro-plating, mainly in continental Europe. Not extensively used in Britain, but some wholesale houses advertised argentine wares until late 1850s.

Argy-Rousseau, Gabriel (b 1885). French Art Deco glass artist. Produced wide range of objects in colourful *pâte-de-cristal*, e.g. vases, perfume burners, lamps, cigarette boxes, and medallions, with motifs of poppies, gazelles and flowers, wolves, stylized female heads, etc. Mark: G. Argy-Rousseau, usually impressed.

Ariel glass. Swedish art glass developed c1930 at *Ørrefors (by whom described as 'organized glass bubbles'). Used notably by E. *Hald and E. *Öhrström. Consists of sandblasting patterns into glass core, then enclosing channels of air with second layer of glass. Sometimes combined with colour inlays.

Arita. Japanese ceramic centre in Saga prefecture, Hizen. Porcelain made after discovery of nearby source of kaolin in 1616. Blue-and-white and enamelled porcelains produced to present day, much exported to West through port of Imari. Kakiemon and Nabeshima wares also made at Arita.

Armenian carpets. *See* Caucasian carpets.

Armfelt, Karl Gustav (fl 1895–1916). Swedish-Finnish Master enameller and silversmith. Succeeded J. V. *Aarne as workmaster at St Petersburg branch of *Fabergé (until 1916). Then in Finland. Worked mainly in silver, usually enamelled and often gilded. Specialized in pastiches of Louis XVI objects of vertu, notably snuff boxes, aide-mémoires, and card cases. Favourite motifs: dolphins, central lyres, garlands.

Armstead, Henry Hugh (c1816–1896). English sculptor and silver designer. Trained by father (heraldic chaser) and at School of Design, Somerset House, London. Worked at *Hunt & Roskell, eventually becoming chief designer, and for C. F. *Hancock. Used various surface effects, including oxidation, as well as usual techniques of ornamentation; favoured classical and Renaissance forms and motifs, e.g. story of Meleager and Atalanta on 1857 Doncaster Race Cup, made by Hancock in tazza form with cast, winged figures applied to base. Awarded medals at International Exhibition, 1862 and Paris Exhibition, 1867. From c1870, devoted himself exclusively to sculpture; worked on Albert Memorial, London. *Illustration at* Hancock, C. F.

Arnoux, Léon (1816–1902). Ceramic chemist and decorator in England. Son of French potter at Apt (Vaucluse); worked in Toulouse (Haute Garonne). Employed at Minton factory from 1848, originally to reproduce formula of French hard-paste porcelain; chemist and art director until retirement in 1895. Achievements include improvement of bone porcelain body and glaze, reproduction of ground colours used at Sèvres, e.g. turquoise, *bleu du roi*, and *rose Pompadour*, and development of majolica colours and techniques in 1850s, imitating early Hispano-Moresque and Italian tin-glazed ware; also

Alphonse Arson. Bronze group of theatrical rats, one with walking stick and a small one at his knee. Late 19th century. Height 4in.

responsible for technique used in making *Henri-Deux ware. Signed work includes reproduction of Chinese vase with crackle glaze, shown in International Exhibition, 1862. In 1878, received Order of Francis Joseph and made Chevalier of Légion d'honneur for achievements as potter and documentarist. After retirement as art director, continued occasional work for Minton factory until death.

arrow-back chair. Modern term for *Windsor chair popular in America c1875–c1900. Flat, arrow-shaped spindles in rectangular back; flat arms attached to outside verticals of back. Some models without arms.

Arson, Alphonse-Alexandre (1822–80). Parisian *animalier* sculptor. Specialized in bird studies; made début at Salon in 1859 with bronzes of Hen and Chicks, Laundress and Children, and group of fighting cocks. Later bird bronzes (comparatively rare) include Partridge Surprised by Weasel (1865), Pheasants (1866), Partridge and Young Surprised by Ermine (1867).

Arström, Folke Emanuel (b 1907). Swedish metalwork designer; studied at Linkoping, and Stockholm Technical School and Royal Academy of Arts; painter and graphic designer until 1931. Thereafter designed in silver, pewter, stainless steel, and plastics; noted for stainless steel cutlery designed for *Gense (head designer, 1940–64).

Art Deco. Group of styles appearing in European design; developed from 1910 and continued

until mid 1930s, reaching peak after Exposition Internationale des Arts Décoratifs et Industriels Modernes (1925) in Paris. Work of many countries exhibited, but only France fully represented. Some sources of modern design, e.g. Bauhaus, not included. Until 1928, stylized roses, garlands, fruit, etc., popular motifs; later superseded by Cubist inspired decoration, which became primary influence. Emphasis on geometrical designs, and sometimes symmetry recalling classical style, developed from more austere and abstract variations of Art Nouveau, e.g. work of C. F. A. *Voysey and C. R. *Mackintosh which influenced J. *Hoffmann. O. *Wagner and A. *Loos pioneered style embraced by Bauhaus under W. *Gropius. Artists in France, America, etc., reacted against florid versions of Art Nouveau. Other influences include oriental designs for Ballets Russes in Paris from 1909. By 1918, attempts to create dynamic style which expressed current environment had developed simple, bold forms in cult of 'machine' aesthetic; lines of speed, e.g. racing car, characteristic. Egyptian influence following opening of Tutankhamen's tomb in early 1920s incorporated in jewellery, architecture, and decorative arts. Palm tree and palmette motifs, scarab, pyramid shape, and other Egyptian inspired decoration notable in jewellery, ceramics, and bronze. Increased interest in art of Central America reflected in design of late 1920s and early 1930s; stepped forms and stones, e.g. rock crystal, jade, obsidian, onyx, became popular. Influence of West African art also apparent in 1920s, e.g. in work of P. *Legrain, and in design of rugs, etc. R. *Lalique, A. *Daum, M. *Marinot, J. *Dunand, E. *Brandt, and J. *Puiforçat among French designers inspired by abstract style of Cubism. Grouping of artists continued and workshops formed, e.g. in French department stores, notably *Atelier Primavera; also studio of A. A. *Rateau. In Germany and Austria, *Deutsche Werkbund and *Wiener Werkstätte provide expression of Art Deco.

In general, furniture characterized by harmonious relationship with setting. Linear design with restrained curves controlled in geometrical patterns. 18th century shapes sometimes used, especially those of Louis XVI style, e.g. *bergère en gondole*. Armchairs heavily upholstered, often with oval, square, or octagonal backs. Many pieces wide and low. Tables often stand on square or circular pedestals. Desks sometimes stepped or asymmetrical in form; lacquer, metal, etc., often incorporated. Many designers used rich, expensive woods and materials – macassar (e.g. M. *Coard), ebony (e.g. C. *Rousseau), rosewood (e.g. E. *Printz), amboyna, sharkskin, and inlaid fruitwoods. Mahogany used by L. *Majorelle in fluid shapes. Lacquer featured; also ivory, mother-of-pearl, or tortoiseshell inlay, and marble tops for tables, cabinets, etc. L. *Jallot incorporated nails of ivory or bronze and emphasized natural grain of wood. M. *Dufrêne associated with workshop, La Maîtrise at Galeries Lafayette. P. *Follot worked in graceful, curving style, using lacquer, marquetry, or decorative plaques in bronze. *Süe et Mare established Compagnie des Arts Français (1919); employed designers G. *Jaulmes, Marinot. Work of A. *Groult and E. *Ruhlmann based on traditional forms with ornamentation in Art Deco idiom. Architect, *Djo-Bourgeois designed simple furniture in *architectural style. P. *Chareau among pioneers in use of plastics; made austere furniture, e.g. in mahogany and

rosewood without further decoration. J-M. *Frank relied on natural colour tones of wood, leather, straw, and unbleached textiles. Couturier Paul Poiret employed e.g. P. *Iribe in design of interiors characterized by use of floral and leaf designs in bright colours. Work of Hoffmann, architect Bruno Paul, J. *Leleu, and G. *Ponti exhibited in America by late 1920s; inspired American designers. F. L. *Wright designed furniture for own houses. Radio City Music Hall built at Rockefeller Center, New York City, embodies typical expression of Art Deco, both in architecture and decoration. In England, work of A. *Heal and G. *Russell notable. Much furniture made in wrought iron e.g. by Brandt and R. *Subes in France. Other metalwork includes andirons, fire backs and screens, and door furniture designed e.g. by Ruhlmann, Puiforçat, and Dufrêne. Tubular metal furniture made by M. *Breuer at Bauhaus.

Other metal furniture made by *Thonet Brothers from designs by *Le Corbusier, L. *Mies van der Rohe, and Breuer.

Many French decorators, e.g. Ruhlmann, Dufrêne, Djo-Bourgeois, designed own textiles to harmonize with furniture. Rugs and tapestries initially feature floral designs, e.g. by Dufrêne, Groult, and Süe et Mare; later designs inspired by Cubism or African art, e.g. by R. *Mallet-

Below right
Art Deco. Varnished wood tea-table by Louis Sorel. c1910.
Below left
Art Deco. Ebony table designed by Rose Adler. Centre inlaid with shagreen and with metal mounts. 1920s.
Bottom
Art Deco. Cupboard designed by Paul-Louis Mergier. Green morocco leather covering with eggshell lacquer mounts and ivory feet. Interior lined in parchment. 1928–29. Height 30in.

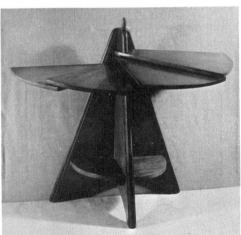

Stevens, or artist Fernand Léger. Tapestries of *Aubusson, *Beauvais, and *Gobelins designed by contemporary artists. J. *Lurçat led group designing rugs made in Cogolin (Var); other artists include Joan Miró. Bauhaus developed tapestry design with abstract compositions; texture emphasized with use of wide range of fibres.

Below
*Art Deco. Liqueur set, possibly by *Baccarat. Small decanter and three small glasses with black enamelled decoration. 1920s.*

Right
Art Deco. Gilt metal and marble table.

Bottom
Art Deco Quenvit Glass. Bowl. Hand-painted with enamels under clear glass surface. Signed. c1925.

Designers in England include E. *McKnight Kauffer and American M. *Dorn.

Ceramics includes work of artist potters and industrial manufacturers. In France, E. *Decoeur, E. *Lenoble, J. *Mayodon, A. *Metthey, G. *Serré among notable potters producing individual work. Ceramics also designed by F. *Jourdain, who sold work in own gallery, J. *Dufy, J. *Luce, and M. *Goupy. *Haviland family notable producers of porcelain with Art Deco ornament. Ceramics sold by Atelier Primavera include lamps and vases with painted decoration; some work commissioned from *Longwy factory. *Sèvres factory exhibited in Paris, 1925, porcelain decorated by Ruhlmann, Dufrêne, Jaulmes, R. *Dufy, S. *Lalique. Paris dealer, Robj, commissioned wide range of objects in porcelain. Some Austrian design followed styles set by Hoffmann, M. *Powolny, and B. *Löffler; later adopted more whimsical decoration. German ceramics inspired by Bauhaus design; producers include M. *Läuger and P. *Rosenthal & Son. Other ceramics in Art Deco idiom made by *Royal Copenhagen and *Bing & Grøndahl factories in Denmark, *Zsolnay factory in Czechoslovakia, at Doccia in Italy, and by *Boch frères in Belgium. In England, Wedgwood factory produced designs of D. *Makeig Jones, and A. and L. *Powell. Lustre patterns also among work of S. *Cooper for A. E. *Gray & Co. Ltd. Work of C. *Cliff notable. Matt glazed pottery made by *Carter, Stabler & Adams and at *Pilkington's Tile & Pottery Co. Pottery designed by F. *Brangwyn for *Doulton & Co. *Carltonware painted with floral designs in gold and bright enamels. Animal figures in Cubist style designed by L. *Wain.

R. Lalique among foremost makers of French glass in 1920s and 1930s. Designed vases with relief decoration of insects, figures, etc. Figures often incorporate hidden light bulbs. Clock cases decorated with nudes, or birds, butterflies, etc. Also made scent bottles, seal stamps, car radiator caps, etc. Opalescent glass much imitated, e.g. by Hunebelle. Series of animal figures made in early 1930s by *Baccarat. Individual glassworkers include Marinot, who made heavy, textured vases, etc.; work imitated e.g. by Daum company, H. *Navarre, A. *Thuret, and Dutch designers C. *Lebeau and A. D. *Copier. Among makers of *pâte-de-verre* were A. *Walter, G. *Argy-Rousseau, F. *Décorchement, C. *Schneider and, in America, F. *Carder, who also made glass for table use. In England, glass with cut designs produced by J. *Powell & Sons. Spanish artist S. *Ysart worked for *Moncrieff & Co. Table glass of Goupy and Luce painted with floral and geometrical designs in enamel. Work of M. *Sabino, also sometimes painted, includes table and toilet ware, and opalescent figures of animals, birds, dancers inspired by Lalique. Austrian glass designed by Hoffmann, noted for *bronzite decoration, D *Peche, and other artists of Wiener Werkstätte; also W. *von Eiff, and J. and L. *Lobmeyr. Work of B. *Mander in Germany influenced by Vienna Secession. In Scandinavia, glasshouses working in styles of Art Deco period include *Ørrefors, *Kosta, and *Hadeland; *Venini and *Barovier working in Italy, and *Leerdam in Holland.

Art Deco styles treated with caution by silversmiths. Allied designs stem from early 20th century work of Mackintosh, H. C. *van de Velde, K. *Moser, and Hoffman. P. *Wolfers among pioneers in Belgium. In France, work of Puiforçat and G. *Sandoz important. *Christofle produced designs of Italian G. *Ponti. Swedish silversmiths inspired by Cubism. In Germany, E. *Riegel made boxes and sculptural pieces, e.g. deer with plant, made in silver and coral.

Jewellery followed general trend towards more geometrical designs, with Aztec temple and sun motif popular. Production flourished in 1920s in France; neglected by English artist craftsmen as opposed to industrial manufacturers. Prominent designers include R. *Templier, Fouquet, who used white gold, silver, platinum with black jet

lacquer, or enamel, eggshell lacquer - crushed eggshells set in lacquer - sometimes set with diamonds, used for reflective quality rather than value. Bakelite and other non-precious materials, e.g. wood, stained ivory, cheaply enamelled metals used with silver and stainless steel for cheaper costume jewellery similar to designs carried out by *Cartier, *Van Cleef & Arpels, in calibré-cut, coloured gemstones, carved hardstones, and pavé-set diamonds with platinum. Statuettes in bronze, etc., influenced by dynamic motifs (figure with flowing hair or clothes, gazelles, greyhounds), from early 20th century. Animal and human figures became very stylized. American work of *Gorham Manufactures important in 1920s. Chryselephantine figures represent sports, fashionable costume, and feature dancers, etc. Interest in Art Deco period revived by commemorative exhibition Les Années '25 (1966) in Paris at Musée des Arts Décoratifs. *Illustration also at* cameo glass.

Artels. Cooperatives, *c*20 in number, of Russian silversmiths and enamellers, created in pre-revolutionary period to enable craftsmen to compete with mass-production of larger firms. Work, sold through large retail companies, includes sugar tongs, kovschi, Easter eggs. Marks, e.g. 11A (signifying 11th Artel).

Arte Vetraria Muranese. Venetian glasshouse founded by Giulio Radi (d 1952) in *Murano. Noted chiefly for decorative ware with metallic surface effects. Employed V. *Zecchin.

Artěl. Association of architects and designers formed (1908) in Prague to promote decorative arts in various media. Ceramic workshops produced earthenware decorated with geometrical motifs influenced by Cubist style of painting, from designs by V. *Hofman and P. *Janák.

Art furniture. Furniture popular in Britain and America *c*1870–*c*1890. Combined styles of W. *Burges, T. E. *Collcutt, C. L. *Eastlake, and E. W. *Godwin. Typified by black or ebonized woods, e.g. walnut, or light oak stained green or left unpolished; slender, turned legs, supports, and uprights, sometimes gilded; formal carving with incised and gilt lines; painted decoration. Term used during 1860s to distinguish products of firms employing designers from trade pieces; adopted by manufacturers to promote own products. American pieces also characterized by Egyptian and Moorish motifs; stiles, rails, and spindles emphasized with incised, gilt lines and centred by painted or marquetry panels (often with stylized floral designs); sabre legs tapering to slender brass ferrules. Designers and manufacturers include *Collinson & Lock, *Herter Brothers, J. *Moyr Smith, B. *North & Sons, and H. *Ogden.

Art Furniture Alliance. Short-lived London firm, selling furniture, metalwork, pottery, glass, and fabrics; started by C. *Dresser in 1880s. Merchandise designed mainly by Dresser, or executed under his supervision.

art glass. Coloured glassware, usually shading from one colour to another, and sometimes with novel surface effects. Popular 1870s–1890s, when major feature of British and American glass production, but continuing in some cases into early 20th century. Used for both blown and pressed glass; usually confined to vases, lamps,

and other decorative items, occasionally tableware. Major glasshouses concerned in development: *Mount Washington Glass Works, *Hobbs, Brockunier & Co., *Boston & Sandwich Glass Co., and *New England Glass Co., in America; T. *Webb & Sons, *Stevens & Williams, and *Sowerby's Ellison Glass Works, in England. Some art glass developed in Europe (e.g. *Tortoiseshell glass), especially Bohemia. *See* Agata, Albertine, Alexandrite, Amberina, Aurene, Burmese, Coralene, Crown Milano, Kewblas, Onyx, Peachblow, Pearline, Peleton, Pomona, Vasa Murrhina.

Artificers' Guild Ltd. London firm of metalworkers, founded 1901 by artist craftsman, N. *Dawson, and others. In 1903, firm taken over by Montague Fordham, and E. *Spencer succeeded Dawson as chief designer. Produced e.g. bowls, goblets, in hammered silver and copper, stamped Edward Spencer in circle surrounding DEL; work sold through showrooms in London (open until 1942), Oxford, and Cambridge.

Artigas, José Llorens (b 1892). Spanish Catalan artist potter; worked in Paris. In 1920s, produced ceramics decorated by painters R. *Dufy and, later, Pierre-Albert Marquet. From early 1940s, produced tiles, ceramic sculpture, and vases in Barcelona; collaborated with painter, Joan Miró. In 1954, settled in Gallifa. Own stoneware relies for effect on carefully controlled glazes and simple forms.

artist potters. Individual artists who use ceramics as medium for creation, expressing traditional oriental respect for ceramic art, only fully recognized in Europe in 19th century. Include studio potters, taking full responsibility for work from design to completion, producing individual pieces; designers controlling execution of work by others; and craftsmen manufacturing everyday ware in quantity. T. *Deck, regarded as pioneer, made ornamental ware in Paris from 1856. Other early French artist potters include A. *Delaherche, E. *Chaplet, J-C. *Cazin – who later worked with R. W. *Martin in England – and J. *Carriès. In England, work of French potters with high-temperature glazes followed in early 20th century by e.g. B. *Moore and W. H. *Taylor. Other potters encouraged by development of craft teaching in regional colleges of art. D. *Billington studied and later taught at Royal College of Art in South Kensington, London. R. *Fry, W. *Staite Murray, C. *Vyse, and R. *Wells all received early training at Camberwell School of Art. B. *Leach established studio, producing own work and teaching other potters, e.g. M. *Cardew, K. *Pleydell-Bouverie, and N. *Braden. L. *Rie worked in London from 1930s, after studying under M. *Powolny in Vienna. Powolny followed by R. *Obsieger as teacher in Viennese School of Arts & Crafts. Styles of Hungarian artist potters set by I. *Gador, M. *Kovacs, and G. *Gorka. In Germany, ceramics department of Bauhaus encouraged artist potters, e.g. O. *Lindig, T. *Bogler, and M. *Wildenhain, under direction of G. *Marcks. Rosenthal factory, although industrial concern, applied ideals of Bauhaus in use of designs produced by students. Arabia factory in Finland employed individual designers, e.g. T. *Muona – former pupil of A. W. *Finch – A. *Siimes, F. *Kjellberg, B. *Kaipiainen and M. *Schilkin, providing them with facilities to carry out own

work. Gustavsberg, Rörstrand, and Royal Copenhagen factories followed policy of encouraging individual potters. Danish Saxbo pottery produced combined work of E. *Staehr-Nielson and founder, N. *Krebs. Dutch pottery dominated by work of B. *Nienhuis. Influences in work of American artist potters include ideals of Bauhaus, as expressed in work of e.g. Wildenhains in California, and early trends in France, e.g. in work of C. *Volkmar. Teaching of C. F. *Binns at Alfred University, New York, regarded as important in developing concept of potter as individual; pupils include A. E. *Baggs and English potter, S. *Haile. Many artist potters have worked in association with artists in other fields, e.g. P. *Gauguin's use of workshop of Chaplet in making his pottery, work of A. *Metthey in early 20th century, and collaboration of J. L. *Artigas with R. *Dufy, Pierre-Albert Marquet, and, later, Joan Miró.

Art Nouveau. Decorative style of late 19th and 20th centuries in Europe and America, regarded as reaching peak at Paris Universal Exhibition in 1900. Ornamental innovation, characterized by use of natural forms as source of inspiration, contains elements of fantasy and eroticism; primarily expressed in rhythmic, plant-like motifs, elegantly extended and convoluted, integrated with design of object as a whole. Typically seen in wrought iron entrances to Paris Métro stations designed by H. *Guimard. More severe treatment e.g. of C. R. *Mackintosh or J. M. *Olbrich not necessarily incompatible and often combined with florid elements. In part, reaction against excessive imitation of earlier styles, which had begun by mid 19th century; had strong affinities with both Naturalist and Symbolist movements in painting and literature; also influenced by vogue for Japanese art. In Universal Exhibition, Paris 1889, floral decoration revived (e.g. in furniture), and changes evident in design inspired by W. *Morris (who had prepared way with Arts and Crafts movement for changes in England, first country to abandon traditions in architecture) and A. H. *Mackmurdo, H. *van de Velde in Belgium, L. C. *Tiffany in America, E. *Gallé and German dealer, S. *Bing, working in France. Bing established Paris shop, La Maison de l'Art Nouveau, originally for sale of oriental art, and developed collection of paintings, furniture, textiles, etc., for interior decoration. Name came to denote style, also called *Jugendstil, Nieuwekunst and, in Italy, *stile Floreale* or Liberty. In Belgium, arose against background of political independence, achieved in 1830 and followed by artistic, literary, and scientific activity by 1880s. Magazine, *l'Art Moderne* (established 1881), rejected eclecticism and concessions to public taste. Exhibitions of avant-garde group of artists, Les Vingt, started early 1880s in Brussels, soon included applied arts. P. *Wolfers, pupil of I. *de Rudder, worked as sculptor; attracted by flower and insect motifs in 1890s, began to concentrate on jewellery design by 1897. In contrast, van de Velde worked in wide range of interior decoration, designing furniture, wall paper and textiles, silver, jewellery, and ceramics, creating integrated setting. Functional doctrines balanced Symbolism of V. *Horta, G. *Serrurier-Bovy, also designers in *Architectural style. German proponents of style include J. M. *Olbrich, R. *Riemerschmid, and A. *Endell, admirers of architect, C. R. *Mackintosh, and designers of *Glasgow School. Austrian designers of Vienna

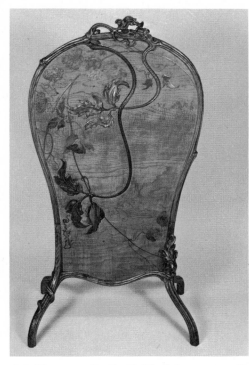

Art Nouveau. Emile Gallé. Ash screen with marquetry of various woods.

*Art Nouveau. René Lalique. Left to right: 1) Pendant female figure in ivory with gold and *plique-à-jour enamel, and pendant baroque pearl, c1898–1900. 2) Pendant, glass, gold, and plique-à-jour enamel, c1900–01. 3) Pendant of two heads surrounded by stylized wheat ears; ivory, gold, enamel, diamonds, and sapphire pendant drop; c1900–02.*

Secession, especially J. *Hoffmann and K. *Moser, also admired controlled style of Mackintosh, and work of C. F. A. *Voysey and M. H. *Baillie Scott. Developed towards more purist style c1900; flowing plant forms began to be replaced by geometrical motifs.

Furniture construction typified by long, undulating curves, following sculptural pattern, often treating wood as if it were malleable material. In France, elegant, sophisticated furniture, sometimes gilded, produced by Parisian designers, e.g. P. *Follot, L. *Jallot, G. *de Feure, E. *Gaillard, and E. *Colonna contrasts with rather heavier work of *Ecole de Nancy, characterized by use of local fruitwoods, with plants of region (thistle, cow parsley, etc.) included in decoration. Designers influenced by Gallé include L. *Majorelle, E. *Vallin, J. *Gruber, and V. *Prouvé. British versions, *Quaint style and that of Glasgow School, characterized by legs on sideboards, tables, desks, cabinets, which terminate under upper cornice or moulding, or are designed as free-standing square columns with overhanging architectural caps. Chair and table stretchers low in position, sometimes almost at floor level. Style had little effect on American furniture design, although appears in some products of *Gorham Manufacturing Co., and in some designs by C. *Rohlfs. Belgian furniture designers, following van de Velde, prominent in aim to create effect of unity in setting. Natural woods used initially; later, fine-grained woods imported from Congo. In Spain, A. *Gaudi y Cornet derived form and ornament from components of human skeleton. A. *Wallander, leading Swedish designer in variety of media, combined Art Nouveau decoration with earlier furniture shapes.

Much glass of Art Nouveau period features iridescent surface effects, e.g. in pioneering work of L. C. *Tiffany, imitated by V. *Durand in France, M. R. *von Spaun at Loetz Witwe glasshouse, A. *Zasche, companies of J. *Pallme Konig, and *Bakalowits & Söhne. Iridescent effects found in work of German K. *Koepping, Belgian glass of *Val Saint-Lambert, also producers of cameo glass inspired by Gallé. In France, Gallé noted for attempt to make glass and its decoration more atmospherically expressive. Early historical styles replaced in c1884 by motifs observed in nature. Also in Nancy, firm of A. and J. *Daum decorated glass with flowers, fruit, grasses, etc. Other makers influenced by Gallé include D. *Christian & Sohn, Müller Brothers and E. *Michel in Germany. Austrian Art Nouveau glass pioneered by L. *Lobmeyr; firm of L. *Moser & Söhne still survives. Enamelled cameo glass made by *Legras, near Paris. High quality glass made by English artist, F. *Carder, in America. Experiments in *pâte-de-verre and *pâte-de-cristal carried out by H. *Cros, F. *Décorchement, G. *Argy-Rousseau, and A. *Dammouse.

Style affected all branches of ceramics, though not adopted by all designers. Generally expressed in decoration, but associated with elongated or contorted shapes. Includes work of small independent workshops as well as industrial producers. For several years in late 19th and early 20th centuries, influenced production of several Scandinavian factories, e.g. *Royal Copenhagen Porcelain Factory, and *Bing & Grøndahl. Also from Scandinavia came work, e.g., of T. *Bindesbøll (Denmark) and A. W. *Finch (Finland). In Germany, *Meissen, *Nymphenburg and other established firms produced ceramics designed by eminent architects, e.g. P. *Behrens, R. *Riemerschmid, and van de Velde; other Jugendstil pottery includes work of M. *Läuger and some Mettlach ware by *Villeroy & Boch. Similar pattern prevailed in Austria, where leading designers, e.g. Hoffmann and K. *Klaus worked for makers of ceramics. Wiener Keramik established in 1905 by M. *Powolny and B. *Löffler. Other Austrian wares include work of *Amphora Porzellanfabrik. Bohemian potter, E. *Wahliss, produced Serapis-Fayence decorated by Klaus. In Hungary, Zsolnay factory produced lustre decorated ware in experimental workshop under V. *Wartha. Painted pottery produced in Holland by *Rozenburg considered among foremost renderings of Art Nouveau in any medium. Much decoration inspired by *batik-printed motifs, which also affected Dutch graphics of 1890s. In Italy, Art Nouveau ceramics made by firms of U. *Cantagalli and *Ginori family. Art Nouveau stylists, e.g. de Feure and Guimard carried out ceramic designs. E. Gallé produced faience at Nancy; other French makers include C. *Massier and family. Artist potters, T. *Deck, E. *Chaplet, and A. *Delaherche had been among pioneers of style in France; influenced by stoneware of Japan and China. Other potters, e.g. A. *Bigot, J-C. *Cazin, E. *Lenoble, and E. *Decoeur among experimenters who achieved wide range of colours and glaze effects. Architectural ware made by E. *Muller. At Sèvres factory, work of T. *Doat important. Figures depicting work of American dancer, Loïe Fuller, by A. *Léonard, produced in porcelain (also made in bronze) included in Sèvres display at Paris Exhibition, 1900; crystalline glazes, and underglaze painting in style of Royal Copenhagen factory among work of Meissen shown. In America, A. *Van Briggle, Tiffany, and W. H. *Grueby most forcible exponents of Art Nouveau style. Much work produced in related

style, derived more from English Arts and Crafts movement, e.g. by A. A. *Robineau, *Newcombe College Pottery, and English potter, F. H. *Rhead, for Roseville Pottery. In England, stoneware of *Doulton & Co., particularly by M. V. *Marshall and F. *Pope, work of L. V. *Solon at Minton factory, also ware marketed as Sabrina by Worcester factory and some work of J. *Wedgwood & Sons influenced by Art Nouveau.

In silver, e.g. English and Dutch, expression of style rather restrained, partly through influence of Arts and Crafts movement. Work of *Liberty & Co., principally designed by A. *Knox, important. Mackintosh predominant designer in Scotland. More florid versions found in Europe, particularly Spain and Belgium. Accounts of French factory, *Christofle, published in 1900, illustrate many examples of work, both by firm and rivals, in late 19th century.

Jewellery of this period noted for inventiveness and high quality. Most outstanding work produced by French designers and jewellers, e.g. R. *Lalique, G. *Fouquet, and A. *Mucha, also working as painter and designer in other media; Grasset, illustrator, and architect, designed jewellery, stained glass, etc., as well as furniture. Artists used wide range of semi-precious stones, copper, horn, ivory, glass, paste, and enamel (particularly in blue and green). Characteristic motifs derived from flower and leaf forms, insects, and female heads with flowing hair. Strongly influenced by Japanese art. Lalique made jewellery for actress, Sarah Bernhardt; pioneered female nude as decorative motif, before abandoning jewellery for glass making in 1914. Employed E. *Feuillâtre to investigate enamelling techniques on silver. H. and P. *Vever inherited father's firm in 1870s. Survey of 19th century French jewellery published (1908) by H. Vever devotes third (final) volume to Art Nouveau style. English jewellery, in less spectacular version of style, mainly produced by commercial firms, many in Birmingham, and in modified form by Liberty & Co. Otherwise, English work dominated by craft revival inspired by Morris. Leading designers include C. R. *Ashbee, N. *Dawson, A. *Gaskin, H. *Wilson. In Holland, limited amount of jewellery made in gold and enamels by B. *Nienhuis, who was principally potter. Artist jeweller reappeared after eclipse by large retail firms and fashion for precious stones in 19th century. Feature of Art Nouveau was reintegration of arts, e.g. pieces of jewellery, etc., named after works of Symbolist poets.

art pot stand. Type of *jardinière* introduced in Britain c1890. Open, ribbed cup, on three or four legs, holds brass or copper plant pot. Usually oak or mahogany, darkened and French polished. cf aspidistra stand.

art pottery. In Britain, ceramics produced in response to search for aesthetic value which prevailed by 1870s; result of deliberate attempt at artistic creation. Made by established manufacturers, in addition to commercial ranges, or by new potteries established to supply demand. Reflects attitudes of Aesthetic and Arts & Crafts Movements. In 1860s, collaboration with firm of Doulton had enabled students of Lambeth School of Art to decorate salt-glazed stoneware made at Lambeth workshop, London, producing individual, signed pieces of work. Also making ornamental stoneware, *Martin brothers worked

*Art Pottery. Goat's mask vase by William *Ault, with aventurine glaze, designed by C. *Dresser, c1894. Signed, and bearing shape number 318. Height 8½in.*

from early 1870s at Fulham and then Southall, sharing tasks involved in production and retail. W. *De Morgan, friend of W. *Morris and closely associated with Arts & Crafts Movement, carried out underglaze painting inspired by Near-Eastern pottery and revived lustre painting. Painted decoration, fashionable in France, developed in England with employment of French artists, e.g. E. *Lessore and E. *Rischgitz, at Minton factory, Stoke-on-Trent. Minton's Art-Pottery Studio opened (1871) in London for amateur and professional painters under direction of W. S. *Coleman. Doulton introduced painted wares in 1873, followed by most art potteries in late 1870s and 1880s. Watcombe Pottery (established 1869) used local clay decorated with enamel or turquoise glaze and often intricately modelled; amalgamated in early 20th century with Aller Vale Art Potteries, which produced tall vases decorated with autumn crocus flowers. *Barum ware, made in Barnstaple, North Devon, combined elements of fashionable design, e.g. in use of colour, with characteristics of traditional Devonshire slipware. Effects of glaze and colour stressed in pottery made from 1880 at Linthorpe, Yorkshire, by H. *Tooth and designed by C. *Dresser. Partnership of Tooth and W. *Ault (1883–86) in Bretby Art Pottery produced ornamental ware with coloured glazes and applied decoration; later work includes finishes which imitate metal, bamboo, etc. Ault continued experiments with glazes at own pottery at Swadlincote and, in 1890s, used designs by Dresser. In work of E. *Elton, raised floral motifs in coloured slip used with streaked grounds predominantly in blue; metallic, crackle-glaze used in early 20th century. Della Robbia Pottery, established by H. *Rathbone in 1890s, produced work signed by individual artists. By c1900, market sufficiently well established to attract many commercial firms into production of art pottery. W. *Moorcroft responsible from 1898 for art pottery department of J. *Macintyre & Co., later estab-

lished own company. Pilkington Tile & Pottery Co., founded in mid 1890s, noted for lustre decoration (from 1903). Much work by external designers, e.g. L. F. *Day, C. F. A. *Voysey, and W. *Crane. Pottery made from 1898 by W. H. *Taylor often relied for effect on high-temperature glazes. In early 20th century, art pottery gradually eclipsed by work of artist potters produced in studio conditions. Moorcroft, among few who continued manufacture of art pottery, forced to introduce variety of experimental lines. In America, Chelsea Keramic Art Works (established 1866) alone produced art pottery before 1879, making earthenware with *barbotine* decoration from 1876. Philadelphia Centennial Exhibition (1876) inspired H. C. *Robertson to attempt reproduction of oriental glazes. Several potteries established in period 1879–89, centred on area of Cincinnati, Ohio, but only Rookwood survived after 1890. Pottery of W. A. *Long, founded at Steubenville, Ohio, in 1892, produced pottery resembling standard ware of Rookwood; acquired by S. A. *Weller. Long himself moved to Zanesville and, briefly at J. B. *Owens Pottery Co., continued use of underglaze decoration. Later, in Colorado, Long produced matt glazed pottery decorated in Art Nouveau style. *Rozane art ware made at Roseville (established in 1892) and, by 1900, Zanesville. Newcomb College Pottery, organized in 1897 to provide practical training in ceramics, also produced pottery inspired by Rookwood wares. W. H. *Grueby made pottery covered with matt enamel after seeing dull glazes of A. *Delaherche at Chicago World's Fair. Work imitated by other potters. A. *Van Briggle introduced matt glazes at Rookwood (1896) and later made art pottery in Colorado Springs; work characterized by careful relationship of glaze and form, and style influenced by Art Nouveau. In more general terms, art pottery refers to work of *artist potters as opposed to industrial wares.

Arts & Crafts Exhibition Society. Association of artists and designers (development of *Art Workers' Guild) founded 1888 to interest public in decoration of artistic merit. Gave name to Arts & Crafts Movement. W. *Crane first chairman, W. *Morris and E. *Burne-Jones among committee members. Designers and craftsmen of equal importance, each piece credited to both. Furniture usually expensive, often decorated with metalwork, gesso, and marquetry. Members included C. R. *Ashbee, S. *Barnsley, W. A. S. *Benson, R. *Bloomfield, W. *Cave, L. F. *Day, E. *Gimson, G. *Jack, A. W. *Jarvis, R. S. *Lorimer, A. H. *Mackmurdo, C. F. A. *Voysey. Exhibitions held in 1888, 1889, 1890, 1893, 1896, 1899, and into 20th century.

Arts & Crafts movement. Artistic movement originating in late 19th century England; with W. *Morris as central figure, urged return to medieval standards of craftsmanship and design in face of industrialism. Religious implications of Gothic Revival and work, e.g. of A. W. N. *Pugin, G. E. *Street replaced by political and social considerations contrasting with insistence of *Aesthetic movement on Art for Art's sake. Pragmatic view earlier held by H. *Cole. Formation by craftsmen and designers of co-operative associations, often influenced by socialist principles, characteristic of movement; *Century Guild of A. H. *Mackmurdo and C. R. *Ashbee's *Guild and School of Handicraft both formed in 1880s. Movement also featured many

Arts & Crafts Movement. Casket with hinged lid, designed and made by members of Newcastle Handicrafts Company. Decorated with enamel plaques and silver-gilt wire. Birmingham hall mark for 1906.

articulate expositions of philosophy of design, in form of contemporary lectures, essays and books by artists. Ideas implied in foundation (1850) of North London School of Design by T. *Seddon to offer study of art and design to working craftsmen. Firm, *Morris, Marshall, Faulkner & Co., formed 1861, and subsequent *Morris & Co. designed and produced decorative objects and materials. Early furniture, made according to ideals of movement, simply and solidly constructed, using natural beauty of wood to decorative effect; expensive, because hand-made. Later examples inspired by precisely drawn furniture in Pre-Raphaelite paintings and tapestries, e.g. sturdy oak chairs in 'Holy Grail' tapestries of E. *Burne-Jones. Century Guild and Guild of Handicraft made more elaborate pieces in which designers and craftsmen cooperated. Favourite woods English – oak, walnut, elm, etc. Acacia sometimes used. Inspired *cottage furniture in England. Influenced American designers and craftsmen, e.g. S. R. *Burleigh, E. *Hubbard, *Prairie School, G. *Stickley. European designers, including K. P. C. *de Bazel, H. C. *van de Velde, G. *Serrurier-Bovy, H. *Muthesius, and artists of *Deutsche Werkbund.

Movement became entity with formation of *Art Workers' Guild in 1884, and *Arts and Crafts Exhibition Society in 1886. (Similar Art Workers' Guild formed in America.) Morris and designers, e.g. A. H. Mackmurdo, W. R. *Lethaby, L. F. *Day, W. *Crane, and Ashbee emerged as leading members.

Ruskin Pottery of W. H. *Taylor began commercial production in 1898. Work of W. *Moorcroft among art pottery sold by *Liberty & Co., who also marketed silver (*Cymric) and pewter (*Tudric) – produced in association with W. *Haseler & Co. – and furniture, textiles, etc.

In ceramics, movement inspired development of work of *artist potters, in studio conditions, notably R. *Wells, E. *Elton, and G. *Cox. *Della Robbia Pottery established 1894 by H. *Rathbone, pupil of Brown and cousin of R. L.

*Rathbone, who produced metalwork for Mackmurdo and Voysey.

Ashbee's School and Guild of Handicraft first guild to produce silver. *Birmingham Guild of Handicraft modelled on Ashbee's, although more commercially orientated; designers include A. S. *Dixon. Influence of movement clear in work of some larger firms, e.g. that of A. E. *Jones. Metalwork characterized by functional qualities, simple ornament emphasizing structural techniques, and hammered finish, to suggest hand finishing. In America, English work influenced *Rose Valley association.

Schools of art provided many designers with work. *Keswick School of Industrial Art, originally evening institute, held daytime classes from 1898; H. *Stabler director. R. *Catterson-Smith headmaster of *Vittoria Street School in Birmingham; succeeded by A. *Gaskin. Manchester School of Art reorganized on Arts and Crafts lines by Crane, and progressive Central School established in London with Lethaby and J. G. *Frampton as joint principals. Enameller, A. *Fisher, opened own school in Kensington, London, 1904.

Movement continued into 20th century e.g. by Lethaby, Ashbee, and Voysey, although many earlier doctrines, e.g. rejection of machine, questioned. Pioneering work in late 19th century had placed Britain at forefront of design and production – supplanted by Belgium with development of Art Nouveau. Movement had wide influence throughout Europe and America. Principles followed, notably, in Scandinavia. Work summarized in Paris Exhibition of British Decorative Art in 1914.

art square. Seamless *ingrain carpet square, c9-12ft wide, introduced in 1880 by W. C. *Gray & Sons. Kilmarnock, Ayrshire, became centre of production.

Art Tile Works. *See* Low, John Gardner.

Art Unions. Societies formed in England to promote sale of works of art, chiefly oil-paintings, water-colours, and sculpture, with encouragement of Albert, Prince Consort. First, Art Union of London (established in 1836) organized annual lottery of works of art, for which members eligible on payment of yearly subscription. After legalization of draws (1846), limited editions of parian figures commissioned, e.g. from Minton factory and firm of W. T. *Copeland, as prizes. Unions later formed include Crystal Palace Art Union (1858), renamed The Ceramic and Crystal Palace Art Union (1865), and Royal Irish Art Union. Work commissioned in many branches of ceramics, e.g. majolica and earthenware, as well as porcelain, bears mark of Union.

Art Workers' Guild. Association of English artists and craftsmen developed in London, 1884; expansion of St George's Art Society, informal discussion group of artists who were or had been pupils of R. N. *Shaw. 1888, absorbed The Fifteen, 15 artists including L. F. *Day and W. *Crane, who described aim as 'renaissance of decorative arts, which should act through and towards more humanized conditions for workmen and employers'. Aim also to establish contact through discussion between artists and craftsmen. Members included W. R. *Lethaby, C. R. *Ashbee, W. A. S. *Benson, A. *Heal, G. *Jack, W. *Morris, C. F. A. *Voysey, as well as

furniture makers and designers. Guilds established in Liverpool (1886) and Birmingham (1902); no commercial influence. *Arts & Crafts Exhibition Society developed from it.

American equivalent founded in Providence, Rhode Island, c1885, by S. *Burleigh, C. W. *Stetson, and industrialist John Aldrich. Designed buildings, manufactured hand-made silver and metalware, panel paintings, and furniture. The most important example of work is the Fleur de Lys studio building in Providence, 1885. Little influence.

Asahi wares. Japanese pottery produced near Uji, south of Kyoto, from 17th century. Tea ceremony ware made with brownish body often showing through translucent blue or green glaze streaked with white slip. Production continues to present day, though late 17th century regarded as best period.

Ashbee, Charles Robert (1863–1942). English architect, writer, and designer; articled to G. F. *Bodley, 1883; leading figure in Arts and Crafts

*Charles Robert Ashbee. Silver salt cellar designed by Ashbee and made by *Guild of Handicraft. 1899–1900.*

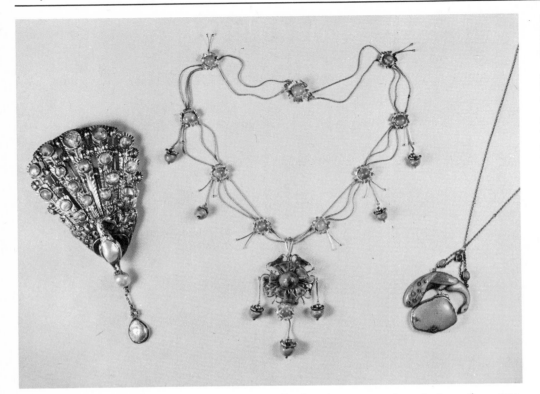

Charles Robert Ashbee. Left to right: 1) Peacock brooch, rose diamonds, blister pearl and ruby, gold and silver base. Made by *Guild of Handicraft, 1901. 2) Gold, enamel and turquoise necklace, 1899. 3) Peacock pendant: gold peacock standing on ball of green jade, set with tiny diamonds, mother-of-pearl, blister pearls, opals and silver. Made by *Guild of Handicraft, c1907.

movement; founded *Guild and School of Handicraft, 1887–88; School discontinued 1895; Guild moved to Chipping Campden in 1902, and continued as The Guild of Handicraft Ltd, to 1908. Aimed to revive medieval craft skills, under influence of writings of John Ruskin and W. *Morris; designed silver, jewellery and some furniture for execution by untrained craftsmen and apprentices of Guild. Silver designs simple; used semi-precious stones and enamel decoration, with Gothic vine ornament, or round lobes and ropework derived from medieval metalwork; characteristic use of silver wire in silver bowl and cover of 1899–1900, with finial of semi-precious stone supported on silver wires, and bowl held on arched wires with ball feet; now in Victoria & Albert Museum, London. Used Celtic and naturalistic motifs in jewellery, with enamelwork, baroque pearls, perle de coq, chrysoprase, moonstones, and turquoises. Furniture combines several techniques, e.g. wood-carving, metal engraving, and leather tooling. Member of *Art Workers' Guild from 1897, Master in 1929; member of *Arts and Crafts Exhibition Society, showed oak cabinet with gilt and red painted decoration in 1899; also exhibited at Vienna Secession; had some influence on Liberty's *Cymric designs, but more significant effect on Vienna Secessionists. Much work untraced. Mark on silver: CRA.

Ashby Potters' Guild. English earthenware potters, organized 1909, at Woodville, Derbyshire, near Ashby-de-la-Zouch, Leicestershire.

Produced ornamental and domestic wares, usually decorated with glazes in two or more colours, e.g. moss-green and blue. Mark: ASHBY GUILD in oval, impressed. In 1922, amalgamated with pottery of W. *Ault at Swadlincote; traded (1923–37) as Ault & Tunnicliffe Ltd.

Ashkabad. *See* West Turkestan.

ashtray. Receptacle for cigar, cigarette, or pipe ash, widely produced in Europe and America following expansion of American tobacco industry (from c1865). Ornate examples made in silver, brass, ceramics, glass, etc.; cheap versions often produced as souvenirs or medium for advertizing cigarettes (popular from c1880), alcohol, etc. Styles frequently reflect current developments in design. Smoking sets, with ash tray, match holder, cigarette box, etc., made by *Tiffany Studios c1895, in bronze and glass. Other examples include beaten copper ashtrays by American Arts & Crafts Movement, e.g. D. *van Erp, *Roycroft Workshops; hemispherical bronze ashtray by M. *Brandt (1924).

ash-tray netsuke. *See* kurawa netsuke.

Ashtead Potters. English pottery established in Sussex after 1st World War, to offer employment to disabled servicemen, with assistance of pottery manufacturers. Original work force of 14 increased to 30 by 1925. At first produced white glazed earthenware; painted decoration of landscapes and linear designs introduced. Figures in white glazed earthenware with touches of colour, characterized by garlands of flowers painted bright blue, yellow, maroon, and light green, made in early 1930s. Mark: printed tree and Ashtead Potters, used 1926–36.

asparagus clip. Instrument for serving asparagus, with broad, flat blade and shorter,

spring-loaded upper jaw opened by pressure of thumb to receive asparagus stalks. Made c1900 in silver and electro-plate, often with ivory handle.

asparagus tongs. Scissor-actioned instrument for eating asparagus; broad blades usually highly ornamented with engraving; introduced late 18th century. Later version in form of spring-bow with wide, pierced, flat grippers; made in variety of patterns to match cutlery, or in sets of six with *asparagus clip; made in silver or electro-plate.

aspidistra stand. Container, often wickerwork, for earthenware pot holding aspidistra plant, supported on three or four varnished wood or terracotta legs; popular in Britain from c1875. Models with 3–4ft high, bamboo, tripod stands made from c1880; bamboo poles (stabilized by stretchers) cross at top providing pronged support for pot, sometimes with small pot suspended by chain from top of each pole. *cf* art pot stand.

Asprey & Co. London firm of retail and manufacturing jewellers producing wide range of luxury items, gold and silver work, objects of vertu, as well as jewellery. Founded 1781 by William Asprey and still run by family. Opened

Ashtead Pottery. Earthenware figure. 1920s.

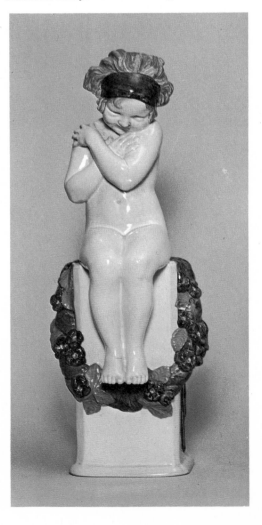

shop in New Bond Street in 1830s with leather, gold, and jewellery workshops above. Established reputation as makers of fine dressing cases containing bottles mounted in chased silver or gold set with gem stones, tortoiseshell, ivory. Examples shown at Great Exhibition of 1851, Universal Exhibition (Paris, 1855), and International Exhibition (London, 1862). Firm expanded throughout 19th century and achieved world-wide reputation for fine craftsmanship. Produced jewellery in conventional style; known for wide variety of specially commissioned and designed presentation pieces in gold, silver. *Illustration at* powder compact.

Associated Artists. *See* Tiffany, Louis Comfort.

Assyrian jewellery. *See* archaeological jewellery.

Left
Asprey & Co. Walnut dressing case with silver gilt fittings, 1850s.

Below
Asprey & Co. Vanity case in gold and silver containing tortoise-shell comb, purse, powder compact. 1936.

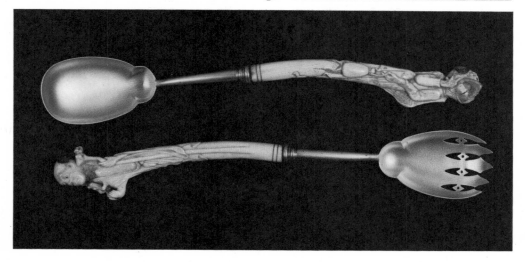

Left
Atkin Brothers. Salad servers with Japanese carved ivory handles. 1883.

Assyrian style silver. Silver with decoration based on illustrations in Sir A. H. Layard's account of his findings at Nineveh, 'Nineveh and its Remains' (1849). Briefly in vogue for electroplated wares during 1860s. Early example of style in pair of electro-plated winecoolers, with barrel-shaped bodies engraved with human-headed bulls and figure of an Assyrian king between borders of winged bulls and anthemions, made by H. Wilkinson & Co. in 1855.

Aston, Jabez (fl c1837–80). English porcelain painter at Coalport factory in Shropshire. Signed work includes delicate naturalistic flowers and fruit painted on large plaques.

Atelier Primavera. Workshop established (1912) at Paris store, Au Printemps, for design and sale of all elements of interior decoration. Noted for work in Art Deco style in 1920s. Ceramic work made to harmonize with other work includes lamps decorated with bold flowers, foliage, birds, and nude figures; also earthenware made e.g. at Longwy, bearing factory marks. Other studios set up in Paris department stores for same purpose, e.g. La Maîtrise at Galeries Lafayette under direction of M. *Dufrêne.

Atkin Brothers. English manufacturers of silver and electro-plate; firm founded c1758 in Sheffield by Thomas Law; passed to son John Law in 1775, becoming John Law & Sons; business closed in 1819 but name retained in firm of Law, Atkin & Oxley 'successors to John Law & Sons' to 1828; name Atkin Brothers adopted by 1853. Produced wide range of ware, mainly cutlery. Truro works bought by T. *Bradbury & Sons in 1947; firm absorbed by *Adie Bros. and C. J. *Vander in 1958.

Atla. *See* Cohr, Carl M.

atlas glass. Opalescent celadon-green art glass popular in Europe for Art Nouveau decorative ware. Uranium based; first made in Bohemia, c1890.

Atmos clock. Self-winding clock with *torsion pendulum, patented (1913) by Swiss, J. E. Reutter; driven by small variations of temperature or barometric pressure acting on aneroid bellows filled with ethyl chloride. Movement of drum or bellows winds mainspring via click advancing a toothed wheel. Movement highly finished in brass, encased in glass dome in arrangement resembling *400-day clock. Manufactured, from 1926, by Swiss firm, Jaeger-le-Coultre.

Aubusson. French carpet and tapestry centre near Lyon, operative from 9th century; factory set up by Louis de Bourbon in 1665. School of industrial art founded 1869, with 30 pupils; formed nucleus of National School of Decorative Arts, inaugurated 1884, to promote textile industries. Throughout 19th century, workshops concentrated on furnishings, especially carpet manufacture, which was adapted to new mechanical processes. Tapestry production confined to imitating past successes, e.g. 18th century designs of Jean-Baptiste Oudry and Charles Lebrun, until c1920, when director,

Augarten. Porcelain figure modelled by Mathilde Jaksch-Szendrö. 1925. Height 6¼in.

J. Leslie Auld. Cup and cover engraved with sea horses, designed as a fishing trophy, 1938. Height 14in.

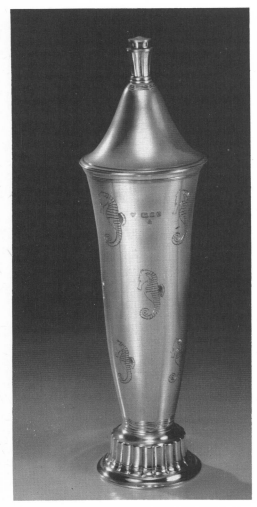

Marius Martin, began employing painters to create original designs, though still allowing weavers little initiative in interpretation. Tapestry renaissance continued under directorship (1930-38) of M. *Cuttoli, who persuaded painters to work at Aubusson and design specifically for tapestry. Measures also taken during 1930s to relieve unemployment caused by modern industrial developments; Guillaume Janneau, administrator of Mobilier National, arranged for renovation and copying of upholstery of state furniture at Aubusson, c1930; in 1935, scattered workshops co-ordinated into single factory intended to employ redundant weavers in area. During 1930s and 1940s, L. *Coutaud, M. *Gromaire, J. *Lurçat, among French artists who created decorative tapestry designs for Aubusson master-weavers.

Augarten. Austrian porcelain factory established (1922) in Vienna. Work influenced by styles of *Wiener Werkstätte. In 1928, produced table service designed by J. *Hoffmann. Also made figures of horses from Lippizaner stud in Vienna. Production continues. Marks include crown over shield and Wien.

Auld, J. Leslie (b 1914). Scottish silversmith; trained at Belfast School of Art and Royal College of Art, London; head of silversmithing department at Glasgow School of Art. Designed trophy (King's Gold Vase) for Ascot races, and dish given by City of London Livery Companies to New York to commemorate New York World Fair of 1939-40.

Ault, William (b 1841). English potter; worked in Staffordshire before establishing art pottery (1882-86) with H. *Tooth at Church Gresley, Derbyshire. From 1887, ran own art pottery at Swadlincote, near Burton-on-Trent, Derbyshire. Ornamental earthenware includes vases (with butterflies and plants painted by daughter, Clarissa), flower pots, pedestals, and grotesque jugs; vases designed by C. *Dresser (c1892-c1896) sometimes covered with aventurine glazes developed by Ault. Also made ware for domestic use. Firm traded as Ault & Tunnicliffe Ltd (1923-37), then Ault Potteries Ltd (from 1937). Marks: tall fluted vase over AULT on ribbon, or monogram of APL.

Aurelian. See Weller, Samuel A.

Aurelian ware. See Moorcroft, William.

Aurene glass. American Tiffany-inspired iridescent glass; patented 1904 by F. *Carder of *Steuben Glass Works. Made in gold, blue, green, or red; plain or painted, usually in gold. *Illustration at* Carder, F.

Aurora colonial furniture. See Rycroft Shops.

Austin, Jesse (1806-79). English pottery decorator. Designer and copper-plate engraver in Burslem, Staffordshire (1826-40). Joined firm of F. & R. *Pratt in 1846 or early 1847; made engravings, original or from work of other artists, for use on pot-lids, table services, toilet sets, etc.; initially printed in two colours, with additional colours hand-painted, later, produced full colour range from use of three-colour plates and key plate. Noted for skill both as engraver and colour analyst. Designs include portraits, views, and genre subjects. In 1859, joined

*Aurene glass. Bowl, gold crackle over alabaster glass. Made at *Steuben Glass Works between 1904 and 1933. Diameter 14in.*

Brown-Westhead, Moore & Co., but returned to Pratts' within a year. Work, normally with key plate printed in brown, signed or initialled.

Australian silver. Mostly handmade until late 19th century; many forms of mark used before 1909, with immigrant craftsmen from Britain generally signing work with initials only, those from Europe with full name. Goldmarking Bill, 1909, created silver standard of .925 parts per 1000 (as Sterling Standard), but did not restrict imports of lower standard. Machine-made borders etc. of .800 standard often imported from Europe and soldered to body of locally produced articles. Emu and kangaroo marks, used to denote Sterling Standard, restricted when symbols were incorporated in Commonwealth of Australia coat of arms.

Auteuil. See Haviland family.

automata and **mechanical toys.** Intricate articulated model animals, figures, animated by clockwork mechanism, developed initially by Swiss *Jacquet-Droz family during 18th century, later made by Swiss and French craftsmen; even more complex by mid 19th century. Acrobats, dancing dolls from c1810; monkey orchestras, musicians and shoe cleaners from c1860; American walking dolls (autoperipatetikoi), with forward, reverse and sideways motion, from c1865; wide range of highly ornate animal automata, e.g. lizard, mouse, caterpillar, in gold, decorated with pearls and enamelwork. These superseded after c1870 by cheap mechanical toys mass-produced by rapidly expanding German tin-plate industry; subsequently adult interest in automata waned, and mechanical toys came to be associated purely with children.

automatic clock winding. System of winding applied to *time switches, domestic clocks, and modern *turret clocks. Synchronous electric motor rewinds mainspring of time switches. Domestic *battery clocks use electro-magnet and ratchet arrangement to rewind small mainspring at short intervals. Weight in turret clocks is wound up about every 15 minutes by electric motor switched on and off by single descending weight suspended from Huygens endless chain; motor often incorporated in weight itself.

autoperipatetikoi. See automata.

Avenard, Etienne (b 1873). French potter, born at St-Brieuc (Côtes-du-Nord). From c1913, sought to renew art of faïence. Using clay from

Automaton. Singing bird in cage. Brass wire cage, beechwood case and penny-in-slot operated movement. French, late 19th century. Height 22in.

own garden, made variety of objects, notably bowls, sometimes covered. Pure white or creamy glaze painted with coloured oxides, e.g. blue, pink, green, violet, or yellow, in geometrical patterns, including plant forms, dictated by shape of article. After 1st World War, director of workshop making faience at Sèvres factory. Work bears painted mark of cypress tree.

aventurine glass. Opaque or clear brown glass with inclusion of gold or copper flakes in glass melt; sometimes iron or brass. Dates from antiquity; accidentally rediscovered in 17th century Venice; revived in 19th century Europe and America for vases and other decorative ware. Produced until c1865. *Illustrations at* Couper, J. & Son, Monart ware.

aventurine glaze. *See* crystalline glaze.

aventurine lacquer. *See* nashiji.

Avisseau, Charles-Antoine (1796–1861). French potter, son of stonemason. Working independently from early 19th century, regarded as forerunner of modern artist potters. Pioneer in revival of *Palissy ware, shown at International Exhibition in London (1851). In 1842, opened workshop in home town, Tours (Indre-et-Loire), with son, Joseph Edouard, and relatives, *Landais family, also working in Palissy style.

From 1850s, developed freer interpretation of original style, including *trompe l'oeil* decoration, e.g. in baskets of fish, or perforations. All work signed or marked with monogram of AV.

Awaji wares. Faience and porcelain made at Japanese ceramic factory established (1831) in Iganomura, on Awaji island. Dishes, etc. glazed with bright orange-yellow and green and decorated with Chinese-inspired designs in low-relief associated with K. *Mimpei. Greyish white, black, tortoiseshell, or green, yellow, and aubergine glazes also used. Work shown at Philadelphia Centennial Exhibition (1876).

Axminster carpet. Term applied to various types of cut pile carpet, with double weft (*cf* Wilton single weft) and single warp, and most of pile yarn on carpet surface. Usually refers to carpet woven on *spool Axminster loom. *See also* chenille Axminster, Donegal, Durham rugs, gripper Axminster, Imperial Axminster, Real Axminster, spool-gripper loom. *Illustration at* McKnight Kauffer, E.

Axminster Carpet Factory (Devon), England. Founded 1755. Fire in 1828 crippled factory; plant bought by *Wilton Royal Carpet Factory and moved (1834) with most of weavers to Wilton. Production revived in 1937 by Kidderminster manufacturer, W. H. Dutfield, who founded Axminster Carpet Co. for production of Axminster carpets only.

Azerbaijan carpets. *See* Caucasian carpets.

Baccarat. French glasshouse in Baccarat, Meurthe-et-Moselle; world-famous for paperweights from mid 19th century. Established 1764 (name, Baccarat, dates from 1822). Under direction of Jean-Baptiste Toussaint (1822–58), high-quality lead crystal glass produced and experiments with colour encouraged, e.g. *verre dichroïde* (green or yellow crystal glass). 1850–70, opal glass in milk or pastel colours made in decorative, often classical, forms (term, *opaline, first used at Baccarat). In 1832, in association with *St Louis, acquired Cristallerie du Creusot, where method of *cristallo-ceramie* had been perfected; led to development of first Baccarat paperweights in 1846. Majority in *millefiori* glass; other groups: overlay weights and bouquet weights; rarer animal weights include caterpillars, snakes, ducks, and butterflies. Some large and miniature weights also made. Many signed B, followed by date and occasionally craftsman's initials. From 1878, fine cut crystal table glass produced in rich and dignified style; also coloured ornamental glass and variety of moulded glass, often in four-piece moulds with name Baccarat impressed on inside. In late 19th century, pressed glass in imitation of cut crystal produced. Factory, which flourishes today, has established large museum in Paris displaying glassware of last 150 years. Mark: Baccarat, France, encircling goblet, decanter, or beaker; stamped or etched. *Illustration also at* paperweight.

Bacchus, George, & Sons. English glasshouse in Birmingham; known earlier as Bacchus Green & Green (to 1834), Bacchus & Green (1834–40). Made first British *pressed ware in 1830s; pressed glass imitating cut glass in 1850s, especially tumblers. From mid 19th century, also produced blown coloured and opaline vases and

bowls, usually in soft, curving shapes; transfer-printed opalines; small objects, e.g. toilet bottles, in plain, transparent glass cut in broad, sharply angular, vertical facets in Bohemian manner; layered work with spaced hollows recalling miniature traceried Gothic windows. Also, fine *ice glass and engraved glass with *façon de Venise* stems of multicoloured canes. Paperweights with *millefiori* canes partly sunk into white glass to resemble melted snow are usually attributed to this glasshouse.

backstamp. Printed mark on underside of English pottery or porcelain; often occurs with transfer-printed decoration, giving title of pattern, maker's mark, and trade name of body.

Baggs, Arthur E. (fl early 20th century). American artist potter. Trained under C. F. *Binns. Worked at Marblehead Pottery, Massachusetts, from 1905. Noted for simplicity of style.

baguette. *See* gem cutting.

Baguette pattern flatware. Flatware design introduced by *Christofle, 1861; still in production in 1960s. Made by several other factories including W. H. *Hutton & Sons, Sheffield, where cost of installing machinery to produce it brought firm close to ruin in 1929 slump. One of most popular designs in Europe apart from Britain and Scandinavia, where considered too large.

Bailey, C.J.C. (fl mid to late 19th century). London potter; in 1864, bought and enlarged Fulham

C. J. C. Bailey. Stoneware vase decorated by E. Bennett. Dated 1888. Height 12in.

Pottery used in 17th century by John Dwight. Earthenware made for domestic, sanitary, and technical use. Terracotta vases, figures, stoves, and architectural ware produced in light pink or red body, sometimes shades combined. Salt-glazed stoneware jugs and mugs, sometimes with heraldic or Japanese inspired designs incised or impressed, designed by J-C. *Cazin in early 1870s. E. *Kettle decorated salt-glazed jugs and vases with foliage and birds, animals, or figures in medieval robes. In late 1870s, J. P. *Seddon designed *jardinières* with incised decoration of leaves in salt-glazed stoneware. Pale, highly refined stoneware made 1873–c1887 from formula used by Dwight. E. Bennett, art director, decorated vases, etc., with designs incised and coloured under glaze. Pottery closed c1889. Marks usually incorporate name of Bailey.

Bailey, Cuthbert (fl 20th century). English ceramic chemist; son of manager of Doulton factory, Burslem, Staffordshire, worked for Doulton 1900–07, and returned to succeed father in 1925. From 1901, collaborated in experiments in production of *flambé* glazes with B. *Moore. *Flambé* glazes produced at Doulton factory under Charles J. *Noke by 1904, and crystalline glazes by 1907.

Baillie Scott, Mackay Hugh (1865–1945). English architect; also designed furniture, metalwork, ceramics, etc. Furniture simple, linear, with colourful inlays, in e.g. pewter, ivory, woods, and copper, and elaborate metal mounts.

Mackay Hugh Baillie Scott. Manxman upright piano made by John Broadwood & Sons, no. 899964. c1898.

Pieces designed for palace of Grand Duke of Hesse in Darmstadt (made by *Guild of Handicraft in 1898) included oak music cabinet with each door ornamented with coloured inlay forming stylized flower, and metal relief work. Much work untraced. Some work for Deutsche Werkstätten, c1910.

Bain, Alexander (c1811–77). Scottish clockmaker; pioneered electric clocks (patents 1845–47) of *long-case type. Magnetized circular pendulum bob enters one or other of two coils mounted on case; on alternate swings, contact is made, giving magnetic impulse to pendulum to overcome energy-loss from friction. Power generated by battery made from zinc and copper plates buried in ground. Also invented *slave clocks, operated by constant electrical signal transmitted every second, minute, or hour (from central, controlled *master clock). Poor electrical contacts made Bain's clocks unreliable; similar but improved linked slave and master clock systems used by British companies c1870.

Bakalowits & Söhne. Influential family of Austrian glass designers and retailers with distribution centre in Vienna. Close contact with products, especially Art Nouveau, of J. *Loetz Witwe glasshouse. Own designs unusual in shape but symmetrical, e.g. tall-necked, shouldered vases, with typical floral festoon decoration; many silver-mounted.

bakelite. Synthetic resin or plastic invented by L. H. Baekeland, 1913. Easily moulded and dyed to form e.g. imitation amber, jet. Much used for cheap Art Deco jewellery and buckles.

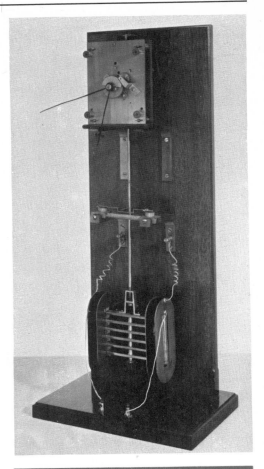

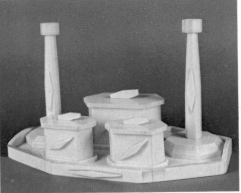

Top
*Alexander Bain. *Electric clock. Mid 19th century.*

Above
Bakelite. Dressing table set in pink and green. Probably English, 1930s.

Bakhmetev Glass Works. Moscow glass factory founded in early 1760s by Bahkmetev family. Specialized in costly ornamental glass, producing fine glassware imitating European styles until 1917. Distinctively Russian black-stained engraving of c1743 revived in 19th century. Closed down during Russian Revolution (1917); subsequently, modernized and reopened under new name, Krasniy Gigant (Red Giant).

Balas ruby. *See* spinel.

Bakhmetev Glass Works. Goblet with stained, engraved and gilded decoration, c1900. Height 5½in.
Right
Bamboo furniture. Dressing table and mirror, made in America. 1870s.

balconet cresting. Late 19th century cabinet-making term (in Britain) for ornamental detail above cornices of wardrobes, cabinets, and bookcases.

Ball, Black & Co. *See* Black, Starr & Frost.

balloon-back chair. Parlour, dining-room or drawing room chair, common in Britain c1840–c1900, in America c1840–c1870. Open, elliptical back narrows towards seat; back and cross rail slightly curved, often carved. Curved back legs; straight, carved, or turned front legs in early models replaced by cabriole legs c1850. Usually in mahogany or rosewood with up-holstered seat, often buttoned; sometimes with oval, upholstered panel above cross rail. Variations include buckle-back, quaker, and round-back chairs.

ball watch. Lady's spherical *fob watch normally suspended from brooch or necklace so that dial faces downwards. From c1860 onwards, particularly in Geneva, often incorporated in jewellery design as e.g. flower head or body of insect; popular in early 20th century.

Baltimore silver. *See* Kirk repoussé.

Balzar-Kopp, Elfriede (b 1904). German artist potter; born in Westerwald region (Rhineland); studied at trade school in Höhr-Grenzhausen near home, then at state factory in Karlsruhe (Baden-Württemberg). From 1927, at own workshop (also in Höhr-Grenzhausen), made earthenware, sometimes for architectural use, ceramic sculpture, and stoneware in traditional shapes with decoration derived from natural

forms, characterized by sensitive use of glazes. Small animal figures made in salt-glazed stone-ware, e.g. hippopotamus.

bamboo furniture. Furniture made from stems of giant, tropical reed. Flimsy, attenuated chairs, tables, whatnots, aspidistra stands, etc., popular in Britain c1875–c1900. Common in America c1870–c1900, although *simulated bamboo used more extensively than less sturdy genuine article.

Bampi, Richard (1896–1966). Artist potter, born in Brazil; worked chiefly in Germany. Studied at polytechnic in Munich; from 1920, at Bauhaus, where influenced by M. *Läuger. In 1923, settled

in Rio de Janeiro, working at own studio until return to Germany in 1927. Early tin-glazed earthenware exhibited in Leipzig (1928). From 1929, inspired by Chinese ceramics at exhibition in Berlin; influence apparent in stoneware, made from late 1930s. Later work includes wall plaque; abstract design in shades of grey with blocks of red and blue, against cream ground, signed Bampi.

Bang, Jacob (b 1899). Danish architect and glass artist in Functionalist style. Industrial designer for Holmegaard glass works, 1925–42. Also made vases and bowls with acid-roughened or corroded surfaces (similar to those of M.

*Marinot), usually engraved with simple linear pattern.

bangle. Inflexible bracelet made of solid gold, silver, or other metal. Fashionable from late 19th century to *c*1910 and again during 1920s and 1930s, when 'slave bangle' worn on upper arm. Circular or oval shape, set with pearls, diamonds, or semi-precious stones in single row, in half-hoop, or forming motifs such as star or crescent, or as single stone with elaborate setting. Plain bangles often engraved with leaves or floral pattern. Hinged bangles worn from *c*1860. Very narrow bangles, worn in sets of six or more, popular *c*1906 onwards.

Banko ware. Japanese pottery developed at Kuwana, Ise province, in 17th century includes, notably, wine ewers with creamy glaze and Chinese-inspired enamel decoration. Version with underglaze blue and enamelled decoration made in 19th century by *Yusetso Mori. Many other potters in Ise province made pottery marked with Banko seal, and styles imitated, e.g. by H. *Kawamoto in Owari province.

Bantam work. *See* Coromandel lacquer.

Bapst. French crown jewellers; carried out commissions for Empress Eugénie and reset many of French crown jewels. Firm founded in Paris, mid 18th century; came into possession of Menière firm when Jacques Bapst married proprietor's daughter (1797). Business continued by sons Constant and Charles-Frédéric. Remounted jewels in medieval style; made much of jewellery worn at Second Empire balls and 'Greek' and 'Russian' diadems shown with other diamond jewellery made for Empress Eugénie at 1867 Paris Exhibition. Charles-Frédéric director of

Barbedienne & Co. Covered container formed from ostrich egg with bronze mounts, parcel-gilt and applied lacquer decoration in Japanese style. c1872.

*Barbotine decoration. Pilgrim vase made by *Haviland & Co., earthenware, c1875. Height 12in.*

workshops for 50 years until death in 1871; sons Jules and Paul, and nephew Alfred continued firm. After Alfred's death, his son Germain left to start separate firm with L. *Falize; Jules and Paul founded new house, Jules et Paul Bapst et Fils (1892).

Baranovka. Polish hard-paste porcelain factory established *c*1801 at Baranovka near Volhynia. Work resembles that of contemporary Russian factories. Noted for production of envelope-shaped snuffboxes, and easter eggs painted with biblical scenes, etc. Generally thought to have closed in 1895, but production may have continued until after 1917. Marks: Baranowka, painted or impressed, or imperial eagle, or three stars, painted.

Barbedienne, Ferdinand (fl mid 19th century). French bronze founder; in association with A. Collas, established foundry in 1839 to produce scale models of full-size sculpture; process made possible by Collas's patent reduction machine. Firm expanded during middle and late 19th century; products, always of high technical quality, ranging from furniture through objects of vertu, exercised strong influence on French bourgeois taste until *c*1900. Output includes edited bronze reductions of work by noted 18th and 19th century French sculptors, e.g. Jean-Baptiste Carpeaux, in editions numbering 24–200; reduction of Neapolitan Improvisatore, by Francisque-Joseph Dürer (1804–65), most popular statuette offered by Barbedienne. Series of *animalier* bronzes started *c*1847 with editions of A-L. *Barye, also P-J. *Mêne, E. *Frémiet, etc. (*see* bronze).

barber's chair. 19th century high-back chair with adjustable head rest above yoke rail rising on ratchet; leather-padded. Used by barbers in Britain. Fitted with adjustable swivel seat from *c*1850.

barbotine (French, 'slip' or 'puddled clay') **decoration.** Use of coloured clay slip, in decoration of pottery; technique resembles oil-

*Barcelona chair. Designed by L. *Mies van der Rohe.*

painting, where colours can be mixed to provide infinite variation in tone. Developed by E. *Chaplet in 1870s; fashionable from *c*1875, but lost favour *c*1890, partly because of difficulties in firing, due to differences in density of body and slip which caused painting to flake. Technique successfully used by M. L. *McLaughlin after experiments inspired by display of *barbotine* decoration in Philadelphia Centennial Exhibition, 1876. Later, characteristic decoration of ware produced at Rookwood Pottery and by American imitators.

Barcelona chair. Designed by L. *Mies van der Rohe for German Pavilion at International Exhibition, Barcelona, 1929; hence name. Side sections of two curved, steel bars are joined by straight bars on which leather-cushion seat and back suspended by leather straps. Now manufactured by *Knoll Associates.

barge, bargee or **Measham ware.** English dark brown glazed earthenware; sprigged relief of birds and flowers in white clay painted with touches of green, blue, and pink. Made *c*1860–*c*1910 in Derbyshire, mainly at Church Gresley, also at nearby Woodville. Sold at Measham, Leicestershire, on Ashby-de-la-Zouch canal. Could be ordered with personal inscription pressed with printer's type on applied white clay before firing. Includes kettles, chamber pots, jugs, tobacco jars and, notably, large teapots (holding up to 1½ gallons), with finial in form of similarly shaped teapot.

Barkentin & Krall. English jewellers and silversmiths; founded by Dane, I. Barkentin (*c*1800–1881), who moved to London *c*1861; joined by Czech, C. C. Krall *c*1868, who became head of firm from 1881. Produced mainly ecclesiastical metalwork and jewellery: made candlesticks for Liverpool Cathedral (1909), and silver altar plate and altars for Sandringham Church, Norfolk. Firm closed 1932.

Barker Brothers. English manufacturers of silverware, electro-plate, Britannia metal ware, and cutlery, founded in Birmingham, 1820, as

Barge ware. Teapot, made in East Staffordshire, c*1900.*

Barker & Creed; became Barker Brothers from c1860. Amalgamated with Levi & Salaman, and Potosi Silver, 1921, and with Ellis & Co., 1931, but retained original name until reincorporated as Barker-Ellis & Co., 1964. Marks include trefoil, with star on each leaf, phoenix, miniature minora candelabrum.

Barlach, Ernst (1870–1938). German sculptor, graphic artist, and poet; modelled work in ceramics. After visit to Russia (1906), figures and groups of Russian peasants produced in stoneware by son of H. *Mutz; stark, expressionistic style betokens suffering and humiliation of many subjects. Russian models also among figures produced in white glazed porcelain (c1908–c1913) by Schwarzburger Werkstätten für Porzellankunst at Unterweissbach in Thuringia.

Barlow, Arthur (c1845–79). English pottery decorator. In London, at Doulton workshop, Lambeth (1871–78), incised or moulded designs of trailing plant forms, often with stamped ground patterns, on stoneware. Some designs carried out by other potters. Mark: monogram of ABB, incised.

Barlow, Florence E. (d 1909). English pottery decorator. From 1873, worked at Doulton workshop in Lambeth, London. Initially, incised designs of birds on stoneware in technique similar to that of sister, H. *Barlow. Later, decoration of birds, foliage, etc., built up in coloured slips. Also painted Lambeth faience. Mark: variants of monogram of FB or FEB.

Barlow, Hannah B. (1851–1916). English pottery decorator. Studied at Lambeth School of Art, London; first female artist to work at Doulton workshop in Lambeth (from 1871). Decorated salt-glazed stoneware with spirited, freehand sketches of horses, dogs, sheep, country scenes. Few lines of design incised and filled with pigment. From c1895, drawings more detailed, with heavy borders. Also painted Lambeth faience. Retired in 1906. Mark: monogram of BHB on base of work.

bar movement. Watch movement, partly machine-made, incorporating bars or bridges instead of plate to hold pivots of train. Used mainly in *Swiss watches, but also in some French and English types. Design attributed to Jean-Antoine Lépine (c1770); most surviving examples date from c1870. Sometimes called skeleton movement.

Barnard, Bishop & Barnard. English metal-workers in Norwich, Norfolk; makers of high-quality ornamental metalwork, and art furniture and fittings in cast-iron. Much of output designed by T. *Jeckyll, e.g. cast brass fire surround, decorated with Japanese-style badges, and incised wave pattern; also, cast-iron Japanese-style pavilion with railings in shape of sunflowers shown at Philadelphia Exhibition (1876).

Right
*Barnard, Bishop & Barnard. Cast and wrought iron sunflower designed by T. *Jekyll, 1876. Height 30in.*

*Hannah B. Barlow. *Doulton & Co. stoneware vase and jug. Vase marked with impressed rosette, artist's monogram incised, and date 1882. Height 12¼in. Jug has scrollwork and harebells outlined in white slip surrounding panel by Florence E. *Barlow. Marked with incised artists' monograms, impressed mark and code for 1903. Height 7¼in.*

Barnard, Edward, & Sons Ltd. Oldest manufacturing silversmiths in London. Firm established 1689 by Antony Nelme; passed into hands of Edward Barnard in 1829; subsequently directed by sons, William (d 1851), Edward (d 1868), and John (retired 1877), and grandsons, Edward, Walter, and John. Throughout 19th century manufactured extensive range of commercial silver, e.g. tea sets, condiment sets, tankards, cutlery, and large quantity of church plate. From 1842, produced electro-plated ware under licence from *Elkington & Co. Also made many elaborate and massive silver centrepieces, candelabra, c1850-90, e.g. as *racing trophies and testimonials. Firm supplied many prominent contemporary retailers, e.g. Rundell's, Braithwaite & Jones, Fisher's. Marks: until 1933, initials of current partners in shield; after 1933 EB above & S. Firm continues in business.

Barnsley, Edward (b 1900). English furniture designer and artist craftsman; son of S. *Barnsley. Established business (1923) in Petersfield, Hampshire, carrying on traditions of Cotswold school. Expanded from c1930, employing 7-10 assistants; pupil assistants from 1946. Introduced power machines in 1950, combining craftsmanship with mechanization. Adviser in woodwork design and production to Loughborough College, Leicester, 1938-65.

Barnsley, Grace (fl 20th century). English pottery decorator. Worked at Wedgwood factory in 1920s and 1930s. With husband, O. *Davies, established *Roeginga Pottery in Kent. Work marked with monogram.

Barnsley, Sydney (1865-1926) and Ernest (1863-1926). English architects and furniture

*Grace Barnsley. Earthenware vase made by *Roeginga pottery and decorated by Grace Barnsley. Matt glazed and painted over glaze with bands of thistles and leaves. c1935. Height 10½in.*

designers; brothers. (S. Barnsley member of *Arts & Crafts Exhibition Society and *Kenton & Co.) Set up workshop with E. *Gimson in Pinbury, Gloucestershire, 1894; moved with him to Sapperton, Gloucestershire, 1903. Members of Cotswold school. Designed and made simple, well-proportioned furniture in oak, walnut, or mahogany, using natural colour and grain of wood for decorative effect.

barograph. Automatic instrument providing continuous graphic record of changes in atmospheric pressure. Readings of *barometer transferred to pen or stylus moving across chart driven by clock movement. Various devices for making record from mercury barometer introduced in 19th century, mainly for observatories etc., but mercury barographs produced commercially by Negretti & Zambra in London from 1864 and by firm of Richard in Paris from c1900. More usual form uses aneroid mechanism with linkage of levers to stylus, and paper chart fitted to vertical drum driven by *8-day clock movement. Early version (1867) by French Breguet Company, has drum connected to separate clock with normal hour and minute dial, and smoked paper chart scratched by stylus. Later type has self-inking pen and paper chart with printed time graduations. M. *Hipp introduced (1871) barograph with electro-magnetic stylus to mark chart at 10-minute intervals; also instrument transmitting electrical impulses to make record at distant point. Barograph assembly usually housed in glass-fronted wooden case.

barometer. Instrument for indicating atmospheric pressure. Standard mercury (in glass) barometer developed by end of 17th century, produced throughout 18th and 19th centuries; two types: direct-reading 'stick' form with scale mounted against upper part of mercury column;

*Sydney Barnsley. Oak coffer with exposed ribbing, panelled inside. Painted floral decoration by A. and L. *Powell. c1905. Length 5ft6in.*

'wheel' form with circular dial and pointer linked to float on mercury reservoir at foot of column. Scales and dials calibrated for height of liquid; domestic barometers often with wording, e.g. fair, changeable, rain. More accurate system of wording introduced c1860 by R. *Fitzroy, allowing for influence of other factors on weather. Refinements by 19th century makers (mainly in instruments for observatory use) include forms of temperature *compensation to counteract expansion of mercury with heat, and improved methods of scale reading. *See also* aneroid barometer.

Barovier, Ercole (b 1889). Italian glass artist. With P. *Venini, responsible for reinstating *Murano as world centre for original glass work in 20th century. In 1920s, reacting against Venetian glassmakers' exclusive concentration on 17th and 18th century imitations, invented new effects and textures, e.g. *vetro rugiado, *vetro gemmato, and *primavera glass. Work usually in subdued colours, with experimental textural effects; sometimes vigorous geometrical decoration. Vases, bowls, and decorative pieces always gently fluid, in simple, but not austere, forms; some work with inlaid gold relief. Co-founder of Barovier & Toso factory, Murano.

barrel chair. Upholstered chair, usually covered in chintz; armless, with high, concave back and round seat. Trade development of rural chair made from barrel; dates from c1850 in America. Laminated examples made by J. H. *Belter.

Barrett, A.J. (fl mid 19th century). English silver designer working for *Hunt & Roskell from 1850s. Designed Royal Hunt Cup for Ascot (1862), depicting stag being brought down by two deerhounds; plinth decorated with classical motifs.

Barum ware. Earthenware art pottery made in Barnstaple, North Devon, from c1879 by C. *Brannam; popular until early 20th century.

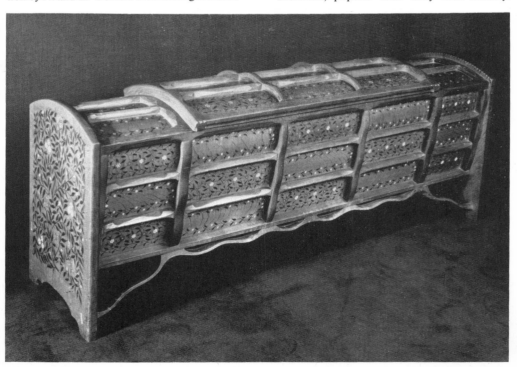

Barum ware. Jug, with incised mark C.H. Brammam, Barum.

Jugs and vases of simple form painted with scrolled designs of flowers, birds, fish, etc., in coloured slip, e.g. muted blue, green, and yellow on white ground, often with outlines incised. Moulded decoration includes dragons or marine life blending with shape of vase. Work usually bears mark C.H. Brannam, Barum, incised on base, often with date. *See also* Lauder, Alexander.

Barye, Antoine-Louis (1796–1875). French romantic sculptor, regarded as founder of *Les Animaliers,* 19th century school of French sculptors specializing in small, vigorously naturalistic animal bronzes. Worked as gold and silver smith, 1823–1831; early pieces anonymously produced for employer, Faucourier. First major success, Tiger devouring Gavial, shown at Paris Salon in 1831. Lion (1833) cast in bronze, placed in Tuileries gardens, Paris. Established own foundry 1838, until bankruptcy in 1848. Prolific output of closely observed bronzes, using *cire-perdue* process, depicting e.g. violent conflict among wild animals; some domestic animals. Models and casts sequestered by creditor E. Martin, used to produce inferior pirated editions of Barye's work 1848–57. Barye financially re-established by 1857; works exported to England and America by 1860. Several full-scale public commissions executed 1860–75, e.g. bronze bas-relief over entrance to Carousel Court, Louvre, Paris; marble figure of St Clotilde, Madeleine, Paris, 1866. Major works include Theseus and Minotaur (1846), Scared Lion (1847), Elephant Crushing Tiger (1847). After Barye's death, F. *Barbedienne edited many of his originals, all with Barye signature and foundry stamp.

basket or **wicker chair.** Chair for indoor or outdoor use in open-plaited wickerwork (of osier or similar material) or case; usually has round seat, continuous back and arms; often with circular base. Some examples without arms. Loose seat cushion, or button upholstery. From *c*1875, term usually referred to canework chair with retractable footrest and adjustable back. cf croquet chair.

basket stand. Work table with central column supporting two circular, galleried shelves. Often in mahogany, rosewood, or bamboo. Common in Britain and America during 19th century.

Antoine-Louis Barye. Bronze figure of African elephant. Signed Barye on base. Late 19th century. Width 8in.
Right
Battery clocks. Left: Bulle clock, height 16½in. including glass dome. Right: another French battery-driven clock with movement on Bulle principle, but with fixed coil and bar magnet forming pendulum bob.

basse-taille enamelling. Intaglio-effect enamelling in which several coats of translucent enamel cover engine-turned or engraved design on metal. Developed in Pisa, Italy, in 13th century for decorating silver plate. Widely used from late 19th century for numerous objects of vertu. Speciality of *Fabergé.

bassinet. Long, hooded, wickerwork basket used as cradle. From *c*1850 in Britain, term also applied to three or four wheeled hand carriage with hooded, basketwork body; for one or two children.

bath chair. Three-wheeled chair invented *c*1750 in Bath, Somerset, by James Heath. Long, steering handle attached to small, pivoting, front wheel allowed chair to be pulled from front, or pushed from back with passenger steering. In Victorian period, painted, decorated, and well-upholstered, sometimes with folding leather hood, apron of two hinged flaps of wood, and shafts for harnessing pony.

Bath metal. Alloy of copper and zinc, similar to brass; used in 19th century for buttons, boxes etc.

batik-printed textile motifs. Stylized patterns of birds, animals, and plant forms inspired by Javanese printed textiles. Feature of Dutch Art Nouveau style in 1880s, comparable to adoption of Japanese decorative elements in England, France, and America. In ceramics, work of T.A.C. *Colenbrander and J. *Mendes da Costa notable.

Batley, Henry (fl 1870–85). English furniture designer; employed by J. *Shoolbred & Co. Known for high-quality, Anglo-Japanese style furniture, with Japanese motifs grafted onto e.g. Early English style. Examples include upright, mahogany piano inset with carved boxwood reliefs (1878), now in Victoria & Albert Museum, London.

Battam, Thomas (1810–64). English pottery and porcelain painter. Trained in London decorating workshop of father, also Thomas Battam. Art director at factory of W.T. *Copeland, *c*1835–*c*1856. Decoration in Etruscan style on ornamental and domestic ware in terracotta and bone porcelain. Also said to have made copies of oil-paintings on large porcelain slabs. Credited with development of parian body at Copeland factory in 1840s. In 1858, founder of Crystal Palace Art Union.

battery or **cordless clock.** Clock with movement powered by electric battery. Current may drive movement directly, or rewind conventional

Above
Bauhaus. Silver tea service with wooden knobs and handles made in Bauhaus metal workshops by Christian Dell. 1925.

Left
Baumgarten tapestry factory. Tapestry in manner of French mid 18th century designs. Height 8ft.

mainspring at intervals. *See* A. Bain, Bulle clock, Eureka clock.

Baudouine, Charles (fl c1829-55). New York furniture maker. Known for rococo style furniture, usually in rosewood; also made some Renaissance revival dining-room pieces in oak, with bunches of fruit, etc., carved on panels. Employed c200 workers, including c70 cabinet makers; pieces made 1849-54 marked: FROM C.A. BAUDOUINE / 335 / BROADWAY / NEW YORK/.

Bauhaus. German school of design formed 1919 in Weimar under leadership of W. *Gropius, using buildings of Academy of Fine Arts and Crafts, and weaving and bookbinding workshops (then privately owned) of former School of Arts and Crafts (developed by H. C. *van de Velde and closed 1915), with new Architecture department and help of some teachers from Academy. Architects, engineers, painters, sculptors, and designers cooperated in application of visual arts

according to demands of machine production. Attempted to reunify artistic disciplines and relate construction to function. Curriculum was to consist of preliminary course, followed by three years of workshop instruction, leading to journeyman's diploma and qualifying student for final architecture course. Students encouraged to carry out research and experiment. Gropius took charge of woodworking shop; commissioned in 1921 to build house near Berlin. Some furniture painted in bright colours, e.g. cradle slung between hoop rockers. M. *Breuer joined as student in 1920; made chairs and tables in geometrical shapes, often in pear or cherry wood, and later introduced use of chrome tubing frame for chairs, initially with canvas seat, arms, back. Some jewellery and religious objects made in metalwork department. Experimental tableware, then jugs, teapots, etc., in form of sphere or hemisphere, e.g. by M. *Brandt, under direction of artist László Moholy-Nagy. W. *Wagenfeld made coffee pots, jugs, etc., often cylindrical in shape, of German silver, and collaborated in design of table lamp with glass stand and hemispherical opalescent glass shade, mounted in brass and silver. Combination of glass and metal regarded as important development in design of light fittings and kitchen equipment. Work of textile department included woven pictures and, later, design of fabrics and experiments in textiles. Some tapestry design attributed to painter Paul Klee, teacher 1920-31. G. *Marcks took charge of ceramics department at Dornburg (20 miles outside Weimer), with O. *Lindig, T. *Bogler, and M. *Wildenhain as apprentices; R. *Bampi employed briefly. Low fired earthenware first used; harder body fired at higher temperature, often unglazed, used to make bold, simple shapes, sometimes with prominent lip or spout for everyday use; beauty of material emphasized. Pottery first Bauhaus department to produce designs which were adopted by industry, e.g. porcelain designs produced by Berlin and Volkstedt factories. On removal of school to Dessau, 1925, ceramic department taken over by Lindig for own production and training of apprentices until 1930s. New Bauhaus buildings in Dessau designed by Gropius, who was succeeded as director (1928) by L. *Mies van der Rohe. School closed by Nazi government in 1933. Work continued by Moholy-Nagy in America from late 1930s. *Illustrations at Bogler, T., Brandt, M., Wagenfeld, W.*

Baumgarten Tapestry Factory. First tapestry works in America. Founded 1893 in Fifth Avenue, New York, by William Baumgarten, with a Mr Foussadier, former weaver at *Royal Windsor Tapestry Manufactory, as masterweaver, and dyer. Low-warp looms used. Initially produced only furniture panels; first piece, a Louis XV chair seat. Moved shortly to Williamsbridge, New York. Foussadier recruited French weavers from Aubusson. Began to make decorative tapestries in Gothic manner and to reproduce François Boucher's Gobelin designs; also repaired old European tapestries. By 1904, highly successful, receiving large private commissions. Closed in 1912.

Bauscher Brothers. German porcelain factory established at Weiden (Bavaria) in 1881; also made ironstone china. Produced table service designed by P. *Behrens (c1901). Firm sold (1927) to *Hutschenreuther family.

*Hilda Beardmore. Porcelain ginger-jar and cover made by B. *Moore; decorated by Hilda Beardmore in red flambé glaze. Marked Barnard Moore, England, and artist's monogram in red flambé. Height 6in.*

Bay State Glass Company. American glasshouse founded 1853 in Cambridge, Massachusetts. Produced plain, moulded, cut and engraved flint glass, lamp chimneys, and mirrors. Closed c1877.

Bazan (1834-97). Japanese netsuke artist, born in Gifu. Worked in Ogaki (Gifu), and Tokyo. Carved wooden netsuke in realistic style from vast range of designs based on nature drawings. *Chomei: Bazan, usually signed in embossed characters.

Beardmore, Hilda (fl 20th century). English ceramic decorator. With J. *Adams and D. *Billington, worked for B. *Moore during period 1905-15. Work signed with monogram includes covered jar painted with dragons in *flambé* glaze on buff ground.

Beauvais (Oise). French tapestry works established 1664. Provisionally amalgamated with Gobelins 1848; re-established 1860-70. Thereafter, worked for state, making e.g. furniture covers for diplomats' houses and state buildings; subjects mainly fashionable military themes, copies of 18th century designs by François Boucher and Jean-Baptiste Oudry, or designs commissioned from popular painters. Wall tapestries secondary product: most imitated well-known paintings or 18th century tapestry panels; occasionally, contemporary designs by academic painters used, e.g. portrait of Jeanne Hachette by Frédéric Cormon, c1900. Jean Ajalbert (director 1917-c1930) opposed continuing reproduction of copies: commissioned cartoons from contemporary painters, e.g. R. *Dufy. Tapestry works granted managerial autonomy by state in 1926, and allowed to undertake private commissions. Several exhibitions of work held in Paris and Beauvais. Artistic committee of Gobelins and Beauvais instituted (1933) to supervise choice of subjects and patterns. Attached to Mobilier National in 1936

(under direction of Guillaume Janneau of Gobelins). Made replicas of Chabal-Dessurgey tapestries in Elysée Palace, Paris, to replace worn-out originals. In 1939, transferred to Aubusson, but building wrecked 1940. Then installed in buildings of Gobelins and Mobilier National until new premises built in 1946.

Becquerel, André-Vincent (fl 20th century). French *animalier* sculptor; pupil of P. *Lecourtier; exhibited at Salon, 1914-22; specialized in studies of racehorses, e.g. group, The Finish, showing two racehorses in close finish.

Bedford Works. *See* Ridgway, Edward John.

Behrens, Peter (1868-1940). German architect and designer. Among members of Munich

Below
André-Vincent. Becquerel. Bronze group of two swallows, gilded. c1920. Inscribed on base. Height 13in.

Bottom
Peter Behrens. Electric kettle designed for A.E.G., c1908.

School. Designed glassware, jewellery, furniture, and porcelain from mid 1890s. At Matildenhöhe artists' colony, Darmstadt, 1899–1903, built, decorated, and furnished own house (1901). Initial metalwork designs, like interior of house, influenced by Jugendstil (e.g. silver cutlery designed c1900 for exhibition at Matildenhöhe). Two porcelain table services (c1901), produced at factory of *Bauscher Brothers; octagonal in form and decorated with simple geometrical designs. By 1902, designed Hessian interior, rectilinear in style, shown at Turin Exhibition. 1903–07: director of Düsseldorf art school. From 1907, chief architect and design director for electrical firm AEG, Berlin. Work includes turbine works (1909), other factories, workers' housing, advertising, and products, e.g. fans, kettles, street lamps, and coffee jug. Designs appear in yearbooks of Deutscher Werkbund as examples of functional objects suitable for industrial mass-production. Professor of Advanced Architecture at Prussian Academy, Berlin, from 1920s; pupils include *Le Corbusier, W. *Gropius, L. *Mies van der Rohe.

Belknap Hardware & Manufacturing Company. American firm in Louisville, Kentucky, flourishing c1900, and still in business. Large-scale maker of wide range of popular hearth furniture, including coal vases, fire irons, andirons, in variety of materials, e.g. gunmetal, brass, iron, bronze; many elaborately wrought and decorated, with ornament and motifs drawn eclectically from spectrum of 19th century styles.

Bell, John (1811–95). English metalwork designer and sculptor; exhibited at Royal Academy, 1832–79. From 1847, commissioned by Felix *Summerly's Art Manufactures to provide original sculpture for reduction and reproduction, e.g. figure, Dorothea, later made in parian ware by Mintons; also designed (1848) bread knife (now in Victoria & Albert Museum, London), engraved with naturalistic figures of children sowing and reaping, with handle in shape of corn-on-the-cob. Showed bronze and ormolu domestic groups of Queen and Prince of Wales at Great Exhibition, London (1851). Commissioned (1850–60) by W. T. *Copeland and Mintons to provide originals for editions in parian ware. Designs marked JOHN BELL, with Minton or Copeland trademark. Public sculpture includes Guards Memorial, Waterloo Place, London (1858–60), and group, America, on Albert Memorial, Kensington Gardens, London (1861).

Bell, John (d 1880) and Matthew, P. (d 1869). Glasgow potters; established company, J. & M. P. Bell & Co., operating Glasgow Pottery from 1842. Made wide range of high-quality earthenware, white, transfer-printed, or enamelled and gilt, shown at Great Exhibition (1851). Parian jugs and vases also on display; figures and busts produced by 1853. Later, porcelain and granite ware introduced. Printed marks include eagle holding name of pattern over J. & M.P.B. & Co., vase with leaf scrolls and name of firm, and later, versions of bell trademark. After 1881, Ltd incorporated in marks. Pottery operated under other companies until 1940.

Belleek factory. Irish porcelain factory, operated from c1863 in County Fermanagh, originally by firm trading as D. McBirney & Co. Version of parian paste, characteristically covered with iridescent glaze, used to make table and ornamental ware, often modelled in shape of shells and other marine forms. Centrepieces, ice pails, and comports frequently combine matt parian paste with nacreous glazed portions. Perforated decoration and strips woven into basketwork occur, with applied flowers and shells. Many original models still in production. Parian ware sometimes marked BELLEEK. CO FERMANAGH, impressed. Printed trademark of Irish wolfhound and harp, over label BELLEEK, appears on tableware; from c1891, sketchier version of trademark over CO. FERMANAGH IRELAND.

'Belleek', or **eggshell china.** In America, delicate, thinly-potted porcelain tableware, similar to that produced by Irish Belleek factory. First made in America at Ott & Brewer factory in mid 1880s, probably by workmen from Ireland. Other makers include Willets Manufacturing Co., Ceramic Art Co., and Columbian Art Pottery.

bellied measure. Baluster-shaped English *ale measure.

bell push. Highly decorative examples as part of electric bell system, used for summoning servants. Produced in Norway and Russia, e.g. in gold, silver, wood and hardstone, decorated with

enamel and gemstones, with particularly fine versions from *Fabergé.

Bell Works. *See* Clementson, Joseph.

Belter, John Henry (1804–63). German-born furniture maker, with salon and workshop in New York by 1844. Known for rococo style parlour and bedroom suites in rosewood. Perfected method of laminating and bending 4–16 layers of rosewood, allowing elaborate carving; motifs included cornucopias, naturalistic flowers, fruit, vines, etc. Employed c40 apprentices, many German immigrants. Furniture made 1856–61 marked: J. H. BELTER & CO./ FACTORY WAREHOUSE/3rd Avenue 76th St 552 Broadway/MANUFACTURERS OF/ALL KINDS OF FINE FURNITURE/NEW YORK.

Beluchi rugs. *See* Afghan carpets.

Benares brassware. Hand-made Indian brasswork, e.g. trays, table tops, salvers, distinguishable from imitations by correct ornament: typically, series of engravings of 10 incarnations of Vishnu. Also, English engraved brass ornamental ware, sold as native Indian work; made mainly in Birmingham during late 19th century; many pieces exported to India, and subsequently re-imported.

Bennett, Edwin (fl mid to late 19th century). American potter, born in England. Established pottery in Baltimore, Maryland (1846). In partnership with brother, William (1848–56), trading as E & W Bennett; work marked with name of company and address, Canton Ave., Baltimore, Md. From 1856, initials EB form

several versions of mark. Unglazed porcelain jugs made in hard green or blue body, with relief decoration, e.g. marine jug with marine motifs, fish etc., in relief. Earthenware teapot depicting Rebekah at the Well in relief, modelled from Staffordshire design, covered with 'Rockingham' glaze. Majolica, made from c1853, includes large jugs with moulded decoration of fish, lobsters, and shells, covered with light blue glaze. Decorative vases, coffee pots, etc., have blue, brown, or olive-green mottled glazes. Tableware made in white earthenware or semi-porcelain, sometimes with transfer-printed designs. Also made parian porcelain in late 19th century.

Benoîton chain. Hair ornament popularized c1865–70 by Victorien Sardou's comedy *'La Famille Benoîton'*. Chain, either plain or decorated to look like string of flowers, attached

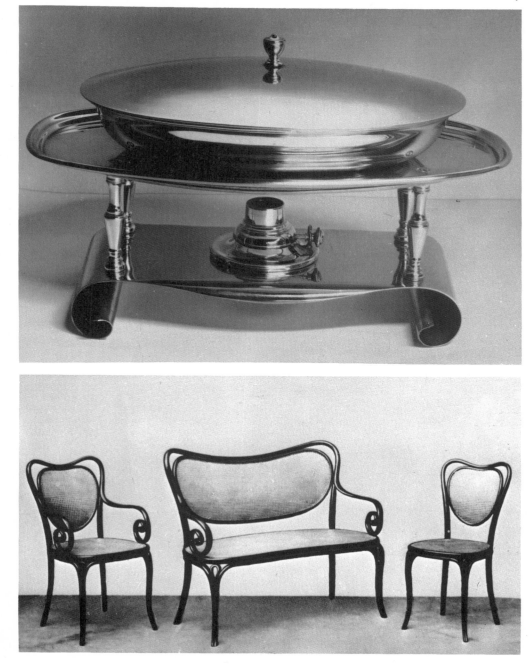

to headdress or hair behind ears, falling like a necklace round front of neck. Originally designed to hang from bonnet.

Benson, William Arthur Smith (1854–1924). English architect, furniture and metalwork designer, In 1880, opened workshop for production of turned metalwork on commercial scale; encouraged by friend W. *Morris, for whom designed decorative metalwork, and some furniture. Opened factory at Hammersmith, London, c1883 (closed after his retirement 1923); showroom in Bond Street, London, from 1887. Produced mainly useful and domestic objects, e.g. tea kettles, fenders, electric lamps, in brass, copper and electro-plate. Simple vessels in brass and copper influenced A. *Dixon and L. *Rathbone. With others, founded *Art Workers Guild (1884), *Arts and Crafts Exhibition Society

(1887); wrote 'Elements of Handicraft and Design' (1893). Designs unique in Arts and Crafts Movement because intended for machine mass-production. Director of furniture department of Morris & Co. from 1896. Furniture, often in rosewood, characterized by inlays (e.g. tulip, ebony, and purple wood) and elaborate metal mounts.

Benten or **Benzai-ten.** One of Japanese *Shichi-fuku-jin. Goddess of knowledge, eloquence, wisdom, education, beauty, talent, music, poetry and fine arts. Only female among group. Usually shown seated (often riding dragon, her messenger), wearing long flowing robe and crown, and holding either lute or sacred jewel (cf takaramono) and key.

bento-bako (Japanese, 'picnic box' or 'lunch box'). In Japanese lacquer, small fitted cabinets (c12×14×6in.), holding matching boxes, trays, *sakazuke and sake bottle. Date mainly from 19th and 20th centuries.

bentwood box. 19th century oval country-style trinket-box, made in Europe and America (particularly Pennsylvania). Thin sheet of light wood soaked in hot water until pliable, then bent round mould and bound with split willow thongs or small wooden pegs. Often varnished and painted in primary colours with stencilled floral motifs.

bentwood furniture. Furniture made from solid or laminated wood, steamed and bent into curvilinear shapes. Technique originally applied to 18th century Windsor chairs; perfected in mid 19th century by M. *Thonet, whose mass-produced, solid, bentwood furniture sold in great quantities in Britain, Europe, and America. Technique widely applied to laminated wood in 20th century, e.g. by H. A. H. *Aalto and M. *Breuer.

Benzai-ten. *See* Benten.

Bergama, Turkey. Traditionally, red rugs of wool or goat-hair hand-knotted by nomads in Bergama region. In late 19th century, new types created for European and American markets, e.g. large, square carpets to fit Western rooms, with central medallions, ornate angles, and overall floral patterns.

Bergé, Henri (d 1930). French painter, sculptor, and glass artist. In collaboration with A. *Walter in Nancy, designed thick bowls and dishes in *pâte-de-verre* decorated with e.g. neat sprays of berries or flowers. Marks: B in shape of a sheep (for work with Walter); Bergé on own pieces.

bergère en gondole. French armchair with upholstered seat, back, and arms, curved to encompass body; narrow, continuous wooden arm rests and back rail. Dates from 18th century;

Above left
W. A. S. Benson. Chafing dish and cover. Silver with brass finial to cover and spirit burner. Made by W. A. S. Benson & Co. Marked Benson on underside of dish and top of stand. Designed c1895. Height 8in.

Left
Bentwood furniture. Set of chair, armchair and canapé by *Thonet Brothers. c1911.

Bergère en gondole. *Giltwood. French, c1920-30. Height 27in.*

modified for coil *spring upholstery in 1830s. By 1860s, framework hidden by cushions and upholstery, but basic outline persisted. Shape used in Art Deco furniture, e.g. by P. *Chareau.

Bergh, Elis (1881-1954). Swedish glass artist in Functionalist style. Designer for *Kosta from 1927. Worked chiefly in restrained cut glass decoration, usually in undulating lines. Made goblets, water jugs; also bowls, vases and other decorative ware.

Berkey & Gay. American furniture manufacturers in Grand Rapids, Michigan; established 1862 as Berkey & Mather. Employed many foreign craftsmen. Known for Renaissance revival style designs in 1870s; showed work at Philadelphia Centennial Exhibition, 1876.

Berlage, Hendrik Petrus (1856-1934). Dutch architect, also designed furniture and metalwork. Published arguments for craftsmanship and logical design widely influential from c1895. Architect in Amsterdam from 1889. Designed metalwork lamps, candelabra, and silver tableware in Art Nouveau style. Mark: B in oval. Furniture pieces have clear structural outlines uncluttered by ornamentation, e.g. oak buffet, c1900, with boldly defined horizontals and verticals, centre panels with animals, birds, and fish carved in low-relief. Many pieces made in Het Binnenhuis (The Interior) workshop, Amsterdam.

Berlin. German porcelain factory purchased (1763) by Frederick the Great and operating as Königliche Porzellan Manufaktur or, from end of 1st World War, Staatliche Porzellan Manufaktur in Berlin. Noted for production of lithophanes (c1830-c1850). Imitations of majolica shown in Paris Exhibition (1867). Among European factories concerned with elaborate glaze effects under oriental influence in late 19th century as seen in work of H. Seeger; also continued work in styles of 18th century. T. *Schmuz-Baudisz, decorator from 1902 and art director 1908-26, introduced large tiles decorated with landscapes. J. *Wackerle employed as modeller from c1910. Table decora-

*Berkey & Gay. Walnut dining table, made at *Grand Rapids. 1873. Diameter 4ft, but can be extended to 12ft3in. long.*

Berlin. Porcelain vase. Marked with transfer-printed blue sceptre and artist's initials. c1900. Height 10in.

tion from models made by sculptor, Adolf Amberg, to celebrate wedding of German Crown Prince (1905), produced for display in Berlin Art Exhibition (1911); procession of figures includes The Bride as Europa on the Bull. P. *Scheurich modelled figures, including Daphne and Apollo (c1925). While producing porcelain e.g. from designs by ceramics department of Bauhaus, and table service designed by M. *Wildenhain, continued to make tableware, etc. with high-quality painted floral decoration. Marks: in mid 19th century, orb or eagle printed, sceptre printed or impressed, all with initials KPM; from 1870, printed sceptre.

Berlin transparency. *See* lithophane.

Berlin woolwork or **German embroidery.** 19th century vogue in Europe and America for canvas work originated in Berlin c1804 with publication of printed embroidery designs, on paper squared up for transfer to canvas. Design worked on canvas squares in tent and tapestry stitches in Berlin wool (sometimes incorporating cut-pile areas), and/or coloured silks and beads; squares then sewn together and finished with border. Complete sets of materials (paper patterns, canvas squares, wool) with instructions manufactured in Berlin by 1830s and exported to France and England (where soon also produced,

Berlin woolwork. Rug, wool on canvas. c1860. 4ft8in. × 2ft9in.

but with designs printed directly on canvas). Also exported to America, rapidly becoming extremely fashionable (known as Zephyrs). Subjects often taken from well-known paintings. Used for e.g. fire-screens, chair seats, cushion covers.

Bernadotte, Sigvard (b 1907). Swedish industrial designer, son of King Gustav VI. Joined G. *Jensen as silver designer (1931); remained until 1947. Designs, e.g. for flatware, angular, with straight lines and sharp points; characteristic ornamentation of incised parallel lines.

Bernardaud & Cie. *See* Limoges.

berry bowl. *See* fruit bowl.

berry spoon. Spoon with broad bowl for eating small soft fruits; larger and heavier than teaspoon; bowls and handles engraved and embossed with fruit motifs. Made in silver, silver gilt, or electro-plate; sold in sets of six; introduced c1870.

Besche, Lucien (d 1901). French-born porcelain painter, worked in England. At Mintons (1871)

Paul Beyer. Stoneware bird, and jug in form of human face. Height 6½in.

and factory of W. T. *Copeland (c1872–85), painted figure subjects in style of Antoine Watteau. Signed work exists. From 1885, painter, illustrator, and costume designer in London.

Beshir rugs. From district adjoining Khiva in West Turkestan. Coarse to medium texture; patterns often floral, unlike most central Asian rugs; predominant colour yellow, also red, brown, and dark blue.

Besnard, Jean (b 1889). French artist potter. Stoneware, exhibited at Salon des Tuileries and Salon d'Automne (1927–37), decorated notably with bold, incised motifs. Marks include scribbled monogram, and balloon-shape containing + V, over Blois and two curved lines.

Bevan, Charles (fl 1860s). English furniture designer and manufacturer; known for Gothic Reform style furniture. Employed by *Marsh, Jones & Cribb, 1865; also designed for J. *Lamb.

Beyer, Paul (d 1945). French artist potter. Regarded as instrumental in revival of salt-glazed stoneware in France in 1920s and 1930s. Stoneware and glass shown at Salon d'Automne (1921–37). Worked at Sèvres, then revived pottery in region of Berry. Figures often thrown, e.g. small rounded duck with bill formed by short pipe of clay, split and opened; feathers represented by streaks of grey and chestnut pigment arranged in bands. Tall, salt-glazed vase (1935) has rounded cover with prominent finial, and stand with four feet made by cutting out semi-circular pieces of clay.

bibelot. Small object of vertu. Term used most often for articles displayed on whatnots, étagères, chimney pieces, etc.

Bichweiler. German earthenware manufacturer working in Hamburg in late 19th century. Among potteries influenced by traditional styles; work includes moulded plates with border of flowers and foliage, and central panel depicting mounted knight with bands of Gothic lettering (1880).

Bichweiler. Earthenware dish with relief decoration. 1880.

Bidri ware. Indian metalwork produced by craftsmen in area of Deccan from 17th century. Name derived from Bidar, one-time capital of Muslim kingdom in Deccan. Objects, e.g. betel-nut box and cover, spice-box, hookah, cast in alloys of zinc, copper, tin, and lead, then chased and inlaid with silver; alloy subsequently blackened by pickling in mixture of sal-ammoniac and saltpetre, giving distinctive black and white appearance. Large quantities exported to England in 19th century.

Big Ben. *See* Westminster Palace Clock.

Bigelow, Erastus Brigham (1814–79). American inventor and industrialist. Invented steam-powered lace loom in 1837, followed by power looms for counterpanes, ginghams, and other figured fabrics. Commissioned (1939) by Lowell Manufacturing Co. of Boston, Massachusetts, to devise power machinery for carpet industry. Produced first power carpet loom for ingrain carpets in 1841. In 1843, with brother, established gingham factory in Massachusetts, around which town of Clinton eventually grew. Invented power looms for Brussels, Wilton, and tapestry carpets, 1845–51. Founded Bigelow Carpet Mills at Clinton c1860.

Bigot, Alexandre (1862–1927). French artist potter from 1892, formerly chemist. Technical adviser to J. *Carriès. Some work in earthenware (c1895) has silver mounts by E. *Colonna. From c1896, specialized in stoneware with *flambé* or greenish-yellow glazes. Also made stoneware for architectural use.

Bijar or **Bidjar rugs.** *See* Persian carpets.

billiards clock. Coin-triggered *time switch operated by clock mechanism; switches on lights over billiards table for predetermined time. In bar billiards, similar mechanism controls release of balls and thus duration of game.

*Alexandre Bigot. Enamelled stoneware jug, mounted in silver by E. *Colonna. c1895. Height 8¾in.*

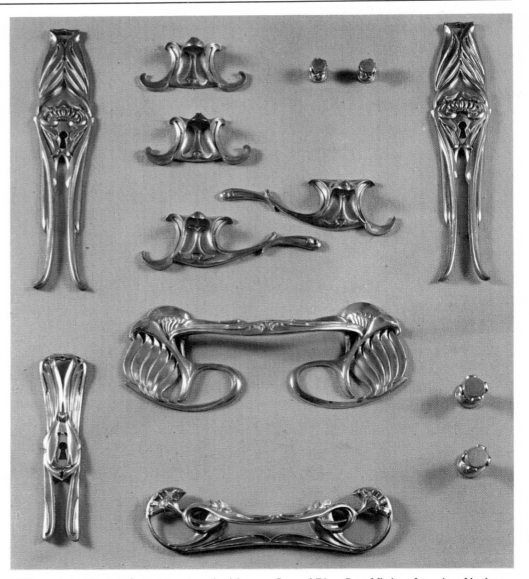

Billies and Charlies. Spurious antiquities supposedly recovered from bed of river Thames, London; in fact, made by William Smith and Charles Eaton during second quarter of 19th century, following their discovery of genuine 15th century medal in Thames, sold to British Museum for large sum. Smith and Eaton subsequently made own medals, seals, goblets, weapons, etc., distributing them to other shore-rakers to pass off as discoveries. Objects, cast in cock metal (cheap alloy of lead), have pseudo-Latin inscriptions, and dates in Arabic instead of Roman numerals, yet not proved to be spurious until trial of dealer accused of selling fakes in 1858; despite this, several respected experts identified them as genuine. After trial notoriety of pieces caused demand, so more produced. Less than 1000 objects made by Smith and Eaton, but many more attributed to them; both fake and real Billies & Charlies (usually indistinguishable) now collected as curios.

Billington, Dora (fl from early 20th century). English artist potter and teacher. Studied at Hanley, Staffordshire, and South Kensington, London. Teacher, and later head of pottery department at Central School of Arts & Crafts,

*Samuel Bing. Set of fittings for suite of bedroom furniture, made by G. *de Feure for La Maison de l'Art Nouveau. 1900.*

London. In early 1930s, designed and decorated pottery for industrial firms, e.g. J. & G. Meakin. Work includes stoneware coffee set hand-painted with grassy leaves. Mark: monogram of DB, incised.

Bimann, Dominik (1800–57). Bohemian master glass engraver; specialist in portrait engraving, chiefly as flat medallions or on drinking glasses and goblets. Also engraved horses and hunting scenes. Worked first in Prague, then Franzen-bad. Marks: D. Bimann; DB; Bi; Biman; Bimann; D. Biemann, and, after 1830, Biemann.

bim-bam clock. *See* ting-tang clock.

Bindesbøll, Thorvald (1846–1908). Danish designer; pioneer artist potter in 1880s. Working alone, made ornamental earthenware, e.g. plate, signed and dated (1893), and vase with bold, flower-like motifs in cream glaze on black glaze ground (also 1893).

*William Birch. Oak armchair decorated with ebony inlay; rush seat and back panels. Designed by E. G. *Punnett. 1901.*

Biscuit tins. Left: casket tin, 'Watteau', produced in 1903. Right: Motor van, produced for children in 1920s.

Bing & Gröndahls Porcellaensfabrik. Danish porcelain factory established (1853) in Copenhagen. Also produced stoneware and earthenware; frequently followed styles of Royal Copenhagen factory. Original, progressive work includes *heron service designed by P. *Krohn, art director (1888). Painting in blue which combines with glaze during firing used from c1910, usually on porcelain, sometimes on stoneware for household use. Figures made in porcelain and, later, mainly stoneware, e.g. by K. *Nielsen and J. *Gauguin.

Bing, Samuel (1838–1905). German connoisseur, publisher and art dealer who did much to promote French Art Nouveau. Encouraged interest in Japanese art. Introduced H. *van de Velde to Paris. In 1895, opened shop, La Maison de l'Art Nouveau, selling furniture and wide range of decorative arts including glass by E. *Gallé and L.C. *Tiffany, jewellery by R. *Lalique and E. *Grasset, posters by Aubrey Beardsley, furniture and jewellery by E. *Colonna. Bing had special Art Nouveau pavilion at 1900 Paris Exhibition, with rooms designed and furnished by E. *Colonna, G. *de Feure and E. *Gaillard.

Bingham, Edward (b 1829). English potter, working (c1864–99) with family at *Hedingham Art Pottery in Essex. Made over pottery to son, who worked as manager after selling works (1901), then emigrated to America (by 1905).

Binnenhuis workshop. *See* Berlage, Hendrick Petrus.

Binns, Charles Fergus (1857–1934). American potter and teacher, born in England. From 1900, director of *New York School of Clay Working. Book, The Potter's Craft, published in 1922. Fostered concept of artist potter, working alone. Austerely styled stoneware, influenced by Ch'ing dynasty wares, made in coal-burning kiln at Alfred University, New York.

Birch, C.B. (fl late 19th century). English sculptor and silver designer. Race trophies designed for *Hancocks in 1880s and 1890s usually with circular panel of relief sculpture in centre, surrounded by bands of moulding and chased or engraved ornament, sometimes interspersed with small panels in low relief or with portrait medallions. Some purely classical, e.g. Royal Hunt Cup for Ascot (1885), with head of Amazon in centre surrounded by frieze of Amazons on horseback.

Birch, William Ltd. English chair makers, established 1840 in High Wycombe, Buckinghamshire; specialized in versions of traditional Windsor chair; also made other types, e.g. Oxford chair. Later added cabinet making to repertoire. Pioneered use of machinery in chair manufacture in 1870s; exported to Europe and America. Made Quaint style furniture designed by E. G. *Punnett.

birchwood. Fine-grained wood; light brown with silver streaks in Britain and Europe, yellow in America. Used for country furniture during 18th century; cheap, mass-produced pieces from c1850. Veneers used extensively for plywood after 1890. In 1930s, used notably by H. A. H. *Aalto.

birdcage. Many large and small decorative examples, e.g. in brass or copper wire, made throughout 19th century; designs reflected current tastes, e.g. versions in Gothic and Moorish styles.

birdcage hook. Curved or angular piece of metal, secured to wall or ceiling, from which birdcage suspended; made from antiquity. 19th and early 20th century American versions in e.g. cast-iron, brass, bronze, bronzed wire; wide variety of design and ornament. Mass-produced by large American foundries, and advertised in catalogues as part of vast range of cast-metal fittings, fixings, and furnishings.

Birley, Samuel (fl 1850–60). English designer and furniture maker; worked in *Derbyshire marble at Ashford, Derbyshire. Won medals in furniture and mining classes of International Exhibition in London, 1862, for marble-topped pedestal table: black top, inlaid with different coloured marbles, etc. depicts flowers, foliage, and birds.

Birmingham. Important English glass making centre. Known especially for fine engraved glass, decorative ware, and novelties in coloured glass. Made earliest British *pressed glass; also, *fairy lights, *paperweights, *Rusticana, and fine *centrepieces. Chief glasshouses from 1851 to early 20th century: G. *Bacchus & Sons, *Lloyd & Summerfield, F. & C. *Osler, and *Rice, Harris & Sons.

Birmingham Guild of Handicraft. Cooperative association of metalworkers founded 1890 by A. *Dixon; modelled on C. R. *Ashbee's Guild of Handicraft. Limited company from 1895; worked in silver and base metal. After merging with two other firms of metalworkers in 1910 and 1919–20, employed almost 300 workers by 1921. Silver, in simple shapes with little decoration, usually hammered and lightly burnished; lathe only machinery used. Work includes silver chalice for Coventry church of St John Baptist. Produced architectural work in 1930s, e.g. decorative and semi-structural ironwork in Selfridge's London store and gates for Government House in Delhi. Variety of products ranged from iron fire grates to jewellery; firm now specializes in agricultural machinery and light engineering plants. Mark: BGHLD. *Illustration at* Dixon, A.

biscuit tin. Tin container, usually rectangular, but also in novelty shapes, e.g. octagon, heart, animal, book, produced c1861–1939 by biscuit manufacturers. Process of transfer-printing on to tin plate, patented 1860 by Benjamin George, soon adopted on biscuit boxes to replace paper labels. Huntley & Palmer, at own tin works, produced commemorative box, designed by O. *Jones, to celebrate granting of royal warrant (1868). Improved method of offset litho printing

(introduced 1875 by John Doyle Fry and Robert Barclay) gave more robust transfer, so possible to emboss and shape tin. New designs usually introduced at Christmas; reflected events of previous year, e.g. Queen Victoria's Diamond Jubilee (1897), or current decorative styles, e.g. picture-frame version by Mackenzie & Mackenzie (c1900) with Art Nouveau motifs.

Bishamon. One of the *Shichi-fuku-jin; god of masculinity, strength, power and martial spirit. Guardian of north quarter of heavens; patron of soldiers. Portrayed in full armour with spear in right hand, pagoda in left. Sometimes shown overwhelming demon. Messenger, centipede.

Bizarre ware. See Cliff, Clarice, Wilkinson, A.J. Ltd.

Bizen. Japanese pottery centre near Okayama. Unglazed, reddish-brown stoneware produced

from 13th century. Potters maintained traditional styles and techniques.

Blackband, William Thomas (1885–1949). English silversmith; studied at Vittoria Street School for Jewellers and Goldsmiths, Birmingham, while apprenticed to local goldsmith. After scholarship course at Central School of Art, Birmingham, returned to Vittoria Street as part-time teacher, 1909; succeeded A. *Gaskin as headmaster, 1924. In later life concentrated on commissions for Roman Catholic Church; produced many necklaces and pendants. After 20 years' experiment, succeeded in reproducing granulation effect of classical antiquity; claimed (1927) that success was due to reconstructing ancient working conditions, and that ancient craftsmen, using techniques of extreme simplicity, had no special knowledge. Mark: W. T. Blackband.

Black Forest clocks. Inexpensive German wall clocks manufactured by peasant craftsmen in Baden and Württemberg from c1640. Earliest clocks with weight-driven foliot movement entirely of wood; c1730–40, pendulum and striking work incorporated. Typical example has arched dial plate with hand-painted floral motifs; bells initially of glass, later metal. Many types, usually weight-driven, include cuckoo, quail (rare), trumpeter, and *picture-frame clocks; exported throughout Europe by c1830. By mid 19th century, wooden movements replaced by brass; cottage industry superseded by factory production, notably by *Junghans at Schramberg, to compete with mass-produced American exports (e.g. *OG clock). Factory products included enclosed spring and weight-driven shelf and wall clocks imitating American

Left
Bizen. Stoneware cylindrical chawan (tea bowl) glazed red with variations produced during firing.

William Thomas Blackband. Silver bowl decorated with doves and stylized flowers in applied gold. Made in Birmingham, 1929. Width 4in.

designs (c1860–70); decorated automaton and musical clocks; *postman's alarm, exported to England from c1860. Up to 4000 clocks per day produced by 1890. Some reproduction German medieval antique clocks, dated 1492, made for Columbia Exposition, 1893. *Napoleon and *400-day clocks made from c1880 to early 20th century. Industry flourished until World War I.

Black, Starr & Frost. New York jewellers and silversmiths. Founded 1810 by Isaac Marquand as Marquand & Co. (1810); then traded as Ball, Tompkins & Black (from 1839), Ball, Black & Co. (1851), Black, Starr & Frost (1876), Black, Starr, Frost-Gorham Inc. (1929), Black, Starr & Gorham (1940), and Black, Starr & Frost (1962). From 1810 had shop on Broadway which became known as 'The Diamond Palace of Broadway' as reputation grew; patronized by Edward VII as Prince of Wales. Were diamond dealers, but imported currently fashionable jewellery from Europe and stocked pieces made by American manufacturing jewellers.

Blackwood, Morton & Sons, Kilmarnock (BMK). British carpet manufacturers. Thriving late 19th century Scottish *ingrain and *art square industry in Kilmarnock, with several factories active, declined rapidly in 1900s with rise of *spool Axminster carpet. Only factory remaining in 1908, Robert Blackwood & Sons, taken over by Gavin Morton and William Ford Blackwood. Continued ingrain and art square production until 1914, and introduced reversible chenille rugs. After 1st World War, whole plant turned over to chenille square and rug manufacture.

blanc. See ébauche.

blind man's or **braille watch,** or **montre à tact.** For telling time by touch, e.g. at night. Pocket watch has studs or touchpieces set at hour points on band of case; approximate time found by rotating single pointer on outside of back cover until stopped by internal mechanism, then checking position relative to touchpiece. Devised by A-L. Breguet c1790; also made in early 19th century, e.g. by J.F. *Cole. Other versions have touchpieces graduated in five-minute intervals, or unglazed dial encircled by swivelling outer ring with pointer which catches at hour hand.

blinking eye clocks. See novelty clocks.

Blomfield, Sir Reginald (1856–1942). English architect; member of *Kenton & Co., designing rosewood furniture based on 18th century designs. Member of *Arts & Crafts Exhibition Society, exhibiting in 1890.

bloodstone. Dark green chalcedony flecked with spots of blood-red jasper. Used mainly for signet rings.

bloomed, matted or **dead gold.** Gold dipped in acid solution, which slightly pits surface, giving delicate, matt appearance; very popular in late 19th century jewellery. Known in America as dead gold.

blotter. Mount for absorbent blotting paper used to soak up excess ink when writing. Main 19th century form, small solid piece of hard material having flat back with stub handle and convex,

Boch Frères. Stoneware vase with applied decoration. Mid 19th century.

curved bottom to which blotting paper attached. Mould made of wood, or plain or embossed silver, with elaborately ornamented metal (brass, silver, or gold) back, often encrusted with semi-precious stones, or inlaid with various materials; most common late 19th and early 20th centuries. Also made entirely in metal, in polished woods, Tunbridge ware, papier mâché, porcelain, etc. Sometimes with two lidded compartments in top for postage stamps. In early 20th century, form largely replaced by large, flat picture-frame style designed to rest on desk or writing table and fitted with sheet of blotting paper. Made of metal, wood, etc.; with decorative sides and corners of leather, ivory, tortoiseshell, porcelain, etc., securing paper in place. Both forms often made as items in matching desk sets.

Blue Amberina. *See* flashed glass.

blue john, or **Derbyshire spar.** Colourful variety of crystalline fluorite from Castleton, Derbyshire. Banded in white, blue, purple, and yellow. First mined by Romans, then largely unused until 1743 when mine reopened. In late 18th century and again in late 19th century, blue john fashionable material for candelabra, vases and small objects of vertu, particularly *hand-coolers, *scent-bottles, *walking stick and parasol handles.

boatswain's whistle. Shrill whistle used to pipe naval officers aboard ship. Usually made in base metal. Presentational or ceremonial versions made of silver in 18th and 19th centuries; most examples 1850-80. Normally decorated with bright-cut engraving. Still used in Navy.

Boch Frères. Belgium firm, branch of German company, Villeroy & Boch; established Keramis pottery (1841) at La Louvière (Hainault). Made transfer-printed earthenware for table and toilet use. Imitations of Delft and Middle Eastern tin-glazed ware also made. Produced designs of A. W. *Finch and, later, M. *Goupy. Tiles made from 1880s at branch factory in France, established (1861) at Maubeuge (Nord).

Boch, Jean-François (d 1858). German potter; manufactured faience at Septfontaines, Luxembourg, and established business at Mettlach (Rhineland) in 1809, which became part of association *Villeroy & Boch (formed 1836).

Boch, William (fl mid to late 19th century). American potter, born in Germany. With brother, opened kiln at Greenpoint, Long Island. Using bone porcelain, made door furniture, etc. Involved with number of firms, e.g. reopened (1857) factory of C. *Cartlidge (had closed in 1856). Firm sold in 1861 and traded thereafter as *Union Porcelain Works.

Böck, Joseph (fl early 20th century). Viennese porcelain manufacturer; in early 20th century, commissioned designs inspired by prevalent Art Nouveau (*see* Vienna Secession) style. Artists include D. *Peche. Marks usually incorporate name or initials.

bodkin case. Small, usually cylindrical, case for bodkins (small pointed instruments with large eye used to draw tape through hem or loop). Made in 18th and 19th centuries. Materials and designs as *needlecase.

Bodley, George Frederick (1827-1907). English architect and designer, born in Hull; studied under George Gilbert Scott, 1845-50. Architectural practice, in partnership with Thomas Cramer, from 1859; first architect to commission decorative work from *Morris & Co., 1862. Instrumental in setting up Watts & Co., for whom designed fabrics, wallpapers, furniture and metalwork in Gothic style strongly influenced by W. *Morris, and Arts and Crafts movement, e.g. chalice and paten made for St Mary's Church, Hendon, London, 1893, in silver gilt, with engraved and pierced decoration.

bog oak. Hard wood, stained dark brown from centuries buried in peat bogs. Used for inlay work in 16th century. Carved bog oak objects popular after Great Exhibition, London, 1851, when examples shown, until c1885. Widely used in Ireland for mourning jewellery carved with motifs popular in jet jewellery, e.g. brooches with flowers and crosses.

Bogler, Theodor (fl 20th century). German potter; apprentice under G. *Marcks at Bauhaus department of ceramics. Work includes covered jugs and jars in stoneware, sometimes highly glazed in dark colours; forms often tall. Mark: B

*Theodor Bogler. Earthenware teapot, cup and saucer and sugar bowl, made at *Bauhaus. 1920s.*

with upright formed by shaft of arrow, or below two short lines (like equals sign).

Bohne, E. *See* Volkstedt-Rudolstadt.

Bojesen, Kay (1886-1958). Danish silversmith and silver designer; trained at G. *Jensen and at Royal Craft School for Precious Metals, Württemberg, Germany. Worked as craftsman in Paris and Copenhagen (own workshop there from 1913). From late 1910s, progressively abandoned florid styles in favour of neo-classicism, and then functionalism. c1928, criticized silver makers for giving products spurious air of hand craftsmanship. Silver functional and undecorated with polished surfaces, but differs from early functionalist silver as forms not geometrical, and rounded rather than sharp edged. Designs for cutlery and flatware often reached by modification of existing forms. Grand Prix pattern of silver cutlery and flatware (1938) also made with slight adaptations in stainless steel.

bois durci. Shiny, imitation ebony, patented 1855 in France; introduced in England, c1860. Widely used until c1900 (especially in France). Made from powdered sawdust, usually rosewood, mixed with animal blood and water, then hardened under heat, and die-stamped into e.g. plaques, rosettes, and medallions for ebonized cabinets.

Bokhara rugs. *See* West Turkestan.

Bolin, W.A. Swedish crown jewellers. Firm founded in St Petersburg, c1845, by Carl Edward Bolin; later opened in Moscow. Exhibited at Great Exhibition, London, 1851. Russian crown jewellers until 1915, when Wilhelm Bolin opened shop in Stockholm. Entire remaining stock lost 1917 in Russian Revolution. Produced fashionable, expensive diamond jewellery. Firm continues as Swedish crown jewellers.

bolster arm. Stuffed, cylindrical arm rest, sometimes used on sofas and easy chairs (e.g. Turkish chair) from c1850, in Britain and America. End plain or centrally buttoned.

bonbonnière, or **comfit box.** Small, ornate, box with lid for holding sweetmeats; dates from 18th century in France. Usually round, diameter c3in., sometimes e.g. egg or barrel shaped. Made in gold, silver, porcelain, ivory, tortoiseshell, etc., richly decorated with e.g. enamel, mother-of-pearl, or gold and silver *piqué* work. Popular in France and England throughout 19th century. Unusual example made (1903) in form of drinking horn (c8in. high) by English silversmith, J. P. Cooper: silver-mounted walrus tusk set on oval base encrusted with lapis lazuli beads (to resemble jellyfish) and supported on bifurcated coral branch entwined with twigs of textured silver; other section of coral branch holds two detachable silver cups of irregular shape, beaded and embossed at rim.

Bonniksen, Bahne. *See* karrusel watch.

bookcase. Case or cupboard with shelves for books, usually with glazed doors. Dates from 18th century. Long examples, 4–5ft high, increasingly popular in Britain until c1850; top often leather-covered and used for ornaments; bookshelves below, sometimes silk-lined;

fronted by ormolu or brass grilles (also found in taller models). Also, low breakfront models. Both types made throughout 19th century. Gothic style examples popular, usually c4ft6in. high; other styles also made, e.g. Elizabethan, Early English. Some papier-mâché examples. Also, heavy-based pieces in walnut, low and square, with three shelves, on turned or carved columns. American examples sometimes open-fronted with three or four shelves graduating in height, or adjustable; plain flat tops with moulded edges; also, with glazed doors and scrolling. *See* revolving bookcase.

Boote, T. & R., Ltd. Staffordshire pottery established (1842) by Thomas L. (retired, 1879) and Richard Boote (d 1891) at Kiln Croft Works, Burslem. Produced earthenware with inlaid decoration, mainly sets of jugs; process patented in 1843 by R. Boote. In 1850, firm moved to Waterloo Works. Parian figures and groups, made from 1850, shown at International Exhibition, 1851. Also produced jugs and tall vases in blue parian ware with white relief decoration of vines or flowers and foliage. From c1850, made ironstone china, hand-painted for domestic use; much exported to America. Majolica tiles made in great quantities in late 19th century; patented (1863) method of moulding encaustic decoration from clay dust. Produced plain tiles for lining of Blackwall Tunnel, London (completed 1897); decorated tiles include set of Seasons by Kate Greenaway, with central hand-painted design and transfer-printed border. Marks: T&RB impressed, or printed greyhound between laurel wreaths.

Booths Ltd. Staffordshire earthenware manufacturers established (1864) in Burslem; traded under names Thomas Booth (from 1868) and Thomas G. Booth (from c1876); firm became T. G. & F. Booth (1883–91), then Booths, and Booths Ltd (c1898–1940s). Operated Church Banks, Tunstall, from 1870. In late 1880s, advertised ironstone china for use on ships and in hotels. In late 19th and early 20th centuries, made imitations of early Worcester porcelain in earthenware or semi-porcelain. Some copies marked with crescent-shaped device. (Firm traded as Booths & Colcloughs Ltd, 1948–54.)

Booz bottle. American whiskey bottle in shape of two-storey house; usually of quart capacity. Made from 1860 (but often deliberately antedated by as much as 20 years) by Whitney Glass Works, New Jersey, for Edward G. Booz (d 1870), wine and spirits dealer of Philadelphia, Pennsylvania. Name, address, year, and either Whiskey or Bitters, moulded on roof. Continued in production after Booz's death; imitations made c1931, and more recently in coloured glass.

Bor (near Nigde), Turkey. Greek school of carpet knotting active in late 19th and early 20th centuries. Copied early Ushak garden and hunting carpets, Ghiordes and Kula prayer rugs.

borne. French version of ottoman; circular or quatrefoil. Characterized by fringed or box-pleated edges to seats, covered in damask, cretonne, or plush; often with *jardinière* or vestigial flower stand containing palm in centre. Many exceeded 6ft6in. in diameter. Popular during 1860s; c1900, replaced in private houses by corner sofa.

Bosselt, Rudolf (1871–1938). German sculptor; studied in Frankfurt-am-Main, and Paris (1891–97). Joined artists' colony at Darmstadt, Germany, in 1899. From 1904, professor at academies of decorative arts in Düsseldorf (1904–11), Magdeburg (1911–25), and Braunschweig (1928–31). Produced mainly small sculptures, bronzes, medallions, plaques, and jewellery.

Boston rocker. First chair made specifically for rocking; manufactured in and near Boston, Massachusetts, from early 19th century, becoming standard American rocking chair. Ogee-shaped arms, and curved seat dipping from back and scrolling over in front, complement curves of bends and facilitate rocking. High spindle back has ornamental panel with paintings or stencils of fruit and flowers on comb-shaped yoke rail.

Boston & Sandwich Glass Company. American glasshouse (previously known as Sandwich Manufacturing Co.) incorporated under new name in 1826 by D. *Jarves. Made large variety of pressed glass novelties, becoming known for paperweights and miniature fruits of N. *Lutz; also, decorative ware in *canary, *crackle, *Ruby, and *Tortoiseshell glass. Produced some of best American cameo-cut glass lamps* and ornamental ware of later 19th century, especially *Smith Brothers vases and lampshades; also, threaded glassware with plants and marshland scenes engraved above threading. Ceased production 1888.

Boston Watch Company. *See* Dennison, Aaron L.

bosun's whistle. *See* boatswain's whistle.

Bott, Thomas John (1854–1932). English porcelain painter; son of Worcester factory painter, Thomas Bott. Apprenticed (c1870) and employed at Worcester factory until 1885 or 1886. Painted with white slip in style of Limoges enamel. Thought to have worked as freelance painter, 1886–89. Artist at London workshop of Brown-Westhead, Moore from 1889. Art director at Coalport factory, 1890–1932.

bottle holder. Frame with handle for holding wine bottle: circular plate at base, joined by crook-shaped handle to collar round neck of bottle. Made in late 19th and early 20th centuries, notably by *Elkington & Co. Usually in electro-plate; also made in silver.

bottle opener. Device for levering metal caps from bottles; dates from introduction of these, c1900. Usually made of steel. Many novelty shapes; some examples very ornate, e.g. with silver, jewel-set handles.

bottle ticket or **wine** or **decanter label.** Rectangular, oval, circular, or shield-shaped label, e.g. in silver, Sheffield plate, enamel, porcelain, or pinchbeck, with metal chain, e.g. in silver, to hang round neck of bottle or decanter, and inscribed according to contents, e.g. port, sherry, claret. From c1720, used to specify contents of opaque bottles of the period. Larger, more elaborate examples after c1840 decorated with, e.g. fauns, masks, or engraved or chased with naturalistic floral and foliate motifs; some versions in 1840s appear with pierced inscrip-

Boucheron. Brooch designed by Charles Massé. Platinum setting with coral and onyx. Signed and dated. 1925.

tion. Widely manufactured c1730–c1860, after which licensing act allowed single bottles of wine to be sold, and paper labels substituted. Numerous modern die-stamped silver reproductions, easily distinguishable from heavier hand-made and cast originals.

Boucheron. French court jewellers with branches in Paris, London, Biarritz, and New York. Founded by Frédéric Boucheron (1858); still run by family. Expensive novelties shown at international exhibitions in Paris (1867 and 1900) and Philadelphia (1876) attracted rich customers (particularly American). Famous for elaborate diamond jewellery during late 19th century. Designers included Octave Loêuillard, specialist in fine diamond flower sprays, much more delicate than florid styles popular in 1860s; Jules Debût, designer of pieces for actress Sarah Bernhardt in 1880s. Also Jules Brateau and Louis Rault, both of whom opened own workshops c1900 and established reputations as Art Nouveau designers. Firm made jewellery in Art Nouveau style entirely in diamonds and precious stones unlike work of pioneering designers e.g. R. *Lalique and G. *Fouquet. Perfected technique for engraving diamonds with flowers and other designs. In 20th century, reputation for diamond jewellery based on late 18th century forms, e.g. feathers, stars, and sprays or bouquets of flowers.

boudeuse. French *cushion furniture; back-to-back side-chair for drawing room. Back, of two cylindrical stacked cushions, separates occupants.

boudoir clock. *See* strut clock.

bouillon spoon. *See* soup spoon.

Boulle or **buhl work.** Type of marquetry using mainly tortoiseshell and brass, sometimes also pewter, copper, mother-of-pearl, etc. Technique developed by 18th century French cabinet maker André-Charles Boulle; popular in France during 18th and 19th centuries. In Britain, c1860–c1880, commonest form, brass inlay, usually with tortoiseshell backing dyed red or green; cheaper turtle-shell widely used on commodes and cabinets. Many pieces have ormolu mounts.

Boullemier, Anton or Antonin (c1840–1900). French porcelain painter, born in Metz (Moselle). In decorators' workshops in Paris, and at Sèvres factory, painted delicate figures, notably cupids in style of François Boucher. In Staffordshire, from 1872, employed at Minton factory. Later worked independently, chiefly for

Minton's, also for Brown-Westhead, Moore. Painted portraits and miniatures; exhibited at Royal Academy, 1881–82. Sons, Lucien (1876–1949) and Henri (fl late 19th century) also worked in similar style as decorators at Minton factory; former also designed and modelled for pottery in Newcastle before going to Hanley in 1932.

Boulton & Mills. English glasshouse in Stourbridge, Worcestershire. Known for fine centrepieces, e.g. flower stands with straight or curved trumpet-shaped holders (from c1864), and plateaux centrepieces with long, leaf-shaped components arranged in circles around central flower holders; also, vessels with threaded glass decoration in form of ribbed handles.

Bourg-la-Reine ware. *See* Chelsea Keramik Art Works.

Bourne, Joseph (d 1860) and son, Joseph Harvey (d 1869). Derbyshire potters, founders of firm Joseph Bourne & Son (Ltd), operating at *Denby from 1809 to present day and incorporating (by 1861) equipment and workers from potteries at Belper, Shipley, and Codnor Park.

Bouval, Maurice (d 1920). French metalwork designer; among pupils of J-A-J. *Falguière. Exhibited ormolu candleholders, silver paper knives, at Paris Exhibition in 1900. Flowing forms and sleek finish of work, e.g. young girl metamorphosed into flower, typical of contemporary preoccupation with Art Nouveau.

Bovey Tracey. *See* Leach, David.

box ottoman. Ottoman with hinged seat; receptacle below.

box setting. Earliest known type of gem setting: metal box with edges rubbed over to grip stone above girdle. Used in Victorian jewellery for cabochon cut stones; popular with Arts & Crafts movement jewellers.

bracket clock. Term loosely applied to spring-driven table clock in wooden case, generally with carrying handle on top, made after invention of pendulum (1657); despite name, not necessarily intended for mounting on bracket. Today, generally refers to modern reproduction, or any pendulum clock other than long-case. French version, known as mantel clock (*horloge de cheminée*), often includes wall bracket of same material as clock case.

bracket and overmantel style. *See* Free Renaissance style.

Bracquemond, Félix (1833–1914). French painter, engraver, and ceramic designer. Designed table service made (1866–67) at Creil-Montereau factory in cream-coloured earthenware. Wavy-edged plates with streaky, brushed enamel decoration at rim, have enamelled motifs, cocks with flowing tail plumes, small plants, insects, etc., after original Japanese motifs, notably by Hokusai, on wide expanses of white ground. Regarded as one of earliest examples of Japanese stylistic influence in late 19th century France. Worked in studio of T. *Deck in late 1860s and briefly at Sèvres factory (c1870). Art director of Auteuil (Paris) workshop of C. F. *Haviland, 1872–80. Later, opened own studio.

Bradbury, Thomas, & Sons. English manufacturers of silver, Sheffield plate, and, from 1840, electro-plate. Company founded by Thomas Bradbury (b 1763), who worked for Matthew Fenton & Co.; after death of Fenton, 1795, business sold to Thomas Watson; firm became Watson and Bradbury, then Thomas Bradbury and Sons after interest of Watson ceased, c1832. Produced commercial items, tea sets, tureens, entrée dishes etc. Took over *Atkin Bros., 1947. Marks include: TB &S (from 1832); JB above EB (1863); TB above JH (1878); JB

Felix Bracquemond. Faience tureen made by Leboeuf and Milliet, decorated by Eugène Rousseau after Bracquemond's designs.

Thomas Bradbury & Sons. Silver hot water jug. London, 1870. Height 11in.
Below
Nora Braden. Stoneware vase with green and rust red glaze. c1935.

(1889); TB above &S (1892). *Illustration at* electro-plate.

Braden, Norah (b 1901). English artist potter. After studying drawing at Royal College of Art, London, pupil at pottery of B. *Leach in St Ives, Cornwall. Worked with K. *Pleydell Bouverie, 1928–36. Stoneware of high quality in austere

E. Brain & Co. Two teacups and saucers. Painted by Paul Nash (left) and Freda Beardmore (right). c1930–34.

shapes, sometimes painted with few, careful brush strokes. Little pottery made since 1936.

braille watch. *See* blind man's watch.

Brain, E., & Co. Staffordshire porcelain manufacturer; from 1903, operated The Foley pottery (established mid 19th century in Fenton), formerly run by Robinson & Son (from 1880s). Noted for simplicity of design. In 1930s, work commissioned from contemporary artists and produced in association with Royal Staffordshire Pottery of A.J. *Wilkinson Ltd, shown (1934) in exhibition of tableware at Harrods, London. Work, e.g. of Vanessa Bell, F. *Brangwyn, G.M. *Forsyth, Duncan Grant, Dod Procter, Laura Knight, and Graham Sutherland, painted by C. *Cliff; marked with maker's name and signatures of artist and decorator. Marks include brand name PEACOCK POTTERY with peacock in rectangle, and Staffordshire knot, containing initials E.B. & Co. F. with Established 1850, Foley China. Initials E.B. & Co used from 1903.

Brandt, Edgar-William (b 1880). Notable French designer and craftsman working in wrought iron. Produced numerous decorative screens, panels, gates etc.; also, furniture, e.g. tables, chairs, lamps, consoles, decorative covers for central-heating radiators. Showed work at Paris Exhibition, 1900; with collaborator, Henri Favier, built and furnished (1921) house in Rue Erlanger, Paris, to exhibit work. Decorative panels, *Les Cigognes d'Alsace*, c1923, show central octagonal cartouche of birds within framework of rays and spiral cloud forms; replicas in interiors of lifts at Selfridges store, London. Notable five-fold screen, *L'Oasis*, shown at Paris Exhibition of 1925, incorporates iron, brass, copper, and other metals; stylized cascade in central panel surrounded by geometrical floral and foliate forms. With Raymond Sukes, contributed (c1927) much decorative ironwork to French liner, Ile-de-France. Earlier work displays decorative debt to exuberant Jugendstil motifs of D. *Peche and others, but later examples (c1928) show more frankly geometrical designs of crosses, diamonds, etc. Surfaces generally show decorative use of hammer marks to impart texture. Furniture includes ornamental and occasional pieces, e.g. rectangular fire-screen in burnished wrought-iron, showing symmetrical, openwork stylized

Edgar-William Brandt. Wrought iron wall light, painted silver with sand-blasted glass shade. 'E. Brandt France' punched at the foot of the frame. c1922. Height 24in.

fountain, with flowers and leaves, surmounting pierced frieze ornamented with regular wave pattern, right and left sides stepped, terminating in plain, scrolled feet; marble-topped console, with decorative gilt edging, supported by two broad S-shaped stepped wrought-iron strips, resting on squared iron feet, decorated with regular lobate forms; also round, marble topped occasional table, with tripod supports resting on marble base.

Brandt, Marianne (b 1893). Noted German metalwork designer; studied at Kunstakademie, Weimar, from 1911; student at Weimar Bauhaus (1923–28), working in metalwork shop on design of lamps, etc. from 1924; assistant master of metalwork shop (1928); designer for metal goods factory at Ruppelberg (Thuringia), 1929–32; subsequently free-lance designer; also taught at Dresden and Berlin universities (1949–54). Metalwork designs for Bauhaus explore relationships between sphere and plane surface, e.g. bronze teapot and strainer, c1924: hemispherical body set into four plain, triangular feet; lid, of cylindrical section, surmounted by disc-shaped ebony finial; semi-circular solid ebony handle. Also, bronze ashtray: hemispherical body set on triangular feet, with tilting cigarette holder (c1924).

brandy saucepan. Small, shallow-lipped saucepan for 'burning' brandy in the preparation of

Above left
Marianne Brandt. Silver teapot and strainer, made at *Bauhaus. 1920s.

Left
Frank Brangwyn. Two side plates, and jam pot and cover. Made at *Doulton & Co., Burslem. c1930.

Above
Frank Brangwyn. Four-fold marquetry screen designed for Rowley Gallery. c1920. Height 6ft2in.

Below
Charles H. Brannam. Collection of earthenware vases, all with sgraffito decoration. Second from left by James Dewdney. 1883–89. Height 20in.

punch. Made from 17th century, usually of silver; plain design with baluster-turned wooden handle. Unusual in Victorian period.

Brangwyn, Sir Frank (1867–1956). Painter, graphic artist, and designer; born in Bruges, Belgium; educated in England. Assistant to W. *Morris, designed tapestry cartoons, 1882–84. Designed textiles, tapestries, stained glass, carpets, and rugs for S. *Bing, 1895–96. Designed first complete set of furniture and interior decoration scheme, 1900. Early work influenced by Arts & Crafts Movement, e.g. cherrywood cabinet (c1910) with recess in base, full-width drawer below cabinet carcase; doors decorated with carved and coloured gesso depicting medieval scene. Designed pottery for Doulton & Co., e.g. vase with incised and painted design of grapes and vines (probably c1926), marked Brangwynware, Royal Doulton. Dinnerware with cane-coloured earthenware body, underglaze decoration, dates from 1930. Knighted in 1941.

Brannam, Charles H. (1855–1937). English potter, working in Barnstaple, North Devon.

From mid 19th century until 1890s made kitchenware and ovens; from 1879, also made art pottery (*Barum ware), at first small jugs and vases decorated with simple designs in white slip over brownish clay body. Work usually signed, often dated.

brass furniture. Chairs, beds, etc., made in drawn brass tubing, or cast brass; popular from 1851 Great Exhibition to c1900, particularly work of Birmingham manufacturers, R. W. Winfield, including Renaissance-style four-poster bed, with massive openwork ends, pillars surmounted by Corinthian capitals topped by urns; child's cot with brass angel supporting canopy; also brass rocking-chair, and curtain-rod terminals, door furniture, locks, keys, lamps, and chandeliers.

brassware. English hand beaten, cast, and die-stamped articles made largely in Birmingham area from c1760. By c1850, output included oil lamps and *brass furniture. Also stamped watch stands, drawer handles, *door furniture, picture frames and *horse brasses; cast inkwells, *fenders, *andirons, *fire irons, decorative mould-

ings, etc. Expensive items burnished and coated with shellac varnish to protect shine. Alloys related to brass also used, e.g. Dutch metal, *Bath metal, gunmetal, pinchbeck, prince's metal.

Brateau, Jules. *See* Boucheron.

bread fork. Short, broad, three-tined fork for holding loaf while slicing. Made in America from c1870, in silver or electro-plate; handle often ivory. *cf* toast fork.

breakfront or **broken front.** Popular design for bookcases until 1870s in Britain and America: central section projects slightly in front of flanking sections. Also used for cabinets.

breloque. Tiny ornament (usually gold or enamel) attached to watch-chain or chatelaine.

Bretby Art Pottery. English pottery established (1883) at Woodville, Derbyshire, near Burton-on-Trent, by H. *Tooth in partnership – until 1886 – with W. *Ault. Produced figures, umbrella stands, *jardinières*, bowls, jugs, vases, etc. Early earthenware decorated with coloured

glazes, notably *sang-de-boeuf*, and applied flowers, foliage, insects, etc. in light coloured clay. Later, earthenware decorated in imitation of hammered copper or steel, or bronze with applied ceramic jewels. Bronze effect also used in combination with imitation wood in 'carved bamboo' ware. From c1912, produced Clantha ware, decorated with geometrical designs and matt, black glaze. Art pottery made until 1920. Mark: from c1891, sun rising behind BRETBY, impressed.

Breuer, Marcel (b 1902). Hungarian-born architect and furniture designer. Joined Bauhaus, 1920; studied industrial design and specialized in interior design; became 'master of interiors', 1926. Inspired by G.T. *Rietveld, designed wooden furniture, including circular table with five square legs projecting above top; also armchair (1922) of square laths set at right angles to each other, with canvas seat and two narrow canvas strips across back. Head of cabinet-making workshop from 1925. Inspired by bicycle handlebars, designed first tubular steel chair: armchair with chrome-plated steel tubing frame, and runners replacing legs; canvas seat, back and arm rests; manufactured (1925) by *Thonet Brothers. Version of cantilevered chair (1928), with attached wood or cane panels forming seat and back, widely imitated; originally made by craftsmen, at Thonet Brothers factories from 1934. Left Bauhaus for Berlin, c1930; lived in Britain, 1935–36. Designed coffee tables, and, for firm Isokon, *chaise longue* in bent plywood with latex foam upholstery. Joined W. *Gropius in America at Harvard Graduate School of Design, 1937; moved to New York, 1946, practising as architect and industrial designer.

Brierley Hill (Staffordshire). English glasshouse founded c1779 near Stourbridge, Worcester-

Left
Bretby Art Pottery. Earthenware jardinière with impressed mark, Bretby England. Height 9in.

Below
Marcel Breuer. Nest of plywood tables made by Isokon Furniture Co. Designed by Breuer, 1936.

shire, by Richard Honeybourne. Noted for glass cutting and intaglio work. Flourishes today. From 1850s, term, Brierley Hill, sometimes refers to glass-making district near Stourbridge, especially products of *Stevens & Williams. Mark: BRIERLEY, stamped or etched.

brilliant cut. *See* gem cutting.

brin (on fan). Decorated part of fan stick between pivot and leaf.

Brinton. British carpet manufacturing firm, founded 1783 in Kidderminster, Worcestershire. First Kidderminster manufacturers to secure rights to use *tapestry process (c1844), and *Crossley's and E.B. *Bigelow's power looms (c1851). Became Brinton & Lewis in 1857; partnership dissolved 1870, and factory switched completely to steam power. Installed French Wilton loom 1879, in preference to Royal Axminster loom (*see* spool Axminster) offered by *Tomkinson & Adam. Patented *gripper Axminster loom in 1890 and maintained monopoly until c1900. Introduced Beacon quality Wilton carpet (less densely tufted) c1890. First European company to install 15ft broadloom (1904), weaving gripper Axminsters. In 1906, established Canadian subsidiary in Peterborough, Ontario, which became independent in 1910. In 1920, bought rights to *Grosvenor-Picking loom.

briolette. *See* gem cutting.

brisé fan. Folding *fan composed entirely of overlapping sticks radiating from pivot, and bound by ribbon threaded through slots in tops of sticks.

Britannia metal. Alloy of c90% tin, 8–10% antimony, and fractional percentage of copper or bismuth; devised c1769 by John Vickers, who called it Vickers metal; later known as French metal, or hard pewter; increasingly replaced pewter for domestic ware, e.g. plates, spoons, mugs, from c1830. Objects machine-stamped or cut from flat sheets; roughly shaped, then spun into form on lathe; seams soldered (never rivetted). If handles, legs, etc., required, cast separately, then soldered to body. When new, metal is silver-white with bluish tinge, but tarnishes easily, so frequently electro-plated (*see* E.P.B.M.).

British hardware industry. By 1862, increased efficiency in manufacturing and smelting process had greatly increased production. Invention of Bessemer converter (1857) had made possible large scale manufacture of mild steel. Many centres of production included Birmingham, Walsall, Coventry, Wolverhampton, Rotherham, and Sheffield. Output included brass beds, furniture, e.g. by R. *Winfield, Peyton; brass cornice poles, door furniture, e.g. by C. Mackay & Co.; brass *chandeliers, *lamps, *gasoliers, in Moorish and Gothic styles, e.g. by Messenger & Co., Birmingham: numerous examples of stoves, *grates, *fenders, *fire irons, in brass and steel, from Rotherham and Sheffield; japanned metal furniture, trays, *coal vases, etc., e.g. by H. Laveridge & Co., and E. Perry & Co., Birmingham. In London, *jelly moulds, coffee urns, *gasoliers, *teapots, *coal scuttles, fire irons, manufactured, e.g. by Hulett & Co.; Gothic metalwork and ornamental wrought ironwork,

e.g. by Hart & Son; many ornamental and decorative *locks, e.g. by J. Chubb, Bramah & Co., Hobbs & Co.

British horological industry. 19th century saw decline and virtual extinction of British clock and watch industry, once world's biggest, in face of competition from American and European mass-production. Lancashire *ébauche* trade declined 1800–50; at London Exhibition of 1862, Rotherham & Sons of Coventry only British firm to exhibit watches made by steam-driven machinery. Cause of decline was refusal of craftsmen in Prescot (Lancashire), Coventry (Warwickshire), and Clerkenwell (London) to accept new mechanization techniques and assembly line production; P. *Ingold's attempt to introduce watch-making machinery in 1843 violently opposed by Soho (London) craft workers. C. *Frodsham and J. F. *Cole produced fine watches, clocks, and *chronometers for exclusive market in association with London finishers Nicole Nielsen, S. Smith & Son, Usher & Cole, etc. Edward Prior of London made watches for Turkish market. *Turret clocks manufactured e.g. by *Dent's of London, Smith's of Derby, Joyce of Whitchurch, Thwaites & Reed of Clerkenwell (London). Double three-legged gravity escapement invented by E. B. *Denison for Westminster Palace Clock, 1853. *Skeleton clocks made widely from 1851; also many *dial clocks, some by local makers, up to c1920 generally, and into post-war period in London. B. Bonniksen produced *karrusel movement in 1893 in response to challenge from Swiss-made precision watches. Chronometers made notably by V. *Kullberg and E. Loseby. Frederick Hope-Jones patented *synchronome clock in 1895, W. H. *Shortt's free pendulum invented c1920. J. Harwood patented *self-winding wrist watch in 1924.

British Horological Institute. Association founded 1858 to maintain standards and encourage development of horology. Members included many eminent 19th century horologists and clockmakers e.g. G B. *Airy, E. B. *Denison (Lord Grimthorpe), C. *Frodsham, V. *Kullberg. Institute's premises (Upton Hall, near Newark, Nottinghamshire), houses collection of clocks, watches, and tools, and world's largest horological library.

Broad, John (fl late 19th, early 20th centuries). English pottery decorator. At Doulton factory, Lambeth, London (c1873–1919) made candlesticks, vases, etc., in salt-glazed stoneware, with carved, incised, and modelled decoration, e.g. of plants, birds, insects, and serpents. Modelled figures and portrait busts in salt-glaze, terracotta, or biscuit porcelain. Work signed with monogram.

broadloom. See wide power loom.

Brocard, Joseph (d c1895). French glass artist known for rich enamelling in Islamic style. Made lamps, vases, footed platters, bowls, etc. Late work chiefly moulded glass enamelled with stylized flower designs in more subdued colours. Mark: Brocard, 23 R. Bertram, Paris; some pieces, Brocard et Fils, in gold.

Brocot, Achille (1817–78). French clockmaker. Invented pin pallet form of dead beat *escapement for pendulum clocks; pins of agate or

Joseph Brocard. Hanging lamp with gilded and enamelled decoration in Islamic style. 1878. Height 5¼in.

hardened steel. Also devised Brocot (adjustable) suspension: key inserted in dial regulates timekeeping by altering length of pendulum spring. Many Brocot clocks with calendar work, some fully perpetual, i.e. allowing for leap-year.

brocs à glace. See ice glass.

Brogden, John. English goldsmith and jeweller. Partner in London firm of Watherston & Brogden, manufacturing jewellers of Covent Garden, 1846–60. Watherston and son then moved to Pall Mall, London; Brogden continued to use Covent Garden workshop on his own until 1880s. Showed at Great Exhibition, London (1851), 1867 and 1878 Paris Exhibitions. Among first English jewellers to copy Etruscan style of *Castellani family. Highly skilled in filigree and granulation techniques of archaeological jewellery; work included neo-Gothic and Egyptian-style jewellery, and Assyrian jewellery based on Nineveh sculptures.

broken front. See breakfront.

bronchite decoration. See bronzite decoration.

bronze. Dense, hard alloy of copper and tin; other metals, e.g. lead, zinc, may also be added in small quantities. Used from antiquity for weapons, utensils, etc. Particularly suitable for casting because of great fluidity in molten state and minimal contraction during cooling, hence crisp retention of detail. Also suited to hand-finishing, e.g. with chisel. Bronze founding industry developed in France by c1800 in response to demand for ormolu furniture mounts, clock cases, etc.; Paris art bronze founders formed Réunion des Fabricants de Bronze in 1818, at time of invention of sand-casting process. By mid 19th century, founders including F. *Barbedienne, *Susse Frères, A-E. *Carrier de Belleuse, were producing wide range of hand-finished *bronzes d'édition*, clock cases, etc.; in England, c1850, Art Unions edited

statuary, reduced by *Collas process, in bronze and parian ware; sculptors included Royal Academicians John Henry Foley, J. *Bell, Charles Bell Birch. In America, L. C. *Tiffany established Tiffany Studios c1900, producing bronze desk sets, clock cases, table and standard lamps.

bronzes d'art. French ornamental bronze figures produced throughout latter half of 19th century, in editions of 24–200, by Paris bronze founders, e.g. F. *Barbedienne, Susse Frères. Success of original association between Barbedienne and A. *Collas in reproducing scale copies of full-size sculpture in bronze, led to wide-scale imitation by other foundries. Many 19th century *bronzes d'art* editions of original work by *animalier* sculptors, including A-L. *Barye, P-J. *Mêne, E. *Frémiet; casts carry signature of artist and foundry stamp. Quality of work may be judged by crispness of surface detail and richness of patination.

bronzite or **bronchite decoration, bronzit dekor, bronchit decor.** Glass painted with matt black geometrical designs or stylized flower, figure, or animal motifs. Characteristic of Vienna Secession style of decoration – forerunner of Art Deco; developed c1910 for J. & L. *Lobmeyr by J. *Hoffman.

Brooks, Thomas (1811–87). New York cabinet maker, active from c1841. Made Louis XVI style pieces from c1865; also known for Eclectic furniture.

Brough, Charles (fl late 19th, early 20th centuries). English pottery and porcelain decorator. Painted flowers, birds, fish, and figure subjects on porcelain made at Copeland factory. Worked at Doulton factory, Burslem, Staffordshire, 1903–11. Work includes decoration of table service made for King Edward VII.

Brouwer, Theophilus A. Jr (1865–c1932). American artist potter, formerly painter. At own

Thomas Brooks. Armchair, made in Brooklyn, New York. c1870.

studio, Middle Lane Pottery, in East Hampton, Long Island, established c1893, experimented with lustre glazes and developed use of gold-leaf under glaze. Early work includes vases decorated with flowers and butterflies; glaze effects increasingly used alone. Rich, iridescent glazes with variety of textures fired under carefully controlled conditions. Vases normally of simple shape, occasionally animal or plant forms. In 1910, abandoned pottery to make sculpture in concrete. Mark: M beneath whalebone arch, impressed or incised.

Brouwer, William Conraad (1877–1933). Dutch sculptor and potter. In Gouda, made vases in low, rounded shapes with decoration incised in coarse clay body, covered in yellow or green glaze. Later, produced terracotta sculptures for architectural use at own pottery, established in 1901 at Leiderdorp.

Brown, Alfred. English silver designer. From 1850s, principal designer for *Hunt & Roskell. Designed and modelled many race cups and presentation pieces, e.g. Royal Hunt Cup for Ascot (1851), vase with wide base and narrow concave neck on baluster stem, three hunting dogs on base, stags on neck and Highland deerstalker and dog on cover. Remainder of cup covered with naturalistic oak branches, guns and hunting weapons. This typifies Brown's trophy designs: shape almost obscured by mass of sculptural decoration. Designs characteristically embody scenes from classical stories.

Brown, Ford Madox (1821–93). English Pre-Raphaelite painter; also designed furniture. Worked for C. Seddon & Co. during 1850s; founder member of *Morris, Marshall, Faulkner & Co., 1861, associate until 1874. Designed functional, joiner-made furniture, with no veneering or excessive decoration. Many designs in commercial production until well into 20th century. Examples include chest of drawers (shown by *Arts & Crafts Exhibition Society in 1890), with sunken finger-holes instead of drawer handles. Originated green stain for oak c1860; applied to cheap, bedroom furniture and chests of drawers, produced by Morris, Marshall, Faulkner & Co.; also used for Art furniture.

brown gold. *See* gilding.

brown oak. Rich brown, inner wood of English oak; widely used by craftsmen designers for cabinets, c1900–25.

Brownfield, William (d 1873). English potter and porcelain manufacturer in Staffordshire. Partner in pottery producing earthenware at Cobridge from 1836. Sole proprietor from 1850 until son, William Etches Brownfield, became partner (1871); firm then traded as W. Brownfield & Son. High-quality earthenware, e.g. toilet sets and tableware, often has underglaze transfer-printing, further enamelled and gilded. Also made moulded stoneware jugs, and majolica for ornamental or domestic use. Porcelain, made from 1871, includes table services with elaborate centrepieces, dessert stands, etc., vases, jugs, and parian figures. L. *Jahn art director from 1872. Factory employed over 600 workers in 1880s; much export to Europe and America. Co-operative Company, trading as Brownfields Guild Pottery Society Ltd, formed soon after retirement of W. E. Brownfield (c1890), failed in

1898. Early printed earthenware marked with initials W & B, WB, or W B & S; later earthenware and porcelain bear printed mark of double globe with BROWNFIELD & SON, CO-BRIDGE STAFFS on ribbon. Staffordshire knot, impressed, with initials WB used on majolica; also BROWNFIELD, impressed. *Illustration at japonisme.*

Brown-Westhead, Moore & Co. English company operating Cauldon Place Works, Hanley, Staffordshire; initially traded as Bates, Brown-Westhead, Moore & Co (from 1858), then T. C. Brown-Westhead, Moore & Co. (1862–1904). Made earthenware table and toilet services, as well as ornamental ware. Services made in high quality porcelain include tea service with handles in form of looped cord, sometimes knotted to provide four feet at base, and dessert service decorated with hunting scenes commissioned by Edward, Prince of Wales. Other services decorated with illustrations of La Fontaine fables, etc. Ornamental ware includes vases, candelabra, and animal figures; firm noted for modelling of flowers. Gilding often lavish. White porcelain, very thinly potted, often lined with pink. J. *Rouse employed as decorator in 1860s. Parian ware also produced. Printed pot lids, introduced in 1855 by previous owners (J. Ridgway, Bates & Co.), produced until 1860s; J. *Austin employed in 1859. Majolica shown at Paris Exhibition of 1878 includes vases and plaques; flower-holders decorated with animals. Marks include name in full, or initials B.W.M. with or without & Co. From 1904, firm traded as Cauldon Ltd, and later Cauldon Potteries Ltd, until bought (1932) by John Rose & Co. Ltd.

Bruckman, P., & Söhne. Silver manufacturers in Heilbronn, Germany; founded by G. P. Bruckman, 1805; introduced mechanical press, 1820; son, E. D. Bruckman succeeded on death of father, 1850. Production of spoons and forks mechanized in 1864. Few original designs before

end of 19th century, when Jugendstil introduced (*see* Art Nouveau); school then founded to train artist craftsmen, later becoming Professional Bruckman School for designers, chasers, engravers and silversmiths; influenced Deutscher Werkbund. Factory rebuilt 1944; firm still in production.

Bruff, Peter Schuyler (fl late 19th century). English porcelain manufacturer, formerly engineer. Owner of Coalport works from 1880, succeeded (1889) by son, Charles Bruff.

brûle-parfum. *See* pastille burner.

Brunkhorst, A.L. (marks recorded 1885–1896). Australian silversmith working in Adelaide; produced Art Nouveau silver and electro-plate, including hand-made set of ewers and side vases. Style more advanced than most contemporary Australian work. Mark: BRUNKHORST ADELAIDE, sometimes with crown added.

Bryant Vase. Silver vase in Renaissance revival style, decorated with engraving, applied masks, and beaded ornament, designed 1874 by American J. H. *Whitehouse for Tiffany & Co.; presented to poet R. C. Bryant on his 80th birthday 'by his countrymen'.

Bugatti, Carlo (1855–1940). Italian furniture designer and craftsman; born in Milan. Known for imaginative, original designs. Early pieces, c1888, characterized by diagonal back panels, asymmetrical uprights, tassels, fringes, stamped brass, vellum-covered wood, Japanese style decoration, e.g. stylized asymmetrical floral motifs and medallions. From c1895, designs more symmetrical and sculptural; continued to

Carlo Bugatti. Table/cabinet. Hardwood with brass, white metal and ebony inlaid geometrical patterns; tabletop and shields on sides covered in vellum. c1900. Height 27in.

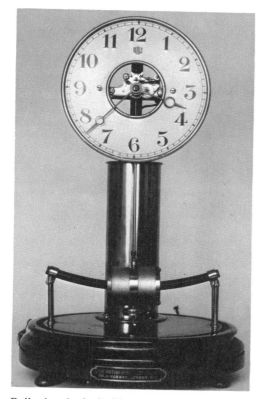

Bulle electric clock. Glass case not shown.

use earlier ornamental motifs, also Egyptian style decoration, e.g. circles, palmettes, wheat ears. Showed work at Turin Exhibition, 1902. Signature: Bugatti. Settled in Pierrefonds, France, in early 1900s.

Bugatti, Rembrandt (1885–1916). Notable Italian *animalier* sculptor, younger brother of motor car designer, Ettore Bugatti. Studied painting and sculpture under father; moved to Paris (1902) to study and model animals; worked in Antwerp (1906–16). Widely acclaimed in both Belgium and France; awarded Légion d'Honneur in 1911. Bronzes cast from c60 animal sculptures modelled in increasingly impressionistic style include studies of wild animals, e.g. lion, tiger, elephant, rhinoceros; and large birds, e.g. pelican, ostrich, cassowary. Few domestic animals. Committed suicide, 1916.

Buck, D. Azro. *See* Waterbury watch.

buckle-back chair. Balloon-back chair with cross rail and back forming outline of belt buckle; carved motif at centre of cross rail.

buckles and clasps. Used to decorate and/or fasten belts, cloaks, capes, shoes, etc. in 19th and early 20th centuries. First worn at the waist, c1820–30. Shoe buckles out of fashion in early and mid 19th century; revived c1880–90. Often made of gold or silver set with diamonds or semi-precious stones. Also cut steel, marcasite, oxidized silver, faceted jet and paste; decorated with *repoussé* designs, scrollwork, cameos and portrait medallions. Fine examples by H. *Wilson and designers of *Cymric range. Reached peak with elaborate designs of Art Nouveau jewellery, particularly those of R. *Lalique and E. *Grasset.

Buffalo Pottery. American pottery established (1903) to make free gifts to maintain sales of flourishing soap firm in Buffalo, New York. In addition to gifts, products sold by mail through soap company. Also made articles advertising other firms, and tableware for sale commercially. In 1908, introduced tableware with olive-green body, transfer-printed and hand-decorated with hunting scenes, sold as Deldare. Emerald Deldare, produced c1911, decorated with Doctor Syntax subjects; borders in style influenced by Art Nouveau. Most products marked Buffalo Pottery and, until 1940, dated. Porcelain, made from 1915, marked Buffalo China.

buhl work. *See* Boulle work.

built-in or **fitted furniture.** Cupboards, wardrobes, cabinets, bookshelves, sofas, etc. fixed in recess or corner. Feature of smaller British houses from c1880. Examples designed e.g. by C. R. *Mackintosh. Increasingly popular during 20th century, e.g. furniture by F. L. *Wright, *Djo-Bourgeois. *See also* convertible furniture, unit furniture.

Bulgari. Italian court jewellers; firm, Gioielleria Bulgari, founded 1881 in Rome by Greek, Sotirio Bulgari (1857–1932); still run by descendants. In 20th century, became known for large, exotic pieces in vivid colours, made of mixture of precious and semi-precious stones, and gold.

Bulgarian carpets. Knotted carpet industry introduced c1900 by two Armenians who founded workshop at Panagiurishte, specializing in copies of Persian types. 20th century industry mainly imitations of 16th and 17th century Persian, and 17th century Turkish, Caucasian, and East Turkestan carpets. Carpet weaving co-operatives, founded in first half of 20th century, also make traditional, regional rugs: woven rugs with sharply outlined geometrical patterns made in Kotel; tufted rugs in the Rhodopes; warmly coloured carpets with stylized plant and animal figures in Chiprovtsy.

Bulle clock. French battery clock with uncased movement under glass dome. Invented by Professor Favre-Bulle and Marcel Moulin, c1920. Pendulum bob containing wire coil swings over curved permanent magnet. Pin on pendulum rod makes electrical contact on alternate swings, energizing coil. Runs on 1½ volt battery, for c800 days. *See* electric clocks.

bull's eye or **bullion.** Circular scar in centre of blown and spun glass pane; often used to glaze doors of *cottage furniture cabinets in Britain.

bundai. *See* suzuri-bako.

Burch-Korrodi, Meinrad (b 1897). Swiss silversmith, enameller, jeweller, and metalworker, born in Zurich; apprenticed as goldsmith in Lucerne; studied at London Central School of Arts & Crafts; worked as jeweller in London, 1922–24, in New York 1925. Opened workshop in Lucerne, 1925; moved to Zurich, 1932. Won Grand Prix at Milan Triennale (1936). Made wide range of jewellery, but best known for church plate, e.g. chalices, often with enamelled decoration.

Burges, William (1827–81). English architect, antiquary, and designer of furniture, metalwork,

William Burges. Decanter made by R. A. Green. Silver set with semi-precious stones; neck inset with malachite. 1865–66.
Below
William Burges. Tulip vase designed for Cardiff Castle. One of pair. Porcelain, unmarked. 1874. Height 14½in.

and jewellery. Exponent of Gothic Reform style. Enthusiast of medieval ideals of craftsmanship; paid as much attention to rarely seen parts of objects as to visible ones. Worked with M. D. *Wyatt from 1849, contributing drawings to 'Metalwork' (published 1852). Designed plate for St Finbarr's Cathedral, Cork, Ireland. With W. Slater, mounted *Medieval Court at International Exhibition, London, of 1862. From 1864, superintendent of Ecclesiological Society's metalwork scheme; commissioned *Barkentin & Krall (1867) to execute Society's manufactures, and continued to design for them after Ecclesiological Society wound up (1868). Inspired by medieval metalwork: favoured elaborate combinations of silver, gilding, coloured glass, semi-precious stones, and engraving. Dessert service in silver and silver-gilt with enamelled decoration, set with semi-precious stones and beads, now in Victoria & Albert Museum, London.

Almost all furniture elaborately painted, e.g. rectangular cabinet entirely covered in paintings by E. J. *Poynter, illustrating battle between wines and beers; shown at International Exhibition in London, 1862; now in Victoria & Albert Museum. Rebuilt and furnished Cardiff Castle, Glamorganshire, 1865, designing Moorish style smoking-room which inspired many imitations, e.g. by *Liberty & Co.; also Castell Coch, Wales, 1875. Both for Marquis of Bute. Furniture, designed mainly for himself or clients, had little effect on furniture trade. Book 'Art Applied to Industry' (1865).

Bureau, Léon (b 1866). French *animalier* sculptor; studied at Ecole des Beaux-Arts; worked in studio of J-A-J. *Falguière. Exhibited at Salon from 1884; specialized in bronzes of exotic sub-

Sydney Richmond Burleigh. Chest. Panels painted with characters from Shakespearean plays. Oak enamelled black. Late 19th century. Length 42in.

jects,' e.g. Abyssinian Lion and Lioness, exhibited at Salon in 1897; other works include Wild Stallion and Stalking Tiger.

Burgess, Leigh & Co. English earthenware manufacturers, operating part of Hill Pottery (c1867–89) and Middleport Pottery from c1889, in Burslem, Staffordshire. Produced ornamental and domestic wares for home and overseas market. Mark: beehive flanked by rose bushes, with ribbon label showing name of pattern, and initials B.L.& Co. Burleigh occurs in printed marks from 1930s.

Burleigh, Sydney Richmond (1853–1931). American artist; born in Providence, Rhode Island. Founder member of American *Art Workers' Guild, c1885. Designed cabinet, c1894, with doors in base painted by C. W. *Stetson.

Burmantofts. Pottery of Wilcock & Co., established 1858 in Leeds, Yorkshire. Produced architectural ware in terracotta. From 1880, hard buff-coloured earthenware fired to high temperature, with feldspathic glaze (Burmantofts faience) used to make tiles, and (1882–1904) art pottery. Vases, bowls, *jardinières*, pedestals, some tableware, and figures modelled after oriental or Middle-Eastern forms, covered with coloured glazes, e.g. *sang-de-boeuf*, orange, yellow, lime-green, or turquoise. Other decoration includes underglaze designs trailed in slip, painted, or incised; copper or silver lustre used on dark red or blue ground colours. After 1904, firm again specialized in terracotta; later traded as Leeds Fireclay Co. Marks: name in full, or monogram of BF.

Burmese glass. American art glass, shading greenish-yellow to delicate pink, in matt or glossy finish. Produced by mixing uranium and gold oxides with glass metal. Patented 1885 by *Mount Washington Glass Works, where used

Burmantofts. Earthenware vase. Marked Burmantofts Faience. c1880–91.
Below
*Burmese glass. Candlestick, made by *Mount Washington Glass Company. c1890. Height 7½in.*

for wide range of table and decorative ware. *See also* Queen's Burmese glass.

Burne-Jones, Sir Edward (1833-98). Pre-Raphaelite painter and designer. At Exeter College, Oxford, with W. *Morris; founder member of *Morris, Marshall, Faulkner and Co. (1861). Designed furniture, e.g. grand piano in oak with gold and silver gesso decoration on dark ground, c1883. Painted panels of furniture designed by W. *Morris, F. *Webb, J. P. *Seddon, etc. Designed stained glass for Morris's companies and e.g. *Whitefriars Glass Works. Chief designer of tapestry figure compositions at *Merton Abbey; important works include *Angeli Laudantes* (Victoria & Albert Museum), completed 1878; The Star of Bethlehem (Exeter College Chapel), completed 1891; Botticelli's Primavera, 1896; The Quest of the Holy Grail set, for Stanmore Hall, Middlesex. Designed tiles: panel of six scenes, Beauty and the Beast (1862), among first tile designs produced by Morris, Marshall, Faulkner & Co.; other panels included Cinderella, and designs for Morris & Co. Member of *Arts and Crafts Exhibition Society. *Illustrations at* Merton Abbey, Morris & Co.

Burton, Joseph (1868-1934). English pottery chemist. With brother, W. *Burton, ran Pilkington Tile & Pottery Co.; sole manager from 1915 until death. Succeeded G. M. *Forsyth as art director; introduced more restrained style. Encouraged experiments in matt glazes, and responsible for development of *Lapis ware.

Burton, William (1863-1941). English ceramic chemist. Schoolmaster in Manchester, then entered Royal School of Mines, with scholarship. In Staffordshire, chemist at Wedgwood factory (1887-92), also teaching pottery in Burslem and Hanley. With brother, J. *Burton, ran Pilkington Tile & Pottery Co. Ltd, until retirement (1915). Examiner in ceramics for City and Guilds of London, and adviser to Board of Trade on problem of lead poisoning suffered by potters. Wrote several books on history and manufacture of porcelain and pottery (1902-10), and work of Josiah Wedgwood I (1922).

Buthaud, René (b 1886). French painter and artist potter; in 1920s made pottery in Art Deco style. Strong enamel colours used to decorate vases in simple forms with foliate designs or, notably, female figures with firm outlining.

Butler, Frank A. (fl late 19th to early 20th centuries). English pottery decorator and designer; deaf and dumb. In London, at Doulton workshop, Lambeth (1872-1911), carved and modelled designs with relief pattern against ground of dots, circles, or interlaced lines, on stoneware. Mark: monogram of FAB, incised.

butler's or **satin finish.** Matt surface obtained on silver or electro-plate by wire-brushing, dipping in hydrofluoric acid, buffing with emery grit, or sandblasting. Style of silver with satin finish patented in America, 1870, by J. R. Reilly of Brooklyn Silver Co.

butter dish. Container for serving butter at table. Early 19th century versions usually consist of silver or electro-plate saucer with glass liner, and cover, frequently with finial in shape of reclining cow. Straight-sided dishes with two

*Butter dish. Made by C. and G. *Fox. Silver with frosted glass base. 1857.*

handles and engraved glass or silver lid fashionable from mid to late 19th century; other popular types include tub shaped dish, often footed or with pedestal. In America, footed dish with domed revolving lid made in electro-plate from c1860.

Butterfield, William (1814-1900). London architect and designer. From c1840, built and restored Gothic style churches, designing interior fittings and details. Appointed (1843) by Cambridge Camden Society as agent for scheme to manufacture church furnishings; designed much church plate in Medieval manner for them (made by J. Keith & Son of London). In 1850, designed silver-gilt chalice for Ecclesiological Society; decorated with pierced, engraved, and applied ornament, set with semi-precious stones and foiled crystals (now in Victoria & Albert Museum, London).
Designed small amount of domestic furniture: simple pieces in walnut, with ebony and sycamore inlays. Style anticipates well proportioned, constructional furniture of P. *Webb and E. *Godwin.

butter knife. Small slice with broad, asymmetrical blade (similar to fish knife), for serving butter; introduced c1830. Made in silver or electro-plate; entire blade may be decorated; handles sometimes mother-of-pearl, etc. Wide range produced in 19th century, e.g. by J. *Round & Son of Sheffield.

butter spreader. Small knife with rounded, spatulate blade, for spreading butter. Handle usually ivory, blade silver or electro-plate; introduced as part of table setting, c1885.

button hook. Instrument for fastening buttons, usually on boots and shoes; introduced in England with fashion for ladies' high buttoned boots, c1880; also used to fasten buttons on starched shirts etc. Hooked shaft normally of steel, up to 13in. long, with handle of e.g. ivory, mother-of-pearl, or inlaid wood. Solid silver examples also made, in animal, bird, human, or tree shape. Sometimes incorporates penknife or other tool in handle. Produced widely in America, particularly by B. F. Norris and Alister & Co. Simple hooks given away to customers carry stamped name of shop or dealer. Companion sets sometimes made containing button hook, glove hook (smaller version), and shoehorn. Not made after c1914.

button-upholstery. Upholstery attached to seat furniture by deeply sunk buttons. Produces raised, quilted effect emphasizing thickness and curves of upholstery, e.g. chesterfield, lady's easy chair. Popular from c1840.

cabinet table. Flat-topped cabinet with double set of four or five shallow drawers; table height, with cabriole or square, tapered legs. Popular in Britain c1860-c1880.

cabochon. *See* gem cutting.

cachos. Spanish tapestry technique similar to appliqué. Panels have hand-woven ground with design built up with superimposed, cut-out worsted shapes.

cachou box. Small gold or silver box (c1-1½in. long) with hinged lid for pills to sweeten breath (often used by smokers). May have ring attached for hanging from chatelaine. Usually decorated, e.g. chased and enamelled. Made in Britain from c1850; popular until c1910.

caddy ladle or **spoon.** Short-handled (*c*3in. long, 1½in. wide) silver or electro-plate scoop for tea; kept in tea-caddy. Introduced *c*1770, often in form of scallop shell, hence also called caddy shell. Other shapes include eagle's wing (rare), jockey's cap, and fish. Large numbers mass produced from thinly rolled plate, designed as cheap presents; most bear Birmingham hallmark. Examples from after *c*1880 often larger and heavier (above 10dwt).

cage cup. *See* diatreta vase.

cagework box, or **tabatière à cage.** Snuff box with lid, sides, and base formed by panels of various materials (particularly enamel or hardstone) fitted into metal (usually gold) frame. Made from *c*1750; form allowed quicker production needed to meet growing demands of snuff-box vogue. Numerous reproductions of 18th century examples made in late 19th century.

Cain, Auguste-Nicolas (1821–94). French *animalier* sculptor; style strongly influenced by father-in-law, P-J. Mêne, whose foundry he shared from 1852. First exhibited at Paris Salon in 1846. Some wax models (1846–52) coated in metallic oxide to give appearance of bronze. Many bronze animal groups edited personally (1852–68), e.g. Eagle Pursuing Vulture (1887), Cock Fight (1861), Saharan Lion (1865), Lioness (1868). Thereafter, concentrated on monumental pieces e.g. statue of Duke Karl von Braunschweig (1879), in Geneva.

cake basket. Swing handled metal basket for cakes, fruit, etc., on legs or pedestal; dates from 17th century, but originally known as bread basket; edges and handle usually pierced; larger versions decorated with cast flowers, foliage, etc. Made in silver to *c*1880, then in other materials, e.g. electro-plate. Produced widely by all leading

Auguste-Nicolas Cain. Bronze group of lion and lioness attacking boar. c*1870–90. Height 14½in.*

British and American manufacturers until present day. Popular variant shell-shaped with allegorical figure on top.

cake fork. *See* cutting fork.

cake or **pie knife.** Silver or electro-plated slice for serving cake: large, flat, oval, highly decorated blade, often with gold inlays, sometimes pierced, or with one serrated cutting edge; handle often ivory. Made from *c*1870 in Britain and America.

Caldas da Rainha. *See* Mafra & Son.

Caldwell, J. E., & Co. American jewellers and silversmiths, founded in Philadelphia, 1835, by James E. Caldwell (1805–81), watchmaker and jeweller. Formed partnership with James Bennett from 1843 to 1848; pioneered staff welfare scheme and use of advertising techniques. Firm headed by son J. Albert Caldwell 1881–1914; executed work commissioned by U.S. Navy. Second son, J. Emott Caldwell succeeded 1914, died 1919. Jewellery manufacture temporarily discontinued due to slump, 1932. Company currently one of largest Philadelphia jewellery manufacturers, with wide range of products.

calendar clock or **watch.** Calendar work showing date through aperture in main dial appears in public clocks from 14th century, in domestic clocks from 16th century, in watches from *c*1630. More elaborate versions show day and month. Semi-perpetual work allows for months of less than 31 days and fully perpetual work allows for leap-years. Made notably by A. *Brocot. Numerous designs in popular watches from mid 19th century, e.g. by V-A. *Pierret.

calibré. *See* gem cutting.

Cambridge chime. *See* Westminster Palace Clock.

caméléon or **changeant glass.** Art Nouveau Bohemian iridescent glass developed by F. *Heckert glasshouse. Changes colour with play of light on surface.

Cameo. *See* Rookwood Pottery.

cameo. Small picture carved in shallow relief in stone or shell composed of two or three different coloured layers, e.g., heat-treated banded agates, helmet shells (e.g. *Cassidaria echinophora*) layered in white against brown, and giant or Queen conch shell (*Strombus gigas*), white on rose-pink. Other stones used include amethyst, emerald, garnet, jasper, and (in late 19th century) opal. Reintroduced in early 19th century Italy; made fashionable by Empress Josephine, *c*1805; continuously popular until 1880s. Shell cameos imported from Italy to France, England, and America (small amount of cameo making done in France). Other varieties include Wedgwood jasper ware cameos, glass cameos by James Tassie, and imitation cameos painted on enamel and porcelain. Settings range from gilded base-metal to gold. Used for brooches, bracelets, and

Top
Cameo glass. Pair of Bohemian vases, blue and opal glass on crystal. Late 19th century. Height 6in.
Above
Cameo glass. Czechoslovakian Art Deco lamp. c*1930.*

necklaces; often surrounded by pearls and linked with pearls or gold chain. Subjects usually taken from classical sources; *Gothic revival led to fashion for subjects from medieval sculpture.

Cameo china. *See* La Belle Pottery Co.

cameo, cased or **overlay glass.** Ornamental glass of two or more coloured layers in which glass surrounding decoration is carved or cut away, leaving pattern in high relief. Technique developed by Romans; most famous example, Portland Vase. Much used in 18th century China, particularly for snuff bottles. Technique revived in Britain in mid 19th century, achieving great popularity with work of J. *Northwood (Bohemian *flashed glass technique also adopted at same period). Popular for German and Bohemian glass throughout 19th century. Art Nouveau version, contrasting opaque masses, clear glass with coloured, and opaque glass with clear, perfected by E. *Gallé and subsequently applied by contemporaries. *See also* E. Rousseau, A. and A. Daum, G. and T. Woodall, and J. Hodgetts. *Illustration also at* Stevens & Williams.

cameo encrustation. *See* cristallo-ceramie.

camera clock. *See* travelling clock.

Campbell Tile Co. Altar tiles. Encaustic pattern inlaid in white clay. c1885.

camp chair. American folding chair with upholstered seat and back, with or without arms, sometimes with bends. Armchair has concave back and plain, fabric-covered yoke rail; side-chair has flat back and shaped yoke rail supporting framed, upholstered panel. Common c1870–c1885. Included in term, nomadic furniture.

campaign furniture. Portable furniture used (on campaign) by British officers in 18th and 19th centuries. Usually teak, with brass corners, recessed handles, and removable, turned feet. Three-tiered wash-stand, supported on metal columns which unscrew for packing flat, widely used from c1856. *See* military chest of drawers, military desk.

Campbell Brick & Tile Co. Staffordshire tile manufacturer; firm established 1875 in Stoke-on-Trent by C. M. *Campbell in partnership; prevented by court injunction from using name Minton in title. Tiles, made by encaustic process, glazed in several colours; also majolica tiles. Some hand-painting influenced by Japanese styles. Geometrical tiles often have relief decoration of flowers and fruits. Mark: points of compass surrounded by CAMPBELL BRICK & TILE Co./ STOKE ON TRENT. From 1882, traded as Campbell Tile Co. Ltd.

Campbell, Colin Minton (1827–85). English potter working in Staffordshire. In partnership with uncle, H. *Minton, and M. D. *Hollins from 1849. Succeeded former as managing director of firm; continued production of earthenware and porcelain separately from tile manufacture which passed to Hollins. Partner in Campbell Brick & Tile Co. from 1875.

canary glass. Late 19th century American art glass produced by *Boston & Sandwich Glass Co. Rich clear yellow in colour (produced by adding uranium oxide to glass melt) with canary-green fluorescence. French version, *verre canari*. *See also* chrysoprase.

candelabrum. Decorative candlestick, with two or more branches or arms fitted with sockets for holding candles. Made throughout 19th century, e.g. in silver, as part of *testimonial pieces; other versions, e.g. in glass and ormolu, characterized particularly by pendant droplets at sockets.

candle box. Cylinder with curved hinged lid for storing candles; hung horizontally on wall; also, less common rectangular type with sliding front. Made of brass, with *repoussé* ornament, or in japanned or painted iron. Produced until c1900.

candle snuffer. Used only to trim wick (cf extinguisher). Originated in early 15th century. Earliest surviving pair 16th century. Action scissor-like; after 1660, often had small attached container to receive the candlewicks. Declined with introduction of self-trimming wicks in mid 19th century.

candlestick. Victorian cast silver candlesticks made in reproduction 18th century or earlier styles, e.g. versions resembling Queen Anne style, based on German models of c1700, by Robert Garrard & Co, from c1840. Corinthian column candlesticks c12in. high made during classical revival of 1870s. Small cast reproductions of George II styles made c1890–c1910. Cheaper versions in electro-plate, generally die-stamped, with loaded base, e.g. dwarf Corinthian columnar form, c4in. high, fashionable in 1870s; reproduction Commonwealth, Charles II, and Louis XVI styles produced c1890–c1910. Ecclesiastical candlesticks, in e.g. brass or ormolu, made in neo-Gothic forms from c1840, notably by J. *Hardman, F. *Skidmore, E. *Barnard & Sons; simple 13th century style brass domestic candlestick designed by P. *Webb for *Morris & Co., c1865. *See* chamber candlestick.

canework. Split cane strips from rattan palm, interwoven to form mesh; introduced in Europe by Dutch East India Co. in late 17th century. Popular seat and back material for chairs in Britain during 19th century, e.g. Derby, lounge, and sewing chairs. cf rattan furniture.

Cantagalli, Ulisse (d 1901). Italian potter. In 1878, inherited family factory at Doccia, near Florence; firm traded as Figli di Giuseppe Cantagalli. Produced copies of early Italian maiolica made e.g. at Urbino, Faenza, Gubbio, and Deruta, and at Della Robbia workshop. Also imitated tin-glazed earthenware in Isnik and Persian styles. Tall, earthenware vases decorated with elongated plant motifs, e.g. daffodils (1899), influenced by Art Nouveau style. Later specialized in decorative tableware, although reproductions of earlier wares continued. Work marked with rebus of crowing cock. In

1901, factory produced vase and dishes from designs by W. *De Morgan, marked DM over C with anchor, from mark of firm responsible for painting.

canteen, nécessaire de voyage, or **travelling set.** Originally, decorative fitted travelling case (usually leather) for eating utensils. 19th century form, large fitted box with tableware, toilet set, sewing and writing implements. Usually wood, often covered in *shagreen or other leather. Declined in popularity from 1890s. *See* nécessaire, workbox.

canterbury. Low, ornamented stand with partitions for books and sheet music. Dates from early 19th century in Britain. Usually square or rectangular, sometimes surmounted by shelf supported on corner-posts; decorated with openwork carving, frets, etc. Usually mahogany, also bamboo or papier-mâché. Term also used for rectangular music-stool with hinged seat for music, c1850.

cantilevered chair. Based on cantilever principle; U-shaped floor-section rises at front, curving back to support seat and back of leather, cane, canvas, etc.; frame originally tubular steel, later also laminated wood. M. *Stam's prototype (1924) revolutionized chair design, proving chairs need not have three or more legs. Examples by H. A. H. *Aalto, M. *Breuer, and L. *Mies van der Rohe.

Cappellin, Giacomo (b 1887). Italian businessman; with P. *Venini, founded Cappellin-Venini glasshouse in *Murano, 1921, initiating 20th century Venetian glass revival. With V. *Zecchin as artistic director, produced simplified versions of vases, urns, ewers, and basins from old

*Canterbury. *Papier-mâché. English, c1860. Height 19in.*

Venetian paintings, in colourless or pastel-tinted transparent glass; subsequently turned to free forms.

captain's chair. *See* firehouse Windsor.

carboy. Large (usually round but sometimes gourd or pear shaped) stoppered clear glass bottle filled with coloured water; used as symbol of pharmacy from medieval times; regular feature of chemists' window decoration from last decades of 18th century. Capacity normally one gallon. Round carboys are of green bottle glass; pear or gourd shaped bottles (usually with matching stoppers) are mostly colourless glass; occasionally light green; rarely bottle green. Some carboys have swan stoppers and long swan necks or short squat necks; both made in various sizes. Some very large carboys from 1830. Show globe (serving similar decorative purpose) is one, two, or (in America) sometimes three tiered spherical carboy, designed to be suspended from ceiling or beam, or mounted on decorative iron brackets or stands; many have feet; some have globular stoppers filled with contrasting coloured liquids. Term, carboy, also applied to large bottle of heavy glass (with basketwork or other casing) for storing dangerous chemicals. *See also* pharmaceutical glass.

carbuncle. *See* garnet.

card case. Slim, rectangular box for visiting cards; fashionable throughout 19th century. Often lined in watered silk or velvet. Lid either hinged or sliding. After c1850, forms included: gold or silver cases with decoration ranging from

Top
Cardeilhac. Coffee-pot with ebony handle and finial. Height 5in.
Above
Cardeilhac. Ivory and gilt metal powder box, exhibited in Paris, 1900.

delicate filigree to heavy embossing; leather cases, tooled or painted in book-binding styles, stained to resemble tortoiseshell, or with embroidered panels on front and back. Also various other materials, e.g. tortoiseshell and ivory *piqué, papier-mâché, *Tunbridge ware, horn, mother-of-pearl, Japanese export *Shibayama style inlaid ivory, and lacquered wood.

Cardeilhac. French silver manufacturer founded 1802 by Vital-Antoine Cardeilhac; important traders in silver and *Britannia metal by 1823. Under direction of Ernest Cardeilhac (joined firm 1860) made notable Art Nouveau work in silver, designed by Bonvallet, c1890, e.g. sugar basin decorated with carved ivory flower buds; silver chocolate pot with carved wooden handles, and chased silver leaves entwining wooden flowerbuds. Much work now in Musée des Arts Décoratifs, Paris. Firm amalgamated with *Christofle, 1941.

Carder, Frederick (1864-1963). English Art Nouveau glass artist. Associated with J. *Northwood at *Stevens & Williams, 1881-1902, for whom for many years chief designer. Founded *Steuben Glass Works in Corning, New York, 1903, where created art glass, e.g. *Aurene, and experimented with lost-wax technique for production of *diatreta vases. Also made gold-ruby and tinted opaque glass, as well as *Peachblow items (often signed Steuben in the pontil). *Illustration at* diatreta vase.

Cardew, Michael (b 1901). English artist potter, pupil of B. *Leach (1923-26). In 1926, rented pottery at Winchcombe, Gloucestershire; made slip-decorated earthenware for domestic use. Early slipware generally light in colour, often with *sgraffito* decoration; later work often covered with black slip, with trailed decoration in white; copper-green also used. Products, often large, include bowls, dishes, and cider jugs fitted with wooden taps. In 1939, built kiln at Wenford Bridge near Bodmin, Cornwall. Experimented with production of tin-glazed earthenware, then stoneware. After returning to Winchcombe in 1941, taught pottery at Achimota College, Gold

*Frederick Carder. Gold *Aurene glass vase with trailed and millefiori decoration. c1920.*

Michael Cardew. Earthenware dish with slip decoration under clear glaze. 1938.

Coast (now Ghana). Following closure of college in 1945, opened pottery at Vumé-Dugamé on Volta River. Used local materials to make stoneware, usually covered with deep green or bluish glazes containing wood ash, with brushed iron decoration fired to bright orange-brown; motifs often African-inspired. At Wenford Bridge from 1948, continued to make stoneware, often pale in colour, e.g. cream or bluish grey, with brushed decoration. As Pottery Officer, working for Nigerian Government (1950-65), established training centre at Abuja, Northern Nigeria (1951). Work marked with initials and impressed seal associated with pottery.

Carlton ware. Staffordshire earthenware and porcelain produced from c1890 at Carlton Works, Stoke-on-Trent, by firm which traded as Wiltshaw & Robinson until 1957. Ornamental ware includes porcelain vases made in 1920s

Carltonware. Group of vases, and jar and cover made at Carlton Works, Stoke-on-Trent. c1907-35. Height of tallest vase 13in.

with bright enamelled and gilded decoration of flowers, fan motifs, etc. Black often used as ground colour. Work normally bears circular printed mark with W & R/ STOKE ON TRENT enclosing swallow and topped by crown. Mark, Carlton ware, sometimes occurs over name and address of firm, hand painted. (Firm retitled Carlton Ware Ltd from January, 1958.)

car mascot. Ornamental badge, figure, device, mounted e.g. on car radiator cap, introduced c1905. Mascots generally of cast metal, e.g.

Car mascot. Bronze with movable china head. By John Hassall. c1912. Height 4½in.

silver, brass, bronze, pewter, stainless steel, chromium, or electro-plate; some examples in glass, wood. Designs frequently also produced as e.g. paperweights or *objets d'art*. Early manufacturers' own mascots include, notably, Rolls Royce's Spirit of Ecstasy, commissioned by firm from sculptor Charles Sykes (1875–1950); all casts signed; each one checked by artist, 1911–1928, subsequently by daughter, Jo, until 1948. Other distinctive mascots from American companies, e.g. greyhound from Lincoln and bird from Duesenberg. As car ownership increased, commercially produced mascots became popular; expensive examples, e.g. bronze Art Deco figure, Speed (1928) by Harriet Frishmuth for *Gorham Corporation; glass birds of prey by R. *Lalique, c1930; glass dragonfly, butterfly, and other insects, from Sabino. More generally available models include caricatured figures of policemen, politicians etc., or novelty animal figures; many examples in this genre by manufacturer John Hassell. Mascots commissioned by individuals range from naturalistic modelled domestic pets, horses, to highly personal *jeux d'esprit*, e.g. birds with articulated wings simulating flight, model lighthouses with authentically revolving light. Family coats of arms or crests common in Germany, less so in England, until 1935.

carnet-de-bal. Ornate 19th century *aide-mémoire with hinged lid fitted with removable ivory or card leaves (usually 6) and lead pencil for inscribing dancing partners' names. Cases made in gold, enamel, ivory, horn, mother-of-pearl, etc. Often inscribed with engraved, inlaid, or encrusted words: *carnet-de-bal* or *souvenir*.

Carr, Alwyn Charles Ellison (1872–1940). English silversmith. Studied at Sheffield School of Art, where met O. *Ramsden. In partnership with Ramsden from c1898; provided finance. Partnership lasted until 1918; produced many ceremonial presentation pieces and ecclesiastical crosses, chalices, etc. Own studio after 1919; active in 1920s as silversmith and designer of wrought ironwork. Mark (joint): Omar. Ramsden. &. Alwyn. C. E. Carr Me Fecerunt, usually with date.

Carr, James (fl mid to late 19th century). American potter, born in England. After leaving Shelton, Staffordshire, in 1844, at first made domestic and pharmaceutical ware. Worked in Jersey City and at South Amboy, New Jersey. In partnership, established New York City Pottery (c1853), sole proprietor from 1871 until retirement in 1888.

Carrara. English stoneware made at Doulton workshop, Lambeth, London, c1887–c1896. Jugs, etc., made with white body usually covered with thin, matt glaze; enamel decoration and gilding or lustre painted over designs in slight relief. Mark: Carrara on shield, in addition to normal Doulton Lambeth and mark of artist (e.g. M. V. *Marshall). Matt-glazed architectural ware, made 1885–1939, also called Carrara.
  Parian ware produced by J. *Wedgwood & Sons Ltd (from c1848) sold under same name because of similarity to white marble quarried at Carrara in northern Italy.

carriage clock. Spring-driven travelling clock, made from c1850, mainly in France. Rectangular ormolu case surmounted by handle, glass panels and top; hinged door at back, sometimes glass, opens for winding. Made with striking, repeating, and alarm work, also Grande Sonnerie. English and American versions strike hours and halves, but lack complicated striking mechanism. In France, escapement and balance wheel mounted on separate platform, made by specialists at Besançon; movements mass-produced by factories at St Nicholas (Dieppe) and Lyon; cases, gongs, etc. made by out-

workers; assembled and finished to required standard in Paris. Completed clock would then be sold to vendor, whose name appears on dial. Numerous modern reproductions.

carriage lamp. Rectangular or ovoid oil lamp, front and sides with glass panels, mirrored or polished reflector behind burner, usually with columnar reservoir, and ornamented finial chimney; mounted at each side of front of carriage, at dash, or on front roof corners. Made in e.g. burnished brass, japanned, gilded or electro-plated metal, finials often silver mounted, by saddlery manufacturers, particularly in Birmingham, Wolverhampton, and Walsall. Wide range shown by John & Henry Lowe & Sons, Birmingham, at Great Exhibition of 1851, including elaborate silver mounted and gilt versions designed for South American market.

Carrier de Belleuse, Albert-Ernest (1824–87). French sculptor (noted for work in terracotta) and porcelain modeller. Studied at Ecole des Beaux-Arts, Paris (1840). Made pastiches of 18th century sculpture from c1845; highly successful – established large studio to reproduce original statues, in marble and terracotta; assistants included A. *Rodin. By 1860 had reproduced or imitated work of most notable 18th and early 19th century sculptors as small groups and statuettes; occasionally these mistaken for originals. Many reproductions cast in bronze; all signed Carrier-Belleuse. Modelled figure of

Left
*Carrara. Stoneware jug, made by *Doulton & Co., Lambeth, decorated by M. V. *Marshall, c1890.*

Below
Carriage clocks. French, c1870, with enamel decoration.

Carriage lamp. Brass with bevelled glass panels, silvered interior, on truncheon holders with cast iron brackets. One of pair. English, c1860.

Jean Carriès. Stoneware vase with gold and brown glazes over dark brown body. Late 19th century.

*G. A. Carter. Silver candlestick representing Knowledge, made by *Hunt and Roskell, 1887. Height 11¼in.*

Charity in parian ware for Wedgwood, shown at Great Exhibition in London (1851). Among foreign artists employed in production of parian ware at Minton factory. Modeller from early 1850s, e.g. of cupids supporting vase with *pâte-sur-pâte* decoration by M-L. *Solon. Returned to Paris after three or four years, but continued to fulfil commissions for Minton. Work for W. *Brownfield includes large globe vase shown in Paris Exhibition (1888). Also modelled work for firm of W. T. *Copeland. Art director at Sèvres factory from 1870s. Worked signed A. CARRIER. Son, Louis-Robert (1848–1912), became art director of earthenware factory at Choisy-le-Roi (Seine); work includes terracotta busts and mythological subjects.

Carriès, Jean (1856–1894). French artist potter, initially sculptor, born at Lyon (Rhone). Made stoneware from 1888 at Saint-Amand-en-Puisaye and Montriveau, near Nevers (Nièvre). Work includes figures with human head on body of frog, etc., busts with smiling or frowning faces, a series of Bohemians *'les Désolés'*, and stoneware for architectural use; some shapes of vases, etc., in imitation of fruits or vegetables. Variety of colour effects achieved with glazes using cinders (grey), wood ash (bluish), or feldspar

(wax-like glazes, ranging from white and brown to greenish tints).

Carter & Co. English earthenware and tile manufacturer, working at Poole, Dorset, from 1873. Supplied tiles for decoration, e.g. by W. *De Morgan; also decorated tiles and murals, sometimes by hand. Took over nearby Architectural Tile Co. in 1895. Owen Carter, son of proprietor, responsible for range of ornamental pottery, primarily experimenting with glaze effects, until matt, cream glaze developed, characteristic of *Carter, Stabler & Adams, formed, 1921. Mark: versions of Carter/Poole.

Carter, G.A. (fl mid 19th century) English silver designer, working for *Hunt & Roskell from c1850. Many designs, e.g. silver racing plate and ewer engraved with formal plant motifs and scenes from Ballad of Chevy Chase, displayed by Hunt & Roskell at 1871 South Kensington Exhibition, London.

Carter, Stabler & Adams. Partnership formed (1921) at Poole, Dorset, by J. and T. *Adams,

Carter, Stabler & Adams. Candlestick with hand-painted decoration over crackled matt ground. Impressed mark 'Carter Stabler Adams Poole England'. Diameter 3½in.

Carter, Stabler & Adams. Earthenware vase. c1930. Height 6in.

and H. *Stabler with Owen Carter, of *Carter & Co. Hand-thrown and hand-decorated pottery, chiefly designed by Stabler and wife, Phoebe, or J. and T. Adams, includes earthenware in simple shapes for table use and, notably, stoneware painted in fresh colours, often in bold, sketchy style under creamy matt glaze. Candlesticks, etc., made in Art Deco style c1930. From 1963, traded as Poole Pottery Ltd.

Cartier, François-Thomas (b 1879). Minor French *animalier* sculptor; exhibited at Salon from 1900; awarded gold medal in 1927. Best known for small bronzes of dogs, e.g. retrievers, bull terriers.

Cartier. French court jewellers; founded by Louis-François Cartier, 1857; helped by patronage of Princesse Mathilde Bonaparte. Shop moved to Rue de la Paix, Paris, c1900. In 1903, Edward VII, frequent client, encouraged Pierre Cartier to open London branch - established in New Bond Street, 1909, under Jacques Cartier. London workshops started, 1921. Identified with expensive precious stone Art Deco jewellery during 1920s; exotic African-inspired jewellery based on animal forms, e.g. panthers, made of enamel and strange precious stones, designed by Mlle Toussaint in 1930s. *Illustrations at* pearl, powder compact.

Cartlidge, Charles (d 1860). American potter, born in England. In America from 1832, worked at pottery in Jersey City, and as distributor for J. *Ridgway. Partner in pottery, Charles Cartlidge & Co., established at Greenpoint, Long Island, in 1848. Among early American porcelain manufacturers. Made buttons, then tableware, door furniture, etc., in bone porcelain and earthenware. Busts and small figures in parian ware. Production ceased in 1856; resumed (1857) by W. *Boch.

Cartlidge, George (b 1868). English ceramic modeller and decorator. In 1882, apprentice tile decorator at *Sherwin & Cotton tile works. Until 1924, modelled miniature relief portraits and portrait tiles. Signed or initialled tiles decorated with portraits of figure designs in *émaux ombrants* in 1890s. From 1890s to early 20th century, decorated and signed Morris ware for S. Hancock & Sons, earthenware manufacturers in Stoke-on-Trent, Staffordshire; plant forms outlined in trailed slip after style of W. *Moorcroft. In America (1919), continued ceramic portraits and designed for tile manufacturer in Newport, Kentucky; some designs sent to England for production. Also worked as painter.

carton pierre. Mixture of paper pulp, whiting, and glue, very hard when dry; can be moulded and painted to look like carved wood. Extensively used in Britain, 1870s-1880s, for ornate decoration on furniture panels and cornices. *See also* bois durci and papier-mâché.

carved lacquer. Oriental lacquer technique in which design (pattern usually diaper or repetitive floral or geometrical) carved out of up to 100 very thin layers of lacquer applied over prepared base. Originated in China (tiao ch'i) where perfected in Sung and Yuan dynasties (960-1368) as *cinnabar lacquer. Introduced into Japan (choshitsu) in Muromachi period (1334-1573); imitated and modified there. In China, carved lacquer most popular and highly developed lac-

Cartier. Brooch in lapis lazuli set with turquoises and diamonds and striped with turquoise enamel. Cigarette holder set with diamonds, amber mouthpiece. Both c1925.

quer style worked in wide colour range and used on huge variety of objects. In Japan, however, never as popular as *makie; used mainly on small objects, particularly tea and incense ceremony utensils. Varieties named according to decoration, depth of carving, colours of ground, intermediary layers and surface. *See* chinkin-bori, Coromandel lacquer, katakiri-bori, guri, kebori, tsuikoku, tsui-o, tsuishu, zokoku-nuri, zonsei-nuri.

carver chair. Armchair or elbow chair, in set of dining chairs, used at head of table by carver.

cased glass. *See* cameo glass.

cassolette. *See* pastille burner.

Castellani, Alessandro (1824-83) and Augusto (1829-1914). Italian goldsmiths and archaeologists, sons of goldsmith and jeweller Fortunato Pio Castellani (1793-1865). Lived outside Italy 1848-58 for political reasons. Workshops closed on father's retirement (1851) until sons' return to Italy. Augusto reopened workshops, 1858; Alessandro collected and dealt in antique jewellery. Firm continued making *archaeological jewellery, expanding range to include pieces copied from English and Italian medieval pieces, probably under influence of patron, Michel Angelo Caetani, Duke of Sermoneta. First exhibited in London, 1861, when Augusto lectured on revival of Etruscan techniques to Archaeological Association; started vogue for archaeological jewellery in England; pieces copied by R. *Phillips shown at International Exhibition, 1862, when Castellani also exhibited. Also shown at international exhibitions in Paris (1867) and Vienna (1873). Style widely copied in England and America. Built up notable collection of classical jewellery (part now in British Museum, London). Augusto wrote 'Antique Jewellery and its Revival' (1862), and 'Della Orificeria Italiana' (1872), both very influential in spreading Italian archaeological style. Mark: crossed capital Cs.

Alessandro Castellani. Gold brooch and earrings. Late 19th century.

cast iron. Type of iron produced by blowing air through molten ore in blast furnace; resulting pig iron may be easily heated to melting point and cast in moulds. Technical improvements during early 19th century continually cheapened cost of process, leading to eclipse of more costly *wrought iron. Concentration of all stages of mining, smelting, manufacturing and transport in one ironworks led to great increase in production, e.g. *Coalbrookdale works, employing over 5,000 men by c1820; cast iron in its Great Exhibition display in 1851 included structural and decorative metalwork, garden

ornaments, and furniture; hall, coat, and *umbrella stands; interior chairs, tables, mantel-pieces, *plant stands, *door knockers, *door porters, bootscrapers.

Castle Hedingham. *See* Hedingham Ärt Pottery.

cathedral clock. *See* skeleton clock.

cat's eye. Name for various chatoyant minerals (i.e. which shine like cat's eyes), particularly variety of chrysoberyl: translucent honey to greenish or brownish colour, with streak of light running across stone. Cabochon-cut to show this. Used in rings and brooches.

Catterson-Smith, Robert (b 1853). English silver-smith and teacher; trained at Dublin School of Art and Royal Hibernian Academy Schools; early career as assistant to W. *Morris at Kelmscott Press. Studied silversmithing with Art Worker's Guild; won national recognition for execution of The Music Panel, hammered silver plaque designed by E. *Burne-Jones, shown at Arts & Crafts Exhibition, London, 1896. From 1901, headmaster of Vittoria Street School for Jewellers & Goldsmiths, Birmingham. Principal of Central School of Art, Birmingham, 1903–20; teaching influenced whole generation of silver-smiths. Large silver-covered cross, made for Rochester Diocesan Deaconess Institution at Clapham Common, London, now in Victoria & Albert Museum, London.

Caucasian carpets (including Armenian, Georgian, and Azerbaijan carpets). Traditional carpet making industry disrupted *c*1890 by im-portation of synthetically dyed, fast fading, deep orange wool. From 1920s, aniline dyes generally used in Armenian Erivan (Yerevan) rugs; Karabagh rugs often chemically rinsed to con-vert characteristic bright purplish-reds to buff. Soviet factories introduced socialist-realist picture and portrait carpets, commemorating heroes and industrial advances. Throughout 20th century, traditional peasant and nomad patterns increasingly hybridized by motifs from factory carpets and dispersal of hitherto local patterns. Kuba and Shirvan regions, in Azerbaijan, now produce bulk of Causasian carpets; several thousand rugs a year also made in Erivan since 1920s.

Cauldon Place Pottery. *See* Brown-Westhead, Moore & Co.

Cave, Walter (fl 1890s). English architect; also, furniture designer in style of Arts & Crafts Movement, e.g. rush-seated oak chair with curved arms and seat rails, low stretchers, and flat splats (shown by *Arts & Crafts Exhibition Society in 1896). Best-known for polished rose-wood piano resembling cupboard, 1893; music rack falls into place when doors open, drawers conceal candle sconces.

Caxton chair. *Wycombe side-chair with cane seat and turned front legs and stretchers; back has top and centre rail, with uprights slightly splayed. Made from *c*1850 for homes, schools, church halls, etc.

Cazin, Jean-Charles (1841–1901). French potter; also painter and engraver. Teacher from 1866, became director of Ecole des Beaux-Arts and curator of museum at Tours (Indre-et-Loire) in

Caucasian carpets. Left: Sumak saddlebag, woven in Caucasus. Late 19th century. Right: bird design carpet. Mid 19th century.

Below
Walter Cave. Oak upright piano designed for Bechstein. c1900. Width 4ft8in.

1869. Worked as painter in Paris from 1875, exhibiting in 1876. In London, as art teacher, from 1871, worked with R.W. *Martin; pupils included W. *Martin. At Fulham pottery, made stoneware jugs and mugs with incised or impressed decoration of flowers, heraldic emblems, etc. Some designs in style showing Japanese influence. Work often signed.

celadon glaze. Greenish feldspathic glaze, used in southern China in 6th century, and widely imitated. Among oriental glazes which inspired European potters in late 19th century. Produced e.g. at Royal Copenhagen Porcelain Company and, later, in America at Rookwood pottery.

celery glass or **stand.** Tall cut-glass vessel for sticks of celery. Cylindrical body with flared rim, usually engraved. May have wire net at top. Bottom half with short stem and low foot, or may be encased in decorative cylinder made of electro-plate. Popular from 18th century in England and America.

Celtic jewellery. *See* archaeological jewellery.

Central Pottery. *See* Wilkinson, A.J. Ltd.

centrepiece, épergne, or **flower stand.** Large British glass table ornament popular from 1860s until early 20th century. Often of curious shape, e.g. grouped hollow bamboo sticks (*see* Rusticana) or employing bizarre colour effects. Although intended as decorative pieces, many combined practical functions (e.g. fitted as candelabra, or with multiple flower holders, or equipped with bowls and dishes as fruit or bon-bon stands); also found as loose baskets hanging from twisted arms. Centrepieces with mirror bases known as plateaux centrepieces (first registered 1871 by *Boulton & Mills glasshouse). Fine crystal centrepieces with tall, trumpet-shaped vases and twisted decoration made 1860s–80s by D. *Pearce for T. *Webb & Sons. Also made by J. *Powell & Sons and *Richardson & Sons. Many cheap cranberry glass specimens, expecially as flower stands.

Century Guild. First English Arts & Crafts society, association of designers, artists, and metalworkers, founded c1882. Founders included A. H. *Mackmurdo, Herbert Horne, Frederick Shields, C. *Heaton, S. *Image. Aimed to promote craftsmanship and involvement of artists in industrial design, and to bring building, decoration, glass-painting, pottery, wood-carving, metalwork, and all applied arts to level of painting or sculpture, instead of to that of trade. Carpets, textiles, furniture, wallpaper, etc., designed and manufactured in workshop in contemporary styles; Mackmurdo chief designer.

All furniture made by established manufacturers. Pieces with decoration by individual members, e.g. S. Image, attributed to Guild in catalogues. Many examples in satinwood with inlay decoration, probably designed by Mackmurdo. Introduced uprights terminating immediately under desk surfaces, cornices, etc. in early 1880s; characteristic of English Art Nouveau furniture.

Metalwork in copper, brass, and pewter made by George Eshing and Kellock Brown. Designs subordinate decoration, including sinuous and stylized plant forms, to strong formal requirements, e.g. standing lamp in brass, stem rising from circular base to chalice shaped holder

*Century Guild. Screen designed by A. H. *Mackmurdo. Satinwood frame; two silk panels embroidered in silks and gold thread. Letter CG embroidered in bottom left-hand corner of right-hand section. 1884. Height 4ft.*

Right
Ernest Chaplet. Porcelain bottle. Late 19th century.

formed from *repoussé* petals of stylized tulip. Guild disbanded in 1888 but many of members continued to maintain close association. *Illustration at* Mackmurdo, A. H.

Century Vase. Porcelain vase made in America by Union Porcelain Works and shown at Philadelphia Centennial Exhibition in 1876. Commemorates events in American history, depicted in six relief biscuit panels around lower part of vase. Other decoration includes paintings of machinery, relief portrait of George Washington, gilded eagle, modelled heads of indigenous animals, and bison's head handles. Marked UPW, with eagle's head holding letter S.

Ceramic Art Company. Pottery established (1889) in Trenton, New Jersey, by J. Coxon and W. *Lenox. Among early American manufacturers of 'Belleek' porcelain; techniques learned at Ott & Brewer factory. Some original models still in production. Marks include overglaze stamp of CAC in circle with palette and brushes at top left and Belleek printed below; also company name with Trenton, N.J. printed in wreath.

cha-dansu. *See* tea ceremony utensils.

chagama. Japanese iron tea kettles decorated with low-relief; lids usually of copper or bronze and often inlaid, with wrought-iron rings for lifting. Cast since 15th century, middle of Muromachi period (1334–1573). Increasing numbers produced as tea ceremony gained in importance. Produced mainly in Ashiya, Chikuzen Province and in Sano, Shimotsuke Province.

chair-bedstead. Metal armchair convertible into bed; utilitarian, with button-upholstered arm rests, seat, and back; front legs usually brass.

Popular in Britain during latter part of 19th century.

chair-table, table-chair, or **jump-up.** Variation of *high chair; chair legs fit into corners of rimmed table top. Pieces could be used separately. Term used by High Wycombe (Buckinghamshire) manufacturers from c1850. Made until early 20th century.

chakra. *See* rimbo.

chamber candlestick or **chamberstick.** Candle-holder in silver, Sheffield plate, Britannia metal, or brass, with carrying handle (scroll, loop, etc.): has short, moulded socket attached to broad greasepan which serves as base. Various forms, square, octagonal, circular, etc., often decoratively engraved; may have long, straight handle giving appearance of small frying-pan. Cylindrical glass shade fits into pierced gallery at base of stem on some early 19th century examples. Often made *en suite* with conical extinguisher (*see* douter) and trimming scissors.

chamber chair. *See* fancy chair.

Chamberlain & Co. *See* Worcester.

chamfer. Planed or smoothed-off angle. May be concave, moulded, or recessed. Feature of Gothic Reform style furniture.

champlevé enamelling. Medieval enamelling technique; metal surface chased, stamped or cast into cellular depressions, or *champs*, which are then filled with enamel to level of original surface. Craft revived in mid 19th century; in 1860 John Ruskin offered prize for best piece of *champlevé* enamelling. *Illustration at Elkington & Co.*

chandelier. Branched central light suspended from ceiling; gas-powered versions, in brass, date from 1851 Exhibition in London. Kerosene chandeliers date from *c*1865 in America; made e.g. by Mitchell, Vance & Co., and shown at Philadelphia Centennial Exhibition, 1876. See gasolier.

Chang glaze. Thick, opalescent or brightly-coloured glazes produced at Doulton factory, Burslem, Staffordshire, from early 20th century. Three or more glazes used together in layers; characteristically, top glaze crackled and trickling down surface.

changeant glass. *See caméléon* glass.

chao-hung. *See* cinnabar lacquer.

Chaplet, Ernest (1836–1909). French artist potter. Apprentice at Sèvres from age of 13. Worked on development of *barbotine* decoration in 1870s at *Laurin factory and, later, as manager of Haviland studio. Work includes vases decorated with flowers in low-relief under copper-red glaze. From 1886, produced stoneware made by P. *Gauguin. Started small stoneware workshop in 1882, for Haviland family; in full control from 1885 until succeeded by A. *Delaherche in 1887. Made jugs, bottles and vases in brown stoneware, painted with flowers, fruit or figures in coloured glazes. Work marked with H & Co impressed, within a chaplet. In 1885, began work also for manufacturer of earthenware and porcelain in Choisy-le-Roi (Seine), using as mark monogram of HB (Hautin, Boulanger et Cie) Choisy le Roi; carried out own research there from 1887. Attempting to reproduce glazes used by Chinese, achieved successful *flambé* glazes and distinctive matt white; also turquoise, mauve, and white. All work characterized by extreme simplicity of form.

Chareau, Pierre (1883–1950). French architect, interior decorator, and furniture designer. Designed reception hall of French Embassy stand at Exposition Internationale des Arts Décoratifs, Paris, 1925, with R. *Mallet-Stevens, *Süe et Mare, P. *Follot, etc. Furniture in Art Deco style characterized by lack of superfluous ornament and fine proportions emphasized by surface texture of woods, e.g. oak, rosewood, sycamore. Chairs often based on *bergère en gondole*.

Charles, Richard (fl *c*1860–*c*1880). English furniture designer. Started Cabinet Makers' Monthly Journal of Design in 1860; pioneer of Early English style furniture, applying motifs to contemporary shapes. Pieces include sideboards, half-tester beds, davenports, bedside cupboards, towel rails, etc.

Charpentier, Alexandre (1856–1909). French sculptor and metalwork designer; specialist in commemorative bas-reliefs, often reduced and

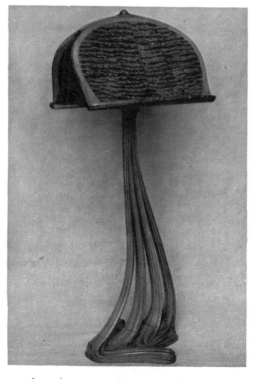

Pierre Chareau. Desk of purple wood veneer. Chair of lacquered and varnished beech with leather upholstery. 1925.
Below
Alexandre Charpentier. Reading desk in hornbeam. Late 19th century.
Right
Chatelaine. Makers' mark W.N. Made in Chester, 1902.

struck as bronze medals. Original models for door furniture show naturalistic nude figures in low-relief, of almost molten appearance. Also designed furniture in Art Nouveau style, characterized by heavily moulded woodwork and use of plaques in bas-relief. Member of *Ecole de Nancy.

chatelaine. Hooked ornament carrying watch, small scissors, keys and seals, often designed *en suite*. Worn at waist or suspended from waist by long chain or belt. 18th century fashion for chatelaine died out by early 19th century; revived in elaborate, purely ornamental form in Europe and America at time of Renaissance re-

Chaumet. Tiara of diamonds mounted in platinum. Oval clusters can be removed and worn as brooches. c1930.

vival, 1870s and 1880s. Made of enamelled gold with precious stones; c1890–1900, made of gold, pavé-set with small diamonds. Modified form carrying only watch or *vinaigrette worn throughout 19th century.

Chaumet. French jewellers, founded 1780 by Etienne Nitot in Paris. Became jewellers to Napoleon Bonaparte. London branch opened in 1875. Firm, still in operation, run by Marcel Chaumet and family from 1928; specializes in production of tiaras and jewelled ceremonial clothing.

chawan. *See* tea ceremony utensils.

cheffonier. *See* chiffonier.

Chelsea Keramic Art Works. American pottery established by A. *Robertson; from 1872, made art pottery near Boston, Massachusetts. Products include reproductions of Greek vases, tiles, ornamental plaques, and flask-shaped vases with decoration in high or low relief. Soon after 1876, H. *Robertson initiated production of earthenware with underglaze decoration in coloured slip, sold as 'Bourg-la-Reine' ware, and introduction of oriental glazes and design. Products impressed with CKAW, or name in full, with marks of artists incised. Firm failed in 1888. New company, *Chelsea Pottery, formed in 1891, removed to Dedham, Massachusetts (1896), trading as *Dedham Pottery.

Chelsea Pottery. American company formed (1891) in Chelsea, Massachusetts, by H. *Robertson, manager, with help from group of Boston businessmen, after failure of *Chelsea Keramic Art Works. Art pottery often covered with oriental-inspired crackle glaze. Because of soil's humidity, which caused steam in kiln, business moved in 1896, afterwards trading as *Dedham Pottery.

chemist's jar. *See* pharmaceutical glass.

chenille Axminster or **Patent Victoria Axminster.** Axminster carpet made by adaptation of chenille silk velvet technique. Velvet made by two-loom process; cloth for pile woven first, with warps spaced at twice required height of pile. Cloth with e.g. ½in. between warps then sliced into bands consisting of warps with ¼in. fringe each side, twisted to give round cross-section; these used as wefts in weaving chenille cloth, which thus has pile on both sides. Un-

Chelsea Keramic Art Works. Two green glazed earthenware bottles decorated in high relief. Designed by Isaac Scott. Impressed mark: Chelsea Keramic/ Robertson & Sons; incised signature, Scott, on front. 1879. Height 8⅝in.
Below
Chenille carpet. Made by James Templeton & Co. c1870 depicting 'Christ in the Temple'.

*Serge Chermayeff. Silvered wood cabinet with vertical band of small drawers. Made for *Waring & Gillow. 1930s.*

Right
Chinese carpet. Decorated in centre with long life symbols and cloud bands in blue, ivory, and salmon-pink. c1900.

limited colour range possible: wefts can be made any shade, or parti-coloured, at first stage of process. Weaver at J. *Templeton's shawl factory in Glasgow suggested pressing fringed threads in V-shaped grooves instead of twisting them, to keep pile on one side of chenille cloth and give designs sharper definition. Templeton applied idea to furnishings and carpets backed with flax or jute; began production on handlooms in 1839. Second chenille carpet factory founded 1855 in Glasgow by John Lyle, Templeton's foreman. Chenille power loom, invented by William Adam of *Tomkinson & Adam, patented in 1869. (Rights shortly afterwards extended to Templeton and Lyle.) Chenille carpets made more than 12ft wide; monopolized seamless carpet market until introduction of *art squares in 1880, and continued dominant until 1900s, when both superseded by wide *spool Axminsters. General production in England continued until 1957: made more recently at Templetons in Glasgow. Still made in Switzerland, and on handlooms in Chile.

Chermayeff, Serge (b 1900). Russian-born architect; also designed furniture. Educated in England, studied art and architecture in Germany, Austria, France, and Holland. Co-director with P. *Follot of *Waring & Gillow's department of modern French furniture, 1929. Practised independently as architect from 1930 in Britain; in America 1933-36. Known for Jazz Modern style furniture, characterized by strongly marked veneers; also used costly materials, e.g. silver. Designed Modernist style furniture in early 1930s; examples shown at

Exhibition of Industrial Art in Relation to the Home (London, 1933). Chairman of department of design, and professor of architecture at Brooklyn College, New York, 1942-46; became American citizen, 1946. *Illustration at* cocktail cabinet.

Chesapeake Pottery. American pottery, established c1880 in Baltimore, Maryland, to make domestic earthenware, sometimes with Rockingham glaze. From 1887, traded as Chesapeake Pottery. Parian ware, made from 1885, includes series of medallions representing Seasons, relief plaques decorated with cats' heads, and portrait busts. Also made majolica, sold as Clifton ware, marked Clifton Decor B, on crossed crescents, with monogram of DHF (D. F. Haynes, proprietor).

chess clock. Timer for chess players, introduced internationally in 1860. Two clocks linked, so that stopping one automatically starts the other, e.g. following each move. Standard dials record time expended by players in hours and minutes. Red flag on each dial gives player warning of completion of each hour's play.

chesterfield. Large sofa popular in Britain in late 19th century. Wooden frame padded with thick stuffing; many springs. Often button-upholstered.

chestnut roaster. Shallow, usually rectangular, sheet-iron box with perforated lid and long wooden handle; chestnuts placed in box and

pushed into glowing coals of open fire. Also, lidless shovel-shaped variety, usually in brass. Numerous modern reproductions, mostly brass.

chest of drawers. Storage furniture; fitted with three or four drawers. British examples during 19th century often flat-fronted with turned, wooden handles, bold moulding outlining drawer fronts. Attached plinth moves with bottom drawer (characteristic of 19th century examples). Topmost tier may contain two half-width drawers. High, narrow chest with six drawers also popular during 19th century. Often matched bedroom furniture. American models, c1840-c1865, often have overhanging tops with plain backboard, or gallery; sometimes with 3in. high recessed cases containing shallow drawers, connected by backboard. Top drawer may overhang in three-drawer examples. Fronts sometimes serpentine. *See also* military chest of drawers.

ch'i. *See* lacquer.

chia-chu. *See* dry lacquer.

chicken-skin. Trade name for supple skin of newborn lamb, used e.g. for leaves of fans.

chiffonier or **cheffonier.** During latter part of 18th century, open shelves for books, with drawer or cupboard below. From c1835, usually cupboard base with one or two shelves on wooden back; often in mahogany, some models in papier-mâché. More elaborate from c1850, e.g. with bow-fronted cupboard section flanked by shelves; ornately framed mirror back.

children's can. *See* christening mug.

child's chair. *See* high chair.

child's mug. *See* christening mug.

chiming clock. Clock playing tune on bells or gongs at quarter and half hour intervals; distinct from striking clock, which strikes only one gong or bell at hour. Many domestic clocks from mid 19th century combine striking and chiming work in Westminster chime, played on rod gongs; these incorporate three separate mainsprings and trains, for timekeeping, chiming, and striking.

chiné ware. English salt-glazed stoneware (made 1886-1914), or earthenware (until c1908) decorated at Doulton workshops in Lambeth and Burslem by process developed and patented by J. *Slater. Netted texture obtained by pressing moistened fabrics, e.g. lace, on to surface of clay before firing. Moulded scrolls, borders, and floral decoration then applied and glazed in several colours. With gold decoration, ware known as *chiné* gilt.

Chinese carpets. Traditional carpets, with symbolic design and coarse weave of two or more wefts between each row of tufts, made until c1860. Thereafter, gold and silver thread, machine-spun wool, and aniline dyes increasingly used; carpets made with finer weave, single weft threads, deeper pile, and up to 30% more knots to 1 sq in. by c1900. Embossing technique widely used: furrow clipped round designs with curved scissors at last stage of manufacture. Embossed carpets sometimes self-coloured, so

pattern formed solely by embossing. Increased in popularity c1930. Industrial school for carpet weaving established at Tsinan, Shantung, c1900. First rugs sold in America after Boxer Rising (1908); thereafter, designs influenced increasingly by Western market. Numerous factories founded in Tientsin and Peking; cheap labour organized for large-scale production of export 'Chinese' carpets, decorated with e.g. lanterns, pagodas, lakes with boats, Great Wall symbols. New sizes created to fit Western rooms. Manufacture in Ningsia and Paotow (near Mongolian border) in *East Turkestan style, expanded by Chinese traders to meet foreign demand. Western market flooded during 1930s with chrome dyed, chemically rinsed carpets with 1in. pile, and Persian, Japanese, Savonnerie, or American designs. Chinese carpets became second only to Persian in popularity with West.

Chinese duplex. Swiss watch with type of duplex *escapement invented by C-E. Jacot (1830) for watches exported to China; elaborate case, in e.g. enamel and gold set with jewels; movement decorated with Chinese-style motifs, and centre-seconds hand appearing to register true seconds.

Chinese lacquer. See aogai, carved lacquer, dry lacquer, heidatsu, lacquer, raden.

Chinese snuff bottles. Small, narrow-necked bottles (2–6in. high) of late Ch'ing period China. First used for aromatics and drugs, then also for snuff. Tightly-fitting stopper often attached to long spoon reaching to bottom inside bottle. Shapes range from simple, rounded forms to elaborately carved or relief-modelled butterflies, human figures, blossoms, fruits, etc. Materials include glass, ivory, jade, and agate. Many glass bottles have delicate designs painted on inside surface. From 18th century, porcelain bottles popular, often enamel-painted and gilded. Fine examples bear mark of Chia Ch'ing or Tao Kuang. Great quantity of all types exported to West; some decorated with Western-style motifs, many refitted with silver caps in England.

Chinese style. Furniture style popular in Britain c1920–c1930. Typical are red lacquer cabinets with ornate brass hinges and locks, resting on carved, silver stands based on Carolean designs; often used as cocktail cabinets.

Ch'ing or **Manchu dynasty** (1644–1912). Chinese period beginning with invasion by Manchus, causing collapse of Ming dynasty. Achievement of technical perfection in ceramics, lacquer-work, jade, etc., towards end of period resulted in loss of simplicity and spontaneity in expression. Increase in trade with other countries accompanied by lowering in standards of work for export and eclectic approach to design. T'ai P'ing rebellion (from 1850) caused e.g. destruction of Imperial Factory (ceramics). Fall of Manchu dynasty followed by formation of republic.

chinkin-bori (Japanese, 'sunken-gold carving'). **sokin,** or **ts'ang-chin** (Chinese, 'cut-out gold'). Oriental *carved lacquer technique, originated in China as ts'ang-chin; adopted in Japan as chinkinbori or sokin in Muromachi period (1334–1573); still used. Fine-line decorative pattern, usually stylized geometrical or floral diaper, engraved into prepared lacquer base, often with a rat's tooth, then filled to highlight design, at first with gold powder or foil; later various coloured lacquers used.

chip carving. Woodworking technique: pattern (usually geometrical) created by chipping small triangular wedges out of surface of object. Popular c1900 for decorating small articles, Colonial reproduction in catalogues. Typified by lyre-back chairs with horsehair seats, slim-toilet sets.

Chippendale style or **Colonial reproduction furniture.** Reproduction furniture based on designs of Thomas Chippendale, 18th century cabinet maker. Popular in Britain from c1870; in America during 1890s, where sometimes called colonial reproduction in catalogues. Typified by lyre-back chairs with horsehair seats, slim-legged tables, and straight, diamond-paned, mahogany bookcases with brass handles. Name often used loosely for furniture in dark red wood.

Chlidema Carpet Company. British carpet manufacturers in Kidderminster, Worcestershire; firm called Winnal & Fawcett until 1887. Pioneered use of steam in British carpet industry; power looms in operation in 1850. Henry Fawcett invented *Chlidema squares and patented them in England and America in 1882. Manufactured first *crush-resistant carpet c1937.

Chlidema square. Carpet width designed for assembling into large carpet with uniform pile, to rival seamless *chenille and *art squares. Patented 1882 in England and America by Henry Fawcett of Winnal & Fawcett (later *Chlidema Carpet Co.). Before general adoption of wide power looms (c1900), all power made carpets (except chenille and ingrain) woven in 27in. or 36in. widths, joined to form carpets of required size. Originally assembled from widths woven from only two Jacquard cards, for central field and border designs. Border sections for complete carpet thus woven with only one pile 'brush'; when attached to four sides of central field, pile lay in four directions, only one coinciding with 'brush' of field. Chlidema system overcame this, and avoided awkward mitred joins where border strips met at carpet corners. (Said to have been first used in 1863, for Prince of Wales's wedding carpet, but not generally adopted until c1885, with extension of Fawcett's patent.) Five Jacquard cards used (instead of two), weaving five different pattern sections: one of central field, other four of border pattern with adjacent central field, for top, bottom, and two sides, plus corners. Method used for patterns with central medallions as well as overall designs. Large numbers of Wiltons made in Chlidema squares in 1920s and 1930s; also some Axminsters, by firms without wide looms. Still used occasionally for carpets with awkwardly shaped borders, e.g. for ships and hotels.

chocolate muddler. Long-handled electro-plated or silver spoon for stirring chocolate (served in tall pot); used in America from c1895. Served same function as stirring rod or molinet used in Britain since mid 18th century.

Choisy-le-Roi. French factory producing white earthenware and porcelain from 1804, at Choisy-le-Roi (Seine). Table services and toilet sets printed in red or, later, black, with classical scenes or French views, often surrounded by garlands of stylized flowers or simple black line. Later, decoration in relief includes swans or scenes with figures. Some pieces have yellow rim decoration, designs of foliage and flowers, printed hunting scenes, or Persian-inspired flowers. Earthenware body developed and refined in 1830s. Transfer-printing continued in black, sometimes with touches of colour or, rarely, printed in white on blue ground. Subjects increasingly sentimental. In 1860s, work with relief decoration often enriched with colour and covered with brilliant glaze; reverse often turquoise-blue. Other work includes architectural ware, tiles, and trompe l'oeil pieces in form of ducks, pigs, and plates of oysters or asparagus. Henri-Deux ware also made. Factory traded as Hautin & Boulanger from 1836; still in operation. Marks incorporate Choisy, or Ch le Roy, and sometimes HB & Cie.

Chokusai, Miyagi (b 1877). Japanese netsuke artist of Osaka. Favourite form, *katabori netsuke, carved in uncoloured wood or ivory, sometimes with inlaid details. *Na: Masanosuke; *Chomei: Chokusai.

Chomei (Japanese, 'carved signature'). Name, including inscription of Japanese carver or sculptor embossed or engraved on work.

choshitsu (Japanese, 'carved lacquer') or **tekishitsu.** Japanese generic term for *carved lacquer. Corresponds to Chinese tiao ch'i.

christening mug, child's mug, or **child's can(n).** Small mug of c½ pint capacity used by infants from 17th century, given as christening present by godparents mostly from Victorian period. Silver or electro-plate, usually straight-sided, tapering slightly from base; some decorated with chasing, repoussé work, or fluting. Child's can(n), American term; smaller version of ¼–⅓

*Christening mug. Decorated with children being protected by Guardian angels. By R. *Redgrave, 1865.*

Christofle. Pitcher and three beakers of different designs. 1925.

pint also called orange juice cup in America. *Illustration at* Adams, G. W.

Christian, D., & Sohn. French glass factory in Meisenthal, Lorraine, active in promoting Art Nouveau glass. Founded by Désiré Christian (1846–1907), who was in charge of decor workshops of Burgen, Schverer & Co. glass factory (also in Meisenthal) 1885–96, where there was close co-operation with E. *Gallé. Produced much fine iridescent glass, e.g. vases, bowls, and lamps. Marks: medallion with D. Christian & Sohn, Meisenthal, below cross; also same words as circular freehand signature with Loth., i.e. Lothringen (German, 'Lorraine'), below Meisenthal.

Christofle (L'Orfèvrerie Christofle). French goldsmiths, silversmiths, and jewellers, founded in Paris, 1829, by Charles Christofle (1805–63) in partnership with brother-in-law Calmette; firm carried on by Charles Christofle alone from 1831. Household silver produced from *c*1839. Bought rights to plating process patented by chemist Ruolz, for 150,000 francs, 1842, but due to prior patent by *Elkington, was forced to pay further 500,000 francs for monopoly of electroplating in France. Nephew Henri Bouilhet (b 1830) joined firm, 1852; introduced new machinery for mass production. Firm patronized by Napoleon III and Prince Joseph-Charles (1853). By 1859, employed 1500 staff; plated dinner service in Louis XVI style for Tuileries mostly destroyed in fire, 1871: remnants now in Musée Nationale de la Château de Compiègne, France.

Business expanded after Charles succeeded by son Paul and Henri Bouilhet in 1863; most of output derived from Louis XV and Louis XVI silver styles and from Japanese metalwork; outside designers included A. *Carrier de Belleuse. In 1890s, firm made cautious use of Art Nouveau style, but after World War I more adventurous designers e.g. C. Fjerdingstad, Jean Serrière, Gaston Dubois, Maurice Daurat, employed in 1925 Art Deco style. Current production of gold, silver, and electro-plate includes Baguette pattern wares, first made in 1861; factories in Switzerland, Buenos Aires, Milan, and New York. *Illustration at* cloisonné enamelling.

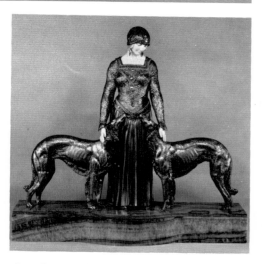

chromium plating. Thin sheet of chromium (metallic element) electrolytically deposited on metal to increase resistance to corrosion; characterized by brilliant silver sheen. Feature of *Modernist furniture during 1930s, marking popular acceptance of tubular steel construction, pioneered by *Le Corbusier, L. *Mies van der Rohe, and M. *Breuer in early 1920s.

chronograph. Term strictly refers to recording timekeeper, but generally applied to watch used for measuring short time intervals, e.g. in sport from 18th century. Centre-seconds mechanism with provision for starting, stopping, and returning to zero by single knob or pendant patented (1862) by A. *Nicole. Split-seconds form (timer) has two concentric seconds hands, which can be stopped independently, showing seconds and minutes only. *See* stopwatch.

chronometer. Balance-controlled exact timekeeper, pioneered by John Harrison, developed by John and J. R. Arnold, Thomas Earnshaw in England, A-L. Breguet in France. Further refinements by E. J. *Dent and V. *Kullberg. Standard form of marine chronometer, with detent escapement, and brass-cased movement mounted on gimbals in wooden box, established during late 18th century. One, two, or eight day movement, often with up and down indicator hand on dial to show state of winding. Box

Chryselephantine sculpture. Dancing girl by C. J. R. Colinet, gilt bronze and ivory on onyx base. Height 20½in.

*Left
Chryselephantine sculpture. Gilt bronze and ivory group by Demètre Chiparus,* Toujours les Amis. *Signed on marble base. Height 16in.*

usually mahogany, with observation glass covered by lid. May include *tourbillon. Later improvements include more effective temperature compensation, with various materials, e.g. palladium and eventually *elinvar, for balance spring. Partly superseded by introduction of wireless time signals in 20th century. Pocket chronometer is watch fitted with detent escapement. Term now used for all timepieces passing official timekeeping tests.

chryselephantine sculpture. Sculpture produced from *c*1900 onwards, incorporating cast bronze – frequently with coloured patination – and hand-carved ivory. Developed through Belgian government's desire to create European market for Congolese ivory; Brussels Salon, Libre Esthétique, ran regular chryselephantine section, displaying carved ivory statuettes in naturalistic style, and hieratic objects in neo-Gothic manner (e.g. Jean Dampt's Silver Knight in full armour, embracing jewelled ivory maiden).

Genre of chryselephantine sculpture in Art Deco style developed 1910–30; statuettes on onyx or marble bases, with clothes or draperies in cast bronze, and hands, heads, legs, etc. in hand-carved ivory. Subject matter ranges from ambivalent cat-suited figures by Austrian, Bruno Zach, through fashion models, night-club danseuses, gamines, to sporting figures, e.g.

golfers, tennis players. Signed figures mounted on onyx plinths, circular, square, triangular, or stepped; by various artists, notably Demetre Chiparus, Friedrich Preiss, P. Philippe.

During 1920s, cheap copies (in e.g. zinc), also signed, made by various artists working for Paris firm of sculptor, Max le Verner (Objets d'Art Fontaines, Luminaire); produced in quantity as lamps, incense holders, book-ends, etc.

chrysoprase. Pale green opalescent glass. Developed 1831 in Bohemia. Similar to American *canary glass; obtained by adding uranium oxide to glass metal. French version, *verre dichroïde*, developed by *Baccarat.

chu-ch'i. *See* cinnabar lacquer.

Church Banks. *See* Booths Ltd.

church plate. Vessels and utensils for liturgical use, e.g. chalice, censer, paten dish, flagon, ewer, ciborium. 19th century church plate reflects high standards of craftsmanship demanded by designers closely involved in High Church revival c1840–c1880. Early Victorian designs, e.g. by Edward Barnard & Sons, display application of Gothic motifs to classical forms; more rigorous historical accuracy proposed by A.W.N. *Pugin in book 'True Principles of Pointed Architecture'; designs in 14th century style executed by J. *Hardman & Co. from 1838, in silver gilt, set with gems and hardstones, according to Pugin's belief that only precious materials suitable for sacred use. Non-Catholic designers highly influenced by High Church theoretical group, Cambridge Camden Society, e.g. W. *Butterfield, W. *Burges, G.E. *Street; designed ornate, accurately detailed plate in 13th and 14th century styles, made in Birmingham by e.g. F. *Skidmore. Freer treatment of Gothic theme and motifs seen in work of J.D. *Sedding; his pupil, H. *Wilson (1864–1939), designed plate c1890–1900 in early art Nouveau style, with stylized natural motifs. Examples by *Arts & Crafts designers from c1880, e.g. Bainbridge Reynolds, N. *Dawson, E. *Spencer, C.R. *Ashbee, in hammered silver, display simplified forms and restrained ornament.

Churchyard Works. *See* Wilkinson, A.J. Ltd.

chutney or **chutnee spoon** or **scoop.** Spoon c6in. long, often with twisted handle, for serving chutney from jar. Made from c1860, mainly in America, in silver or electro-plate; bowl often embossed and engraved, with e.g. floral motifs or classical flatware patterns.

cigar cases. Originally cigar manufacturer's wooden boxes from Spain and Portugal, painted, or transfer-printed. In Europe, from early 19th century, personal cigar cases made in various woods, decorated with carved, painted, poker work, or transfer-printed ornament. English versions, from c1830, decorated e.g. with sporting scenes, landscapes, literary characters, famous buildings; subdivided into individual compartments for cigars until mid 19th century, when increased production made cigars cheaper. Ornate examples, e.g. in tortoiseshell and mother-of-pearl; gilded or painted papier-mâché; embroidered Morocco or Russian leather on metal frame. Frequently combined with e.g. wallet, match compartment, notebook,

visiting card holder. Rectangular silver models with hinged lid, rounded corners, owner's initials engraved on shield on lid or body, popular c1880–c1910. Large numbers imported to Britain from Europe, notably France.

cigar cutter. Instrument used to make hole in end of cigar for easier drawing; appeared in mid 19th century Britain and America with introduction of larger cigar. Large number of designs: some cut end off cigar, some pierced it, some made V-shaped nick. Made in silver or gold, with leather carrying case. Table versions, bladed with wooden handle, used in American tobacco stores to cut 'chaw' off block of tobacco.

cigar holder. Popular from mid 19th century. Basic form: short unornamented tube. Earliest examples in clay (made mainly in France); later materials included amber, hardstones, horn, ivory, porcelain. Usually unornamented or with single plain gold band. From c1875, much more elaborate holders of cut glass, enamel, porcelain, lacquered wood, and ornately carved ivory. Also *meerschaum holders varying from straight tubes, either plain or with simple figure carving along length, to s-curve shaped tubes and elaborately carved miniature pipes. Centres of production: Austria (particularly Vienna), Germany and France. In 1890s, bird and animal bone holders fashionable.

Cin. Pottery Club. *See* Women's Pottery Club.

cinnabar lacquer, Pekin lacquer, chu-ch'i or **tchou-ts'i** (Chinese, 'cinnabar lacquer'), or **t'i hung** (Chinese, 'carved red'). Chinese carved red lacquer, introduced in Sung period (960–1278). Peak production in Ming period (1368–1644), particularly in Peking. Made until 20th century, often for European and later American export trade. Technique: numerous layers of red lacquer applied to prepared, usually wood, base, then carved in highly conventionalized floral, plant or abstract designs. Imitation cinnabar lacquer, known as tui-hung ('painted-red') or chao-hung ('plastered-red'), widely produced in 19th and 20th centuries. Effect simulated by coating pre-carved base with cinnabar lacquer. *See* tsuishu, Kamakura-bori.

cire-perdue or **lost wax process.** Method of reproducing original model in metal, often bronze; used from antiquity. Mould, taken from original, lined with wax, and then filled with core of refractory material. Molten bronze poured in to replace wax as it is melted out. Casting finished by hand when cool, after removal of mould and core. Process increasingly superseded by *sand-casting method, c1820–c1850, because of high cost. Used in manufacture of experimental pieces of art glass by F. *Carder at *Steuben Glass Works in early 20th century, and occasionally in production of *pâte-de-verre.

*Cire-perdue glass. Vase by R. *Lalique, made in Paris. Early 20th century.*

Above
Claret jugs. Left to right: 1) With frosted glass base. John Foligno, London, 1857. 2) With ebony handle. *Walker & Hall, Sheffield, 1901. 3) With jasper ware base by J. *Wedgwood &

Sons. E.K.R., London 1873.

Below
Clarice Cliff. Coffee set. Bizarre. Made at Newport pottery. 20th century.

Wax, coating shaped core, carved in minute detail and covered with several layers of clay. Channels cut in clay cover provide outlet for melted wax, which is then replaced by molten glass. When mould removed after cooling, glass given required finish.

citrine. *See* topaz.

Clantha ware. *See* Bretby Art Pottery.

claret jug. Large pear-shaped flagon, with handle, to hold wine at table; English versions, *c*1800–*c*1850, mostly in silver, with corked necks; numerous later examples, *c*1850–*c*1900,

in clear or coloured glass, silver mounted, with hinged lid, reflect eclectic, naturalistic, and Gothic styles of mid 19th century. Animal jugs e.g. as walrus, or swan, designed as novelties, particularly by G. *Fox. Late 19th century versions, e.g. with cut glass body, silver mounts richly chased or engraved, lid surmounted by tall, ornate finial. Highly functional glass and silver claret jugs designed by C. *Dresser for *Hukin & Heath, *c*1880, e.g. with clear glass body, star-cut at base, mounted with two plain silver bands and square handle supports, wide upper band, with spout, hinged to flat circular cover. Straight square handle flares gently outwards at top. *Illustration at* Fox, G.

Clarke, W.E. (fl mid 19th century) English silversmith working for E. & E. Emanuel in 1860s; designed silver dessert service for International Exhibition, London, 1862, including candelabrum with basket at top for fruit or flowers, and base formed as large group of Britannia seated on lion, attended by allegorical figure of Industry, distributing rewards to the representatives of various nations who are laying their products at her feet. Also showed silver tazza, ornamented with bas reliefs of Richard Coeur de Lion and the Saracens.

Classical style. *See* Grecian style.

claw setting. In jewellery, open-backed setting in which stone held in place with minute claws. Used for gems, particularly diamonds, to allow maximum light to enter stone.

Clementson, Joseph (1794–1871). English potter, born in Cumberland, apprentice in 1820. In partnership, operated Phoenix Works, Hanley, Staffordshire, from 1832. Produced white granite ware and painted earthenware for American and Canadian markets. As sole proprietor, enlarged works in 1845, and purchased nearby Bell Works (1856). Transfer-printed tableware includes services decorated with religious devices for use of Methodist churches in Canada. After retirement in 1867, succeeded by four sons, who traded as Clementson Bros until 1916, maintaining wholesale and retail outlet in Saint John, New Brunswick, until 1890s.

Clesinger, Jean-Baptiste-Auguste (1814–83). French neo-classical sculptor; made début at Salon in 1843 with marble of Vicomte Jules de Valdahon. Worked exclusively in academic tradition, but statues popular subjects for reduction by *Collas process, e.g. Young Fawn (1846), Roman Bull (1859), Combat of Roman Bulls (1864), cast in bronze by F. *Barbedienne and *Susse Frères.

Clevedon Court. *See* Elton, Sir Edmund.

Clichy. French glass works founded 1837 in Billancourt, Paris; made cheap glassware for export. Moved to Clichy-la-Garenne 1844, specializing in cameo, filigree, and *millefiori* glass, and coloured and painted opaline glass. Only French glasshouse represented at Great Exhibition of 1851. Noted for *millefiori* and other brightly coloured paperweights, particularly swirl-patterned weights, often signed C, with rose in design. Merged (1875) with Sèvres glass works. *Illustration at* paperweight.

Cliff, Clarice (b 1900). Staffordshire pottery decorator and designer. Trained at Burslem School of Art. Apprentice at A.J. *Wilkinson Ltd; later, until 1939, art director at Wilkinson's Royal Staffordshire Pottery and subsidiary, Newport Pottery. In 1920s, painted Tibetan ware; large jars painted with floral designs in bright colours and gold. Also painted on pottery designs by artists, including F. *Brangwyn, Paul Nash, and Laura Knight. In early 1930s, carried out designs commissioned from contemporary artists for exhibition of modern tableware at Harrods, London, in 1934; produced by Wilkinson's in association with Foley Pottery. Designed tea ware with yellow glazed surface moulded to resemble surface of corn-on-the-cob (sweetcorn). Painted decoration varies from

*Clarice Cliff. Ginger jar, Tibetan, made at A. J. *Wilkinson Ltd. Designed, painted, and enamelled by Clarice Cliff. Marked with gold transfer printed signature. c1925. Height 15in.*

simple, concentric bands of colour, to stylized trees, flowers, or landscapes, in combinations of bright orange, blue, purple, green, etc., or often black, yellow, and orange or red. Forms often angular, in Art Deco styles. Range of tall shapes have handles of modelled and brightly enamelled flowers (My Garden). Other lines entitled e.g. Bizarre, Inspiration Bizarre, Scarab Blue Inspiration Bizarre, Biarritz, Fantasque. Ornamental vases painted in bright colours with lavish use of gold.

Clifton Art Pottery. *See* Long, William A.

Clifton Junction. *See* Pilkington's Tile & Pottery Co.

Clifton ware. *See* Chesapeake Pottery.

Cloisonné enamel. Old Russian style jug. Height 4in. c1870.

clock jack. Weight or spring driven mechanical spit, of brass, iron, or steel, incorporated e.g. in andiron. When wound up, device automatically turns spit for roasting meat at open fire. May be built into semi-circular heat reflector (hastener), or Dutch oven.

cloisonné enamelling. Decorative technique: fillets of metal soldered on solid back plate form small cells or enclosures, which are then filled with coloured enamel. Method developed in 10th century Byzantium; adopted in China in Yuan (1260-1368) or Ming (1368-1644) dynasties. Revived c1860 by A. *Falize after import of Chinese cloisonné vases into France; continued by son, Lucien. Mainly used in France to imitate Japanese work, both in subject matter and style. Popular with Art Nouveau jewellers. Used by Arts & Crafts movement in England, e.g. C. *Heaton, H. *Stabler, N. *Dawson. *See also plique-á-jour.*

clothes hook. Came into general use in Europe and America during 1850s; usually in iron (often bronzed or lacquered), also brass. Made in wide variety of shapes, and decorated e.g. with ceramic or gilt ornament; during Art Nouveau period (1890-1910), many elaborate designs incorporating stylized plant forms, human figures, etc.

clous d'or. Gold or silver nail points used in *piqué point.*

club chair. Deeply sprung easy chair with inclined back and seat, open sides and upholstered arm rests. Usually button-upholstered in leather. Popular from c1835 in Britain. *cf* club divan.

club divan. Easy chair with open sides, low, inclined back, and long seat projecting beyond wide, upholstered arm rests; popular in Britain during 1890s. Deeply sprung, usually button-

*Cloisonné enamel. Teapot designed by Tard and made by *Christofle. 1867.*

Below
*Clutha glass. Three vases designed by *Dresser for J. *Couper & Sons. Two outer vases acid-etched with C D; central vase marked only with manufacturer's name. All c1890-95. Height of tallest vase 16in.*

upholstered in leather; sometimes with drawer beneath seat for metal spittoon.

club fender. Continuous padded seat on vertical metal bars rising from fender curb; usually upholstered in leather. Dates from c1860 in Britain. *cf* seat curb.

Clutha glass (Old Scottish, 'cloudy'). Scottish glass; cloudy yellow, green, amber (rarely black), with variegated bubbles and streaks; sometimes with patches of aventurine. Developed by J. *Couper & Sons and made c1885-1905. Shapes of Clutha vases, bottles, bowls, etc., often based

on antique models. Designers include C. *Dresser and G. *Walton. *Illustration also at Couper, J., & Sons.*

Coalbrookdale Company. Shropshire iron foundry; in 19th century, Britain's largest manufacturer of ornamental cast-iron furniture, mainly hall stands and garden seats. Designs registered from 1839. Exported to America and France. Realized designs by C. *Dresser.

coal cabinet. Wooden receptacle for coal; popular during 1890s in Britain. Front section slides down or pulls out revealing metal coal container. Often carved, with front inlaid.

Coalport Porcelain Works. English porcelain factory established at Coalport, Shropshire, 1796. In 1862, last member of Rose family, original proprietors, retired. Work from this period generally imitates 18th century porcelain from France, Germany, etc. Decoration in Sèvres style painted e.g. by J. *Rouse. Plaques decorated with delicate flower painting by J. *Aston. Business declared bankrupt (1875–80), then acquired by P.S. *Bruff. T.J. *Bott art director from 1890. Tableware decorated with panels of landscapes, flowers, etc., or lightly decorated with pink or green grounds. In late 19th century, artists began to sign work. Parian used in combination with glazed porcelain in modelled comports, centrepieces, etc. Enamel jewelled decoration in imitation e.g. of topaz, pearls, used on tall vases, painted also with landscapes or views. In 1924, firm bought by Cauldon Potteries Ltd (formerly *Brown-Westhead, Moore & Co.) and moved (1926) to Staffordshire. (Coalport China Ltd now operates at Crescent Works, Stoke-on-Trent.) Marks, usually in underglaze blue, C, S, and N, in loops of monogram of CS (1861–75), Coalport A.D. 1750 (1875–81) and crown (from 1881), with England (from 1891) or Made in England (from c1920).

coal scuttle. Container for coal, made from 18th century; often in copper with brass handles, also in brass, bronze, or lacquered tin; helmet shape particularly popular. Gradually superseded by coal box or vase during 19th century.

coal tar dyes. *See* aniline dyes.

coal vase. American term for rectangular metal coal bin with foot and sloping lid; similar to purdonium. Often japanned, and painted with scenes, figures, scrollwork, etc. Mass-produced in copper, brass, gunmetal, bronze, steel, and iron after c1860, e.g. by Belknap Hardware & Manufacturing Co., Louisville, Kentucky.

Coard, Marcel (b 1889). French interior decorator and Art Deco furniture designer; trained architect. Furniture characterized by veneers emphasizing structural components. Worked only for individual clients, e.g. art patron, Jean Doucet; exhibited at salons. Used rare materials, e.g. lapis lazuli, sharkskin. Examples include flat-topped, square-legged desk in macassar ebony veneer on oak, top covered in crocodile skin.

Coates, Wells Wintemute (1896–1958). Architect, engineer, and industrial designer; born in Tokyo, educated in Canada; settled in London, 1924. Established architectural practice,

Marcel Coard. Sofa in rosewood carved in imitation of basketwork and decorated with two bands of ivory. 1920s.

*Cocktail cabinet. Designed by S. *Chermayeff, in coromandel ebony and walnut veneer on mahogany frame. Height 38½in.*

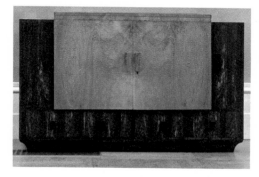

1929–39. Designed Modernist style furniture; also light, graceful, metal-framed chairs and tables. Showed furniture at Exhibition of Industrial Art in Relation to the Home (London, 1933). (Practised in Vancouver, Canada, from 1956.)

cochin. Small cartouche or vignette showing contemporary event or vista. Found as decoration on objects of vertu.

Cocker, George (1794–1868). English potter. Apprenticed at Derby factory c1808; modelled figures until 1817. Worked at Coalport and Worcester, 1817–21. In partnership, established pottery in Derby, c1826. Ornamental ware includes figures, some in biscuit, portrait busts, small animal groups, and modelled baskets of flowers. Tea and dessert services also produced. Biscuit figures sometimes bear incised signature. 1840–53: worked in London. From 1853, at Minton's and other Staffordshire potteries.

cocktail cabinet. Cabinet containing bottles, glasses, etc., for cocktails. During 1920s, antiques (e.g. lacquer cabinets) often adapted by replacing interiors with glass shelves. Modernist style examples popular during 1930s, with lead-lined ice containers, compartments for bottles and glasses, and mirrored interior often lighting up when doors open. *Illustration at* amboyna wood.

cocktail ring. Heavy, elaborate ring (often of unusual design). First appeared in 1920s; worn for cocktail and dinner parties after wearing of evening gloves abandoned. Term now used to describe any large, vulgar ring made in 1920s.

cocktail watch. Lady's ornamental wrist-watch, fashionable in 1920s; distinguished by abnor-

mally thick, raised glass; boldly styled and sometimes set with paste or jewels. Swiss examples generally from Geneva.

Codman, William C. (fl late 19th and early 20th centuries). English silver designer; chief designer for Cox & Son in London. From 1891, worked in Providence, Rhode Island, for *Gorham Manufacturing Co., for which designed *Martelé range of Art Nouveau silver.

coffee pot. Made *en suite* with matched tea service by c1835. Variety of styles, including tall, tapered shape derived from 18th century, with hand engraved body, spout, and lid; also larger, full-bottomed pyriform shape, decorated e.g. with heavy *repoussé* work and human mask at base of spout. Handles e.g. of ivory, with silver mounts, and finial in form of e.g. cherries, pineapple, surrounded by foliage. Manufactured throughout 19th century, e.g. by *Elkington, Barnard, *Hukin & Heath.

coffee spoon. Smaller version of teaspoon, c4in. long, introduced in mid 19th century; made in silver and electro-plate, sometimes enamelled or embossed.

Cohr, Carl M. Danish manufacturing and retail silversmiths, founded 1860 in Fredericia by D. Cohr, producing flatware and engagement rings. Silver hollow-ware added in 1895, electro-plate (trade name, Atla) in 1921, and stainless steel in 1930. Exports started 1921. Large output of cutlery: Old Danish pattern, with threaded edge, introduced 1860, remains among best-selling lines.

cold meat fork. *See* cutting fork.

Coldrum Pottery. *See* Wells, Reginald.

Cole, Sir Henry (1808–82). English designer and artistic reformer. Early official work includes organization of Public Records Office with records salvaged from fire at Palace of Westminster, reorganization of Post Office, and railway administration. Published series of children's books with help of artists, e.g. William Mulready, Richard Redgrave. Under pseudonym, Felix Summerly, won award from Society of Arts, 1846, for design of earthenware tea service made at Minton factory; appointed to Society's council in same year. Established *Summerly's Art Manufactures, 1847, with aim of improving aesthetic value of objects in everyday use. Established monthly Journal of Design and Manufacture (1849–52). Contributors include O. *Jones, M.D. *Wyatt, and G. *Semper, as well as colleagues from Summerly's Art Manufactures. Campaigned for reform of Schools of Design; as secretary, until 1872, introduced classes in applied arts. Instrumental in organization of Great Exhibition in London (1851); with Redgrave, A.W.N. *Pugin, and O. *Jones formed committee selecting objects from Exhibition to form basis of collection of ornamental art for benefit of design students. Also responsible for organization of South Kensington Museum, later Victoria & Albert Museum. Memoirs, 'Fifty Years of Public Work', completed and published by son (1884).

Cole, James Ferguson (1799–1880). Notable British maker of high-quality signed clocks and

watches. One of few craftsmen remaining after 1850 with skill necessary to make a complete watch from start to finish. Devised many forms of lever *escapement. Showed at International Exhibition, 1862.

Coleman, William Stephen (1829–1904). English pottery painter and designer. Worked at factory of W. T. *Copeland and, from 1869, at Mintons. Art director of Minton's Art Pottery Studio (1871–73). *Japonaiseries* and nude figures painted on biscuit porcelain plaques, bowls, etc. supplied by Minton factory, at first in underglaze colours, later mainly in bright enamel over glaze with brown outline under glaze. Also designed work for painting by other artists at Mintons. From 1873, worked as illustrator and painter in oils and watercolours.

Colenbrander, Theodorus A.C. (1841–1930). Dutch pottery and porcelain decorator. Director of Rozenburg Plateelbakkerij from foundation in 1885. Early tin-glazed earthenware painted with stylized clouds, scrolls, and geometrical motifs, e.g. in pale yellow, pink, and blue, with large areas left white. Thinly-potted plates and vases light in weight. Some decoration apparently inspired by Javanese batik-printed fabric. Later, director of Zuidhollandsche Plateelbakkerij in Gouda, continuing style developed at Rozenburg, and Ram pottery at Arnhem, where mark, with ram's head, incorporates name COLENBRANDER. In early 20th century, painted linear designs, predominantly in blue and brown; in 1920s, often left work unglazed.

Collas process. Method of producing exact scale copy of large piece of sculpture; invented c1839 by Frenchman A. Collas, and used by him in association with F. *Barbedienne to reproduce original works in bronze editions of 24–200.

Collcutt, Thomas Edward (1840–1924). English architect and furniture designer. From c1870, designed light, finished versions of Early English style furniture, e.g. ebonized mahogany cabinet with bevelled glass decoration, painted and coved panels on top and base, turned supports, and corner shelves (now in Victoria & Albert Museum, London); made by *Collinson & Lock in 1871; shown at International Exhibition in London in same year, also at Centennial Exhibition in Philadelphia (1876). Influenced Art Furniture in both countries. Collcutt mainly responsible for Collinson & Lock catalogue of 1871. Dining chairs (made by Collinson & Lock c1872), with sturdy turned legs, stretchers, row of turned balusters on back, were prototypes until 1890s. *Free Renaissance style pieces in 1880s characterized by bevelled glass decoration and broken pediments. Also designed for *Gillow.

Collier & Plucknett. English furniture makers in Warwick; development of firm founded by W. *Cookes. Furniture influenced by Gothic Reform style; also made some pieces in Old English style. Some examples bear metal label.

Collingwood Ltd. British court jewellers founded by Joseph Kitching in London, 1817. Joined by partner Richard Abud (1837); appointed jewellers to Queen Victoria: firm still holds Royal Warrant. Traded as Kitching and Abud until their retirement in 1855. Firm left to Henry Collingwood who began as apprentice in late

*Thomas Edward Collcut. Cabinet in painted mahogany made by *Collinson & Lock. Painting by Albert Moore. c1871.*

Below
E. Collinot. Enamelled earthenware bottle with 'Persian' decoration. c1869. Height 11¼in.

1830s. Continued firm with son, Robert Nelson Collingwood as Collingwood Ltd. Produced high-quality jewellery in currently fashionable styles.

G. R. Collis & Co. Electro-plated six-light candelabrum. c1875. Height 13in.

Collinot, E. (fl mid to late 19th century). French potter. Made earthenware at Boulogne-sur-Seine (Hauts-de-Seine). Noted for enamel decoration in Persian style with grotesques, arabesques, etc., outlined with black in manner of *cloisonné* enamel, often on shapes of European derivation. Work marked with painted initials.

Collinson & Lock. London cabinet makers closely associated with Art furniture movement. Firm established 1870; realized designs by T. E. *Collcutt, B. J. *Talbert, J. *Moyr Smith, E. W. *Godwin. Absorbed *Jackson & Graham, 1885; taken over by *Gillow, 1897. Stamp: Collinson & Lock, London. *Illustrations at* Collcutt, T. E., Mackmurdo, A. H.

Collis, G. R., & Co. English firm of silversmiths founded 1835 by George Collis, in partnership with George Whitgrave; mark registered at Birmingham Assay Office. Collis withdrew, 1837, and registered individual mark. Firm's output includes hollow-ware and centre-pieces displayed at Great Exhibition, London, 1851.

Colman, Samuel (1832–1920). American painter; exhibited at New York Academy of Design (c1850), associate of National Academy (1859). Collector and connoisseur of oriental art. Partner in Louis C. Tiffany & Co., Associated Artists (see Tiffany Studios).

Colonial reproduction furniture. *See* Chippendale style.

Colonna, Edward, sometimes mistakenly called Eugène (b 1862). German designer and decorative artist. Trained as architect in Brussels; emigrated to America in 1882, working in Dayton, Ohio during 1880s designing railroad car interiors; designed furniture for Canadian Pacific Railways in Montreal, also some East-

lake style furniture. Worked with Associated Artists, L. C. *Tiffany's interior decorating firm. Lived in Paris in 1890s, designing furniture and jewellery for S. *Bing's shop; jewellery featured baroque pearls set in gold scrolls. Serpentine motifs also used in furniture; style that of *Ecole de Paris. Designed furniture for Bing's room settings at Paris Exhibition, 1900: attenuated satinwood furniture, lightly carved with scrolls; table tops and cabinet panels inlaid with stylized floral motifs. Designed ceramic table ware decorated with flowing plant forms in green, mauve, and grey, made in Limoges in 1899; also provided silver mounts for stoneware jug, glazed blue and brown, made by A. *Bigot c1900. Returned to America in 1905; settled in Newark, New Jersey. *Illustrations at Bigot, A., Limoges.*

colour combing. Decorative treatment for painted furniture, e.g. cupboards. Combs drawn across paint surface form zig-zags and waves. Developed by A. *Heal; popular in Britain during 1920s and early 1930s.

Columbian Art Pottery Company. American pottery, established at Trenton, New Jersey, in 1893, year of World's Columbian Exhibition in Chicago. Among early manufacturers of 'Belleek' in America; made tableware and toilet sets.

comb. Worn as ornament. Jewelled heading, either hinged and designed to be worn just above forehead with prongs lying flat on head, or with heading and prongs in one piece, worn in chignon; decorated with gold, coral, or rows of gemstones. Very popular 1860–80. In America, very elaborate combs with large 'waterfall' mounts worn in 1860s. Some comb-mounts equal in size, shape and decoration to *tiara. Large Spanish combs made of tortoiseshell decorated with pierced work fashionable 1870s, popularized by Bizet's opera, 'Carmen' (first produced 1875). Simpler combs in plain gold or silver decorated with punched or engraved designs worn at turn of century. Fine Art Nouveau examples, e.g. by R. *Lalique, using ivory and horn. Comb abandoned after World War I, when long hair out of fashion. *Illustration at horn.*

combination clock. Type of *travelling clock with additional mechanism and dials for e.g. calendar, barometer, thermometer, hygrometer. Popular as *novelty and presentation clock from c1880.

comfit box. *See bonbonnière.*

commemorative objects. Large number of objects, e.g. mugs, pipe stoppers, plaques, door porters, plates, biscuit tins, vases, tobacco jars, made to mark or celebrate individuals or occasions of national or local significance, e.g. coronations, royal anniversaries, jubilees; political or military events or personages; notorious crimes, criminals. Many objects carry portraits, insignia, or names of royal family. *Coalbrookdale Co. produced many commemorative plaques in cast-iron; other articles in wide variety of materials including ceramics, pewter, brass.

commercial silver. Term used to describe mass-produced plate for domestic use.

commesso di pietre dure. *See Florentine mosaic.*

commonsense chair. *See Sinclair's American commonsense chair.*

Comoléra, Paul (1818–97). French *animalier* sculptor; pupil of F. *Rude. First work exhibited at Salon (1847), study of Golden Pheasant. Subsequent bronzes include: Quail caught in a Snare (1849), Partridge and Thrush (1851), Heron Wounded by an Arrow (1852), Hare (1859), Pheasant (1863), Wounded Partridge (1865), Dead Partridge (1866); bronze editions by *Susse Frères, and A. Gouge.

compact. *See powder compact.*

Compagnie des Arts Français. *See Süe et Mare.*

companion chair. Three, upholstered, double seats with curved, horizontal back rails meeting in centre, forming conjoined S plan. *See tête-à-tête.*

compendium. Wooden travelling box divided into compartments for e.g. jewellery, valuables, personal effects, writing or painting materials, often also with secret drawer or compartment often opened by concealed catch in lock mechanism. Examples, frequently footed, made from mid 19th century e.g. in wood, ornamented with tortoiseshell and ivory inlay, frequently with brass carrying handles at sides, and brass nameplate. Superseded earlier writing boxes, lap boxes, by virtue of greater capacity.

compensation (in clocks and watches). Means of maintaining accuracy despite temperature changes. Rate of going of uncompensated clock or watch affected by expansion and contraction of pendulum rod, or variation in elasticity of balance spring. Materials with different degrees of expansion combined in many forms of pendulum compensation designed to keep centre of oscillation constant. Simplest arrangement: wooden rod with cylindrical lead bob. John Harrison's 'gridiron' of parallel steel and brass bars (invented c1720) still generally used during 19th century, especially in France and Austria. Many cheap factory products made with imitation gridiron pendulums. George Graham's mercurial compensation widely used for *precision clocks throughout 18th and 19th centuries: jar or jars containing mercury form pendulum bob; upward expansion of mercury counteracts lengthening of steel rod. Variant, patented (1899) by S. *Riefler, has hollow steel rod part-filled with mercury, and plain bob. Concentric tubes of iron, or steel and zinc used from c1860, mainly in turret clocks, e.g. Westminster Palace clock. Compensation devices largely superseded by introduction of *invar for pendulum rods.

Compensation balances for watches, chronometers, etc., in many forms; most use differing expansion of steel and brass to bend rims of balance inward or outward with temperature changes. Degree of compensation adjusted to equalize behaviour of balance spring by series of screws in rim. Cheaper late 19th and 20th century watches have screws in balance rim to imitate true compensation balance. Various auxiliary compensations applied to *chronometers from c1845, as basic compensation strictly accurate at two temperatures only. 20th century introduction of alloys with almost constant elasticity for balance springs, e.g. *elinvar and nivarox (beryllium alloy), allowed use of plain nickel balance.

Changes in barometric pressure also affect rate, but to extremely small degree. Resulting errors avoided in observatory clocks by placing them in airtight containers at constant low pressure.

complicated watch. Any watch that gives more information than time of day. Examples include astronomical watches, chronographs, repeaters; stopwatches and calendar watches generally considered too numerous to qualify.

comtesse. *See pouf.*

Comtoise clock. Provincial French clock made in Franche-Comté, chiefly in towns of Morbier and Morez, from late 17th century. Mostly weight-driven long-case and wall-bracket types; some spring-driven 'bull's eye' wall-mounted versions, with raised dial surrounded by circular moulding. Movements characterized by crude iron frames with train pivoted in brass bushes, and verge *escapement, gradually replaced by anchor in 19th century; escapement and pendulum sometimes mounted near front of movement. Striking work, where fitted, arranged to repeat strike at two minutes past hour. Pendulums ornate and shaped in e.g. violin form, often embodying simulated gridiron compensation. Enamel dials generally surrounded by decorative gilt castings. Long-cases of various woods may be painted or inlaid, with glazed aperture to reveal pendulum. Comtoise clocks sold throughout France after supplanting other provincial types by 1800; signature on dial usually denotes retailer, not maker. Production continued into 20th century, possibly to 1914.

Comyns, William, & Sons. English firm producing hand-made silver since 1848, when founded by William Comyns. Still trading in Tower St, London. Mark: WC in shaped oval.

condensed milk can holder. Container to hold can of condensed or evaporated milk for use at table. Consisted of cylindrical container, lid with finial, and plate at base to catch drippings; sometimes with one or two handles, and repoussé decoration. Made in America during 19th century in electro-plate and porcelain; wide variety of electro-plate versions made by *Adelphi Silver Plate Co. Some French porcelain ones imported from Limoges.

confidante. Comprehensive term in Britain and America for multiple seat on which two or more couples could sit side by side. Dates from c1870. Button-upholstered seating divisible into sofa and four easy chairs. *See also companion chair, tête-à-tête.*

confortable. French armchair dating from 1838. Contours softened, cushion and mattress quality stressed; examples from c1880 have cylindrical cushions for arm rests, low, squat proportions, and low back. Upholstery (often of oriental carpeting) decorated with pleats, tassels, and fringes. Often companion piece to sofa. *See cushion furniture.*

Conta & Boehme. German porcelain manufacturers in Pössneck, Saxony. Made hard-paste porcelain for ornamental and domestic use, also novelties, claiming establishment in 1790. Noted for *fairings, made chiefly c1860–c1890, previously attributed to firm Springer & Lockett in Ellbogen, Bohemia, using similar mark. Some

small groups, intended as match-holders, have small patch of surface roughened at back or side. Firm continued operation well into 20th century. Mark: shield bearing upraised arm holding dagger, impressed. Fairings often also have numbers incised; later, impressed.

contre-émail. Plain plaque of enamel, applied on reverse of enamelled decoration on e.g. copper, porcelain, to ensure opacity of colour.

conversation chair. See tête-à-tête.

convertible furniture. Wardrobes, chairs, chests, etc. convertible into other pieces, often beds; dates from medieval period. Also type of American *patent furniture, developed simultaneously with *adjustable chairs, etc. Common c1860–c1890. See chair-bedstead, couch-bedstead, piano-bed, sofa-bed, and wardrobe-bed.

Cook, William (c1800–76). English porcelain painter. At Coalport factory, from c1840, painted flowers and fruit; noted for delicacy of style. Work includes flower panels on dessert services and vases in Sèvres style shown at Great Exhibition of 1851. Later work, including painted plaques, sometimes signed.

Cook Pottery Company. American pottery established (1894) at Trenton, New Jersey; succeeded Ott & Brewer at Etruria Pottery. Produced porcelain and earthenware marked with versions of lion and unicorn flanking shield with monogram of C.P.Co. over name of firm Mellor & Co, SEMI VITREOUS/MELLOR & CO around four leaved clover, versions of mark with three ostrich plumes, circular mark MADE BY COOK POTTERY CO/ TRENTON N.J. with year of patent, etc. Also made copies of Dutch Delft ware, adopting mark of Delft factory. The Porcelain Bottle, rounded bottle over F/Delft/D.C., painted in script (from 1895).

Cookes, William (fl 1850s). English wood carver, member of *Warwick school of carving. Work characterized by narrative detail, e.g. Kenilworth buffet, made of Kenilworth oak, depicting scenes from visit of Queen Elizabeth I to Kenilworth Castle (Warwickshire); shown at Great Exhibition of 1851, London. Responsible for carving on sideboard designed (1853) by H. *Protat. Also made household furniture, e.g. chairs, mirrors, firescreens. Firm taken over by *Collier & Plucknett.

Coolidge, Charles A. (1858–1936). American architect in Boston, Massachusetts; also designed furniture, e.g. desks, chairs, and tables in Romanesque and American Colonial styles.

Cooper, Henry (fl 1870s). English furniture maker; from c1875, specialized in Moorish style interiors. Author of The Art of Furnishing, 1876.

Cooper, John Paul (1869–1933). English architect, silversmith, and jeweller; articled to J. D. *Sedding (1887) and H. *Wilson (1891); under latter's influence took up metalwork in 1897. Revived use of shagreen for boxes mounted in silver, material neglected since early 19th century. Head of Metalwork Department, Birmingham School of Art, Margaret Street, 1904–07; then set up jewellery workshop in

John Paul Cooper. Silver cigarette box with shagreen sides. Lined with wood. Marked JP on inside of lid. 1928.

Below
Susie Cooper. Large dish. 1930s.

Maidstone, Kent, where succeeded by son, Francis. Style strongly influenced by Wilson, to lesser degree by Birmingham colleagues A. *Gaskin and B. *Cuzner. In 1906 made number of pieces of silver jewellery decorated with copper by Japanese *mokumé technique. See also bonbonnière.

Cooper, Peter (1791–1883). American industrialist and philanthropist, credited with making America's first metal rocking chair at Trenton, New Jersey, c1860–c1870. Frame of strap metal painted to imitate tortoiseshell; continuous button-upholstered seat and back, padded arm rests (see digestive chair); based on British prototypes, e.g. tubular metal rocking chair shown at Great Exhibition of 1851, London.

Cooper, Susie (b 1903). English pottery designer. Studied at Burslem Art School, Staffordshire,

from 1922. Made jugs, bowls, and vases in stoneware with incised designs in style influenced by Art Nouveau, using forms and techniques of Northern celadons. From 1925, designer for A. E. Gray & Co. Ltd, at Hanley, Staffordshire; geometrical patterns in bright greens, orange, and reddish-brown, or abstract patterns of foliage produced in silver or copper lustre on cream ground. Designed tableware for own company (established 1932), using mark of deer; decoration echoes style of 1920s, though colour and patterns more restrained. Children's ware and cocktail trays decorated with animals. Designs from 1930s later carried out in bone porcelain by firm, now part of J. Wedgwood group. All work signed.

Copeland, William Taylor (1797–1868). Staffordshire potter; in 1833, bought firm developed by Josiah Spode I and descendants from 1762. Firm traded as Copeland & Garrett soon after purchase until 1847, then W. T. Copeland late Spode (1847–67), and W. T. Copeland & Sons. Products shown at Great Exhibition in London (1851) include parian figures; tableware with painted, gilt, and jewelled decoration; also porcelain slabs with floral decoration, notably by D. *Lucas II, who also painted vases and dessert services with landscapes. Terracotta includes busts of Juno and Minerva, made in late 1850s. In 1860s, tableware painted with flower panels, e.g. by C. F. *Hürten. G. *Eyre art director (1864–65), succeeded by R. F. *Abraham (1865–95). Other artists include S. *Alcock, L. *Besche, C. *Brough, and W. *Yale. Firm noted for variety of tableware produced in porcelain and earthenware. Styles adapted from Japanese in 1870s and 1880s. Porcelain vases, bottles, etc., often lavishly ornamented. Ground colours include turquoise, green, and vermilion. Tiles hand-painted, e.g. by R.J. *Abraham, or transfer-printed; sometimes (1870s and 1880s) printed outlines filled in by hand. Tiles, usually handmade, sometimes produced in majolica. Parian ware made until 20th century. Variety of marks used. From 1847, number of versions of Copeland, late Spode; Copeland, sometimes enclosed in wreath surmounted by crown; crossed C's over Copeland; bee over label W. T. Copeland & Sons; SPODE/ COPELAND with C superimposed on pseudo-Chinese seal (c1875–89); ship with sail bearing crossed C's and Copeland late Spode along top (1804–1910). COPELANDS CHINA/ENGLAND printed from 1875. (Firm trades as Spode Limited from 1970.) Illustration at parian ware.

Copeland & Garrett. See Copeland, William Taylor.

Copier, Andreas Dirk (b 1901). Leading Dutch glass artist in Art Deco and Functionalist styles. Joined *Leerdam as designer 1917, where engaged in creation of *Unica and *Serica models. Also designed many new drinking glasses. Work distinguished by purity of line and pared simplicity. Subsequently, appointed artistic director. Mark: C. in right angle, with number and date letter, engraved on all Unica glass to his design.

copper. Used by American and French jewellers in *mixed metal techniques for Japanese and Indian style jewellery to damascene silver and gold jewellery. Theoretically not allowed in England because of assay laws, but these were

frequently ignored. Some enamelling on copper in Art Nouveau jewellery, e.g. pieces by Marcel Bing. Used by English Arts and Crafts jewellers, i.e. T. *Morris, for buckles (sometimes combined with steel or pewter), and by American craft revival designers.

Coralene glass. Late 19th century American art glass with coral-like growths enamelled on surface, then picked out with minute beads of crystal, coloured, or opalescent glass. Objects finally furnace-finished to fix enamels and fuse beads on. Developed by *Mount Washington Glass Works. Later, also popular in Europe and Britain.

Corbyn bottle. *See* specie jar.

cordless clock. *See* battery clock.

corkscrew. Implement used since mid 17th century for drawing cork from bottle. Commonest type, from *c*1850: steel spiral attached at right angle to oblong wooden handle. From late 19th century, more elaborate forms developed, particularly in early 20th century America. Main ornamentation on handles made of chased, embossed, or inlaid silver, gold, or brass; or of carved and inlaid ivory, mother-of-pearl, horn, and hardstone. Simple transverse bar replaced by variety of shapes, including objects, plants, human, and animal forms. Some made with frame for steadying bottle, some with arms for levering out cork. Also, from early 20th century, numerous combination corkscrew-and-bottle-openers, often with attached pen-knives, wire cutters, etc.; most lavish examples date from 1920s.

carnelian or **cornelian.** Type of chalcedony; flesh red to deep clear red. Used for seals, signet rings, and beads.

corner divan seat. *See* Turkish corner.

corner settee. *See* cosy corner.

Corning Glass Works. American glasshouse established 1875 in Corning, New York State, by reorganization of several earlier companies. Made decorative and table ware, especially glasses. Assimilated with *Steuben Glass Works in 1918. Still flourishes. The Corning Museum of Glass, Corning, houses one of world's major glass collections.

Coromandel lacquer or **Bantam work.** Chinese lacquer, used mainly on screens or furniture. Prepared wooden base coated first with layer of chalk, then layers of black lacquer. When dry, lacquer layers carved in intaglio to expose chalk layer. Finally, carved portions painted with bright-toned coloured lacquer. Main production centre, Honan Province. Coromandel lacquerware widely exported to Europe (particularly England and Holland) from late 17th century. Names taken from two major export centres on eastern (Coromandel) coast of India.

Corona Pottery. *See* Volkmar, Charles.

corset-back chair. American armchair with high upholstered back curving in at sides to give waisted effect. Popular *c*1850.

*Cottage furniture. Dresser made by *Heal & Son. Elm with black framing, interior painted white. 1914. Width 4ft.*

costrel. Ancient form of pilgrim bottle in flattened ovoid shape with loops at shoulder for carrying strap. Popular shape for Victorian silver and ceramic ornaments; many modern reproductions.

cosy corner or **corner settee.** Development of Moorish corner during 1880s; combination of seats and shelves fitted into corner. From early 1890s in Britain, seat free-standing, upholstered, and surmounted by shelves, brackets, mirror, and sometimes miniature cabinet.

Cothurne, La. Most popular of series of eight Art Nouveau female figures of Greek dancers (name derives from cothurnus, thick-soled boot worn by actors in Greek tragedy). Modelled for Sèvres by French sculptor, A. *Léonard, as dining table ornaments. Originally made in white biscuit porcelain; success at Paris Exhibition of 1900 led to *Susse Frères buying right to cast versions in metal; some produced with pose and draperies altered so as to incorporate small electric light bulb.

cottage furniture. Simple bedroom furniture popular in America *c*1850–*c*1880. Proponents included A. J. *Downing. Polished, painted surface, usually white, grey, lilac, or blue, sometimes with painted decoration, e.g. flowers. Tables with plain or spool turned legs; matching spindle-back chairs with cane seats. Also hoop-back Windsor chairs. Alternatively, in Britain *c*1900–*c*1913, name for simple, unstained, unpolished furniture inspired by Arts & Crafts Movement; commercially produced, e.g. by

*Heal & Son. Usually in oak, especially *limed oak, or ash. Cabinets may have *bull's eye glazing on doors.

cottage piano. Upright piano with projecting keyboard supported by legs or consoles (bracket supports); development of upright grand piano with keyboard enclosed by doors. Patented in America and England in 1800; name dates from *c*1825, commonly used by *c*1850. Often has fretwork panel (backed with pleated silk) above keyboard lid; More expensive examples may have carved or painted panel.

Cotswold school. Association of furniture designers and craftsmen in the Cotswolds, Gloucestershire; led by S. and E. *Barnsley and E. W. *Gimson from 1893. Development of *Kenton & Co., linking traditional rural craftsmanship with Arts & Crafts Movement. Craftsmen included P. *Waals and Henry Davoll. Tradition continued during 20th century by E. Barnsley.

Cotterill, Edmund (1795–1858). English silver designer; principal designer for *Garrard & Co. from 1833. Worked in naturalistic style, with great attention to surface detail and high degree of realism; favoured equestrian subjects on e.g. table fountain in oxidized silver, gilt and enamel (in Royal collection), and English historical scenes, e.g. centrepiece depicting Battle of Lansdowne in Civil War.

couch-bedstead. Term used in Britain from *c*1850 for couch with hinged end folding down level with seat to give additional length.

Couper, James, & Sons. Scottish glasshouses in Glasgow. Developed *Clutha glass *c*1885, with designs by notably C. *Dresser and G. *Walton.

*James Couper & Sons. *Clutha glass bowl with *aventurine inclusions made between 1885-1905 and set into *Tudric pewter stand.*
Right
Lucien Coutaud. Tapestry, Travestis, signed and dated in bottom right-hand corner, 'L. Coutaud 39'. 6ft6in. × 7ft2in.
Below right
Cranberry glass. Vase with handles and frill in clear glass. c1885.

Dresser's Clutha pieces sometimes marked with flower (for Couper) followed by CLUTHA DESIGNED BY C.D. *Illustration also at* Clutha glass.

Coutaud, Lucien (b 1901). French artist. Introduced to tapestry in 1930s by M. *Cuttoli, who commissioned cartoons from him for Aubusson. Early tapestries include Paul et Virginie (1935), Travestis (1939). (Main output, 1940-60.)

Cox, George (fl 20th century). English artist potter. Experimented with high-temperature glazes. Work made at Mortlake, Surrey (c1910-c1914) and sold in London (c1912). Teacher at Columbia University Teachers' College, New York. Book, Pottery for Artists, Craftsmen and Teachers (published 1914), stresses importance of artistic as opposed to scientific values in relation to pottery. *Illustration at* Mortlake Pottery.

Crace, J. G. & Sons. London interior decorators and furniture manufacturers, founded 1745; known for Elizabethan style furniture, but particularly associated with Gothic style furniture of A. W. N. *Pugin, with whom John G. Crace worked closely from c1847, continuing to design furniture inspired by Pugin's designs after latter's death. Made furniture for Abney Hall, Cheshire, Chatsworth House, etc. Son, J. D. Crace, joined firm in 1854. Firm ceased trading, 1899.

crackle or **craquelle glass.** Popular late 19th century American clear art glass with crackled appearance but smooth outer surface. Produced by plunging red-hot finished objects into cold water. Modified version of 16th century Venetian *ice glass technique. Made chiefly by *Hobbs, Brockunier & Co. (who first employed term, craquelle, 1883) and *Boston & Sandwich Glass Co.

Craftsman furniture. Simple, comfortable, and durable furniture (usually oak) designed by G. *Stickley. Popular throughout America

c1900–c1915; characterized by square, structural elements with visible mortise joints. Upholstery and table coverings in canvas (often green), or leather; copper or iron fittings. Trade mark: words, Als Ik Kan, within joiner's compass. Copied by manufacturers after exhibition in Grand Rapids, Michigan, 1900. *cf* Mission style furniture.

cranberry glass. Late 19th century British glass; clear, pinkish-red. Originally, designed to soften austerity of *pharmaceutical glass jars; in 1880s, became fashionable for tableware, e.g. fluted bowls and vases with frilled rims, often enamelled with *Mary Gregory children. Made as cheap line by most leading glasshouses of period.

Cranch, E. P. (1809–92). American pottery decorator. Lawyer in Cincinnati, Ohio; employed as artist at Rookwood Pottery. Noted for series of tiles illustrating tales or rhymes.

Crane, Walter (1845–1915). English artist, designer, writer. Associate of W. *Morris; leading figure in *Arts & Crafts Movement. 1884, one of original members and first president of Art Workers' Guild, in which he was Master. Chairman of *Arts & Crafts Exhibition Society, 1888–90, 1895–1915. From 1893, director of design, Manchester Municipal School. Art director, Reading University College, 1896. Principal, Royal College of Art, 1898.

Designed pottery and tiles for Wedgwood factory (1867–77), Mintons (c1870). For Maw & Co., designed printed and moulded tiles, also some vases decorated with ruby lustre. Designs commissioned in early 20th century by Pilkington Tile & Pottery Co. include elaborately decorated lustreware. Some vases painted with figures in lustre by R. *Joyce (c1905–c1908). Mark: C surrounding crane, sometimes in square.

Designed first tapestry woven at *Merton Abbey, Goose Girl (1881). Furniture designs include cabinet and stand in ebonized wood, with embroidered panels showing days of week behind glass; lined with stamped leather wallpaper; shown by *Arts & Crafts Exhibition Society, 1888. *Illustration at* tube-lining.

crapaud. *See* pouf.

craquelle glass. *See* crackle glass.

Craven Dunnill & Co. English tile manufacturer at Jackfield, Shropshire (1872–1951). Tiles decorated with abstract floral designs, e.g. in green, brown, and ochre or pink, and copper lustre, under glaze (c1880). Decorative techniques include hand-painted stencils and lithography. Vases also produced in same style. Circular marks incorporate line drawing of works and JACKFIELD.

cream jug. Generally larger during 19th century than previously; 3–5in. high. Commonly found with handle squared off at top level with rim. Among most popular styles was melon-shaped body frequently embossed or chased with naturalistic motifs. George I pear-shaped jug remained in prolific production until early 20th century. Hexagonal or Elizabethan pattern popular; also squat baluster with bulging curves on low moulded foot, often embossed with mechanical raising or deeply engraved and

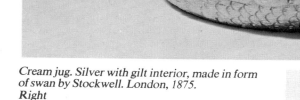

Cream jug. Silver with gilt interior, made in form of swan by Stockwell. London, 1875.
Right
Henri Cros. Polychrome pâte-de-verre vase.

chased. Made in silver or electro-plate; also in cut glass or porcelain.

Creil-Montereau. French *faïence fine* made at Montereau (Seine-et-Marne) from 1749, initially by English workers, and at Creil (Oise) from 1796; factories united, 1818–25 and again, from 1840, produced tableware, etc., transfer-printed with historical and legendary scenes, illustrations of crafts, contemporary costume, songs, dances, etc., or Chinese-inspired decoration. In late 19th century, delicate sepia transfer-printed designs heightened with touches of colour. After closure of Creil workshops (1895), name, Creil-Montereau, retained. Variations of mark usually incorporate Creil et Montereau and LM & C (proprietors: Lebeuf et Millet).

Creole earring. Earring in form of hoop with lower half thicker than upper, crescent shaped in appearance. Fashionable from 1860s, after French colonization of Africa; based on shape frequently found in slave jewellery. Made in gold, or in hair, coral, or jet mounted in gold.

Crescent Pottery. *See* Jones, George.

Crescent Works. *See* Coalport.

cristallo-ceramie, sulphides, sulphures, or **cameo encrustation.** Method of enclosing cameo or medallion of unglazed white porcelain, or other refractory material, within transparent glass mass. Technique tried unsuccessfully in Bohemia and France in late 18th and early 19th centuries; perfected and patented 1819 by A. *Pellatt, who found flint glass best for displaying enclosed items. Used for glass balls, paperweights, door handles, portrait medallions, decanters, and occasionally tableware and jewellery. Method copied by *Baccarat, *Clichy, and *St Louis, particularly for paperweights.

Croix de Lorraine. Cross with short cross bar above main one. Sometimes added to signature in E. *Gallé's glass, and almost always as factory trade mark on glass by A. and A. *Daum; also used by other Lorraine glass makers, particularly after Franco-Prussian War (1870–71), when Lorraine annexed by Germany.

Cromargen. Trade name for *stainless steel alloy used for tableware by *WMF in Germany in early 1920s.

croquet chair. Larger version of *basket chair; button-upholstered, with semi-circular seat, and continuous arms and back.

Cros, Henri (1840–1907). French sculptor; employed by Sèvres porcelain factory during Art Nouveau period. Re-discovered ancient Egyptian technique of *pâte-de-verre* after nearly 30 years of experiment. Used it for coloured sculpture. Masterpiece, 6ft high low relief, *L'Histoire*

du feu, formed central item in Sèvres exhibit at Paris Exhibition, 1900. Also made numerous decorative masks and plaques in same material.

Crossley. British carpet manufacturing firm in Halifax, Yorkshire. Pioneers in mechanizing industry. Bought and improved Richard Whytock's *tapestry process in 1844. Employed George Collier, developer of power-driven cloth mills, to devise power loom for tapestry and Brussels carpets. Loom perfected and patented c1850; factory turned over to Boulton & Watt steam engines. Bought British patent on E. B. *Bigelow's Brussels loom; characteristics incorporated in Collier loom. Bought British patents on Bigelow's Wilton and tapestry looms and installed them in 1851. Licensed other manufacturers to use Bigelow's inventions, and collected royalties. Crossley mosaic carpets invented in 1850; shown at Great Exhibition of 1851; manufactured until 1869. First British manufacturers to install wide Jacquard *Wilton loom (in 1900s); exported large numbers of wide Wiltons to America before 1st World War. Installed *gripper Axminster loom in 1920s. Obtained world patent outside America for *Karvel machine, installed 1931.

Crown Devon. *See* S. Fielding & Co.

Crown Milano glass. Late 19th century American art glass made by *Mount Washington Glass Works. Core of pattern-moulded or pressed (characteristically ribbed) milk glass first rough-finished with acid, then lavishly enamelled (usually in beige or pink, but sometimes vivid) and gilt. Objects sometimes further embellished with prunts and finials. Mark: CM as monogram, with crown over. *See also* Albertine glass.

crumb lacquer. *See* gyobu lacquer.

crumb tray and brush. Small tray, with matching brush, for brushing crumbs from table after meal. Tray made in silver, electro-plate, brass, copper, or pewter; brush frequently curved, and made of wood with inlaid metal fillets to match tray. Produced c1860–c1926; later ones made in chromium-plated steel.

crush-resistant carpet. Developed during 1930s vogue for plain carpeting (especially susceptible to shading and plushing). Manufactured from over-twisted yarn: curls up instead of standing upright, so cannot mat or crush. Made first by *Chlidema Carpet Co. (c1937), then also by J. *Templeton.

crystal ball clock. Table or desk clock with pocket watch movement, produced in early 1900s. Dial magnified by hemispherical glass; similar glass fitted at back, flattened at base to form stand.

crystalline glaze. Ceramic glaze in which crystals, due to presence of mineral salts, produced during slow cooling process; final result difficult to predict. Often contains iron, lime, zinc, or rutile (titanium dioxide), and alkaline flux. Crystals may occur in clusters or, in case of aventurine glaze (resembling aventurine quartz), be evenly spread, e.g. in *tiger-eye glaze produced at Rookwood pottery from 1884. Other crystalline glazes developed at Royal Copenhagen Porcelain Factory from 1886, and by

*Crown Milano. Cracker jar, made by *Mount Washington Glass Company. c1890. Height 5¼in.*

c1900 at many other factories; included in Meissen display at Paris Exhibition (1900). Produced from 1909 at University City Pottery near St Louis (Missouri), under direction of T. *Doat. At time of development, many artist potters were concentrating on glaze as sole means of decorating both porcelain and stoneware. *Illustration at* Rorstrand.

cuckoo clock. *See* Black Forest clocks.

Cumberworth, Charles (1811–52). French sculptor; first exhibit at Salon (1833), portrait bust of young child. Specialized in portrait busts and allegorical statuary; also some minor animal bronzes, e.g. signed, lidded ink-well in form of Turtle, c4in. high.

Cundall, Charles E. (b 1890). English pottery decorator. At Pilkington Tile & Pottery Co. (1907–14), painted flowers and other plant forms, usually in formal arrangements, occasionally trailing. After service in Royal Fusiliers (1914–17), returned briefly to Pilkington factory, then worked in London as portrait painter.

cupping glass. *See* pharmaceutical glass.

Curnock, Percy Edwin (1873–1956). English porcelain decorator. At Doulton factory, Burslem, Staffordshire (1886–1954) painted figures in landscapes, or flowers, notably roses. Made MBE in 1954.

curricle armchair. Low armchair with continuous, curved back and arms; projecting seat enables chair to fit slightly under table. Based on shape of open carriage (hence name). Used in Victorian dining-rooms in Britain.

curtain holder. Metal arm designed to hold back full length curtain, sometimes in form of semi-circular bracket. Made from mid 19th century in gilded or lacquered brass.

cushion furniture. Furniture with framework hidden by over-stuffed fabric upholstery, usually built around spiral springs. Popular in France from c1830. *See confortable, boudeuse.*

Cuthbertson, Thomas (b 1890). English silver designer and teacher; studied at Central College of Art, Birmingham, returned as teacher after 3 years work in industry; head of Silver and Jewellery Department, 1916–46, when moved to Vittoria Street School as headmaster. Stressed importance of quality over fashion, and knowledge of characteristics of metals etc. Own work finely detailed, showing medieval influence, particularly in early years, includes badges of office, clock cases, stud boxes, and christening mugs; examples in Birmingham City Museum and Art Gallery.

cuticle knife. Manicure knife with short, curved blade sharpened at tip; made in silver and electro-plate; often found in étuis from early Victorian period.

cutting fork. Fork with one tine broad and sharpened to act as blade. Patented in America by *Reed & Barton (1869). Originally made in dinner and dessert sizes; later became standard form for small cake or pastry fork (still used today), and larger cold meat fork; made in silver or electro-plate.

Cuttoli, Marie (Mme Paul Cuttoli). Patroness of French tapestry renaissance, c1920–c1940. Friend of J. *Lurçat; first commissioned tapestries from him in 1921. As directress of Aubusson tapestry works, c1930–c1938, commissioned cartoons or adaptations of paintings for tapestry from contemporary painters, including L. *Coutaud, R. *Dufy, C. *Le Corbusier, J. Lurçat, Henri Matisse, Joan Miró, Pablo Picasso. Designs included tapestries for French pavilion at New York World Fair, 1939.

Bernard Cuzner. Bowl with niello decoration. Made in Birmingham, 1933. Height 3¾in.

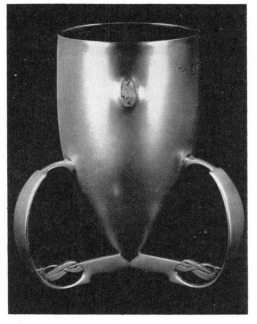

*Cymric Silver. Bullet-shaped vase designed by *Knox. Inset with turquoise matrix cabochons. Dated 1902, made in Birmingham, sold by *Liberty & Co. Height 8½in.*

Cuvelier, Joseph (d 1878). French *animalier* sculptor; small animal bronzes exhibited at Salon 1868, mainly of horses and ponies.

Cuzner, Bernard (1877-1956). English silversmith and jeweller; apprenticed to watchmaker father; studied watchmaking at Redditch School of Art, then took up silver work; studied under A. *Gaskin and R. *Catterson-Smith at Vittoria Street School, Birmingham 1896-1900, where later taught. Designed jewellery for Liberty's *Cymric range, 1900. Head of metalwork department at Birmingham School of Art, 1910-42; wrote 'A Silversmith's Manual', 1935. Work incorporates floral motifs of Art Nouveau, but generally closer to style of C. R. *Ashbee and Arts & Crafts movement, whose ideals he retained throughout life; used enamel, cabochon-cut semi-precious stones, and mother-of-pearl, with Celtic ornamentation. His workshop on display at Birmingham Museum of Science & Industry. Mark: Bernard Cuzner.

Cymric. Trade name for range of silver and jewellery launched by *Liberty & Co. in 1899, incorporating features current in Arts and Crafts movement. Name chosen to suit Celtic inspiration of many designs. Most pieces produced by Birmingham firm W. H. *Haseler, in which Liberty's had shareholding. Examples include hammered silver caskets with broad scrolling strapwork and prominent rivets, candlesticks decorated with enamel and semi-precious stones, brooches, bracelets, chains, earrings, hatpins, lockets, necklaces, and rings. Various stones used in jewellery, e.g. turquoise, lapis lazuli, amethyst, green Connemara marble, and freshwater pearls. Designers anonymous; since identified as including Oliver Baker, A. H. Jones, B. *Cuzner, A. *Gaskin, J. M. *King, R. *Silver, and A. *Knox. Liberty-Haseler agreement ended in 1926; some designs continued until early 1930s. *Illustration at Haseler, W. H., & Co.*

Cyprus glasses. 19th century Bohemian coloured glassware with matt surface and elaborate enamel decoration. Produced by F. *Heckert glasshouse from 1898. Wide range of colours, e.g. green, bronze, violet, and azure blue; often decorated in neo-classical style and given elaborately descriptive names, e.g. Princess of Green Cyprus. *Illustration at Heckert, F.*

Czechoslovakian carpets. Large export industry developed after 1st World War in Czech section (former Bohemia and Silesia). Produced chiefly chenille carpets, then other Axminsters, Wilton, and Brussels; most made to designs ordered by country of delivery. World market glutted in 1920s with quantities of Czechoslovakian *hair Brussels carpets. Exceptionally fine Turkish-knotting machine developed in 1920s; produced carpets of hand-knotted quality, e.g. Persian types, mostly Tabriz, Isfahan, and simple hunting designs.

Czechoslovakian tapestry. Dates from *c*1895 when painter Rudolf Schlattauer, impressed by Scandinavian cottage textile industry, founded first factory at Zašova pod Radhoštěm (village in Wallachian district noted for embroidery). Later moved to Valašske Meziřiči. Designs (by Schlattauer and fellow painters) in illustrational, Secessionist style, with subtle colour schemes; executed on upright looms using kelim technique. Schlattauer's attempts to engage notable artists and attract large furnishing companies unsuccessful.

Second factory founded 1910 at Jindřichůr Hradec by artist Marie Teinitzerova (had studied tapestry in Europe, notably at *Merton Abbey). Supported from start by government commissions; approach to design and technique more experimental than at Schlattauer's factory; produced stylized, angular designs in sharply contrasting colours, woven on horizontal looms. Both factories now state controlled: several tapestries made for state buildings.

Czeschka, Carl Otto (1878-1960). Austrian painter, architect, designer, and artist craftsman. Taught at Wiener Kunstgewerbeschule 1902-08. Member of Wiener Werkstätte; co-director 1904-08. Taught at Hamburg Kunstgewerbeschule, 1908. Metalwork includes set of cutlery designed for Wiener Werkstätte, *c*1910, now in Museum für Kunsthandwerk, Frankfurt-am-Main, Germany. Mark: OCC in monogram (O and first C in ligature) in square. Designed jewellery made by craftsmen at Wiener Werkstätte; similar in style to work of J. *Hoffmann and K. *Moser. Collaborated with Hoffmann on design and decoration of Palais Stoclet, Brussels.

da Costa, Josef Mendes. *See* Mendes da Costa, Josef.

Daigueperce, Albert (fl 1890s) French Art Nouveau glass artist. Assistant to E. *Gallé, with whom exhibited at Paris Exhibition of 1900.

Daikoku. Among most popular of Japanese *Shichi-fuku-jin. God of wealth and prosperity; like *Ebisu, a kitchen deity. Portrayed as plump jovial man wearing long, baggy jacket, soft cap with high crown and high, loose-fitting boots. Carries magic mallet in one hand; has large sack with 'treasures' (*takaramono) on back or at side. Usually shown standing on or near rice bale(s), often with messenger, a rat, at feet.

Salvador Dali. Hands chair. Carved walnut with purple leather seat, made by Arthur English. c1936.

Dalgas, Frederick (1866-1934). Danish potter and porcelain maker. In 1902, succeeded P. *Schou as director of Aluminia and Royal Copenhagen Porcelain Factory; stressed importance of artistic values and good design.

Dali, Salvador (b 1904). Spanish artist; also designed surrealistic jewellery, glass, and furniture, e.g. sofa in shape of Mae West's lips, *c*1925, upholstered in pink satin; original drawing also showed sideboard in shape of nose. Manufactured by Green & Abbot, London. Also 'hands' chair, *c*1936; back supports resembling up-stretched arms and hands, meet at base to form V-shaped central support; made in French walnut with purple leather seat. Also designed lifelike composition lobsters covering telephone receivers.

Dalou, Aimé-Jules (1838-1902). French naturalist sculptor; trained in Paris. Escaped to London after fall of Paris Commune, 1871; exhibited at Royal Academy, 1872-79. Professor of modelling (*c*1873) at South Kensington schools, London, exerting considerable influence on English sculpture until return to Paris in 1880. Work in England includes many portrait busts in terracotta, marble, and bronze, often using unpretentious subjects, e.g. French peasant woman with child, exhibited at Royal Academy (1872). After 1880, executed number of public monuments of historico-allegorical nature, e.g. Triumph of the Republic, Place de la Nation, Paris; series of peasant figures drawn from paintings of Jean-François Millet, intended for Monument aux Ouvriers, Paris. All cast in bronze after his death.

Dalpayrat, Adrien-Pierre (b 1844). French artist potter. Among potters associated with E. *Chaplet, working on development of glaze effects on stoneware and porcelain; achieved soft yellow, blue, and opaque blood-red. Shapes influenced by Art Nouveau, often asymmetrical.

*Above
Adrien-Pierre Dalpayrat. Stoneware bottle. Late 19th century.*

*Below
Damascening. Steel tazza and cover damascened with silver and engraved. Joseph Falloise, Liège, Belgium. 1851.*

Dari. The Garden of Paradise. Late 19th century. 11ft5in. × 10ft4in.

damascening. Decorative technique: gold and silver wire inlaid into base metal. Ancient oriental origin; particularly used by early goldsmiths in Damascus, hence name. Wire hammered into fine grooves of previously undercut design, and planished flush with surface. Technique revived in Spain during mid 19th century; in England, used in many racing trophies, testimonial shields etc., e.g. *Milton Shield, by *Elkington & Co.

Damm. German pottery at Damm, near Aschaffenburg; made cream-coloured earthenware and faience. In 1840, acquired moulds of Höchst porcelain factory (operating 1746-98); many models closely resembling originals bear wheel mark of Höchst factory, sometimes with letter D. Moulds resold in 1880s, and subsequently used at Nymphenburg.

Dammouse, Albert (1848-1926). French potter. At Sèvres factory, where father was modeller, initialled work with *pâte-sur-pâte* decoration. Later, at Haviland factory, style influenced by Japanese; work signed or initialled. From 1892, made stoneware in simple shapes with coloured decoration of flowers, e.g. iris, thistle, and vegetable forms. Also made Art Nouveau decorative

glassware, chiefly in *pâte-de-verre*, decorated with trailing seaweed or flowers in soft browns, blues, and greys. Mark on glass: A. DAMMOUSE, encircling large S (for Sèvres), impressed. *Illustration at* Sèvres.

Danforth, Josiah (1803-72). American pewterer, working in Middletown, Connecticut. Mark: J. DANFORTH.

Danish rugs and tapestries. Hand-weaving tradition lapsed in 19th century because of industrial revolution. Revived in early 20th century by pioneers such as G. *Henning, who derived inspiration from old Danish textiles, hangings, and rugs.

Dantesque style. Furniture style popular in Italy from c1850. Revival of 15th and 16th century designs, e.g. heavily carved wooden tables, and X-chairs upholstered in red plush.

dari or **durry.** Smooth, pileless, reversible cotton drugget, made in India or Pakistan; intended for cheap bed or floor covering. Patterns mainly

simple, rectilinear: usually incorporate stripes, sometimes with flower or animal designs. Made for home market throughout 19th century, especially in Punjab (in Delhi and Multan jails). Woollen daris also made in late 19th century Darjeeling, Nepal, and East Tibet. In 1910s, Ambala (East Punjab) probably only district exporting daris; shortly afterwards, became fashionable in Europe and large numbers made for foreign market. Navalgund (Mysore) became chief centre of production; also made in Shikarpur and Hyderabad (Pakistan); Bhavani (Madras), where dari weavers' organization formed 1931; Obra (Bihar); Jobat (Madhya Pradesh). Coir - coconut fibre - daris, or mourzucks, made in several places in Kerala.

Darmstadt. Artists' colony in the Matildenhöhe founded by Grand Duke Ernst Ludwig of Hesse in 1899 to integrate all arts on basis of social and aesthetic criteria. Members included P. *Behrens, T. *Olbrich. Style strongly influenced by C. R. *Mackintosh and *Vienna Secession. Designers used by T. *Fahrner for jewellery.

Darmstadt service. See Rosenthal, Philip.

dashboard clock. See motor car clock.

date letter (on gold and silver). Letter of alphabet stamped by British assay offices to indicate year of assay (not necessarily year of manufacture); practice introduced from France to London in 1478. Letter is stamped within shield: style of letter is changed after each alphabetical cycle; shape of date shield is also altered to distinguish between cycles using same letter style. London uses twenty letter cycle a–u, e.g. 1896–1915, changing on May 30th. Birmingham: twenty-five letters changing on July 1st, originating in 1773, with twenty-six letter cycles including j used 1798–1823 and 1849–74, to run e.g. 1875–99. Sheffield: twenty-five letters changing on day after Annual Meeting of assay office in July. Edinburgh: twenty-five letters changing on third Tuesday in October.

Daum, Auguste (1853–1909) and Antonin (1864–1930). French glass craftsmen, brothers, followers of E. *Gallé, working in similar style and technique. Generally, work technically coarser, less extravagant, and designs more traditional, e.g. cameo-cut floral decoration; mottled or streaky backgrounds favoured. Members of *Ecole de Nancy. Founded Art Nouveau factory at Nancy producing Gallé-inspired works, and concentrating on enamelling; later, also worked in pâte-de-verre. In 1930s, factory produced number of pieces in etched, geometrical glass in style of M. *Marinot. Employed many fine artists, notably A. *Walter. Factory flourishes today as Cristallerie Daum. Mark: Daum, Nancy, with Croix de Lorraine motif.

Davenport's. Staffordshire pottery established at Longport (1773), in control of John Davenport and family from c1793. Made earthenware, ironstone china, and porcelain. Dessert services often decorated with landscapes. Many tea services produced in 1880s, when Japan patterns, in imitation of earlier decoration at Derby factory, a speciality. Notable producers of tableware for use in ships, as earthenware strong and of high quality. Porcelain plaques decorated both at factory and by independent artists; marked Davenport Patent, impressed. Marks include

Daum Frères. Cameo glass vase on gilt-bronze mount. c1900.

Below
Davenport's. Porcelain jardinière, enamelled and gilt, c1850–65. Height 7in.

DAVENPORT printed in blue, over anchor (on porcelain) from c1850, and crown over DAVENPORT / LONGPORT / STAFFORDSHIRE (c1870–87). Firm failed in 1887.

Davenport. Mid-Victorian walnut cylinder davenport. Width 22in.

davenport, or **pulpit** or **lady's desk.** English writing desk, probably named after maker. Escritoire top with sloping writing surface conceals drawers, often with hidden spring locks, pigeon holes, etc. Front rests on e.g. turned supports, back on base section containing larger drawers, usually down one side only; special drawer for pen and ink, and side flap, also common. Made from late 18th century, popular throughout 19th. Exported to America, where copied by factories and cabinet makers; popular c1860–c1975; called pulpit desk, or lady's desk.

davenport bed. American term for *couchbedstead; dates from late 19th century.

davenport table. Loose term, sometimes used in America to describe long, narrow table.

Davidson, George, & Company. English glasshouse founded 1867 by George Davidson as Teams Glass Works in Gateshead, County Durham, to produce glass chimneys for lamps. By 1877, also made wine glasses and small bottles. Warehouse destroyed by fire, 1880. Rebuilt (1881) as Davidson & Co. Major British producer of *pressed and *slag glass. By 1886, established large export trade to Australia, as well as home market, in jugs, dishes, compotes, salad bowls, salvers, butter dishes, sweetmeat glasses, and water sets. Patented Pearline glass c1889 and Primrose glass in 1890s. Mark (on pressed glass): lion on rampant, facing right.

Davies, Oscar (fl 20th century). English potter. Patented design of combined milk and coffee pot, produced c1935 by Wedgwood factory as part of earthenware coffee set, decorated by wife, G. *Barnsley. In 1930s, with wife, established *Roeginga Pottery.

Davis, Alexander Jackson (fl 1840–60). American architect, associate of A. J. *Downing. Influential exponent of Gothic style in architecture and furniture, e.g. furniture for Paulding Manor c1841 (New York mansion, renamed Lyndhurst in 1864). Examples include pair of chairs with rose-window pattern adapted for backs.

Davis, Greathead & Green. English glasshouse in Stourbridge, Worcestershire. Known at first as Wheeler & Davis. Made some of earliest British *pressed ware, usually dishes and plates in lacy style; also, coloured ware and painted glass versions of Greek pottery.

Davis, Harry (fl late 19th, early 20th centuries). English porcelain painter. At Worcester Royal Porcelain Factory from 1898; painted animal subjects, etc.

Dawson, Nelson (1859–1942). English designer, painter, silversmith, and metalworker. Trained as architect; studied painting at South Kensington Schools. In 1891, took up metalwork and enamelling as pupil of A. *Fisher. Set up workshop with wife, Edith Robinson, specializing in silverwork with enamelling by her until work damaged her health (due to poisonous fumes from gas-fired kiln). Gave up metalwork entirely in 1914. Enamelling technique, e.g. on pendants, buckles, and plaques, clearly derived from Fisher. Also produced hand-made jewellery, often set with wife's jewel-like enamels in Arts and Crafts style. Among founders of *Artificers' Guild (1901); Art Director until 1903. Mark: maple leaf device incorporating initials ND.

Day Dreamer chair. Easy chair with visible parts of frame covered in papier-mâché and decorated with allegorical illustrations of happy and unpleasant thoughts (Hope, etc.). Twisted back supports ornamented with poppies, convolvulus, etc.; apron has central shell with cherub head; back deeply button-upholstered. Shown at Great Exhibition of 1851, London, by *Jennens & Bettridge.

Day, Lewis Foreman (1845–1910). English designer, lecturer, and writer. Educated in France and Germany. Started business in 1870, designing and manufacturing carpets, textiles, embroidery, wallpaper, book-covers, pottery, stained glass. Also designed tiles, e.g. for Maw & Co. and Pilkington Tile & Pottery Co. Leading member of Arts and Crafts Movement; founder member of Art Workers' Guild, 1884; founder member of Arts and Crafts Exhibition Society. Also designed simple, well-proportioned furniture, e.g. oak cabinet with painted panels

Above left
*Harry Davis. Pair of covered vases in Royal *Worcester porcelain painted with highland sheep and decorated with gilding. Marked with Registration no. 437172, shape no. 2330, date mark 1910–11, painter's signature, all in puce. Height 14½in.*

Left
Nelson and Edith Dawson. Top: waist ornament in patinated silver, decorated with enamel and set with garnets; marked with D in maple leaf, c1905. Bottom: pendant and chain, silver set with enamel, 1908–12.

Lewis F. Day. Earthenware dish with painted decoration, dated 1877.

depicting 12 zodiac signs framed in ebony and satinwood; shown at Arts and Crafts Exhibition Society in 1888.

dead gold. *See* bloomed gold.

Dean, J.E. (d 1935). English porcelain decorator; noted for animal, fish, and game subjects at Minton factory, during 40 years from c1882. Work normally signed.

Dearle, John Henry (1860-1932). W. *Morris's assistant and successor as director of *Merton Abbey. Taught tapestry weaving by Morris in 1878. *Illustration at* Merton Abbey.

debased wriggling. Zig-zag pattern mechanically engraved on pewter ware from mid 19th century; imitates simple ornament applied by itinerant pewterers in 17th century, using chisel with rocking or wriggling motion.

de Bazel, K.P.C. (1869-1923). Dutch furniture designer; apprenticed to joiner; became architect. Early furniture designs influenced by Egyptian and Assyrian art. From c1890, pieces reflect Arts & Crafts Movement theories; examples include rectangular oak tea table with projecting shelf below top, geometrical inlay on skirt, and pierced stretchers.

Debût, Jules. *See* Boucheron.

de Camarsac, Lafon (1821-1905). French porcelain manufacturer. In 1854, invented method of reproducing photographs on porcelain; awarded medal for examples shown at International Exhibition of 1862.

decanter label. *See* bottle ticket.

de Castro, Daniel (d 1863). Leading 19th century Dutch glass engraver. Worked in classical style, with vine garland motifs, figures in landscapes, etc., in diamond point, usually on English crystal glassware. Some humorous pieces.

Above
Lafon de Camarsac. Porcelain cup and saucer printed with photographic portraits. French, c1860.

Below
Théodore Deck. Enamelled earthenware dish with decoration painted by Albert Anker. Signed Th. Deck on reverse. c1867.

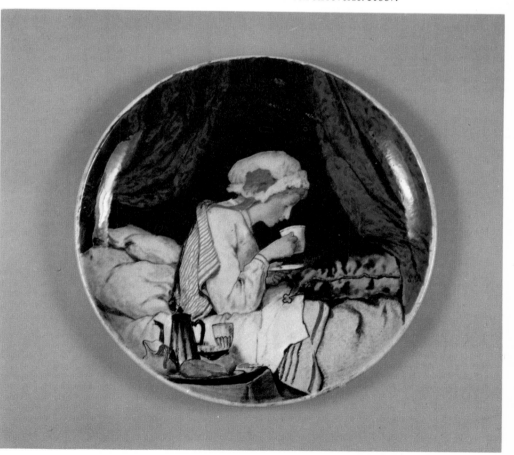

Deck, Théodore (1823-91). French pioneer artist potter. Apprentice potter at age of 19. Worked in Strasbourg (Bas-Rhin), and later Paris, before returning to home district in Alsace (1848). From 1856, made ornamental earthenware in Paris. Early pottery decorated with scenes commissioned from painters. Work influenced by styles and glazes of 16th and 17th century Persian and Near-Eastern pottery. Isnik inspired ware shown at Exhibition of Arts & Industries in

Emile Decoeur. Stoneware vases. Left and centre: c1910. Right c1920. Height 6¾ in.

Paris, 1861. Work in 1870s includes earthenware with glazes of different colours contained within raised outlines of clay, sometimes with lavish use of gold, inspired by Byzantine mosaics in Venice. From c1875, made tin-glazed earthenware, e.g. plaques, for architectural use. Later, experimented with stoneware and porcelain; high quality *flambé* glazes achieved. Work influenced other French potters, e.g. A. *Dammouse, A. *Delaherche, J. *Cazin, and later B. *Moore in England. As art director at Sèvres factory (1887–91), encouraged development of stoneware for architectural use; responsible for introduction of new underglaze colours. Book, *La Faïence*, published 1887.

deck chair or **hammock chair**. Outdoor chair with light, folding, wooden frame (notched at back for adjusting angle) and continuous seat, usually canvas. Dates from c1850 in Britain and America.

Decoeur, Emile (1876–1953). French artist potter. In early 20th century, made faience, then stoneware (from c1905) and porcelain (from c1907). Decorated stoneware (c1910–c1920) with floral or geometrical designs, carved and sometimes painted. From 1920s, produced stoneware in simple shapes covered with matt glazes in ochre, blue, green, or violet.

Décorchement, Françoise-Emile (1880–1971). French Art Nouveau and Art Deco glass artist, working in Conches, Normandy. Made vases, bowls, and other decorative ware in *pâte-de-verre* and *pâte-de-cristal*, of which was one of greatest and most important exponents. Mark: DECORCHEMENT as horseshoe, impressed, with date code engraved on pontil.

Dedham Pottery. American art pottery; former *Chelsea Pottery moved to Dedham, Massachusetts, in 1896. Tableware, at first only plates, decorated with underglaze blue border patterns of e.g. rabbits, crustaceans, insects, dolphins and, rarely, elephants, alternating with foliage motifs; covered with white crackle glaze and marked with painted stencil, DEDHAM POTTERY. Porcelain vases coated with streaked glazes in

François-Emile Décorchement. Plaque of pâte-de-verre. *Impressed with stamp 'Decorchement'.* c1935. Height 5¾ in.

several colours, e.g. crimson, orange, grey, and green, or white, brown, and olive-green, sometimes with iridescent effect, or rough bubbled surface, marked with DEDHAM POTTERY, incised, and painted cypher of potter, H. *Robertson (manager). Robertson succeeded by son, William. From 1908, chiefly crackle-glazed tableware made until operation ceased, 1943.

de Feure, Georges (1868–1928). Designer of furniture and ceramics. Born in Paris; grew up in Netherlands. Associate of S. *Bing. Designed furniture in *Ecole de Paris style of Art Nouveau. Known for light, fragile pieces, often gilt, sometimes lacquered, or in pale woods combined with panels veneered in figured wood, e.g. birch, sycamore. Decorative use of interplaying lines based on plant forms. Chairs and sofas usually upholstered in embroidered silks, damasks with floral motifs, *femme fatale*, and greyhound figures. In ceramics, designed tableware for S. *Bing; porcelain vase, painted with

plants, swans, and curved lines, in grey, lavender, and green, produced at Limoges (c1898–1904). *Illustration at Bing, S.*

de Forest, Lockwood (1850–1932). American artist. Partner in Louis C. Tiffany & Co., Associated Artists (*see* Tiffany Studios) established 1879. In 1881, founded workshops in Ahmadabad, India, producing ornaments, and carved and inlaid furniture for own decorating studio in New York.

Degas, Hilaire-Germain-Edgard (1834–1917). Noted French Impressionist painter; produced no bronzes in lifetime, but 72 terracotta studies of horses, modelled in rough impressionist manner, edited posthumously in bronze by P. Durand-Ruel and founder A. A. Hébrard using cire-perdue method. Editions of 20, plus 2 held by editors; bronzes carry incised signature of Degas and raised name of founder; each edition, marked alphabetically A to T, has own serial number.

Delabrierre, Paul-Edouard (1829–1912). French *animalier* sculptor, pupil of painter, Delestre. Worked in terracotta and plaster, producing mainly groups, of e.g. animals, hunting scenes, edited in bronze. Works include Stags Fighting (1849), Family of Dogs (1851), Lion and Crocodile (1855); large composition, Equitation, for façade of Louvre in Paris, best-known full-scale sculpture.

Delaherche, Auguste (1857–1940). French artist potter, one of family of stoneware potters near Beauvais (Oise). Early experiments carried out nearby. From 1883, worked at Goincourt. In 1887, succeeded E. *Chaplet in Paris workshop of Haviland & Co. Later, worked chiefly in Oise area at Armentières (from 1894) and La-Chapelle-aux-Pots. Early work consists of plain forms, sometimes with sparse relief decoration of flowers, birds, leafy twigs, etc. Later, used shapes with simple ribbing or moulding. Experimented with running colour of metallic oxides; developed good red or brown glazes, sometimes with iridescent effects. Until 1904, designs usually executed by other potters. Work marked with name incised on circular band, or monogram of A.D.; small objects marked with initials A.D.L.H. in lozenge, with number at centre.

Below
Georges de Feure. Carved pearwood chair upholstered in silk. Copy of original designed by de Feure, c1900.

Georges de Feure. Chocolate pot in *Limoges porcelain. c1900. Height 11½in.

Paul-Edouard Delabrierre. Bronze group of two tethered hounds, one sniffing a lizard. Signed on base. Late 19th century. Width 18in.

Right
Della Robbia Pottery. Earthenware dish with sgraffito and painted decoration. c1885. Height 15½in.

Auguste Delaherche. Stoneware vase, enamelled with thick glaze. Signed and dated 1893. Height 7¼in.

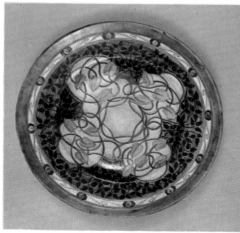

Deldare. *See* Buffalo Pottery. ·

Della Robbia Pottery. English pottery established in 1894 at Birkenhead, Cheshire, by H. *Rathbone and sculptor, Conrad Dressler. Vases, bottles, jars, plates and dishes, with *sgraffito* and painted decoration and, sometimes, elaborate modelled relief, inspired by Italian maiolica. Relief plaques and architectural earthenware also made. Works closed (1901) but reopened until c1906. Mark: DELLA ROBBIA incised or impressed with ship device and initials of decorators.

demantoid. *See* garnet.

Demidoff. Russian gold and silversmith firm established in St Petersburg in early 19th century. Owner of most productive malachite mines

in Urals, giving it virtual monopoly of material. Specialists in monumental urns, architectural devices, set with silver, gold, completely veneered in malachite; notable exhibitor at Great Exhibition, London, 1851.

demi-parure. *See* parure.

De Morgan, William Frend (1839-1917). English ceramic designer. Trained as painter at Royal Academy Schools in London. Designed stained glass (1864-69), and tile decoration (from 1869). Using undecorated tiles bought, e.g. from Architectural Pottery Co., developed method of decoration in which tissue paper, painted with design, laid on biscuit tile covered with white slip, then sprinkled with powdered glaze; paper burned away during firing. In 1872, established pottery and showroom in Cheyne Row, Chelsea; began to produce own tiles. Experimented with lustre decoration in attempt to reproduce red lustre of maiolica painted in Gubbio. Designs, influenced by friend, W. *Morris, include flowers, birds, fish, ships, or mythical beasts. Dishes in cream-coloured earthenware decorated with red lustre. Sunset and Moonlight Suite of dishes decorated in gold, silver, and copper lustre by C. *Passenger. From c1875, introduced decoration in 'Persian colours': predominantly purple, blue, and green, imitating 15th and 16th century Isnik tiles. With Morris (1882-88) at Merton Abbey, near London, continued production of tiles; also made dishes, vases, etc. In partnership with H. *Ricardo (1888-1908), established factory at Fulham, London; produced pottery, tiles, panels, and murals, painted by C. and F. *Passenger (partners from 1898), J. *Juster and J. *Hersey. From 1892, spent increasing periods in Italy for health reasons, while continuing to send designs to workshop, some executed by Italian artists. After retirement from pottery (1905), worked as novelist. Factory closed in 1907. Early tiles unmarked; work at Fulham marked DM over tulip with two leaves, or WILLIAM DE MORGAN & CO/ SANDS END POTTERY FULHAM, surrounding tudor rose. Other marks include initials DM over two figures of year (e.g. 98) in circle, and WdeMerton Abbey in rectangle, with A forming steeple of sketched abbey.

Denaura. *See* Long, William.

Denby Pottery. English pottery established in 1809 at Denby, near Ripley, Derbyshire. Taken over (1912) by J. *Bourne, owner of pottery making stoneware bottles. Firm absorbed workers and equipment of Belper pottery (1834) and of works at Shipley (1856) and Codnor Park (1861), both nearby, trading as Joseph Bourne & Son (Ltd) until 20th century. Stoneware, at first chiefly salt-glazed, used for production of medical and domestic utensils, preserving jars, candlesticks, foot-warmers, etc.; also jugs with relief decoration, handle sometimes in form of hound. Terracotta made for domestic and ornamental use includes butter coolers, cheese dishes, boxes, vases, pedestals, fonts, and garden ornaments. Terracotta body improved and refined (c1883), then also used in plaques. Firm now noted for stoneware for kitchen and table use. Marks include versions of name, Bourne, or Denby.

Denison, Edmund Beckett (**Lord Grimthorpe**) (1816-1905). Lawyer, amateur horologist, and

Top
*William de Morgan. Earthenware tiles. Top, left to right: 1) Lustre decoration on Dutch Delft tile, before 1880. 2) Designed by William *Morris, impressed mark, Merton Abbey; 1882-1888. 3) Impressed mark, DM 98, made in Fulham, 1898-1907. Centre row: 1) and 2) Both with impressed mark, DM98, made in Fulham 1898-1907. 3) Impressed mark for Merton Abbey. Bottom row: 1)*

Impressed mark, William de Morgan, Sands End, Fulham, made 1888-97. 2) Impressed mark, Merton Abbey. 3) Decorated with lustre on Dutch Delft tile.

Above
Denby. Group of stoneware objects from 1912 catalogue, including oven-to-table ware.

scientist; designed *Westminster Palace clock (Big Ben), for which he invented double 3-legged gravity *escapement. Also designed great clock at Great Exhibition in London, 1851. Made peer in 1886.

Dennison, Aaron L. (1812–95). Pioneer of American machine-made watches; together with E. *Howard, opened first factory at Roxbury, Massachusetts, in 1849; designed tools, jigs, etc. for machine production. First watches produced in 1853, under name of Warren Manufacturing Company. Moved with Howard to Waltham, Massachusetts, in 1854, trading as Boston Watch Company; by 1856 still producing only 30 watches a week; company taken over (1857) by Tracey & Baker, case manufacturers, with Dennison as works manager. Travelled to Switzerland (1863) to supervise manufacture of Swiss movements for his American watches. Emigrated to England (1870) and established Dennison Watch Case Co. in London; this ceased trading in 1967.

Dent, Edward John (1790–1853). English clock and watch maker. In partnership (1830) with John R. Arnold; started own business in 1840, later joined by stepson, Frederick; firm still active. In 1851, E.J. Dent & Son undertook to build Westminster Palace clock to design of E. B. *Denison; completed 1854.

Derby. After closure of original porcelain factory in 1848, equipment sold to Staffordshire manufacturers. Several former workmen, led by W. *Locker, established small factory at King Street, Derby. Work, all painted by hand, continued established models and patterns of early factory. Marks include names of managers, e.g. Locker & Co. Late Bloor (until 1859), subsequently Stevenson & Co., Stevenson, Sharp & Co., and Stevenson & Hancock, or crossed baton mark of early factory, with (from 1862) initials SH. Company traded as The Old Crown Derby China Works until 1935; under management of S. *Hancock until 1898. Decorators include J. *Rouse. Derby Crown Porcelain Company, established in 1876 by former director of Worcester factory, in production at Osmaston Road from 1878. Work in tradition of early Derby factory, e.g. Japan patterns, with addition of new shapes for vases, and original figure models. Noted for richness of gilded decoration of printed or hand-painted tableware, etc. Much exported to America. Vases, decorated in Persian or Indian influenced styles, also lavishly decorated with raised gilding. Cups and saucers made in exceptionally thin porcelain with delicate gilded decoration. Porcelain paste sometimes tinted, e.g. mauve or green. Painters include Rouse (from 1882), and D. *Leroy. In 1890, obtained royal privilege to use title, The Royal Crown Derby Porcelain Company. Later, earthenware body occasionally used in production of tableware. In 1935, bought King Street factory. Printed mark: crown over double D, with addition, from 1890, of ROYAL CROWN DERBY, and, in 20th century, Made in England. Year symbols indicate date. Impressed mark, DERBY, used inearly 20th century, gives month and last two figures of date or, after 1911, date in full.

Derby or **steamer chair.** Folding chair with six curved legs and slatted or canework back and seat; with or without arms. Sometimes padded,

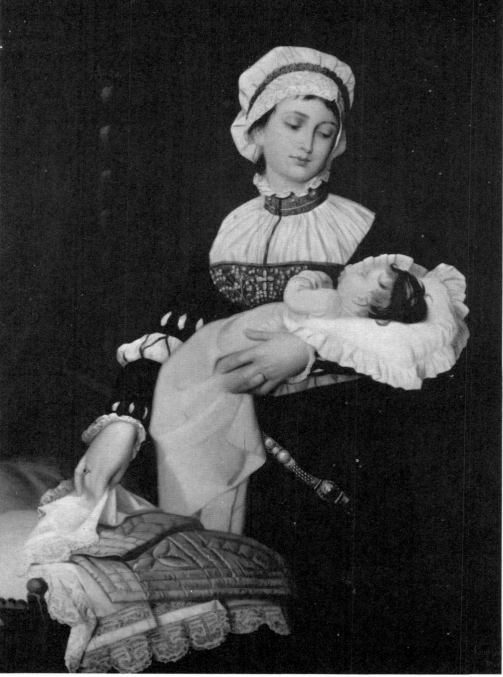

Derby Crown Porcelain Company. Plaque painted by G. Landgraf. Printed mark on back; signed 'Landgraf Derby'. c1884. Height 21½in.

cushioned, and covered in chintz or other fabric. Used extensively on passenger liners from 1860s.

Derbyshire marble tables. Tables with tops made from marble mined in Derbyshire; popular in England during 1840s and 1850s. Local craftsmen (e.g. S. *Birley) copied Florentine marble work, and evolved individual designs often incorporating English flowers; examples made by c30 firms. Industry declined in late 1850s because of high price, but continued until 1905.

Derbyshire spar. *See* blue john.

de Rudder, Isidore (fl late 19th, early 20th centuries). Belgian potter. Operated own kiln in Brussels, then worked for Brussels porcelain manufacturer. Made (c1900) masks of theatrical or traditional Belgian characters in porcelain or stoneware; either unique or in limited editions. Also painted panels with designs of female figures in Art Nouveau style in blue, pink, and white. Some work produced by Boch Frères, and E. *Muller. Pupils include P. *Wolfers.

Descomps, Jean-Bernard (b 1872). French Art Deco sculptor and glass artist. Worked with A.

*Walter in Nancy, where made vases, bowls, etc., in *pâte-de-verre*.

Design & Industries Association. Private association of British designers and manufacturers established (1915) in England. Modelled on *Deutscher Werkbund. Aim: promotion of art in industry; expressed functionalist principles and encouraged controlled use of machinery. Members included H. *Stabler, A. *Heal, W. R. *Lethaby. Forerunner of Council of Industrial Design.

desk, hand, letter or **library seal.** Free-standing instrument with round, flat base for sealing letters with sealing wax; for desk or writing table. Usually 2–5in. high with heavy, ornamental handle in gold, silver, pinchbeck, brass, hardstone, ivory, or porcelain; embossed, carved, mounted with mother-of-pearl, etc. Popular from early 19th century, largely as substitute for *fob seal. After *c*1850, very fashionable; large quantity produced in variety of fanciful shapes and designs, lavishly ornamented. Swivel seal has stirrup-shaped mount holding revolving matrix engraved with design on both sides. Another form has series of interchangeable matrices mounted on short, screw-on bases. American examples made in late 19th and early 20th centuries. Use declined with improvement of postal services. Desk seals made until present time, though little used since World War I.

Despres, Jean (b 1889). French goldsmith and jeweller. Known for fine Art Deco jewellery in style of J. *Fouquet and *Cartier.

Despret, Georges (1862–1952). Belgian Art Deco glass artist and manufacturer, nephew of Hector Despret, founder (1859) of Glaceries de Seumont. Director from uncle's death until factory's closure in 1937. Produced ornamental ware, chiefly in *pâte-de-verre*.

dessert, jelly, and pudding moulds. Large versions made throughout 19th century in tinned copper, brass, and pewter; some with hinged centre section to assist removal of contents, others made in sections, allowing for variations of surface ornament on e.g. jelly. Pewter moulds used for freezing. Cheap stoneware versions produced from *c*1840. Variety of types displayed by Watts & Harton at Great Exhibition in London (1851).

De Stijl. Association of artists, painters, and sculptors formed 1917 in Leyden, Holland, by Dutch artist and writer, Theo van Doesburg and others; van Doesburg published magazine, *De Stijl* (1917–31), in which group explained aims. Propounded rejection of ornament, use of primary colours, abstract rectangular forms. Ideas adopted and incorporated in Bauhaus teachings. Association disbanded 1931. Furniture designed by G. *Rietveld exemplifies group's ideas.

Deutscher Werkbund. Association of manufacturers, architects, artists, and writers established in Munich in 1907 by H. *Muthesius. Aimed to create synthesis between art, craftsmen, and industry, producing functional designs characterized by honest use of materials and working processes. Early supporters included H. *van de Velde, R. *Riemerschmid, J. *Hoffmann. Produced influential illustrated yearbooks and

Jean Despres. Left: buckle, silver and gold, 1930. Right: pendant, silver and gold, 1936.

arranged exhibitions, e.g. Cologne Exhibition, 1914. Built exhibition settlement at Stuttgart, 1927, under leadership of L. *Mies van der Rohe; designers included M. *Stam, *Le Corbusier, W. *Gropius. Inspired similar associations in Austria in 1910, Switzerland in 1913; also *Design and Industries Association in Britain, 1915. Closed by Nazis; recommenced activities in 1947.

Deutsche Werkstätten. Workshop established 1898 in Dresden by cabinet maker Karl Schmidt to produce furniture; among first groups to design specifically for mechanization. Showed inexpensive pieces at Exhibition of Industrial Art at Dresden, 1899–1900; machine-made furniture by R. *Riemerschmid shown at Dresden Exhibition, 1905–06. Designed unit furniture, *c*1910. Products shown in yearbooks of *Deutscher Werkbund, 1910–15.

devil's workball or **puzzle ball.** Concentric, free-moving spheres with delicate pierced-work design, carved from small, solid ball of ivory. Made in China, particularly Canton, from 14th century. From 19th century, produced in quantity for export to West; some examples have ivory stand.

devotional chair. *See* prie-dieu chair.

Devreese, Godefroid (b 1861). Belgian naturalist sculptor; first exhibited at Nationale des Beaux-Arts, 1895, thereafter regularly at Salon. Specialized in human figures; also produced some small bronzes of animals, particularly horses, e.g., bronze equestrian group on shaped and moulded bronze base (1886), showing female figure in full riding habit, mounted side-saddle on horse.

dewdrop glass. *See* hobnail glass.

Dewsberry, David (fl late 19th, early 20th centuries). English ceramic decorator. Trained at Hill Pottery, Burslem, Staffordshire. Plates and vases painted with flowers, notably orchids, at Doulton factory, Burslem (1889–1919).

dial clock or **English dial.** Clock with circular dial concealing rectangular wooden case; made in England from *c*1740, until superseded by *electric clocks in 20th century. Used in shops, offices, schoolrooms, stations, etc. Earliest examples have flat dial in wood or silvered brass with wooden bezel (rare), later brass. Painted iron dial, flat or convex, replaced wood *c*1800. Late examples also found with silvered brass dial, e.g. Metcalfe dial *c*1880 (rare). Movement with verge escapement and fusee replaced *c*1800 by anchor escapement; many verge movements converted. Pendulum may be long or short, e.g. drop dial clock has case extended below dial to accommodate long pendulum. Inlaid octagonal case popular from *c*1830, usually in wood, also black papier-mâché painted with flowers (rare in England, but many American versions); name of maker, retailer, or owner usually appears on dial between 11 and 1, place of manufacture between 4 and 8. *Black Forest weight-driven imitation imported to England from *c*1870 (*see* postman's alarm).

diamond. Crystalline form of pure carbon, hardest known substance, found chiefly in South Africa, India, and Brazil. Colourless or tinted yellow, pink, green, and blue; 'blue-white' most prized. Stones always faceted, using various cuts. In 19th century, brilliant cut replaced rose cut in popularity – shows off stone to greatest advantage; popular in France from mid 18th century, but established in England after Queen Victoria decided to have the Koh-i-noor (Indian diamond given to British Crown, 1849, and shown at Great Exhibition, 1851, in original rose cut form) brilliant cut. Rose cut revived *c*1900. Emerald and baguette cuts also developed. First stones from South African mines reached Paris early 1870s. Introduction of electricity in public places brought desire for less garish, more brilliant stones. Diamond most popular stone from 1880s to World War I; worn particularly in *tiaras, *rivières, and bracelets; sometimes combined with pearls, opals and moonstones. Often set in silver mounted with gold; in late 19th century, with platinum. Settings became less elaborate; more attention paid to quality of stones. *Cartier made break with traditional designs fashionable since late 18th century, e.g. bouquet, star,

feather, crescent; started to experiment with geometrical Art Deco forms in 1920s.

diamond mark. British *registry mark, used 1842–83 for all classes of product, including ceramics, metal, textiles, and glass. Device printed, impressed, or incised on objects of which form or decoration registered at Patent Office, London, to prevent imitation for initial period of three years. Class IV, in Roman numerals enclosed in portion of circle outside top corner of diamond outline denotes earthenware and porcelain. Other information, in coded form as letters or digits contained inside corners of diamond. Until 1867, top corner refers to year of first registration (1842–68 coded X, H, C, A, I, F, U, S, V, P, D, Y, J, E, L, K, B, M, Z, R, O, G, N, W, Q, T, respectively); right corner digit denotes day of month; bottom corner digit, parcel number; letter in left corner shows month. From 1868, different order of information: top, day of month; right, year (1868–83 coded X, H, C, A, I, F, U, S, V, P, D or W, Y, J, E, L, K); bottom, month; left, parcel number. All diamond marks contain RD at centre. Months in both sequences coded (from January) C or O, G, W, H, E, M, I, R, D, B, K, A. Exceptions were 1st–8th December 1860 lettered K, and 1st–19th September 1857 lettered R. Information on these marks stored at Public Record Office, London.

diatreta vase or **cage cup.** Double layered glass vessel with outer layer cut away to form delicate, intricate trellis over lower (usually transparent) layer, but remaining attached to it by small decorated struts; many with lettered inscriptions undercut in same way below rim. Cups usually ovoid in shape. Technique dates from Roman times. Some pieces produced as *tours de force* in second half of 19th century; also vases on same principle, but employing *cire-perdue* method, by F. *Carder.

digestive chair. Mid 19th century rocking chair with continuous, button-upholstered seat and back, padded elbow rests, and frame of bent, steel strips. Recommended for invalids and women. Associated with a Dr Calvert (possibly Frederick Crace Calvert, F.R.S. [1819–73], an industrial chemist interested in industrial design). Never patented; exported to America, where also manufactured.

d'Illiers, Gaston (b 1876). French *animalier* sculptor specializing in small bronzes of horses. First exhibited at Paris Salon in 1899; subjects include plough-horse, group of hunters from Louis XV period, and studies of horses on battlefield during 1st World War, e.g. Artillery Team, Wounded Cavalry Horse, Dead Mule; also modelled racehorses, many edited in bronze.

DIM or **Entreprise de Décoration Intérieure Moderne.** French interior decorating firm established 1919; opened shop in Paris, 1925. Furniture characterized by linear design, fine woods, absence of ornament. Examples include writing table, c1925, in walnut with apron in amboyna; amboyna and ivory top with leather covering; three drawers, central one recessed. Among first furniture firms to show modern pieces in Britain (at exhibition held by J. *Shoolbred & Co. in 1928). Known for Modernist style tubular steel and glass furniture. Represented in London from 1929.

dish. Made in great variety of sizes and shapes, in copper, brass, and pewter. Those intended for use in oven usually made of tinned copper or brass.

dispensing bottle. *See* pharmaceutical glass.

*Diatreta vase. Made by F. *Carder.*

*Arthur S. Dixon. Kettle stand and spirit burner. Silver-plated copper, hand-raised, with cast handle and stand. Made by *Birmingham Guild of Handicraft, c1905–10.*

Ditisheim, Paul (1865–1945). Swiss inventor and horologist; collaborated with C-E. *Guillaume in developing special alloys for precision timekeeping. Introduced epilame, to improve lubrication by watch oils. Produced signed watches of exceptional quality for Swiss Solvil Co. Invented (1920) type of temperature-compensated balance for use with *elinvar hairspring.

divan. Ottoman without arms or back, supported on castors or feet with no visible underframing. Popular in America from c1840; essential item of Turkish style furnishing. From c1918, used as couch by day, bed at night. During 1920s, became part of decorative scheme when surrounded by low bookshelves.

divan bench. Upholstered bench set against wall. First used c1830 in Parisian literary cafés; common in public places from c1850.

diver's watch. *See* elapsed time indicator.

Dixon, Arthur S. (1856–1929). English designer and silversmith; one of chief designers of metalwork at *Birmingham Guild of Handicraft from 1895. Designs characterized by simplicity: decoration usually limited to hammered surface; christening mug designed for Birmingham Guild of Handicraft c1895 now in Victoria & Albert Museum, London.

Dixon, James, & Sons. English manufacturers of Sheffield Plate, Britannia wares, silver, and electro-plate in Sheffield. Founded (1806) as Dixon & Smith for production of Britannia wares and Sheffield Plate. Made electro-plate after acquisition of licence in 1848; developed technique of electro-plating Britannia metal. Registered teapot of leaf form 1850 and produced complete service from design in electro-

plated Britannia metal; large amounts of Britannia and plated wares exported to America from 1830s to 1860s. Made some silver and plated goods for *Felix Summerly's Art Manufactures; continued production of Sheffield Plate into 1860s. Marks: D&S in rectangle (from 1829); JD&S in banner (from 1867); JD&S in border with STERLING SILVER (on exported pieces); bugle with banner and PLATED SILVER; DIXON and bugle in border; 'electroplated' used instead of *E.P.N.S. or *E.P.B.M. All work simply marked DIXON is of Britannia metal. Firm still in existence. *Illustration at Dresser, C.*

Djo-Bourgeois (fl 1920s and 1930s). Architect and interior decorator, active in France. Designed furniture characterized by stark, angular lines; often built-in, e.g. divans framed by surrounds, beds with wall-fixed bedheads, shelves attached to wall for sideboard. Used metal in furniture from 1926.

Doat, Taxile (b 1851). French potter, born at Albi (Tarn). Work at Sèvres factory (1875–1905) includes small plaques modelled with animals' heads in porcelain or stoneware, and vases in shapes influenced by Art Nouveau style. Work signed Doat or marked with monogram. In

America from 1909, taught at *University City Pottery; work with high temperature glazes had widespread influence on artist potters. Book, *Les Céramiques du Grand Feu,* translated in America (1903–06).

Doccia. Italian porcelain factory established in 1735 by *Ginori family. Also produced earthenware, notably imitations of early Italian maiolica produced in 1870s. Some tin-glazed ware decorated in enamel colours. Merging of company with Società Ceramica Richard followed by introduction of Art Nouveau style. White porcelain pitcher made in early 20th century has

Above
Doccia. Earthenware vase with applied white decoration, made by Ginori-Lisci, Doccia, 1862.
Left
*Taxile Doat. Paperweight designed and made by Doat at *Sèvres. Porcelain with incised and applied relief decoration. 1900.*
Below
*Dog-collar. Glass and diamonds, mounted in gold, engraved with floral and animal motifs, made by R. *Lalique. c1906–12.*

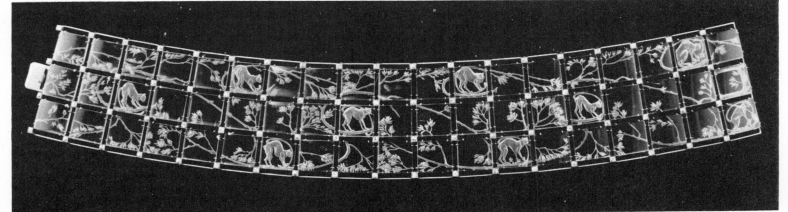

handle in form of heron. After 1st World War, faience and porcelain in Art Deco styles includes fluted bowls decorated with dancing figures, or sea with dolphins and small sail-boats. Porcelain plates painted e.g. with winged nude. Earthenware vases in 1930s have sharp, flat shoulder, or horizontal bands in contrasting colour. Under influence of designer, G. *Ponti, neo-classical decoration occurs, e.g. in vases with acanthus scroll handles. Ribbed forms include porcelain bottles with spiral ridges, thinly-potted and covered with pale glazes. Jars with vertical ribbing covered with matt black glaze, or red alternating with greyish-blue. Portrait plaques printed with photographs in gold. Decoration of vases occurs in gold and underglaze blue, or in matt and polished gilding, e.g. design of female figures riding dolphins. Tableware painted with landscapes etc. in purple. Marks include Richard Ginori with three stars, N under coronet, or coronet with Richard Ginori.

dog-collar. Close fitting necklet worn at end of 19th century and during Edwardian period; popularized by Queen Alexandra when Princess of Wales. Up to 2in. deep, with five or six rows of diamonds or pearls; fitted with gold bar stiffeners at intervals to make collar stand up around neck. Sometimes worn with longer necklace in contrasting stones. Led to fashion for similar collars in semiprecious stones.

Dohachi, Ninami (1783–1856) and **Dohachi III** (c1810–79). Japanese potters; successors to Dohachi I (d 1793). Ninami thought to have learned production of faience in Awata. Still working in Kyoto area, made raku and other types of tea-ceremony ware, ornamental figures, and incense burners in form of human or animal figures. Noted for work in style of 17th century potter, Ninsei. Also made blue-and-white porcelain. In early 1840s, established kiln at Momoyama in Fushimi. Son, Dohachi III, worked in Momoyama and, from 1848, in Satsuma; noted for blue-and-white porcelain.

dollar watch. Cheap watch first produced (1892) in America by R. *Ingersoll, sold by mail order; cost 1 dollar (in England, 5 shillings). Strong mainspring and robust case; manufactured by *Waterbury Company; by 1920, over 70 million sold. Many Swiss and German imitations.

Domestic style. See Eastlake style.

Donatello service. See Rosenthal, Philip.

Donegal. Irish carpet manufacturing district, with weaving tradition dating from establishment of Flemish colony in 1339. First carpet factory founded 1898 by A. *Morton at Killybegs, to relieve local unemployment; specialized in Real Axminsters. Followed by others in Kilcar, Crolly, and Anagerry. Industry declined after 1939, until only Killybegs factory remained (now only hand-knotted carpet factory in Britain and Ireland).

door furniture. Term embraces *door knocker, closing ring, finger plate, *escutcheon, hinges, *door porter. Door knockers in brass or cast iron; finger plates, escutcheons, and handles often made *en suite* e.g. brass, ormolu, or ceramics. Indoor door furniture reflects developments in current styles, e.g. in organic schemes of interior design (1870–20th century), in which all

*Door furniture. Finger plates and door handles designed by S. & A. *Charpentier, made by Fontaine Frères and Vaillant, c1900.*
Below
Door porters. English, cast-iron. Left: head of jester. Right: Punch and dog Toby. Mid 19th century.

effects and fittings of house designed to illustrate one theme. In America, silvered-glass door-knobs manufactured by New England Glass Works.

door-handle (in glass). See millefiore.

door knocker. Many designs from early 19th century in copper, brass, wrought iron, and cast iron (particularly by *Coalbrookdale Co). Forms include flowers, ropes, heads of animals, birds, and humans, also casts of royal children's hands.

door porter or **stop.** Heavy object, commonly in cast-iron or lead, for holding door open; widely produced in 19th century. Decorative Victorian examples, e.g. in form of lion couchant, elephant, or caricatures of popular contemporary figures; these lack wooden handle found on early 19th century models. Numerous cast-iron versions bear trademark of *Coalbrookdale Co. Smaller porters sometimes made of glass.

doorstop or **dumpy** (in glass). Late 19th century glass weight of crude green glass (3–6in. high), sometimes in tall beehive shape. Many enclose rough flowers; others, brightly coloured animals or birds. Also found with spaced air-bubble decoration. Chiefly associated with north of England glasshouses. *Nailsea doorstops with air-bubble decoration made 1873–1920; also some with enclosed plaster figures or flowers.

Doria, Carlo (fl late 19th century). Italian goldsmith and jeweller working in England, c1860–80. Worked for R. *Phillips in London, making

pieces in style of F. P. *Castellani. Known for high quality Etruscan style jewellery and enamel-work. Mark: stylized fleur-de-lys with monogram C.D.

dorine box. *See* powder compact.

Dorn, Marion (fl 1920s and 1930s). American rug and curtain designer living in London. Wife of E. *McKnight Kauffer. Designs less angular and geometrical than those of contemporaries. Colours carefully selected: shades of cream, beige, brown, and grey, with six tones of white. Each rug designed for particular setting, usually in private patron's modern house; larger commissions included rugs for café of Orient liner, Orion. Designs executed by *Wilton Royal Carpet Factory. Work often bears woven signature, Dorn.

Doughty, Susan Dorothy (1892–1962). English porcelain modeller. Noted for birds in limited editions produced from 1935 in bone porcelain at Worcester Royal Porcelain factory. First model, Redstarts on Hemlock, taken from Audubon's Birds of America; later models from life. Second series begun in 1950. Visited America in 1953 and 1956 for study of more birds in natural surroundings. Also modelled flowers: named botanical specimens.

Doulton, Sir Henry (1820–97). English potter; son of J. *Doulton; joined father's firm in 1835, trading as *Doulton & Co. Took out patents for improvements to kilns (1854), earthenware jars and bottles (1859), and vats and tanks (1861). In 1877, acquired factory of Pinder, Bourne & Co. in Burslem, Staffordshire to produce earthenware for domestic use, adding new wing (1884), for manufacture of bone porcelain.

Doulton, John (1793–1873). English potter. Worked at Fulham pottery, London. In partnership, acquired interest in pottery at Vauxhall Walk, Lambeth. Firm, trading as Doulton & Watts, sole owners of pottery from 1820; moved to Lambeth High Street in 1826. From 1854, with sons, traded as Henry Doulton & Co. As well as Doulton factory, Lambeth, operated tile and fire-clay potteries at Rowley-Regis and Smethwick, Birmingham, and St Helen's, Lancashire.

Doulton & Co. Pottery firm established (1815) by J. *Doulton and J. *Watts, succeeded by H. *Doulton. Operated at Lambeth High Street, London, from 1826. Until 1860s, specialized in commercial and industrial stoneware, although household articles and ornamental flasks, jugs, etc. made from 1830s. Terracotta used for production of vases and, in pale shade, chimney pots, shown at Great Exhibition in London (1851). Art department, formed through association of H. Doulton with John Sparkes, head of Lambeth School of Art, employed many students in decoration of stoneware. Products unique, and invariably signed with name or monogram of artist; considered early examples of English art pottery. Firm among first to employ female labour on large scale. Artists include A. B. *Barlow, F. *Barlow, H. B. *Barlow, F. *Butler, J. *Eyre, E. *Lupton, M. V. *Marshall, E. *Simmance, G. *Tinworth. *Lambeth faience introduced in 1873, *Silicon ware, 1880, *chiné, 1886, *Carrara, c1887, *marqueterie ware, patented 1887, and impasto

Above
*Doulton & Co., Lambeth. Left to right: 1) Tripod vase in *silicon ware, decorated by E. *Simmance, dated 1885. 2) Stoneware vase decorated by Louisa Edward, dated 1877; height 10in. 3) *Impasto ware decorated by Dora Keen, dated 1887. 4) Faience painted by M. M. Arding, dated 1897.*

Left
Doulton & Co., Burslem. Flambé vase, earthenware decorated with bands of stylized floral ornament under red flambé glaze. Marked with Royal Doulton device over Flambé, transferprinted. c1925.

Below
Doulton & Co. Porcelain figure, The Bat Girl. c1927. Height 8in.

decoration developed in late 1870s. In 1901, King Edward VII granted royal warrant and authorization to use title, Royal Doulton. V. Huggins employed in 20th century. Production ceased at Lambeth in 1956. In 1877, acquired Staffordshire firm of Pinder, Bourne & Co., producing earthenware and porcelain in partnership with proprietor until firm became Doulton & Co. in 1882. New wing added in 1884 for production of bone porcelain. Charles J. *Noke, employed from 1889, art director from 1914 until retirement (1936), introduced *Holbein, *Rembrandt, and *Titanian wares, succeeded (1936) by son , Cecil J. Noke, as art director. Chemist, C. *Bailey contributed to development of glaze effects. Glazes include *Sung, *Chang, *sang-de-boeuf*, and clear, monochrome *rouge flambé*. Tableware, etc., painted by P. *Curnock, D. *Dewsberry, H. *Mitchell, C. *Hart, J. *Slater, also art director. Naturalistic figures also made in porcelain. From 1955, firm traded as Doulton Fine China Ltd. Marks (Lambeth): normally include DOULTON LAMBETH (from 1856) and often name of ware, e.g. marqueterie, silicon,

Carrara, with artist's mark. From 1902, marks incorporating lion over coronet often used on earthenware and porcelain made at Burslem; lion appears on stoneware from 1922. *Illustrations also at* Barlow, H.B., Brangwyn, H., Carrara, Marshall, M.V., Noke, C.J., Simmance, E.

douter. *See* extinguisher.

Dovecot Studios or **Dovecot Tapestries.** *See* Edinburgh Tapestry Co.

Doveston, Bird & Hull. English furniture makers. Employed B.J. *Talbert, 1862–65. Furnished Manchester Town Hall, 1876–77; pieces include Grecian style sofas. Became Doveston Davey, Hull & Co., 1882; active until c1900.

Christopher Dresser. Black lacquered pine wardrobe by unknown manufacturer. Matt bronze-green panels stencilled with conventionalized owls, lotuses and zig-zag designs. c1879–80. Height 6ft 10in.

Downing, Andrew Jackson (1815–52). American architect and landscape gardener; associate of A.J. *Davis. Author of influential books on gardens, buildings, e.g. The Architecture of Country Houses (1850), and interior decoration. Wrote on classical, rococo, Gothic, Elizabethan, and Renaissance revival style furniture. Advocated specific styles of furniture for particular rooms, e.g. Gothic style for halls, libraries. Suggested cottage furniture for rural surroundings.

Dragon lustre. *See* Makeig-Jones, Daisy.

dragon style silver. Scandinavian silver inspired by old Norse art and stimulated by discovery of Oseberg ship burial in 1914; made by D. *Andersen, G. *Gaudernack, Theodor Olsen, and others in late 19th and early 20th centuries; includes pieces in form of Viking ships and drinking horns. Covered cup made for visit of King Oscar II to Trondheim, 1897, decorated with heads of king and bishop, and scenes from Norse myths and sagas to illustrate roles of church and monarchy in Norse history; now in Royal Palace, Stockholm.

Dresser, Christopher (1834–1904). British botanist, designer, and writer; born in Glasgow. Studied in London at School of Design, Somerset House, then trained as botanist and lectured (1860) at Department of Science and Art. Articles published in Art Journal (1857–58) examine significance to design of relationship between structure and function in plants. Designed silver from early 1860s. Work characterized by simplicity of style, relationship of form to use (e.g. careful calculation of balance and handling properties in jugs, teapots, etc.), and emphasis on inherent beauty of metal; constructional features, e.g. cut edges held by rivets, constitute only decoration. Early collector of Japanese art; absorbed and adapted elements from Japanese design (clearly seen in form of handles, etc.) in own work. Designs in silver or electro-plate for Hukin & Heath (c1878–1890s) include tripodal tureen with ladle, glass claret jug with electro-plated silver mounts, and cubic silver teaset (in 1890s). Mark: Designed by Dr. C. Dresser sometimes occurs with manufacturer's mark. For J. *Dixon (1879–82), designs include tea service (1880), consisting of teapot, jug, and sugar bowl in rounded shapes, with cast metal feet held by rivets; facsimile signature occurs in mark. Work produced by Elkington & Co., c1885–88, severe and often angular. Fire dogs, kettle, jugs, etc. produced in copper, sometimes combined with brass, by London manufacturer, Benham & Froud (c1895–1904). Also designed wallpaper and textiles and, for Coalbrookdale Co., cast-iron hall stand with bronzed finish. Art editor of Furniture Gazette in early 1870s. After government-sponsored visit to Japan, 1876, which resulted first in imports and then imitations of Japanese metalwork, organized Art Furniture Alliance in 1880; metalwork, etc. (often designed by Dresser), displayed in Bond Street, London; shareholders include Arthur Lasenby Liberty. Instrumental in establishment of *Linthorpe Pottery (1879); supplied many shapes and designs, drawing inspiration from Egyptian, Greek, Roman, wide range of earlier cultures, e.g. Moorish, Indian, pre-Columbian, Celtic, and Chinese, as well as Japanese. Work marked Chr. Dresser (impressed). Ceased active

*Christopher Dresser. Electro-plated tea service with gilt interiors designed for J. *Dixon & Sons. Marked with Christopher Dresser facsimile signature, design registry mark for 25th November 1880 and retailer's mark, K. & Co. Height of teapot 5in.*

Below
Christopher Dresser. Painted copper, brass and wood candlestick designed by Dresser. Made by Perry & Co. Signed and with design registry mark for 30th October 1883. Height 5¾in.

participation in pottery, 1882. Designs for pottery of W. *Ault in 1890s often incorporate animal or grotesque masks. Associated with J. *Couper & Sons; designed glass coffee jugs and other table ware (often silver-mounted); also Clutha glass vases, bowls, etc. in 1880s, with initials C.D. incorporated in Clutha trademark. Opened design studio working in all media, at Sutton, Surrey (from 1882), then in Barnes, London (from 1889). Stylistic theories expressed in books, e.g. 'Art of Decorative Design' (1862), 'Principles of Design' (1873), 'Studies in Design' (1875–76), 'Japan, its Architecture, Art and Art Manufactures' (1882), and 'Modern Ornamentation' (1886).

dressing or **toilet table.** Table designed to display and contain toilet necessities. Dates from 17th century; surmounted by fixer mirror from early 18th century. During Victorian period, matched wardrobe, wash stand, etc. Mirrors small (often flanked by jewel drawers), or full-length, pivoting on pedestal drawers. Low-based models surmounted by three, tall, swivelling mirrors popular from 1920s.

drinking horn. Ceremonial drinking vessel of ancient origin; made of ox or buffalo horn with ornamental silver bands and cover surmounted by finial; sometimes footed. From mid 19th century, many reproductions of 'Gothic' style 16th century English, German, and Dutch horns. Fine examples include cut glass horns in enamelled silver mounts from Vienna and Paris; hardstone and enamelled silver from Russia (in *Old Russian style). Medieval style silver-mounted horn by G. *Fox with gilt interior, and silver foot cast in shape of eagle's talon; made c1865 for London silversmiths, Lambert & Rawlings.

Driscoll, Clara (fl 1900). American Art Nouveau glass designer of vases, bowls, lamps, and other decorative pieces for *Tiffany Studios. Noted especially for Dragonfly lampshade designs shown at Paris Exhibition, 1900.

drop dial clock. *See* dial clock.

drum clock. Standard clock movement with cylinder or lever escapement fitted inside drum-shaped glass-fronted brass case, usually set in wooden outer case. Mostly French: manufactured e.g. by V-A. *Pierret, and *Japy Frères of Beaucourt.

dry lacquer. Oriental lacquer technique used in both China and Japan for making small sculptured figures, Buddhist images, and utensils. Hemp or linen, soaked in lacquer, wrapped around or within removable wooden framework or clay mould; when fabric dry and hard, core removed and exposed surfaces relacquered and decorated. Chinese dry lacquer (chia-chu, kia-chu, kia-tchou, or *étoffe insérée*) used from 4th century A.D. Japanese copy (kanshitsu or kyocho) made from 7th century A.D., but became obsolete from 10th to 18th centuries; revived in 19th century by several netsuke and okimono artists, including *Kyusai.

Dubucand, Alfred (b 1828). French *animalier* sculptor; first exhibit at Salon (1867): Dead Pheasant, modelled in wax. Later works include

Valet Restraining Dogs (1868), Griffon Attacking a Duck (1868), Spaniel and Hare (1869), Egyptian Gazelle Hunt (1873), Hunting in the Sahara (1874), Ass-driver of Cairo (1876), Persian Hunter (1878). Many works originally exhibited as wax models, subsequently edited in bronze; also produced bronzes of famous race-horses, e.g. Niger, Koalin.

Dufrêne, Maurice (1876-1955). French designer of furniture, metal, ceramics, carpets, glass, etc; progenitor of Art Deco. From c1910, furniture distinguished by simple lines and well-proportioned forms, resulting from re-appraisal of 18th century techniques; also designed Modernist style furniture, sometimes in tubular metal. In 1921, started shop, La Maîtrise, within Galeries Lafayette (cf Atelier Primavera).

Dufy, Jean (b 1888). French porcelain decorator, painter, and water-colour artist; brother of R. *Dufy. Worked at factory of T. *Haviland. In 1920s, decorated tableware, e.g. with heads of corn painted and in relief, roses painted in pink and blue, or turreted castles, sometimes with horsemen; edge often gilded; usually signed.

Dufy, Raoul (1877-1953). French painter and designer. In 1920s, collaborated with J. L. *Artigas in production of pottery. Commissioned to design tapestry cartoons for Beauvais and Gobelins; set of furniture pieces entitled Paris (screen, upholstery for sofa, six armchairs, four chairs), executed at Gobelins 1929-30. Also designed for Aubusson, e.g. Fine Summer (1941-42).

dumpy. See doorstop.

Dunand, Jean (1877-1942). Swiss sculptor, metal, and lacquer worker in Paris from c1904; studied with Art Nouveau sculptor Jean-Auguste Dampt; c1904, exhibited undecorated vases hammered from single copper sheet; by 1910, simplicity of forms contrasted with inlaid surface patterns of various alloys and lacquerwork; commissioned to make decorative helmet as subscription gift to Marshal Foch (1920). Revived art of Japanese lacquer; leading Art Deco lacquer artist, noted for furniture and screens designed in 1920s and 1930s; pieces often decorated with stylized motifs, e.g. animals, geometrical shapes, in gold or silver on black or occasionally coloured grounds. Also used eggshell lacquer on furniture and *objets d'art*, e.g. cigarette cases. Designed smoking room for Exposition Internationale des Arts Décoratifs, Paris, 1925, with L. *Jallot and Charles Hairon. Worked mainly for private clients; also designed furniture and panels for ocean liners Normandie and Atlantique, and dining room for Crocker apartment building in San Francisco, during 1920s. *Illustration at* lacquerwork.

Dunfermline Carpet Factory (Fife), Scotland. Short-lived French hand-weaving factory set up c1938 to make Aubusson carpets, taking advantage of price protection maintained by Allied British Carpet Makers, constituted in 1937.

Dunn, Constance (fl 20th century). Studied at Cambridge school of art and, from 1924, at Royal College of Art under D. *Billington and W. *Staite Murray. Taught pottery in Middlesbrough, Yorkshire, and worked independently from c1933 at Billingham, Durham. With

Durand Art Glass Company. Iridescent vase. Peacock feather design with applied thread decoration. Made between 1924 and 1931. Height 8⅜in.

Below
Leslie Durbin. Cup and cover made to commemorate accession of George VI, 1936. Maker's mark: Central School, London. Height 14in.

husband, experimented in stoneware until 1939; resumed work after 2nd World War. Thinly potted vases, bowls, etc., in rounded shapes, have simple, brushed decoration.

Durand, Victor (1870-1931). French-born Art Nouveau glass artist. Emigrated to America with father (who had worked at *Baccarat) and took over management (1897) of Vineland Glass Manufacturing Co. (established 1892 and then called Vineland Flint Glass Works). Employing workers from *Quezal Art Glass & Decorating Co., experimented with decorative techniques, making decorative ware in similar style, which marketed as Durand Art Glass. Work includes much fine, Tiffany-inspired iridescent glass, though shapes in general less inventive. Factory taken over and ceased production of art glass, 1931. Mark: Durand.

Durbin, Leslie (b 1913) English silversmith, studied at Central School of Art, London; subsequently established studio and workshops in Camden Town, London. Specialist in ceremonial silver, ecclesiastical plate, Badges of Office, and Maces, e.g. plate for Hudson's Bay Co., centrepiece and coat of arms for Worshipful Company of Grocers. Many other pieces commissioned by City Livery Companies, banks, societies and organizations. Fishing Trophy in form of silver cup and cover, with straight sides, fluted base, ivory handles, and carved ivory mermaid finial; engraved with fish swimming among waterweed; made for Goldsmiths' and Silversmiths' Co. (1935); purchased for 1938 Exhibition at Goldsmiths' Hall. Marks: Central School London 1937. Other work marked e.g. LG Durbin, and manufacturer's name.

Durham rugs. Heavy hand-knotted rugs made in Durham, England, until c1920, first by Hendersons (founded 1814, in liquidation 1903), then by Hugh MacKay, who re-established factory.

durry. See dari.

Dutch carpets. Production dates from foundation of first factory at Amersfoort in late 18th century, followed in 1797 by Royal Deventer Carpet Factory. Royal Carpet Factory of Rotterdam founded 1865; at first made only coconut matting, then, from 1887, hand-tufted woollen carpets. Hague Factory for hand-made rugs founded 1900. In 1919, Deventer, Hague, and Rotterdam factories combined to form Royal United Carpet Factories; hand-tufted work done largely at Rotterdam and Hague, machine-made carpets at Deventer (new mill added in 1900 for production of Wiltons). Designs commissioned from contemporary artists, or adapted from old oriental patterns.

Dutch metal. Brass alloy used as substitute for gold-leaf, e.g. in powder form to decorate papier-mâché.

Dutch tapestry. Production revived c1900 by Belgian tapestry designer, J. F. Semey de Gand; brought three weavers from Malines, Belgium, to train young Dutch weavers, then set up factory with new recruits. Closed this after 1st World War, but three others opened, making furnishings and hand-knotted carpets as well as tapestries. Designs broke with 18th and 19th century tapestry traditions. Semey de Gand made

artistic director of Hague School of Tapestry in 1920. In 1935, his factories made series of six tapestries for Utrecht University; in 1940, major commission for Leyden Town Hall. Other Dutch designers involved in tapestry revival include Jan Bons, Gisele von der Gracht, and Hans van der Norden.

du Tremblay, Baron A. (fl mid 19th century). French potter. Inventor of *émaux ombrants* technique, and owner of earthenware factory at *Rubelles until 1855.

duty mark. On British gold and silver, sovereign's head mark, indicating that duty had been paid on piece bearing it. On all gold and silver articles made between 1 December 1784 and 30 April 1890, except those not liable to compulsory hallmarking and on watch cases after 1798. During the period, tax, varying from time to time, levied on all silver assayed in Great Britain. At Dublin assay office, sovereign's head as duty mark not introduced until 1807; at Glasgow, not until 1819.

Duxer Porzellanmanufaktur A.G. Porcelain factory established 1860 in Dux, Bohemia (now Duchov, Czechoslovakia). Noted for portrait busts and lavishly decorated vases exported to America. Marks include E (proprietor: E. Eichler) in oval surrounded by Royal Dux Bohemia.

Dyer & Watts. London furniture makers; specialists in bedroom furniture from c1860. Pioneered use of cheap woods, e.g. pine, stained and grained to resemble more expensive material such as satinwood; also used woods with painted decoration resembling inlay. Examples include pine wardrobe stained and painted to resemble maplewood, exhibited at Universal Exhibition, Paris (1867), and bought by Empress Eugénie of France.

Eagle Works. See Meakin, J. & G. Ltd.

Early English, English Gothic or **Old English Gothic style,** or **Eastlake furniture.** Furniture style in Britain c1865-c1871. Typified by solid, well-proportioned rectangular designs using pegged joints instead of glue; sideboard and bookcase backs made of narrow boards set vertically or diagonally; prominent hinges; absence of veneers, French polishing, etc. Best-known proponents: C. L. *Eastlake, B. J. *Talbert, and R. *Charles. Characteristic features include chamfered and shaped rails and stiles, carved roundels, tracery. Exponents include T. E. *Colcutt, W. *Morris, and P. *Webb. American version known as *Eastlake style.

Easter egg. Early Christian symbol of eternal life promised by Resurrection; hen's egg, painted red, traditional Russian Easter gift. Ornamental 18th century eggs in wood, ivory, and porcelain, decorated with religious motifs. Still more ornate 19th century examples produced e.g. by Imperial Porcelain Factory, Morozoff, and *Fabergé; mounted in gold, silver and decoratively enamelled, incorporated e.g. into women's necklaces, men's watchchains. Fabergé made first of famous series of 56 elaborately jewelled Imperial Easter eggs in 1884; presented by Tsar Alexander III to wife, Maria.

East or **Chinese Turkestan carpets.** First reached Europe in 19th century with opening of trade routes. Khotan rugs (from Khotan oasis [Sin-Kiang], principal weaving area) became known in Europe in 1860s; called Samarkand or Kansu carpets, depending on whether exported to West via West Turkestan or China respectively, and wrongly attributed to West Turkestan or Chinese craftsmen accordingly. Traditional designs retained throughout 19th century: principally, framed guls, vase and pomegranate tree motif, and one, two, or three circular blue medallions on red ground with scattered motifs. Water and clouds design and swastika meander became more prevalent in borders. Synthetic dyes introduced c1870, but vegetable dyes, mostly imported from India, still used. After 1875, stronger Chinese influence apparent in border designs, and lily-shaped yun-t'sai-t'ou motif introduced. Designs with Muslim-Indian and West Turkestan influence appeared, e.g. tendril tracery and stylized animals. Organized export to Russia, China, and British India established in late 19th century. By early 20th century, Chinese-influenced realism was replacing traditional stylized designs; also, European fashion increasingly influential: uniformly subdued colour schemes replaced traditional practice of outlining each design element with most contrasting colour. 1928-34, Russia (under Stalin) supplied European and American markets with quantities of old and antique rugs from East and West Turkestan.

East India Carpet Company. Offshoot of East India Co. (which first established carpet weaving in Mogul court at *Agra, then Lahore and *Amritsar, c1600; sent first carpet to England in 1584). In Agra, took over German company, Otto Weylandt, on expulsion of owner in 1914. Built up chain of factories in northern India. In 1922, bought up and amalgamated numerous small companies, e.g. in *Gwalior, *Amritsar, *Srinagar, Mirzapur, Jaipur. Bought in turn by *Oriental Carpet Manufacturers in 1924, but retained name and separate identity. Specialized in reproductions of Savonnerie and Aubusson designs. Introduced graph paper system in factories for transcribing traditional designs, instead of talim method.

Eastlake, Charles Lock (1835-1906). English architect and furniture designer, chief theorist of Art furniture movement. Hints on Household Taste (1868) roused interest in Early English style in Britain; eight editions published in America, generating Eastlake style. Propounded method of holding furniture together by pegged joints instead of glue. Recommended marquetry, shallow carving, and incised gilt lines to achieve richness: features of Art furniture in America. Condemned use of French polish. Designed light, simple, rectangular furniture.

Eastlake, neo-Gothic, modern English Gothic, Domestic, or **Homelike style.** Furniture style popular in America c1870-c1880. Inspired by writings of C. L. *Eastlake. Characterized by straight lines; square or turned tapering legs; beds with rectangular, panelled head and foot boards and moulded cornices; cabinets, bookcases, etc., often with large, rectangular, recessed panels framed by stiles and rails, and moulded bases; narrow, recessed shelves; arched or flat moulded cornices; scroll-cut brackets supporting marble or wooden tops. Ornamentation includes

chamfering; shallow, geometrical carving; incised lines framing drawer fronts, etc.; tiles, scrolls, and rosettes. Woods (often ebonized): ash, cherry, oak, chestnut; also black walnut. High-quality examples made by *Herter Brothers; many pieces, often inferior quality, mass-produced. cf. Early English style. Illustration at Herter Brothers.

Eastlake furniture. See Early English style.

easy chair. High-backed, upholstered, winged armchair dating from 17th century. After introduction of spring upholstery in 1830s, seats became deeper, backs more inclined, wings uncommon, and legs shorter - only feet on castors being visible - e.g. lady's easy chair, Wolsey chair. Upholstery materials included velvet, plush, tapestry work, leather, and panels of oriental carpeting. After c1880, seats became shallower, structure lighter, e.g. grandfather chair; standard shape of upholstered armchair with inclined back continued until c1940. See also lounge chair.

ébauche or **blanc.** Incomplete watch movement or 'frame'; basis of Swiss factory-made watch industry. Ebauche goes to series of specialist factories where escapement, dial, hands, etc., added; finally cased and finished to specific designs of individual manufacturers. In England, ébauche trade in Lancashire served Liverpool watch industry c1800-50; such movements described as 'in the grey', i.e. unpolished.

Ebisu. One of Japanese *Shichi-fuku-jin; god of fishermen and daily food. Like *Daikoku, a kitchen deity. Portrayed as short, chubby, bearded man wearing fishing clothes; often carrying fishing pole and woven basket. Always seen with messenger, a sea bream; often accompanied by Daikoku.

ebonized wood. Wood stained black and polished to resemble ebony. Dates from 18th century. Popular in Britain from c1870, for cabinets, etc. Feature of Eastlake style in America.

Echizen-bori. See Kamakura-bori.

Eckmann, Otto (1865-1902). German artist, designer and, until 1894, painter. Among group of artists in Munich, working in Jugendstil in late 19th century. With H. *Obrist, initiated use of plant motifs.

Eclectic furniture. Combines styles and decorative motifs from different periods in single piece. Popular in Britain from c1850, in America from c1840. Usually commercial pieces, e.g. Gothic style inlay on Louis XVI forms, Renaissance motifs on 18th century forms. Best examples well-proportioned with restrained decoration, high standards of craftsmanship; made e.g. by *Gillow, *Holland & Sons, *Johnstone & Jeanes, *Wright & Mansfield. American examples include bookcase made by T. *Brooks, presented to Swedish singer, Jenny Lind, in 1850, combining rococo, baroque, Caroline, and Renaissance motifs. Term also applies to named styles, e.g. American Colonial, Elizabethan, Jacobethan, Queen Anne, Old World.

Ecole de Nancy. Name given to group of French Art Nouveau artists who drew inspiration from

Ebonized wood. Corner cupboard with painted panels. c1880.

work of E. *Gallé in Nancy during 1890s, adopting his techniques and style of decoration, some working in workshop he established there. Notable among them, V. *Prouvé, A. & A. *Daum; later artists in same area (e.g. A. *Walter) worked in *pâte-de-verre*.

Ecole de Paris. Art Nouveau furniture style characterized by slender lines, abstract, stylized use of plant motifs, occasional use of gilt wood. Designers include E. *Colonna, G. *de Feure, E. *Gaillard.

Edgewater Tapestry Looms (New Jersey). One of first American tapestry works (operated in 1920s); made inexpensive tapestries in loose texture on low-warp handlooms. Also furnishings imitating cross-stitch needlework.

Edinburgh Tapestry Company (popularly called **Dovecot Studios,** or **Dovecot Tapestries**). Non-profit-making workshop projected by W. *Morris and 3rd Marquess of Bute; established 1912 in Edinburgh by 4th Marquess, with two weavers, formerly of *Merton Abbey, who trained Scottish apprentices. First tapestry, Lord of the Hunt, begun 1912. Until 1940 (with break during 1st World War), large, finely woven, high-warp tapestries made to commissions, e.g. monumental series of scenes from Scottish history for Marquess of Bute. (Since 1946, work, for general sale, concentrates on smaller panels, with coarser weave and fewer colours, designed by contemporary artists.)

Edo period (1615-1868). Japanese period beginning with establishment of Tokugawa shogunate. In late Edo period (19th century), porcelain industry developed rapidly, although quality declined as quantity of production increased. Shogunate insisted on policy of isolation, and

port of Imari sole means of communication with West until restrictions relaxed in 1853. Japanese art shown in International Exhibition, London, 1862. Collapse of shogunate (1867) followed by restoration of imperial government and accession of emperor Mutsuhito (1868), starting Meiji period.

Edwards, Emily J. (d 1879). English pottery decorator, at Doulton workshops, Lambeth, London, from 1872. Trained other artists in stoneware decoration. Stamped designs, often of natural forms, on elaborately diapered grounds; used colour to emphasize relief effect. Work characterized by use of classical motifs, e.g. acanthus leaf, and freely drawn foliage. Mark: monogram of EJE.

Egermann, Friedrich (1777-1864). Bohemian glass artist and manufacturer. Highly innovative. Developed fine new glass imitating precious stones, notably *lithyalin (1829). Also, special *red and *yellow staining decorative processes for ornamental ware (1820, 1840). His inventions and decorative techniques remained widely popular during second half of 19th century.

eggshell china. See 'Belleek'.

egg stand, frame or **cruet.** Silver, electro-plate, or ceramic holder for egg cups, formed as 4 or 6 rings grouped around central pedestal and handle, with smaller rings for spoons; introduced in 1777; 19th century examples often decorated with scroll-work, foliage, piercing, and beading; type designed by *Mappin & Webb has cups enclosed in casket, opened by half turn of handle. made in silver and electro-plate.

egg steamer. Vessel for cooking eggs in steam. Spherical or ovoid, with hinged or removable lid. On frame, with spirit lamp underneath. 4-6 eggs supported above water on frame inside. Made in silver and Sheffield plate from 1790s; electroplated versions being produced by *Elkington & Co. by 1850.

egoro. In Japanese Buddhist metalwork, a long-handled censer.

Egyptian carpets. First loom recorded 2000 B.C. Major period of production 1400-1600. Weaving tradition declined after 1700; during 19th century, cotton kelims main product. In 20th century, carpets knotted in imitation of Persian types at Heluan (near Cairo), and hand-woven kelims in natural wool colours made increasingly for export.

Egyptian jewellery. See archaeological jewellery.

Egyptian revival or **neo-Grec style.** Furniture style in America c1820-c1840 and c1860-c1880; reflects interest in Egyptology aroused by collection of Egyptian antiquities, including furniture (shown in New York City, 1852), and archaeological discoveries, e.g. at Giza, Egypt. Furniture in later period characterized by application of Egyptian motifs, e.g. brass sphinx heads on sofas and armchairs, animal feet, palmettes, and lotus on Renaissance revival style furniture. Never widely popular. Manufacturers included *Pottier & Stymus. Egyptian style furniture also fashionable in Britain following discovery of

*Egyptian Revival style. Armchair, possibly by *Pottier & Stymus. Original upholstery. c1870.*

Tutankhamun's tomb by Lord Caernarvon in 1922.

Eichler, E. See Duxer Porzellanmanufaktur.

8-day clock. Clock that runs for eight days. Should be wound once a week.

Eiraku, Hozen (1795-c1855) and son, Wazen (1823-96). Japanese potters, 11th and 12th in succession of Zengoro family working at Omuro in Kyoto. Hozen Eiraku succeeded adopted father in 1841. Noted for porcelain in Chinese styles of reign of Yung Lo (1403-25), e.g. blue-and-white and kinrande, also influenced by work of 17th century potter, Ninsei. Made celadon ware, and faience decorated in gold, red, white, silver, and black. Moved (1850) to Otsu by Lake Biwa. In spite of success as potter and extensive patronage, died in poverty. Wazen Eiraku, Zengoro XII, continued father's work, adapting and developing styles. Revived kiln of Ninsei at Omuru (1855) and later, with brother, established kiln at Yamashiro in Kaga province. Contributed to revival of Kutani wares, specializing in kinrande style. Adopted Eiraku (Japanese reading of Chinese characters, Yung Lo) as family name, using father's inscription and mark, Ko Kutani, in gold. Tokuzen Eiraku, Zengoro XIII, worked in Kyoto from c1875.

Eisenloffel, Jan (1876-1957). Dutch metalworker and silversmith; from c1896, head of metalwork department at Atelier Amstelhoek; in 1908, worked at Werkstätte für Kunst und Handwerk (workshop for Arts and Crafts), Munich. Made Art Nouveau tableware (c1900) for *van Kempen & Begeer; later made tea and coffee services in simple style suggesting influence of Vienna Secession; also made metal lamps, vases, spirit kettles, etc. Mark: 1900-03, JE above plus sign in rectangle; 1903-45, JE in monogram.

ekagami. In Japanese metalwork, mirror with long handles, cast in bronze. Originally based on Chinese form, but Japanese style evolved later, in Heian period (794-1185). In vogue during Momoyama and Edo periods (1574-1869), when

Electric lamp. American, made by P. J. Handel in ormolu, shade in *Steuben glass.

Electric lamp. Bronze lamp by Gustav Gurschner, incorporating a nautilus shell. Signed Gurschner. c1900.

great numbers produced. Later shape often circular, with inner inscribed circle and designs in centre extending into frieze area. Typical motifs; flying cranes, fir branches, sparrows, chrysanthemums.

Ekholm, Kurt (b 1907). Finnish ceramic artist. Trained in Stockholm. Art director of *Arabia factory from 1931. Work in stoneware includes tall, cylindrical vases, glazed, and decorated only with slight horizontal ridges formed by throwing. In Sweden again as principal of School of Applied Art in Gothenberg from 1948.

elapsed time indicator. Accurate watch for use by sportsmen, skin-divers, etc; has rotating bezel with extra set of minute markings reading anticlockwise. Bezel set with required time interval, say 20 minutes, opposite minute hand. Hand proceeds to zero on bezel, showing minutes remaining. If bezel set at centre-seconds hand, shows remaining seconds.

electric clocks. Four main types: electrically driven by impulse to pendulum (*Bain clock, *Hipp clock); electrically wound, with conventional movement or turned e.g. by weighted lever (*Hope-Jones clock); secondary or impulse

type, in which *slave clock is advanced by regular impulses transmitted from controlled central *master clock; mains driven synchronous rotor clock, with revolutions of electric motor geared down to provide motive power for hands (Warren *synchronous clock).

electric lamp. Electric light bulb invented by American, Thomas Alva Edison, in 1880; brightness of light (16 candlepower), and flexibility of wires, rather than gas tubes, promoted new designs. Edison worked with L. C. *Tiffany from 1880; Tiffany workshops produced great variety of forms in search of beautiful and effective design, notably five-branch lily lamp by Philip J. Handel, in which cluster of lights, in form of lilies, point in different directions, thus eliminating own shadows. American Arts & Crafts Movement designed lamps in *Mission style, with beaten copper shades, by D. *van Erp and *Roycroft copper shops. In Europe, Art Nouveau standing, wall, and ceiling lamps made e.g. by R-F. *Larche, V. *Horta; functionalist lamps by *Bauhaus; Art Deco designs by E. *Brandt and R. *Lalique.

electro-gilding. Method of producing gold design on silver or other metal surface by electrolytic deposition; replaced old process of mercury-gilding which was harmful to health. Article masked leaving design to be gilded exposed, then electro-plated with gold, and masking removed. Introduction of electro-gilding is usually attributed to Arthur Smee in 1840; taken up by *Elkington & Co. in same year; process was patented by A. Parkes, firm's chief metallurgist, 1845. The process is still used.

electro-plate. Silver-plated ware produced by electrolytic deposition of layer of silver on base metal; process developed commercially by G. R. *Elkington c1840 after experiments in electrolysis by Sir Humphrey Davy, Michael Faraday and others in early 19th century. All patents relating to electro-plating bought by Elkington, Mason & Co., who sold licences to other manufacturers. Largely replaced Sheffield plate by mid 1850s through lower production costs, although some articles were marked 'Sheffield Plated' to mislead. Introduction of electro-

plating also coincided with fashion for naturalistic designs not easily produced by other processes. Base metal initially copper; Britannia metal and *nickel silver, used later, match colour of silver and show less if plating wears thin. Marks EPBM and EPNS, indicating electro-plated Britannia metal and electro-plated nickel silver, found from c1850. Similar process of electro-gilding superseded dangerous method of mercury gilding. *Illustration at* Stevens, A.

electro-typing. Extension of principal of *electro-plating for production of accurate facsimile from solid objects. Plaster mould taken of original, and coated with plumbago (graphite). Coated mould placed in electro-plating trough. Layer of metal electrolytically deposited on plumbago, forming exact duplicate of original object. Accuracy of reproduction depends entirely upon faithfulness of mould. Process introduced in 1840 by *Elkington & Co.

elinvar (from French, '*élasticité invariable*'). Non-magnetic alloy of steel, nickel, chromium, manganese, tungsten, invented c1920 by C-E. *Guillaume for use in watch balance springs. Provides constant elasticity regardless of temperature, eliminating need for additional compensation devices. *See also* invar.

Elizabethan style. Furniture style popular in Britain during 1840s and America c1830–c1860. Continued to be used for hall furniture in Britain until c1870. Combines elements of Tudor, Jacobean, and Stuart designs, e.g. spiral-turned legs, stretchers and back uprights, applied split balusters, and elaborately carved back panels, e.g. by W. *Rogers. In Britain, also typified by grotesque, strapwork carvings, faceted figures, and needlework seats. Manufacturers include J. G. *Crace & Sons.

Elizabethport Carpet Factory (New Jersey). One of earliest American hand-tufted carpet factories, founded 1891 as branch of Wilton Royal Carpet Factory; worked by English weavers. Made Real Axminsters. Commercial failure: closed after a few years.

Elkington & Co. (Birmingham). English silversmiths, founded by George Richard Elkington (1801–65), who inherited gilt toy and spectacle factory, and cousin Henry Elkington (c1810–52). 1830–1840, George developed processes of *electro-plating and electro-gilding, collaborating with Alexander Parkes and John Wright; intended to maintain toy-making concern and profit from electro-plate by selling licences to firms throughout Europe, but gradually devoted all resources to manufacture of silver and silver plate; took Josiah Mason as partner, 1842 till Mason's death in 1859; mark EM & Co for Elkington, Mason & Co., retained until 1864. Firm also used electro-typing method of producing copies of silver articles etc. Factory in Newhall Street, Birmingham, mechanized in 1851–52, with steam-operated presses to stamp out nickel silver pieces. Exhibited at Great Exhibition, London, 1851, where jury commended electro-gilding but questioned durability of electro-plate. Business expanded with introduction of mass-production techniques, and use of designs by French sculptors Aimé Chesneau, P. E. *Jeannest, Albert Wilms, and L. *Morel-Ladeuil; Milton Shield designed by Morel-Ladeuil awarded gold medal at Paris

Above
Elkington & Co. Pair of vases in cloisonné *enamel designed by Albert Willms. c1875. Height 9½in. (without base).*

Below
Elkington & Co. Brass covered bowl with *champlevé *enamel decoration. c1870. Height 4in.*

Elkington & Co. Silver biscuit box with Japanese decoration. Made in Birmingham, 1881.

Exhibition, 1867; commissions executed by Elkingtons for Prince Consort and aristocracy.

Success of Elkington & Co. continued after death of George in 1865, when firm employed c1000 people; experimented with *champlevé* and *cloisonné* enamelling, including pieces in Japanese style in early 1860s, with similar style applied to silver c1870, e.g. jug now in Victoria & Albert Museum, London; adaptations of Japanese Komai patterns produced c1875. Designs purchased from C. *Dresser, 1880; representatives visited Russia, 1880–81 to make electro-type copies of antique silverware, including English pieces from 16th to 18th centuries. Firm still in existence, though merged with *Mappin & Webb and others in 1963 to form British Silverware Ltd.

Ellis, Harvey (1852–1904). American architectural draughtsman; also designed furniture. Employed by *United Crafts, 1903–04, designing oak furniture characterized by inlays in darker woods, copper, and pewter. Motifs include stylized flowers and Viking ships.

Ellore. *See* Eluru.

Ellwood, George Montague (fl 1890–1910). English furniture designer. Noted for Quaint style pieces for J. S. *Henry and *Trapnell & Gane. Also designed Arts & Crafts Movement furniture, e.g. side-chair with studded leather seat, two splats in top of back, vase-shaped piercing below.

Elmslie, George Grant (1871–1952). Scottish-born architect and designer. Worked in same office as F. L. *Wright and G. *Maher in Chicago, Illinois, from 1887; member of Prairie School. Chief draughtsman (1895–1909) for architect, Louis Sullivan. Furniture characterized by rich, flowing ornamental detail, often with geometrical motifs as organic parts of structure.

Elton, Sir Edmund (d 1920). English artist potter. After experiments beginning in 1879, made art pottery known as Elton ware in Sunflower Pottery at family home, Clevedon Court, Somerset, from 1881. Lead-glazed jars, jugs, vases, and bowls produced in simple shapes from local clay, decorated with coloured slips, e.g. red

George Grant Elmslie. Tall clock, mahogany with brass inlay. Face modelled by Kristian Schneider, hands made by Robert Jarvie of Chicago, movement and chimes imported from Germany. Designed 1912. Height 7ft4in.

Right
Sir Edmund Elton. Earthenware vase, designed 1882.

and purple or green, or violet and grey; outlines incised. Relief designs of flowers, etc., applied to surface and then modelled, covered with transparent glaze. Monochrome glazes also occur, e.g. in dark bluish green, on shapes inspired by plant forms. From c1900, produced vases, jugs, etc., decorated with metallic glazes given crackle effect. Mark: ELTON, incised.

Eluru or **Ellore** (Andhra Pradesh [formerly in Madras]), India. Woollen carpets produced in late 19th century, with bold (usually floral) designs on white ground, and coloured border. Small rugs made for local market; large carpets for European export firms. Native dyes used until aniline introduced c1900, when nearly all carpets made for export, to patterns supplied by buyers. By 1940 (when market no longer dominated by European firms), c10 major workshops in operation, e.g. Eluru Pile Carpet Weavers' Co-operative Society, founded 1937 with c200 members to make carpets in Persian tradition (dating from 16th century Muslim invasions).

Emaux de Longwy. *See* Longwy (Meurthe-et-Moselle).

émaux ombrants. Ceramic decoration carved, moulded, or impressed in unfired clay and flooded with coloured transparent glaze; depth of colour varies with contours of relief design. Introduced c1844 by A. *du Tremblay on cream-coloured earthenware made at *Rubelles. Glaze generally green, although blue, violet, yellow, or

turquoise occur; two colours sometimes together. Designs normally landscapes, or scenes with figures. At first used for plates, later also on tiles, panels, etc.; G. *Cartlidge made tiles with portraits and figure subjects in 1890s. Applicable only to level surfaces. Technique used at Wedgwood factory in 1860s.

embedded or **inlaid lacquer.** Japanese lacquer decoration: wide variety of materials cut into small flat sheets or flakes cemented to thin layer of lacquer applied over prepared *honji. Surrounding area then coated with layers of lacquer until embedded pieces flush with surface. Most important forms: *heidatsu, *kanagai, *Somada work.

Emerald Deldare. *See* Buffalo Pottery.

Empire clocks. Term usually given to fine French ormolu clocks made 1800–15; also used for reproductions from 2nd Empire period (1850–70) with standard French *drum movement, e.g. by *Japy Frères or S. Marti & Cie. Cases made separately by specialists; early bronze cases fire-gilded, later examples in electro-gilded lead spelter or, rarely, aluminium. Japy Frères made complete Empire clocks for 1889 Paris Exhibition.

Enamel Porcelain. *See* Meigh, Charles.

e-nashiji. *See* nashiji.

encaustic tiles. Tiles with inlaid design fused to main body of tile in firing, originally used to cover and decorate floors in medieval France and England. From mid 19th century, made in England; few made for domestic decoration after *c*1900. Patent for mechanized production process bought in 1830 for use at Minton factory; pattern, impressed in tiles with plaster mould, filled with clay slip. Commercially produced from mid 1830s, and in general use by 1850s. Early, simple figure subjects and heraldic motifs imitated designs of medieval tiles; geometrical patterns also occur. Often white used on red ground, later buff and brown. Blue popular ground colour in 1860s; combination of up to six colours (e.g. black, white, gold, pink, blue, and green) possible by 1880s. Designs commissioned by Maw & Co. from artists, e.g. J. P. *Seddon in early 1870s. Production process, using clay dust to fill designs pressed in dry clay body of tile, employed by T. & R. Boote Ltd from early 1860s, made tiles at lower cost than method using moist clay and slip, but best results produced with relatively simple designs of one colour in addition to ground.

encrusted lacquer. In Japanese lacquer, any variety of lacquer ornamented with elaborate patterns composed of chips and thick flakes; numerous materials (e.g. gold, silver, copper, metal alloys, mother-of-pearl, tortoiseshell, ivory, faience, wood, hardstones). Technique: precarved chips sunk through lacquer after all other decoration done, then given finish. Encrusted work extremely popular in Meiji and Taisho eras; used on huge range of objects, often made for European and American export markets. *See* *aogai, *raden, *Somada work, *Shibayama.

Endell, August (1871–1925). German architect and designer; exponent of Jugendstil furniture.

*En plein enamelling. Detail from Russian silver centrepiece in *Old Russian style. Late 19th century.*

Pieces contribute to total effect of room interiors, each detail harmonizing with object beside it. Used traditional materials, e.g. elm; also steel. Pieces characterized by contrast between curves and straight lines, often emphasized by natural wood grain, and curved, often abstract, ornament. Examples include washstand, *c*1899, with concave back echoing lines of drawers and skirt, contrasting with rectangular top and straight verticals.

end-of-day glass. Small ornaments or useful items, e.g. sugar shakers, mugs, and tumblers, made by American glass blowers in spare time. Usually mottled. Popular *c*1885–1905. Term sometimes used as alternative for *slag glass. *See also* friggers.

engine clock. *See* novelty clocks.

engine-turning. Semi-mechanized metal engraving technique developed in mid 18th century: pattern applied to object while being rotated on lathe. Characteristic patterns include chevrons, chequers, fluting; irregular basketwork pattern produced by attachment, called rose-engine, causing eccentric movement of cutting point on surface to be engraved.

English Gothic style. *See* Early English style.

English mosaic. 19th century English veneer cut from block composed of slivers of various coloured woods (black, white, brown, red, yellow, grey and green). Peak popularity *c*1850, mainly for decoration of small boxes, trays, desk sets, etc. Commonest on *Tunbridge ware; also manufactured elsewhere, particularly London. Early patterns geometrical, from parquetry work; later ones often copy intricate *Berlin woolwork designs, frequently enclosed in floral, bird, or animal motif borders and bands. Also souvenir views surrounded by floral borders. In 1920s, numerous reproductions of 19th century work produced by Tunbridge Wells Manufacturing Co.

engraved glass. Five basic methods used: wheel engraving (dating from antiquity), diamond en-

graving (from Roman times), stippling (Dutch 18th century technique, later enjoying a limited revival), acid engraving (from *c*1670), and sandblasting (invented 1870). In wheel engraving, copper wheels ranging in diameter from 4in. to pin's head rotated by small, foot-operated lathe produce greyish white marks on glass surface; in diamond engraving, design scratched on surface with hand-tool tipped with diamond or other hard substance. *See* acid engraving, sandblasting, stippling.

en grisaille. Technique of grey monochrome painting representing objects in relief and giving appearance of depth. Enamel painting *en grisaille* developed and popularized by French Limoges enamellers in 16th century. Design laid on in layers of white enamel over dark ground. Shading produced by varying thicknesses of white layers. Often combined with coloured translucent enamel painted over *grisaille* work. During revival of Renaissance styles after 1850, *grisaille* enamelling popular mainly for reproductions of earlier work. Main centres of production, Vienna and Paris.

en plein enamelling. Technique in which entire surface of object covered with highly finished, usually translucent, enamel. Perfected by 18th century French goldsmiths; used most often on snuff-boxes. After almost a century of disuse, revived late 19th century by *Fabergé, whose sumptuous objects of vertu characterized by *en plein* translucent enamelling over *guilloché* base of gold or silver.

en résille enamelling. Goldsmith's term for *champlevé enamelling on very small scale, used primarily on jewellery.

entrelac. Form of interlaced decoration inspired by Celtic jewellery of 9th and 10th centuries excavated in 19th century. Used on pieces copied exactly from ancient jewellery, and by Arts &

Crafts designers, e.g. A. *Fisher, and A. *Knox; in modified form on some *Cymric designs.

Entreprise de Décoration Intérieure Moderne. See DIM.

Eocean ware. See Weller, Samuel A.

Eosian. See Weller, Samuel A.

E.P.B.M. Electro-plated *Britannia metal; mark found on English objects made from c1840 in metal electro-plated with silver. Die-marked letters in separate shields to simulate hallmark.

épergne. See centrepiece.

E.P.N.S. Electro-plated nickel silver; mark found on English objects made from c1840 *nickel silver electro-plated with silver. Die-marked letters in separate shields to resemble hallmark.

Erivan rugs. See Causasian carpets.

ermine mark. See Mintons Ltd.

Escallier, Eléonore (1827–88). French earthenware and porcelain decorator. Worked at studio of T. *Deck; influenced by Japanese design. Plates dated 1867 feature asymmetrical arrangements of birds with fluffy crests and long tail plumes sitting on branches over sprays of flowers or rhubarb; signed or initialled with first E reversed. Employed at Sèvres factory, 1874–88; painted or designed decoration, notably fruit, flowers and birds.

escapement (in clocks and watches). Device which locks and unlocks train, simultaneously passing impulse to pendulum or balance to maintain oscillations. Oldest form, verge, obsolete by 19th century, though still found in watches to c1860. Other early forms continued in use throughout 19th century, e.g. cylinder, duplex (in watches), anchor, dead beat (in clocks). English lever escapement, invented c1765, perfected by 1820; very widely used from mid 19th century. Swiss factories, using mass-production techniques, made cylinder watches to c1950. Factory production led to introduction of cheaper materials and methods, e.g. bent steel strip replacing solid steel pallets in anchor escapements of American clocks; steel pins substituted for jewelled pallets in G. F. *Roskopf's lever watches; simplification of duplex escapement in *Waterbury watches.

19th century technical developments mainly limited to improvements in existing escapements. Swiss industry evolved own form of lever type: club-shaped escape wheel teeth, pallet arms and lever in approximate Y-form; arbors (axles) of escape wheel, pallets and balance in straight line, instead of English-style, triangular layout. A. *Brocot's pin pallet form of dead beat escapement used from c1840 in small domestic clocks, mostly French, e.g. with escape wheel and pallets mounted visibly in centre of dial (See also *skeleton clocks). Gravity escapement in turret clocks from 1854, e.g. E. B. *Denison; in original double three-legged form, pair of escape wheels with three extended teeth or 'legs' each locked by pallets acting on tips of teeth; pallets lifted by pins near axis of wheels and, in falling back, give impulse directly to pendulum. Distance through which pallets fall constant, so

Lever escapements. Movements of two deck watches. Left: by A. Johannsen & Co., London, three quarter plate movement with free-sprung compensation balance. Case marked Birmingham 1894. Right: bar movement by Ulysse Nardin, Locle, Switzerland. Compensation balance, micrometer-type 'wishbone' regulator adjustment. Watch fits into brass outer case in wooden carrying box, c1920. Both movements 1¾in. diameter.

impulse independent of power applied to train and of external influence, e.g. wind or snow on exposed hands. Variants produced by turret clock makers in late 19th century include 6 and 15 legged forms, some with separate pallets for locking and impulse. Four-legged type used in some *regulators (rare).

Escapements devised for high-precision clocks include S. *Riefler's (1893), with pendulum connected to pin pallets through suspension spring only, pallet assembly being supported by knife edges on jewelled blocks, and acting on two concentric escape wheels for locking and impulse. Pendulum receives impulse through suspension spring, thus influence of escapement on regularity of vibrations minimized. Development of mechanical escapements lost impetus in 20th century with introduction of electrical systems, e.g. in W. H. *Shortt's free pendulum clock.

escutcheon plate. Metal plate fitted round keyhole for protection and as ornament. Elaborate 18th and early 19th century examples in ormolu or brass; later versions simpler, set flush with surrounding surface. Many imitations of early designs. See door furniture.

Esser, Max (b 1885). German sculptor. Before 1st World War, worked as figure modeller for M. *Pfeiffer at Schwarzburger Werkstätten für Porzellankunst (Thuringia) and, after war, at Meissen factory.

Essex Art Pottery. See Hedingham Art Pottery.

'Essex' crystal. See sporting jewellery.

étagère. See whatnot.

eternity ring. Ring set all round with evenly spaced gemstones as symbol of continuity; usually worn on fourth finger of left hand with wedding ring; particularly fashionable in 1930s – 20th century version of *keeper and *regard rings. Set with diamonds alone or combined with rubies, emeralds, or sapphires.

etiquette spoon. See moustache spoon.

étoffe insérée. See dry lacquer.

Etruria factory. See Wedgwood, Josiah & Sons Ltd.

Etruria Pottery. See Cook Pottery Co., Ott & Brewer.

Etruscan jewellery. See archaeological jewellery.

Etruscan Majolica. See Griffen, Smith & Hill.

Etruscan style silver. Silver designs based on forms and decoration of Graeco-Roman antiquities: symmetrical, formal, controlled, with decoration subservient to form of article. Fashionable from 1850s to 1870s.

etui, or **lady's companion.** Small case made to carry or hang on chatelaine; partitioned for manicure or sewing sets, snuff spoon, etc. Usually flattened, tapering, cylinder with upper third hinged as lid; cube-shaped version, similarly fitted, now usually distinguished as nécessaire. Made up to end of 19th century in gold, silver, porcelain, painted enamel, pinchbeck, and onyx and other hardstones.

Eureka clock. Electric *battery clock, controlled by large visible balance-wheel instead of pendulum. Invented 1906 in England by T. B. Powers with G. H. and H. Kutnow; made by Eureka Clock Co. Examples rare.

European glass. Continuing popularity throughout 19th century for both plain and decorated *opalines (especially in France), and for brilliantly coloured glassware with enamel and gilt decoration; also, enormous output of *flashed and *overlay decoration with elaborate geometrical cutting (especially in Bohemia); revival of Renaissance Venetian styles throughout Europe. From 1830s to end of century, much new glass in imitation of marble, jasper, and other semi-precious stones, e.g. *lava glass, *agate glass, and many versions of *lithyalin glass developed by F. *Egermann. Many Old German techniques revived in Bohemia, e.g. *Altdeutsches enamelled glass and versions of *Waldglas*. In France, *Baccarat, *Clichy, and *St Louis glasshouses continued with traditional output, with emphasis on elegant, restrained versions of Renaissance, Venetian designs; but more elaborate Oriental-style decoration later in century; also some fine deep engraving on thick glass by *Pantin in late 1870s, as well as traditional Bohemian engraving to end of century. Some Bohemian art glass developed, e.g. *Tortoiseshell glass. Spun glass ornaments and silvered glass also popular. But essentially period was of stagnation and revived styles. See also Art Nouveau, Art Deco.

extension table. See telescopic table.

extinguisher. Candle snuffer, made in two forms: douter, formed like sugar nippers, has flat plates or discs at ends of scissor arms to pinch wick of candle or kettle lamp, etc.; earliest silver examples from late 17th century. Conical form, lowered over flame, more convenient, and popular in 19th century; small examples attached to *chamber candlesticks by lug or hook; larger versions with long handle for

*Henry Eyles. Carved and inlaid walnut chair. Back has inset *Worcester porcelain plaque enamelled with portrait of Queen Victoria. Original seat cover of silk cross-stitch. Exhibited at Great Exhibition, London, 1851.*

church candles, sconces, and chandeliers, produced widely during Gothic revival.

eye bath. Small cup with oval bowl for bathing eye. Commonly made of blue glass; also found in gold, silver, enamel, and electro-plate, often with embossed decoration. Usually part of toilet service. Made in Britain from late 18th century. Some European examples can be reversed for use as salt cellar or egg cup.

Eyles, Henry (fl 1850s). English furniture designer and manufacturer in Bath, Somerset. Known for elaborately carved, naturalistic decoration; marquetry inlays. Pieces include side-chair in walnut, with porcelain plaque portrait of Queen Victoria in back; shown at Great Exhibition of 1851 (now in Victoria & Albert Museum, London).

Eyre, George (1818-87). English ceramic decorator and designer. Painted figure subjects on earthenware. At Minton factory, from 1847, designed pavings for construction in encaustic tiles. Later, designed dessert service made in porcelain and parian ware at Hill Pottery, Burslem, Staffordshire, shown at International Exhibition of 1862. Art director at factory of W. T. *Copeland, 1864-65.

Eyre, John (1847-1927). English pottery designer and decorator. Worked at Minton's Art-Pottery Studio, then designer at factory of W. T. *Copeland (c1874-80). At Doulton workshop, Lambeth, London, from c1885.

Fabergé. Russian firm of goldsmiths and jewellers, founded 1842 in St Petersburg by Gustav Fabergé (1814-93), who retired to Dresden in

*Fabergé. Box, in interwoven gold and platinum with diamond clasp, c1900. Green enamel scent bottle, mounted in gold, top set with ruby and diamond cluster, made by H. *Wigstrom, c1905. Blue enamel pencil and paper knife, and oyster enamel pencil, both by V. Soloviev, c1905-10.*

1860. Left firm in care of silversmith, Zaiontchovsky, until succeeded by sons Peter Carl Fabergé (1846-1920) in 1870 and Agathon (b 1862), who joined firm in 1882. Specialized in production of objects of vertu from 1882; in that year won medal at Pan-Russian Exhibition. Work, always of high quality, often contained indigenous Russian stones, combined with precious metals and enamel. Associated with fantasy objects, e.g. Easter eggs (first, made 1884, presented to Empress Maria Fedorovna). Established Moscow branch with jewellery workshops. Firm operated system of workmasters in which entire production of any given piece from Fabergé design supervised by one craftsman, who also initialled finished work. Chief workmasters in St Petersburg jewellery workshops were A. W. *Holmstrom and adopted son, Albert (Holmstrom mark: AH). Peter Carl Fabergé became jeweller to Russian Imperial court; firm commissioned by royal family to make jewellery for personal and state occasions, e.g. brooches to commemorate coronation of Czar Nicholas II (acceded 1894) and tercentenary of Romanoff rule (1913) in diamonds, pearls and other gemstones. Jewellery distinguished by superb craftsmanship and design; used semi-precious stones found in Russia e.g. tourmaline, moonstone, Siberian amethyst and, notably, translucent chalcedony, set as brooches and pendants cut en cabochon, and surrounded by small diamonds, rubies or emeralds. Pieces sometimes set with translucent enamel, rather than stones. Decorative objects include Russian peasant figures. Also made tea and dinner services. Commissioned by King Edward VII to make models in England of his livestock, from which carvings made in hardstone. Firm opened branches in Odessa, Kiev, and London, but dissolved when goods confiscated by Bolsheviks in 1918.

face-to-face loom. Weaves two carpets at once, face to face, sharing same frames, with yarn passing in one movement through both. Circular knife moves across breast of loom and slices

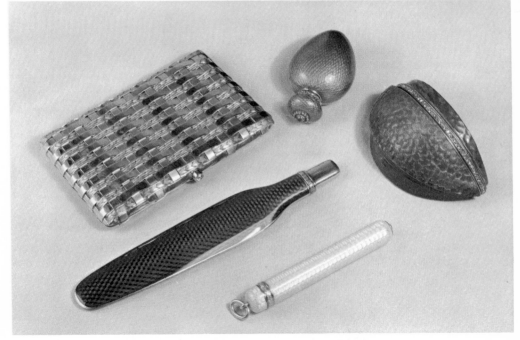

carpets apart. Developed simultaneously (1924) in Britain, by T. F. *Firth & Sons, and Germany, by Uebel, Tefzet, and other carpet manufacturers, in response to 1920s fashion for plain carpeting.

façon de Venise. Term used for 19th century glass made in imitation of Venetian Renaissance styles, e.g. with threaded and applied decoration, gadrooning, elaborate handles, frilled and crimped edges and spouts; or in *latticinio, vetro a reticelli*, filigree, mosaic, and other glass of Venetian inspiration.

Fahrner, Theodor (1868–1928). German jewellery manufacturer in Pforzheim, Germany. Made cheap, mass-produced jewellery of low-carat gold or silver, set with semi-precious stones, mother-of-pearl, even glass. Range of jewellery similar to Liberty's *Cymric, but much more geometrical, in spirit of Jugendstil. Used designers connected with Matildenhöhe artists' colony set up (1889) by Grand Duke of Hesse at Darmstadt; e.g. J.M. *Olbrich; also used designs of H. *van de Velde.

Faience Manufacturing Company. American porcelain manufacturers at Greenpoint, New York. Plates, centrepieces, etc., with elaborate raised gilt designs of flowers and foliage against e.g. glossy dark blue or matt cream ground, made by *Lycett family (1880–92).

Faïencerie de Nancy. *See* Gallé, Emile.

fairings. Small porcelain groups illustrating everyday situations, chiefly made c1860–c1890, by Conta & Boehme of Pössneck, Saxony, for export to Britain; often prizes or souvenirs obtainable at fairgrounds. Subjects include amusing or risqué courtship and marriage scenes. From c1857, children appear in adult situations and animals carry out human activities; political subjects also occur. Early examples (1860–70) generally slightly larger and of higher quality than later figures. Those from 1870s and 1880s generally show signs of mass-production. Often rather clumsily moulded, with flat bases. After 1890, colours more garish and gilding often used. Examples light in weight, with hollow bases.

Fairing. Inscribed Can can. Late 19th century. Height 3½in.

fan. Folding frame of ribs held together at one end by pin or rivet. Outside pair of ribs, thicker than inner, protects folded fan from damage. Segment of circle, known as leaf, e.g. of paper, silk, lace, attached to ribs at equal intervals, to provide stiffening when open, and ensure even folding when flat. 19th century versions and modifications to traditional fans include lorgnette, or Dubarry fan, with peep holes; mirror-fan, used for make-up, or covert observa-

Alexis Falize. Rock crystal, gold, and enamel bowl, c1870. Plique-à-jour and cloisonné enamelling. Height 10in.

Fairyland lustre. *See* Makeig-Jones, Daisy.

fairy or **night light.** Small, individual glass candle shade popular in Britain and America in 1880s. Patented c1885–89 by Samuel Clarke & Sons, London. Usually made of Queen's Burmese glass with daisy pattern. Sometimes in form of flower, cottage, comic figure, or other novelty.

Falguière, Jean-Alexander-Joseph (1831–1900). Notable French realist sculptor; awarded *médaille d'honneur* at Salon in 1868. Commissioned to undertake considerable amount of public sculpture, e.g. Triumph of the Republic (1878). Small bronzes include bust of Diana, and Fighting Cock. Work signed; cast e.g. by Thiébaut Frères.

Falize Frères (Paris). French silversmiths and jewellers; founded c1860 by Alexis Falize (1811–98), chiefly noted for work on revival of Japanese cloisonné enamel techniques; pieces made by him at Paris Exhibition, 1867. Son Lucien studied under Barbet de Jouy in Louvre, specialized in translucent enamel work; Lucien, in partnership with silversmith Germain Bapst, took over firm c1880; made mainly jewellery and enamel work, also some table silver; 1888, commissioned to make toilet service in rococo style for wedding of Princess Laetitia Bonaparte, now in Bibliothèque Nationale. Cup made in 1896 for exhibition of Union Centrale des Arts Décoratifs, Paris, of Renaissance style in three-colour gold. After Lucien's death in 1897, firm continued by son André, eventually joined by brothers Jean and Pierre. Made wide range of Art Nouveau and other jewellery to mid 1920s. Mark: AF in lozenge with flail.

tion; telescopic fan, to fit easily into purse. Lace fans with mother-of-pearl mounts, from c1860; large silk versions decorated with birds and flowers in Japanese style from c1870, e.g. humming bird fan (fashion introduced to England by Empress Eugénie). Sequinned fans, of black and white lace mounted on gold or silver net, from c1890. Many late 19th century novelty and souvenir fans, e.g. as give-away advertising medium for shops, hotels and restaurants; or trick versions, designed to disintegrate if opened wrong way. Lettered fans for teaching alphabet to children also popular. Fan declined in use from c1910; revived briefly c1925–c1930; Art Deco examples by Paris designers, e.g. Georges Bastard, Plumereau, Paul Follot. Ostrich plume fans also fashionable in this period.

fan-back chair. Chair with fan-shaped back, e.g. *Prince of Wales lady's easy chair. Also round-seated, Windsor side-chair with crested yoke rail, back spindles inclining outwards, and shaped back uprights; usually beech with elm seat; popular in Britain during 19th century; variants still made. Also American Windsor chair with straight splat flanked by outward-inclining spindles.

Fanciful style. *See* Quaint style.

fancy or **chamber chair.** Loose term for balloon-back chair in plain or japanned light wood, e.g. birch, often with cane seat. Common in Britain from c1850. In America, term, fancy chair, applied to open-back, painted, side-chair with cane seat; popular c1835–c1855.

fancy pieces. American trade term for pieces of silver flatware ordinarily sold singly, e.g. serving pieces.

Fantasque ware. *See* Cliff, Clarice.

fantasy or **form box.** Snuff-box of unusual shape, e.g. animal, human figure, article of clothing, musical instrument, furniture.

farmhouse clocks. Popular name for Scandinavian long-case clocks made in Finland, Sweden, Norway, and Denmark from 18th to mid 19th century. Movements resemble English

*Favrile glass. Plate designed by L.C. *Tiffany. New York, 1902.*

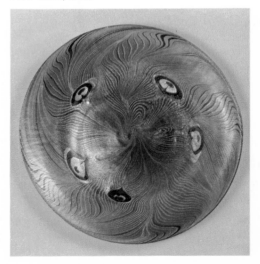

Eugène Feuillâtre. Cup in silver gilt and plique-à-jour *enamel, designed and made c1900.*

A. E. Finch. Earthenware dish and mug, made at Iris factory at Porvoo. c1900.

long-case type, but cases reflect contemporary French taste. Also, some Swedish *bracket clocks, in French style. Swedish long-case clocks probably influenced American brass clock designs, e.g. lyre and girandole (*see* American horological industry).

Farnham, Paulding (fl late 19th century). American silver designer; worked for *Tiffany & Co. in 1890s. Designed *Adams Vase (1891).

Favrile. *See* Tiffany, Louis Comfort.

Favrile glass. American Art Nouveau iridescent glass. Term derived from Old English, fabrile, meaning hand-made. Developed 1893 by L. C. *Tiffany; later widely imitated in Europe, e.g. by J. *Loetz Witwe. Wide range of vivid colours, e.g. purple, peacock-blue, golden-brown; also transparent pastels. Weathered, iridescent effect achieved by subjecting hot glass (usually thin-blown) to metallic vapours, which form iridescent film on absorption; also, by direct application of metallic lustres, or by corroding glass surface with acids. Many variations on basic technique developed. *Illustration at* Loetz Witwe, J.

feeding bottle. *See* pharmaceutical glass.

Felix Summerly's Art Manufactures. *See* Summerly's Art Manufactures.

fender. Hearth surround made of brass, cast-iron, burnished steel, etc.; prevents damage from hot embers falling from open fire. Most mid 19th century examples in revivalist styles, e.g. rococo, neo-classical. *Club fender common in late 19th century. Kitchen fender often fitted with broad, flat top-rail used to keep plates warm.

Fenton Potteries. *See* F. & R. Pratt & Co.

Fentonia ware. *See* A. G. Harley-Jones.

Feraghan carpets. Firm-textured, west Persian carpets woven in Feraghan (near Arak) from late 18th century. Short, finely Persian-knotted wool

pile on cotton or cotton and wool foundation. Most incorporate herati pattern in blues, reds, and greens on blue or dark red ground. Main border has herati motif in characteristic celadon green. Corrosive dye produces relief effect in pattern. *See also* Sultanabad.

Ferenczy, Noémi (fl early 20th century). Hungarian artist, tapestry weaver and designer. Learnt weaving techniques in France c1910, studied tapestry design in several European countries. First exhibition in 1916. Taught at Budapest School of Decorative Arts. Designs experimental, worked out directly on loom rather than in cartoons; typically, composed of flat, decorative figures, in rich colours.

fern, leaf or **flower decoration.** Popular motifs on e.g. silver or electro-plate in mid-19th century. From c1860, engraved ferns (and revival of late 18th century bright-cut work) found on e.g. trays, flatware and boxes.

ferrule. Ring or cap placed over tip of walking stick, parasol, etc., to strengthen and protect it. Also, ring attaching handle to stick.

Feuillâtre, Eugène (1870–1916). French sculptor, goldsmith, and enameller. Employed by R. *Lalique, then set up alone, 1899. Made extensive experiments in enamelling on silver, later perfecting technique of applying enamel to platinum for jewellery; specialized in *plique-à-jour enamelling. Jewellery, similar to that of Lalique, uses combination of materials, e.g. glass, gold, and silver. Also made Art Nouveau hollow-ware in similar materials. Exhibited in Paris (1900) and Turin (1902). Mark: Feuillâtre.

Fielding, S., & Co. (Ltd). Staffordshire pottery manufacturers working at Stoke-on-Trent from 1870. Wide variety of products includes majolica, sometimes with hand-modelled flowers, etc., terracotta and, later, high quality earthenware for domestic use. 'Majolica argenta' with white body and glaze introduced in early 1880s; decorated with high temperature colours and designs in relief. Later work sold notably under trade name, Crown-Devon (from 1913), includes lustre ware in Art Deco styles. Marks

include FIELDING, impressed, and SF & Co printed with title of pattern.

filigree. Decoration created by curling and twisting silver or gold wires in open patterns. Used since antiquity; revived in 17th and 19th centuries. Much filigree work, e.g. jewellery, silver elephants, imported from India in 19th century.

filigree or **lace glass** or **vetro-di-trina.** General term for decorative glass made with milk-glass canes interwoven in crystal or clear coloured glass. Technique, which dates from Roman times, revived in 16th century Venice, when *latticinio* and *vetro a reticelli* variations first developed. Enjoyed second revival in 19th century, when became popular decorative feature throughout Europe.

filled gold. *See* rolled gold.

Finch, Alfred William (1854–1930). Ceramic artist, noted for influence on Finnish ceramics through work as teacher. Born of English extraction in Belgium. Among pointillist painters working in style of Georges Seurat in Paris. Early earthenware simple, influenced by Art Nouveau style, made at Keramis workshop of *Boch Frères. Signed vases, dishes, jugs, and candlesticks in rough, red earthenware body, covered with slip and glazed in ochre, blue, bottle-green, or fawn, with incised linear decoration and dots of light coloured glaze. Some work sold through friend, H. *van de Velde. Invited (1897) by L. *Sparre to take charge of ceramic department of *Iris factory. Work includes cheese dish with crocus flowers in yellow against blue ground, and vases decorated with wave pattern in dark brown with mottled green glaze and wavy rim, echoing motif, or with handles arranged in pairs, resembling outline of butterfly wings and marine design in blue, white, and brown over green ground. As teacher of ceramics at Central School of Arts & Crafts, Helsinki, worked in stoneware and experimented with complicated glaze effects. Pupils include T. *Muona.

Finnish rugs and tapestries. Standards of design and production declined during late 19th century under impact of industrialization, until founding of Finnish Handicraft Association (1879) to reinstate old peasant patterns and revive ancient techniques, e.g. takana (double-weave method using only four heddles). In 1920s, *ryijys became popular in Europe as wall-hangings. New generation of painter-designers emerged, e.g. Eva Brummer, Uhra-Beata Simberg-Ehström, and Maija Kolsi-Mäkela, producing vividly coloured abstract designs, and experimenting with modern fibres.

fireback. Metal shield at back of open fire to protect chimney wall and reflect heat. Made from 17th century in cast or wrought iron; often decorated e.g. with heraldic device, foliage motifs. Reproductions of old styles made in England until c1934.

fire-dogs. See andirons.

firehouse or **kitchen Windsor,** or **captain's chair.** Low-backed Windsor chair common in America from c1850. Vertical, ring-turned front legs joined by rectangular stretcher; spindle back, side stretchers, and back legs straight-turned. Continuous horseshoe-shaped arm with low cresting, terminating in rounded ends. Pine, maple, or ash often used. So called because used extensively in volunteer fire companies' quarters, and in pilot boats. cf smoker's bow chair.

fire irons. Sets may include shovel, tongs, poker, blowing tube or bellows, and hearth brush. Long-handled irons made from mid 19th century, e.g. in wrought-iron, brass, copper, steel; may be decorated, e.g. with knopped or moulded shanks, ornate finials. In latter part of 19th century, fire irons rested either on ornamental andirons, or against specially designed sections of fender.

fire opal. See opal.

fireplace front. Decorative metal shutter for fireplace when not in use. Often designed to match grate, in bronze, nickel, brass, copper, or iron; many have embossed ornament. Manufactured in quantity in late 19th century America.

Firth, T. F., & Sons. Carpet manufacturers, founded 1822 in Heckmondwike, Yorkshire; moved shortly to neighbouring Brighouse. Made hair Brussels, Wilton, and Axminster carpets. Developed *face-to-face loom in Brighouse c1924, and introduced face-to-face piece goods (textiles woven to standard lengths) in Britain in 1928. Founded early American carpet and tapestry factory in New York State, 1888 (under American management from 1944); made tapestries, tapestry carpets, rugs and piece goods.

Fischer, Maurice (1800–80). Hungarian porcelain manufacturer. Established factory at Herend (c1839). Noted for high-quality reproductions of oriental and 18th century European porcelains. Products shown at Great Exhibition, London (1851). After closure of Vienna factory (1864), received right to use models and patterns selected by Emperor Franz Joseph for continued use. Retired in 1873; succeeded by sons, but factory failed in following year, and underwent

Top
Alexander Fisher. Silver plaque with enamel centrepiece. Signed and dated 1898.

Fish servers. Made in Exeter by J. Whipple & Co. Pierced and engraved silver blades with carved ivory handles. 1880.

series of changes in ownership. Marks include variations on arms of Hungary.

Fisher, Alexander (1864–1936). English painter, sculptor, and silversmith; studied painting at South Kensington Schools, London, 1881–86; took up metalwork and enamelling 1886, studied in Italy and in Paris under M. Dalpayrat; set up workshop in London; from 1896 in charge of enamelling section at Central School of Arts & Crafts, London, where met H. *Wilson; exhibited with Arts & Crafts Exhibition Society in 1896, at Royal Academy, and in many international exhibitions; wrote on enamelling in many art journals; made silver decorated with Celtic *entrelac motifs from c1896, which influ-

enced *Cymric range; peacock sconce in steel, bronze, brass, silver with enamelled decoration, shown at Arts & Crafts Exhibition Society, 1899, now in Victoria & Albert Museum, London. Created technique of using foil base with several layers of translucent enamel to give illusion of depth; widely copied. Art Nouveau bronze statue, Adoration, 7ft6in. high, with figure embracing heavens, made for Earl Gray and presented to Queen Alexandra on her birthday, 1903.

fish knife and fork. Decorative utensils for fish course of formal dinner, rarely en suite with dinner service, made in sets of 6, 12, 18. Introduced in mid 19th century England and America. Knife with scrolled, dull-edged blade, frequently with pierced floral, or marine motifs, in silver, or electro-plate, with e.g. flat handle in mother-of-pearl; en suite with fork, distinguished from dinner fork by shorter tines and long ornamental shaft.

Fishley, Edwin Beer (1832–1912). English potter, making traditional earthenware pitchers etc.,

covered with brown or mottled green lead-glaze, at Fremington, near Barnstaple, North Devon. Vases in brownish earthenware, coated with white slip, have *sgraffito* designs in Etruscan style. Puzzle jugs, fruit dishes, and candlesticks also made, as well as kitchenware and fireclay ovens. Pottery closed in 1912.

fish server. Utensil in silver or electro-plate, with broad pierced·or engraved blade, rolled silver or mother-of-pearl handle. Asymmetrical blade common *c*1820–*c*1880 in England and America. Often with matching fork, *en suite* with fish knives and forks.

Fitzroy, Robert (1805–1865). British hydrographer, meteorologist, and subsequently admiral; accompanied Charles Darwin on voyage of Beagle. Devised extremely detailed forecasting system for use with mercury column barometers. Fitzroy barometer, named after him, has glazed rectangular oak case, 36 × *c*6in.; paper labels give details of weather; 36in. glass column contains mercury. Instrument usually incorporates thermometer and storm glass; sometimes also inexpensive clock movement. Popular in 2nd half of 19th century.

Fjerdingstaad, Christian (fl 1920–30). Danish designer and silversmith; designed silver tea service and other pieces for *Christofle, Paris, in restrained, geometrical Jugendstil. Work exhibited at Paris Exhibition (1925). 12-sided goblet and sauceboat (1925) now in Musée des Arts Decoratifs, Paris.

flambé glaze. Ceramic glaze first found on Chinese Chün ware in Sung period, with splashed and streaked effects of brilliant red or purple caused by oxidation of copper in iron-based glaze. Among oriental glazes which European potters tried to emulate in late 19th century. In Germany, achieved by H. *Seeger at Berlin Porcelain factory, and in France (in 1880s) e.g. by T. *Deck and E. *Chaplet. Experiments in England by B. *Moore with Clement *Bailey led to commercial production at Doulton & Co., under direction of Charles J. *Noke. Also produced by W. H. *Taylor, G. *Cox, W. *Moorcroft, and at Pilkington works. In America, revived at Rookwood Pottery in 1920s.

Flammarian ware. *See* Moorcroft, William.

flashed glass. Technique for producing cheap parti-coloured shaded glassware; originated in Bohemia, but in common use throughout 19th century. Glass object (usually of plain glass) allowed to cool then dipped in molten coloured glass of intense colour, usually cobalt or ruby-red. Thin outer layer then sometimes decorated with etching or simple cut design. In more elaborate version, base of opalescent glass flashed with second colour, then pattern-moulded and reheated to form raised opalescent surface design. Very popular decorative technique for Bohemian glass of period. English flashed glass of period includes Rubena Verde, Rubena Crystal, and Blue Amberina.

flat-backs. Earthenware figures made in Staffordshire, England, also Scotland, from mid 19th century, especially in 1850s and early 1860s. Press-moulded and decorated in underglaze colours or enamel and gilding; intended for

Flat-back. The Prodigal's Return. Made in Staffordshire. Late 19th century.

viewing from one side only. Simple form could be produced at low cost. Many examples portrayed personalities or events of contemporary interest. Small proportion marked, mainly by S. *Smith, thought to have been main producer.

flick clock. *See* ticket clock.

flint enamel ware. American variant of *Rockingham ware; streaks and blotches of green, orange, yellow, and blue added to brown glaze by oxides sprinkled on surface before

firing. Developed at United States Pottery (patented 1849) for use e.g. on animal figures, bell-shaped cover for change on counters in form of figure wearing crinoline, and toby jugs.

Florentine mosaic or **commesso di pietre dure.** Popular term of mosaic of semi-precious stones (*See* hardstone). Patterns include pictorial scenes, figures, floral and plant forms, and geo-

metrical designs. Found particularly on table-tops, and on boxes and other objects of vertu. Technique used in 17th century Italy; revived mid 19th century in England.

Florian ware. *See* Moorcroft, William.

florid Italian style. *See* French style.

flower or **plant stand.** Wire, cast iron, wrought iron, or carved wooden stand for flower arrange-ment or pot plant; common in Britain and America during 19th century; usually has tripod base, with top recessed to hold container. Wooden examples *c*18-*c*24in. high date from 17th century in Britain; 3-4ft high examples date from *c*1750. Display area generally increased from *c*1830; table form also common. Top often fitted with tin pan to hold wet sand, and trellis work or pierced cover to support flowers; loose wooden top may fit into recess, converting stand into small table. Increasingly ornate during 19th century, e.g. with naturalistic carving around tripod base or table legs. Large numbers of Japanese-style stands made in America after Philadelphia Centennial Exhibition, 1876. *cf jardinière.*

flower stand (in glass). *See* centrepiece.

flushed glass. Art Nouveau glass developed by E. *Rousseau and E. *Léveillé; glass objects coated with coloured glass dusts, then fired to produce faint flush of surface colour.

Flutina box. *See* musical box.

flying pendulum clock. Rectangular, flat-topped American table or shelf clock surmounted by two vertical pillars flanking central spindle. Cord and ball pendulum attached to spindle,

Paul Follot. Chair in carved sycamore wood, inlaid detail in ebony and kingwood. c1913. Height 3ft1in.

which is rotated back and forth by clock move-ment; pendulum swings in half-circle, succes-sively winds and unwinds about each of the two fixed pillars. Patented 1883 in New York by P. Closon; possibly derived from Willard rope escapement (*c*1250). (Revived in Germany as novelty clock in 1959).

fob seal. Small seal worn from early 18th century on chatelaine, watch chain, or watch Albert; usual form, small mount of low carat gold sup-porting hardstone, steel or glass matrix. Early 19th century examples made with larger mounts of gold, silver, hardstone, or pinchbeck in shapes including animal or human head, shell, or flower. Declined in use *c*1830, replaced by *desk seal. Renewed demand for fob seals in mid 19th century with revival of fashion for chatelaines. Remained in vogue as decorative accessory until World War I. Produced in great quantity; many forms modelled on older styles, but large variety of new, often fanciful designs.

fob watch. Ornamental lady's watch suspended from short chain or strap, e.g. from brooch in lapel; dial sometimes inverted for ease of reading. Made particularly in Switzerland from *c*1870.

folding biscuit box. Hinged container on stand, with two compartments for biscuits. When not in use, compartments could be folded together like butterfly wings. Numerous versions made in late 19th century in silver or electro-plate. Version e.g. by *Mappin & Webb in shape of scallop shell.

Foley Art China. *See* Brain, E. & Co.

Foley China Works. *See* Brain, E. & Co.

folk art ware or **mingei.** Japanese hand-crafted pottery made, ideally, by local potters for every-day use. Appreciation of folk pottery, important development of Taisho (1912-26) and present Showa periods, fostered by S. *Yanagi. Mashiko, north of Tokyo, became main centre of move-ment from early 1920s, when S. *Hamada settled there. K. *Tomimoto, in early work, among potters associated with folk art movement. Folk art ware also produced at traditional pottery centres throughout western half of Japan.

Follot, Paul (1877-1941). French interior decorator and designer of furniture, carpets, textiles, and metalwork. Early work in Art Nouveau style; one of progenitors of Art Deco. From 1923, associated with shop, Pomone, in Bon Marché department store, designing Pomone stand for Exposition Internationale des Arts Décoratifs, Paris, 1925, as well as reception hall of French Embassy stand (with P. *Chareau, R. *Mallet-Stevens, *Süe et Mare, etc.). Co-director, 1929, with S. *Chermayeff of *Waring & Gillow's modern French furniture depart-ment. Furniture distinguished by use of fine materials, e.g. lacquerwork and bronze, and expensive techniques, e.g. marquetry in olive, rosewood, ebony, etc. Work from 1920-25 retains curves of neo-rococo French Art Nouveau within simplified forms; 1925-28, new emphasis on cubist geometrical shapes in response to shift in public taste. Turned to Modernist style, 1929.

Fomin factory. Russian porcelain factory esta-blished by 1830 in Kusajevo, near Bogorodsk.

Produced tableware, enamelled and gilded; also faience. Operation ceased in 1883. Marks include full name of founder, Petra Fomina, in Cyrillic characters.

Fontana, Lucio (b 1899). Italian artist and, from 1930s, ceramic sculptor, working in Milan. Among artists concerned with revival of ceramic art in Italy. Work includes plaques coated with slip, sometimes with scratched line and/or per-forations characteristic of painting.

Fontanille et Marraud. *See* Limoges.

Fontenay, Eugène (1823-87). Parisian jeweller noted for Etruscan style jewellery inspired by Campana collection bought by Napoleon III in 1860 (now in Louvre). Made diadem of diamonds, pearls and emeralds for Empress Eugénie (1858), and pieces for King of Siam, Shah of Persia, and Said Pasha of Egypt (1860-67). Etruscan style necklaces, bracelets, demi-parures, and chatelaines, first shown at Paris Exhibition of 1867; decorated with pearls, lapis-lazuli, coral and enamel. Favoured oat and corn motifs. Also carved insect jewels in jade. After retirement (1882), published book, 'Les Bijoux Anciens et Modernes' (1887).

footman. *See* trivet.

foot-warmer. Portable hot-water container with watertight screw top; made in copper, stoneware, etc. in various shapes, e.g. flattened cylinder. Carpet-wrapped versions provided by English railway companies for comfort of travellers. Continental variety, for domestic use, has inner metal container for hot coals or charcoal burner, and pierced outer case; Swiss, Scandinavian, Russian, and Polish examples often with wooden outer case, intricately fretted and painted; in France, Germany, Austria, and northern Italy, case more often of wrought-iron, copper, or brass.

Ford, Edward Onslow (1852-1901). English sculptor; studied in Antwerp and Munich (1870-72). Exhibited in London at Royal Academy (from 1875) and at Grosvenor Gallery (from 1879). With A. *Gilbert and Hamo Thorneycroft, leading figure in English New Sculpture. Series of bronze statuettes (1876), e.g. Peace, Folly, hand cast and finished using cire-perdue process. Member of Art Workers' Guild from 1882. Public sculpture includes statue of Rowland Hill (1882), monument to General Gordon (1890), and Shelley Memorial in Oxford (1892). Adopted polychromy in later works, e.g. Singer, bronze set with turquoises and garnets, exhibited at Royal Academy in 1889.

form box. *See* fantasy box.

Forsyth, Gordon Mitchell (1879-1952). English pottery decorator, designer, and teacher. Trained at Royal College of Art, London. Art director at Minton factory (1903-05). From 1906, art director at Pilkington Tile and Pottery Co. Work includes five large vases, shown at Franco-British Exhibition (1908), depicting Ride of the Valkyries (cobalt-blue and silver lustre), Orpheus and the Beasts (blue), Ship (dark green), Eumenides (scarlet with gold lustre), George and the Dragon (pale blue). 1916-19, worked as designer in Royal Air Force, returning briefly to Pilkington's. From 1920, principal of Stoke-on-

Above
Edward Onslow Ford. Bronze figure of Folly. Stamped: Published by Earnest Brown and Phillips, The Leicester Galleries, Leicester Square. c1900. Height 20in.

Below
Gordon Mitchell Forsyth. Two-handled earthenware goblet decorated in lustre, made by *Pilkington's Tile and Pottery Co. Marked with impressed 2793, Pilkington trade mark, and Forsyth's rebus of four scythes. 1908. Height 9in.

Trent Schools of Art; pupils include S. *Cooper and C. *Cliff. Noted for efforts to relate training of designers to demands of industry. Meanwhile designed pottery, e.g. for E. *Brain & Co. Published work includes 20th Century Ceramics (1936). Retired in 1945. Work marked with four interlaced scythes, or GMF, incised.

Foster, Herbert Wilson (1848–1929). English porcelain decorator. At Minton factory from 1872, specialized in portraits of contemporary personalities, including royal family. Also painted animals and birds. Exhibited paintings at Royal Academy and in Europe. Teacher at Nottingham School of Art from 1893. Work normally signed.

fountain clock. Ornate French automaton clock, introduced c1845; made to resemble a fountain. Rotating glass spirals give appearance of streams of water emptying into receptacle containing e.g. water (in which goldfish may be kept). Whole assembly typically mounted on rectangular plinth containing mechanism for illusion, and (usually) separate clock movement. Other versions use coloured glass spirals to show e.g. stream of wine emptying into flagon. Highly elaborate examples produced in France during mid 19th century; cheaper versions in Germany, c1900.

fountain pen. First pen with ink reservoir invented by Bartholomew Folsch (1809), quill pen with reservoir devised by J. H. Lewis (1819). Introduction of vulcanizing process for rubber, 1844, provided non-corrodible plastic, vulcanite, suitable for pen barrels; subsequent developments led to large scale manufacture from c1890 in Britain and America of fountain pens with 14 carat gold nibs tipped with iridium. These

Right
Georges Fouquet. Left: brooch, gold, light green plique-à-jour enamel, baroque pearl, and sapphire, c1900. Right: comb, horn, gold, enamel, and diamonds, designed by Charles Desroziers, 1914.

Below
Alphonse Fouquet. Bracelet with theme of Diana, goddess of hunting. Enamel plaques by Grandhomme. Mid 19th century.

versions needed to be filled manually: self-filling lever action model with rubber reservoir introduced during World War I.

Fouquet, Alphonse (1828–1911). French jeweller in Paris, famous for renaissance revival pieces decorated with painted enamels. Modelled statues, medallions and busts before opening own business (1860); quickly successful. Designer rather than craftsman: designed motifs to be carved on amethysts and topaz, fantasy forms in onyx, and turquoise jewels set with diamonds and pearls. Diamond jewellery modelled on lace forms; also designed sphinx, dragons, and sirens in diamonds. Also jewels in human form. Joined by son G. *Fouquet in 1880; retired 1895.

Fouquet, Georges (1862–1957). French jeweller in Paris, son of A. *Fouquet; joined family business in 1880. Created style known as *'Milleneuf-cent'*, combination of coloured stones, diamonds, pearls and enamel. Designed jewellery himself and carried out designs by A. *Mucha (for Sarah Bernhardt), Tourrette, Charles Desrosiers. Mucha also designed interior of Fouquet's shop in Rue Royale, Paris, centre for Art Nouveau jewellery, Paris. Mark: Gges. Fouquet.

Fouquet, Jean (b 1899). French jewellery designer; founder member of Union des Artistes

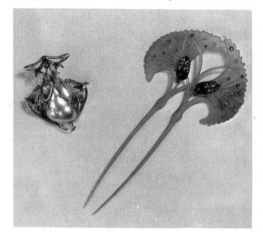

Modernes. Son of G. *Fouquet; joined family firm, 1919. Work shown at Paris Exhibitions of 1925 and 1937. Work characterized by impersonal, geometrical, Art Deco style: large, solid, with stark lines often with *pavé set diamonds and coloured stones.

Fourdinois. Parisian cabinet making and upholstery firm established by Alexandre Fourdinois (1799–1871) in early 1850s. Known for wide range of high-quality pieces using rich materials. Examples include carved ebony cabinet based on 16th century design, ornamented with lapis lazuli, bloodstone, jasper, and ivory inlay, and carved silver masks; shown at International Exhibition of 1862. (Firm showed at all major exhibitions from 1855.) Son, Henri, first showed at Universal Exhibition in Paris (1867). Firm active until 1900. *Illustration at* Renaissance revival style.

four-glass clock. English clock with wooden case and glass sides, top, and back; up to 12in. high. Made from c1820, in walnut, rosewood, satinwood, or mahogany; has pendulum movement with fusee, sometimes with striking work; some examples with platform escapement. Also, French four-glass regulator: larger version of French carriage clock with pendulum movement, made c1850 e.g. by Leroy or S. Marti & Cie. Gilt metal frame, sometimes with marble top or base, glass sides, highly finished movement with visible *Brocot escapement, and *compensation pendulum (e.g. Harrison gridiron) purely for decorative purposes. Exact copy produced in America by *Ansonia Clock Co.

400-day clock. Dial and movement, surmounting *torsion pendulum, mounted on circular wooden base and encased in glass dome; introduced in Europe c1880 by German, Anton Herder; runs for one year on a single wind. Metalwork brass, highly finished; pendulum is balance spring bearing ornamental bob, or horizontal disc, which swivels about vertical axis. Rare examples strike the hours. First developed commercially by Aaron D. Crane in America; later made in quantity in German factories, e.g. *Junghans, until 1914. Production subsequently declined until 1945, after which popularity revived. Limited modern manufacture continues.

Fox, George (fl mid 19th century). Noted English silversmith, probably son of George Fox of Rundell, Bridge and Rundell. In partnership with Charles Fox (Junior) from c1838, when latter inherited father's silver works. Both worked for *Lambert & Rawlings; produced many pieces for Great Exhibition, 1851, including large wine flagon in silver and parcel gilt, with melon-shaped body, and tall neck embossed with naturalistic foliate ornament, now in Victoria & Albert Museum, London. Work marked by novel designs, e.g. claret jugs in shape of walrus, military drum; also drum mustard pots and goblets. *Illustration at* butter dish.

Frampton, George James (1860–1928). English sculptor, designer, and craftsman. Studied at Royal Academy Schools, London, 1881–87; worked in Paris (1888). Took up applied arts on return. Joint Principal, with W. R. *Lethaby, of Central School of Arts & Crafts, London, 1896. Master of Art Workers Guild, 1902. Designed

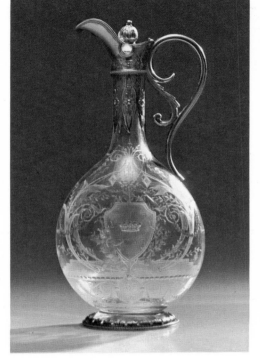

*George Fox. Silver-gilt mounts on engraved glass *claret jug. 1866.*

and produced number of silver presentation pieces, e.g. casket (1901) in silver and ivory, with embossed, chased, and cast ornament, for Merchant Taylor's Company to be presented to Field Marshal Earl Roberts; now in Victoria & Albert Museum, London.

Frank, Jean Michel (fl 1920s). French Art Deco interior decorator and furniture designer. Worked on Templeton Crocker apartment, San Francisco, California. Furniture characterized by simple, clean lines, neutral colours, e.g. beige, grey, and cream, and natural materials, e.g. sharkskin, parchment, and rock crystal.

Frankl, Paul (1886–1958). Architect and furniture designer. Born in Vienna; educated in Vienna, Berlin, Paris, and Munich. Settled in America in 1914; became American citizen in 1925. In 1920s, designed furniture to harmonize with urban landscape, e.g. cupboards and bookcases in Californian redwood based on skyscraper silhouette. Also known for curvilinear designs, often finished in silver leaf, e.g. dressing-table with curved base narrowing towards top, surmounted by larger circular mirror.

Fratin, Christophe (1800–64). German-born sculptor working in Paris. Studied under painter Théodore Géricault. Exhibited at Paris Salon, 1831–39 and 1850–63. Produced notable bronzes of horses, deer, domestic and game animals, modelled with lively surface, clearly derived from Géricault's characteristic impasto. Early plaster models cast by *Susse Frères, later personally supervised casting in workshops of E. Quesnel, A. Daubré. Received medal at Great Exhibition of 1851 in London and citation describing him as foremost animal sculptor of day. Large group, Two Eagles Guarding their Prey (1850), now in Central Park, New York.

freedom box or **freedom casket.** Round or octagonal box of silver, or sometimes wood with inscribed silver plaque, containing certificate presented to freeman of borough or city; usually engraved with civic coat of arms; made from 17th to 20th century in Britain. Some large examples have been converted to inkstands: smaller boxes were often used for snuff.

free pendulum clock. Most accurate pendulum clock ever made; based on principle developed 1921 by W. H. *Shortt. Consists of two pendulums: one in vacuum chamber, free to keep time with minimum interference, is periodically monitored by second 'slave' pendulum which provides impulses and controls dials. *See* synchronome clock.

Free Renaissance or **bracket and overmantel style.** British furniture style for cabinets, sideboards, chimney pieces, etc., c1870–c1900. Restrained examples by T. E. *Collcutt. Commercial pieces (often large scale) typified by numerous brackets, recesses, cupboards, and shelves, and dominated by architectural members, e.g. moulded cornices, pillars, and arches. Decorative motifs include carved and inlaid garlands, heads and figures, arabesques, etc. Manufacturers include *Gillow, and *Collinson & Lock. *See also* Renaissance revival style.

Frémiet, Emmanuel (1824–1910). French sculptor; apprenticed as lithographer to watercolourist, Jacques-Christophe Wemer, 1840–42; then studied under uncle, sculptor François Rude. Animal sculpture from 1843 includes studies of cats, dogs and fox, *Renard d'Egypte* (1848), all modelled with characteristic detailed naturalism founded on precise anatomical research. Further figures (1850–60) of cats, dogs, horses, culminated in six horse groups in 1859: *Cheval de Troupe, Cheval au Rigeur, Cheval Arabe, Cheval de Saltimbanque, Cheval de Chasse, Cheval au Corbeau.* c32 autographed bronzes, 1860–80, mostly of domestic animals at play, feeding young, etc. Some classical subjects,

Christophe Fratin. Bronze of eagle and vulture with dead sheep. Marked with founder's stamp, Daubré Editeur. c1880.

Freedom box. Silver-gilt and enamel. Made for City of Exeter. Maker's mark, D. & F. Birmingham, 1899. Width 7¾in.
Below
Emmanuel Frémiet. Bronze figure of Roman centurion on horseback. Signed. c1850–75. Height 16½in.

e.g. Centaur. Succeeded A-L. *Barye as Professor of Drawing at Jardin des Plantes, Paris, from 1875. Monumental pieces executed from 1860 include sculptural decoration for Louvre (c1862), Joan of Arc (1872; Place des Pyramides), Velasquez (1891; Jardin du Louvre), Colonel Howard (1903; Baltimore, Maryland). Bronze, Seated Hound, now in Victoria & Albert Museum, London.

Fremington. *See* Fishley, Edwin Beer.

French antique style. *See* rococo style.

French horological industry. Factory production of clocks developed by c1840; plates and wheels (*rouages*) machine cut at factories, e.g. *Japy Frères, S. Marti & Cie., both in Beaucourt (Jura), then sent to Paris craftsmen for finishing to necessary standard. Inventiveness and perfectionism of early pioneers (Julien and Pierre Leroy, A. Lepaute, J-A. Lépine, A-L. Breguet) reflected in accuracy and quality of factory products. Important centres of production at St Nicolas d'Aliermont, near Dieppe, and Besançon, on Swiss border. *Carriage clock French speciality from c1850 to early 20th century; has highly finished, visible movement. Output included *four-glass regulators, *marble, *Empire, provincial *Comtoise, *mystery, and *novelty clocks. Many reproductions. From 1871 (following Franco-Prussian War) industry suffered from removal of tariffs on imported German clocks. *Bulle electric clocks introduced early 20th century. Trade revived 1920–40, following 1st World War; bronze-cased clocks made in Art Deco style, and domestic shelf and alarm clocks.

French jet. Black glass used as cheap substitute for real jet. Takes high polish; often sharply faceted.

French modern style. *See* rococo style.

French polish. Transparent gum solution applied to wood to harden surface and give additional lustre; popular in Britain in early 19th century. Condemned by C. L. *Eastlake and W. *Morris, because practice of staining wood before polishing (common c1850) obliterated wood's natural colouring.

French, Louis XIV, Old French, or **florid Italian style.** Contemporary terms for furniture style popular in Britain c1835–c1900 and America c1845–c1860. British pieces characterized by scrolls and curves, asymmetrical design (in early pieces), gilt and white paint, and sometimes mid Georgian rococo motifs. Often in rosewood in 1890s. Widely made in Britain, e.g. by H. *Ogden. American examples usually large and heavy, with broken pediments, classical decoration, free-standing heroic figures, and geometrical detail. Shown at Crystal Palace Exhibition in New York, 1853. Few examples survive. *cf* rococo style.

fretwork. Thin wood cut with fretsaw to form patterns such as frets or trellis-work; may be applied to drawer fronts, panels (e.g. on cottage piano), used as frieze, etc. Sometimes backed by fabric (often silk); also applied to wooden surfaces to create effect of relief carving. Feature of English and American Victorian furniture. Home fret-carving machines popular c1865–c1880 in Britain, c1876–c1880 in America. *See also* A. H. Mackmurdo.

friggers or **whimseys.** Walking sticks, pipes, trumpets, bugles, toys, and other small glass

Frigger. Bird fountain. Late 19th century.

William Fritsche. Goblet in amber-cased glass engraved with portrait medallion of Edward VII. Early 20th century.

novelties; made by British glass blowers in spare time from leftovers. Often of coloured glass, decorated with *latticinio* or enamelling. From 1860s, produced commercially, chiefly in Nailsea, Stourbridge, and Alloa. *See also* end-of-day glass.

Fritsche, William (fl 1870s). Bohemian-born glass engraver at T. *Webb & Sons. Worked in classical style, with both floral and figurative subjects, employing *rock crystal engraving.

Frodsham, Charles (1810-71). English clock maker and businessman. Founded London firm of Charles Frodsham & Co.; in association with finishers Nicole-Nielsen, produced slim watches in Breguet style; also fine clocks, *chronometers. Took over Arnold & Son after death of J. R. Arnold in 1843. Acquired Vulliamy & Son, 1854, with Royal Warrant for care of Buckingham Palace clocks. In 1868, designed make-and-break device for electrically recording time shown by chronometer. Writer on horological subjects. Firm still active as division of Dent's.

frosted glass. *See* ice glass.

fruit bowl or **berry bowl.** Ruffle-edged bowl of coloured glass in metal frame. Usually without handle, and with pierced or embossed decoration on silver or electro-plated frame.

fruit spoon. Spoon with fluted silver-gilt bowl, and chased stem and handle; size between that of

tea-spoon and dessert spoon. Usually sold in pairs or sometimes fours during 19th century.

Fry, Laura Anne (1857-1943). American pottery decorator. Simultaneously member of *Women's Pottery Club and employee of Rookwood Pottery. Early work includes incised decoration in style of English decorators, e.g. H. *Barlow, on wing-handled pitcher made at Rookwood, though bearing mark of Women's Pottery Club; design of ducks and water lilies, picked out in blue glaze, initialled. In 1883, introduced application of ground colours of Rookwood Standard ware with atomizer, to achieve smooth blending of colours. Later, worked with W. A. *Long.

Fry, Roger (1866-1934). English painter, art critic, and artist potter. In 1913, started *Omega workshops. First learned pottery making from flower-pot maker in Mitcham, Surrey (1913), then studied pottery. Began pottery training at Camberwell School of Arts and Crafts, London. Made tin-glazed earthenware; simple shapes, usually with white, sometimes green or blue glaze, and without further decoration. Domestic ware and ornamental plates in white, or deep blue, sold at Omega Workshops until closure (1919), marked with Greek character omega in rectangle. Worked at Poole Pottery in effort to improve body of his earthenware; experiments curtailed by outbreak of World War I. Also designed dining chair (1914), painted red, with cane seat and back. *Illustration at* Omega Workshops.

fubako or **fumi-bako** (Japanese, 'letter-box'). Long, rectangular, Japanese lacquer box ($c3 \times 9 \times 4$in.), usually with two metal rings through which silk cords passed and tied. Used for carrying letters or messages; often made to match suzuri-bako. Widely exported to West from early 19th century. Extremely popular in Victorian and Edwardian England as glove boxes.

fuchi. *See* sword furniture.

fude. *See* yatate.

fudetate. Japanese metalwork brush stands, used with mizuire (metal water holders) for writing. Kept in *suzuri-bako (writing case).

Fujina. Japanese folk pottery produced near Matsue, Shimane prefecture. Products in 19th century include tea bowls with bluish-green glaze and domestic ware glazed in white, yellow, or bluish-green. Later work, for urban sale, continues to foster taste for folk art.

Fukurokuju. One of Japanese *Shichi-fuku-jin; god of good fortune, learning, wisdom, prosperity and longevity. Portrayed as serene elderly scholar with elongated head (indicating wisdom). Shown standing, either reading from ancient scroll, or holding staff in one hand and fan in other. Often caricatured.

Fulham Pottery. *See* Bailey, C.J.C.

fully jewelled movement. *See* jewelled bearings.

Fulper Pottery. American pottery established in 1805 at Flemington, New Jersey; at first, made drain tiles, using local clay. From 1860, also

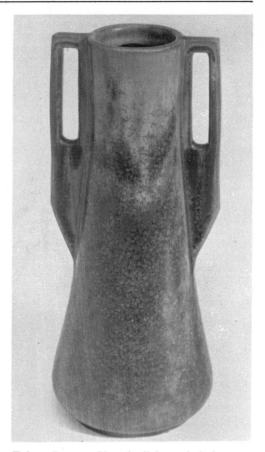

Fulper Pottery. Vase in light and dark green crystalline glazes. Stamped on base, Fulper in rectangle. c1915. Height 11in.

made variety of domestic wares. Art pottery, made from 1910, inspired by Chinese decoration, e.g. close imitation of *famille rose* style. Lamps produced with pierced pottery shade concealing bulb. Wide range of glazes, e.g. brownish-black intended to resemble dark oak. Vases often angular in shape. In 1926, took over pottery in Trenton, New Jersey, and in 1929 transferred to Trenton, retaining showroom in Flemington.

fumed oak. Oak exposed to ammonia fumes in airtight chamber before polishing; resulting greyish-brown colour gradually fades to yellowish-brown shade resembling antique oak. Used for Quaint style furniture; also by Sir A. *Heal.

fumi-bako. *See* fubako.

Funaki, Michitada, and son, Kenji (fl 20th century). Japanese potters working at Matsue in Shimane prefecture. Michitada among potters of folk art movement; influenced by Korean pottery and English slipware. Noted for frequent use of yellow or cream glazes. Work of Kenji characterized by painted decoration of animals, e.g. horses, fish, cockerels, octopus.

Functionalist modern furniture. *See* Modernist style.

Functionalist style in glass. European glass made in 1920s and 1930s in style inspired by later work of Vienna secession, functionalist ideals of

Bauhaus (glass department under direction of J. *Albers), etc. Characterized by discipline and simplicity in design, which was determined by use. Decoration, seldom used, emphasized geometrical aspects of form. A. *Loos designed glass for Viennese firm of J. & L. *Lobmeyr in 1920s. Also among pioneers in application of style to glass design, R. *Süssmuth founded own factory in Dresden in early 1920s. *Ikora glass made at *Württembergische Metallwarenfabrik. W. *Wagenfeld left Bauhaus in early 1930s to concentrate on design of glass and ceramics. C. *Lebeau and A. D. *Copier worked in functionalist style at Dutch *Leerdam factory. In Sweden, Ørrefors factory employed designers, e.g. E. *Hald, who worked in *Ariel and *Graal glass, S. *Gate, E. *Strömberg and, later, V. *Lindstrand. Other Scandinavian makers include *Kosta, *Hadeland, and Danish designer, J. *Bang. Italian glass artists E. *Barovier and P. *Venini at Murano influenced by simplicity of style.

fundame (Japanese, 'powdered ground') or **ikakeji** (Japanese, 'richly-covered ground'). Flat, matt gold Japanese lacquer ground: finely powdered gold dusted on to lacquer base or mixed into lacquer and applied with brush. Widely used as both background and design technique from Fujiwara period (895–1192), particularly on inside and bottom surfaces of lacquer boxes, and on insides and risers of inro. Term, ikakeji, used for work done after 17th century.

Furnival, T. & Sons. Staffordshire pottery firm established 1851; operated two factories at Cobridge. Produced earthenware and ironstone for domestic use. Tableware decorated with e.g. delicate linear designs, impressed and filled with glaze to produce flat surface. Transfer-printed decoration often hand-enamelled and gilded. Much work exported, often with appropriate decoration, e.g. transfer-printed beaver and maple designs for Canada. Some unglazed ware sold for painting or (from c1865) crayoning by amateur artists. Early mark: FURNIVAL, impressed. Variety of printed marks from 1890 usually include trademark of crossed sword and anchor. Firm traded as Furnivals Ltd, 1913–1960s.

fusee box. See match-holder.

Futagawa. Japanese folk pottery kiln in Fukuoka prefecture, Kyushu. Products include storage jars with white glaze under brown trickled glaze, with decoration of wavy lines around base, and, notably, large bowls for use in wax-making, with green and brown brushwork painted on white slip, made until production declined in 20th century.

GAB (Guldsmeds Aktiebolaget). Swedish silver manufacturers, founded 1867 in Stockholm. J. *Angman, designer from 1907, established firm's reputation as producers of modern silverware. Merged with *Gense AB (1964) forming largest silver production unit in northern Europe.

gabba. Kashmiri floor covering made by appliqué technique: shapes, cut out of various coloured woollen fabrics, inserted in embroidered ground.

Gado, Naniwa (b 1888). Japanese wood and bamboo carver of Takamatsu. Graduate of Kanagawa Prefectural Arts & Crafts School. Made numerous *tea-ceremony utensils and some netsuke. *Na: Shikazo; *Chomei: Gado.

Gádor, István (b 1891). Hungarian artist potter. Studied under M. *Powolny; work shown at first Wiener Werkstätte exhibition in 1910. Subsequent work in Vienna influenced by expressionist sculpture. From 1927, in Hungary, increasingly influenced by Hungarian folk art, made e.g. tin-glazed earthenware. Later taught at School of Applied Art in Budapest.

Gaillard, Eugène (fl 1895–1911). French furniture designer. Associate of S. *Bing, designed bedroom and dining-room suites for Paris Exhibition of 1900. Work in *Ecole de Paris style characterized by bold, plain outlines, balanced proportions, and sometimes elaborate, abstract decoration.

Gaillard, Lucien (b 1861). French jeweller and silversmith. First won reputation as silversmith (1889), but persuaded by R. *Lalique to change to jewellery. Used unusual materials (e.g. ivory, horn), and uncommon semi-precious stones; designs based on *insect and flower forms.

Below
Lucien Gaillard. Combs. Left: horn with ivory flowers and brilliants, 1902, length 6in. Right: horn with enamelled detail on the bees, 1904, length 7in. Both stamped L. Gaillard.

Eugène Gaillard. Chair. Mahogany, upholstered in leather stamped with design. c1900. Height 3ft2in.

Visited Japan; adopted Japanese *mixed metal techniques. After 1900, employed Japanese craftsmen in Paris workshop. Exhibited at International Exhibitions, Paris (1900), Glasgow (1901). Work strongly influenced by Lalique; continued to work in style abandoned c1900 by Lalique until c1910. Mark: L. Gaillard.

Gale & Son. American silverware manufacturers in New York, founded in 1821 by silversmith William Gale. Became Gale & North, 1860; subsequently Gale, North & Dominick, 1868, then, Dominick & Hogg, 1873; finally absorbed by *Reed & Barton. Division of company established, 1833, to produce close plate ware; became Gale, Wood & Hughes (c1836–c1890), later Graff, Washburn & Dunn (1890–1960). Firm now part of *Gorham Corporation.

Gallé, Emile (1846–1904). French glass artist and technician; also designed ceramics, furniture, etc. At small workshop, established 1874 in Nancy (Meurthe-et-Moselle), made earthenware, first exhibited c1890. Later, experimented with stoneware and porcelain. Decoration includes heraldic motifs, and scenes recalling those of Delft ware. Plant designs, dandelions, chrysanthemums, orchids, etc., echo decoration of glass. Flowing, opaque glazes used, sometimes with several colours mingled. Forms simple, sometimes slightly clumsy; use of some of his shapes acknowledged by *Rookwood Pottery. All ceramics marked, with initials E.G. impressed, Em. Gallé Faiencerie de Nancy, or versions of signature.

Theorist and leader of *Ecole de Nancy, inspired generation of followers and imitators. Regarded as one of most influential figures in modern glassmaking. Evolved many new techniques, e.g. *marqueterie sur verre. Early pieces in 1870s in enamelled glass, based on historical styles and themes, or with floral or insect motifs. Experimented with addition of metal oxides to glass melt, colouring glass in imitation of semiprecious stones. Exhibited clair-de-lune glass (with opalescence turning sapphire blue in certain lights, produced by cobalt oxide) in 1878. By 1889, perfected both enamelled and coloured glass techniques, with wide range of colours and effects. Noted for *cameo glass, drawing inspiration from many sources, e.g. Chinese and Japanese arts, and nature. Produced *vases de tristesse and *verreries parlantes. From 1899, as well as individual hand made pieces, produced cameo glass on commercial scale in factory at Nancy, allowing use of standardized designs, acid etching, etc. Began decorative application of glass to electric lighting in 1900, producing lamps e.g. in form of flowers with light fittings concealed by half-open petals. All own work, as well as that of factory (employing c300 workmen by 1900) signed. Firm continued after Gallé's death; after interruption in work (1914), reestablished and continued in production until 1935.

Made furniture from mid 1880s; summarized theories in Revue des Arts Décoratifs (1900). Designs, often based on 18th century forms (e.g. Louis XV), characterized by restrained lines and naturalistic ornament. Limbs and cross-sections of mouldings often based on shapes and outlines of plants; marquetry decoration in natural fruitwoods on flat surfaces. Work sometimes inlaid with inscriptions (e.g. quotation from Baudelaire on desk, 1900) and often titled. Major pieces for private clients include table and display cabinet

Above
Emile Gallé. Silver-mounted glass ewer, c1870, and bowl of later date.

Left
Emile Gallé. Chair made in beechwood, moulded and sculpted. Designed 1902.

supported by dragonflies carved in full relief, with blown-glass eyes; bed with marquetry panels shaped like butterflies, carved in relief and inlaid with mother-of-pearl and glass. Also designed bedroom incorporating cow parsley motifs on bed head, chair backs, and bedside tables.

Gallia metal. Type of plated ware introduced by *Christofle at Paris Exhibition of 1900. Heavier than electro-plate, and more sonorous when struck. Christofle catalogue of 1904 includes some Art Nouveau objects in Gallia metal.

Gambone, Guido (b 1909). Italian artist potter. Working alone in Naples until c1949, made brightly-coloured pottery vases, etc. in extravagant shapes, often with extensive flat surfaces

and sharp edges. Stoneware frequently covered with white speckled glaze and simple linear decoration, e.g. in blue. Decoration of earthenware sometimes recalls early Etruscan pottery. Figures, etc. also produced. From early 1950s, ran workshop in Florence, supervising manufacture of articles in series, as well as own unique works.

garden furniture. Wooden outdoor furniture dates from c1750. Chairs, tables, garden seats, etc., in cast and wrought iron popular from 1851 Great Exhibition, London, where first displayed, to end of 19th century; early designs show Regency influence, later designs more massive, giving way to Gothic rusticity; originally painted black, brown in imitation of oak, or bronzed; much metal garden furniture in variety of styles made by *Coalbrookdale Co. American examples made c1860-c1880 by e.g. Boston Ornamental Iron Works, J. W. Fiske Co., New York, and Samuel S. Bent & Co., New York. Wooden garden furniture made during period of Arts & Crafts movement, also in terracotta by Doulton & Co., c1905.

garnet. Gemstone in colours including reds, green, and yellow, widely used in secondary jewellery throughout 19th century. Small dark red pyrope garnet from Bohemia, usually facet cut and set in clusters, particularly popular. When cabochon cut, known as carbuncle; much used in Victorian medieval and Gothic pieces, and as central stone in brooch or ring. Other varieties: almandine (violet-red), rhodolite (pale violet), and demantoid (olive-green).

Garrard & Co. (London). English silversmiths and jewellers; firm descended from 18th century partnership between silversmiths George Wickes and Edward Wakelin; Wakelin's son passed business to employee Robert Garrard on retirement in 1802; Garrard died 1818, succeeded by sons Robert (1793-1881), James, and Sebastian. Followed Rundell, Bridge & Rundell as Royal Goldsmiths in 1830; became official crown jewellers in 1843; patronized by visiting royalty including Russian Czar, but derived prosperity from domestic trade; with Hunt & Roskell, were leading makers of presentation silver; made Ascot and Doncaster racing trophies and many large centrepieces. Chief designer, E. *Cotterill; some designs by Prince *Albert for royal commissions. Showed Assyrian jewellery inspired by Nineveh sculptures at 1851 Great Exhibition, London (see archaeological jewellery). After death of Cotterill in 1860, less ambitious designs by W. F. Spencer. In 1911, Garrards opened new factory and showrooms in Albemarle Street, London, for coronation of George V; Albemarle works closed in 1952 after acquisition by Goldsmiths' and Silversmiths' Company; now part of British Silverware Ltd.

Garrison Pottery. See Sunderland Pottery.

Gaskin, Arthur Joseph (1862-1928). English painter, illustrator, and metalworker. Trained and later taught at Birmingham School of Art. Illustrator of Hans Christian Andersen's Stories and Fairy Tales (1893), and Grimms' Household Tales (1899). With wife, Georgina Cave France (1868-1934), designed and made jewellery from 1899. Necklace and pendant (c1912) made in silver, with plaques set in chain; three pendant

Garrard & Co. Silver-gilt table candlestick. London, 1874. Height 12in.

Below
Arthur and Georgina Gaskin. Silver pendant and chain. Pendant set with emerald and semi-precious stones. Early 20th century.

drops decorated with silver wire in filigree scrolls, set with cabochon-cut pale amethyst and mother-of-pearl. In 1902, succeeded R. *Catterson Smith as headmaster of Vittoria Street School of Jewellers and Silversmiths, Birmingham.

gasolier. Branched gas lighting centrepiece, resembling *chandelier, for domestic and public use; made in e.g. brass from mid 19th century. Gas pipe forms centre shaft, distributing gas to upright burners inside spherical shades of plain or coloured glass, frequently decorated with foliate or floral motifs. Early burners inefficient, hence introduction of water slide gasolier, c1860: fitting counterbalanced, so can be lowered to working level; telescopic shaft has water seal to prevent escape of gas. Incandescent gas mantle, introduced c1887, enabled development by c1900 of gasolier with burners and globes directed downwards, giving more efficient light distribution.

Gassan (1815-78). Japanese tsuba maker. Excelled in depicting subjects from nature, e.g. wolves.

Gate, Simon (1883-1945). Leading Swedish glass artist in Functionalist style. Appointed designer at *Ørrefors 1917, where, with master glass blower, Knut Bergqvist, developed *Graal glass. Early work, tall, slim vases in tinted glass; later vessels in Graal glass, often with multicoloured decoration and human figures in motion. Also, designed heavy vessels deeply engraved with biblical or mythological figures. Marks: SG-KB, engraved; also G, followed by Ørrefors or Øf (on all engraved glass to his design); GA (on cut glass; GU (on furnace-finished glass).

Gaudernack, Gustav (1865-1914). Norwegian silversmith and designer; studied in Austria. Designed glass for Christiania Glasmagasin, Oslo (1891). Worked for D. *Andersen, 1892-1910, then started own workshop. Silverwork at first in *dragon style, then in Art Nouveau style; worked in neo-classical forms in last years. Bowl in filigree and enamel with dragonfly handles, made 1907, now in Kunstindustrimuseet, Oslo.

Gaudí y Cornet, Antonio (1852-1926). Spanish architect; exponent of Catalan version of Art Nouveau. Designed furniture characterized by undulating curves in original designs, e.g. wooden chair with back shaped like pelvic girdle.

*Simon Gate. *Ørrefors glass bowl, The Bacchus Festival. 1925.*

Paul Gauguin. Pottery dish, made 1887-88.

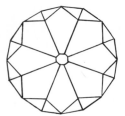

Above and right:
Brilliant cut

Below:
Pendeloque

Below right:
Marquise

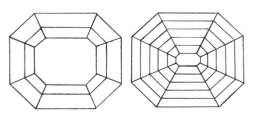

Above and below left: Step cut
Below right: Mixed cut

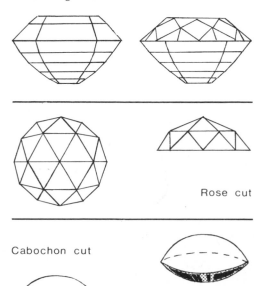

Rose cut

Cabochon cut

Gauguin, Jean-René (1881-1961). Potter and ceramic modeller. Son of P. *Gauguin, born in France. In Denmark from 1884; naturalized Dane from 1909. As modeller and chief designer at Bing & Grøndahls Porcellaensfabrik, noted for sculptural work in hard red porcelain and stoneware. Figures, e.g. of bulls and a satyr riding an ass, characterized by power and action. Large jars have animal finials.

Gauguin, Paul (1848-1903). French painter, sculptor, and graphic artist. Made stoneware at workshop of E. *Chaplet from 1886; about 60 pieces known. Freely modelled jugs, vases, etc., unglazed, and decorated with moulded figures, often have loops of clay attached like handles. Similar strips of clay frequently join separate vessels forming part of same work. Made *jardinières*, etc., thrown and glazed; cylindrical vases decorated with scene of trees and sheep, or Breton figures, in coloured glazes between bands of yellowish speckled glaze. After return from Martinique in November 1887, made portrait vases with painted slip decoration and incised designs; also bowls, etc., with modelled figures. Self-portraits in stoneware, with trickles of red colouring in glaze, and figures (Eve, Black Venus, etc.) date from 1888/89. During brief visit to Paris from South Seas (1893-95), again made figures, e.g. Hina, Tefatou, and Oviri. Work, signed P. Go, or P. Gauguin, sometimes bears mark of Chaplet; earliest pieces also have mark of Haviland factory.

Gebrüder Thonet. *See* Thonet Brothers.

gem cutting. Transparent stones usually cut with facets for use in jewellery to display them to best advantage. Portion of stone above point of greatest width (girdle) known as crown; uppermost, central facet, table. Portion below girdle termed pavilion; surface corresponding to table known as culet.

Among main styles of cutting, brilliant used on finest diamonds to catch most of 'life' and 'fire' in stone. Style perfected in late 17th century Venice, popular in France from 18th century, and England from mid 19th century. Perfect brilliant cut has 33 facets above girdle and 25 below. 1/3 total depth of stone should be above level of girdle, 2/3 below. Variations include marquise, in shape of pointed ellipse, and pendeloque, drop or pear shaped.

Step or trap cut displays full colour of stone; used for large, valuable diamonds and other gemstones. Rows of facets on crown slope from table to girdle, facts on pavilion slope from girdle to culet. Finished stone square, hexagonal, or octagonal when viewed from above. Eight-sided cut often used for emeralds, therefore known as emerald cut. Variation, baguette, used for small diamonds, developed in 19th century, but particularly associated with 20th century jewellery. Mixed cut, with crown cut as brilliant and pavilion in steps, used to bring out colour and brilliance of small stones.

Rose cut, developed in mid 17th century Holland and France, although superseded by brilliant cut, underwent minor revival in late 19th century. Normally has 24 facets; six star facets forming crown surrounded by 18 cross facets (dentelle). Pavilion usually has broad, flat face, but may also be rose cut; style then double rose. Variations: briolet (drop-shaped) and

cushion-shaped (square).

Calibré stones cut in shapes to fit specific design. Facets sometimes curved to fit small boat shaped or half moon settings developed c1900. Also refers to small, square stones used in *eternity rings.

Translucent or opaque stones usually cut *en cabochon* (with rounded surface); some transparent stones, in particular garnets, also cut in same style. Popular in Gothic and neo-Renaissance jewellery. Simple cabochon oval or circular with flat base, double cabochon domed below, although less steeply than top. Hollow cabochon given shell-like form; inside of stone ground away at base.

gem inlay. Furniture decoration used in Britain from c1850. Inlay of glass stones or paste, sometimes used instead of mother-of-pearl on papier-mâché pieces.

Gense AB. Swedish firm founded in Eskiltuna (1886) to produce stove shutters and ventilators. From c1900, produced silver and nickel plated tea and coffee sets and cutlery. One of pioneers of stainless steel tableware in 1930s. Merged with *GAB in 1964.

Georgian carpets. *See* Caucasian carpets.

German carpets. Traditional rug craft regenerated in 19th century; became experimental in technique and materials. Chief product: hand-tufted Turkish-style 'Smyrna' carpets. Hand-knotted carpet making became commercial industry in mid 19th century; factories founded in Lähn (Riesengebirge, northern Bohemia) in 1854; Wurzen (near Leipzig); Cottbus and Görlitz; Schmiedeberg (1857), and elsewhere in Silesia and the Spreewald. Seamless hand-knotted carpets made up to 40ft wide. Schmiedeberger carpets gained international reputation; particularly popular in America. Chenille carpets also made from 1877. Industry rapidly mechanized during late 19th century; extensive power loom industry by 1914. German synthetic dyes led market. *Face-to-face loom developed in 1924.

German embroidery. *See* Berlin woolwork.

German horological industry. Black Forest continued to be main European centre of production of popular domestic clocks, e.g. made cuckoo clocks, trumpeter clocks, *picture frame and *novelty clocks, *postman's alarm, *Napoleon clocks, all widely exported 1850-1914. Industry suffered from American competition 1845-60; revived 1861 by E. *Junghans, who reorganized it on American pattern. Many imitations of American shelf and wall clocks by Teutonia Clock Co., Hamburg America Clock Co., Congress Clock Co., etc. Mass-production established in factories at Schramberg, Schwenningen, Furtwangen, and Lenzkirch (Baden-Württemberg) by 1870. Copies of *Vienna regulator made e.g. by Gustav Becker Uhrenfabrik, Lenzkirch Uhrenfabrik. *Precision clocks and *chronometers manufactured in Hamburg-Altona, northern Germany; *precision watches, made e.g. by Adolf Lange Uhrenfabrik, at Glashütte, near Dresden. Industry's exports to France and Switzerland

benefited from removal of tariffs during 1870s. Ornamental *clock cases produced by porcelain factories at Meissen, Frankenthal, Ludwigsburg, and Berlin. *400-day clock with torsion pendulum patented by Anton Herder c1880. Industry flourished up to 1914, revived c1920-40.

German silver. *See* nickel silver.

German tapestry. Weaving tradition, dating from 15th century, stimulated c1900 by contemporary Scandinavian tapestry revival. Small factory founded 1896 at Scherrebek in North Schleswig (now Denmark), supported by artists designing specifically for tapestry (e.g. Otto Eckmann, Hans Christiansen, Alfred Mohrbutter, Otto Ubbelonde). Tapestries shown at Paris International Exhibition (1900). Factory closed 1903, but others opened in Kiel and Meldorf. German Expressionist painters Franz Marc, August Macke, and Ernst Kirschner, also experimented privately with small tapestries. Bauhaus involved in modernizing both tapestry and carpet design for industry.

German Workshops. *See Deutsche Werkstätten.*

Gien. French faience factory established at Gien (Loiret) in 1822. Early work often left in white, or rimmed with acid yellow. Printed decoration depicts local views, scenes from Parisian life, or illustrates traditional French tales. From 1860, imitated 18th century faience, e.g. *style rayonnant* or *décor à la corne* of Rouen, work of Moustiers, or 16th century Italian maiolica. Blue painting picked out in colours. Produced chiefly tableware, also door furniture, sugar sifters, wall brackets, and inkstands. From c1880, decoration includes monochrome hunting subjects, panels *en camaïeu*, imitations of jasper, agate, or mother-of-pearl. Experimented with application of *flambé* glazes to faience. Mark (from 1864): castle and label, GIEN.

Gilbert, Sir Alfred (1854-1943). English sculptor and metalworker, best known for statue of Eros in Piccadilly Circus, London. Studied at Royal Academy Schools, and in Paris and Rome. Designed ceremonial badges and chains, most notably Mayor's badge and chain for Mayor and Corporation of Preston, Lancashire, and President's badge and chain for Royal Institute of Painters in Watercolour, London. Also designed some other jewellery. Denied connection with Art Nouveau, but designs often in this style. Designed and made maquettes for necklaces, brooches, and rings in silver, steel wire, and coloured glass paste; completely abstract, based on continuous flowing line; some made as late as 1930s.

gilding. In ceramic decoration, techniques in use from mid 19th century include raised gilding, with gilding applied to relief designs. Brown gold evolved in 1853, but little used before late 1860s: thin paste containing gold chloride, bismuth oxide, and borax; when fired, produced dull gilded surface which could be polished. Delicate, intricate patterns possible with use of design transfer, printed in ink consisting of asphalt, oil, and gold size over gold-leaf, applied on coating of isinglas painted on glaze. Unprotected gold-leaf washed off with water leaves gold decoration under ink, cleaned off before firing. Liquid gold, seldom used before 1850s, depends on ability of

some oils containing sulphur to dissolve gold or hold it in suspension; resulting decoration brilliant, but not resistant to wear. Fire-gilding, developed in late 18th century, using amalgam of powdered gold painted over glaze, continued in use. *See also* acid gilding.

Gilet & Brianchon. French porcelain manufacturers working (1855-80) at various addresses in Paris. Porcelain, with iridescent glaze containing bismuth, became very fashionable. Specialities include pink *trompe l'oeil* shells. Marks include GB/breveté/Paris, enclosed in oval formed by small v's.

Gillow. English furniture makers founded 1695 in Lancaster by joiner, Robert Gillow. London branch established 1761. Made all types of furniture, in many styles, e.g. Free Renaissance, Eclectic; also realized designs by leading 19th century designers, e.g. T.E. *Collcutt, B.J. *Talbert. Exponents of New Palace Westminster style, making furniture for Houses of Parliament, New Law Courts, etc. in London. Employed resident designers; over 500 workmen by 1873. Most pieces made after 1820 stamped: Gillow & Co., or Gillow, and numbered. Acquired Collinson & Lock in 1897. Name changed to *Waring & Gillow after amalgamation with S.J. Waring & Sons c1900. Showed at major exhibitions. *Illustration at* Talbert, B.J.

gilt clocks. Clocks with wooden or metal cases finished in gold. Gold or water-gilding (gold-leaf applied with size, or direct on to gesso surface) used on, e.g. *sunburst clocks, cartel (*Comtoise or Swedish) clocks. Fire gilding (powdered gold and mercury paste applied to metal base, then fired to evaporate mercury) used e.g. for *Empire clocks. Both techniques gradually superseded c1840 by electro-gilding (gold layer deposited by electrolysis).

gimmel or **gimmal flask.** Double flask, with spouts facing in opposite directions, pourable from one side without disturbing the other. Usually of clear or lightly tinted transparent glass, often with combed or *latticinio* decoration. Many *Nailsea specimens.

Sir Alfred Gilbert. Badge and chain made for Mayor of Preston. Silver, gilt, and enamel. 1888.

*Ernest Gimson. Box and cover in ebony and figured walnut with painted decoration by A. and L. *Powell. c1905. Width 7¾in.*

Carlo Giuliano. Enamel butterfly brooch, and enamel and diamond necklace. Both signed.

Gimson, Ernest William (1864–1919). English architect and furniture designer; follower of W. *Morris. Articled to J. D. *Sedding, 1886–88; learnt to make traditional turned ash chairs with Herefordshire chair maker. Member of *Kenton & Co. and *Arts & Crafts Exhibition Society; later became leader of Cotswold school. Set up workshop with S. & E. *Barnsley at Pinbury, Gloucestershire, in 1894; started Daneway House workshop at Sapperton, Gloucestershire, in 1902, settling permanently in Sapperton in 1903. Designed furniture in conjunction with craftsmen, often making modifications as work progressed. Made use of decorative qualities of untreated English woods, e.g. oak, ash, yew, elm, and walnut, for individual pieces of furniture. Designed chairs with turned legs and rails, slat-backs, spindle-backs, and rush seats, drawing on traditional woodworking methods and craft processes; also cabinets, chests, and sideboards with burr elm veneer, and inlays of holly, ebony, cherrywood, ivory, bone and mother-of-pearl. *Illustrations at andirons, Kenton & Co.*

Ginori family. Italian manufacturers of porcelain and earthenware. Owners of *Doccia factory since establishment by Marchese Carlo Ginori in 1735. In 1896, porcelain factory incorporated with Società Ceramica Richard in Milan, trading as Società Ceramica Richard-Ginori.

giobu lacquer. See gyobu lacquer.

Gioielleria Bulgari. See Bulgari.

Giuliano, Carlo (d c1912). Italian goldsmith and jeweller best known for *archaeological jewellery in Etruscan style. Sponsored by London jeweller R. *Phillips; opened business in Piccadilly in late 1860s. Outstanding enameller; work characterized by delicacy and subtle use of colour. Holbein-inspired pendants and fringe necklaces set with cabochon or rose-cut stones and pearls in gold decorated with fine enamel work. Pendants often have drop of polished amethyst or baroque pearl. Also worked in Renaissance, oriental and Art Nouveau styles. Work signed C. & A. G., C. & E. G., C. G. Sons Federico and Ferdinand opened own business in London as manufacturing jewellers and worked in father's style.

Glasgow Pottery. See Bell, John and Matthew P.

Glasgow School. Group of architects and designers led by C. R. *Mackintosh in association with Glasgow School of Art. Style, characterized by floral and foliate motifs (e.g. tulips on extended stems, conventionalized roses, sym-

Glass furniture. Coffee table in peach-coloured glass on wood frame. London, c1925. Height 2ft1½in.

metrical trees), spectral figures, and use of painted, inlaid stained glass, or applied metal-work ornamentation in furniture, constitutes British expression of Art Nouveau. Furniture generally designed as part of total decorative scheme with straight or curved lines attenuated. Members included Francis H. Newbery, principal of Art School, Mackintosh's wife, M. *Macdonald, who designed and made metal-work and jewellery with sister, F. *Macdonald, and brother in law, J. H. *McNair, who also made some jewellery; also T. *Morris and J. M. *King. Exhibited at Liège in Belgium (1895), Vienna Secession Exhibition (1900), Glasgow Exhibition (1901). Style, influential in Europe, especially after Turin Exhibition (1902), affected Jugendstil and Vienna Secession style; also imitated in America.

Glass beads. See pharmaceutical glass.

glass furniture. Contemporary or antique-shaped tables, stools, cocktail cabinets, chest-of-drawers, etc. covered with mirror glass. Popular in Britain during 1930s. Often peach-coloured; artificially antiqued mirror glass, etched and gilded with linear and calligraphic ornamentation, also used. Dining-table centrepieces, obelisks, etc. often decorated with faceted mirrors.

glass walking stick. Plain, twisted, solid or hollow glass rod in shape of walking stick; made from c1860 with other glass objects, e.g. bells, by workmen at Bristol glass factories in their spare time, as presents for wives, families, friends; practice possibly stemmed from old West Country belief that glass rod protected against illness. Designs included hollow version, filled with confectionery called 'hundreds and thousands'; engraved, decorated examples

R. M. Y. Gleadowe. The Sea Beaker. Engraved by George Friend. Maker's mark Murphy and Falcon, London. Designed 1929. Height 5½in.

common. Eventually commercial production instituted, e.g. as commemorative objects.

glaze. *See celadon glaze, flambé glaze, crystal-line glaze, matt glaze, Moonstone glaze, oriental glazes, sang-de-boeuf glaze, temmoku glaze.*

Gleadowe, R.M.Y. (1888-1944). English designer, worked with various silversmiths including H. G. *Murphy, *Barnards, and *Wakely & Wheeler from c1929 to his death; art master at Winchester College and Slade Professor of Art at Oxford. Evolved linear style, with use of fluting etc., e.g. on chased Romanesque-based alms dish in form of radiating sun, now at Goldsmiths' Hall, London.

Glebe Street Works. *See* Robinson & Leadbeater.

Glienitz. German faience factory, established 1753. Produced cream-coloured earthenware, c1830-70. Marks include GLINITZ over M (owners: Mittelstadt family), and G impressed.

Gmündener Keramik. *See* Schleiss, Franz.

Go (Japanese, 'art name' or 'pseudonym'). In Japanese arts, professional name chosen by artist, unconnected with ordinary names. Often directly or indirectly derived from name of art family, master, or speciality. Appear on works of art either alone or with other names of artist. May be changed several times during career.

Gobelins. French tapestry works in Paris, state-owned from 1662; from 1825, also made carpets (*see* Savonnerie). Later 19th century tapestry continued to emulate painting; quality lowered by introduction of *aniline dyes, use therefore suspended in early 20th century. During 2nd Empire (1852-70), factory produced many full-length and bust portraits of royalty after Franz Winterhalter and other court painters, also

copies of well-known paintings. Made panels for Paris theatres in 1880s and 1890s, e.g. eight panels for buffet at Théâtre de l'Opéra in 1872. Gustave Geoffroi (director, 1919-25) tried to free tapestry from slavish imitation of painting: commissioned cartoons from contemporary painters, e.g. Jean Weber (series illustrating fairy stories, 1919-25), R. *Dufy, but still allowed weavers little initiative. Guillaume Janneau (director 1935-45) continued tendency, giving weavers greater scope for interpretation, and re-introducing (improved) synthetic dyes.

Godwin, Edward William (1833-86). English architect and furniture designer. Known for Anglo-Japanese style furniture, e.g. ebonized wood sideboard with silver-plated fittings, inset with simulated embossed leather panels; made by W. *Watt, 1877. Designs based on detailed research, e.g. structural details from medieval furniture or manuscripts. Pieces often in square-section laths, easily adapted to mass-production; chairs and coffee tables, in favourite ebonized oak, extensively copied. Art Furniture, catalogue of his designs manufactured by W. *Watt (published 1877), influenced Japanese style furniture and art furniture in America. *Illustration at* Aesthetic movement.

gohana. *See* jogahana.

*Edward William Godwin. Sideboard made by W. *Watt in ebonized wood. c1867.*

gold. Highly malleable precious yellow metal. Most popular metal for jewellery in 19th century. Purity of gold based on 24 units, e.g. 22 carat gold is 22 parts pure gold, two parts alloy. 22 and 18 carat gold used until 1854, when 15, 12 and 9 carats made legal. 15 and 12 replaced by 14 carat in 1932. Coloured gold widely used: dark red in late 1860s, green, orange, and yellow. Colour varied by proportion of alloy, e.g. copper produced red gold, silver or cadmium, green. White gold, alloy of silver and gold, used as forerunner of platinum, to set diamonds at end of 19th century; highly reflective and does not tarnish.

Goldsmiths' & Silversmiths' Co. English gold, silver, and jewellery designers, manufacturers, and retailers established in London by William Gibson, 1890. Became public company, 1898: mark registered at Goldsmiths' Hall, 1899. Designs by H. *Stabler for company include set of blue enamel boxes; also die-struck ornamental tea set, 1928, made by *Wakely & Wheeler, now owned by Worshipful Company of Goldsmiths. Firm taken over by *Garrard & Co. in 1952.

gold-stone. *See* tiger-eye glaze.

Goliath clock. Large Swiss pocket watch, used as travelling clock, often has 8-day movement; made from c1880. Normally enclosed in lined outer case of e.g. leather, tortoiseshell, as travelling-case fitting.

*William Henry Goss. *Parian ware portrait figure of Queen Victoria, mid 19th century.*

J. Willis Good. Bronze of hunter with fox mask hanging from saddle. Signed on base, c1906. Height 1ft 3in.
Right
Gorham Manufacturing Co. Four designs for silver butter knives from 1888 catalogue. Left to right: Versailles, Old Masters, Cluny, and St Cloud.
Below
*John Edward Goodwin. Tableware set, Edme, first produced in 1908 by J. *Wedgwood & Sons.*

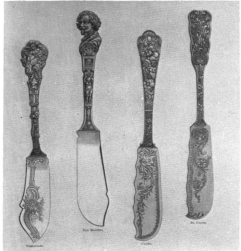

gong. Metal, usually bronze, disc, producing resonant sound when struck with stick. Originally used outside oriental temples to announce prayer time; imported to England, e.g. by returning 19th century Imperial Civil Service and military personnel, and used to summon diners at meal times. Versions intended for domestic use usually hung on wooden frame, with e.g. hook or rack for striker. Many examples display workmanship of high quality.

Good, John Willis (fl late 19th century). English sculptor; exhibited at Royal Academy, London, 1870–78. Best-known work: c16 crisply modelled bronze or terracotta hunting groups, racehorses, and jockeys. Most bronzes produced in matched

pairs; some founded by *Elkington & Co. and bear their stamp.

Goodwin, John Edward (1867–1949). English ceramic designer. Art director at Wedgwood factory (1902–35), succeeded by V. *Skellern. Designed new shapes for production in Queensware, some based on 18th century originals, and still in production.

Gorham Corporation. American manufacturing silversmiths and jewellers. Later produced bronzes and furniture; founded in Providence, Rhode Island by Jabez Gorham, c1815. Made jewellery with Stanton Beebe until 1831, when Henry Webster joined firm to make silver spoons; in 1841 joined by Gorham's son John who installed steam machinery for finishing hand made articles, and broadened scope of business. 1861, company opened New York sales office and began making electro-plate; became corporation, 1865. In 1868, adopted Sterling Standard for silverware, and introduced trade mark of lion, anchor, and capital G; 1878, opened branches in Chicago and San Francisco; 1887, Edward Holbrook became head of firm and brought over W. C. *Codman from Cox & Son, London, as designer. Later merged with *Black, Starr & Frost. Under trade mark Martelé, made jewellery in French Art Nouveau and craft revival style, popular in America from c1890, but were also one of first silver manufacturers to use mass production techniques. Established bronze foundry in Providence c1925, with exhibition galleries at 5th Avenue and 42nd Street, New York; produced small human and animal figures (formed e.g. as bookends) in editions from 24 to 200; modelled by various artists; figures with green patination by Harriet Frishmuth, on black Belgian marble bases, particularly popular; bronzes marked with name of artist and stamp: rectangle divided in three, with initials G and C flanking panther. Company also made Art Nouveau style furniture, usually of ebony, inlaid with silver, mother-of-pearl, and ivory; often with cabriole legs; motifs include

twining vines, leaves, mermaids with swirling hair, etc.

Gorka, Géza (b 1894). Hungarian artist potter. Initially learned skill from folk potter, then trained in early 1920s, e.g. under M. *Läuger. Glaze important feature of work, e.g. tin glaze streaked with white on graceful earthenware vase with rounded belly and slender neck.

Goss, William Henry (1833–1906). English potter and porcelain manufacturer. Modeller and designer for W. T. *Copeland & Sons, 1857. Started factory in partnership (1858); later established own factory, moving to Falcon Works, Stoke-on-Trent, in 1870. From 1858, made parian ware, notably portrait busts; also produced household ware in terracotta with bands of painted decoration, e.g. in blue, green, yellow, or black and white; usually unmarked. By 1873, patented method of applying jewelled decoration to recesses cut in clay before baking; used in making trinkets. Also made small, openwork porcelain baskets decorated with flowers, and modelled flower brooches or clips. Small souvenirs with heraldic decoration made in ivory-coloured porcelain from 1880s until 1st World War; at first, simple shapes, later models of historic houses, fonts, crosses, lighthouses, etc. Printed marks include W. H. Goss, with goshawk, wings outstretched. Succeeded by sons Victor Henry (d 1913) and William Huntley. Firm, trading as W. H. Goss & Sons, and later W. H. Goss Ltd, absorbed into Cauldon Potteries (formerly *Brown-Westhead, Moore & Co.).

Gothic Reform style. British furniture style based on 13th century examples; development of Gothic style. Popular c1860–c1870. Typified by simple, sturdy forms decorated with narrative paintings; often large, with bobbin-turned legs, stump columns, and chamfering. Principal exponents include C. *Bevan, W. *Burges, W. *Butterfield, R. N. *Shaw, J. P. *Seddon, and P. *Webb. First shown at International Exhibition of 1862, London. Made commercially by *Collier & Plucknett.

Gothic revival and **neo-Renaissance jewellery.** Jewellery in Gothic and Renaissance styles introduced by mid 19th century. Victorian Gothic designs based on medieval ecclesiastical metalwork and sculpture. French designs, very sculptural, used silver. English jewellers used enamel and gold set with cabochon stones. French and English Gothic and neo-Renaissance jewellery shown in Great Exhibition, London, 1851, includes work of A. W. N. *Pugin, whose medievalism inspired style that remained in fashion until 1870s. Many examples made by *Hardman & Co., and by makers of *archeological jewellery, e.g. A. G. *Castellani, R. *Phillips, J. *Brogden and, in France, A. *Fouquet. Neo-Renaissance designs closely followed Italian and German pieces of 16th and 17th centuries. Designers include A. *Gilbert and C. *Ricketts.

Gothic style. Furniture style popular in Britain c1840–c1860 and America c1840–c1865. Principles expounded by A. W. N. *Pugin; summarized by O. *Jones in Grammar of Ornament (1856). In Britain, style generally typified by application of 14th century ornament to con-

Marcel Goupy. Bowl decorated with enamel painting. c1920. Height 5in.

temporary forms; in America, to classical forms (inspired by A. J. *Davis). Decorative devices include pointed, arched panels and chair backs, often filled with tracery; flying buttresses; pinnacles, gables, and angular crockets; steeple-turned finials; incised or pierced quatrefoils and trefoils; medium-relief carving, often foliate or floral; heraldic devices; overhanging cornices; deeply cut spiral turnings; chamfering and raised mouldings (latter always applied in America). Popular for architectural cabinets, bookcases, standard-sized chairs with high backs, etc. in America; in Britain, for bookcases and hall chairs. Favourite woods, dark oak in Britain, mahogany, rosewood, or walnut in America. Manufacturers and designers include J. G. *Crace & Sons, J. *Jelliff, J. Lamb, A. *Roux, and J. P. *Seddon. Developed into Gothic Reform style. *See also* Abbotsford style.

Gouda, Dutch pottery centre. Tin-glazed earthenware made from 17th century. Modern factories include Zenith pottery (established in 18th century), making tile panels, figures, and domestic ware, and Zuid-Hollandsche Platteel-bakkerij, where work includes tableware, figures, vases, and imitations of Rozenburg pottery made in early 20th century under direction of T. A. C. *Colenbrander.

Goupy, Marcel (b 1886). French artist and designer of glass and ceramics; worked in transitional Art Nouveau/Art Deco style in 1920s. Made glass vases, bowls, and other decorative pieces, many with stylized flowers in enamel; designed for several glass firms, including *St Louis. Ceramic work includes earthenware services, decorated notably in ochre and blue, pro-

duced by Keramis factory; services also designed for production in porcelain by factory of T. *Haviland, e.g. with polychrome decoration of birds and stylized flowers, sometimes gilded. Work usually signed.

Government schools of design. British centres for training craftsmen and attempting to raise standards of public taste. First school established at Somerset House, London, in 1837; followed by others in Manchester, York, Birmingham, Glasgow, etc. Emphasis on ornamentation – often based on subjects from nature – and earlier styles. Many *Jennens & Bettridge decorators trained at London or Birmingham schools.

Graal glass. Swedish art glass developed at *Ørrefors by S. *Gate and E. *Hald c1920. Effect similar to E. *Gallé's cameo glass, although decoration not cut in relief. Objects decorated, then furnace-finished to give surface glassiness and more fluid pattern.

Grachev Brothers. With Fabergé, leading Russian silver firm. In St Petersburg (1866–1917). Established by G. P. Grachev; directed from 1873 by sons, Michael and Semen; granted Imperial Warrant, 1895. Specialized in *Old Russian style silver and enamel: made tableware, objects of vertu, and jewellery.

Graf Harrach'sche Glasfabrik. Bohemian glass factory in Neuwelt. Produced iridescent Art Nouveau glass, particularly at turn of century. Made both table and decorative ware.

Grainger, G. & Co. *See* Worcester.

gramophone. Mechanical device reproducing sound from flat discs, patented 1887 by Emil Berliner in America; development of phono-

Grand Rapids furniture. Bed by John E. Brower, made by Sligh Furniture Company at Grand Rapids. Gumwood stained green. c1907. Width 51½in.

Grape scissors. Silver-gilt with chased vine pattern. Made by Francis Higgins. London, 1855–56.

Below
Eileen Gray. Lacquer screen. Made in Paris, 1913.

graph patented 1877 by Thomas Alva Edison. Characterized by large, trumpet-shaped horn, sometimes harmonizing with furniture styles, e.g. petal-like form in Art Nouveau style. From c1920, mechanism concealed by large box or cabinet.

Grand-Ducal Fine Glass Company (Groszherzogliche Edelglasmanufaktur). German glass factory associated with Grand Duke Ernst Ludwig of Hesse, in Darmstadt, producing fine iridescent glass 1907–11 and active in pioneering Art Nouveau style. Employed J. L. *Schneckendorf. Marks: EL with coronet above, either enclosed within circle or free-standing.

grandfather chair. High-backed, winged, easy chair; traditional design, revived in Britain c1875. Term dates from c1880.

grandfather clock. Long-case clock usually over 6ft6in. Name coined in 1876 from first line of American song: My grandfather's clock was too tall for the shelf. Smaller version, c4ft. called grandmother clock.

Grand Rapids furniture. Loose term for inexpensive, mass-produced furniture made in Grand Rapids, Michigan, from c1850. City became important manufacturing centre during 1870s, employing many foreign craftsmen and producing commercial adaptations in variety of styles, e.g. American Colonial, Craftsman, Louis XVI, and Art Nouveau; numerous Renaissance revival style examples made c1870–c1900, e.g. by *Berkey & Gay. Exported to South America, Canada, Philippines, Hawaii, and Europe. Illustration also at Berkey & Gay.

grape scissors or **shears.** Scissor-actioned instrument with thick, stepped blades for splitting bunches of grapes; elaborate looped handles. Handles and blades frequently decorated with embossed designs of grapes and vine leaves. Made in Britain from c1850 of silver, silver gilt, and electro-plate. Introduced c1870 into America, where called grape shears.

grape stand. Oval dish with overhanging upright, usually modelled on grape vine: bunch of grapes hung from projection at top of branch. Made in silver or electro-plate from c1860.

Grasset, Eugène Samuel (1841–1917). Swiss architect, writer, illustrator, and designer; settled in Paris in 1871. Helped to popularize French Art Nouveau. Attracted by medievalism of architect Eugène Viollet-le-Duc; interested in Japanese art. Original jewellery designs for *Vever based on flower, fish, and bird forms. Edited 'La Plante et ses Applications Ornamentales', pattern book of flower designs, very influential in decorative arts.

grate. Fire-basket, normally of cast iron or polished steel. Early Victorian examples generally plain, later becoming more elaborate and culminating in massive Gothic versions of late 19th century.

gravity escapement. See escapement.

Gray, A.E., & Co. Ltd. Staffordshire pottery producing earthenware working at Hanley (c1912–33) and Stoke-on-Trent (1934–61). Produced e.g. by S. *Cooper (1925–32). In 1960s, combined with firm of W. *Kirkham, subsequently trading as Portmeirion Potteries Ltd. Marks, usually printed, incorporate versions of galleon and Gray's pottery England.

Gray, Eileen (b 1879). Irish architect and furniture designer. Studied fine art at Slade School, London; settled in Paris in 1907. Started workshop for wood and lacquer furniture c1912. Exhibited at 14th Salon des Artistes

Décorateurs, 1923, and Pavillon de l'Esprit Nouveau at Exposition Internationale des Arts Décoratifs in Paris, 1925 (her work shown by *Le Corbusier). Designed decorative pieces, e.g. earthenware, mainly for domestic use, designed lacquered screen oranamented with human figures; table with lotus flower legs (one of a number of pieces commissioned by art patron, Jean Doucet). Later phase characterized by totally plain, linear forms in luxury materials – usually lacquer – e.g. screen made from lacquered cubes. Also Modernist style furniture reduced to structural elements, e.g. collapsible folding chair (1926), based on deck chair, with level arm rests and self-adjustable panel at shoulder height. *Illustration at* screen.

Gray, William C., & Sons. Scottish firm of carpet manufacturers, founded 1876 in Kilmarnock, Ayrshire. Introduced *art square in 1880 to compete with *chenille Axminster squares for seamless market. Wide ingrain power loom – first wide power loom – developed 1886. Major Scottish ingrain production centre grew up round factory by end of century.

Greatbach, Daniel (fl mid 19th century). American pottery modeller, born in England. In Jersey City and at South Amboy, New Jersey, with J. *Carr; introduced hound-handled pitcher, derived from Hungarian and English forms, and continued to produce versions at United States Pottery. Also made animal figures, etc., some derived from Staffordshire models. After c1858, went to South Carolina, then Peoria, Illinois.

Great Exhibition of the Works of Industry of All Nations. International exhibition open May-October 1851 at Hyde Park, London; housed in Crystal Palace (first large building constructed entirely of glass and metal in prefabricated units). Proposed (1848) by H. *Cole and organized by Society of Arts under president *Albert of Saxe-Coburg-Gotha to promote foreign trade. British exhibits formed four main categories: minerals and raw materials, machinery, manufactures, and fine arts. Other exhibits (almost half total number) classed under country. Jury's report regretted absence among British exhibits of design which relied on fine proportions, materials, and workmanship; over-ornamentation regarded as worst fault. Ceramic entries emphasized technical mastery of material. *Parian ware shown by many manufacturers, and *majolica by L. *Arnoux introduced in Minton display. Garden seats, jars, jugs, etc., made in *ironstone china. Transfer-printing in colour appeared in display of F. & R. *Pratt & Co. Main English exhibitors include *Mintons Ltd, firms of W. T. *Copeland and J. *Wedgwood & Sons, C. *Meigh, T. & R. *Boote Ltd, Grainger and Chamberlain factories in *Worcester, *Coalport Porcelain Works, and T. J. & J. *Mayer. Glass manufacturers who exhibited include T. *Webb & Sons. Much cut glass on display. High quality of craftsmanship and technical achievement in English furniture not extended to design. Decoration, primarily naturalistic carving, often used on shapes which combined elements of more than one historical style, e.g. cabinet furniture with semi-classical carcases on rococo legs or supports. Sofas, easy chairs, armchairs, rosewood and walnut stands, and inlaid floorings included in display of M. *Thonet. Work e.g. of W. G. *Rogers, *Jennens & Bettridge, W. *Cookes, H. *Eyles also shown. Influential furniture shown in Medieval Courts organized by A. W. N. *Pugin. Yorkshire firm of *Crossley showed examples of *mosaic carpet. The *Ladies' carpet also shown. *Indian carpets and Kashmir carpets from *Srinagar found new market in West as result of display. Exhibition made considerable profit; contributed to endowment of South Kensington (later renamed Victoria & Albert) Museum and design education under aegis of Cole. Stimulated attempts to improve standard of design and craftsmanship in England. Followed by other *International Exhibitions in Britain, Europe and America.

Grecian or **Classical style.** British furniture style based on Regency pattern books; fashionable in London c1835–c1855, continuing later in rural areas. Typified by well-proportioned, symmetrical design with restrained ornament, e.g. bead moulding and formalized honeysuckle or palmette cresting. Popular for library and dining-room furniture; also used in bedrooms.

Greek carpets. Carpet industry dates from c1916, when small plants established in Megara and Hydra. Given great impetus c1923 by influx of Greek and Armenian refugees from Turkey and Asia Minor – 4 factories in 1922, 80 in 1926 – and continued to expand. Cottage industry also developed. Main products: barely distinguishable copies of Turkish and Persian types, e.g. Smyrna, Sparta (known as 'Greek Spartas'), Isfahan, Tabriz, and Feraghan. In 1920s, also produced 'Chinese Spartas', again very similar to originals, but colours slightly inaccurate. Particularly high quality carpets made in 1930s, but export trade, relying heavily on American, British, and French markets, badly affected by Depression.

Green, A. Romney (1872–1945). English poet, writer, mathematician, and furniture designer. Follower of W. *Morris; produced sturdy pieces of high craftsmanship in London workshop. Designs mathematically calculated rather than worked out on drawing-board.

Greene, Charles Sumner (1868–1957). American architect; practised in Pasadena, California, with

Left
Charles and Henry Greene. Chair, made for the Gamble house. 1908.

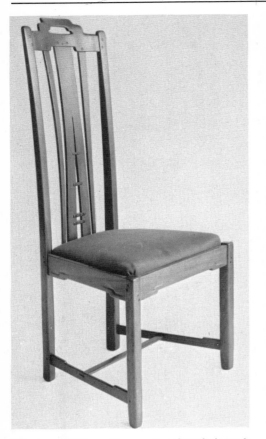

Charles and Henry Greene. Another chair made for the Gamble house, 1908.

brother, Henry Mather Greene, from 1893; also designed furniture influenced by Japanese and Mission styles. Pieces (often in walnut or mahogany) characterized by square ebony pegs, brass screw fastenings, and wood and semi-precious stone inlays in floral motifs.

Greener, Henry, & Company. English glass-house in Sunderland, County Durham. Known especially for *pressed ware in *slag and other glass in latter decades of 19th century, especially vine pattern designs in 1870s and stipple work and dot designs in American lacy style in 1870s and 1880s. Firm taken over 1885 by James Jobling (though listed under own name in Sunderland until 1920). Flourishes today as James A. Jobling & Co. Pressed glass trade mark: lion rampant with axe.

Greenwood Art Pottery Company. American pottery, established 1861 at Trenton, New Jersey, and incorporated (1868) as Greenwood Art Pottery Company. Made ironstone china, marked with coat of arms, G. P. Co, and name of pattern. Later made thinly-potted porcelain in imitation of Worcester Royal styles.

Grenzhausen. *See* Merkelbach, Rheinhold.

gridiron pendulum. *See* compensation.

Griffen, Smith & Hill. American pottery at Phoenixville, Pennsylvania, making majolica (1879-90). Ornamental mugs, etc. with relief decoration of leaves, flowers, marine life, etc., covered with monochrome glazes. Marked with

Greenwood Art Pottery Co. Porcelain ewer made at Trenton, New Jersey, c 1885.

monogram of GSH, impressed, or ETRUSCAN MAJOLICA; sometimes combined to form circular mark, with label surrounding monogram.

Grimthorpe, Lord. *See* Denison, Edmund Beckett.

Grinsell & Bourne. Birmingham manufacturers of electro-plate. Displayed goblets, jugs, cups, etc., in classical and Renaissance styles, at 1871 South Kensington Exhibition, London.

gripper Axminster. Name of loom, and carpet woven on it. Gripper invented and patented by H. *Skinner; together with Jacquard mechanism, incorporated in modified Axminster tufting loom, patented by *Brinton of Kidderminster in 1890. Gripper (narrow steel beak) seizes yarn, selected and raised for pile tufts by Jacquard, inserts it in warp where weft thread secures it, then opens, releasing it, and seizes next tuft. Pile yarn held in bobbins behind loom as in *Wilton process, but all used in tufts, eliminating dead yarn, so carpets much cheaper to produce. Also cheaper than *spool Axminsters (no lengthy preparation of spools needed for each new design), but colour range much narrower; early gripper looms used only six frames, one for each colour. Brinton sole users until c1900, when licence extended to German company, Vorwerk, who sold invention in America. More generally adopted in 1920s, e.g. by *Crossley and Hugh Mackay (in England), and Besmer and Posner (in Germany). Brinton installed 15ft gripper loom in 1904; wide gripper looms not adopted by other British and German firms until 1929, starting with 9ft, then 10ft6in. in 1932, and 15ft after 2nd World War.

gripper-spool loom. *See* spool-gripper loom.

Below
Griffen, Smith & Hill. Shell and seaweed pattern Etruscan Majolica platter. Made at Phoenixville, Pennsylvania, between 1881 and 1892.

Gromaire, Marcel (1892–). French artist; participated in French tapestry revival from 1939. Worked for M. *Cuttoli at Aubusson. Designs include Spring in Paris (1939); Summer, or Brittany; Autumn (1940); Woodcutters of Mormal; Winter (1941).

Gropius, Walter (1883–1969). German architect, founded Bauhaus, 1919; director until 1928. Designed furniture on modular basis, 1927, enabling separate units to be combined in various ways; principle used by many designers, e.g. Charles Eames, Eero Saarinen. Left Germany, 1934, for England; settled in America, 1937. Ideas on modern ceramic design, expressed in work of Bauhaus ceramic department e.g. by G. *Marcks, O. *Lindig, T. *Bogler, and M. *Wildenhain, influential not only in 1920s and 1930s, but also since World War II.

grosse porcelain. *See* Sèvres.

Grosvenor-Picking loom. Invented and patented in England in 1919 by William Thomas Picking, tuner at *Woodward Grosvenor in Kidderminster. Knitting machine principle adapted for cut pile carpets: hooks with retractable blades (replacing usual slow-moving steel strips) secure and loop warp pile threads, then cut loops to make velvet pile. Rights sold to *Brinton and several American firms.

Groszherzogliche Edelglasmanufaktur. *See* Grand-Ducal Fine Glass Co.

Groult, André (b 1884). French interior decorator. Designed Art Deco furniture characterized by undulating silhouettes, harmonizing colours and wood tones, and fine materials, e.g. ivory, velvet upholstery, and, especially, sharkskin (some pieces completely upholstered in latter). Decorative motifs include geometrical flowers, ropes, tassels. Exhibited at Exposition Internationale des Arts Décoratifs, Paris, 1925. Examples of work include small round table with mosaic sharkskin top, four fused legs resting on ivory ball feet.

Gruber, Jacques (1870–1936). French furniture designer; member of Ecole de Nancy. Pieces characterized by plastic, sculptural forms, using interplay of line and volume to decorative effect.

Grueby, William H. (1867–1925). American potter. Trained at tile works of J.G. *Low. Partner in short-lived company making tin-glazed earthenware for architectural use; concentrated on development of glazes. In 1894, formed Grueby Faience Co. at East Boston, Massachusetts, incorporated in 1897. Made tiles, e.g. in Hispano-Moresque style, and plaques inspired by 15th century work of Della Robbia family; also vases, at first designed by G. *Kendrick. From c1898, used matt glazes of opaque enamel in shades of yellow, brown, blue and, occasionally, red; most characteristic is dark green with veined effect resembling skin of water melon. Vases hand-thrown and, though thickly potted, said to have been inspired by work of A. *Delaherche. Some plain or ornamented with simple geometrical patterns; most decorated with plant forms in low-relief. Leaves of varying shapes, set in rows, often alternate with long-stemmed buds or flowers; treatment frequently severe. Rarely, *cloisonné* style decoration occurs, with glazes of different

Grueby Faience Co. Yellow vase with matt glaze, c1900. Height 11in.

colours contained within raised outlines of clay. From 1904, glazed paperweights made in scarab form. Art pottery usually bears incised signature of artist, and often GRUEBY POTTERY BOSTON USA impressed in circle surrounding lotus blossom motif. Tiles hand-decorated with floral designs, animals, forest scenes, knights, etc. From 1899, name, Grueby Pottery, used for section of firm producing art pottery, incorporated as separate entity in 1907, although still closely associated with rest of company. Grueby Faience Co., unable to withstand competition of imitators, declared bankrupt in 1908; new firm, Grueby Faience & Tile Co., formed to continue manufacture of architectural ware. Production of vases virtually ceased by 1911, although probably not entirely until 1913. Tile manufacture, sold in 1919 and transferred to Perth Amboy, New Jersey, ceased operation c1930.

guards (of fan). Outer sticks, usually more elaborately decorated than inner sticks.

Gueyton, Camille. French silversmith working in Art Nouveau style c1900; works featured symmetrical outlines with naturalistic floral decorations asymmetrically arranged in relief; favourite motifs, palm fronds and marguerites, front of flower, with gold centre, modelled on one side of object, the back on reverse.

Guild of Handicraft. Guild of artist-craftsmen founded by C. R. *Ashbee, 1888, as development of School of Handicraft founded by him, 1887 (closed, 1895). Aim: to create working conditions of medieval guild with several craftsmen co-operating on one piece - small workshop in which knowing each other's limitations was

thought to facilitate working together. Apart from Ashbee, no one had any experience: considered a disadvantage. Reacted against mechanical decoration of commercially manufactured products. Established workshops in Mile End Road, London, and Mayfair retail premises (1890). Limited company from 1898. Moved workshops to Chipping Campden, Gloucestershire, 1902. Showed at exhibitions of *Arts & Crafts Exhibition Society, *Vienna Secession, etc. Production continued until 1908 when Guild went into voluntary liquidation.

Designs by Ashbee and L. F. *Day. Undertook painting and decorative work in wood and metal, also silver, jewellery, furniture, leatherwork, and later, books (using type and presses of Kelmscott Press acquired after W. *Morris's death, 1896). Also work for palace of Grand Duke of Hesse at Darmstadt, to M. H. *Baillie Scott's designs.

Silverwork in simple shapes, often with serpentine handles, etc.; surface retains hammer marks, burnished to soft, grey sheen. Much of jewellery in Art Nouveau style, e.g. peacock pendant in Victoria & Albert Museum, or based on Celtic designs with enamel and semi-precious stones set in heavy mounts, e.g. altar cross designed by Ashbee, made by Guild, presented to Lichfield Cathedral (1907), made of silver, partly enamelled and set with moonstone and pearl clusters. Furniture simple, well-proportioned; each piece credited to named designer, painter, and craftsman. Marks were CRA (1896), G. of H. Ltd. (1898); CRA mark retained for certain pieces after 1898; before 1896, work not marked regularly, though some pieces bore Ashbee's initials. *Birmingham Guild of Handicraft modelled on Guild. *Illustrations at* Ashbee, C. R.

Guillaume, Dr Charles-Edouard (1861–1938). Swiss metrologist; director, International Bureau of Weights & Measures in Paris. Nobel prizewinner (1920) for revolutionizing precision timekeeping with invention of *elinvar and *invar.

Guild of Handicraft. Silver-mounted green glass decanter. 1901. Height 8¼in.

Guimard, Hector (1867–1942). French architect and decorator; known for individualistic interpretation of Art Nouveau. Often made clay maquettes of designs for craftsmen to translate into wood. Many pieces designed to sweep over fireplaces, fill corners, etc. Early work, c1896–99, often hard, dark mahogany, characterized by

Hector Guimard. Corner cupboard in carved pearwood. Height 5ft 5in.

asymmetrical motifs and fluid forms. Used soft pearwood, c1900–10, for simpler furniture with pure lines, often gently curved, and restrained ornament. Known for Paris Metro entrances, 1900.

Gulbrandsen, Nora (fl 20th century). Norwegian potter. Art director of Porsgrund porcelain factory from mid 1920s. Developed individual factory style based on functionalist principles. Among artists working to promote artistic aims in Norwegian crafts and industry, in reaction against romantic concentration on folk art.

gunstick. *Walking stick, e.g. in malacca, incorporating air gun mechanism, for firing pellets or cartridges, made from c1855, popular during 1880s. Stick divided into two threaded portions; top third is compressed air reservoir, remainder contains breech, barrel, and detachable ferrule. Once loaded, two portions screwed together and ferrule removed, revealing muzzle; firing mechanism operated by concealed trigger in handle; pellets fired by direct air pressure, cartridges via pressure-activated firing pin. When air pressure in reservoir is exhausted, must be repressurized by accompanying hand or foot pump.

guri (Japanese, 'crook-ring') or **guri-bori.** Japanese *carved lacquer, copied from Chinese *tsuishu lacquer. Up to 40 coats of coloured lacquer (usually red and black) applied in alternating layers to prepared lacquer base; when dry, deeply carved in V or U shaped channels to reveal various colours. Patterns usually stylized geometrical designs or stylized cloud-scrolls. Variety known as hashika-bori has pattern of stylized ears of corn ('hashika'). Most often used on small lacquer objects, particularly netsuke and inro.

Gustavsberg. Swedish factory, established 1827 on island of Farsta; produced faience and, later, creamware transfer-printed in English style. Decorative majolica introduced in 1860s. Bone porcelain made from early 1860s to present day,

Gustavsberg. Faience plates decorated by Wennerberg. Marked with signature and date, 1909.

and parian ware, also from 1860s, to late 19th century. W. *Kåge employed from 1917, later art director, produced domestic ware in earthenware and porcelain, and individually designed stoneware. Marks include GUSTAVSBERG with anchor (1820–60); version used on hardpaste porcelain (1910–40). Initials, SSF, printed within circle from 1930.

gutta-percha. Dried sap of tree *(Dichopsis gutta)* from Borneo. Greyish-brown, tough, and impervious to water; malleable when heated, hardens on cooling. Can be coloured and moulded to resemble woodcarving; used for moulded decoration on furniture from mid 19th century.

Guzhev, N.A. (fl mid to late 19th century). Russian potter and porcelain manufacturer; proprietor of factory at Cherniatka near Tver (1860–79), making decorative ware in faience and porcelain.

Gwalior (Madhya Pradesh), India. Carpet factory established 1902 by G. P. *Stavrides (amalgamated with Austrian factory at *Amritsar, 1920). Produced copies of Persian and Turkish carpets; Chinese designs introduced later. Patronized by Maharajah and court. Bought by East India Carpet Co. in 1922. Several Amritsar companies moved to Gwalior after partition (1947).

gyobu, giobu, gyobu-nashiji, or **crumb lacquer.** Japanese lacquer technique named after originator, Gyobu Taro, 18th century Tokyo lacquer artist. Large, irregular flakes of gold arranged on prepared lacquer surface to create mosaic effect. Used mainly as background technique; particularly fine examples on inner surfaces of *Kajikawa inro.

Gyokuso, Ouchi (b 1879). Japanese mastercarver and netsuke artist. Pupil of M. *Joso; 1920–24, studied netsuke-carving daily with M. *Soko. Netsuke carved in ivory and wood (often combined in same piece), sometimes encrusted with tortoiseshell, *raden, *aogai, etc., and often tinted. Shared work at various Japanese exhibitions. *Na: Jiemon. *Chomei: Gyokuso.

Gyokuzan, Asahi (1843-1923). Self-taught, Japanese ivory master-carver and netsuke artist of Tokyo. Among first professors of Sculpture Department at Tokyo Academy of Fine Arts; founding member and later head of Tokyo Carvers' Association. Made finely-carved figures in detailed, realistic style. Early subjects include toads, crabs, monkeys, and snakes; later specialized in skulls. Best-known for Meiji and Taisho period ivory skull netsuke, and small okimono.

Hadeland. Norwegian glass factory established 1757 to manufacture bottle glass. Large output of bottles and spirit flasks during 19th century. By early 20th century, only remaining factory making table and decorative glassware in Norway. Produced some crude cameo glass in imitation of E. *Gallé c1911 and some pieces of heavy glass decorated by sandblasting process during 1930s. Employed S. *Pettersen as artistic director from 1928. Production continues.

Hadley, James (1837-1903). English ceramic modeller and designer. Work at Worcester factory (c1870-75) in variety of styles, notably Japanese; many pieces with reticulated decoration, others in imitation of Japanese Shibayama technique on ivory. Japanese figures, and vases with relief decoration depicting lacquerwork, silk-making, or series of pottery processes, shown at exhibitions from early 1870s. Pottery also subject of reliefs on sides of pair of vases decorated in Renaissance style, shown at Paris Exhibition of 1878. Worked independently from 1875, supplying models to Worcester Royal Porcelain Co. until 1896; work includes series of figures after Kate Greenaway, often for table use, carrying baskets and enriched with gilding in variety of shades. Later, produced own porcelain, sold as *Hadley ware. Succeeded by sons until firm sold to Worcester Royal Porcelain Co. in 1905.

Hadley ware. Porcelain, chiefly vases, made by J. *Hadley from 1896; resembles work of Worcester Royal Porcelain Co.; ivory-coloured body often used. Characterized by moulded

*James Hadley. *Worcester porcelain in Japanese style. c1875.*

relief decoration, of e.g. scrolls, in tinted clay, notably bluish-green, used with polychrome or monochrome painting of flowers. Marks: impressed or printed monogram of JH & S, or printed monogram with HADLEY'S WORCESTER, crossed (1897-1900) with ribbon label FAIENCE, or (1900-02) without ribbon; from 1902: HADLEYS/WORCESTER ENGLAND.

Haematin. Dark red Bohemian marbled glass; opaque, with bright red streaking, imitating mineral haematite. Popular for decorative ware, boxes, and novelties to c1860s. Often gilded, painted, cut, or engraved.

Hagi wares. Japanese pottery made in Nagato province, associated with Yamaguchi Hagi. Greyish or yellowish white ware with crackle glaze, inspired by Korean Ido ware made by Korean potter, Korai Saiemon, in late 16th century. Tea bowls with salmon-pink glaze characterized by cuts in foot rim. Production continued until 1880s by eight generations of descendants of Korai Saiemon.

Haile, T. Sam (1909-48). English artist potter; studied under W. *Staite Murray at Royal College of Art, London (1931-34). From 1935, taught pottery in Leicester and then London. Work influenced by painting of Pablo Picasso and surrealist school. In America in 1938, taught and studied at New York State College of Ceramics; later taught at University of Michigan, Ann Arbor. Stoneware with brushed decoration sometimes inspired by Pre-Columbian sculpture and Pueblo Indian pottery. In England, after army enlistment (1943-45), made slip-decorated earthenware at Sudbury, Suffolk. Jugs, dishes, etc., have linear decoration, often with eye motif prominent. From 1947, worked at Shinner's Bridge near Dartington, South Devon. Killed in road accident; pottery continued by wife, Marianne de Trey. Work marked with monogram of SH within rectangle, impressed.

hair Brussels carpet. Extremely tough, cheap, machine-made carpet, with pile of 60-80% horse-hair (imported from Russia or Argentine), developed in early 20th century. Stippled appearance results from uneven dyeing of hair

and wool mixture. Made by T. F. *Firth before 1st World War; *Wilton Royal Carpet Factory became main British manufacturers. Large quantities, made in Czechoslovakia, glutted market in 1920s. (Rising cost of horse-hair in 1950s reduced proportion in pile to nominal amount.)

haircord carpet. Like hair Brussels carpet, but with uncut pile. (By 1950s, pile almost entirely wool cord because of cost of horse-hair.)

hair jewellery. Mourning or sentimental jewellery decorated with hairwork. Hair woven into plait and used for bracelets, as border for central stone in brooches, or as an oblong surrounded by seed pearls, tiny diamonds or garnets in brooches and rings. Also worked to form scenes or flowers, used under crystal cover for rings and brooches. Ingenious examples shown at Great Exhibition, London (1851). Particularly popular, not only as mourning jewellery, during late 19th century, after death of Prince Consort (1861).

hair work. Memorial pictures woven by mourners from locks of hair belonging to deceased; depict e.g. weeping figure standing by funeral urn. Frequently incorporated into gold brooch. Popular from 18th century to c1880.

hakeme (Japanese, 'brush-marked'). Japanese lacquer imitating Korean ceramic technique, Punch'ŏng, in which brushstrokes of white and grey stripes painted on glaze remain visible. Used in Japan from early 19th century by numerous lacquer artists, including S. *Zeshin. Effect obtained by mixing egg-white or gelatin into lacquer, which is then brushed on black, or occasionally gold, lacquer ground.

hako (Japanese, 'little box') **netsuke** or **kaku** (Japanese, 'angular') **netsuke.** Form of *manju netsuke: small, square or rectangular hollow box of lacquer, wood, metal, or ceramics, decorated with variety of techniques.

Hald, Edward (b 1883). Leading Swedish glass artist; studied under Henri Matisse in Paris. Appointed designer to *Orrefors in 1917, where, with S. *Gate, laid foundation of modern Swedish glass industry. Known for cut and engraved crystal glassware, e.g. bowls, vases, goblets, heavily engraved with abstract or figure subjects. Also worked in tinted glass, and *Ariel and *Graal glass. Marks: H, followed by Ørrefors or Øf (on engraved glass); HA (on cut glass); HU (on furnace-finished glass).

*Edward Hald. *Ørrefors glass pipe bowl made for Stockholm Exhibition, 1930.*

hall chair. Hard-seated side-chair for entrance hall; dates from early 18th century in Britain. Grecian style in mahogany, or Elizabethan style in yellow polished oak common c1835–c1865, latter also in stained, carved, black oak; also chairs with Gothic style backs. May have coat of arms (often false) on centre back.

hallmark. Symbol or device struck at assay office on gold or silver indicating that article conforms to legal standards of manufacture established by monarch, local guilds, government etc. Literally, mark applied at Goldsmith's Hall (London assay office since 1300) but extended to cover e.g. all five stamps found on Victorian silver until 1890: assay office mark specific to each assay office; date letter, letter of alphabet denoting year when article was assayed; maker's mark, usually initials of one or more partners of firm, occasionally with additional symbol; assay mark, indicating metal is up to required standard; duty mark (tax levied on all English silver, 1784–1890 – sovereign's head stamped on article to show tax paid). For gold, carat content also marked on article.

hall stand or **hatstand.** Combined hat and umbrella stand for entrance hall; often with matching chair. Made from early 19th century. Early example, free-standing pillar with turned pegs for hats, cloaks, etc. at top, circular supports at appropriate height to hold umbrellas, and base tray to catch drips. Also, wall-standing model with flat wooden arms branching from central upright. Became increasingly ornate, with framed mirror, shelf for vase, etc. Models with brush drawer and central table for card tray common c1850–c1900. Table sometimes replaced by bench. Rosewood, mahogany, and oak usual woods. Also made in cast iron; from c1870, sometimes highly decorative, painted and marbled. Bentwood examples with curved arms popular in offices, restaurants, etc. Gothic style examples common in America.

Hallin, F. August (fl late 19th century). Danish porcelain decorator; pupil of A. *Krog. Painted vases at Royal Copenhagen Porcelain Factory and, later, at Bing & Grøndahls factory. Vases decorated with plant forms exhibited in Paris, 1893–94.

Hamada, Shoji (b 1892 or 1894). Japanese artist potter. Early work influenced by Korean ceramics of Yi dynasty; studied glazes of early Chinese wares. Then, working mainly in stoneware, produced vases and articles for everyday use in strong, simple shapes with soft colours, usually brown, olive, grey, and black. Designs abstract, or derived from natural forms, with strong, free brushwork. Accompanied B. *Leach to England (1920), and took part in experiments with lead-glazed slipware. After return to Japan (1923), joined country pottery community in Okinawa. Later, lived in Mashiko, working and experimenting with local clay. Founder member of Japanese Craft Movement (1929). After visit to England (1929–30), built own kiln in Mashiko. Recent use of angular, slab-built and moulded forms, in late 1950s and 1960s, influenced younger Japanese potters. Mark, Japanese seal in rectangle, impressed, used only briefly, at Leach's pottery in early 1920s.

Hamilton & Co. English silversmiths working in Calcutta, India 1808–1969; founded by Robert

Shoji Hamada. Stoneware vase with sgraffito decoration. Made at St. Ives. c1925. Height 8¼in.

Below
Hamilton & Inches. Wine cooler. Made in Edinburgh, 1923.

Hamilton, who became millionaire and left firm, 1818; produced wide range of silverware and jewellery, including military silver, travelling sets, badges, buttons, buckles, and ceremonial pieces (e.g. trappings for elephants). Mark: H & Co with elephant.

Hamilton & Inches (Edinburgh). Scottish silver manufacturers and retailers, established 1866 by James Hamilton and nephew Robert Kirk Inches as jewellery retailers; produced silverware from 1880s; took over Robert Bryson & Son, 1887, and received Royal Warrant to supply clocks and watches. Most of firm's silver made in traditional Scottish styles. Mark: H & I in

rectangle with truncated corners, or in bifoliate leaf shape.

Hammersmith. *See* Stabler, Harold.

Hammersmith rugs. Fine quality English hand-knotted rugs and carpets: heaviest on English market. Woven 1878–80 at Hammersmith workshop of W. *Morris. Still produced at *Merton Abbey, but name dropped.

hammock chair. *See* deck chair.

Hammond, Henry Fauchon (b 1914). English artist potter and painter; studied under W. *Staite Murray at Royal College of Art, London. Until 1939, worked mainly in stoneware, often with celadon glazes in grey or blue-green and brushed decoration, e.g. of fish or ducks. Appointed teacher at Farnham School of Art, Surrey, in 1939. Work interrupted by army service. From 1946, in Farnham, at first made earthenware with slip decoration of fish, abstract foliage, etc. Stoneware made from c1951 with brushed designs of grasses, bamboo, etc., in cobalt or iron, sometimes covered with wax resist to restrict coating of coloured glaze. Mark: monogram of HH, impressed, within rectangle.

hamon. *See* Japanese swords.

Hampshire Pottery. American pottery established (1871) at Keene, New Hampshire. Made earthenware for domestic use; also souvenirs for sale at holiday resorts. Decoration often transfer-printed in black. Also produced majolica. Marks: HAMPSHIRE/POTTERY and signature of J. S. Taft (proprietor); circular variations give same information.

hanaike. Flower vases used by Japanese schools of Ikebana (flower arrangement) for ceremonial bouquets; usually pottery or bronze; also in bamboo and cast iron.

hanagai. *See* raden.

Hancock, Charles Frederick. English silversmith, worked with Storr & Mortimer; left 1843, and founded own firm in late 1840s; employed Marshal Wood as chief modeller, and various designers including H. H. *Armstead and Eugene Lami; favoured French styles. Competed with *Garrards and *Hunt & Roskell in 1840s and 1850s for commissions to make presentation pieces and silver sculpture then in fashion. Display at Great Exhibition, London, 1851 described as impressive. Armstead's Tennyson Vase shown by Hancocks at Paris Exhibition, 1867, depicted stories of Guinevere and Merlin in high relief. Firm, now Hancock & Co., still in existence as retailers.

Hancock, Sampson (d 1898). English porcelain manufacturer. Worked at original Derby factory and took part in establishment of works at King Street, Derby, under W. *Locker. As last remaining employee of original factory, manager of King Street works until death.

Hancock, S., & Sons. *See* Cartlidge, George.

hand (as ornament). Model of female hand, fingers gracefully curved, rising from shallow dish or flat base; made in brass, pottery, marble, earthenware, porcelain. Popular ornament,

c1840–c1900. Less common version, showing girl's hand resting on pillow, supposedly reproduction of cast made during Queen Victoria's childhood.

hand cooler. Solid sphere of glass or minature paperweight in *millefiore*, floral, animal, and other designs, imitating balls of glass used as hand coolers in Roman times. 1½in.–2in. in diameter; elaborate examples made by *Baccarat, *Clichy, and St *Louis glasshouses. Stone, e.g. agate, marble, alabaster, carved into size and shape of egg and highly polished. Often found in work box for use as darning egg. Made in England, France, and America from late 18th to late 19th century.

handkerchief ring. Ring with loop attached for carrying handkerchief. Usually gold with engraved or *repoussé* decoration; similar *vinaigrette ring used in same way for carrying small vinaigrette. Popular in England during 1860s and 1870s.

hand seal. *See* desk seal.

Above
*Hammersmith rug designed by W. *Morris. Hammersmith mark on border of upper left-hand corner. Woven c1880.*
Above right
*Charles Frederick Hancock. Parcel-gilt ewer designed by Raphael Monti and O. *Jones. 1863. Height 31in.*
Right
*Charles Frederick Hancock. The Doncaster Cup, from designs by H. H. *Armstead. Made 1857. Height 25in.*

hand-warmer. Pierced copper or brass container for heating element, e.g. piece of heated iron; used by sportsmen, travellers, doctors, etc.

hanko. *See* in.

Hardman, John, & Co. Birmingham firm manufacturing ecclesiastical plate and church furnishings. Founded in 1838 by John Hardman the Younger (1811–67) in association with A. W. N. *Pugin, chief designer. Produced church plate and ecclesiastical furnishings e.g. pews, rood screens, and all trappings associated with

funerals. Ornate chalices, censers, monstrances, ewers, bowls, etc., in silver, silver-gilt, silver plate, set with gemstones. Interior furnishings, e.g. screens, candlesticks, lamps, chandeliers, made in brass. In 1847, firm made jewellery designed by Pugin for intended third wife, Miss Lumsden. Work subsequently shown in Medieval Court of Great Exhibition, London, 1851. Pieces in same style exhibited by firm at International Exhibition of 1862; some possibly based on drawings by Pugin, others designed by his son in law, John Hardman Powell, nephew of John Hardman, who succeeded Pugin as chief designer (1852). Firm still exists. *Illustration at Pugin, A. W. N.*

hardstone. Term applied to various relatively common rocks and minerals whose colour and structure make them particularly suitable for decorative inlay or ornament. Includes lapis lazuli, turquoise, opal, feldspar, agate, amethyst, rock crystal, jade, flint, beryl, emerald, tourmaline, zircon, topaz, chrysoberyl, spinel. All except emerald often described as semi-precious stones. Victorian fob and desk seals usually carved from hardstone e.g. bloodstone, *carnelian.

Harley Jones, A.G. Staffordshire pottery operating (1907–34) at Fenton. Made earthenware and porcelain. Printed marks incorporate initials HJ, often with name of ware, e.g. Fentonia ware, Wilton ware, Paramount.

A. G. Harley Jones. Lustre jar and cover. Wilton ware. Made at Fenton-on-Trent, c1925. Height 11½in.

*W. H. Haseler & Co. Tea service made for *Liberty and Co., marked W. H. Haseler, Birmingham. 1904.*

*A. E. Harvey. Pepper mill in ivory and silver. Makers' mark *Hukin and Heath Birmingham. Designed 1934. Height 4in.*

Harradine, A. Leslie (fl early 20th century). English modeller of pottery and porcelain. At Doulton factory, Lambeth, London, from 1902; work includes figures of Dickens characters in cream salt-glazed stoneware, brown salt-glazed flasks depicting contemporary politicians, and some porcelain figures. Later, worked as freelance modeller, and, c1914–17, modelled figures for reproduction in bone porcelain at Doulton factory in Burslem, Staffordshire. Work initialled.

Harris, Kate (fl c1890–1910). English silver designer, working in Art Nouveau style, for W. Hunter & Sons.

Harrison's Patent Hygenic Teapot. English teapot, made e.g. of Britannia metal from late 19th century. Internal infuser in form of perforated chamber can be raised or lowered by turning knob on top of lid; device intended to prevent tea over-brewing.

Hart, Charles (fl late 19th, early 20th century). English porcelain decorator. At Doulton factory, Burslem, Staffordshire, painted naturalistic designs of fish, game birds, or flowers on bone porcelain.

Hart, George Henry (b 1882). English designer and silversmith; one of final members of *Guild of Handicraft, after its move to Chipping Camden, Gloucestershire; continued to work there after Guild ended (1908). Designer of church plate, restorer of many old buildings in locality 1902–14, metalcraft master to Gloucestershire County Council; taught at teachers' summer schools in Chipping Camden, 1934–44.

Harvey, Arthur Edward (b 1893). English architect and industrial designer, educated Paris, Dijon and Vienna; studied at Royal College of Art, Slade School, and Royal Academy School, London. Active in scheme for improving gold plate for Worshipful Company of Goldsmiths; later head of School of Industrial Design, Birmingham School of Art. Silverware designs,

W. H. Haseler & Co. Cymric silver butter dish. Chased flower decoration on bowl and top; glass container inside. Marks Liberty and Co. (Cymric) Ltd Birmingham. 1926. Width 6½in.

c1933, for *Mappin & Webb, *Hukin & Heath display spare functionalism similar to that of C. *Dresser, e.g. faceted, cylindrical ivory pepper mill, with plain silver cap sloping back in concave mouldings to central turned finial; made for Hukin & Heath, 1934.

Harwood, John (1893-1964). English watchmaker and jeweller from Bolton, Lancashire. Patented first self-winding wrist watch (1924). Wound by small weight, pivoted at centre of movement, and oscillated by normal activity of wearer. Hands set by rotation of knurled bezel surrounding dial. First 36 movements made under Harwood's supervision. Set up in business with Swiss firm, A. Schild, c1930: venture failed during 1931 Depression. (Personally awarded *British Horological Institute Gold Medal in 1957.)

Haseler, W. H., & Co. English manufacturers of silver, jewellery, and pewter; founded 1870 in Birmingham. In partnership with Liberty & Co. until dissolved in 1927. Manufactured *Cymric silver from 1901, and *Tudric pewter from 1903. Mark: WH, sometimes combined with Liberty trademark. *Illustrations at* King, J. M., Liberty & Co.

hashi-ire. *See* sagemono.

hashika-bori. *See* guri.

hatpin. Pin, 4-5in. long, with jewelled or enamelled head, for securing hat. Fashionable in late Victorian and Edwardian periods, when large hats worn. Made in pairs, or sets of three or four. Designs of head include fans, crescents, shells, figures, insects and flowers; also represented sports, e.g. golf, archery and fishing. Well suited to semi-abstract Art Nouveau designs in enamel.

hatstand. *See* hall stand.

Hattori, K., & Co. *See* Japanese Horological Industry.

Hautin & Boulanger. *See* Choisy-le-Roi.

Haviland family. Porcelain manufacturers owning several factories at Limoges (Haute-Vienne). Robert I (b 1803) worked in America until 1830s and at Limoges from mid 19th century. Son, Charles Field (b 1814) worked in 1850s at Haviland & Co (established late 19th century) and married into Alluaud family, also manufacturers of porcelain at Limoges. Established own factory, using mark CH FIELD HAVILAND/LIMOGES. Firm, Ch. Field Haviland opened (1870) in New York. Proprietor of Alluaud factory from 1876 until retirement in 1881. Grandson, Robert, established own firm in 1924, and bought right to use Haviland trademark from father's successors in 1942. David (1814-79), brother of Robert I,

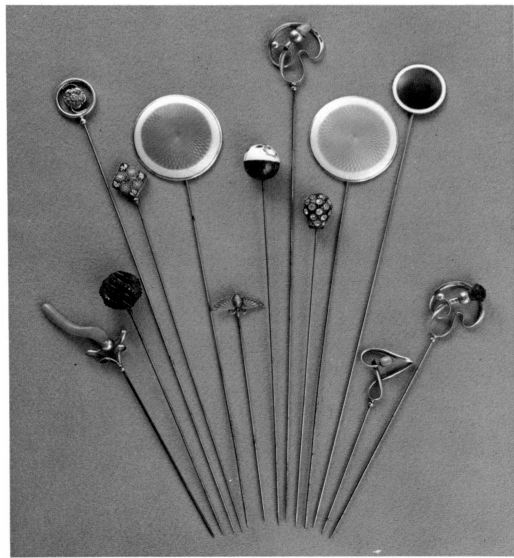

Hatpins. Collection of late Victorian and Edwardian hatpins, decorated tops of silver, guilloché enamel, paste, hand-painted glass, enamel, jet, and coral.

Haviland & Co. Stoneware jug. Late 19th century.

worked as importer and retailer of English porcelain in New York (1839). Established factory (1842) in Limoges to make porcelain for export to America. Artists include A. *Dammouse. Made table service decorated with American subjects, e.g. indigenous animals, birch bark, making of maple sugar, commissioned (1879) for use at White House, Washington. Copies and adaptations made for retail include Canadian edition, marked with arms of Dominion in polychrome. Succeeded by son, Théodore (b 1842), who established own factory in 1892 and featured, notably, tableware designed by J. *Dufy and S. *Lalique in Paris Exhibition of 1925. William, son of Théodore, produced porcelain in America. At Haviland design studio in Auteuil, Paris, under direction of F. *Bracquemond, pottery painted in style of Barbizon landscape painters. *Barbotine* decoration, shown at Philadelphia Centennial Exhibition of 1876, inspired underglaze painting carried out in America, e.g. by M.L. *McLaughlin. Studio moved (1881) to Rue Blomet, Paris; directed by E. *Chaplet, who started small stoneware workshop, and took over control in 1885. *Illustration at* barbotine decoration.

Heal, Sir Ambrose (1872–1959). English furniture designer and artist-craftsman; member of Art Workers' Guild; vice-president of Design & Industries Association. Served cabinet-making apprenticeship from 1890, joining family firm of *Heal & Son in 1893. Designed all furniture from 1896. Became managing director in 1907, chairman in 1913. Furniture simple, well-proportioned; early pieces reflect principles of

Arts & Crafts Movement. Examples include simple bedroom furniture (1898) in *fumed oak with wrought steel handles and hinges. Also chest of drawers in holly-wood, painted green with details outlined in vermilion (1899). Favourite inlay materials included ebony, pewter. Showed at Paris Exhibition, 1900, and Glasgow Exhibition, 1901. Initiated painted furniture with colour-combed, hand-painted decoration c1917 to overcome hardwood shortage caused by 1st World War; from 1918, developed new finishes, e.g. weathered oak, to replace unpolished surfaces. Active until 1939, experimenting with new materials, e.g. steel, aluminium. Knighted in 1933. Publications include London Tradesmen's Cards of the Eighteenth Century (1926); The Signboards of Old London Shops (1947); London Furniture Makers, 1660–1840 (1953).

Heal & Son. London furniture makers, established 1810 by John Harris Heal; specialized in bedroom furniture. Heal & Son Ltd from 1907; managing director A. *Heal. Showed at Paris Exhibition of 1900. Most pieces stamped or labelled. *Illustration at* cottage furniture, painted furniture, wash-stand.

hearth furniture. Includes *andirons, *fireback, fire guard, *grate, *fender, *fire irons, blowing-tube, bellows.

Heaton, Clement J. (1861–1940). English craftsman designer; studied stained-glass and metalwork techniques in father's firm, Heaton, Butler & Bayre. Associated with A. H. *Mackmurdo's Century Guild (1882–88); carried out a number of Mackmurdo's designs in *cloisonné* enamel. One of few craftsmen using *cloisonné* technique at that time; set up own firm, Heaton's Cloisonné Mosaics Ltd. Settled in Neuchâtel, Switzerland, in early 1890s; carried out commissions for stained-glass and *cloisonné*, including decoration of Neuchâtel Museum. Emigrated to America in 1912.

Heal & Son. Pedestal writing table made in weathered oak with writing surface and chamfers veneered in brown oak. Made 1931. Width 5ft.

*Fritz Heckert. Iridescent glass vase with enamelled design by Max Rade. One of Cyperngläser series (*Cyprus glasses). 1898.*

Heckert, Fritz. Bohemian glass factory founded 1866 in Petersdorf. Specialized in enamelled neo-classical glassware, notably *Cyprus glasses from 1898. Also, large quantities of *Altdeutsches glass, e.g. Humpen with enamelled and gilt decoration, *Waldglas* imitations, and iridescent *caméléon* glass. Employed L. *Sütterlin and Max Rade (1840–1917) as designers.

Hedingham Art Pottery. English pottery in Essex owned by E. *Bingham succeeded by son, c1864–1901. Moulded earthenware with slip or applied relief decoration, sometimes in white clay, of coats of arms, classical motifs, etc., made from local clay. Coloured glazes occur in blue, grey, green, or brown. Specialized in reproductions of German stoneware and early English earthenware; 17th century dates sometimes occur. Marks: small relief of Hedingham Castle

Robert Hennell. Silver tea and coffee pot. Made in London, 1868.

above scroll with E. BINGHAM, or incised signature; Royal Essex Art Pottery Works incised, c1901.

heidatsu or **p'ing-t'o.** Oriental lacquer technique: layers of transparent lacquer cover design made from minute sheets of gold or silver embedded in brown, grey, or red lacquer ground. Originated in China as p'ing-t'o. Widely used by 8th century; introduced to Japan in Nara period (710-95), where variety, heidatsu, developed in second half of 17th century. *See* kanagai, Owari ware.

Heimburg (Berne). Swiss potters at Heimburg made dishes etc. for domestic use in traditional styles from 18th century. Chocolate or brownish-black glaze decorated with designs in bright red, green, yellow, and white slips. Vase with floral decoration shown at Paris Exhibition of 1878.

Heinrich & Co. German porcelain factory operating in Selb, Bavaria, from 1896 to present day. Porcelain for ornamental or everyday use includes tea and coffee services; much exported to America before 1st World War. Marks incorporate H & Co, Selb, Bavaria, Germany, and sometimes crown.

Hendery, Robert (fl 19th century). Canadian silversmith working in Montreal, c1837-1897; made silver cutlery, prize cups, presentation plate, tea sets, etc. Mark: R. HENDERY, or RH.

Henk, Christian (d 1905) and John (1846-1914). Ceramic decorators. Christian Henk, born in Germany, worked in England. At Minton factory from c1848, painted landscapes with figures after Jean-Antoine Watteau. Son, John Henk, also at Mintons (from 1863) became chief modeller; made animal figures, notably in majolica.

Henkels, George (fl 1850-70). American cabinet maker in Philadelphia, Pennsylvania. Known for rococo and Gothic style furniture. Favourite woods: rosewood, walnut, mahogany, satinwood, and maplewood. Made low bed with ornate side canopy and draped hangings for Swedish singer, Jenny Lind.

Hennell, R. C. T., & Sons. Jewellers founded 1839 by Robert Hennell, continued by his sons. **Henry, J. S.** London furniture makers, active settings of pearls and fine gems. Family interest sold out in 1906, but name of firm still retained.

Henning, Gerda (1891-1951). Danish; designed and wove rugs, tapestries, textiles. Led 20th century Danish design in these fields. Influenced by austerity of contemporary Danish architecture, and by medieval Danish textiles and weaving techniques. Used stripes, lozenges, and simple geometrical shapes; or single repeated motif, e.g. stylized bird. Often worked in only two colours. Experimented with reversible designs, one side negative of other.

Henning, Gerhard (b 1880). Swedish sculptor. Modeller for Royal Copenhagen Porcelain Factory from 1909. Work includes nude female figure sitting cross-legged on cushioned pedestal; head sways from side to side in manner of *nodding figures. Influenced by oriental styles. Enamel colours used in decoration.

Henri-Deux ware. English earthenware made in mid 19th century; follows designs of French 16th century lead-glazed earthenware with inlaid decoration made at Saint-Porchaire near Poitou (Charente-Maritime). Painting sometimes used to give effect of inlaid patterns. Ewers, etc., elaborately decorated at Minton factory, notably by C. *Toft, and at Wedgwood factory. 19th century French examples made at Choisy-le-Roi.

Henry, J.S. London furniture makers, active c1880-c1900. Specialized in light, ornamental furniture, e.g. harewood desk with linear inlay of pale blue wood, c1900. Best-known for Quaint style furniture designed by E. G. *Punnett, G. M. *Ellwood; examples, of their designs, and others by C. F. A. *Voysey, shown at Paris Exhibition of 1900.

Hepplewhite style. Reproduction furniture style based on designs of George Hepplewhite, 18th century cabinet maker. Popular in Britain from c1870. Typified by shield-back chairs, serpentine

front chests of drawers, and chairs with curved legs, arms, and seat and back rails.

Hereke, Turkey. Carpet factory founded 1844; made copies of Ghiordes and Persian carpets. Second workshop opened c1910 by former factory designer, Zareh Penyamin, under Sultan; made huge Isfahan silk carpets, silk prayer rugs (clipped very short for folding and carrying), silk Brussa carpets, Pandermas, and other fine quality copies of old Turkish and Persian types. Closed c1940.

Herend. Hungarian porcelain factory established c1839 by M. *Fischer. In 1873, passed to Fischer's sons, who went bankrupt in following year. Continued under various owners. (Present production mainly imitates Meissen porcelain of 1760s.)

Herez or **Heriz carpets.** *See* Persian carpets.

heron service. Porcelain table service designed by P. *Krohn and made (1888) at Bing & Grøndahl factory, Copenhagen. Decoration in underglaze colours and gilding includes elaborate ornamentation in low relief at scalloped rim, and painted panels with asymmetrical designs of herons, standing or dancing, against background of coiled forms.

Hersey, J. (fl late 19th, early 20th centuries). English pottery decorator, employed at pottery of W. *De Morgan. Initialled work.

Herter, Albert (fl early 20th century). American painter, tapestry weaver and designer, general

*Henri-Deux ware. Ewer made by C. *Toft at *Mintons. Height 9¼in.*

Herter Brothers. Chest of drawers with matching mirror of inlaid ebonized wood, in *Eastlake style. c1876. Height of mirror 4ft4in.

artist craftsman. In 1908, founded high-warp-loom tapestry factory in New York. Specialized in 16th century Flemish subjects and style; also contemporary designs, e.g. A History of New York (26 panels).

Herter Brothers. New York furniture manufacturers, established c1865 by G. *Herter and C. *Herter. Chairs often have bulbous-topped front legs, tapering to ring-shaped ankle and trumpet-like foot. Many tables marble-topped, with shallow floral carving on end panels. Made numerous slipper chairs, often in ebonized maple with inlaid breaking-wave, floral, and leaf motifs, swan's head finials, grooved front legs, deeply cushioned round seats, and small backs. Known for Eastlake and Japanese style furniture during 1870s and 1880s. Also made Art furniture. Often used cherrywood.

Herter, Christian (1840–83). German-born furniture designer; established *Herter Brothers with half-brother, G. *Herter, in New York, c1865. Studies with decorative artist, Pierre Victor Galland, in Paris, 1868–70; took over Herter Brothers in 1870. Retired c1880.

Herter, Gustave (fl 1848–80). German-born furniture designer and maker; silver designer for *Tiffany & Co., c1848. Established Gustave Herter, Decorations, c1851. Started *Herter Brothers with half-brother, C. *Herter, c1865. Returned to Germany c1870.

hibachi. Japanese charcoal basins with perforated lids, used for warming hands and lighting pipes. Usually cast in bronze or cast iron. Used in tea ceremony.

Hida ningyo. See ningyo netsuke.

Hidehira or **Nambu ware.** Japanese coloured lacquer with floral or plant designs in red, or red and gold, on black ground. Most often found on soup bowls and *sakazuke but also used on other lacquer utensils and small objects.

high chair or **child's chair.** Chair with foot rest, hinged tray or bar, and elongated legs enabling child to sit level with table top; often based on Windsor chair. Development of chair designed 1835 by Sir Astley Paston Cooper to train children to sit upright. cf chair-table.

high-warp or **vertical loom.** Tapestry hand-loom widely used in Europe from 14th century. Vertical frame has heavy uprights carrying horizontal roll at top and bottom on which warps are stretched. Each warp passes through loop of cord; even numbered loops attached to one cylinder, uneven numbers to other. Weaver pulls forward each set of warps in turn in order to pass bobbin carrying weft thread behind. Finished section of work rolled up and further length of warps unrolled on cylinders, so that section being worked always in convenient position. Cartoon hangs beside weaver, who works from back of tapestry and checks work in progress by looking in mirror behind unwoven warps, or by walking behind loom. Most tapestries woven at right angles on loom, so that warps run horizontally in finished work. Though result of high aesthetic quality, method creates inherent weakness in fabric. Production on vertical loom extremely slow and therefore costly compared with that on *low-warp loom, which uses treadle, thus freeing both weaver's hands to work bobbin.

hikite. Japanese metal finger plates set in sliding doors of rooms and cupboards to facilitate opening. Very decorative; sometimes enamelled after 1600.

Hill, Oliver (1887–1968). English interior decorator and furniture designer. Known during 1930s for Modernist style interiors complemented by specially designed furniture, e.g. finished in ivory lacquerwork or steel. Designed shaped plate glass *chaise longue*, dressing-table, stool, and small table for Pilkington stand at Dorland House Exhibition, 1933, anticipating similar furniture in plastics.

Hill Pottery. See Burgess, Leigh & Co.

Hingelberg, Frantz. Danish manufacturing and retail silversmiths and jewellers, founded 1897 by Frantz Hingelberg, succeeded by son Vilhelm. Firm still produces wide range of silver in modern styles and supplies jewellery to Danish court.

Hingre, Louis-Théophile (c1835–1911). French *animalier* sculptor; first exhibit at Paris Salon (1863), Marsh Heron. Later works include Chicken (silvered-bronze, 1868), English Cat (1869), Dromedary (1872), Family of Partridges (1877), and plaster bas-reliefs of fruit and flowers.

hip, sitz or **Oxford bath.** Portable, oval bath with high, inclined back; sometimes with projecting lugs for lifting. In japanned or enamelled tin or zinc. Hand-filled with hot water and used in bedroom. Common in Britain from c1850.

Historical flask. Aquamarine Pike's Peak flask with hunter on reverse, quart capacity, made in Midwest after 1859.

Hipp, Matthäus (1813–93). Swiss clockmaker, pioneered *electric clock. Invented Hipp toggle (patented 1842) attached to pendulum rod, which brushes to and fro over notch on two open electric contacts; as pendulum arc shortens, toggle engages in notch and completes circuit giving impulse to pendulum. His clocks made by Telegraph Manufacturing Co. in Neuchâtel. Devised Hipp chronoscope, c1850, recording short intervals (to within $6/1000^{th}$ second) on wax or paper drum.

hirame (Japanese, 'flat-eye'). Japanese lacquer technique used from Fujiwara Period (895–1195) mainly as ground decoration, with simple designs. Irregular, largish flakes of sheet gold sprinkled on to still wet, usually black, lacquer ground, and covered with several layers of clear lacquer. When dry, surface polished to reveal edges and points of flakes as sparkling flecks. Popularity declined in 19th century: often replaced by *nashiji.

hiramakie (Japanese, 'flat-sown picture'). In Japanese lacquer, *makie flush with or only slightly raised above surface ground. Originated in Heian period (795–1192); widely used from 12th century on whole range of lacquerware. From 19th century, used increasingly in combination with various types of inlaid or encrusted lacquer decoration. Technique: outline of desired design transferred to prepared lacquer base and portions dusted with gold powder. When dry, surface covered with layers of clear lacquer, then dried and polished. Process re-

*Joshua Hodgetts. Wheel-engraved vase of cameo glass, made for *Stevens & Williams. Late 19th century. Height 8¼in.*

peated until complete design appears. Finally, details added with shading lacquer, and object given finishing coats of lacquer and high polish. *Illustration at kobako.*

historical or **pictorial flask.** American whiskey bottle decorated with relief portrait of president, state or commemorative emblem, goddess of victory, etc. First free-blown specimens made in 1780; metal-moulded versions in numerous shapes, sizes (½ pint, pint, quart) and colours (mainly clear glass), produced in quantity 1816-75; fashion spread to Europe. *See* Booz bottle, Jenny Lind bottle, violin flask.

hitori koro. Squat, flat-bottomed miniature Japanese box, with openwork metal cover, used for burning charcoal needed in incense ceremony. Usually bronze or celadon; occasionally lacquer with silver or copper lining.

hiuchi-bukuro (Japanese, 'tinder-pouch'). Oldest known Japanese *sagemono, worn from 8th to 19th centuries; production continues into 20th century. Late examples either elaborated ornamented brocade silk, leather or cloth pouches; or more frequently small boxes, similar to *tonkotsu in shape and ornamentation, but often provided with piece of exposed steel on bottom for striking light.

Hizen. Province in north-west of Japanese island of Kyushu. Porcelain made at Arita and nearby, e.g. at Mikawachi, and Okawachi (site of production of Nabeshima ware), exported through port of Imari.

Hobbs, Brockunier & Company. American glasshouse founded c1844 by James B. Barnes in Wheeling, Virginia. Known at first as Hobbs, Barnes & Co. Made fine cameo glass and developed and patented much new art glass in late 19th century, e.g. *Spangled glass, and own version of *Peachblow (known as Coral glass); also made *crackle glass, glass with applied decoration, and many pressed or blown novelty items, e.g. egg-shaped salt and pepper shakers, rose leaf bowls.

Hobby Horse. Magazine of *Century Guild; started 1884 by A. H. *Mackmurdo. Only one issue in first year, with cover by S. *Image and woodcut decorations by Image, A. H. *Mackmurdo, and designer, Herbert Horne. Reappeared under their editorship, 1886-92. Horne sole editor of second series from 1893; magazine taken over by Bodley Head.

hobnail, dewdrop, or **opalescent dewdrop glass.** Late 19th century American art glass with raised decoration. Widely used from 1880s for tableware, pitchers, and especially bottles. Wide range of colours. Objects first pattern-moulded, then expanded, finally further expanded and

shaped by hand. Process patented 1886 by *Hobbs, Brockunier & Co.

Hodgetts, Joshua (1858-1933). English cameo glass engraver; employed in workshop of J. *Northwood and by *Stevens & Williams (1880-1900). Amateur botanist; engraved fine vases, dishes, etc., in classical style (inspired by work of Northwood) or with naturalistic flower motifs.

Hoentschel, Georges (1855-1915). French artist potter. Formerly architect; began ceramic work, mainly in stoneware, in 1890s. Associated with J. *Carriès, used similar style; influenced by oriental glazes, while developing characteristic forms and decorative techniques. Also made stoneware bath, backed with flowing plant forms surrounded by arch, in Art Nouveau style.

Hoffmann, Josef (1870-1956). Austrian architect and designer. Studied in Munich and Vienna. With teacher, O. *Wagner, K. *Moser, and J. *Olbrich, involved in *Vienna Secession, 1897-1905. Teacher at School of Decorative Arts (Vienna), 1899-1941. With Olbrich, designed Austrian pavilion at Paris Universal Exposition (1900). Among founders of Wiener Werkstätte (1903); one of principal designers of metalwork. Jewellery in geometrical style set with unusually coloured, often opaque stones, e.g. malachite, coral. Metalwork often decorated with chequerboard pattern, and sometimes incorporates gold, pearl, ivory, or enamels. Furniture characterized by linear, cubist design, e.g. chair (c1903) with two square-sectioned splats in open back, square runners joining front and back legs. Oak desk and armchair made c1905 in rectilinear design; white colouring rubbed into grain of stained, waxed wood; white metal handles recessed. Later furniture more refined, e.g. cabinet (early

Left
Georges Hoentschel. Glazed stoneware vase. c1902.

Below
Josef Hoffmann. Metal baskets, enamelled white. Designed c1905.

Joseph Hoffmann. Chair in stained mahogany, upholstered in red leather. Designed 1903-06.

1910s) with tarsia strips of mother-of-pearl, and boxwood and ebony panels in front. Also designed furniture for *Thonet Brothers. Black and white linear designs in squares and rectangles used on porcelain vases and tableware. Even earliest work foreshadowed styles characteristic of Art Deco. Also provided geometrical designs linked with Cubist style for black and white majolica made at Wiener Keramik (established 1905). From 1910, drinking glasses and other vessels with bronzite decoration produced by J. & L. *Lobmeyr. Most important work regarded as design of Palais Stoclet in Brussels (1904-11), including interior fittings and furniture, in collaboration with C. *Czeschka. Founder of Österreichisches Werkbund, 1912, leaving in 1920 to lead Viennese section of *Deutscher Werkbund. Designed porcelain table service (c1928) for *Augarten factory. Ribbed shapes decorated with vertical stripes of colour; coffee pot, covered bowl, etc. in shape of gourds, saucers have wavy edge. Curvilinear metalwork designs for Wiener Werkstätte influenced silver design of 1920s. Work usually commissioned by patrons, and examples rare; marked with monogram JH.

Hofman, Vlatislav (fl 20th century). Czechoslovakian architect and ceramic designer. Work with decoration influenced by Cubism produced at Artel workshops, Prague, includes earthenware vase with lobed form tapering to square rim, covered with yellow glaze (c1911).

Hogarth chair. Armchair with curved, inclined back and vase or baluster shaped back splat. Scroll-over arms form continuous curve with back uprights; seat usually upholstered. Type dates from early 18th century; name (introduced after 1850) derives from use by 18th century English painter, William Hogarth, in self-portrait and other paintings; side-chair versions also shown.

hogen. *See* ho-in.

ho-in or **hoin.** Honorary title granted to outstanding Japanese artists; third ecclesiastical rank in Buddhism (fourth is hogen; fifth hokkyo). Appears on work as calligraphic symbol following signature and *kakihan.

Hojitsu, Yamada (d 1872). Japanese netsuke artist, established last famous 19th century Tokyo netsuke school. Most famous pupil, M. *Joso. Made realistic carved ivory and boxwood *katabori netsuke in painstaking, elegant style. *Na: Izaemon or Iueman. *Go: Meikeisai. *Kaimyo: Zekoin Myotatsu. *Chomei: Hojitsu, or *kakihan derived from Hojitsu.

hokkyo. *See* ho-in.

Holbein ware. Vases, plaques, and bowls, in very hard earthenware body, decorated usually with one or more portraits inlaid in contrasting clay and covered with slightly uneven glaze. Introduced by Charles J. *Noke at Doulton factory, Burslem, Staffordshire, and produced 1895-1914.

Holland & Sons. London furniture makers founded in early 18th century. Made high-

Holland & Sons. Bookcase designed by G. E. Street. Made in solid oak with incised and inlaid decoration and brass mounts. Stamped Holland & Sons. 1865. Height 8ft 7in.

quality furniture throughout 19th century. Furnished Queen Victoria's residences at Osborne (Isle of Wight), Balmoral (Aberdeenshire) and Sandringham (Norfolk); won many exhibition awards. Many pieces inspired by 18th century design, e.g. Sheraton, Adam, Chippendale. Designers include G. *Semper, G. E. *Street, and B. J. *Talbert. Also known for Eclectic furniture. Sideboards, writing tables, etc., often satinwood, characterized by urns and swags inlaid with contrasting woods. Known for floral marquetry. Some pieces stamped: Holland and Sons. *Illustration at* Semper, G.

Hollins, Michael Daintry (1815-98). English potter. Grandson of Samuel Hollins, partner in New Hall porcelain factory. Formerly surgeon, in partnership with uncle, H. *Minton, from 1845. After partition of Minton, Hollins & Co. (1868), took control of tile manufacture, retaining use of name Minton for production and sale of tiles.

Hollming, August Fredrik (1854-1915). Finnish jeweller, goldsmith and enameller. Apprenticed in St Petersburg, 1876; workmaster at St Petersburg branch of *Fabergé from c1880. Specialized in gold, enamel and hardstone objects of vertu. Also made some jewellery. Mark: A*H.

hollow-ware or **holloware.** Generic term for all types of hollow metal vessels, e.g. *spirit kettle, *teapot, sugar or *fruit bowl, *butter-dish, *christening mug. Originally all hollow-ware beaten out by hand, but factory production by spinning on lathe, or stamping by mechanical press. Term has particular currency in America.

Hollywood style. Interior decoration and furniture style in 1930s films. Anonymous period furniture in rooms based on 18th century traditions; contemporary designs rare. Period décor also popular for film stars' private homes, e.g. Louis XIV for Mae West, Victorian for Ida Lupino.

Holmström, August Wilhelm (1829-1903). Swedish-Finnish jeweller; apprenticed in St Petersburg. From 1857, chief jeweller and workmaster at St Petersburg branch of *Fabergé. After death, workshop continued under son, Albert (1876-1925). Mark A. H.

Homelike style. *See* Eastlake style.

Homyo. *See* Kaimyo.

Hongo. Japanese folk pottery kiln in Fukushima prefecture. Noted for production of square dishes with trickled glaze for use in salting herring, and other kitchen ware glazed in greyish blue, brown, or green. Long-established production continues to present day.

honji (Japanese, 'real basis'). In Japanese lacquer, prepared wooden core for decoration. Complex process of priming wood, and applying initial coats of branch lacquer mixed with rice starch and chopped hemp, then layers of mixed clay and lacquer, and finally numerous thin coats of black lacquer. Each application followed by lengthy drying period and careful polishing.

hooded chair. Bedroom chair designed by C. F. A. *Voysey, shown by Arts & Crafts Exhibition Society, 1896. Fined-down version of

sedan chair, with upholstered seat and back, turned uprights, curvilinear sides, roof.

hoop-back or **loop-back Windsor chair.** High-back chair with back spindles; bow-shaped yoke rail continuous with uprights. With or without arms. Common from c1750 in Britain and America; feature of *cottage furniture in America.

Hope-Jones, Frank. *See* synchronome clock.

horizontal loom. *See* low-warp loom.

horloge de cheminée. *See* bracket clock.

horn. Animal horn can be worked to produce wide range of colour. First used in 19th century jewellery by R. *Lalique (1896). Used by him and L. *Gaillard for combs. Carved horn pendants with Japanese style designs popular c1910.

horn furniture. Chairs, sofas, etc. made with whole animal horns, e.g. steer, buffalo, elk, stag. Mid Victorian examples made for Balmoral Castle, Scotland. With opening up of West, popular in America c1880 to early 1900s. Upholstered in hide (e.g. prairie dog or alligator), velvet, damask, etc. Horn chairs presented to Presidents, Abraham Lincoln and Theodore Roosevelt. Also feature of European hunting lodges, mainly in Bavarian Alps.

horns. *See* drinking horn, hunting horn.

Horová, Julie (b 1906). Czechoslovakian artist potter. Studied at Prague School of Applied Art, then under R. *Lachenal in France among others. Work, as teacher in Bratislava, Slovakia,

influenced by knowledge of folk ceramics. Later work, often decorated with scraped texture, in rounded shapes, e.g. vase with turquoise glaze, or unglazed sculpture of llama (c80in. high) thrown on wheel.

horse brasses. Decorative brass ornaments attached to show harness; possibly originated as heraldic devices on medieval horse armour, later awarded as prizes at agricultural shows, ploughing competitions, etc. Made by hand until introduction of cast brass versions c1830. Variety of patterns include wheatsheaf, elm tree, acorn, knot of flowers etc., later superseded by more abstract designs incorporating diamond, star, and wheel shapes. Portrait and commemorative brasses, fashionable c1840–c1860, depict e.g. royalty, politicians; also county symbols, e.g. Staffordshire knot, Suffolk windmill. Machine-stamped examples (from c1870), lighter in weight and in cruder decorative style, commemorate public events, military victories, etc.

Horse brasses. Below: three unmounted English 19th and 20th century brasses. Above: head-pieces, known as swingers (centre) and flyers (either side).

*Horn. Group of three *combs, French. c1890–1900.*

Below
Horn furniture. Armchair probably from western United States. Steer horn with leather seat. Brass claw feet holding glass balls. c1900.

Sets of three or four brasses, mounted on leather, commonly sold by harness makers; sets of five or two fairly uncommon, sets of six, rare. Genuineness may be indicated by signs of wear on reverse of brass from contact with harness; modern reproductions abound.

Horsley, John Calcott (1817–1903). English painter; contributed some metalwork designs to Felix *Summerly's Art Manufactures; c1847, designed series of decanter stoppers in silver, silver-gilt, and electro-plate made by Benjamin Smith.

Horta, Victor (1861–1947). Belgian architect and designer; pioneer of Art Nouveau style. Designed Architectural style furniture, often with wood tones harmonizing with colours of door frames, panelling, etc. to create harmonious interior style. Pieces characterized by sinuous lines, use of space to emphasize contrasting curves highlighted by restrained use of moulding; curves often represent stems of flowers. Ornamentation of wrought iron, curved metalwork, and inlaid woods. Designed furniture and fittings for Hôtel Solvay, 224 Avenue Louise, Brussels, 1895–1900.

Hotei. One of Japanese *Shichi-fuku-jin; god of constant good-humour and contentment. Patron of children, comparable to Western Santa Claus. Portrayed as bald, jovial, huge-bellied old man. Carries huge hotei ('hempen sack', or 'cloth bag'), bulging with toys or *takaramono. *Illustration at* kozuka.

hotel china. *See* semi-porcelain.

hot stamping. Technique for die-stamping pattern on to metal article, e.g. spoon handle, without losing temper of shaft; invented 1895 in America by E. Talman. Area to be stamped is heated, while rest of object kept cool by constant stream of water.

hot-water bottle. Gradually superseded warming pan for heating bedclothes in mid 19th century; early versions made of brass, copper, or tinware, with embroidered flannel cover to protect feet; later versions of earthenware.

Houn, Takahashi (b 1824). Japanese sculptor and netsuke artist. Worked in Tokyo, where established own netsuke school at Kanda. Awarded honorary title, *hogen, for carving of Buddhist images. *Na: Seijiro. *Go: Shokosai.

hound-handled pitcher. *See* Greatbach, Daniel, United States Pottery.

hour-glass seat. Circular, upholstered seat with round base of equal size, and pinched waist.

Victor Horta. Dining room in Horta's house. Furniture executed c1900.

Sometimes in straw for outdoor use. Popular c1850 in Britain.

household gods. *See* Shichi-fuku-jin.

Howard, Edward (1813–1904). Pioneer of American machine-made *precision watch industry. Opened domestic and *precision clock factory at Roxbury, Massachusetts, in 1842. Partner of A. L. *Dennison, 1850–57. Began trading on own in 1857 (still as Boston Watch Co.); expanded to Howard Clock & Watch Co. in 1861; became E. Howard Watch & Clock Co. in 1881. Produced many precision watches of exceptional quality. Retired 1882.

Howell & James. English pottery and porcelain retailers in Regent Street, London, in late 19th century. From 1876, held annual exhibitions of painted pottery including work of *amateur decorators on pottery and porcelain vases, plaques, etc., bought undecorated from manufacturers, notably Mintons Ltd, sometimes with maker's mark impressed. Paper labels, which sometimes still survive, gave name of artist, title of design, and date. Much amateur work sold at exhibitions, judged by Royal Academicians, and reviewed in contemporary periodicals.

Howell & James. Two plates painted by J. Edith Cowper for Howell & James exhibit at Paris Exhibition, 1878. Both signed. Diameter 8in.

Hubbard, Elbert (1856-1915). American writer and craftsman; promoted Arts & Crafts Movement in America. Settled in East Aurora, New York State, establishing first *Roycroft Shop in 1895. Bought printing press after visit to W. *Morris in 1894; printed fine books on hand-made paper, e.g. The Song of Songs, 1895-96.

Huggins, Vera (fl 20th century). English potter. Designed stoneware made at Doulton workshop, Lambeth, London, from 1923 until 1950s. Salt-glazed vases, etc., decorated in delicate colours, still made for export during and after 2nd World War, signed with name in full.

Hukin & Heath (1879-1953). Birmingham manufacturers of e.g. tea and coffee sets, cruet stands, sugar basins, sugar tongs, claret jugs in silver and electro-plate. C. *Dresser artistic director and adviser from c1880; firm consistently responded to new developments in design; also manufactured electro-type reproductions of Persian and Japanese styles. Showrooms in Charterhouse Street, London. Silver in Art Moderne style designed by A. E. *Harvey, c1933-c1936.

*Hukin & Heath. Sugar bowl and sifter spoon. Designed by C. *Dresser. London, 1883. Width 6½in.*

Maker's mark JWH over JTH. *Illustration also at* Harvey, A. E.

Hunebelle, André (fl 1920s). French Art Deco glass artist. Strongly influenced by R. *Lalique. Made vases and bowls of lightly frosted glass decorated with spirals of stylized flowers. Later, turned to geometrical decoration inspired by Cubism, using semi-opaque glass. Mark: A. Hunebelle, impressed.

Hungarian carpets. Thick, shaggy rugs in natural wool colours (suba or racka), and folk designs with Turkish elements main export types; first appeared on European market c1880. Production greatly accelerated c1900, and several new factories opened.

Hungarian tapestry. 20th century production dates from founding of artists' colony and weaving workshop in Gödöllö, near Budapest, by group of painters, including Sandor Nagy and Aladár Körösföi Kriesch. Stimulated other artists, e.g. N. *Ferenczy, to design for tapestry.

Hunt, William Holman (1827-1910). Pre-Raphaelite painter. Painted furniture for *Morris, Marshall, Faulkner & Co., for whom also designed experimental furniture, e.g. chair based on Egyptian example in British Museum, London.

Hunt & Roskell. Large English retailers and manufacturers of wide range of silver and electro-plate articles, founded in London, c1840, as Mortimer & Hunt, by John Mortimer and John Samuel Hunt. In 1843, Mortimer withdrew; firm subsequently styled Hunt & Roskell. Chief designers for firm c1845-c1880 included E. *Cotterill, G. A. *Carter, A. *Brown, A. J. *Barrett, and E. H. Baily. Firm produced many presentation pieces, testimonials, *racing

*Hukin & Heath. Electro-plated soup tureen, cover and ladle with ivory mounts. Designed by Christopher *Dresser. (Other examples known of this pattern with ebony mounts.) Bears design registry mark for 28th July 1880. Diameter 9½in.*

Hunt & Roskell. Silver jug designed by J. S. Hunt. London, 1855. Height 10¾in.

trophies, exhibiting over 60 examples at Great Exhibition of 1851, e.g. Royal Hunt Cup, 1849, made in silver, consisting of tazza, with flattish cover, decorated with stag and hound hunting scene, and chased with Elizabethan strapwork. Continued in business until taken over, c1939. Marks: IM over ISM, or ISH over crown.

hunting horn. Simple, valveless horn, blown by huntsman to indicate various stages of chase; made, e.g. in brass, or copper, frequently with decorative chasing, or damascening. In early 19th century, length of horn reduced from c19½in. to c9in.

Hunzinger, George (fl 1850-90). German-born furniture manufacturer in New York. Noted for chairs, many adjustable, some folding. Patented

George Hunzinger. Walnut side chair. Marked Hunzinger N.Y./Pat. March 30/1869. Height 32½in.

reclining chair in 1861. Often used machine-inspired decorative motifs of wheels, cogs, etc. Some Renaissance revival style models. *Illustration at* patent furniture.

Hürten, Charles Ferdinand (1813-1901). English ceramic decorator, born in Cologne. In France from 1836, worked independently as flower painter; some work commissioned by Sèvres factory. Employed by W. T. *Copeland (from 1859) after painting shown at Paris Exhibition of 1858. Realistic painting of flowers from water-colours or natural specimens includes signed vases and earthenware plaques; work figures in Copeland displays at all major Exhibitions from 1862 until retirement (1897). Also painted panels, e.g. of fruit and birds.

hussif, or **housewife.** Folding fabric or leather case, used as combination pin-cushion and needle-book. Usually 8-12in. long when un-folded; cushion for needles and pins on one side, channels for embroidery threads on the other. Popular from mid 19th century. Precursor of 20th century travelling sewing kit.

Hutschenreuther family. German porcelain manufacturers. Carl Magnus Hutschenreuther (d 1845) established factory at Hohenberg, Bavaria; succeeded by widow and sons, Christian and Lorenz (d 1886). Factory, estab-lished (1857) by Lorenz in Selb, managed from 1860 by Christian, in partnership, succeeded by son Albert (noted for decoration in underglaze blue). Family purchased factories at Altrohlau, near Carlsbad (1909), Altwasser, Silesia (1918), and Arzberg, Bavaria. Also set up decorating workshop in Radeberg, near Dresden. Firm of Lorenz Hutschenreuther bought Bavarian fac-tories in Selb (1917), and Tirschenreuth (1927), and factory of *Bauscher Brothers in Weiden

Oberpfalz. Noted for manufacture of high-quality tableware, figures, etc. (In 1969, branches of firm united.)

Hutton, William, & Sons. Birmingham firm of silver, Sheffield plate, and close plate manufac-turers founded 1800 by William Hutton (1774-1842); known as Hutton & Houghton, 1818-20. Produced various small articles, e.g. candle-snuffers, nutcrackers, in Old Sheffield and close plate. Opened new factory in Sheffield, 1832, production extended to spoons and forks in argentan metal. On death of founder, firm passed to son William Carr Hutton (1803-65). T. Swaffield Brown, formerly of *Hunt & Roskell, head of Art Department 1880-1914; produced large quantities of domestic silver, silver plate, pewter, and Britannia metal ware, including many trophies, military figures and sports shields. Art Nouveau pieces to design of K. *Harris, displayed at Paris International Exhibi-tion, 1900. In association with James Dixon, Walker & Hall, and *Barker Bros, firm launched Sheffield Flatware Company, 1914. After interruption by war, concentrated on mass pro-duction of *Baguette pattern flatware, until pro-duction ceased, 1921. Firm in liquidation 1923; name and goodwill transferred to James Dixon & Son (1930). Makers marks: silver, WH in oval; Sheffield plate, Hutton W-; Close plate, W.H. & S with Greek letter omega.

hyacinth. *See* zircon.

hyomon. *See* kanagai.

hyotan. *See* sagemono.

*William Hutton & Sons. Set consisting of mug, napkin ring, knife, fork and spoon, made 1903 for *Mappin & Webb.*

ice cream fork-spoon. Spoon with bowl divided into three tines at tip for eating ice-cream; made in silver or electro-plate. Produced in America from c1860.

ice glass, frosted glass, overshot glass, or **brocs à glace.** Popular British and European art glass with frosted outer surface and smooth interior. Made by rolling partly inflated glass body over powdered glass fragments, then reheating slightly and blowing to desired shape; or by plunging red-hot glass into cold water, then re-heating and reblowing. Both methods of 16th century Venetian origin; latter revived in Bohemia, but later becoming popular in England (where A. *Pellatt produced Venetian Frosted Glass c1845-50), France, and elsewhere. *See also* crackle glass.

ichiraku netsuke. Netsuke of basketwork design in woven or braided metal, rattan, or bamboo; shaped as box, basket, or gourd. Named after Ichiraku, mid 18th century inventor of technique.

ikakeji. *See* fundame.

Ikonnikov, I.A. (fl mid to late 19th century). Russian porcelain manufacturer. From 1865, proprietor of factory operating at Vsevolozhskoy, near Moscow, from early 19th century. After closure of Popov factory in 1875, bought and used moulds of figures and tableware.

Ikora glass. German Functionalist glass pro-duced by *Württembergische Metallwaren-fabrik. Usually, heavy glass objects with air-bubble decoration in organized patterns and colour encrustations. Has affinities with Swedish glass of same period. *See* Ariel glass, and Graal glass.

Ikora metal. *See* Württembergische Metallwarenfabrik.

Imaemon, Imaizumi (fl 20th century). Japanese potter, member of family traditionally producing Nabeshima porcelain at Okawachi kiln in Arita. Work regarded as equalling quality of best period (18th and early 19th centuries).

Image, Selwyn (1849-1930). English illustrator and designer of embroidery, mosaics, stained glass, etc.; associate of A. H. *Mackmurdo. Designed cover for first issue of *Hobby Horse, 1884; co-editor, 1886-92. Painted panels, inscriptions, and designed inlay decoration, e.g. intarsia on mahogany, for *Century Guild furniture.

Imari wares. Japanese porcelain made in pro-vince of Hizen, chiefly in Arita or at neighbour-ing kilns, shipped through port of Imari for export. In Europe, refers particularly to export ware with rich enamel decoration in designs in-spired by textiles, originally known as 'Old Japan'.

imitation amber and jet. *See* bakelite.

impasto ware. English stoneware developed at Doulton workshop, Lambeth, in late 1870s; made mainly 1879-1906, some 1907-14. Decorated in coloured slips, applied sufficiently thickly to achieve raised effect. Surface lacks

gloss, resembling painting of frescoes; plaques and tiles for wall decoration, made c1890–1914, known as vitreous fresco. *Illustration at* Doulton & Co.

Imperial Axminster. Type of Axminster carpet evolved c1893 by J. *Templeton of Glasgow to counteract flooding, first of American then British markets, by A. *Smith & Co.'s cheap moquette carpets. New Imperial Axminster quality superior to moquette, but more expensive (though cheaper than any contemporary British carpet). Supplanted moquette in Britain and Europe.

Imperial Glass Factory. Russian state glasshouse, in St Petersburg from 1715; production almost exclusively for Tsar until c1865, then sold glass imitating European styles and techniques, e.g. Bohemian *cameo glass. Merged with Imperial Porcelain Factory, 1890.

Imperial Porcelain Factory, St Petersburg. State-owned Russian porcelain factory, established 1744 in St Petersburg (now Leningrad). Noted in mid 19th century for copies on porcelain of paintings in the Hermitage Museum, St Petersburg. Useful and decorative ware produced in wide variety of styles. Continued manufacture of brightly-coloured figures illustrating crafts, peasant costume, etc. Until 1917, products marked with cypher of reigning monarch.

in or **hanko** (Japanese, 'seal'). Small seal with wood, ivory, stone, or metal matrix engraved with distinguishing mark or design. In Japanese

Imperial Glass Factory. Covered goblet, enamelled and gilded decoration in Byzantine style. Mark for Alexander II period gilded on base. c1870.

*Ingrain carpet. Probably designed by C. F. A. *Voysey. c1895–1900.*

decorative arts, stamped on object or document as legal identification of individual maker or art family. Used either alone or with regular signature.

incense boxes (in Japanese lacquer). Miniature boxes for storing incense used to scent rooms of Japanese homes, and burned in tea, incense and religious ceremonies. Among most beautifully ornamented and painstakingly executed examples of Japanese lacquerware, often executed by famous artists. Most important forms: *kogo, *kobako, *kyara-bako, *kojubako, and *jukogo.

Indian carpets. Apart from East India Co. exports, made chiefly for home market until lower-priced specimens, shown at Great Exhibition of 1851, created new Western market; decline in workmanship followed: quicker methods and cheaper materials, e.g. aniline dyes, adopted; designs dictated by demand for cheap copies of Persian, Turkish, and French types. Local peculiarities disappeared with workshops throughout India copying patterns from standard works. Deterioration of standards often blamed on *jail carpet industry. By c1900, production dependent chiefly on export trade. By 1930s, largest centres in northern India, e.g. *Amritsar, *Srinagar, and *Agra; industry controlled mainly by big concerns, e.g. *Oriental Carpet Manufacturers, C. M. Hadow & Company, Amar Dass, and Sheik Sahib, using predominantly Muslim labour force. *See also* dari,

East India Carpet Co., Eluru, gabba, Gwalior, Kashmir carpets, Madras carpets, Mirzapur, Mitchell & Co., Multan, nakhai rugs, namda, Shahjehanpur, G. P. Stavrides, Warangal.

Indian or **sind lac.** Variety of Indian lacquer made from gummy deposit of insect, *Coccus lacca,* and used on numerous household articles, containers, etc. Various layers of coloured lac (mainly black and/or gold) applied by pressing sticks of lac against prepared surface of object as it is turned on lathe. Designs (usually geometrical, floral, or arabesque) then chiselled in dried lacquer to reveal various layers.

Indian Stone China. *See* Meigh, Charles.

Ingersoll, Robert Hawley (1859–1928). American mail-order pioneer who sold first *dollar watch. Advertized as 'the watch that made the dollar famous'. Early lever watches robust, simple, non-jewelled, manufactured by *Waterbury Clock Co., subsequently taken over by Ingersoll. 70 million watches sold by 1922, when company failed because of overwhelming competition from Swiss firms.

Ingold, Pierre-Frédéric (1787–1878). Swiss watchmaker; pioneered mechanized watchmaking, and introduced jewels into Swiss horological industry. Worked for A-L. Breguet in Paris (1817–24). Invented new form of lever escapement and Ingold fraise-cutter for shaping wheels. Moved to London (1839) to help start British Watch Co.; English craftsmen, opposed to his manufacturing methods, sabotaged Soho (London) factory and company failed 1844. Moved to New York (1844), took American nationality; expelled, and started factories in Boston; returned to Switzerland, c1855.

ingrain, Kidderminster, or **Scotch carpet.** Pileless carpet with tapestry-like ribbed surface, woven with coloured warp as well as weft threads. First type of carpet made on power loom (invented by E. *Bigelow in 1841). During late 19th and early 20th centuries, shared bulk of market with Brussels carpets. Woven in 3ft widths until *art squares broke *chenille Axminster monopoly of wide seamless carpets in 1880. Wide ingrain power loom, developed by W. C. *Gray & Sons in 1886, wove 9ft patent 'Akbar' carpets. Ingrain production centred on Kilmarnock, Ayrshire, and Kidderminster, Worcestershire. Superseded in 1900s, together with wide chenille squares, by wide *spool Axminsters. By 1908, on ingrain factory remained in Kilmarnock (became *Blackwood, Morton & Sons); replaced ingrain by chenille production after 1918. Kidderminster ceased ingrain production in 1930s. *Illustration at* Morris, W.

inkpot. *See* inkwell.

inkstand. Container for inkwells, pens, and writing accessories, in use since 15th century; originally known as standish; produced in many materials e.g. iron, pewter, copper, gold, and silver. Examples from Victorian period elaborately ornamented, often incorporating bell to summon servant to post letters. Novelty designs include rowing boat with pens as oars, bowls of fruit, shells, palm trees, emu eggs, cricketing figures. Commemorative inkstand made by *Elkington & Co. for Great Exhibition,

London 1851, as globe, containing inkwell, with base decorated with scenes representing peaceful arts of all nations. Usage declined after introduction of fountain pen in 1886.

inkwell or **inkpot.** Usually made in pairs in 19th century, most commonly of white transparent glass, either cut, plain, or, in some Stourbridge examples, with base and stopper in *millefiore* pattern; air-beaded decoration used late 19th century. Also found in marbled and *slag glass, 1875–90.

inlaid lacquer. *See* embedded lacquer.

inro (Japanese, 'seal case'). Small sectionalized case in which Japanese carried seals and later medicines. Used from late 16th to 19th centuries. Usually 3–4in. wide, 4–5in. long, about ½in. thick, with 3–5 compartments fitting closely together, held by two cords passing up sides of inro through holes at ends of each segment. Worn suspended from *obi, kept in place by *netsuke; held closed by a slip-bead (*ojime) on cord. Often made in matching or complementing set with netsuke and ojime. Usually of lacquer with finely detailed workmanship - inro was only exposed ornament worn apart from sword.

insect jewellery. Necklaces, bracelets, earrings, and brooches with insect motif, e.g. dragonflies, butterflies, beetles, bees, moths, and flies. Popular in Europe and America from late 1860s until c1900. Often treated in Japanese style e.g. by *Tiffany & Co., and J. P. *Cooper. Also by L. *Gaillard, who evolved technique similar to Japanese shakudo which gave fine veined effect on insect wings. Expensive insect jewellery made with body of carved stone (e.g. onyx, cat's eye), wings of engraved gold or pavé-set diamonds; alternatively with jewelled or plain gold bodies and enamelled wings. Dragonflies and butterflies in debased Art Nouveau style produced in quantity in Birmingham. Cheap insect jewellery made of enamelled silver. In 1920s and 1930s, made in enamelled base metals. *See also* animal jewellery.

International Exhibitions. Exhibitions following example of *Great Exhibition (1851) in London, intended as showcases for promotion of international trade and communication. Exhibitions in Ireland at Cork (1852) and Dublin (1853), Crystal Palace Exhibition, New York (1853), and exhibitions at Munich (1854) and Paris (1855) among early examples. English International Exhibition at South Kensington, London, in 1862 featured Japanese display and furniture e.g. of *Morris, Marshall, Faulkner & Co, J. P. *Seddon, and W. *Burges in *Medieval Court; publicized move towards reform in design and attracted attention of manufacturers and designers. Glass reflected revived fashion for engraved decoration. Ceramics included last work of Kerr & Binns before formation of Royal Porcelain Factory at *Worcester, and exhibits from firms of W. *Brownfield and J. *Wedgwood & Sons; *Mintons Ltd showed examples of Henri-Deux ware and designs by A. W. N. *Pugin. Paris Universal Exposition, 1867, featured display by T. *Deck. Designs by F. *Bracquemond influenced by Japanese art. *Satsuma ware introduced to West. English ceramics shown by Mintons Ltd, firm of W. T. *Copeland, Worcester Royal Porcelain Co., and Doulton & Co. Many examples of British furniture based on 18th century shapes in *Queen Anne style. Satinwood with gilt decoration featured by English makers, ebony by French. Annual International Exhibitions held at South Kensington (1871–74). First included influential design for cabinet by T. E. *Collcutt, made by *Collinson & Lock. Universal Exhibition in Vienna (1873) included *pâte-sur-pâte decoration from Minton factory, and porcelain from Worcester imitating Japanese carved ivory. Philadelphia Centennial Exhibition contained Japanese pavilion which inspired e.g. ceramic work of M. L. *Nichols and furniture in Japanese style. Furniture, generally characterized by variety of styles, included work of *Grand Rapids furniture companies, e.g. *Berkey & Gay, and Ohio companies, e.g. *Mitchell & Rammelsberg of Cincinnati; mainly mass-produced versions of *Renaissance revival style. Medieval pieces showed influence of W. *Morris, C. L. *Eastlake, B. J. *Talbert. New England kitchen inspired *American Colonial style. Many cabinets based on British designs in Art or Queen Anne style. *Barbotine decoration in display of C. F. *Haviland inspired M. L. *McLaughlin. Universal Expositions held in Paris, 1878 and 1889 followed by exhibition in 1900, regarded as high point of Art Nouveau; S. *Bing responsible for room settings with furniture by E. *Colonna, E. *Gaillard. English furniture shown by only seven manufacturers, e.g. *Heal & Son and J. S. *Henry. *Sèvres porcelain table decoration by A. *Léonard. Crystalline glazes and underglaze painting shown by *Meissen. Display by W. H. *Grueby in Paris exhibition of 1900 said to have been inspired by work e.g. of A. *Delaherche and E. *Chaplet shown at World's Columbian Exhibition, 1893, in Chicago. Other exhibitions which featured versions of Art Nouveau include German exposition (1897), Vienna Secession exhibition (1900), Glasgow exhibition and Pan-American International Exposition, Buffalo (1901), Turin International Exhibition of Modern Decorative Art (1902), St Louis World's Fair (1904) - celebrating centenary of purchase of Louisiana from French - and fair at Dresden, 1906. Austrian pavilion at Werkbund Exhibition (1914) in Cologne, designed by J. *Hoffmann, included work of H. C. *van de Velde and M. *Breuer. Exposition Internationale des Arts Décoratifs et Industriels Modernes, 1925, in Paris regarded as most comprehensive expression of Art Deco. Included pavilion L'Esprit Nouveau, associated with *Le Corbusier and furnished e.g. by *Thonet Brothers. Commemorative exhibitions, Les Années '25, held in Paris, 1966. International exhibition, 1929, in Barcelona noted for Barcelona chair by L. *Mies van der Rohe, designed for German pavilion.

invar. Alloy of nickel (35.6%) and steel developed 1898 by C-E. *Guillaume. Use for pendulum rods in clocks greatly increased accuracy and simplified temperature compensation systems. Name derived from French, *invariable*, because of negligible expansion at different temperatures. *See also* elinvar.

Iranian carpets. *See* Persian carpets.

Iribe, Paul (1883–1935). French illustrator and designer of jewellery, textiles, furniture, etc. Carried out commissions for art patron, Jacques Doucet; worked with film director, Cecil B. De Mille, in America from 1914; returned to Paris,

Paul Iribe. Armchair. c1925. Carved wooden arms and legs. Original African-inspired velvet upholstery. One of pair. c1925.

1930, to make jewellery for Mme Chanel. Designed feminine, boudoir style Art Nouveau furniture characterized by sinuous legs, use of rich upholstery materials (silk, figured velvet), carved floral and foliate motifs, and use of colour contrasts. Examples include chest of drawers, c1912, with black marble top, mahogany interior, flower garlands at apron, ebony knobs; two drawers covered in green sharkskin inlaid with stylized vase of flowers in ebony. Also mahogany easy chair, 1913, with geometrical ebony inlay on front and side seat rails; front legs fluted, sabre back legs; upholstered in mauve silk. Noted for illustrations of clothes designed by couturier, Paul Poiret.

iridescence. Surface lustre caused naturally in ancient glass by long exposure to damp soil or air. In 19th century, imitated by application of metallic lustres.

iridescent or **lustre glass.** Late 19th century art glass imitating decomposition of ancient Middle Eastern glass. Effect achieved by subjecting glass body to metallic vapours at furnace mouth, or by direct application of metallic oxides or acids. Major feature of Art Nouveau glass; principal exponents: in America, L. C. *Tiffany and F. *Carder; in Austria, Bakalowits & Söhne and J. *Loetz Witwe. *See* Aurene and Favrile.

Iris. *See* Rookwood Pottery.

Iris factory. Small Finnish industrial art firm established 1896 at Porvoo (Borgå), east of Helsinki, by L. *Sparre. Intended to make furniture designed by Sparre and, from 1897, pottery made by A. W. *Finch, who was invited to form ceramic department. Emphasis on good design, rather than financial gain. Work sold in Helsinki and St Petersburg and some exported to Germany and England. However, factory closed in 1902 because of insufficient demand for progressive styles.

iroe-togidashi (Japanese, 'coloured-picture togidashi'). In Japanese lacquer, multi-colour *togidashi used from 18th century, mainly for pictorial elements in lacquer decoration. Design

produced either by usual togidashi method or by painting design in coloured lacquers and then sprinkling with gold dust.

ironstone china. In England and America, hard, white earthenware body resembling that patented by Staffordshire potter, Charles J. Mason, in 1813, purporting to contain iron slag. Resembles stone china made at Spode factory from c1805. Produced by many American manufacturers c1860–1900. *cf* semi-porcelain.

Isfahan, Isphahan, or **Ispahan rugs.** Carpet industry revived in Isfahan, Persia c1870; produced short-pile woollen rugs, typically with blossom, cloud-band, and palmette designs. *See* Persian carpets.

Ishiguro, Masayoshi (1781–1851). Japanese sword furniture maker in Satsuma. Member of Ishiguro family of sword furniture makers. Noted for fine engraving, with delicate execution of plant and animal motifs, and exquisite colour combinations in relief work.

Ishiguro, Munemaro (fl 20th century). Japanese potter, working in Kyoto. Imitated ceramics of Chinese Sung dynasty; noted for high quality of temmoku glazes.

ishime (Japanese, 'stone ground'). Japanese metalwork technique: metal hammered, chiselled, or engraved to produce irregular rough surface imitating coarse-textured stone. Also, Japanese lacquer technique used to create same effect.

Islington Glass Works. *See* Rice, Harris & Sons.

Isolde service. *See* Rosenthal, Philip.

Isparta. *See* Sparta.

Italian rugs. Hand-knotted woollen rugs, used more often as bed covers than floor rugs; made by peasants principally in Abruzzi district. Made on narrow looms by knotted, tapestry-weave process, resembling Spanish *Alpujarra weave: weft wound over rods or pins forms loops on surface. Usually self-coloured (often white), with pattern formed by looped pile against flat background. Craft declined with development of machine-made carpets, but several exhibitions of Italian peasant crafts, c1910–30, awakened outside interest. Society (Industrie Femminili Riunite) formed to revive traditional crafts, studied ancient methods of weaving and dyeing, and old designs.

Italian tapestry. Papal factory founded 1710 by Pope Clement XI in Hospital of San Michele, Rome, to teach tapestry, drawing, and painting. Erulo Eruli (fl late 19th century) trained there; after closure of San Michele in 1870, founded own factory in Rome, which remains active. Tapestry school founded 1935 at Esino Lario, near Como, and factory at Asti (made panels e.g. for transatlantic liner, Leonardo da Vinci).

Itaya, Hazan (b 1872). Japanese potter, working in Tokyo. In Meiji era (until 1919), influenced by European styles; later work Chinese-inspired. Noted for high-quality white porcelain, and celadon glazed ware, often with low-relief decoration of flowers, etc.

itto-bori (Japanese, 'single-knife carving'). Japanese wood-carving technique using only one implement, so that surface has rough, faceted appearance. Widely used throughout 19th and 20th centuries, particularly for *ningyo. Speciality of carvers at Takayama in Hido, and of *Toen.

ivory. Hard, white substance of elephants tusks; whiter, more expensive variety from African elephants, yellower from Indian. Term sometimes applied to items made of teeth and bone. Dieppe, France, popular centre for carved ivory jewellery from early 19th century. Used as carved decoration on mourning jewellery and carved into most of popular decorative motifs of 19th century, e.g. crosses, flower brooches, Gothic motifs. Ivory necklaces fashionable in 1880s when coloured stones out of fashion. Also used by Art Nouveau jewellers, e.g. R. *Lalique and P. *Wolfers, and by Wiener Werkstätte designers, e.g. J. *Hoffmann, D. *Peche.

ivory porcelain. Ivory-tinted porcelain paste introduced at Worcester factory in 1856. Figures, groups, busts, and other decorative ware left in biscuit or covered with soft glaze. From mid 1860s, sometimes coated with film of silver, bronze, etc. Decorated in Japanese styles from 1873, notably by J. *Hadley. Also used for production of *Raphaelesque porcelain from c1860. Very thinly potted ivory-toned paste used by W. H. *Goss. Jewelled decoration applied to ivory-toned paste by E. *Wedgwood.

Jack, George (1855–1932). American-born architect and furniture designer; worked for P. *Webb from c1880. Became chief furniture designer of *Morris & Co. in c1890, designing costly pieces

in high-quality walnut and mahogany; furniture plain in outline, often with metal mounts and elaborate panels of floral marquetry. Member of *Arts & Crafts Exhibition Society and *Art Workers' Guild. Took over Webb's practice in 1900.

Jackson & Graham. London cabinet makers, established 1840. Known for ornate, lavishly decorated furniture. Won many exhibition awards, e.g. gold medal at Paris Exhibition of 1855, for cabinet, c14ft high, with carved, chased, and inlaid enrichment; base, ornamented with ormolu caryatids, surmounted by massive mirror; designed by E. *Prignot; ornament by foreign craftsmen including H. *Protat. Firm mechanized in early 1850s: employed 600 workmen by 1875. Designers include O. *Jones. Taken over (1885) by *Collinson & Lock.

Jacobethan style. Eclectic furniture style popular in Britain during 1930s. Combines elements of Elizabethan, Hepplewhite, Sheraton, Adam and other styles. Widely used for three-piece and dining-room suites.

Jacobus, Pauline (fl late 19th century). American artist potter. Established Pauline Pottery Company in Chicago, Illinois. Firm operated (1888–c1894) at Edgerton, Wisconsin. Made art pottery with underglaze decoration in bright colours, e.g. yellow, peacock-blue, green, and creamy tones, marked with crown containing C (for Chicago), impressed or, later, printed in black.

*George Jack. Escritoire and stand made by *Morris & Co. Marquetry of sycamore and various other woods. 1893.*

Jacquard mechanism. Device used in carpet and textile weaving for selecting and raising threads required to form pattern; developed progressively by several 18th century French inventors. Most important single invention applied to hand-loom and, later, power-loom, allowing large and complex patterns. Warp threads lifted by rows of vertical wires bent at ends (hooks), with horizontal needles attached. These selected by block of wood (cylinder) with perforations on each side corresponding to each needle. Cards, perforated by special machinery from painted design (number of cards equals number of weft threads) placed in succession between cylinder and needles; those without corresponding holes in card tilt upwards, while remainder, carrying warp threads, are lifted for insertion of weft thread. On removal of card, all needles and hooks return to normal position. New card then brought forward and process repeated with different combination of warp threads raised. Jacquard mechanism may incorporate 100-1200 hooks and needles; several machines may be mounted on same loom.

Jacquemart, Henri-Alfred-Marie (1824-96). French *animalier* sculptor; first exhibit at Salon (1847), plaster model of heron. Contributed regularly until 1879; principal works include Tunisian Horse (1848), Watching Tiger (1851), Lion (1855), Menagerie Lion (1857), Prisoner Delivered up to the Beasts (1865), Dog-handler (1866), Camel-driver of Asia Minor (1877), Nubian Dromedary (1879), and some bronzes of domestic animals. Also supplied designs for *Christofle, e.g. decorations on Bull shrine, Vatican (Rome). Bronzes signed A-J or A Jacquemart. Public sculpture in Paris from c1858 includes two winged gryphons on St Michel fountain (1860-61), and rhinoceros on fountain in front of Trocadéro (c1862).

Jacquet-Droz family. Swiss family of watch and automaton makers established in Geneva from early 18th century, by Pierre Jacquet-Droz; son, Henri-Louis Jacquet-Droz (1752-1791), invented *singing bird musical box, also draughtsman automaton, which executed drawings in baroque style. Family produced ornate musical snuff boxes, singing bird boxes, *precision watches throughout 18th and 19th centuries; London premises from 1785.

Jahn, Louis (d 1911). Ceramic decorator, born in Thuringia. After working in Vienna, moved to Staffordshire, England. At Minton factory (1862-72), painted vases in Sèvres style, e.g. with cupids and child figures after Jean-Antoine Watteau. Art director for W. *Brownfield (1872-95) and at Minton factory (1895-1900). From 1900, curator of Hanley Museum.

jail carpets. First made in Indian prisons in 17th century. Industry promoted throughout India by British government in early 19th century; made in e.g. Agra, Lahore, Mirzapur, Bangalore, Vellore, and Jeroda (Poona). Some examples, e.g. from Agra and Jeroda, among finest carpets produced in 19th century India. Jail industry often blamed for decline of workmanship in late 19th century Indian carpets, though many businesses catering for rapidly expanding cheap export trade probably more to blame.
In 20th century, jail carpet industry introduced

in *Sparta, Turkey, and in Portuguese women's prisons.

Jallot, Léon (b 1874). French cabinet maker; progenitor of Art Deco. Director (1899-1901) of S. *Bing's Paris workshops; early pieces with fruit and animal relief decoration. Later, well-proportioned pieces made in polished oak, with uncluttered lines emphasized by high-quality veneers, e.g. tall, drop-front writing desk, c1914, with green leather lining, two drawers at top, ormolu feet, and projecting moulding emphasizing horizontal and vertical lines. Showed work at *Exposition Internationale des Arts Décoratifs*, Paris, 1925.

Janák, Pavel (b 1882). Czechoslovakian architect and ceramic designer. From 1909, designs decorated with geometrical motifs produced at Artěl workshops, Prague.

Japanese button. *See* manju netsuke.

Japanese horological industry. Japanese system of time measurement operated until adoption of Western method in 1873. Day and night each divided into 6 equal periods numbered 9 to 4, so that 9 stood for midnight and mid-day. Thus, as year proceeded, daylight 'hours' lengthened and night 'hours' became shorter. Japanese produced indigenous version of weight-driven lantern clock with foliot, c1700-1873, originally introduced by European traders. Has rectangular case, surmounted by deep bell secured with decorated nut; movement often with unique double escapement to accommodate differing length of day and night hours; after 1830, with free-standing corner pillars of turned brass and shallower bell; placed on conical stand, or table with cabriole legs. Two other distinct types of clock (with many interesting variants) made after c1830: spring-driven table clock with glazed sides and visible plates elaborately engraved or pierced; light, wooden glued case c8-9in. high, with carrying handle; moveable dial figures allow for change from day to night; movement with balance wheel and balance spring, rarely pendulum; distinctive striking work. Also, weight-driven pillar clock to be hung from central pillar of Japanese house. Has rectangular wooden case 1-4ft high; movement in glazed section at top of clock, plates decoratively engraved or pierced, with single foliot, balance wheel, or (rarely) pendulum. As weight moves down, attached pointer appears through slit in case front, indicating time on adjustable sliding scale of numerals on outside of case. Striking versions use spring-driven striking train as weight; during descent, train engages with pins set at numerals. All clocks with striking work mark hours and half hours according to Japanese striking sequence i.e. 9,1; 8,2; 7,1; 6,2; etc. Japanese precision watch industry founded 1873 by Seiko Watch—K. Hattori & Co., using American and Swiss methods of assembly line production (now world's largest manufacturer of high precision jewelled lever watches).

Japanese lacquer. *See* aogai, carved lacquer, dry lacquer, embedded lacquer, encrusted lacquer, fundame, hakeme, hirame, honji, jogahana, Kamakura-bori, kanagai, keiran-nuri, kinji, lacquer, makie, mokume, nashiji, negoro-nuri, raden, roiro-nuri, sabiji, same-nuri, zogan-nuri.

Japanese style. Furniture style popular in America c1870-c1885. Inspired by commercial contacts between Japan and America, Anglo-Japanese style, Japanese exhibits at Centennial Exhibition in Philadelphia, 1876, and designs of E.W. *Godwin. Typified by application of Japanese decoration to simple, rectilinear shapes broken up by mouldings, incised lines, marquetry panels, and large undecorated areas. Also applied to Anglo-Japanese style forms. Motifs include loosely composed marquetry designs of chrysanthemum-like flowers on stylized branches; pierced fretwork in skirts; polychrome tiles painted with Japanese bird and flower scenes. Manufacturers include *Herter Brothers.

Japanese swords. In Japan, weapons traditionally venerated and collected as works of art. Sword guards are *tsuba. Sword blades include some of finest Japanese metalwork, seen in unique construction, great subtleties of structure in surface of steel, and ways that these fit into shape of blade. Jihada, surface steel, has delicate pattern, sometimes like wood grain, from folding and welding of original steel; very many layers make up finished blade. Hamon, edge pattern, of hardened cutting edge appears as milky-white area along blade; its shape and width vary according to tradition of school and skill of swordsmith. 19th century swordsmiths, e.g. T. *Naotane, inherited set tradition. Blades of different lengths named tachi, tanto, katana, and wakizashi. Tsuka, or hilt, of wood with pommels at both ends; wrapped in raw silk and taped with silk, leather, cotton, or cord, held in place by kashira (hilt pommel). Classical tachi (slung sword) style developed by Goto Yujo (1435-1512): black fish roe ground (shakudo-nanako) with raised gilt borders and badges (*mon). Remained correct for court ceremonies until wearing of swords forbidden by national decree, 1876. Shin-shinto (very new sword) period of swordmaking was 1781-1868. Sword-making revived from 1926 (*see* showa-to).

japanned metalware. Black or tin-plated iron (occasionally other metal, e.g. copper), coated with lacquer, and decorated with motifs loosely drawn from oriental lacquerwork. Technique consists of applying lacquer, then firing in kiln; quality depends on number of coats and stovings. Quality improved during 19th century, when used on wide range of metal objects, e.g. purdonium, plant-stand, clock dial.

japanning or **japan work.** Wood, metal, or papier-mâché surfaces treated with paint and varnish to resemble lacquerwork, painted with coloured designs. Process dates from 17th century in Britain; also used in America. Early examples characterized by black background; scarlet, blue, yellow, or cream from c1700. Often applied to furniture. Up to 12 coats of spirit varnish used for high-quality pieces, oil for cheaper models. Each coat is allowed to dry, harden, and become transparent; final coat polished in expensive pieces. Term generally interchangeable with papier-mâché in Britain c1850.

japan patterns. European ceramic decoration adapted, notably, from brocade patterns, predominantly in dark underglaze blue with red enamel and gilding, found on Japanese porcelain exported from port of Imari (Arita) in 18th and

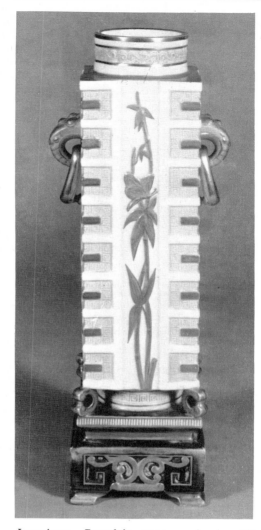

*Japonisme. Porcelain vase made by W. *Brownfield & Son and based on Yatsushiro ware. c1880. Height 10¾in.*

early 19th centuries. Fashion revived in England in 1850s. Used on porcelain made at Derby and Worcester factories and by firm of W. T. *Copeland. Also decorative feature of Mason's patent ironstone china.

japan work. *See* japanning.

Jap Birdimal. *See* Weller, Samuel A.

japonisme. Adoption of Japanese decorative styles, previously seen in use of *japan patterns, influenced design of European ceramics from 1860s. After displays of Japanese art and craftsmanship at Exhibitions in London (1862) and Paris (1867), styles and treatment rapidly adopted in England and France, possibly as reaction against traditions of classical design, since freedom from symmetrical arrangement of motifs and confinement of border patterns implied, and opportunity to leave expanses of background undecorated. Feature of aesthetic movement in England. Most primitive application consisted of use of Japanese motifs, roundels, prunus blossom, pine branches, birds, etc., on traditional European shapes. However, high standards of craftsmanship and imaginative

design, notable in Japanese work, inspired porcelain made at Worcester after Japanese models in ivory, lacquerwork, and metal; work of J. *Hadley includes vases with modelled figures of Japanese craftsmen. Bowls, tea ware, candlesticks, and pairs of vases produced with Japanese forms and decoration, sometimes using ivory porcelain body. Some Minton porcelain inspired by *cloisonné* enamelled ware. Japanese influence on work of W. S. *Coleman at factory and Minton's Art-Pottery Studio. At Doulton workshop, Lambeth, decorative styles e.g. of H. *Barlow, F. E. *Barlow, and M. V. *Marshall show study of Japanese styles. Incised designs of birds and foliage used in decoration by firm of C. H. *Brannam in 1880s and 1890s. Factory of W. *Brownfield produced gourd-shaped teapot with Japanese figure; table and ornamental work in stoneware or porcelain decorated with cranes, bamboo, butterflies, Japanese figures, and geometrical motifs, often also based on Japanese shapes. In 1880s, birds, bamboo, geometrical, and floral motifs painted on inkstands, vases, and tableware made in porcelain at Coalport. *Martin Brothers made vases with decoration e.g. of cranes and flowers, or geese and foliage; gourd shapes often used. Some work shows influence of J-C. *Cazin. Other examples seen in jugs produced by Pinder, Bourne & Co., vases of Japanese form made at Watcombe Pottery, and vases decorated with foliage, fruit, flowers, etc., made at Wedgewood factory. Designs and work of C. *Dresser influenced by travel in Japan. Japan, its Art, Architecture and Art Manufactures published in 1882. Unglazed earthenware plates, etc., with moulded decoration in Japanese styles made at Linthorpe Pottery.

In France, Japanese influence seen in work of F. *Bracquemond and E. *Escallier in 1860s, followed in 1870s by A. *Dammouse. T. *Deck worked in Japanese style, e.g. plate painted in enamel with large flowers against floral diapered ground, shown in Universal Exhibition in Paris (1878), although influenced more by *oriental glazes than by decorative elements that affected his artists. Cazin, among potters influenced by Japanese style, made relief decorated stoneware before teaching in London (in 1870s). Work of A. *Dalpayrat and T. *Doat show elements of transition from Japanese to Art Nouveau style.

Reorganization at Royal Copenhagen porcelain factory, following union with Aluminia factory under direction of P. *Schou, included introduction of oriental and particularly Japanese treatment of European scenes in underglaze painting by artists led by A. *Krog. Work also affected by oriental glazes. Pupil of Krog, F. A. *Hallin, introduced similar work at Bing & Grøndahl factory.

In America, Japanese display at Philadelphia Centennial Exhibition (1876) inspired asymmetrical flower decoration in coloured slips, and figured grounds and glazes used at Rookwood pottery; widely imitated by American art potteries. *See also* Anglo-Japanese style, Japanese style.

Japy Frères. In 19th century, largest French manufacturer of *drum clocks, machine-made brass movements (*rouages*) and watches. Company established *c*1770 by Frédéric Japy (1749-1812), at Beaucourt, in French Jura mountains. Business continued by sons, Fritz, Louis, and Pierre; over 6 million movements manufactured 1810-88, all sent to Paris clock finishers. Made complete clocks from 1889, in response to

Japy Frères. Mantel clock with ormolu case and white enamel dial. c1860. Height 18½in.

competition from mass-produced *Black Forest clocks. Products stamped JAPY.

jardinière. Metal, earthenware, or carved wooden support for cut flowers or house plants; elaboration of *flower stand, dating from early 19th century in Britain and America. Became increasingly ornate, e.g. examples incorporating aviaries from *c*1830. Also pedestal models with elaborate carving, of birds, flowers, plants etc. around base. *See also* art pot stand.

jargon or **jargoon.** *See* zircon.

Jarves, Deming (1790-1869). American glassmaker from Boston, Massachusetts; founded *New England Glass Co., 1818. Left to establish *Boston & Sandwich Glass Co., 1826; also founded *Mount Washington Glass Works (1837), where encouraged production of high-quality mould-blown glass, and Cape Cod Glass Co. (1858). Credited with inventing American glass-pressing machine (which he disclaimed); also said to have made first pressed drinking glass. Revolutionized world glassmaking with pressed ware of fine quality lead glass.

Jarvie, Robert R. (1865-1940). Metalworker and silversmith in American Arts & Crafts movement. From 1905, ran Jarvie Shop, known for its copper and brass candlesticks. After 1912, designed and made number of silver trophies awarded at cattle shows in and around Chicago. Mark: Jarvie (in script on brass and copper).

Jarvis, A. Wickham (fl 1900s). English architect; also designed furniture. Member of *Arts & Crafts Exhibition Society. Furniture character-

ized by simple form, joined construction, architectural proportions, and straight lines contrasting with restrained ornament. Examples include walnut armchair with tall, straight-splatted back, closed arms with flat arm rest, upholstered seat; stylized floral motifs on arms and deep yoke rail. Shown by Arts & Crafts Exhibition Society, 1896.

jasper ware. Hard, unglazed stoneware perfected *c*1774 by Josiah Wedgwood and associated with Wedgwood firm. White body stained throughout (solid jasper), or coated with colour wash (jasper dip). Production of solid jasper lapsed; revived in 1856. Usually decorated with motifs moulded in white jasper body applied to coloured surface. Designs normally in classical style, although jugs and vases with all-over designs of plants, displayed at Exhibitions in London (1851) and Paris (1855), made until *c*1860. *Illustration at* claret jug.

Jaulmes, Gustave (1873-1959). French painter and designer of furniture, tapestries, etc.; studied architecture. Exhibited regularly from 1910, designing Art Deco furniture characterized by fine woods and logical construction. Designed Sèvres pavilion for Exposition Internationale des Arts Dècoratifs, Paris, 1925; decorated

Paul Jeanneney. Stoneware bowl with lid of turned ivory. Exhibited at Paris Exhibition, 1900. Height 5¾in.

Musée des Arts Dècoratifs with E. *Ruhlmann in same year. Associate of l'Atelier Français (*see* Süe et Mare). Examples include rectangular fire screen, *c*1919: lacquered framework, with oval tapestry panels depicting wreaths of fruit.

Jazz Modern style. Loose term for furniture style popular in Britain, France, and America during 1930s. Cubist and geometrical forms emphasized by strongly patterned wood veneers, e.g. by S. *Chermayeff: also depictions of contemporary scenes and fashions, e.g. Cubist representation of negro jazz band.

Jeanneney, Paul (fl late 19th, early 20th centuries). French artist potter; pupil of J. *Carriès. Stoneware, influenced by Japanese styles, includes spherical vase; brownish body covered with blue-tinged white crackle glaze. Work bears incised signature on base.

Jeanneret, Charles-Edouard. *See* Le Corbusier.

Jeannest, Pierre-Emile (1813-1857). French ceramic and silver designer working in England; son of sculptor Louis-François Jeannest; produced designs for *Mintons, *c*1845-1852; joined *Elkington & Co. *c*1850. First work for Elkington, silver group of Queen Elizabeth I entering Kenilworth Castle, shown at Great Exhibition, London, 1851; appointed supervisor of Elkington's French workers in 1853, 'with liberty to design for others of dissimilar trades', i.e.

*Pierre-Emile Jeannest. *Parian and glazed porcelain vase, painted and gilded. Made by *Mintons, c1954.*

ceramic manufacturers. Contemporaries attributed much of Elkington's success to Jeannest's designs, and admired his versatility and attention to detail in figure modelling.

Jeanselme, Charles-Joseph-Marie (b 1827). French cabinet maker and upholsterer. Made high-quality cabinets, also companion chairs, etc. Active until 1870.

Jekyll, Thomas (1827-81). English architect; also designed furniture, metalwork, and embroidery. Began as architect working in Japanese style, influenced by Japanese art at 1867 Paris exhibition; became associated with Aesthetic movement. Decorated several houses in Japanese taste, e.g. Peacock Room in Frederick Leyland's house, *c*1867; designed cast iron pavilion in Japanese style for *Barnard, Bishop & Barnard; displayed at Philadelphia Centennial Exhibition in 1876; subsequently adapted elements of pavilion, notably sunflower motif, in designs for cast ironwork, including fire surrounds (some in cast brass), stoves, *grates, and *firedogs; with numerous other designs, produced for many years by Barnard, Bishop & Barnard. Furniture closely based on Japanese originals; characterized by asymmetrical top drawers in desks, lattices behind turned front columns, moulded decoration, and oriental brackets; examples include bookcase and whatnot in ebonized wood, with carved, incised, and moulded decoration; panels of mirror glass, porcelain plaque painted with flowers and birds. *Illustration at* Barnard, Bishop & Barnard.

Jelliff, John (1813-90). American cabinet maker in Newark, New Jersey. Made furniture in

John Jelliff. Gothic side-chair designed by Mary Peshine. Rosewood. c1855. Height 4ft 10in.

Right
Jenny Lind bottle. Quart capacity in aquamarine glass. Possibly made at Isabella Glass Works, New Brooklyn. c1855.

Gothic, rococo, and Louis XVI revival styles. Also known for Renaissance revival style armchairs in rosewood, with trumpet-shaped legs and broad, button-upholstered seats. In 1870s, made small parlour tables with intricate marquetry decoration on tops.

jelly mould. *See* dessert mould.

Jennens & Bettridge. English manufacturers of papier-mâché furniture; took over factory of Henry Clay. Active 1816–64 in Birmingham. Showed tables, chairs (e.g. *Day Dreamer chair), tea trays, etc. at Great Exhibition of 1851. Also made cabinets, bookcases, pianos, and bedsteads. Name stamped on reverse and underside of most pieces; exhibited as Bettridge & Co. (after death of Jennens) at International Exhibition of 1862, London.

Jenny Lind bottle. American whiskey flask decorated with commemorative portrait of the Swedish singer. Made in wide variety of sizes and colours during late 1850s.

Jenny Lind furniture. *See* spool-turned furniture.

Jensen, Georg (1866–1935). Danish silversmith, sculptor and potter; apprenticed to goldsmith;

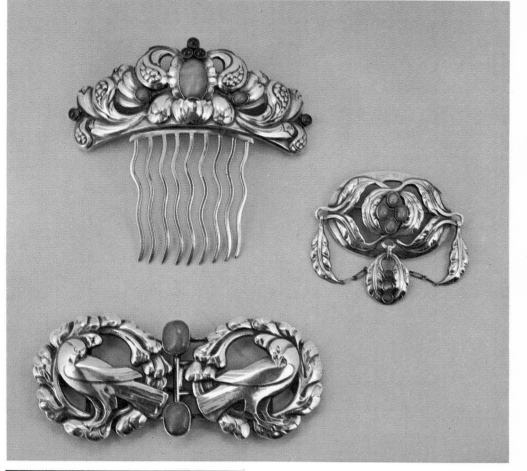

Georg Jensen. Jewellery designed in 1906. Left: brooch (no 26). Above: comb (no 52). Below: buckle (no 8). All in sterling silver set with amber and green onyx.

studied under Mogens Ballin, and at Copenhagen Royal Academy; exhibited first silver piece in 1892; visited France and Italy; won honourable mention for ceramics shown in Danish pavilion at Paris Exhibition in 1900; on his return opened unsuccessful porcelain factory with Joachim Peterson; joined Ballin as foreman of jewellery concern in 1901. Opened own workshop in Copenhagen in 1904; first exhibition of silver in 1905; began collaboration with painter J. *Rhode, 1907; opened shop in Berlin in 1908, producing mainly silver pieces, e.g. handhammered coffee pots and milk jugs; received international recognition after gaining gold medal at Brussels International Exhibition in 1910; expanded activities, employing craftsmen including Inger Møller and Mrs Just Andersen. Limited company formed in 1916; designers included G. *Albertus and H. *Nielsen; marketed Nielsen's Pyramid cutlery. Opened shops in Paris (1919), London (1920), and Stockholm (1930); Jensen shop opened in New York, 1920, by Jost Lunning. Created market for high quality, mass-produced silver jewellery, characterized by heavy style, and set with amber and semi-precious stones. Firm acquired in 1922 by initial commercial backers, Hostrup-Pedersen family. Mark: JENSEN. *Illustration at* opal.

Jerndahl, Aaron (1858–1936). Swedish metal-worker; work in Swedish Jugendstil includes The Dance (1903), and pewter bowl of undulating form with sinuous motifs.

Jerome, Chauncey (1793–1868). American; pioneer of New England clock export industry. In 1842, exported first consignment of factory-made *OG clocks to England. Rectangular wooden cases (*c*26 × 15in.), painted glass tablet in door, weights enclosed so that clock may be stood on table or hung on wall. Within five years, trade extended throughout Europe, outselling cheap *Black Forest wall clocks.

jet. Form of fossilized wood (i.e. variety of coal) found in bituminous shale, particularly at Whitby, Yorkshire. Mass production of jet jewellery introduced in Whitby, 1826; grew in popularity in 1850s. Only jewellery allowed at English court during periods of mourning. Widely worn throughout England following death of Prince Consort (1861). Popular in 1880s, when coloured stones out of fashion. Carved, engraved, or faceted for pendants, brooches, necklaces, earrings, and bracelets. Outstanding craftsmen included E. H. Greenbury, Isaac Greenbury, H. Barraclough, W. H. Crane, Thomas Jose, T. Kraggs, and W. Lund, who initialled work. *See* French jet.

jewelled bearings (in watches). Watch has bearing surfaces, e.g. pallets, arbors, made from hard gemstones to minimize wear. From late 18th century, ruby, sapphire, and garnet used; later, synthetic substitutes. 'Fully jewelled' movement has minimum of 15 jewels.

jihada. *See* Japanese swords.

jinchu-yatate. *See* yatate.

Joachim, Christian Hans (b 1870). Danish artist and ceramic decorator. Studied painting in Copenhagen; portraits exhibited from 1893. Art director (from 1915) at Aluminia and Royal Copenhagen Porcelain Factory. Underglaze painting includes earthenware plate with design of pair of birds and broad decoration at rim. Noted for lively style and rich colours.

Joel, Betty (b 1896). English furniture designer; with husband David Joel, founded firm Betty Joel Ltd., *c*1919. Designed simple, functional pieces for smaller houses. Often used teak and oak, also Empire woods, e.g. Queensland walnut; Indian laurel, silverwood, and greywood; *macassar ebony for edging plinths, handles. Designed bed with curved headboard sloping to form circular bedside pedestals, *c*1930; shown at Exhibition of British Industrial Art, 1933. Designed unit furniture for G *Russell in 1934. Retired in 1937. Firm's pieces bear date and signature of designer and craftsman on card fixed behind glass.

jogahana or **gohana.** Japanese lacquer painting technique attributed to 15th century Jogahana lacquer artist. Painting done with coloured lacquers mixed with oil; green, white, red, and brown used from 15th century, gold from 18th. Used to decorate lacquerware and miniature shrines as well as paintings.

Johnstone & Jeanes. London cabinet makers (formerly Johnstone, Jupe & Co., 1835–38);

active 1842–*c*1880 and 1880–1900, as Johnstone & Norman. Known for simply styled satinwood and walnut cabinets in 1860s, e.g. walnut cabinet with quarter-circle curves each side of square, central section, and stylized flat-patterned inlay decoration. Made furniture designed by L. *Alma-Tadema, 1884; supplied furniture for Windsor Castle, 1889. Stamp: Johnstone and Jeanes.

joint handle or **leg-of-mutton holder.** Carving accessory introduced in early 19th century and popular in Britain and America to *c*1890; consists of ivory handle and silver tube, attached by thumbscrew to bone in joint of meat.

Jones, A.E. English silversmiths in Birmingham developed by A. Edward Jones (1879–1954) from family firm of blacksmiths in 1902; Jones was active in Arts & Crafts movement, and friend and collaborator of Howson Taylor of Ruskin Pottery. Bought trade mark of St Dunstan, patron saint of silversmiths, from L. *Rathbone, 1905. Products include water jugs, caskets, tea sets, candlesticks, and tobacco boxes, often hammered and hand-raised to high standard.

Owen Jones. Dressing table designed for Eynsham Hall, Oxfordshire. c1873.

Company still in existence, re-organized in 1950s after wartime difficulties.

Jones, George (d 1893). Staffordshire potter; worked at Minton factory. Established Trent Pottery (1861) at Stoke-on-Trent, trading from 1873 as George Jones & Sons. As well as white and transfer-printed earthenware for domestic use, made majolica (exhibited from 1867); also candelabra, table centrepieces, shell-shaped flower vases, etc., in Palissy ware. Ornamental earthenware with *pâte-sur-pâte* decoration (from 1872) includes wall pockets, and vase with modelled figures and gilded relief decoration. From 1876, made porcelain, e.g. flower holders in form of baskets, or curled water-lily leaf with modelled stems and flowers, covered with white and celadon glazes. Vases with coloured earthenware body introduced *c*1880, with painted decoration and gilt relief. Marks: initials, GJ, impressed or painted, later enclosed by crescent bearing & SONS (factory renamed Crescent Pottery in 1907).

Jones, Owen (1809–74). English architect, designer, and illustrator; influential theorist of principles of ornamental design; after visit to Islamic palace in Granada, Spain, in 1834, published illustrated book, 'Plans, Elevations,

Sections and Details of the Alhambra' (1842–45), radical in subject matter of non-classical ornament and architecture, and in emphasis on mathematical structure of Islamic design. Superintendent of Works at Great Exhibition, London, 1851; in series of publications, e.g. 'Grammar of Ornament' (1856, with M. D. *Wyatt), and 'Examples of Chinese Ornament' (1860), prescribed that ornament should be based on geometry; with Henry Warren, designed and illustrated 'Paradise and the Peri', published 1860, in Near Eastern manner. Influence extended through Victorian Gothic, exotic, and utilitarian styles (e.g. Arts and Crafts movement), and abroad to J. *Hoffman and *Vienna Secession, where theories of Jones and W. *Crane turned Austrian Jugendstil to more rigorous formalism. In own work, furniture characterized by naturalistic floral and foliate wood inlays in formal flat patterns; designed Egyptian, Greek, Roman, and Alhambra Courts in Crystal Palace on its move from Hyde Park to Sydenham; designed range of oriental furnishings for *Jackson & Graham, 1874. *Illustration at* Hancock, C. F.

Joso, Miyazaki (1855–1910). Japanese sculptor and netsuke artist of Tokyo. Specialized in small carved objects, e.g. netsuke, kiseru-zutsu,

okimono. Style closely based on that of teacher, Y. *Hojitsu. Member of Japan Art Association; founding member and examiner of Tokyo Carvers' Association; received numerous commissions and honours from *Meiji Imperial household. Pupils included M. *Soko and O. *Gyokuso. *Na: Seitaro. *Kaimyo: Shakufugaku Senshu Shenshi. *Chomei: Joso.

Jourdain, Francis (1876–1958). French designer, formerly painter. From c1912, made glazed earthenware thrown in austere shapes, with simple geometrical decoration in coloured slips, e.g. bottle with bands and rectangles of trailed slip in white, ochre, and blue on black ground, and large dish with blue circles on red ground, covered with yellow glaze; both date from early 1920s. Work initialled in slip on base.

Joyce, Richard (d 1931). English pottery decorator and designer. At first, worked at Bretby Art Pottery in Derbyshire. From 1905, at Pilkington Tile and Pottery Co. in Lancashire, carried out painted and relief decoration, also

*Jugendstil. Chest of drawers designed by J. *Hoffmann and made by M. & W. Niedermoser. Boxwood inlaid with ebony and mother-of-pearl, 1910–14.*

characterized by neo-rococo elements of French of animal and fish motifs. Painted vases designed by W. *Crane, shown in Franco-British Exhibition (1908), e.g. with draped figures holding garlands against green ground, alternating with torches in silver lustre with deep red fires. Also modelled pair of vases designed by G. M. *Forsyth depicting St George and the Dragon.

jubako (Japanese, 'tiered boxes'). Large, usually square, Japanese lacquer box used for storing mainly foodstuffs and household accessories. Usually composed of several (two to four) tiers of separate shallow cases; form an adaptation of basic *inro design, in vogue since early 19th century. Produced in large numbers both for domestic use and for export market.

Jugendstil. General term for German and Austrian design in Art Nouveau style 1896–c1900, named after theoretical magazine, Jugend, published in Munich from 1896 with contributions from O. *Eckmann. Style, as seen in work of artists of Munich school, initially characterised by neo-rococo elements of French Art Nouveau, e.g. languid, writhing line metamorphosed into stylized flowers or figures, later (after c1902 e.g. at Darmstadt) featured more geometrical style derived from work of C. R. *Mackintosh.

jukogo. Miniature Japanese lacquer-covered incense container ($c2\frac{1}{2} \times 4 \times 3$in.), similar to *kojubako, but with interior divided into three sections and fitted with boxes to hold talc squares, incense packets, and ashes.

jumping dial. Digital recording dial for clocks and watches: hour and minute numerals 'jump' into view through small apertures in dial plate. Popular from 19th century.

jump-up. *See* chair-table.

Junghans, Erhard (d 1870). German clockmaker; with brother, Xavier, transformed family straw-hat business into Junghanssche Uhrenfabrik, Schramberg, in southern Germany (1861), employing American techniques by mass-production. Developed German factory-made clock industry, starting with imitations of American movements and cases. Firm continues.

Jurojin. One of Japanese *Shichi-fuku-jin; god of longevity and wisdom. Characterization closely resembles that of *Fukurokuju, but more dignified and solemn. Often shown wearing small hat with emblem of sun. Carries fan and staff with ancient scrolls. Often accompanied by deer. Messenger usually dove.

Juster, Joe (fl late 19th, early 20th centuries). English pottery decorator, employed by W. *De Morgan. Initialled work.

kagamibuta (Japanese, 'mirror-lid') **netsuke,** or **kanabuta netsuke.** One of three basic forms of *netsuke. Shallow, usually plain bowl ($c1\frac{1}{2}$in. diameter) of ivory, wood, horn, or bone; fitted with ornamental metal (or very rarely ceramic) disc. *Sagemono or inro cords passed through small hole in bottom of bowl and attached to eyelet on inside of lid. Made from late 17th century; huge numbers produced since 1860s, at first to meet domestic demand created by 1854

Edo earthquake, then primarily for export trade. Late 19th century and early 20th century discs often executed by famous metalwork artists. mainly in gold, silver, or copper alloys, with elaborate designs engraved, embossed, carved, or encrusted in high or low relief. Referred to as kanabuta netsuke only in Kyoto and Osaka.

Kåge, Wilhelm (1889–1960). Swedish ceramic artist. Trained as painter in Sweden, Denmark, and Germany. Associated with movement to improve design of articles in everyday use. Joined Gustavsberg factory in 1917; later art director (until 1949). Designed tableware with flowered rims, and oven-proof pottery, e.g. with single central flower, fluted sides and lids, and curved decoration at rim. Ornamental ware includes sculptural stoneware, and dishes or vases with green glaze and nude figures or merfolk in silver lustre. Devised wavy shapes of Soft forms service (1940) and designed earthenware vases, etc., fired at high temperature with figured glazes.

Kähler Ceramics. Danish pottery established 1839 at Naestved, Seeland; at first made earthenware stoves. Herman A. Kähler inherited pottery in 1872; later introduced lustre decoration, painted in designs of flowers, etc., on earthenware vases. Herman J. Kähler (b 1904) glazed and fired salt-glazed stoneware bowls and jars, designed by brother Nils A. Kähler (b 1906), sometimes with sketchy brushed decoration, e.g. of figures and landscape. Pottery still in production; stoneware made for architectural use.

Kaigyokusai, Kwaigyokusai, or **Masatsuga** (1813–92). Self-taught Japanese master ivory and wood carver of Osaka. Made mainly *okimono and *netsuke, but also *ojime, *inro and *kiseruzutsu. 70–80% of carvings exported to West. Early works executed in simple, strong styles of old masters; later used highly individual style. Favourite designs small animals and insects, executed in finest materials from numerous life-drawings, with scrupulous attention to details (e.g. fine hair-lines for hairs, realistic-looking inlays for eyes, noses, claws), and given fine polish and finish. Representation deft and sensitive, both anatomically correct and animated. Exerted profound influence on later artists in both Osaka and Tokyo; styles and designs widely copied. *Go: until aged 20, Masatsugu; until 30, Kaigyokudo; until 50, Kaigyoku; then Kaigyokusai. *Kaimyo: Takuo Kaigyoku Zenjoman.

Kaimyo or **Homyo.** Posthumous name conferred by Japanese Buddhist priests on followers and inscribed on their funeral tablets.

Kajikawa. Large family of outstanding Japanese lacquer artists, established early 17th century by heads of upper-class families as legal many lacquered netsuke. Work extremely detailed and meticulously executed in wide range of techniques; distinguished by excellent gold lacquerwork, particularly *gyobu, on linings of inro. From early 19th century, inro increasingly ornate, often executed in conjunction with *Shibayama artists; joint works elaborately encrusted with metal or mother-of-pearl on gold lacquer grounds. Kajikawa artists generally signed works only with family name and seal: small red vase, or two-handled, two-footed perfume bottle.

Kakiemon ware. Japanese porcelain with delicate enamelled decoration made at Nangawara kiln, Arita, by line of potters established by Sakaida Kakiemon I (1596–1666). High quality copies of early work made by present Kakiemon (13th generation). Some industrial copies made by companies, notably in same province.

kakihan or **kao** (Japanese, 'written seal'). Simple, Japanese calligraphic mark, comparable to Western monogram or initials. First used in 17th century by heads of upperclass families as legal identification on documents. In Japanese decorative arts, adopted by heads of art families as part of identification on various works. Art family kakihan passed down from master to best pupil; sometimes also used by other pupils in deference to master, or simply forged. By 19th century, kakihan of individual artists often seen. Both types found on metalwork, lacquer, netsuke and ceramics, either as sole identification or after *Chomei. Characters derived from family name, artist's first name, or Chomei; often forming rebus of all or part of any one of them.

kaku netsuke. *See* hako netsuke.

Kalo Shops, The. American silversmiths founded in 1900 by Clara Barck Welles at Park Ridge, Illinois, with sale rooms on Michigan Avenue and Adams Street, Chicago; moved to Chicago Fine Arts Building, 1918; closed 1970 on deaths of silversmiths Daniel Penderson and Yngre Olsson. Produced silverware of simple design and fine finish.

Kamakura-bori, Echizen-bori, Odawara-bori, or **Yoshino-bori.** Japanese lacquer imitation of *carved lacquer. Developed in 13th century. In disuse from 16th to 18th centuries; revived in 19th century. Most often used on small objects, particularly sword-stands and dagger scabbards. Wood core (usually gingko, ho, or katsura) carved in low relief, then covered with numerous layers of coloured lacquer (at first red and black, later additional colours), ending with red. Patches of coloured underlying layers gradually revealed as surface rubbed down with use. Designs mainly stylized floral patterns, particularly peonies and plum blossom, on diapered ground. Names of technique taken from centres of production.

kanabuta netsuke. *See* kagamibuta netsuke.

kanagai (Japanese, 'gold shell' or 'metal foil') or **kani-gai.** Japanese lacquer technique: pieces of metal foil (mainly gold or silver) cut and embedded as design in soft lacquer ground. Varieties include *kirigane and *heidatsu. Also hyomon: pre-cut designs in sheet gold or silver applied to lacquer ground and covered with layers of ground-colour lacquer; surface then rubbed down to reveal foil design.

Kandern Pottery. *See* Läuger, Max.

Kaneije style. *See* tsuba.

kangaroo sofa. Small reclining sofa with high, scrolled and curved back; lower curve elevating legs and feet. Dates from c1830 in America; popular during mid 19th century. Anticipates *Le Corbusier's *chaise longue*.

kani-gai. *See* kanagai.

Kanishege, Toyo (fl 20th century). Japanese potter working at Bizen, near Okayama. Vases, bowls, jars, plates, etc., made with local clay, in traditional styles of region.

Kano, Mitsuo (fl 20th century). Japanese potter of Showa period (from 1926). Angular pottery vases, etc., decorated with vertical and spiral ribbed lines.

kanshitsu. *See* dry lacquer.

Kansu rugs. *See* East Turkestan.

kao. *See* kakihan.

Kaolin. *See* Southern Porcelain Co.

Karabagh rugs. *See* Caucasian carpets.

Karaja rugs. Persian. Runners and small rugs; 19th century design similar to traditional Herez carpets but more geometrical, with shorter pile. *See* Persian carpets.

Karhula Iittala. Finnish glasshouse founded 1881 for manufacture of cheap household items. More ambitious work from 1930s. Now one of world's major centres for artistic glass production.

karrusel (Swedish, 'merry-go-round') **watch** Precision movement, designed 1894 in Coventry, Warwickshire, by Swede, Bahne Bonniksen; reduces positional errors, accurate to within one second per day. Essentially, more compact version of *tourbillon movement; has fourth wheel of train mounted on cage carrying complete escapement, which revolves continuously about once every 52½ minutes. Produced in response to high-quality Swiss factory-made watches.

Karvel machine. Makes carpets directly from carded wool, eliminating spinning and weaving. Invented c1930 in America; world patent (excluding America) obtained by *Crossley of Halifax, who installed machine in 1931. Wool or other fibre dyed, carded, treated to form 'bat' of required thickness, folded into trough, and pressed by large rotating drum with sharply grooved surface to create corded effect on bat. Spray guns spread rubber solution on side of bat pressed in grooves, while heated presses bond hessian, coated with strong adhesive, to other. Bat comes away covered with looped pile of wool or fibre, resembling plain Brussels carpet. Cut pile also produced, by shearing at end of process. Similar machines patented in Australia, Holland, France, and Switzerland.

Kasaoka. Japanese pottery centre in Okayama prefecture. Vases, plates, and tea ware made at kiln operating from 1907 to present day, following traditional styles of region.

kashi-bako. *See* kashiki.

kashiki or **kashi-bako** (Japanese, 'sweetmeat box'). Small Japanese lacquer sweetmeat box (c6×4×4in.). Many shapes: mainly rectangular, square, or circular, but also quatrefoil, oval, cylindrical, or hexagonal, kidney or fan shaped, etc. Some composed of two intersecting or tiered

boxes, some fitted with tray. Decorated in numerous techniques, mainly on gold or black-and-gold grounds. Peak production, 19th and 20th centuries.

kashira. See Japanese swords and sword furniture.

Kashiwaya, Buhei. See Mokuhaku.

Kashmir carpets. Carpet industry, established by Prince Shahi Khan in mid 15th century, ceased c1750, when Khani shawl weaving became most important industry. When overseas demand for shawls fell in mid 19th century, redundant weavers diverted to carpet making. Talim method of pattern notation adopted from shawl weaving. New industry stimulated by European manufacturers, e.g. *Mitchell & Co., *East India Carpet Co. Carpets shown at Chicago World Fair (1893); by 1900, export market was developing in America, Canada, and Britain. Numerous copies of famous 15th and 16th century Turkish and Persian carpets (e.g. Ardebil Vase Carpet) produced. Also local specialities: chainstitch carpets in very fine wool, decorated with intricate flower and animal motifs, and *gabba rugs. Industry prospered until 1930s, when badly affected by Depression and competition from machine-made carpets. Situation critical until 1935, when state subsidy aided gradual recovery. *Srinagar chief centre of production.

katabori (Japanese, 'figure-carved') **netsuke.** Most popular of three basic *netsuke forms; miniature sculptured figures. Subject range enormous, includes variety of gods (e.g. *Shichi-fuku-jin), demons, humans, birds, animals, insects, fish. From early 19th century, secular and animal subjects most popular, usually realistically carved with designs often drawn from sketches of popular artists, particularly Hokusai. Category includes miniature dolls (*ningyo netsuke) and various miniature masks: favourite subjects, goddess Ofuku, Bukgaka, and Noh and Kyogen drama characters. During Meiji and Taisho periods, katabori netsuke often carved as models for fashionable *okimono.

katakiri-bori (Japanese, 'side-cut engraving'). Japanese carved lacquer technique imitating varying thicknesses of brush-drawn lines (cf chinkin-bori). Often found with contrasting *kebori technique.

katana. See Japanese swords.

Kato, Hajime, and family (fl 20th century). Japanese potters working in Seto district. Early work in traditional local styles: Shino, Oribe, yellow Seto, etc.; recent experiments with brushed decoration under modern influences.

Kawai, Kanjiro (b 1890). Japanese potter; associated with S. *Hamada in formation of Japanese craft movement (1929). Noted for wide range of high-quality glazes used, e.g. Chinese-inspired temmoku or celadon. Stoneware often moulded or hand built. In 1930s, made jars and vases in soft grey, brown, or blue, with firmly brushed designs. Relief decoration also used under glaze.

Kawamoto, Goro (fl 20th century). Japanese potter of Showa period (from 1926). Work includes dried flower holders: hand-built

Kayser Sohn. Pewter tea service with relief decoration, designed by Hugo Leven, 1900. Mark, Kayserzinn, 4515, in raised letters within raised circle.
Right
Kelim. Showing detail of weave. Caucasian. Late 19th century.

earthenware boxes with top perforated by square hole.

Kawamoto, Hansuke, and Masukichi (fl late 19th century). Japanese potters working in Owari province. Hansuke noted for Banko ware. Masukichi decorated large plaques with landscapes, birds, etc., exhibited in Vienna (1873). Also made blue-and-white porcelain tableware, vases, slabs, etc., painted with flowers, insects, fish, figures, etc.

Kayseri (central Anatolia), Turkey. Carpets produced in large quantities for export in late 19th century. Made of silk or jap silk, usually imitating old Turkish or Persian patterns.

Kayser Sohn. German metalwork firm, founded 1885 at Krefeld-Bochum, near Düsseldorf, by Jean Kayser (1840–1911). From 1896, manufactured pewter objects in Jugendstil (e.g. ashtrays, dishes, lamps, beakers, vases) known as Kayserzinnwaren ('Kayser pewter wares'); designed by H. *Leven and sold at Atelier Englebert Kayser, Cologne. Pieces usually decorated with flowing floral motifs, etc. Many examples in Berlin museums. Marks: KAYSERZINN, with number above and below, or with number in oval or round stamp.

kebori (Japanese, 'hair-carving'). Japanese *carved lacquer technique, similar to *chinkin-bori, but more deeply-carved and without gold infilling of sculptured designs. Often used with contrasting katakiri-bori.

keeper ring. Wide gold ring, so called because worn above wedding ring. Usually covered with engraved designs of hearts, flowers, or ivy; sometimes with word *Mizpah, carved in relief. Introduced c1830; popularity continued throughout 19th century.

keiran-nuri or **tamago-ji** (Japanese, 'chicken-egg lacquer'). Japanese eggshell lacquer. pressed on to prepared lacquer base and broken; after five or six day drying period, surface painted over with *sabi until eggshell covered; after second drying period, surface lightly polished until shell reappears. Technique rarely used in modern period until 1920s, then increasingly popular through 1930s for decorating wide variety of small lacquered objects.

kelim. Reversible tapestry-weave carpet woven by particular technique. Weft thread of given colour worked to and fro in own area of pattern; next colour continues pattern from adjacent warp thread, so that no weft thread runs across full width of piece. Resulting slits (between differently coloured areas of pattern) reduced to minimum by indenting outlines of design.

Kendall, Thomas (1837–1919). English furniture designer and manufacturer; member of

*Warwick school of carving. Known for sideboards; also made elaborately carved fire screens, loo tables, chairs, etc., c1850-c1870. Founded Kendalls of Chapel Street, Warwick; firm continued at same address until his death.

Kendrick, George P. (fl late 19th, early 20th centuries). American potter. In 1890s, designed art pottery made by company of W. H. *Grueby; also director of company. Left 1901.

Kent & Parr. Staffordshire potters working at Burslem c1880-94; made earthenware figures, hens on nests, dogs, etc. From c1894, traded as William Kent, and after 1st World War as William Kent (Porcelain) Ltd, using original moulds. (Production ceased in 1962.)

Kenton & Company. Association of furniture designers and makers in Bloomsbury, London.

Formed 1890 by S. *Barnsley, R. *Bloomfield, E. W. *Gimson, W. R. *Lethaby, and M. *Macartney. Precursor of Cotswold school. Furniture made under supervision of designer, sometimes stamped with initials of designer and craftsman. Held successful exhibition at Barnard's Inn, London, 1891, but bankrupt 1892.

Kenya, Miura (1820-99). Japanese potter, nephew of Kenzan V, Myakuan Nishimura (d 1853); worked in Kenzan tradition. Also made beads, and small decorative objects in form of flowers, grass, insects, etc., in close imitation of 17th century originals. In Kenzan line of succession, but allowed title to pass to *Kenzan VI, Ogata Shigekichi.

Kenzan VI or **Shigekichi,** Ogata (fl mid 19th century). Japanese potter; in 1853, inherited title of 6th descendant of Kyoto potter, Kenzan I

(1663-1743). Taught techniques of raku and stoneware to B. *Leach in Tokyo (1911-12), later choosing Leach and K. *Tomimoto as joint successors.

Kernan. See Kirman.

Kerr, william B. & Co. American goldsmiths, silversmiths, and jewellers. Established 1885 in Newark, New Jersey, by William Kerr. Specialized in silver tableware, silver and gold toilet articles, and silver jewellery. Silver jewellery mass-produced by stamping process to imitate *repoussé work. Much influenced by French Art Nouveau jewellery of c1900: designs lifted from continental periodicals, e.g. *Die Perle* and *Le Bijou,* illustrated with line blocks which gave no idea of colour and stones employed in original pieces; designs were reproduced entirely in silver. Firm bought by *Gorham Corporation in 1906; moved to Providence, Rhode Island, 1927.

Kerr & Binns. See Worcester.

Keswick School of Industrial Art (Keswick, Westmorland). Founded as evening institute in 1884; daytime classes begun in 1898 with appointment of full-time director; produced small objects e.g. coffee spoons, rose bowls, and tea caddies, in hammered silver and copper, sold through Home Arts and Industry Association, and Rural Industries Co-operation Society. Mark: KSIA.

Kettle, Edgar (fl late 19th century). English pottery decorator. Relief designs incised on stoneware vases and jugs at Fulham pottery of C. J. C. *Bailey in 1870s, marked with monogram of E.K.

Left
Kenton & Co. Cabinet on ebony stand. Designed by E. *Gimson. Decorated in palm, ebony, and orangewood marquetry. Silver handles hallmarked 1891. Height 4ft 7in.

Below
William B. Kerr & Co. Silver cigarette case embossed with mermaid chasing lobster. c1909.

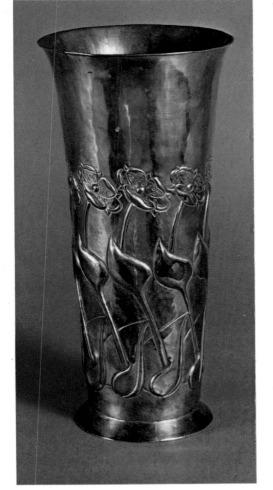

Keswick School of Industrial Art. Copper vase with repoussé *decoration. c1900.*

Kewblas. American art glass made by *Union Glass Co. in 1890s. Vessels composed of two layers, usually clear and *milk glass with coloured surface design (usually abstract leaf or feather pattern); dishes and tazzas have design on interior. Not unlike some *Tiffany glass, by which influenced.

Kew Certificate. Performance certificate awarded in England to timepieces successfully tested over wide range of position and temperature, e.g. 'A' Certificate covers eight five-day periods with mean variation in daily rate not exceeding two seconds. System instituted 1885 at Kew Observatory (Surrey); since 1912, tests conducted at National Physical Laboratory, Teddington, Middlesex. *See* rating certificate.

Khiva rugs. *See* West Turkestan.

Khlebnikol, Ivan (fl late 19th century). Russian silversmith and enameller. Among leading adherents of Pan-Slav movement. Specialized in *champlevé* enamelling and filigree work on silver executed in *Old Russian style. Worked in St Petersburg at Gasse firm; in 1869, established Moscow branch (under own name). This operated until 1918. Marks: either initials or full name in Cyrillic characters.

Khotan rugs. *See* East Turkestan.

kia-chu. *See* dry lacquer.

kia-tchou. *See* dry lacquer.

Kidderminster carpet. *See* ingrain carpet.

Kiev. Russian faience factory established near Kiev in 1798. Mid 19th century products decorated with transfer-printed or perforated designs. Some porcelain also made.

Killybegs carpet factory. *See* Donegal carpets.

Kiln Croft Works. *See* Boote, T. & R., Ltd.

kimono tray or **midare bako.** Large, oblong, deep-sided lacquer tray, made as dressing-room accessory for Japanese ladies. Usually covered with *roiro-nuri lacquer and often decorated with gold family crest or monogram.

kinchaku. *See* sagemono.

King, Jessie M. (1876-1949). Scottish designer, illustrator, and potter. Studied at Glasgow School of Art, 1894-1900. Became prominent member of *Glasgow School group. Designed jewellery and silverwork for Liberty's *Cymric range.

King Street. *See* Derby; Hancock, Sampson; Locker, William.

kinji (Japanese, 'gold ground'). In Japanese lacquer, highly-polished gold lacquer ground. Finely-powdered gold either painted or sprinkled on to prepared lacquer base, then covered with several layers of transparent lacquer. Finally, surface polished with powdered

Right
S. Kirk & Son. Silver soup tureen with chased decoration and cast stag finial. c1865. Height 7½in.
Below
*Jessie M. King. Buckle. Silver and blue enamel, made by W. H. *Haseler for *Liberty & Co. 1905-06.*

hartshorn and oil. Also, generic term for all types of gold lacquer grounds, including fundame and nashi-ji.

kinrande. In Japanese ceramics, gold decoration on red ground associated with porcelain of Chinese Ming Emperor, Yung Lo (1403-25); reproduced in 19th century, e.g. by H. *Eiraku in Kyoto and W. *Eiraku in Kyoto and Kutani.

kin-shi. *See* tsuishu.

kirigane or **kirikane** (Japanese, 'cut metal'). Japanese *embedded lacquer technique used from 15th century: minute sheets of gold or silver arranged in mosaic-like design. Also, old-fashioned term for okibirame, in which larger, irregular metallic pieces used to produce same effect. Alternatively, in lacquer painting, technique using very fine threads of gold leaf for lines in design.

Kirk, S., & Son (Baltimore). American silversmiths, founded by Samuel Kirk (b Doylestown, 1793, d 1872) after apprenticeship to James Howell, Philadelphia; son Henry Child Kirk

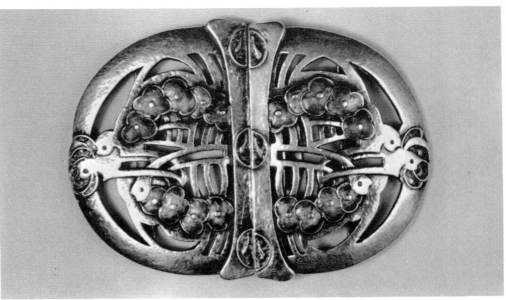

Above
S. Kirk & Son. Silver wine ewer, inspired by original excavated at Pompeii, engraved with heraldic shield of Bonaparte family. Height 6½in.

Right
Thomas Kirkby. Plate made at *Mintons with decoration after Giulio Romano. 1862.

became partner in 1846 (firm named Samuel Kirk & Son), succeeded by Henry Child Kirk Junior in 1914. Firm noted for *repoussé* style of ornament developed in 1828, often called Baltimore pattern. 48-piece flatware service made in 1905 for US cruiser Maryland, is decorated with nearly 200 scenes of history of State of Maryland; now in State House, Annapolis.

Kirk repoussé, or **Baltimore silver**. American silverware covered with intricate floral *repoussé* pattern; introduced 1824 by Samuel Kirk, and still made by S. *Kirk & Son Inc.

Kirkby, Thomas (1824-90). English ceramic decorator. In Staffordshire, at Minton factory (c1845-87), painted figure subjects on majolica; also noted for panels of flowers or figures in Sèvres style on porcelain tableware.

Kirkham, William (fl mid to late 19th century). Staffordshire potter. Bought manufacture of roof and floor tiles, etc. (established 1856) at London Road, Stoke-on-Trent. Products (1862-92) include earthenware and stoneware, chemical and technical utensils; water bottles, jugs, spill jars, pedestals, etc., made in hard, fine textured terracotta, decorated with printed Etruscan figures or groups of flowers. Some enamelled borders, etc., and gilded decoration. Fern patterns also occur. Mark: W. KIRKHAM, impressed. Firm, subsequently Kirkhams, then Kirkhams Ltd, combined with A. E. Gray & Co. Ltd, trading as Portmeirion Potteries Ltd from 1961.

Kirman or **Kerman,** Persia. Carpet making centre, and type of carpet produced there. Became most popular Persian rug on American and European markets, c1870, with widest range of designs apart from *Tabriz. By 1920, short pile rugs with traditional patterns no longer made; new pastel colours and naturalistic designs, unlike other Persian types, evolved: medallions, flowering trees, birds, animals, portraits, gardens, and hunting scenes. Pattern of large flower-strewn medallions, pendants, and floral corners, devised especially for export trade by Kirman weavers working for Tabriz merchants: known first - confusingly - as Kermanshah (another rug-making city), then Kirman. Several Western companies (mainly American and British) active in Kirman by 1925; carpet industry continued to expand until Depression in 1930s.

Kiselev. Afanasii Leontevich (fl mid 19th century). Russian potter and porcelain manufacturer. Operated porcelain factory near Moscow from early 1830s. Established own factory in early 1850s, also near Moscow, making high-quality porcelain tableware, figures, porcelain for everyday use, and faience. Patterns often inspired by local peasant art. Work marked with name or initials.

kiseru (Japanese, 'pipe'). Japanese tobacco pipe, used from introduction of tobacco by Portuguese, probably in late 16th century. Produced in great quantity in 19th and early 20th centuries. Tiny bowl, holding pinch of tobacco, and long, thin stem. Materials and styles range from simple unadorned clay to highly ornamental examples with chased, inlaid or engraved metal bowls and mouthpieces fitted on decorative bamboo or occasionally lacquered wood stems. Kiseru carried inside *kiseru-zutsu, worn tucked under obi.

kiseru-zutsu (Japanese, 'pipe sheath'). Case in two sections for *kiseru. Many beautifully executed and ornamented; some carved in ivory, wood, or horn by netsuke artists, others made in metals by sword furniture artists, or in lacquered wood by renowned lacquer artists, including S. *Zeshin. Existing kiseru-zutsu date mainly from 19th and 20th centuries.

kitchen Windsor chair. *See* firehouse Windsor chair.

Kirman. Carpet depicting story of Lela and Majnun. c1850. 7ft8in. × 4ft6in.

Kjellberg, Friedl (b 1905). Finnish ceramic artist, born in Austria. Worked at Arabia factory from 1924. Specialized in bowls and coffee sets in thin porcelain with perforated decoration, resembling Chinese rice grain pattern. Undecorated table services made in bone porcelain.

Other work includes use of intensely coloured glazes, e.g. peacock-blue, *sang-de-boeuf,* celadon, on porcelain or stoneware.

Klaus, Karl (b 1889). Austrian architect and designer, working in Vienna. Designed furniture and ceramics produced by Wiener Werkstätte, 1911. Also designed vases, etc., decorated with bold, intricate painted patterns, produced by E. *Wahliss.

Kaare Klint. Collapsible chair. 1933. Height 32in.

Kleitos. Wide, seamless carpet square (up to 9ft), woven on wide *spool Axminster loom, patented by A. *Smith & Co. in America in 1896.

Klimt, Gustav (1862–1918). Austrian painter and designer. Studied mosaics, ceramics, and glass painting in Vienna. Associated until 1905 with Vienna Secession, and provided friezes, mosaics, etc., for exhibitions. Mosaic frieze designed for interior of Palais Stoclet of J. *Hoffmann, executed in marble and enamelled metal, inset with ceramics and glass, completed 1911.

Klint, Käre or Kaare (1888–1954). Danish architect; appointed professor of furniture design at Academy of Fine Arts, Copenhagen, 1924. Used traditional forms and construction (e.g. from Chippendale and Shaker furniture), tailored to needs of human body; influenced much Scandinavian design; also adapted modern designs, e.g. teak deck chair, 1933, derived from *Le Corbusier's *chaise longue.* Used wax-polished, but unvarnished, woods.

kneeling chair. *See* prie-dieu chair.

knife cleaning machine. Circular wooden case, c18in.–c24in. in diameter. Apertures on circumference bound e.g. in brass, receive knife blades, which enter between counter-rotating interior discs, set with bristles, turned by external handle. Case and handle mounted on stand in e.g. cast iron, fixed to stable surface by clamps or screws. Number of rotary knife cleaners introduced at Great Exhibition, 1851; subsequently became standard equipment in Victorian households.

knife rest. Horizontal bar on two low supports (usually X-shaped) to support blade of carving knife when not in use. Made in silver or electroplate. Widely used since c1850.

Knowles, Taylor and Knowles. Porcelain pot-pourri, made in East Liverpool, Ohio. Dated 1897.

Right
*Frederick Kny. Claret jug made at Dennis Glasshouse of T. *Webb & Sons. Wheel-engraved with figures from Elgin Marbles. c1880. Height 14½ in.*

Above
*Kobako. Irregularly shaped and standing on four feet. Cover decorated with mallet, hat, tama, and cloak of invisibility in gold *takamakie. Sides decorated with lakeside landscapes in *hiramakie. Unsigned.*

Knöchel, Franz (fl 2nd half of 19th century). Bohemian master glass engraver. Worked with C. *Pietsch and F. *Ullmann for J. & L. Lobmeyr in Steinschönau, where fine work led to renewed interest in Bohemian cut and engraved glass.

Knoll Associates. American furniture manufacturing firm established in New York in 1946; development of Hans Knoll, founded by Hans Knoll in 1939. Made furniture designed earlier by L. *Mies van der Rohe, e.g. *Barcelona chair, from c1953.

Knowles, Taylor & Knowles. American pottery, established 1854 in East Liverpool, Ohio. Traded from 1870 as Knowles, Taylor & Knowles; organized as company in 1890. From 1872, made cream-coloured earthenware; semi-porcelain introduced c1890, marked with star-shaped device, or with bison and KT & K in rectangle or circle. 'Belleek', developed in 1890s, marked Lotus Ware with name of firm in circle with crescent and star, also initials of artist (if decorated). Some sold in white for decoration by amateur painters, until production ceased because of high cost. *Pâte-sur-pâte* decoration shown at Chicago World's Fair in 1893. Tableware, etc., marked with initials or name of company and several designs, some incorporating eagle.

Knox, Archibald (1864-1933). English designer, teacher, and craftsman; associated with *Celtic revival within Arts & Crafts Movement. Born and educated on Isle of Man. Moved to London (1897), and worked as designer for *Liberty & Co; made over 400 designs for *Cymric range of silverwork and jewellery and *Tudric pewter. Designs employ *entrelac designs, sometimes enriched with blue and green enamel. Taught at Kingston-on-Thames School of Art, Surrey, until teaching criticized as over-advanced. Many discarded silver and jewellery designs salvaged by pupils.

knurling. Mechanical form of decorative embossing, originally employed by goldsmiths; repeated pattern separated by fine indentations, e.g. milled edge of coin.

Kny, Frederick (fl 1870s–1920s). Bohemian-born master glass engraver. Settled in Stourbridge area, working for T. *Webb & Sons from 1880s at own Platts Workshop. Noted for *rock crystal engraving and cameo glass. Employed team of engravers, including sons.

kobako (Japanese, 'incense box'). In Japanese lacquer, miniature covered box (c3 × 3 × 4 in.) for holding incense powders and tablets. Materials, shapes, and decoration similar to shallow *kogo.

Koch, Mogens (b 1898). Danish architect; also designed furniture characterized by light-coloured woods and constructional form. Upright beech-framed chair (1933) folds from side to centre, has canvas seat and back rest, leather arm rests (first manufactured 1959).

*Above and right
Karl Koepping. Two flower glasses. c1900.*

kodansu (Japanese, 'small box-chest'). Japanese lacquered cabinet (c13 × 15 × 12in.). Cabinet doors open to reveal nests of small drawers for storing personal accessories. Often found with carved metal fittings (particularly silver or gold).

ko-dogu. *See* sword furniture.

Koehler, Florence (1861-1944). American artist-craftsman, leader of craft revival movement in America. Worked in Chicago, where Arts & Crafts Society formed, 1897. Jewellery close in style to English work in Arts & Crafts vein, e.g. silver set with cabochon-cut coloured stones. Work much admired in American artistic circles in early 20th century.

Koepping, Karl (1848-1914). Foremost German Jugendstil glass artist. Produced extremely fragile ornamental glassware in iridescent glass, characterized by flat base and leaf-like forms emerging from tall, sometimes contorted, stems. Mark: Koepping.

kogai. *See* kushi, tsuba.

kogatana. *See* tsuba.

kogo (Japanese, 'incense box'). Very shallow miniature Japanese covered box (c2½ × 2½ × ½in.) for storing incense powders and tablets. Made for aristocracy from mid 12th century, often as part of set of incense ceremony or tea ceremony utensils. Peak production 19th century. Usually square or round, but also in e.g.,

quatrefoil, octagonal, diamond, fan, and shell shapes. Most made of lacquered wood, decorated by master lacquer artists in wide range of techniques. Most elaborate work often found on underside of cover. Rarely signed. Among finest and most highly-prized miniature Japanese lacquer objects. Also made in porcelain and metal. *Illustration at* Zeshin, S.

Koishibara. Japanese pottery centre in Fukuoka prefecture; originally parent kiln of Onda (Oita prefecture), and work hard to distinguish. Covered pots and jars made in rounded shapes with trickled glazes, e.g. in black, brown, green, grey, and white.

Kojitsu, Saito (1833-93). Japanese master ivory-carver and netsuke artist of *Hojitsu's school. Carved numerous Buddhist images. *Na: Yataro. *Kaimyo: Bonshakuengyo Shinshi.

kojubako (Japanese, 'nest of boxes for incense'). Japanese lacquer. Flat, miniature, covered *incense box (c2½ × 3 × 4in.), made for aristocracy from 12th century as incense ceremony utensil. Most square or rectangular, but also in e.g. single or double fan, quatrefoil, bird-cage, or shell shapes. Fitted with two to four smaller matching boxes and occasionally a tray. Bottom

surface of outer box often has circular hole to facilitate removal of inner containers. Rarely signed.

Kok, J. Jurriaan (1861-1919). Dutch ceramic designer. At *Rozenburg factory; from c1900 designed porcelain vases, tea ware, etc., in which Art Nouveau style pervaded form as well as decoration. Enamel painting by J. Schellink. Work marked with monogram.

koka-ryokuyo. *See* zonsei-nuri.

kokoshnik. Traditional Russian peasant-woman's headdress. Profile of head of woman wearing kokoshnik adopted c1896 as Russian hallmark on all silver and gold articles.

Kokusai, Ozaki, or **Takeda,** Kokusai (fl late 19th century). Japanese netsuke artist of Tokyo. Specialized in deerhorn carving, particularly *katabori and *sashi netsuke. Subjects and designs atypical, often humorous or caricatured animal figures, loosely derived from Chinese models. Technique meticulous; highly individual style (known as kokusai-bori) extremely popular and widely copied by later artists. *Chomei: Koku or Kokusai.

Kollin, Erik August (1836-1901). Swedish-Finnish master goldsmith; worked in St Petersburg. Apprenticed with A.W. *Holmström. From 1870, workmaster for *Fabergé. Specialized in gold filigree work, carving and engraving. Noted for gold replicas of treasures from Kirch, Crimea. Mark: E.K.

Köln-Ehrenfeld. *See* Rheinische Glashütten.

Komei, Ishikawa (1852-1913). Japanese ivory sculptor of Tokyo. Carved numerous *okimono and *kiseru-zutsu, as well as some *netsuke. Professor in Sculpture Department, Tokyo Academy of Fine Arts.

kongo. *See* vajra.

Koninklijke Delftsch-Aardewerk Fabriek. *See* Thooft, Joost.

Koninklijke Nederlandsche Glasfabrik. *See* Leerdam.

Kornilov, Mikhail Savinovich (d 1885). Russian porcelain manufacturer; established factory at St Petersburg in 1835. Succeeded by family. Products, noted for high quality of paste and decoration, sold in America from c1893. Firm traded (1893-1917) as Brothers Kornilov, and marks incorporate name.

koshisage. *See* sagemono.

k'ossu. Chinese tapestry-woven silk fabric used in mandarin squares (worn on back and front of mandarin's coat as badge of office: c1ft square, heavily brocaded). Decorated with elaborate pictorial designs in wide range of colours, usually partly in gold thread. Production declined during 18th century; revived in 19th century, but quality lower. Adversely affected by introduction of synthetic dyes towards end of century.

Kosta. Oldest Swedish glass factory, founded 1742 in Småland, but greatest prominence dates

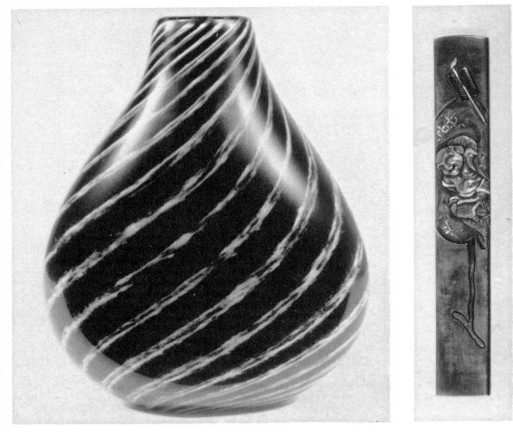

from 1920s and 1930s, when much original table-ware produced. Employed E. *Bergh from 1927. Continues as important glass centre today.

Koum ka Pour rugs. Made by Turkish factory in suburb of Istanbul, Koum ka Pour ('gates to the sands'), operating 1890–1910, under patronage of Sultan. Very fine quality rugs (c1,000 knots to 1 sq in.) woven in silk with gold and silver thread. Pastel colours; embossed metallic roses feature of some designs.

Koun, Takamura (1852–1934). Japanese master wood-carver, netsuke artist of Tokyo *Houn family, and perhaps greatest Japanese expert on carving during *Meiji and *Taisho periods. From 1888, professor of Sculpture Department at Tokyo Academy of Fine Arts; later, member of Imperial Art Committee. Main output, okimono; many exported.

Kovács, Margit (b 1902). Hungarian artist potter. Studied at Budapest School of Applied Art. Later worked in Vienna, and Munich (1928–29) under A. *Niemayer; work in Expressionist style shown at Budapest Exhibition in 1930. Studied in Copenhagen from 1932, then worked for 1½ years at Sèvres factory. Work, influenced from 1930s by Hungarian folk art, includes large wall plaques with country scenes of horsemen, etc., under monochrome tin glazes, statuettes painted in coloured slips, often of religious subjects, e.g. madonna and child, children, or animals, e.g. lion painted in coloured slips.

kozuka. In Japanese metalwork, long, flat handle of sword knife (kogatana), which was carried in usually rectangular and often highly decorated scabbard. Term sometimes refers to knife itself.

Above left
*Kosta. Glass vase by V. *Lindstrand. Thick cased black glass with internal spiralling lines of white glass. Stencilled mark, Lindstrand Kosta, and engraved number 241159. Height 7 in.*

Above right
*Kozuka. Shibuichi. Carved in low relief with *Hotei holding fan and staff, reclining on his treasure bag. Mid 19th century. Signed Seiriuken Noahiro.*

Introduced during Muromachi period (1334–1573).

Krebs, Nathalie (b 1895). Danish ceramic artist; trained as civil engineer. Worked at Bing & Grøndahls porcelain works (1919–29). Established stoneware pottery (1929) in partnership with G. *Nylund; alone from 1930 (trading as Saxbo). Used coloured glazes to decorate simple stoneware shapes, e.g. bowls, jugs, vases, often designed and finished by E. *Staehr-Nielsen.

Kriegel & Co. Czechoslovakian firm making lead-glazed earthenware at pottery established (1795) in Prague. Products (1836–62), after English styles, marked K & C/P, impressed.

Krog, Arnold (1856–1931). Danish architect, designer, and ceramic artist. Decorator, and, in effect, art director at Royal Copenhagen Porcelain Factory from 1885. Noted for underglaze painting begun in 1885, and won Grand Prix for factory at Paris Exhibition in 1889. Dishes and plaques, without rim decoration, painted with misty Danish scenes with birds or distant figures,

seascapes, or flowers (e.g. iris). Plaque with water-lilies in low-relief modelled in late 1880s. Figures slip-cast in smooth compact shapes and decorated with underglaze colours include pair of owls standing on knotted twigs. Later work includes painting in coloured slip to achieve relief effects.

Krohn, Pietro (1840–1905). Danish painter, illustrator, and porcelain decorator. Art director and artist at *Bing & Grøndahls factory, Copenhagen. Noted for design of *heron service, made in 1888. As painter, specialized in genre subjects and Danish or Italian landscapes.

Kuang Hsü (fl 1874–1908). Chinese Emperor of Ching dynasty. Imperial kilns at Ching-tê-Chên continued use of *famille noire* decoration, *sang-de-boeuf*, peach-bloom, and apple-green glazes. Also reproduced 18th century ware of Ch'ien Lung reign.

Kuba carpets. *See* Caucasian carpets.

kugikakushi. Japanese metalwork. Often elaborate metal pieces set over mortice jointings of beams and vertical posts. Many other parts of temples and dwellings also decorated with metal, e.g. temple pillars stand on bronze footing above base.

Kullberg, Victor (1824–1890). Swedish watch, clock, and *chronometer maker, apprenticed to L. U. Jürgensen in Copenhagen. Visited London, 1851, to see Great Exhibition; soon found employment, and worked in England until death. Made particularly fine chronometers, winning awards for timekeeping at Greenwich trials, 1862, and setting new records in trials in 1872, 1889. Signed watches and clocks of high quality; worked as watch finisher, polishing and casing movements, for Army & Navy Co-operative, later Army & Navy Store, Victoria, London. Active member of *British Horological Institute; work displayed at 1889 Paris Exhibition.

kundika (Sanskrit), or **suibyo** (Japanese). Metal water bottle carried by Buddhist priests.

kurawa or **ash-tray netsuke.** Netsuke designed for use with *tabako-ire or *tabako-bon; serves as ash-tray. Usually made of cast metal; some ceramic. Peak production, 19th century.

Kurliukev, Orest Federovich (fl late 19th and early 20th centuries). Russian master silversmith working in Moscow. Kurliukev's firm flourished 1884–1918; noted for fine enamel done in *Old Russian, Louis XVI, and Art Nouveau styles. Mark: O.K., or occasionally full name in Cyrillic characters.

kuro-makie (Japanese, 'black sown-picture') or **urushi-makie.** Japanese lacquer with highly-polished black ground and low-relief polished black *makie decoration.

kuroe-nuri. *See* negoro-nuri.

kushi or **sashi-gushi.** Japanese ornamental lacquer comb (c4 × 2 × ¼ in.), usually crescent-shaped, oblong, or rounded with triangular-cut sections at either end. Cut and shaped by comb-

artists from tortoiseshell, ivory, wood (boxwood and camellia), and horn. Area above teeth elaborately ornamented with lacquer designs. Worn by Japanese women into 20th century often with matching ornamental hair-bar (kogai).

Kutani. Traditional Japanese ceramic centre in Ishikawa prefecture, Kaga province. 19th century products include imitations of 17th century porcelains, e.g. styles inspired by Chinese porcelain of Ming and Ch'ing periods; or resembling early Imari ware (Ao-Kutani), with green glaze and enamel decoration in black, purple, and yellow; eggshell porcelain; and wide range of pottery. Porcelain with gold scrollwork designs on red ground, inspired by kinrande style developed in 1840s and later made by W. *Eiraku. After late 19th century, porcelain generally mass-produced.

Kuznetsov family. Russian porcelain and faience manufacturers. Iakov Kuznetsov established factory (1810) at Novocharitonowka; operated until 1870s by sons, trading as Brothers Kuznetsov. Other factories at Liszowo (1816–86), Dulow (1830–40). Matvei Sidorovich Kuznetsov owned factories at Riga, Charkow, and Boudy; noted for powder boxes, vases, toilet sets, etc., in blue or pink porcelain, enamelled and gilded. Figures in regional costume made in biscuit porcelain with painted decoration. Products exported to other European countries, India, and Far East. In 1891, firm acquired factory of Francis Gardner, established 1766 at Verbilki, near Moscow. Marks usually incorporate name, M. S. Kuznetsov, with place of manufacture in Cyrillic characters.

kwaichu-yatate. See yatate.

Kwaigyokusai. See Kaigyokusai.

kyara-bako (Japanese, 'aloe-wood box'). Miniature Japanese lacquer box for storing pieces or sticks of scented woods used to scent clothes, rooms, etc., and burned during incense ceremony. Size, shape, and ornamentation very similar to *kobako.

Kyhn, Knud (b 1881). Danish artist potter. In 1920s and 1930s, designed figures in stoneware, sandstone, and porcelain animal figures for Bing & Grøndahl and Royal Copenhagen Porcelain Factory, sometimes enamelled, or covered with celadon glaze. Work usually marked with signature and date, impressed, incised, or painted.

kyocho. See dry lacquer.

Kyoto. Seat of Japanese Imperial court and centre of ceramic production in Edo period (1615–1868). Noted for enamelled and gilt pottery developed by 17th century potter, Ninsei, at Awata (on eastern side of city) and continued from 18th century, notably by Kenzan and successors. Many kilns built in late 18th and early 19th centuries for production of similar pottery. Individual potters worked in other districts of Kyoto; as well as faience, many made porcelain in Chinese Ming styles, e.g. blue-and-white, kinrande, and san-ts'ai (three-colour). N. *Dohachi made faience, porcelain, and high-

quality raku ware, which originated in Kyoto in 16th century. Artist potters of district include Y. *Seifu in Meiji period (from 1868), and K. *Kawai and M. *Ishiguro (Showa period, from 1926). Work of Kyotu area regarded as influencing ceramics throughout Japan.

Kysela, František (fl 1920s and 30s). Leading Czech tapestry designer; also known for book, textile, jewellery, and stage design, mosaics and painting. Professor at National School of Applied Arts, Prague, from 1917. First tapestry (of national emblem) made for National Assembly in 1921. Designed series of tapestries and carpets for music chamber in castle at Nové Město nad Metují, 1922–23. Produced group of nine vast tapestries (shown at Paris Exhibition of 1925) for exhibition room at National School of Applied Arts. Like many contemporary designers, chiefly inspired by Gothic art. Modelling of form derived from early Gobelin tapestries. Typical designs: stylized animal and fruit shapes in formal arrangements. Inspired school of younger Czech tapestry designers, including Antonin Kybal and Cyril Bonda.

Kyuichi, Takeuchi, Kyuichi, or **Takeuchi,** Kengaro (1857–1916). Japanese master carver, netsuke artist, and scholar. Professor of Sculpture Department at Tokyo Academy of Fine Arts from foundation in 1888. Member of Imperial Art Committee from 1906. Used wide range of techniques and subjects for meticulously executed carvings in ivory, wood, bamboo, horn, etc. *Go: Shusai or Kyuen.

Kyusai, or **Kyusai,** Hirai (1879–1938). Japanese netsuke artist and master-carver of Osaka. Best-known for carving of small objects, e.g. tea-ceremony utensils, okimono, netsuke, and obi clasps. Worked in kanshitsu, bamboo, wood, and *ikkaku. Style greatly influenced by *Kaigyokusai. Many pieces exhibited, both in Japan and at International Exhibitions. Won bronze medal at 1895 Paris Exhibition for bamboo flower vase, Goddess of Peace. *Na: Hirai Shin. Go: until 1915, Tetsugen or Tetsugendo, then Kyusai. *Chomei: Kyusai.

Kyushu. Most southwesterly of main Japanese islands. Ceramic production mainly centred in old province of Hizen, largely originated by Korean potters in 16th and 17th centuries. Work includes tea ceremony ware, but most intended for every-day use and made in large quantities. Kilns include Ryumonji and Naeshirogawa, producers of Satsuma ware in present Kagoshima prefecture; Nishi-shimmachi, Futagawa, Shiraishi, and Koishibara in Fukuoka prefecture; and Onda in Oita prefecture. Porcelain chiefly produced in or near Arita, Hizen province.

La Belle Pottery Company. American pottery company established 1887 by managers of *Wheeling Pottery Co. Made granite ware and Cameo china, thinly-potted tableware decorated, e.g. in blue and gold. Marks include torch, WP, and LA BELLE CHINA.

laboratory glass. See pharmaceutical glass.

lac burgautée. See aogai.

Lacemaker's lamp. Mid 19th century. Height 4in.

lace brooches and **pins,** and **scarf pins.** Small brooches and short pins, like tiepins, worn on scarves, lace at neck of gowns, and to attach shoulder bows to evening dresses, 1885–1901. Set with diamonds, pearls, or moonstones, and in wide variety of shapes, e.g. insects, birds, ships, crescents, horseshoes. Also in form of narrow bar with jewelled motif in centre.

lace glass. See filigree glass.

lacemaker's lamp or **lanthorn.** Two-part glass lamp in which beam from candle or rush in inner chamber is concentrated through water-filled glass globe onto lacemaker's pillow. Made from late 17th century. In some examples, light source positioned behind water-filled globe.

Lachenal, Edmond (b 1855). French artist potter. Among potters active in Paris in late 19th century. Made stoneware and porcelain, sometimes with relief decoration of foliage in Art Nouveau style, under dull, green glaze. Velvety surface texture sometimes achieved with use of hydrofluoric acid on glaze. Also made earthenware with painted decoration.

Lachenal, Raoul (fl early 20th century). French artist potter; trained under father, E. *Lachenal. From 1904, made stoneware with geometrical decoration; coloured glazes contained within raised outlines of clay; patterns sometimes incised. Also made porcelain. Work signed.

Lacloche. Parisian retail and manufacturing jewellers, founded 1897 by brothers Fernand, Jules, Leopold, and Jacques Lacloche. Made expensive jewellery in current fashions. Noted in 1920s for enamelled pieces in oriental style, and

for Art Deco jewellery set with precious stones in tiny geometrical patterns.

lacquer, urushi (Japanese), or **ch'i** (Chinese). Non-resinous sap from type of sumac, the lac tree (*Rhus vernicifera*). When dried in moist atmosphere, emulsion forms extremely tough,

Lacloche. *Powder compact. Gold, jade, diamonds, platinum and lacquer. Designed by Meyer, 1924.
Below
Lacquerwork. Vase by J. *Dunand in eggshell lacquer. Made in Paris, c1929.

heat and solvent resistant surface which takes high polish. Originally used in Orient as simple protective coating for wood and leather objects, lacquering developed into major decorative art of both China and Japan used on large range of objects and materials mainly wood (*cf* honji), also ivory, metal, ceramics, horn, tortoiseshell, etc. Oriental lacquer widely imitated in Europe and America with various varnishes. *See also* Indian lac.

lacquerwork. Chairs, tables, screens, cabinets, etc. treated with up to 40 coats of lacquer (resin from Far Eastern lac tree: *Rhus vernicifera*) each rubbed to achieve smooth surface. Applied to wood previously smoothed with pumice, covered with fine silk pasted with rice gum, and smoothed again by application of powdered stone. Imparts rich, deep, lustrous finish, becoming black (foremost colour) when dry. Brownish-red – called 'tango' during 1920s – green, ochre, yellow, etc. also obtainable through addition of vegetable dyes. Gold and silver foil, powders, mother-of-pearl inlay, sometimes incorporated. Popular variant, *eggshell lacquer. May be applied to metal, and fired. Art practised from c400BC; screens, etc. imported to Britain from China and Japan after c1650. Lacquerwork particularly popular during 1920s, e.g. screens, furniture by J. *Dunand, E. *Gray, P. *Follot, A-A. *Rateau, E. *Printz; also Chinese style furniture, cocktail cabinets.

ladder-back chair. *See* slat-back chair.

Ladies' Carpet, The. Outstandingly large (20×30ft) English *needlework carpet with repeated flower motif. Consists of thousands of squares made by 150 women; organized and made up by firm of W. B. *Simpson for Great Exhibition (1851) in London.

lady's desk. *See* davenport.

lady's easy chair or **pompadour chair.** Small, button-upholstered chair with vestigial arms or none, high back, deep seat, and short, turned legs. Examples include *Prince of Wales lady's easy chair, *Spanish chair. Common from c1850.

lady's fancy sewing chair. *See* sewing chair.

Lalique, René (1860-1945). French jeweller, silversmith, glassmaker, and decorative artist. Apprentice in 1876, studied at Ecole des Arts Décoratifs; became leading Paris Art Nouveau jeweller. Also designed wallpaper and fabrics. Actress Sarah Bernhardt, first important patron, commissioned groups of jewels. Achieved prominence through work shown at Paris Salon, 1894; became freelance designer, working for e.g. *Cartier and *Boucheron. Used semi-precious stones, ivory, glass, enamel, coloured gold, horn etc. Favourite motifs include flowers and insects, particularly dragonfly; also used female face or figure from mid 1890s. Showed work at shop of S. *Bing, Paris Exposition of 1900, and in Turin (1902); exhibitions and one man show in London, 1903 and 1905. Made collection for millionaire Calouste Gulbenkian (1895-1912); 145 pieces, preserved at Paombel Palace near Lisbon, include combs, buckles, pendant, and delicate dragonfly ornament with wing span over 10 ins. Occupied combined house and workshop in Paris from c1902, succeeded by son. Studied glass techniques from 1890s and experimented in

glassmaking c1900. Had incorporated coloured glass in jewellery in 1890s, and eventually abandoned production of jewellery for glass (c1914); influenced by work of E. *Gallé. Experimental work includes statuettes and vases, left without final polishing, etc., after firing. In 1908, commissioned to design range of moulded scent bottles for perfume firm, Coty. Leased (1909) and bought (1910) glass factory; noted for work in 1920s and 1930s. Outstanding technical innovator; developed new varieties of glass, e.g. milky white opalescent glass, and richly coloured glass imitating precious stones. Also worked in brown, blue, and soft peach opalescent glass. Many designs incorporate human figure, usually nude; also animal and insect motifs, often with foliage in relief. Some bottles have elaborate stoppers and deeply moulded or acid-textured decoration. Other work includes lamps of circular or semi-circular sheets of glass, decorative fountains, screens, chandeliers, door panels. Marks: Lalique; Lalique, France; R. Lalique, France; engraved, or stamped and etched.

Lalique, Suzanne (b 1899). French porcelain decorator. Work, produced at factory of T. *Haviland, includes plates painted with design of grapes and vines in black, green, and silver. Designs commissioned by Sèvres factory for display at Paris Exhibition of 1925.

Lallemand, Robert (fl 20th century). French artist potter; worked in Paris in 1920s. Vases, often in angular forms, painted with clouds, geometrical designs, or titled scenes with figures, in black and green or red enamel; also lamp bases and black pottery vases in stepped shapes. Figures engaged in sporting activities represent javelin throwing, running, etc. Work signed Lallemand/Made in France.

Lamb, James. Manchester furniture manufacturer, active c1840-c1900. Made Gothic style

Laminated wood. Armchair designed by Fritz Hansen. Laminated mahogany seat and back, beechwood arms and legs, Danish, c1935.

René Lalique. Figure modelled in opalescent glass, Suzanne au bain. *Base engraved, R. Lalique France No. 833. Height 8¾in.*

furniture, designed e.g. by H. *Protat; Gothic Reform style furniture by C. *Bevan; also Quaint style pieces. Stamp: Lamb, Manchester.

Lambeth faience. English earthenware made at Doulton workshop in London from 1873. Vases, bottles, and tile panels made in fine body, containing kaolin, chinastone, and calcined flint, decorated under glaze with flower subjects, landscapes, portraits, etc. Larger articles include pedestals, flower pots, and architectural relief decoration. Inspired by earlier forms of tin-glazed earthenware, although decoration painted directly on biscuit clay, rather than glaze, before second firing.

Lambeth School of Art. *See* Doulton & Co.

laminated wood. Thin layers of wood, e.g. rosewood, birch, bonded by gluing or compressing under heat. Grain on alternate layers may be at any angle. Can be carved or moulded into complicated curves. Widely used from mid 19th century, e.g. by H. A. H. *Aalto, J. *Belter, and M. *Thonet.

lamp bracket. Right-angled wall fitting acting as support for e.g. Argand oil lamp, kerosene lamp, gas burner and shade, electric light bulb. Numerous forms in brass, copper, wrought-iron, bronze, ormolu, etc. With lamp, common subject for innovations of design and style, particularly by Art Nouveau designers, e.g. *Tiffany Studios, V. *Horta.

lamps. *See* carriage lamp, electric lamp, paraffin lamp, ship's lamp, standard lamp, student's lamp.

Lancashire snuff-box. Robust English snuff-box in brass or copper, made by watchmakers at Prescot, Lancashire; typically, has ingenious combination lock, worked by pointers on dials crudely engraved with e.g. sun and moon. Made during 19th century, but probably not later than c1885.

Lancastrian Pottery. *See* Pilkington's Tile & Pottery Co.

Landais family. C-J. Landais (1829–1908), A. Landais (1829–1912), and J. Landais (1800–83); French potters working in Tours (Indre-et-Loire). Produced *Palissy ware. *Illustration at* Palissy ware.

Landberg, Nils (b 1907). Swedish glass designer at *Ørrefors from 1936. Worked in free-blown and engraved glass, producing elongated vases in subtly shaded colours; also decorated windows and light fittings. Mark: N with Ørrefors, or Øf, on all engraved glass to his design; NA on cut glass; NU on furnace-finished glass (e.g. *Graal).

Langenbeck, Karl (fl c1871 – early 20th century). American ceramic chemist. From early 1870s, experimented with M. L. *Nichols in pottery decoration at Cincinnati, Ohio. Worked briefly at Rookwood, then established own Avon pottery (1886), which lasted one year; products marked AVON. Worked at American Encaustic Tiling Co., and established *Mosaic Tile Co. in partnership with H. *Mueller.

Lanternier factory. *See* Limoges.

lanthorn. *See* lacemaker's lamp.

Lapis ware. Earthenware made (1928–38) by *Pilkington Tile & Pottery Co. Designs of foliage, etc., painted under matt glaze, became mottled, blurred and slightly raised during firing, because of chemical action between pigment and glaze. Few colours, notably green, painted on tinted grounds, generally by G. M. *Rodgers. Dishes, vases, etc., bear mark ROYAL LANCASTRIAN, and artist's monogram.

Laporte-Blairsy, Leo (1865–1923). French designer of silver ornaments and jewellery; studied sculpture e.g. under J-A-J. *Falguière; showed at Paris Exhibition in 1900. Work displays typical flowing, sensuous lines of French Art Nouveau sculpture, in manner of e.g. R. *Larche, A. Léonard. Favoured marine motifs, e.g. silver group, Water Nymph pursued by Triton (c1900): nude figure of nymph carried on breaking wave, escaping grasp of half-submerged triton; group mounted on shaped base of green antique marble, with silver feet.

Larche, Raoul-François (1860–1912). French Art Nouveau sculptor; one of many in 19th century whose main income derived from mass-production of original models by bronze foundries or ceramic manufacturers, e.g. Sèvres. Noted for series of gilt-bronze statuettes of American dancer, Loïe Fuller, many altered to incorporate small light-bulb.

Larsson, Carl (c1850–1920). Swedish painter; published books illustrating house interiors, e.g. *Ett Hem* (A Home), 1899. Light, simple furniture influenced contemporary German and

Latticinio. Vase. English, late 19th century.

Scandinavian designers, and much modern Scandinavian design.

l'Art Nouveau style. *See* Weller, Samuel A.

Lasa. *See* Weller, Samuel A.

latex foam. Upholstery material made by combining chemical - usually zinc oxide - with fluid from rubber plant (latex), and beating to obtain desired density. Process, invented 1928, revolutionized upholstery techniques; complete units can be moulded in single operation for bonding to chair frames. Used notably by M. *Breuer.

latticinio or **latticino.** Decorative glass process by which opaque white canes enclosed in clear or coloured glass to produce lace-like effects. Canes lined round walls of cylindrical pot; by twisting gather, simple or complicated patterns formed. Canes also used for applied decoration, e.g. trailing. Favourite aspect of *façon de Venise. Technique developed in 16th century Venice, remaining popular to late 18th century. Enjoyed second great period of popularity (as decoration for all kinds of ornamental ware) throughout Europe in late 19th century, especially at Choisy-le-Roi, *Baccarat and *St Louis. In 20th century, technique used by P. *Venini. *See also* filigree glass, *lattimo*, and *vetro di trina*.

lattimo. *See* milk glass.

Lauder, Alexander (fl late 19th, early 20th centuries). English potter working (1876-c1914) at Barnstaple, North Devon. Art pottery, marked Lauder Barum, resembles *Barum ware of C. H. *Brannam.

Läuger, Max (b 1864). German architect, engineer and sculptor; artist potter from late 19th century. In Karlsruhe (Baden), led art department at Grossherzogliche Majolika-Manufaktur; also teacher at local school of applied art (Karlsruhe Kunstgewerbeschule).

Alexander Lauder. Earthenware vase with sgraffito decoration. c 1885. Height 15½in.

Made tiles, initially influenced by Art Nouveau style, at Kandern Pottery nearby. Experimented in ceramic sculpture, although chiefly known for glazed bowls, vases, and wall plaques. Jugs and vases, made at Karlsruhe, have slip decoration over contrasting deep colours, influenced by German peasant pottery of Bavaria and Black Forest region.

Laurin factory. French pottery making faience at Bourg-la-Reine (Hauts-de-Seine) in 19th century. Noted for high-quality body and glaze; products often sold in white for decoration by artists and amateur painters. Some ware painted by E. *Lessore. In 1870s, E. *Chaplet carried out early work in development of *barbotine* decoration.

lava glass. Marbled art glass made by mixing volcanic slag with glass metal; purple, with texture of stone. Process developed by French chemist, J. A. Chaptal, in late 18th century. Popular for boxes, candlesticks, and table ornaments in 19th century France, Bohemia, and, from 1880s, Britain (where sometimes known as *slag glass).

Max Läuger. Earthenware jar with slip decoration. Mark MKL in monogram with arms of Grand Duchy of Baden, impressed. c 1900.

layered glass. Glass in two or more superimposed layers. In contrast to *flashed glass, layers are of some thickness. Often decorated by cutting, to reveal underlying glass layers, like cameo glass.

lazy Susan. American circular table surmounted by smaller revolving tray; latter attached to spindle resting on low plinth supported on X-shaped turned stretchers, or to central turned base on table top. Tray usually c24-34in. in diameter, table top 4ft-4ft6in.; larger models unusual. May have two crescent-shaped drop leaves, central portion slightly larger than tray. Legs turned or plain, sometimes with bead-moulded or chamfered edges. Common c1840-c1880.

lazy tongs. Wooden or metal gadget resembling strip of narrow trellis with handles at one end and grippers at other, extendible up to 3ft; used to pick up objects out of normal reach. Fashionable in heyday of crinoline (c1860-c1875), when fullness of skirt restricted movement.

Leach, Bernard (b 1887). English artist potter; born in Hong Kong and brought up in Tokyo, Japan. In England from 1897, studied engraving under F. *Brangwyn (1908); returned to Tokyo in 1909. While teaching engraving and design, learned art of raku and stoneware pottery under *Kenzan VI (from 1911). With Soetsu Yanagi, began to develop influences which led to Japanese folk art movement, officially recognized in 1929. Travelled to Peking (1916-18) and Korea to study sources of oriental art. In 1919, rebuilt stoneware kiln of Kenzan on new site near Tokyo. In 1920, settled in St Ives, Cornwall. With help of Shoji Hamada (until 1923), made stoneware and raku, using local materials; revived art of marbled slip decoration, moulding dishes from slabs of clay, decorated and dried to firm texture. Joined (1922-24) by Tsuronoske Matsubayashi, who designed climbing kiln, still in use (though modified) at St Ives. A Potter's Outlook, published 1928, states economic necessity of producing useful, as well as beautiful, work, and difficulty of reconciling artistic urge for expression with practical needs, suggesting work by team of potters as possible solution. In 1933, established small pottery at Shinner's Bridge, South Devon, while teaching ceramics at nearby Dartington Hall. Returned to Far East (1934-36) to continue work with Hamada and visit Korea for purposes of study. Technical and aesthetic experience expressed in practical guide, A Potter's Book, published in 1940. Writing, teaching and work all equally influential in general development of studio pottery in 20th century. Pupils include wife, Janet, son, D. *Leach, also M. *Cardew, K. *Pleydell-Bouverie, and N. *Braden. Pottery noted for carefully planned relationship of body and glaze, and wide range of decorative techniques, e.g. brushwork, stencils, slip decoration, inlaid clay, stamped relief motifs, and modelled finials. In Japan (1950s), painted decoration used. Work marked with initials impressed within rectangle or painted. Products of Leach Pottery, St Ives, marked with S and I crossed, with two dots, enclosed in square or circle, impressed.

Leach, David (b 1910). English artist potter. Son of B. *Leach. Apprentice in father's workshop at St Ives, Cornwall, from 1930; manager from 1933; later partner. Studied in Staffordshire at Stoke-on-Trent College of Technology. Made vases, bowls, jugs, etc., in simple, practical style. Established small pottery in Bovey Tracey, South Devon (1955); also teacher. Mark: monogram of DL, impressed.

Lecourtier, Prosper (1855-1924). French *animalier* sculptor; pupil of E. *Frémiet; exhibited at Salon in late 19th century; known bronzes include Great Dane, The Forgotten One (figure of braying donkey), and Stalking Lion (1898).

leaf or **mount.** Covering of fan, either stretched across rigid frame of screen fan, or covering and binding sticks of folding fan. Usually made of lace, silk, paper, parchment, vellum, or feathers.

Lebeau, Chris (1878-1945). Dutch designer, potter, and leading glass artist; one of major figures in 20th century development of Dutch art glass. Employed as designer by *Leerdam (1922, 1925), for whom at first designed simple, mass-produced tableware. Also made elongated

*Bernard Leach. *Temmoku glazed earthenware vase. Marked with monogram and St Ives pottery mark. c1925-30. Height 4½in.*

vessels in iridescent glass in Art Nouveau style, as well as plainer vessels in Functionalist idiom with simple outlines and mottled surfaces. Contributed some designs to *Unica studio at Leerdam, and was responsible for Dutch crackle and cameo glass of period.

Lebeuf et Millet. *See* Creil-Montereau.

Le Corbusier, or **Jeanneret,** Charles Edouard (1887-1965). Architect; born in Switzerland, active in Paris; became French citizen, 1930. Used *Thonet bentwood chairs for Pavillon de l'Esprit Nouveau at Exposition Internationale des Arts Décoratifs, Paris, 1925. Designed furniture with C. *Perriand, and cousin, Pierre Jeanneret, from c1926. Reduced pieces, called 'equipment', to standard forms in three categories: chairs, multi-use table, and open or enclosed shelves; all designed for mass-production. Chairs have tubular steel frames, e.g. tilt-back model (1928) with natural hide seat and back supported on straps, strip leather arms; square armchair (1928) with rectangular, leather-covered cushions forming seat, base, arms, and back; adjustable *chaise longue* or cowboy chair (1929), with curves adapted to fit human body in various positions, leather or natural hide upholstery supported on straps. Designs still influential. All manufactured by *Thonet Brothers in France, 1929. Standardized shelves, forming open or enclosed pigeon-hole storage space, may be free-standing or fitted to wall.

Lee, Frances E. (fl late 19th century). English designer and decorator of stoneware; worked at Doulton workshop, Lambeth, London (c1875-c1890). Salt-glazed vases have incised decoration of blackberries, etc. Work initialled.

Leeds Fireclay Co. *See* Burmantofts.

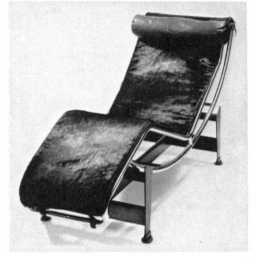

*Le Corbusier. Chaise longue, made by *Thonet Brothers. Chromium-plated steel tube frame, self-adjusting on mild steel base, pony skin upholstery. 1928.*

Leerdam or **Koninklijke Nederlandsche Glasfabrik** (Royal Dutch Glass Works). Dutch glasshouse founded 1765 in Leerdam to make bottles and tableware. (Incorporated today in Verenidge Glasfabricken, Holland.) During 19th century, produced ornamental glass and tableware following current French and German styles, notably Art Nouveau. By 1915, fresh ground broken with plain, heavily faceted crystal, including *Jaarbeckers* (first made 1918), heavy memorial glasses for each year, usually colourless or slightly tinted and decorated with gilt or engraved inscriptions. In early 1920s, C. *Lebeau established factory as one of leading European centres for Art Deco design; finest output in Functionalist glass. Other artists employed include A. D. *Copier; some outside designs also contributed by F. *Lloyd Wright.

Above
Leerdam. Glass vase by De Lorm. c1900.

Above right
Pierre Legrain. Chair of palm-tree wood with lacquer decoration; seat covered in parchment. 1925.

Below
Legras. Vase of white cased glass mottled with brown and etched with frieze of birds. Painted signature, Legras. 1920s. Height 21in.

Factory flourishes today. Mark: some factory pieces marked Leerdam; work of individual artists frequently signed and dated. *See also* Serica and Unica glass.

leg-of-mutton holder. *See* joint handle.

Legrain, Pierre (1889–1929). French bookbinder, interior decorator, and leading Art Deco furniture designer. Active in Paris; opened workshop in 1926. Furniture often reflects African influence, e.g. rosewood stool with oval seat curving upwards from centre, inspired by sacred stool of Ashanti in West Africa. Also influenced by cubism, e.g. oak stool veneered in ebony, with seat supported by rectangular column resting on two-stepped base. Often used unusual, sometimes expensive, materials such as palmwood, banana wood, macassar ebony, silver, sharkskin, lacquer, parchment, etc. Designed glass piano. Carried out commissions for art patron, Jacques Doucet.

Legras. French glasshouse founded 1864 by Auguste Legras at St Denis, near Paris. Noted for ornamental ware in Art Nouveau style, enamelled cameo vases frequently with snowscapes or autumn forest scenes, and Art Deco cameo glass. Amalgamated with *Pantin in c1920. Mark: Legras.

Leistler, Carl (1805–57). Viennese cabinet maker. Opened factory (1842) making furniture, parquet flooring, etc. Partner of M. *Thonet, c1842–49, with whom furnished Liechtenstein Palace in Vienna. Won award for furniture shown at Great Exhibition of 1851, London; examples include Gothic style bookcase presented to Queen Victoria by Emperor Franz Josef. Firm specialized in parquet after Leistler's death, continuing until c1900.

Leleu, Jules (1883–1961). French cabinet maker, showed at major exhibitions from 1922. Furniture usually in dark wood, influenced by E. J. *Ruhlmann. Furnished public buildings,

Pierre Lenordez. Bronze figure of racehorse Saucebox. Mid 19th century. Height 13½in.

Emile Lenoble. Stoneware with incised decoration, 1911-13 (left and centre), and with sgraffito decoration, 1907 (right).

Below
*Agathon Léonard. One of seven figures made by **Sèvres forming table centrepiece, Le Jeu de l'Echarge. Incised marks of Sévres factory and modeller. c1903-05.*

interior of liner, Ile de France. Showed armchair at Exposition Internationale des Arts Décoratifs, Paris, 1925.

Lenoble, Emile (1876-1939). French artist potter. After seven years' study of techniques of faience, worked for E. *Chaplet from 1904. Made stoneware in style influenced by Sung Chinese and Korean ceramics, with frequent use of floral or linear decoration incised through dark brown, blue, green, red, or white glazes, exposing grey body. In 1920s, developed use of geometrical motifs, often incised through coloured slip, and adopted more heavily-potted forms.

Lenordez, Pierre (fl 19th century). French *animalier* sculptor, specializing in equestrian subjects, e.g. Arab horses, racing groups. Exhibited at Salon, 1855-77. Works include Stallion and Brood-mare (1861), Half-breed Mare (1867), Huntsman Sounding Horn (1876), Slave and Sultan on Horseback (1877). Signature, in script: P. Lenordez.

Lenox, Walter Scott (d 1920). American porcelain manufacturer. Apprentice at Ott & Brewer factory and Willetts Manufacturing Co.; later, manager for Ott & Brewer. In partnership, established Ceramic Art Company (1889); in sole control from 1894, until Lenox Company organized (1906). Made 'Belleek' in ivory-toned, translucent porcelain, less glossy than original Irish ware, in simple, graceful designs for dinner services, etc.; sometimes transfer-printed, or etched, and acid gilded. Marks include THE CERAMIC ART CO/ TRENTON N.J., enclosed by laurel wreath tied with bow; CAC in circle with artist's palette and brushes at top left, impressed, with BELLEEK printed in red; later, Lenox monogram in laurel wreath over LENOX.

Léonard, Agathon (fl late 19th, early 20th century). French sculptor and modeller; worked

for Sèvres factory c1900. Modelled biscuit porcelain figures for table decoration, in Art Nouveau style. Series, Le Jeu de l'Echarpe, exhibited in Paris (1900). Dancing figures also produced in bronze. *See also* La *Cothurne.

Léonard, Lambert-Alexandre (b 1821). French *animalier* sculptor; studied under A-L. *Barye; exhibited at Salon, 1851-73. Works include Heron (1851), Fox and Partridge (wax with silvered finish, 1853), Thrushes Fighting (1859), Sparrows Watching Thrushes (1861), Foraging Chickens (1863), Wild Ducks Surprised by a Fox (1863), Wounded Bittern (1865), The Wolf and the Swan (1866), Heron Surprised by Spaniels (1867), Arab Surprised by Lions (1869), Combat of Eagles (1870), Waterhens (1873). Sculptures in plaster, wax, or wax with silver finish, edited in bronze; bronzes signed A.Léonard.

LePrince, Ringuet-Emmanuel (fl c1840-c1860). Parisian decorator; established workshop in New York in 1849. Father-in-law of L. *Marcotte; listed with him as Ringuet Le Prince & Marcotte in 1849-50 New York directories. From 1855, also listed separately as Ringuet, Le Prince & Co. Known for Louis XVI style furniture. Retired 1861.

Leroy, Désiré (1840-1908). Porcelain decorator. Born in France, worked in England from 1870s. Thought to have trained at Sèvres factory. Worked at Minton factory from 1870s; painted birds and flowers in Sèvres style and, notably, in white on blue ground, in style of Limoges enamel. Art director at Royal Crown Derby factory c1890 until death, succeeding J. *Rouse.

les Désolés. *See* Carriès, Jean.

Lessore, Emile (1805-76). French ceramic decorator, formerly painter. Worked at Sèvres factory. In England from 1858, worked briefly at Mintons before joining Josiah Wedgwood &

*Emile Lessore. Vase painted for J. *Wedgwood & Sons. Late 19th century.*

Above
William Richard Lethaby. Oak dresser with inlay decoration. c1900.

Below
Letter scales. Brass. Postal rates engraved on balance. English, early 20th century.

Sons. Painted plates, dishes, etc., with figure subjects in muted colours. Work, often signed, featured in Wedgwood displays at International Exhibition, London (1862), and Universal Exhibitions in Paris (1867) and Vienna (1873). Continued to paint earthenware for Wedgwood after return to France in 1863.

letter opener. *See* paper knife.

letter seal. *See* desk seal.

Lethaby, William Richard (1857-1911). English architect; also designed metalwork, furniture, pottery, etc. Principal assistant to R. N. *Shaw, 1881-93; Professor of Design at Royal College of Art, 1900; founder member of *Art Workers' Guild, 1884, Master in 1911; member of *Kenton & Co., 1890; President of *Arts & Crafts Exhibition Society; member of Design & Industries Association, 1915. Designed simple, unpolished furniture, mainly in oak, often decorated with floral marquetry in e.g. unpolished ebony, sycamore, and bleached mahogany. Also designed pieces in mahogany and rosewood for manufacturers, e.g. *Marsh, Jones & Cribb.

letter rack. Two vertical metal plates attached to opposite sides of flat base, with space between to hold letters. Usually in electro-plate, sometimes silver; usual size c8in. long, c5in. high; some with openwork or pierced designs. Made in late 19th and early 20th centuries.

letter scales. Balance, usually in brass, one end terminating in flat rectangular letter pan, other in weight pan; mounted on rectangular or shaped frame in e.g. cast brass. Variations include balance arm pivoting on central post, with weight and letter pans suspended by chains. Accompanying set of weights, also usually brass,

at ¼oz, ½oz, 1oz, 2oz, 4oz. Examples date from introduction of penny post (1840), when letters charged at one penny per ½oz.

Lettré, Emil (1876-1954). German artist craftsman; worked in Vienna, Budapest, and Paris. Went to Berlin (1912), where joined by H. G. *Murphy. Director of Staatliche Academie, Hanau, from 1933. Small amount of jewellery followed simple geometrical designs, mostly carried out in silver. Principally silversmith; won Grand Prix at Paris Exhibition, 1937.

Léveillé, Ernest (fl 1885-1900). French Art Nouveau glass artist, working in Paris; pupil of

E. *Rousseau, with whom developed *flushed glass. Continued Rousseau's experimental work with other glass surface effects after latter's retirement; as Rousseau-Léveillé, produced many sculptured pieces in crackle glass. Mark: E. Léveillé over E. Rousseau, with 74 Bd. Haussmann below.

Leven, Hugo (b 1874). German sculptor and designer active in Bremen and Düsseldorf in late 19th century; also had workshops in Paris. Designed pewter tea service c1900 for *Kayser Söhne in Art Nouveau style ornamented with enamel plaques, similar to Liberty & Co. *Tudric range. From 1910, Director of Hanau

E. Leveillé. Crackle glass vase. c1889. Height 6 in.

Below
Liberty & Company. Pewter clock case and enamelled face. Stamped 0761. c1900. Height 8in.

Academy. Pewter reliefs at National Museum of Stuttgart; tea-service design at Hessisches Landesmuseum, Darmstadt.

Levien, J.M. (fl 1840–c1865). London furniture designer and manufacturer; visited New Zealand in 1840, awarded Society of Arts medal for introducing New Zealand woods to Britain.

Liberty & Co. Left: buckle, silver with hammered finish, stamped Ly & Co, with Birmingham Assay marks for 1904. Centre: pendant and chain, silver with hammered finish, set with cabochon-cut chrysoprase. Marked WHH, for W. H. *Haseler & Co. Right: buckle, silver with repoussé design, stamped L & C, with Birmingham Assay marks for 1900.

Specialized in geometrical marquetry using natural woods, and Pompeian style furniture, e.g. cabinet incorporating 14 woods, including coconut wood, ebony, orange wood, sandalwood, and amboyna; shown at International Exhibition in London, 1862.

ley, lea, or **lay metal.** Inferior quality pewter with high lead content (up to 40%); used for candle moulds, measures, etc. from Middle Ages until 1907, when permitted lead content of pewter reduced to 10%.

Libbey, Edward (d 1925). American glass maker. Manager of *New England Glass Co. (where patented *Wild Rose Peachblow, and *Plated Amberina). Took over charter at closure in 1888 and moved firm to Toledo, Ohio, re-establishing it successfully as *Libbey Glass Co.

Libbey Glass Company. American glasshouse founded 1888 in Toledo, Ohio, by E. *Libbey, employing workers from defunct *New England Glass Co. Responsible for return to international favour of cut glass in 1880s and 1890s (which became known in America as Brilliant Period of cut glass). Also made vessels in *Amberina glass, usually marked Libbey in pontil mark.

Liberty & Co. English retail firm established 1875 by Arthur Lasenby Liberty, formerly manager of London oriental warehouse, Farmer & Rogers, in Regent Street. In 1880s, commissioned range of Art fabrics. Goods,

harmonizing with Art Nouveau decorative schemes, inspired Italian term for Art Nouveau, stile Liberty. Imported eastern, Egyptian, and Moorish furniture; commissioned designs for Moorish style smoking-rooms inspired by work of W. *Burges. Furniture, influenced by Arts and Crafts movement, often incorporates Quaint style elements, e.g. unvarnished mahogany cabinet on eight tall legs, decorated with three circular panels of inlaid coloured woods, c1905. Sold pieces designed by E. G. *Punnett, manufactured by W. *Birch. Furniture sold in Europe, e.g. by G. *Serrurier-Bovy in Liège, Belgium. Pieces usually stamped or labelled, Liberty & Co. Sold and popularized art pottery made by C. H. *Brannam in Barnstaple and at *Aller Vale Pottery. Work of W. *Moorcroft, friend of A. L. Liberty, sold with printed mark MADE FOR/ LIBERTY & CO. First silver mark, Ly & Co, entered at Goldsmiths Hall in 1894, probably

Liberty & Co. Thebes stool. Turned mahogany frame with leather seat. Copied from Egyptian original. Registered with patent office, 1884.

intended initially for use on Japanese and other imported silver. *Cymric range launched 1899; new company, Liberty & Co. (Cymric) Ltd, formed 1901 with Birmingham firm, W. H. *Haseler, which produced much of Liberty's silver (under mark, L & Co, entered at Birmingham assay office, 1901) and pewter, produced as *Tudric from 1902. Partnership ended 1926, but some Cymric pieces made in late 1920s and early 1930s. Designers, not named in catalogues, included B. *Cuzner, R. *Silver and, notably, A. *Knox. J. M. *King designed silver and jewellery from c1905. Work machine-produced in quantity; given hand-finished appearance by hand beating and inlaid enamelled plaques or semi-precious stones, e.g. turquoise or chrysoprase. Presentation caskets decorated with broad scrolling, strapwork, and prominent rivets.

library seal. *See* desk seal.

Lily pad decoration on blown pitcher, made at the New York, Lancaster, or Lockport Glassworks. c1855. Height 7⅜in.

lighthouse clock. *See* novelty clocks.

Liisberg, C.F. (1860–1909). Danish sculptor and painter. Work at Royal Copenhagen Porcelain Factory, from 1885 until death, includes plaque painted under glaze with lakeside scene, featuring coniferous tree. Style and palette resemble those used by A. *Krog.

lily-pad decoration. In American glass, design tooled from applied layer of glass into three main shapes: slender stem with bead-like pad; wider stem with small, flattened pad; long, curving stem with flat, ovoid pad.

lime glass. Effective substitute for lead glass developed 1864 by American, William Leighton, of Wheeling Glass Factory, West Virginia. Based on usual lime and soda additives, but in improved combination. Cheaper, lighter, and faster cooling, it led to significant increase in pressed glass production, but also to marked lowering of quality.

limed oak. Oak treated with lime coating which is subsequently brushed off, leaving white residue in grain. Popular in Britain from c1900.

Limoges (Haute-Vienne). French ceramic centre, 25 miles from St-Yrieix (main source of kaolin in France). Porcelain industry flourished after establishment and royal patronage in late 18th century. *Haviland family, among best known producers to present day, owned several factories from mid 19th century, selling large quantities of porcelain in America. Pouyat factory, established 1842, and those of Lanternier (1855), Bernardaud & Cie (1863), Vignaud (1911), Raynaud & Cie (1919), Léon Texeraud (1923), and Fontanille & Maraud (1925) all marketed tableware, often for export. Firm of C. *Ahrenfeldt, started as decorating workshop in 1880s, produced porcelain from 1890s. Marks: usually incorporate name or initials of factory, and Limoges, France, sometimes with trade mark or name of ware. *Illustration also at* de Feure, G.

Limoges enamelling revival. Craft of enamelling at Limoges, established in 12th century, declined during 18th century. Revived c1820–c1850 with works from several enamellers, notably Julien Robillard. Exhibitions held in Germany (1863), and Limoges (1866), stimulated by training schemes established by Sèvres porcelain factory, Paris, in attempt to re-create ancient styles. Viennese enamelling by Maria Stemkovska, Auguste Wahrmund, result of research into old techniques by teacher Professor Hans Macht, with view to restoration of national measures. Vogue consistently criticized in England, e.g. by A. *Fisher, for its deliberate archaism, and lack of function.

Limoges ware or **enamels.** Decorative porcelain, rarely earthenware, painted in thick white enamel on dark coloured ground, usually blue; effect resembles cameo. Made in 19th century, imitating 16th century enamels applied to copper in Limoges (Haute-Vienne). Introduced at Sèvres factory by 1840s. In England, speciality of T. J. *Bott at Worcester factory. In Sweden, carried out on earthenware e.g. at Rörstrand in 1880s. *cf* pâte-sur-pâte.

Lincoln rocker. American rocking chair with high, straight, upholstered back continuous with seat, open arms with pierced decoration, and padded elbow rests. Yoke rail sometimes surmounted by carved cresting. Reputedly favoured by Abraham Lincoln; dates from c1850.

Lindig, Otto (b 1895). German artist potter. Learned manufacture of porcelain in Thuringia. From 1913, studied under H. *van de Velde at Weimar, then joined Academy of Fine Arts to learn sculpture. Granted diploma and own studio at Academy in 1917, but joined ceramic department of Bauhaus as apprentice to G. *Marcks, later becoming 'journeyman' potter (1922). Introduced sharp, convex rims, made possible when production changed to hard earthenware fired at high temperature. Large coffee-pots, beer jugs, water pitchers, etc. often have large rounded belly and flared neck; lips and spouts prominent in design. Narrow, graceful shapes also occur, e.g. tall, lidded pitcher in cream earthenware, with purple flecks in glaze, on silver mount, dated 1922–23. Work marked with versions of monogram of OL, incised or in ink.

Lindstrand, Vicke (b 1904). Swedish glass designer in Art Deco and Functionalist styles. At

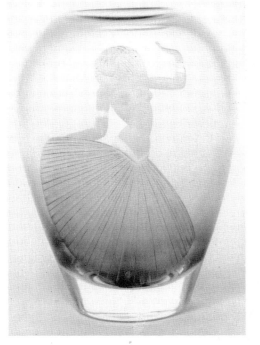

Top
Limoges. Covered porcelain jar, bowl and vase designed by E. *Colonna. c1908.

Above
Limoges enamel. Salt dish designed by G. Fauré. 1920s.

Vicke Lindstrand. Engraved glass vase for *Ørrefors. Base engraved Ørrefors Lindstrand 1648 A4. 1930s. Height 9¼in.

*Ørrefors, 1928–41. Worked first in *Ariel glass with colour inlays. Turned later to thick glassware, e.g. vases, goblets, heavily engraved with pictorial scenes of shark killers, clowns, etc. Also worked in *Graal glass. Mark: L with Ørrefors, or Øf, diamond engraved (on all engraved glass); LA (on cut glass); LU (on furnace-finished glass). *Illustration at* Kosta.

linear engraving. Ornamental pattern or inscription traced in metal with chisel-like tool, graver, which removes fine threads. 19th century repertoire of patterns, scenes, calligraphy, derived from pattern books circulating in Europe and England from 16th century. Varia-

tions include bright-cut engraving, developed in Birmingham in late 18th century to decorate silver, Sheffield plate, and flatware; double edge of graving tool simultaneously removes material and burnishes cut; and related feather-edge engraving: border ornament of fine, oblique lines e.g. on silver flatware (called feather pattern). *See* engine turning.

linen smoother, slicker, or **slick stone.** Mushroom-shaped glass implement with solid base and 5in. long handle for smoothing linen or polishing floor. Made in clear or coloured glass; some *millefiori* specimens made in Stourbridge from mid 19th century.

Linossier, Claudius (1893–1955). French metalworker. Made copper vases, some inlaid with silver, in Art Deco style, e.g. vase in hammered copper with irregular fire patination, decorative border of five narrow lines of inlaid hammered silver, c1925, now in Victoria & Albert Museum, London.

Linthorpe Pottery. English art pottery established in 1879, near Middlesbrough, Yorkshire, with help of C. *Dresser, art director and designer until 1882. H. *Tooth was manager, 1879–82. Early Linthorpe ware in simple, graceful forms, usually with flowing glazes in two or more rich colours. Later decoration sometimes

Linthorpe Pottery. Earthenware pot pourri and cover. One of pair. 1879-81. Decorated by Clara Pringle.

painted in slip or underglaze colours, *sgraffito*, or *pâte-sur-pâte*. Production ceased in 1890. Work marked LINTHORPE, sometimes over outline of squat vase, impressed. Some pieces signed by Dresser and/or initialled with monogram of Tooth.

Lion-Cachet, C.A. (1864-1945). Dutch artist and furniture designer. Introduced Javanese bȧtik designs as decorative motifs on furniture, e.g. armchair, *c*1900, in rosewood with seat and back panel ornamented with batik designs.

liqueur cup. Small cup, with one or two handles, for liqueurs. Made from *c*1860 in sets of six, in solid silver or in glass with silver mounts.

liquid gold. *See* gilding.

lithography. Ceramic decoration; design drawn in acid-resistant wax on lithographic stone, then treated with dilute nitric acid to remove background, leaving details of pattern in relief. Stone then used to print transfer paper for application to ceramic body, over or under glaze. First process patented in England (1839) allowed monochrome printing, at first in blue; later, pink, green, purple, grey, or black used. Polychrome printing, patented in mid 1850s but not perfected until 1870s, employed separate lithographic plate for each colour, printed in varnish on transfer paper and sprinkled with metallic oxide pigment and dried before application of next, lighter, colour. Process used at Wedgwood factory from 1863; notable examples by E. *Ravilious in 1930s.

lithophane, lithophany, or **Berlin transparency.** Translucent panel of biscuit porcelain with intaglio moulded decoration visible by transmitted light. Process using wax original and plaster cast, patented in Paris (1827). Rights of manufacture in Germany bought by Meissen factory; examples made from 1828 include shades for night lights, etc. Also produced in large quantities at Berlin state porcelain factory until *c*1850. After expiry of French patent, made at Sèvres factory by 1850, and later by other European manufacturers, e.g. Royal Copenhagen Porcelain Factory (late 1840s, early 1850s). In England, few made before mid 19th century; views and scenes with human or animal figures made at Minton factory from *c*1848.

Other makers include South Wales Pottery at Llanelly, W. T. *Copeland, W. H. *Goss, and Belleek factory. Process used at Wedgwood factory for manufacture of lamp shades.

lithyalin glass. Polished opaque or translucent marbled glass developed 1829 by F. *Egermann in wide range of strong colours, e.g. blue, amethyst, ruby red, green. Resembles natural gemstones. Vessels sometimes silver-etched, cut, engraved, or painted in enamels or gold. Imitated by number of contemporary and later Bohemian glass factories; also in France.

Llanelly. *See* South Wales Pottery.

Lloyd & Summerfield. English glasshouse in Birmingham. From 1849, made pressed glass and coloured and opaline ware. Drinking vessels with elaborately convoluted stems also distinctive mid century product. Later, like F. & C. *Osler, made novelty glass busts of celebrities or allegorical subjects; also busts in medallion form.

Lobmeyr, J. & L. Austrian glasshouse in Vienna. Period of international importance when under directorship of L. *Lobmeyr from 1864. Thereafter, produced fine cut and engraved glass to close of 19th century; also, original Art Nouveau iridescent glass and, later, fine Functionalist glass. Artists include O. *Haerdtle, J. *Hoffman, F. *Knöchel, C. *Pietsch, and F. *Ullmann. Mark: JLB forming grille, engraved on important pieces after 1860.

Lobmeyr, Ludwig (fl *c*1864-1900). Austrian glass designer and industrialist; in 1864, took over parental factory of J. & L. *Lobmeyr in Vienna. Reacting against current Islamic style revival and mass-produced ware, brought together finest Austrian and Bohemian glass artists to design studio glass, reinstating cut and engraved glass to earlier preeminence. Brought same pioneering enthusiasm to development of Austrian Art Nouveau glass.

lock. Appliance for fastening door, lid, etc., with bolt requiring specific key to work it. Made from antiquity in Egypt, China, etc.; 19th and 20th century examples in cast brass, cast or wrought iron, steel, bronze. Main categories: rim lock, fitted to door surface; mortice lock, fitted within door body; padlock, self contained lock for securing e.g. hasps, staples; cabinet lock, for use on household furniture; safe lock, for high security. Since introduction (1818) of detector

*J. Loetz Witwe. Three vases, designed by M. R. *von Spaun. c1898.*

lever safe lock by English maker, Jeremiah Chubb, no significant improvement in principle of high-security lock. American, Linus Yale, introduced (1848) cylinder rim lock, first mass-produced lock giving adequate security. Keyless locks introduced mid 19th century, e.g. combination lock; dialling numbers in sequence, lifts pins, tumblers, etc. from sockets in bolt, allowing it to be drawn; also time lock: adaptation of clock movement to secure bolt for specified time; both types frequently used in combination with subsidiary, conventional, lock and key system. London, Birmingham, Coventry, Prescot, principal English centres of lock production during 19th century. Improvements in casting processes meant iron locks particularly cheap from c1850.

Locke, Edward (1829-1909). English porcelain painter. Apprentice at Grainger's factory, Worcester, in 1845; painted flowers in *pâte-sur-pâte* style. Vases signed with initials incised on base. In 1895, with family, established factory at Shrub Hill Works, Worcester. Products generally small and decorated with flowers in style of Worcester Royal Porcelain Co.; painted birds or landscapes with animals imitated work of Grainger's factory. In 1902, prevented by High Court injunction from using Royal Worcester name and marks. Firm ceased operation c1904.

Locke, Joseph (fl 1880s). British-born glass artist in Cambridge, Massachusetts. Developed *Amberina glass and *Agata glass for *New England Glass Co.

Locker, William (d 1859). English porcelain manufacturer. Worked in original Derby factory, as clerk and warehouseman, and established small factory at King Street, Derby, continuing work in styles of earlier factory.

locket. Popular piece of sentimental jewellery, to house picture or lock of hair. Returned to fashion in 1860s, when necks bare again. Most popular neckware of 1870s; large and flamboyant. Usually oval, though heart shaped also popular; made of gold decorated with precious stones or enamel, or chased. Also made of crystal, and carved jet. Heavy silver lockets fashionable during 1880s, often decorated with monograms, names, stars, crosses, hearts, flowers, etc., set in jewels or engraved.

Loetz (also **Lötz**) **Witwe,** J. Bohemian glass-making firm. Founded 1836 in Klostermühle; bought 1840 by Johann Loetz. Known for fine quality stone glass (from c1883); coloured glass; painted milk glass; cameo glass with simplified plant forms in blue or black. Under M. R. *von Spaun, made fine iridescent glass, coming closest to L. C. *Tiffany of all his European imitators, for a time even surpassing him in popularity. Designs often more purposeful than Tiffany's, though forms later became stereotyped. Ceased production at outbreak of 2nd World War. Marks: two crossed arrows with star in each intersection; Loetz, Austria; crossed arrows within circle and Lötz; crossed arrows within circle and Lötz, Klostermühle.

Loêuillard, Octave. *See* Boucheron.

Löffler, Bertold (b 1874). Austrian painter, designer, and graphic artist. With M. *Powolny,

established Wiener Keramik (1905). Designs include figures, vases, jars, and tiles.

Long, William A. (fl late 19th, early 20th centuries). American potter; formerly pharmacist in Steubenville, Ohio. Organized *Lonhuda Pottery (partnership of Long, Hunter & Day) in 1892. Helped by L. *Fry, used underglaze process of Rookwood Standard ware to produce pottery decorated with flowers, etc. Mark: LONHUDA, impressed, sometimes with emblem of Indian's head. Sold business to S. A. *Weller and transferred operation to Zanesville, Ohio, in 1895. At J. B. *Owens's Pottery from 1896, made art pottery decorated under glaze, e.g. with portraits of American Indians, animals' heads, or sprays of flowers, painted in coloured slips on shaded, flowing grounds; marked OWENS UTOPIAN. Later, established Denver China & Pottery Company in Colorado. Some work resembles that made at Lonhuda Pottery; also made art pottery with matt glazes, usually green, sometimes iridescent, painted with native flowers of Colorado in style influenced by Art Nouveau, marked DENAURA DENVER in emblem which includes arrow and two fish. In 1905, at Newark, New Jersey, established Clifton Art Pottery. Products include earthenware imitating shapes and decoration of early American Indian pottery.

Longwy (Meurthe-et-Moselle). French faience factory established in 1798; by late 19th century, traded as Société des Faïenceries de Longwy et Senelle. Relief decoration, frequently used, includes vine branches on plates, etc., edged with blue line. *Emaux de Longwy*, introduced c1875,

Longwy. Vase with white, blue, turquoise and gold enamel decoration. c1920.

decorated notably with Persian inspired motifs. Designs outlined with black printed manganese resist, resembling *cuerda seca* (traditionally used in decoration of tiles since introduction of technique in 11th century North Africa), and filled in with brightly coloured glazes, predominantly turquoise-blue. Work imitated by Vieillard family at Bordeaux (Gironde). Marks incorporate LONGWY, impressed or painted under glaze.

Lonhuda Pottery. American art pottery established at Steubenville, Ohio, in 1892 by W. A. *Long in partnership. With help of L. A. *Fry, introduced underglaze decoration in style of Rookwood Pottery. Shapes derived from American Indian pottery with aim of developing characteristically American style. Products shown at Chicago World's Fair (1893) seen by S. A. *Weller, who bought pottery and transferred operations to own works in Zanesville. Style continued under name Louwelsa.

loop-back Windsor chair. *See* hoop-back Windsor chair.

Loos, Adolf (1870-1933). Austrian architect, pioneer of Functionalist style; also designed glass and furniture. Trained in Dresden, Germany, and America, 1893-96 (where met F. L. *Wright). Settled in Vienna, 1896; follower of O. *Wagner. Opposed Vienna Secession, Art Nouveau. Furniture characterized by logical, constructional design, vigorous strong shapes, and absence of ornamentation, e.g. wooden chair, 1898, with yoke rail (supported by two back uprights) curving forward to form vestigial arms, and studded leather seat. Designed glass tableware for J. & L. *Lobmeyr in early 1920s.

loo table. Circular table with central pillar supporting top, resting on three or four footed base; designed for card game, loo, introduced in early 19th century. Ornate decoration popular from 1840s, e.g. carving on pedestal, or open-work scrolls on pedestal base, often incorporating stylized, floral motifs to match inlay on table top.

lorgnettes. Eyeglasses hinged to handle of varying length. First made of ebony or ivory; examples with handles of gold, silver, or mother-of-pearl, set with precious stones, appeared as evening accessory c1857. Also of sculptured rosewood, with medallions encircled by pearls. Fine Art Nouveau designs (e.g. in shape of lizard in gold, enamel, and precious stones), by R. *Lalique.

Lorimer, Sir Robert Stodart (1864-1929). Scottish architect; also designed furniture. Exponent of Arts & Crafts Movement, encouraging revival of Scottish crafts. Member of *Arts & Crafts Exhibition Society, showing drop-front oak desk with cupboard base in 1896; also oak chest with natural grain of wood suggesting details in landscape decoration on upper part.

Losanti ware. American hard-paste porcelain developed in Cincinnati (at one time called L'Osantiville), Ohio, by M. L. *McLaughlin; result of experiments starting in 1898. Exhibited in 1901 at Pan-American Exposition, Buffalo, New York. Painted decoration superseded (c1901) by carved floral and leaf designs in Art

J. & J. G. Low. Earthenware plaque modelled in low relief by A. *Osborne. Yellowish green glaze. 1880–85. Height 11in.

Low, John Gardner (b 1835). American tile maker from Chelsea, Massachusetts; formerly artist. Worked at Chelsea Keramic Art Works. In 1878, with father, established Art Tile Works, trading as J. & J. G. Low. Tiles, decorated with floral or geometrical relief designs accentuated by transparent, coloured glaze collecting in crevices, made mainly for architectural use; ornamental tiles sometimes enclosed in metal frames made by Low company. Developed 'natural' decorative process, moulding tiles from impressions of leaves or grasses. From 1883, firm traded as J.G. & J.F. Low. Portrait panels include series of American presidents. Moulded, hand-finished and glazed plaques, made by A. *Osborne, decorated with portraits, landscapes and, notably, farmyard animals. Operation ceased in 1890s. Marks include J.&J.G.LOW/ PATENT ART TILE WORKS/CHELSEA, MASS., U.S.A. and date, impressed.

low-warp or **horizontal loom.** Tapestry loom developed in Brussels in late 15th century: warp threads stretched on horizontal loom; warp cords moved by heddles; cartoon, beneath loom, reproduced in reverse (weaver cannot see result of work until complete). Both weaver's hands freed for insertion of weft threads, so technique almost doubled production speed of older *high-warp loom method, without reducing quality.

Lucas, Daniel I (1788–1867). English porcelain decorator; trained at Davenport factory. Worked at Derby from early 1830s until closure (1848); landscapes influenced by contemporary painting: subjects often taken directly from J. M. W. Turner in particular. Trained sons, John, William, and D. *Lucas II at Derby.

Lucas, Daniel II (fl mid to late 19th century). English ceramics decorator. Apprenticed to

---

Nouveau style, normally restricted to surface without affecting classical shapes. Vases, covered with glazes in subdued colours, e.g. grey, dull red, or pale green, marked with incised cypher of MCL, and LOSANTI, painted.

lost-wax process. *See* cire-perdue.

lo-tien. *See* raden.

Lotus ware. *See* Knowles, Taylor & Knowles.

Lötz Witwe, J. *See* Loetz Witwe, J.

Louis XIV style. *See* French style.

Louis XV style. *See* rococo style.

Louis XVI style. Furniture style popular in France during 1850s; in America c1865–c1900. Characterized by simple lines, round, tapering legs, straight stiles, oval backs in chairs; ebony, mother-of-pearl inlays; porcelain plaques on

Louis XVI revival style. Satinwood bonheur du jour inlaid with porcelain plaques and mounted with ormolu. Tapering amaranth legs.

large cabinets. Pieces mainly in mahogany, light walnut also used during 1880s and 1890s. Exponents include J. *Jelliff, L. *Marcotte, T. *Brooks.

lounge or **lounging chair.** Deeply sprung easy chair with long seat; usually has bobbin turning on back uprights and horizontal and vertical supports for padded arm rests, sometimes also on legs. May have detachable seat and back cushions. Also made in canework with foot rest; often with broad arms for book, glass, etc. Common in Britain and America; term dates from c1840. *cf* Sleepy Hollow chair.

Louwelsa. *See* Lonhuda Pottery and Weller, Samuel A.

Jean Luce. Two porcelain plates, with gold and silver painting (left), and blue, green, and gold painting (right). c1925.

father, D. *Lucas I, at Derby factory. At Coalport (1830-50), and factory of W. T. *Copeland (1850-70), painted landscapes on ornamental vases and dessert services. Established decorating workshop c1870.

Luce, Jean. French designer. In 1920s, decorated tableware in faience and porcelain for sale at own shop in Paris. Enamelled motifs include stylized flowers and fruit and, notably, rays of light, e.g. crossing wavy lines representing clouds, or arranged with flowers at centre of plate. Mark: crossed LLs in rectangle, painted.

luminous dial. Clock or watch dial on which hour dots, and/or numerals and hands thinly coated with mixture of phosphorus and radium, for visibility in dark. Adopted in America, c1900. Replaced night clock, in which complete dial illuminated from within, or projected on to ceiling.

Lunn, Dora (fl 20th century). English artist potter. Made earthenware at Ravenscourt Pottery in London (1916-28). Work includes tall vases with glossy monochrome glazes. Also specialized in use of matt glazes. Mark: RAVENSCOURT. Later, worked in Shepherd's Bush, London (1943-55), using mark LUNN.

Lupton, Edith (fl late 19th century). English decorator and designer of stoneware at Doulton workshop, Lambeth, London (c1876-89). Work includes vases and jugs with geometrical animal and floral designs. Specialized in stylized designs of flowers and foliage extending over most of surface. Decoration incised, perforated, carved or built up in coloured slips.

Lurçat, Jean (1892-1966). French painter, ceramic artist, frescoist, embroiderer, and leading tapestry designer in French tapestry renaissance of 1930s and 1940s. Born in Bruyères (Vosges) and worked there until 1941, then moved to Lot (bordering Dordogne). Pupil of V. *Prouvé. Took up fresco painting in 1913, tapestry in 1915, while convalescing from war wound. On visit to *Beauvais (1918), dis-

Jean Lurçat. Entrée d'un Cavalier. Tapestry on canvas. 1925. 8ft4in. × 11ft8in.

appointed by attempted reproductions of Odilon Redon and Jean Weber paintings: thereafter, avoided tapestry factories until 1937. During 1920s, made tapestries for M. *Cuttoli, also French and American patrons. Studied tapestry experiments of Nabi artists, Aristide Maillol, Paul Sérusier, and Edouard Vuillard: again disappointed; c1930, turned to methods and materials of Middle Ages. Especially impressed by Apocalypse, in only 24 colours, made in late 14th century Angers. Abandoned embroidery in favour of tapestry. Met François Tabard, Aubusson master-weaver. Began to design coarse-weave tapestries with limited colour range, maximum 20-30 shades (cf possible range of 14,000 at Gobelins in 1925). During 1930s, also produced pottery. In same period, led group of artists (including Joan Miró) designing rugs in bold, colourful, representational style, handknotted at Cogolin. Founded own workshop, 1938. Gave up painting in 1939 to devote time to tapestry. Began collaboration with Aubusson; introduced standardized scale of 34 colours for all his designs. From 1940, worked entirely from black and white cartoons, numbered according to scale. Designed set of tapestries, The Four Seasons, for Mobilier National in 1940. Throughout 1940s designed for Aubusson. 1947, co-founder (with Denise Majorel) and president of Association des Peintres-Cartonniers de Tapisserie. Designs reflect preoccupation with animal symbolism, especially cocks. Major tapestries include The Storm (1928); Garden of Cocks, and Harvests (1939); Liberty (1942);

*Below
Jean Lurçat. Le Jardin des Coqs, woven on *low warp loom by Tabard Frères et Soeurs. 1939.*

Lustre decoration on Royal Lancastrian vase made at *Pilkington Tile & Pottery Co. Early 20th century.

L'Apollinaire (1943); Man (1945); Earth, Air, Water, Fire (1946).

lustre decoration. Technique of painting pottery with metallic film revived in England by W. *De Morgan by early 1870s under influence of Pre-Raphaelite regard for medieval Italian art. Imitated e.g. by Maw & Co., who commissioned designs from W. *Crane, Craven Dunnill, and subsequently Pilkington factory. High quality lustre decoration also achieved, notably by C. *Massier in France from c1870, Zsolnay factory in Hungary, and *Kähler ceramics in Denmark. Monochrome lustre glazes became popular in 20th century. Production of English lustre ware, often with transfer-printed designs, widespread in early 19th century, continued notably in Staffordshire and north-east England; associated with Sunderland Pottery. Tableware painted with designs in lustre by A. and L. *Powell for Josiah Wedgwood & Sons Ltd and by S. *Cooper for A. E. Gray and Co. in Art Deco styles.

lustre glass. *See* iridescent glass.

Lutz, Nicholas (fl 2nd half of 19th century). French glass artist, leading craftsman of period in *latticinio* and *vetro di trina* techniques. Also made threaded glassware. After period with *St Louis glasshouse, emigrated to America in mid 19th century, working first at *Boston & Sandwich Glass Co., where became noted for floral bouquets and miniature fruits resting on *latticinio* beds. Later moved to *Mount Washington Glass Works, and, finally, to *Union Glass Co.

Lycett family. American art porcelain manufacturers; at *Faience Manufacturing Company in late 19th century. Edward Lycett director, sons, Francis and Joseph, modellers and decorators.

Lyman, Fenton & Co. *See* United States Pottery.

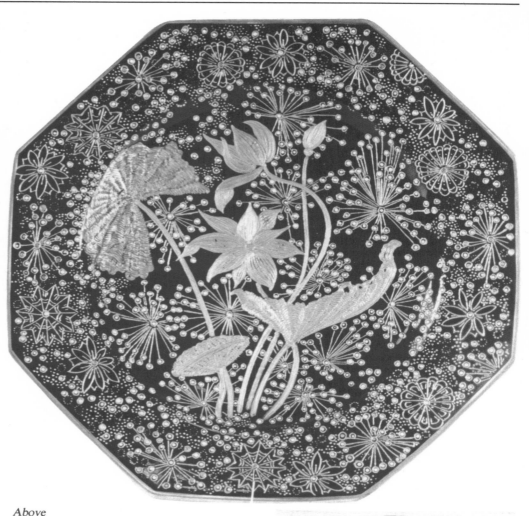

Above
Francis Lycett. Porcelain plate painted by Lycett at Greenpoint factory. c1890.
Right
Frances Macdonald. Candlestick of beaten brass. c1885. Height 20½in.

Macartney, Mervyn (1853–1932). English furniture designer; trained architect. Member of *Kenton & Co. in 1890. Designed mahogany pieces with elaborate marquetry based on 18th century designs for *Morris & Co. from 1890.

macassar ebony. Deep brown Indonesian wood with dark, almost black, stripes. Veneer used for cabinet work; popular Art Deco wood.

Macdonald, Frances (1874–1921). Scottish designer and metalworker; studied at Glasgow School of Art. Worked alone and with sister, M. *Macdonald. Collaborated with husband, J. H. *McNair, in design of furniture and stained glass. Taught enamelling, gold, silver, and metal work at Glasgow School of Art from 1907. Examples of work (e.g. pair of sconces in beaten brass, c1897) in Glasgow Museum & Art Gallery.

Macdonald, Margaret (1865–1933). Scottish designer, metalworker, and embroideress. Studied at Glasgow School of Art. Designed and made decorative metalwork with sister, F. *Macdonald. Collaborated with husband, C. R.

Margaret Macdonald. Gesso panel, one of four. Made in Glasgow, 1909.

Below
Charles Rennie Mackintosh. Oak chair painted white with stencilled canvas back. c1900. Height 45in.

*Mackintosh, in production of furniture, metal-work, etc. Later work includes gesso panels and stained glass.

Machin, Arnold (fl 20th century). English ceramic decorator and modeller. Studied in Stoke-on-Trent, Staffordshire, Derby, and South Kensington, London. Painted figures in enamel colours on porcelain made at Minton (1925–33) and Derby (1931) factories. Worked at Wedgwood factory in 1940s. Modelled figures and groups inspired by Victorian flat-back chimney ornaments, sometimes picked out in colour. Creamware figures of bulls decorated e.g. with lithographic prints of signs of zodiac.

machine-knotting. Industrial technique used in 20th century carpet manufacture to reproduce hand-knotting (usually Turkish knot). First knotting machine (Anglo-Turkey power loom) invented c1900 in England by William Youngjohns at Edward Hughes & Sons, Kidderminster; by 1901, 33 installed. Produced few designs, in limited colour range. More versatile upright loom invented by French firm, Renard Frères of Nonancourt (near Lyon): incorporated grippers and Jacquard mechanism; wove up to 13 colours. Made two qualities of carpet (Smyrna and Persian) up to 10ft6in. wide in wide range of designs. (Loom imported by English firm, *Tomkinson & Adam, in 1910.) Finest knotting machine made in Czechoslovakia in 1920s: quality of carpets approximated to very fine (Turkish) hand-knotting, with range of Persian designs. Many carpets exported to western Europe, but probably no machines. Machine-knotting technique also developed in early 20th century by Austrian, Dr M. Banyai.

machine-tufting. Followed production of hand-tufted rugs in America (inspired by popular revival of candlewick bedspreads, c1900). Machine-tufted cotton bath and bedside mats and small carpets made from c1924, eventually on wide-frame looms. (*See* tufted process.) After 2nd World War, synthetic fibres also used, with rubberized backing for durability.

Macintyre, James, & Co. Staffordshire pottery operating at Washington Works, Burslem, from c1847. Door furniture, inkstands, etc. made with black finish achieved by coating red-brown body with dark blue glaze. Also produced earthenware with rich cream body. Art pottery department, opened 1897, under direction of W. *Moorcroft until closure (1913). Firm then specialized in manufacture of electrical equipment. Transfer-printed marks incorporate name or initials of firm, and sometimes title of ware, e.g. Florian. *Illustration at* Moorcroft, W.

McKeig-Jones, Daisy. *See* Makeig-Jones, Daisy.

Mackintosh, Charles Rennie (1868–1928). Scottish architect, designer, and decorator; leading exponent of *Glasgow School. Studied at Glasgow School of Art while apprenticed to Glasgow architect John Hutchinson. Prize-winning architectural draughtsman; visited France and Italy on travelling scholarship, 1890. Joined Glasgow architect's office, where worked with J. H. *McNair. Began designing furniture c1890; first piece simple, painted cabinet book-case with asymmetrically arranged doors and shelves in base. Won competition to design and furnish new Glasgow School of Art building,

from 1897; library chairs based on traditional Windsor types.

Strongly influenced Vienna Secession; work gained more respect in Europe, especially Germany and Austria, than in Britain; exhibits by him shown by Arts & Crafts Exhibition Society, 1896, were censured.

Furniture all for buildings he had designed, e.g. various tea rooms in Glasgow remodelled for Miss Cranston from 1897, notably Willow Tea Rooms (1904): circular tables with quatrefoil lower shelf dissected by curved supports, meeting at centre; chairs very high or low backed, painted or stained, with plain vertical splats, and horizontal back rails. Many interiors included built-in furniture, e.g. settles against walls.

Furniture characterized by long straight lines complementing gentle curves. Chairs have tall, attenuated backs, low seats; cupboards with projecting cornices; tables with slender legs. Pieces often painted white with symbolic decorative motifs: favourite was stylized rose inlaid in ivory, or coloured glass, e.g. red, lilac, or mauve. Not interested in functionalism or mass-production.

Married (1900) to M. *Macdonald, with whom collaborated to produce The Opera of the Winds, one of twelve decorative panels for Wärndorfer music salon (c1902), Vienna. Designed British pavilion for Turin Exhibition, 1902.

Also designed metalwork, e.g. jewel box (c1897), wood mounted with beaten brass, set with opalescent glass; now in Victoria & Albert Museum, London. Fish knife and fork in nickel-plated silver, now in Museum of Modern Art, New York.

Little architecture after 1904. Moved to London, 1913; settled in France to paint, 1920.

Mackmurdo, Arthur Heygate (1851–1942). English architect and designer of metalwork,

*Arthur Heygate Mackmurdo. Mahogany dining chair designed for *Century Guild, c1882; made by *Collinson and Lock. Height 3ft1in.*

textiles, wallpaper, furniture, etc. Pupil of neo-Gothic artist James Brooks, strongly influenced by John Ruskin, whom he accompanied to Italy, 1874-76. On return to England prime mover in founding Society for the Protection of Ancient Buildings, 1877. 1878-80, visited Switzerland and Italy, notably Florence, and studied the Gothic and Romanesque styles; impressed by the Italian ideals of the union between artist and artisans in Middle Ages and Early Renaissance. While in Europe, also studied plants, which feature in designs from 1881. Member of *Arts & Crafts Exhibition Society. Established *Century Guild (1882) with others, including designer, poet, and architect, Herbert Horne.

Designed wallpaper, 1882 (now in Victoria & Albert Museum, London), with plant and floral motifs, including peacock, symbol of *Aesthetic movement - two face each other; between tail feathers, initials CG of Century Guild. From 1884 his floral and stalk motifs appear in wide range of designs, including brass and silver lamps. Furniture, e.g. chairs, simple and well-proportioned, with characteristic contrast between horizontal and vertical lines, often with fretwork ornament of sinuous seaweed and floral decoration, foreshadowing Art Nouveau. Used classical details, e.g. cornices. *Illustration at Century Guild.*

McKnight Kauffer, Edward (1890-1954). American artist. Trained as painter in San Francisco, Chicago and Paris; worked in England from 1914. Known mainly as poster artist (pioneered Cubist style in posters); also designed murals, interiors, exhibitions, stage sets, costumes, book illustrations, carpets and tapestries. Carpets (from c1928) similar to those of wife, M. *Dorn; influenced by Cubist painting, flat patterned, with colouring kept to subdued tonal range. Usually woven at *Wilton Royal Carpet Factory. Designs signed with initials.

McLaughlin, Mary Louise (1847-1939). American pottery and porcelain decorator. Early experiments (c1876) in underglaze decoration on porcelain made at Union Porcelain Works; painted with cobalt-blue slip. In 1877,

*Edward McKnight Kauffer. *Axminster rug. Designed c1925.*

Mary Louise McLaughlin. Pilgrim jar, 1877. Pottery painted with underglaze decoration of roses. Mark, incised, L Mc L Cin'ti 1877. Height 10¼in.

discovered secret of *barbotine* decoration; vases decorated in style developed by E. *Chaplet at Limoges (Haute-Vienne), later known as Cincinnati Limoges, exhibited in New York and Paris (1878). Organized *Women's Pottery Club (1879). Work in underglaze colours on Rookwood pottery (1880-83) includes large vase (c37in. high) decorated with hibiscus flowers in dull red and yellow on shaded background in tones of sage-green. From 1883, painted in overglaze colours and worked as metal engraver, painter, illustrator, embroiderer, and lace maker. In Cincinnati, Ohio, in 1889 began experiments in hard-paste porcelain, produced as *Losanti ware. From 1901, carved decoration of stylized flower forms and intricate pierced work in restrained Art Nouveau style. Production ceased in 1904.

McNair, J. Herbert (fl c1890-c1910). Scottish architect; designed furniture in Glasgow School style. Married F. *MacDonald. Worked with C. R. *Mackintosh in Glasgow architect's office. Designed well-proportioned furniture often with

curves and stylized naturalistic metalwork decoration, e.g. smoker's cabinet with exaggeratedly curved front, metal panels decorated with appliqué wire and *repoussé* work. Also folding screen with lead panels depicting owls in top section, glass in base.

Madras carpets. Carpet production in Madras (including part of modern Andhra Pradesh) dates from Muslim invasions in 16th century. In south, decline of 19th century wool, silk, and cotton carpet production followed introduction of aniline dyes (c1890) and cheap wool, and rapid expansion of export trade in cheap, low quality carpets. Though adapted for Western market, designs never very successful: Ayyampet, 19th century centre for woollen carpets, employed 107 weaver families c1880, only 12 by 1890. Silk carpet production, centred in Tanjore, moribund by c1890 (supposedly ruined by new jail carpet industry at Vellore). In north, centres at e.g. *Eluru, Masulipatam (and neighbouring *Warangal, Hyderabad) more successful; by 1925, c120 factories active, working exclusively to commissions, mainly for British and American markets.

Madrid, Fabrica Real da (Royal Manufactory of Madrid). *See* Spanish carpets and tapestries.

Mafra & Son. Portuguese pottery established c1853 at Caldas da Rainha. Specialized in Palissy ware. Also made earthenware figures and version of Toby jug. Glaze usually splashed with coloured oxides. Impressed mark: M.MAFRA/ CALDAS/PORTUGAL, with anchor.

magazine stand. Portable rack divided into sections for newspapers, magazines, etc. (published in increasing numbers from c1820-20th century). Examples common from mid 19th century, in variety of materials including bamboo, wickerwork, papier-mâché, drawn brass tubing, or combinations of wood and metal.

magic lantern clock. *See* novelty clocks.

Magnussen, Eric (1884-1961). Danish artist-craftsman and silversmith; studied at Kunstgewerbeschule, Berlin, 1907-08; otherwise self-taught. Own firm, 1901-33 and 1939-60. In America, worked for International Silver Co., c1938-39. Among pioneers of Art Nouveau silver in Denmark.

Maher, George Washington (1864-1926). American architect, also designed furniture; member of Prairie School. Worked in same office as F. L. *Wright and G. G. *Elmslie in Chicago, Illinois, c1887. Designed private houses, sometimes conceiving complete interiors with single decorative motif, e.g. hollyhock, thistle, or lion.

mahogany. Heavy, durable hardwood with straight, close grain; varies from pale red, deepening with age and exposure, to reddish brown, or dark red. From Cuba (Spanish mahogany), Honduras, or San Domingo; also, trade name for African wood. May be plain or figured; flame figure often used for wardrobe doors, occurs in wood taken from tree crotch; series of dark figures called plum pudding. Used in America and Britain from c1730, especially for dining-room tables, and chairs.

mains clock. *See* synchronous clock.

Maison de l'Art Nouveau, La. *See* Bing, Samuel.

Maîtrise, La. *See* Atelier Primavera.

majolica. From mid 19th century, earthenware painted in imitation of 16th century Italian maiolica. In England, made notably by Minton factory, introduced by L. *Arnoux (1850); early decoration by T. *Allen and T. *Kirby, often with figure subjects. Wide variety of products range from garden ornaments to small dishes and figures. In Europe, made notably in Italy at *Cantagalli workshop in Florence and by Ginori family at *Doccia; among other reproductions of early wares made in France at *Gien (Loiret); also, shown at Paris Exhibition (1867) by Berlin State Porcelain Factory. Term also denotes earthenware, usually with buff coloured body, decorated in relief under translucent, coloured glazes. Introduced at Minton factory, again by Arnoux, and shown at Great Exhibition in London (1851); used for vases, dishes, etc., also figures. Work of G. *Jones mainly dessert services with comports or centrepieces, fruit or salad dishes, and tureens; often impressed with monogram of G.J. and (after 1873) & Son. *Wedgwood factory took opportunity to revive own 18th century green glazed ware with decoration of leaves moulded in relief, using white earthenware body. Other English makers include W. *Brownfield & Son, and *Brown-Westhead, Moore & Co. In Sweden, produced from late 1860s by Rörstrand and Gustavsberg factories, e.g. in form of *jardinières,* vases, coffee pots, and small figures. Also made in America, apparently from 1853, by E. *Bennett and, notably, *Griffen, Smith & Hill (1879–90).

Majorelle, Louis (1859–1926). French cabinet maker. Trained as painter in Paris; took over father Auguste's cabinet making workshop in Nancy, 1879, producing reproduction 18th century furniture. Influenced by E. *Gallé, designed Art Nouveau furniture in *Ecole de Nancy style from c1890; leading manufacturer by 1900, producing machine-made pieces in series of workshops specializing in cabinet making, marquetry, etc. Furniture, usually in

Louis Majorelle. Armchair. Mahogany with leather upholstery. Height 30in.

mahogany, characterized by fluid, sculptural forms, fine proportions, often with marquetry decoration. Some pieces in giltwood. Designed custom-made suites e.g. for bedrooms, dining-rooms, drawing rooms; often with ormolu mounts in form of orchids or water-lilies. Flat surfaces, e.g. table tops, shelves, often curve upwards at rim in better quality pieces. Furniture monumental after 1906. Metalwork section of factory produced elaborate mounts for Majorelle furniture and Daum vases and bowls; also staircase balustrades, and lamps e.g. in hammered wrought iron, all in neo-rococo Art Nouveau style. Factory closed in 1915, burnt down in

*Daisy Makeig-Jones. Fairyland lustre plaque, made by J. *Wedgwood & Sons. c1915.*

1916; reconstructed from 1918. Designed Art Deco style furniture, serving on jury of Exposition Internationale des Arts Décoratifs, Paris, 1925. Factory in production until 2nd World War.

makaishi. *See* suzuri-bako.

Makeig-Jones, Daisy (fl 20th century). Porcelain decorator working at Wedgwood factory (1915–32). Designed and painted bone porcelain with lustre decoration; some derived from Chinese and Japanese styles, or influenced by Persian decoration. Birds, butterflies, dragons (Dragon lustre), or, in 1920s, fairy subjects (Fairyland lustre) painted on thinly-potted vases, dishes, etc. Ground sometimes powder-blue or black.

makie (Japanese, 'sown picture' or 'sprinkled picture'). Japanese lacquer in which design created with metallic dustings. Since development in 8th century, consistently most important and widely-used of Japanese lacquer techniques. Technique: Design drawn on prepared lacquer base, dusted with gold, silver, copper or other metallic powders, then rubbed down. Process repeated until design complete. Often used in combination with other techniques, particularly in 19th and 20th centuries, when found with embedded and encrusted lacquer. Major varieties include *hiramakie, *takamakie, *togidashi, *iroe-togidashi, and *kuro-makie.

malachite. Hard, bright green mineral (hydrated copper carbonate) with circular banding in shades of green. Much used in 19th century for inlay work, pebble jewellery, rather flat cabochons, and beads. Very often used as border for Italian mosaic jewellery. Found notably in Russia and Zambia.

Malinowski, Arno (fl early 20th century). Danish sculptor. In 1920s and 1930s, modelled figures in cream-coloured biscuit porcelain for Royal Copenhagen factory, e.g. young girl with plaited hair-style holding flowers and coloured with sepia and gold.

Mallard, Prudent (b 1809). Cabinet maker, active in New Orleans, Louisiana, from 1838. Born in Sèvres, France; emigrated to New York in 1829, when probably already trained cabinet maker. Believed to have worked with Duncan Phyfe in New York. Opened shop in New Orleans, 1838; moved to more spacious quarters, 1841; bought adjoining building, 1860. Frequent visitor to Europe. Known for large-scale furniture in rococo and Renaissance revival styles; pieces cost more than those of local contemporaries, e.g. bedroom suite sold for $3,000. Furniture unlabelled; many pieces attributed to him in existence.

Mallet-Stevens, Robert (1886–1945). French architect, interior decorator, and furniture designer. Hall and music room shown at Salon d'Automne (1913) established reputation as interior decorator. With P. *Chareau, P. *Follot, *Süe et Mare, etc. designed reception hall of French Embassy stand for Exposition Internationale des Arts Décoratifs, Paris, 1925. Designed furniture as integral part of architectural whole, using steel, aluminium, nickel, etc., sometimes painted to look like wood, e.g. metal desk (c1928) painted to look like chestnut; working surfaces lined with leather.

Maltsev Glass Works. Russian glass factory founded 1760 in Moscow by Thomas Maltsev. Made decorative ware with distinctively Russian black-stained engraving until c1850, when turned to tableware imitating current European styles.

Mamontov, Prince Savva Ivanovitch (fl c1895–c1905). Russian art patron, employing woodworkers, painters, and metalworkers on estate at Abramtsevo, near Moscow. Furniture (reflecting Russian interest in crafts revival) characterized by plant motifs and two-dimensional decoration.

manju netsuke or **Japanese button.** Probably earliest of three major forms of netsuke. Named after type of small, round Japanese rice-cake. Usually round, c1½in. in diameter, resembling squashed button; either solid or hollow, and composed of one or two sections. Solid manju made with metal ring on bottom for attaching sagemono or inro cords; hollow variety with hole in bottom through which cords threaded and then knotted inside. Early examples carved from wood, and sometimes lacquered by inro artists. By 19th century, numerous other materials popular, including ivory, horn, and bamboo; decorated with lacquer, etching, and relief carving. Two variations of basic structure, *hako and *ryusa, also popular. Greatest number made after Ansei period (1854–1859) to meet demand created by destruction of Edo in 1854 earthquake: these pre-shaped on lathe before final carving to shorten manufacturing time; decoration minimal.

mantel clock. See bracket clock.

Maltsev Glass Works. Tea caddies, with ruby flash (left) and blue glass (right). Both with brass screw tops and impressed on base with mark of Russian double-headed eagle. Height 4¾in.

mantel mirror. British Victorian term for chimney glass: mirror, usually with arched head and moulded gilt frame, resting on mantelshelf. Good quality examples in carved and gilded wood, less expensive models have *carton pierre* or papier-mâché ornament.

mantel shelves. See shelf-cluster.

manual automata. Large number of 19th century automata without elaborate clockwork mechanisms, driven by simple friction, magnetic, or counterweight devices, requiring to be set in motion by hand. French performing acrobat dolls set going by tipping attached sand container; flow of sand alters centre of gravity. Realistic swimming fish, and doll, powered by twisted elastic band, made c1880 in Paris by Ferdinand Martin. American Tammany bank, c1870, in form of caricatured politician; coin placed on outstretched hand, immediately transferred to slotted 'pocket', head simultaneously gives conspiratorial nod. English flying propeller, late 19th century, demonstrates Archimedean propulsion; formed of detachable airscrew mounted on spindle; when spindle sharply rotated, e.g. by pull cord, airscrew set in flight.

Manzoni, Carlo (fl late 19th century). Architect working in England. Ran Granville pottery at Hanley, Staffordshire, c1895–98. Painted geometrical designs of flowers, etc., within *sgraffito* outlines on earthenware, marked with monogram. In early 1898, business transferred to pottery in Ashby-de-la-Zouch, Leicestershire. Moved to Birkenhead, Cheshire, in late 1890s; associated with Della Robbia pottery.

maplewood. Light, yellowish-brown North American wood with decorative dark brown figure, e.g. bird's eye: small spots linked by undulating lines. Used for ornamental veneers; ebonized in Louis XVI style furniture.

Mappin & Webb Ltd. English engravers, silversmiths, and cutlers, originating with engraver Joseph Mappin (1797–1817) in Sheffield, 1810; engraving business discontinued by elder son, but second, Joseph Mappin the younger, worked as cutler in Norfolk Street, Sheffield; business carried on by his sons as Mappin Brothers; youngest, John Newton Mappin, left to form Mappin & Co., joining with brother-in-law George Mappin as Mappin & Webb, and later buying out Mappin Brothers. Showroom in Regent Street, London, was retained, and name changed to Mappin & Webb Ltd; foreign branches opened before 1914 in Paris, Biarritz, Johannesburg, Buenos Aires, Rio de Janeiro, and Bombay, of which last three were closed in post-war depression. Firm's products included fire irons, grates, and fenders; in mid 19th century, replaced by electro-plate silverware; leather and fancy goods, clocks, watches, etc., added later, with jewellery becoming main present-day concern. Merged with other leading companies to form British Silverware Ltd, in 1963. *Illustration at* Hutton, W., & Sons.

marble clock. Heavy overmantel clock with visible escapement and black (rarely, green or white) marble case, popular c1870–1910. Originally French; incorporates standard 19th century French high-quality factory made movement: circular plates, only slightly smaller than

dial, spring contained in going barrel, teeth of wheels finely cut. Good timekeeper: has comparatively heavy pendulum, and weight of case minimizes accidental vibration. Many exported to England. Widely imitated by American clock industry, but cheaper movements used and black slate, cast-iron, or vulcanite substituted for marble.

Marblehead Pottery. American art pottery, established 1905, originally to provide work therapy for patients in Massachusetts sanatorium; before long, operating as separate venture. Earthenware vases and bowls, sold from c1908, in simple shapes, often straight-sided, covered with matt glazes in muted colours, sometimes mingled. As well as animal and flower motifs, decoration includes subjects related to Massachusetts coast, e.g. seaweed, fish, ships; also geometrical patterns. Mark: impressed M and emblem of sailing ship, with potter's initials incised.

Marcks, Gerhard (b 1889). German sculptor and potter. Modelled figures for production in porcelain at Schwarzburg factory (Thuringia). In 1914, made decorative plaques for restaurant at Deutscher Werkbund exhibition in Cologne. Member of expressionist Novembergruppe. Teacher of modelling in Berlin (1918-20) and at ceramic school of Bauhaus at Dornburg (1920-25). Decorated tile in pale grey earthenware, unglazed, with design of face in incised lines and strips of greyish-brown slip; also painted jug with cubist design of fish, in dark brown, dark green, and blue. Often decorated work thrown by O. *Lindig or T. *Bogler. Marked work with incised cypher. On move of Bauhaus to Dessau (Halle), joined art school at Halle-Gebichenstein (1925-33); later at Hamburg (1946-50), and subsequently Cologne.

Marcotte & Company. New York furniture makers established 1861 by L. *Marcotte. Known during 1860s for Louis XVI style furniture, often finished in black and gilt; chairs with moulded backs. Parlour suites often upholstered in satin; mother-of-pearl set in marquetry often used for back panels. Later examples in Eastlake style. Occasional tables, with sabre legs tapering to slender, brass ferrules, also typical, c1870.

Marcotte, Léon (fl 1850-c1880). French cabinet maker, trained architect. Emigrated to New York, 1854, taking examples of French furniture. Son-in-law of R. E. *LePrince, listed with him in New York directories 1849/50. Known for butterfly motifs in shaded woods, and mother-of-pearl stars on furniture. Established *Marcotte & Co., 1861; leading New York decorator by 1865.

Marinot, Maurice (1882-1960). French Art Deco glass artist. Was *fauve*-painter; started making glass in 1911. At first, worked in enamels, decorating bottles and vases blown to his designs by fellow workers at Viard Fils factory near Troyes. Became fascinated by impure or imperfectly blown glass rejects, developing similar imperfections deliberately. Created large range of work in thick, sculptured glass, deeply acid-etched to give texture of moss, lichens, or bark, with colours trapped between layers of glass. Before returning to painting (1937), produced c2500 original glass pieces and gained reputation as leading glass artist. Mark: Marinot.

Maurice Marinot. Glass jar and lid with trailed and carved collar. Made in Troyes, France. c1935.

Below
Gilbert Marks. Pewter dish, signed and dated 1898.

Marks, Gilbert Leigh (1861-1905). English silversmith and metalworker in Arts and Crafts movement. Worked in firm of manufacturing silversmiths, 1878-85, then set up own workshop producing handmade metalwork. From 1895, had several one-man exhibitions in London; occasionally worked in collaboration with G. *Frampton. Work fashionable during 1890s: typical designs include flat, broad-flanged dishes, tall beakers on baluster stems and round feet, pear-shaped jugs, and tazza forms; work embellished with embossed decoration of flowers, fruit, and sometimes other motifs, e.g. fish.

Marks, Henry Stacy. *See* Stacy Marks, Henry.

Markup, Václav (b 1904). Czechoslovakian artist potter. From 1930s, noted for pottery figures inspired by Czechoslovakian folk art.

marqueterie sur verre. Decorative glass technique perfected by E. *Gallé c1897. Lumps of coloured glass pressed into warm, soft body; object then rolled on marver to smooth insets. On cooling, insets wheel-carved.

marqueterie ware. English pottery with body chequered in contrasting clays, sliced thinly and

then moulded, at Doulton workshop, Lambeth, London. Used to make tea ware, glazed and sometimes gilded. Very light in weight. Process patented in 1887; limited quantities produced until 1906.

marquetry. Furniture decoration dating from late 17th century. Floral or arabesque shapes are cut into sheet of wood veneer and inlaid with other woods or tortoiseshell, ivory, bone, metal, mother-of-pearl, etc. Veneer sheet is then applied to carcase, usually of table, chair, or cabinet. Fret saws used for expensive work; from *c*1870, cheaper examples stamped.

marquise. *See* gem cutting.

marrow scoop. Implement with elongated bowl at one end, stem channelled into narrow flute at other; known as marrow spoon to *c*1830; used to extract marrow from meat bones. Originally made in early 18th century, revived in Victorian period, usually in electro-plate; after *c*1900 formed as single-ended scoop with handle to match other cutlery.

Marsh, Jones & Cribb. English furniture makers in Leeds and London, established *c*1850. Known for Gothic Reform style furniture designed by C. *Bevan; also realized designs by B. J. *Talbert; made rosewood furniture designed by W. R. *Lethaby, 1890.

Marshall, Mark Villars (d 1912). English potter, designer, and sculptor. Trained at workshop of R. W., W. and E. *Martin. At Doulton workshop, Lambeth, London (1876–1912), incised and modelled salt-glazed stoneware in low-relief with rich ornament. Pieces often large, although small jugs, etc., also made with high-relief decoration and openwork. Much work characterized by modelled reptiles, e.g. salamanders, lizards, or frogs, used in decoration,

*Mark V. Marshall. Left to right: 1) Stoneware fish vase, c1880. 2) Stoneware vase for *Doulton & Co., Lambeth, c1880, height 10¼in. 3) Vase with carved ornament, dated 1889.*

and sensitive use of colour; graceful figures also occur. Small articles include door-stop in salt-glaze, modelled in form of cowled head with scowling face. Work bears initials MVM, incised. *Illustration at* Carrara.

Martelé silver. American silverware made by *Gorham Corporation from *c*1900; objects made from silver purer than sterling standard, formed by hammering into shapes reflecting Art Nouveau influence; craftsmen trained by English designer, W. *Codman, working in America from 1891.

Martin Brothers. English potters, partnership of R. W., E., and W. *Martin, regarded as pioneers in production of individual art pottery. Opened studio in Fulham, London (1873), and established workshop at Southall, Middlesex (1877).

Martin Brothers. Stoneware double-face jug. Eyes picked out in white; with stone and biscuit coloured faces. Signed and dated 1–1900. Height 8½in.

Made salt-glazed stoneware, fired in own kiln. Early vases and jugs, in angular forms until mid 1880s, with incised patterns and high-relief decoration, marked with scratched signature, R. W. Martin, date, and place. Shapes gradually became simpler and more rounded; incised decoration more sparingly used. Grey stoneware body decorated with cobalt-blue, or covered with dark brown glaze. Designs include leaves formally arranged in Renaissance style. From *c*1895, range of colours increased; shapes derived from gourds and other natural forms appear, often decorated with glaze effects of Japanese inspiration. Birds, animals, and jugs with leering faces made throughout period of operation; other products include goblets, candlesticks, clock cases and wide range of vases. Marks: R.W. Martin & Brothers or Martin Brothers, with London & Southall, used from 1882 until

Robert Wallace Martin. Stoneware bird with moveable head. Signed on both head and base R. W. Martin and Bros London 1–1889. Height 6¾in.

closure (1914). Management and administration of pottery undertaken by brother, Charles Martin (1846–1910), who also ran retail department in Holborn, London.

Martin family. French manufacturers of automata, in Paris, in late 19th and early 20th centuries, specializing in small figures, e.g. little pianist, barber, messenger boy; all standing *c*6in. high, incorporating unusually complex clockwork and, later, electro-magnetic mechanisms.

Martin, Robert Wallace (1843–1923). English artist potter. Worked as stone carver. In London, studied modelling at Lambeth School of Decorative Art under J-C. *Cazin, and sculpture at

Royal Academy Schools (1864); modelled terra-cotta, fired at Doulton workshop, Lambeth. In 1871, worked as modeller at potteries in Devonshire and Staffordshire. Decorator, with Cazin, at *Fulham Pottery. With W. and E. *Martin, opened studio in Fulham (1873) and organized *Martin Brothers partnership at Southall, Middlesex (1877). Specialized in modelling of animal figures and series of grotesque birds with detachable heads.

Martin, Walter (1859–1912) and Edwin (1860–1915). English artist potters. In London, studied at Lambeth School of Decorative Art and worked at Doulton workshop. In partnership with R. W. *Martin, made salt-glazed stoneware in Fulham, and at Southall, Middlesex, trading as *Martin Brothers. Walter Martin responsible for preparation of clay and throwing vases; also carried out incised decoration. Edwin Martin decorated vases, etc., with incised or relief decoration e.g. of seaweed, fish, flowers, dragons. Later work characterized by use of shapes derived from natural forms.

Mary Gregory glass. Clear or coloured inexpensive glassware, e.g. jugs, decanters, and tableware, enamelled with pink or opaque white figures, usually children. Made in large quantities in Bohemia in 19th century, imitating work of enameller at *Boston & Sandwich Glass Co., who had earlier decorated glass with similar subjects. *See also* cranberry glass.

Masaka, Sawabi (b 1868). Japanese netsuke artist and *okimono carver. Born in Nagoya; worked in Osaka from 1883. Specialized in ivory carvings, distinguished by painstaking technique and realistic style. Favourite subjects, small animals, particularly rats. Numerous carvings for Meiji Emperor and Imperial family. *Na: Risaburo. *Go: Kibodo. *Chomei: Masaka or Kihodo Masaka.

Masatsugu. *See* Kaigyokusai.

Mary Gregory glass. Possibly Bohemian. Fired enamel painting. Late 19th century. Height 7in.

Clément Massier. Earthenware bowl with lustre decoration. Mark, C. M. Golfe Juan A.M. c1890.

Mashiko. Japanese pottery centre, north of Tokyo, traditionally supplying kitchen ware for sale in city. Developed as focus of folk art movement in Japanese pottery after arrival of Hamada Shoji who settled there in 1920s.

Massier, Clément (fl late 19th, early 20th centuries). French artist potter, son of potter at Vallauris (Alpes-Maritimes). At own workshop in nearby Golfe-Juan, produced earthenware with lustre decoration, e.g. wing-handled vase with all over design of lobed leaves (dated 1889). Other plant motifs include rose, cactus, or *Eryngium,* all painted in lustre.

Massoul, Félix (fl 1890s–1930s). French artist potter; with wife, Madeleine, among number of potters active in Paris region in late 19th and early 20th centuries. Noted for use of wide range of styles, often inspired by study of archeology; other influences include Hispano-Moresque ware.

master clock. Controlled central clock which regulates one or more *slave clocks or dials by transmitting constant electrical impulse. Invented by A. *Bain, 1840; subsequently improved, e.g. in *Synchronome system.

matchbox holder. Metal cover for table use to hold box of matches, produced in late 19th and early 20th centuries. Rectangular box shaped, with slots in sides to expose striking surface on matchbox. Three sizes, corresponding to standard sizes of matchbox. Made in silver, plain, or with chased, fluted, or engine turned decoration; some types with ball feet. Cheaper versions in copper. Russian enamel examples, usually in smallest size, made c1900.

match-holder, match-box, or **match-safe.** Small container with striking surface for holding and lighting matches. Also known as vesta or fusee box. Made from late 1830s, either in tiny portable size, or larger standing size placed on desk, table, etc. Basic form, usually in silver or pewter, oblong case c3in. long, with hinged lid at

one end, striking surface (sometimes concealed) of thin parallel ridges (or later glass paper) at other. Early examples, made before widespread use of safety matches, often designed with individual compartments for each match. From mid century, large variety of forms, including many fanciful shapes: miniature letter-box with serrated base and holder for single lit match on top; miniature barrel which unscrewed in middle, fitted with container in one half, striking surface in other; bottles, musical instruments, human and animal figures, articles of clothing. Sometimes sold in presentation case with matching cigarette case. Made also in gold, silver, electro-plate. Most popular materials after metal: Tunbridge ware, enamel, porcelain, papier-mâché, shagreen, and, from c1855, bone china.

match vase or **stand.** Cylindrical match holder rising from circular ashtray base; may have rectangular holder for matchbox. Made in brass, porcelain, etc. from c1880.

Mathews, Arthur (1860–1945) and wife, Lucia (1870–1955). American painters and furniture designers in San Francisco, California; owned furniture shop employing up to 50 craftsmen. Collaborated on pieces, mainly custom-made, Arthur supervising general designs, Lucia responsible for colour and carving. Furniture characterized by brightly coloured decoration, e.g. poppies, leaves, figures in greens and orange, incised on drawer fronts, sides, and perimeters; handles often scarab-shaped. Popularity diminished after 1st World War.

Mathews, Heber (1905–59). English artist potter. Studied painting and design at Royal College of Art, London, then among pupils of W. *Staite Murray (1927–31). From 1932, pottery advisor to Rural Industries Bureau; involved in work of Arts & Crafts Society and Crafts Centre. Work in porcelain and stoneware includes large jars, vases, etc., with swirling brushed decoration. Marked work with initials, incised.

Mathsson, Bruno or Karl Bruno (b 1907). Swedish interior decorator and furniture designer. During 1930s, known for bent,

Bruno Mathsson. T.102 chair. Made at Vänamo, Sweden. Laminated beech frame and hemp webbing. 1934.

laminated wood in fluid, curved shapes, especially in chair frames; often combined with webbing made from paper compound. Tables supported by legs opening at top like petals. Designs also include combination of poles and shelves, braced between floor and ceiling, serving as bookshelves, magazine rack, and writing desk. Widely influential, 1940-50.

Matildenhöhe artists' colony. *See* Darmstadt.

matrix (of seal). Block of hardstone, glass, ivory, metal, etc., intaglio-engraved with device to be impressed on sealing wax.

matted gold. *See* bloomed gold.

matt glaze. Smooth glaze without surface gloss; pleasant to touch. May be achieved by addition e.g. of barium carbonate or aluminium oxide, combined with slow cooling process. W. H. *Grueby, inspired by work of French potters (e.g. E. *Chaplet and E. *Delaherche) exhibited at Chicago World's Fair of 1893, produced opaque enamel glaze with matt surface, c1898. On return to America from France (1896), A. *Van Briggle experimented with reproduction of Chinese matt glazes; achieved some success by 1898, and later produced wide range of colours. Matt glazes in production at Rookwood Pottery from 1901; many other potters followed. Became feature of much European art pottery in 1920s, e.g. Pilkington's Lapis ware, work of Carter, Stabler & Adams, and in France, notably on stoneware of E. *Decoeur.

Mattoni, Andreas (1779-1864). Bohemian master glass engraver of goblets, beakers, etc. Worked in Karlsbad, where L. *Moser among pupils. Mark: A.H. Mattoni.

Mauder, Bruno (1877-1948). German glass artist. Made decorative ware in geometrical Vienna Secession style during early 20th century. Head of Fachschule in Zwiesel, Bavaria, from 1910.

Maw & Company. English tile manufacturers. In 1850, bought premises and equipment of encaustic tile makers on site of Flight, Barr & Barr

Maw & Co. Glazed earthenware vase. Mark: H. & W. Maw & Co. Ltd Jackfield. 1887.

Below
Jean Mayodon. Stoneware bowl and dish. c 1925.

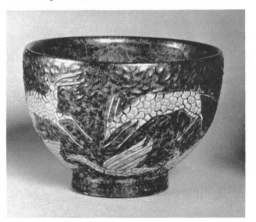

Worcester porcelain factory, then moved (1852) to Broseley, Shropshire. From 1851, made small quantity of plain and mosaic tiles; encaustic tiles often decorated with Roman or medieval designs. After experiments with local and other clays, began rapid development (from 1857), eventually becoming largest single English tile manufacturers. In 1861, started production of tesserae for use in decorative mosaics. Majolica tiles decorated with rich glazes and relief designs in Hispano-Moresque and Italian styles; full range of maiolica colours developed. Examples of transparent turquoise glaze shown at Paris Exhibition (1867). Techniques used for tile decoration include carving of layers of clay to reveal contrasting colour below, painting with overglaze colours over slip decoration, and moulding relief designs for use against ground of contrasting colour. Although mass-produced, tiles noted for high quality; steam-driven press used from 1873. Majolica vases, dishes, etc., with relief decoration also produced, some designed by W. *Crane. In 1883, transferred to new premises in Jackfield, Shropshire; operated until 1967 with several changes in firm after 2nd World War. Marks include MAW, Maw & Co./ Benthall Works/ Broseley/ Salop, or Jackfield/ Salop; name, MAW, also occurs enclosed in circular label FLOREAT SALOPIA.

Mayer, T., J. & J. Staffordshire pottery firm, operating initially in Stoke-on-Trent. In 1843, Thomas, John, and Joshua Mayer took over works at Dale Hall, Burslem. Made transfer-printed earthenware, mainly for table use, with polychrome decoration by process developed by F. & R. Pratt in 1840s; shown at International Exhibition of 1851. Other products include parian ware with elaborately modelled floral decoration. Succeeded (1855) by firm Mayer & Elliot. Marks include T. J. & J. MAYER and MAYER BROS.

Mayodon, Jean (b 1893). French artist potter. In 1920s and 1930s, made stoneware with modelled or painted decoration of figures, also e.g. deer, or birds, influenced by pottery of Near East. Shallow, stemmed bowl with red crackle glaze over delicate ribbing (at rim), decorated with nude figures and gold lustre, shown at Paris Exhibition in 1925.

Meakin, Alfred (fl late 19th century). Staffordshire potter; produced wide range of high-quality earthenware and ironstone china at Royal Albert Works, Tunstall (established 1873). Firm traded as Alfred Meakin (Tunstall) Ltd from 1897; still in operation. Earthenware marked with crown and ALFRED MEAKIN/ ENGLAND, printed.

Meakin, J. & G., Ltd. Staffordshire pottery firm, originally at Longton (from 1845), transferred to Hanley in 1848. When James Meakin retired in 1852, succeeded by sons, James and George; firm traded as J. & G. Meakin. Eagle Works built (1859) and enlarged (1868); branches also at Cobridge and Burslem. Produced earthenware and granite ware, decorated in styles of French porcelain, for American market. Mark: J. & G. MEAKIN, impressed or printed in black, also royal arms, with IRONSTONE CHINA; from 1912, trademark SOL with rising sun. Production continues.

measure. *See* ale measure.

Mecca stone. Cabochon-cut stained chalcedony. Widely used on jewellery and objects of vertu. Often found on *Fabergé items.

mechanical toys. *See* automata.

medicine bottle. *See* pharmaceutical glass.

medallion-back or **mirror-back sofa.** American sofa with serpentine front and top rail; large, upholstered medallion (oval or cartouche) in centre back. Top rail surmounts medallion and curves downwards in unbroken line to enclosed arms; secondary element sweeps beneath medallion. Rococo style models popular c1855–c1870.

Medieval Courts. Displays of furniture, inspired by medieval forms, at London Exhibitions of 1851 (designed by A. W. N. *Pugin and J. G. *Crace & Sons) and 1862 (designed by J. P. *Seddon, W. *Burges, and *Morris, Marshall, Faulkner & Co.). Inspired *Gothic Reform, *Early English styles.

Meeks, Joseph, & Sons. New York cabinet makers established 1797; showroom in New Orleans, Louisiana, by 1835. Prominent during 1850s and 1860s; known for rococo style parlour furniture, often with Renaissance revival style motifs. Ceased trading 1868.

Meerschaum (German, 'sea foam'). Soft, white, grey, or cream-coloured porous mineral, magnesium silicate, mined mostly in Turkey, but occasionally also found floating in Black Sea, giving rise to old belief that it was petrified seafoam. Particularly suitable for carving; exported in large quantities during 18th and 19th centuries to Vienna, Paris, Budapest, where carved, worked, and polished into smoker's requisites, e.g. ornate pipes, smoking bowls, cigar pipes, cigar and cigarette holders. Original white colour turns to mellow gold, or brown, after period of use, as porous substance absorbs nicotine. Most popular c1870–c1900; production declined steeply by 1914.

Meigh, Charles (fl mid 19th century). Staffordshire potter; succeeded father, Job Meigh, at Old Hall works, Hanley in 1835, after some time as manager; company traded (from 1851) as Charles Meigh & Sons, then (from 1861) as The Old Hall Earthenware Company Ltd and (1866–1901) as The Old Hall Porcelain Co. Ltd. Produced wide range of earthenware, white or decorated, for table or toilet use; dessert services enamelled and, sometimes, jewelled and gilded. Vases, figures, groups, and busts produced in parian ware, usually white, although jug (design registered 1862) with moulded insignia on handle and body has relief portrait panel of Prince Albert against blue ground. Water bottles, tea kettles, etc., made in black basalt, often enamelled and gilded. Firm noted in mid 19th century for elaborate relief decoration cast with body, not applied, e.g. on vases and, particularly, jugs. Designs for stoneware jugs include architectural detail in Gothic style, with figures in niches, or vines, and Bacchanalia; widely copied in American parian ware. Early mark: CM; other marks include MEIGH in rectangle, and titles of ware, e.g. OPAQUE PORCELAIN, ENAMEL PORCELAIN, or INDIAN STONE CHINA, and initials OHECL.

Meissen porcelain. Figure of American Indian warrior on white pony. c1898. Height 12½in.
Left
Joseph Meeks & Sons. Gothic revival desk and bookcase, made in New York. 1850s or 1860s.
Below
Meerschaum. Pipe carved as portrait of Rudyard Kipling. Made in Vienna. Block amber mouthpiece.

Meiji period (1868–1912). Japanese period starting with restoration of monarchy in 1868. Ceramics affected by introduction of European techniques and growth of industrialism. Manufacture of porcelain increased; centres include Nagoya and district, Kanazawa (Ishikawa prefecture), Yokkaichi (Mie prefecture), and Kyoto. European styles followed, mainly for export. Traditional Japanese wares, e.g. Imari, Kakiemon, and Nabeshima imitated, notably at Arita. Work of individual potters continued, mainly at Seto, Kyoto, and Tokyo.

Meissen. German porcelain factory established at Meissen, near Dresden, in early 18th century; regarded as foremost German factory until financial difficulty and artistic decline in period afftected by Napoleonic Wars (1814). Technical and financial improvements made, 1833–70; H. G. *Kuhn director from 1849. Many models from 18th century revived; some figures made from original rococo style moulds. New models, 1860–90, include child musicians and mythological groups. From 1870, figures in contemporary costume include soldiers and sportswomen. Technical experimentation resulted in display of crystalline glazes and underglaze painting in style of Copenhagen factory at Paris Exhibition (1900). Shapes echoing earlier forms decorated in style influenced by Art Nouveau, e.g. tall octagonal bottle painted on each side with *Dianthus* flower and long-stemmed bud.

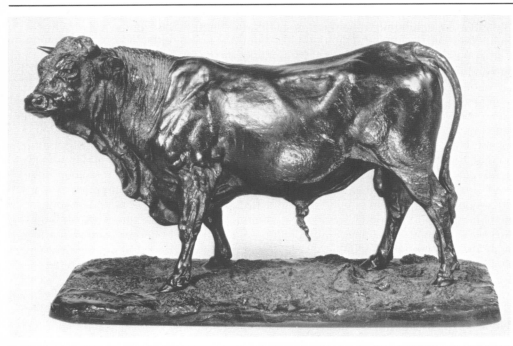

depicting hunting groups, racehorses, etc., executed with lively and meticulous naturalism. First exhibited at Salon in 1838; won awards in 1848, 1852, 1861. Many works designed specifically for British market, notably Derby Winner, exhibited at Salon of 1863, cast in bronze in 1864. After death, many models edited in bronze by son-in-law, A-N. *Cain, later by *Susse Frères and F. *Barbedienne. Casts of high technical standard bear Mêne's signature and foundry stamp. Slightly less fine copies made by English Coalbrookdale Foundry, stamped Coalbrookdale-bronze. Pirated editions, of inferior quality, appeared in early 20th century.

menu holder. Small stand consisting of two vertical plates with small gap to take menu card; or small frame, as for photograph, sometimes fitted with frosted white glass so menu could be written; stand type often in form of animal, bird, etc.; sometimes sold in sets of four. Made from middle of Victorian period in silver and electroplate, often with elaborate enamel decoration c1900. Also made in porcelain from c1860, some with flattened section on which name can be written, instead of slot for card.

menuki. See sword furniture.

Tableware commissioned from contemporary designers, e.g. H. *van de Velde (c1905) and R. *Riemerschmid (c1906). Under direction of M. A. *Pfeiffer (from 1918), figures modelled by artists including P. *Scheurich and M. *Esser. Copies of earlier models still produced. Variations of crossed sword mark include curved guard (1860-1924), addition of dates 1710, 1910 in Jubilee year, dot between sword blades (1924-34).

Mellor & Co. See Cook Pottery Co.

Mendes da Costa, Josef (1864-1939). Dutch sculptor and ceramic artist. Made stoneware vases, etc., from c1898. Figures include religious and family groups, devils, and grotesque animals. Coarse clay covered with grey glaze and

Top
Pierre-Jules Mêne. Bronze figure of pedigree bull, signed on base. Mid 19th century. Height 14in.

Above
Meriden Britannia Co. Silver-plated covered dish, 1869. Mark: Meriden B. Company.

touches of blue and brown pigment. Decorated earthenware plates, etc., with stylized animals, birds, and plants in style inspired by Javanese art, particularly batik-printed textiles.

Mêne, Pierre-Jules (1810-79). Noted French *animalier* sculptor. Son of metal turner; cast work at his own foundry, established 1838. Prolific output (1838-77) of autographed bronzes

Meriden Britannia Co. Ice-water pitcher. 1886.

mercurial compensation. See compensation.

Meriden Britannia Co. (Connecticut). American metalware manufacturers; founded 1852 by H. C. Wilcox and his brother to finish and market electro-plated etc. products of other firms, including articles made by Rogers brothers Asa, Simeon, and William, who experimented with electro-plating processes 1845-47, then began manufacturing with mark '1847 Rogers Brothers'. Meriden Co. expanded in

*Merton Abbey. High-warp woollen tapestry, woodpecker. Designed by W. *Morris, birds by P. *Webb. Woven 1885.*
Right
*Merton Abbey. Tapestry, Angeli Laudantes. Figures designed by E. *Burne-Jones, border and background by J. H. *Dearle. 7ft10in. × 6ft8in.*

1860s and 1870s, acquiring Rogers trademark and reputation; Meriden Britannia mark used for hollow-ware, though 1847 Rogers mark retained from flatware. Rogers family started rival concerns, Rogers Bros., in 1858, and William Rogers & Son, in 1865; William Rogers offered large sum by Meriden Britannia Co. to bring all Rogers companies under single control, but two further businesses were founded with Rogers name; all were finally absorbed in 1898 with establishment of Meriden International group. Meriden products in 19th century included complete range of domestic plated ware, also more specialized items e.g. *marrow scoop and *pump pot. Firm now world's largest tableware manufacturer.

Merkelbach, Reinhold (fl late 19th, early 20th centuries). German potter in Grenzhausen, Westerwald (Rhineland) from 1870s. Made stoneware, traditional production of Westerwald, with design and decoration in modern styles, e.g. by R. *Riemerschmid.

Mersey Pottery. *See* Wilkinson, A.J. Ltd.

Merton Abbey. *See* De Morgan, William Frend, Morris, William.

Merton Abbey (Surrey), England. Factory making stained glass, wallpaper, carpets, tapestry, and printed textiles; founded 1881 by W. *Morris, because insufficient space in London premises for looms and dyeworks. Tapestry looms and natural dyes used; rugs and carpets hand-knotted. Carpet designs mainly formalized plants; tapestries mainly verdures or figures on floral grounds. Plant designs and colour schemes, by Morris and J. H. *Dearle, influenced by Jacobean textile design. Animals often by P. *Webb; figures by E. *Burne-Jones, except in first Merton tapestry, Goose Girl, by W. *Crane (completed 1881), and The Seasons (or Orchard) by Morris (completed 1893). After Morris's death (1896), most designs by Dearle. Tapestry cartoons also commissioned from painters, e.g. John Byam Shaw (The Slaying of Truth), and Heywood Sumner (The Chase, c1908). Factory closed 1940.

Meshëd kelims. Rugs, from Khorassan district in Persia. Often plum-red and dark green, with medallion designs. *See* Persian carpets.

metallized glass. Iridescent glass with near-metallic surface bloom, produced by prolonged subjection to metal vapours, or by direct spraying with metallic oxides. Feature of e.g. some L. C. *Tiffany and J. *Loetz Witwe iridescent glass. Also, trade name for spatter glass developed by Aurora Glass Co., London, 1870.

metal spinning. Process used in mass production of hollow-ware from 19th century. Rotating metal disc forced over wooden or metal revolving chuck of lathe. Smooth tool of wood or polished steel used to force metal over shaped chuck.

Metthey, André (1871–1921). French artist potter, initially stonemason. After serving in army, set up kiln; made stoneware until 1906; exhibited work in 1901. Produced tin-glazed

earthenware decorated by artists of Ecole de Paris. Vases, dishes, and plates, signed e.g. by Pierre Bonnard, Maurice Denis, André Derain, Odilon Redon, Georges Rouault, Kees van Dongen, and Maurice Vlaminck, marked on reverse with initials, AM, shown at Salon d'Automne in 1909. Later, worked alone; style at first influenced by pottery of Near East (exhibited 1909). Then, inspired by Hispano-Moresque ware, experimented with colouring techniques, using geometrical or stylized plant designs; later, scenes with human or animal figures.

Mettlach ware. *See* Villeroy & Boch.

Metuchen. *See* Volkmar, Charles.

Meunier, Constantin (1831-1905). Belgian painter and poster artist; became sculptor in 1880s. Series of statues, depicting workmen of Le Borinage, reproduced as small bronzes; shown at S. *Bing's Exhibition of Art Nouveau (1899) at Grafton Galleries, London.

Meyer, Alfred (1832-1904). French enameller, known for revival of Limoges enamel techniques.

Michel, Eugène (fl 1890s). French Art Nouveau glass engraver; c1885, employed by E. *Rousseau, then E. *Léveillé. From c1900, worked mostly in coloured ice glass, shaped and cameo-cut with convoluted, undulating lines.

Michelsen, Anton. Danish firm of manufacturing and retail goldsmiths and jewellers, founded by goldsmith Anton Michelsen (1809-77) in 1841. Goldsmith and Insignia Jeweller to Danish Court from 1848. Business taken over by son, Carl Michelsen (d 1921), produced many occasional pieces for Court, e.g. 1892 Golden Wedding present for King Christian IX and

Anton Michelsen. Two cups, designed by T. Bindesbøll. Repoussé decoration. Copenhagen hallmarks for 1899 and 1900.

Queen Louise, including three epergnes, one measuring 6ft3in. G. *Jensen worked for firm, 1892-94. Art Nouveau pieces, decorated with stylized leaf forms, designed by Thorvald Bindesbøll, manufactured by Michelsen c1900, now in Kunstindustrimuseet, Copenhagen. Firm continues in business, under direction of Jorgen Michelsen.

midare bako. *See* kimono tray.

Middle Lane Pottery. *See* Brouwer, Theophilus.

Middleport Pottery. *See* Burgess, Leigh & Co.

*Ludwig Mies van der Rohe. MR chair, made in Germany by Joseph Muller from 1926, then by *Thonet Brothers in Vienna. Tubular plated steel frame.*

Mies van der Rohe, Ludwig (1886-1969). German architect; also designed furniture. Designer in P. *Behrens's office from 1908, where met W. *Gropius and *Le Corbusier. Appointed a vice-president of Deutscher Werkbund, 1926; director of Bauhaus, 1930-33. Left Germany for America, 1937. Known for experimental furniture, e.g. cantilevered chair in tubular steel with curved, front supports (manufactured by *Thonet Brothers, 1926) and *Barcelona chair, 1929.

Mikawachi. Japanese ceramic centre in Nagasaki prefecture, to south of Arita. Kilns established in 17th century. Porcelain made from 19th century known as Hirado ware, after port of export. Blue-and-white porcelain includes vases, statuettes, animal figures, and paperweights. Quality declined by late 19th century.

Miklaschewski, Andrei (fl mid 19th century). Russian porcelain manufacturer. Established factory at Volodino, near Kiev (Ukraine) in 1839. Products, including tableware, vases, etc., and figures in peasant style, made by serfs; factory closed (1862), after serfs freed by Czar Alexander II.

Milchglas. *See* milk glass.

Miles. *See* Solon, Marc-Louis.

military chest of drawers. British *campaign furniture: four drawers in two sections; front of top drawer pulls down to form writing surface, revealing small drawers, pigeon-holes. Popular until c1870.

military desk. Knee-hole desk in mahogany, cedar, or camphor wood; British *campaign furniture. Top section has brass carrying handles each side, three one-third width drawers, pull-out section flanked by two small drawers supporting collapsible, sloping writing surface; rests on two three-drawer base sections.

milk churn. Container, usually 8-10 gallon capacity, for transporting milk from farm to bottling plant or retail outlet. 19th century lidded examples conical, with flared rim, and handles;

Military chest of drawers. Mahogany with brass corners and handles; in two separate parts. English, mid 19th century.

or cylindrical, stepped in to circular neck of smaller diameter; versions e.g. in brass, copper; also made in wood, bound with brass strips, and with brass handles and rim.

milk or **opaque-white glass, lattimo, Milchglas, Porzellanglas.** Densely opaque white glass made from antiquity and widely popular throughout 19th century. Made originally by addition of calcified bones to glass body; in 19th century, usually replaced by tin or stannic oxide. Often surface painted, gilded, enamelled, or transfer-printed; found as vases, lamps, etc.; also table-ware. *See also* opal-decorated ware, opalescent glass, opaline.

millefiori (Italian, 'thousand flowers'). Canes of coloured glass rods arranged in bundles so that cross-section forms pattern; design miniaturized when bundle heated and drawn out thinly. Slices of millefiori canes used in glass bead manu-facture, and, set out side by side and fused, moulded into hollow-ware. To produce flower pattern, rods of one colour were cased several times in different coloured glass and marvered on corrugated slab while still ductile, resulting in star-pattern cross-section. Technique of ancient origin, revived first in 16th century Venice, then again in 19th century France and England for paperweights, door knobs, and other ornamental glass. In 20th century, technique used by P. *Venini. *Illustration at* paperweight.

millegrain. Gem setting: pavé-set stones held in place by numerous tiny beads of metal; back left open to increase reflectivity.

Milton Shield. Shield of silver and steel damascened with gold, depicting incidents from 'Paradise Lost'. Designed and made by L. *Morel-Ladeuil for *Elkington & Co., who made and sold copies. Won gold medal at 1867 Paris Exhibition; now in Victoria & Albert Museum, London.

Mimpei, Kaju (fl c1830–70). Japanese potter, trained in Kyoto. From early 1830s, worked at own kiln in Iganomura, on Awaji island. Made porcelain and stoneware with green and yellow glazes and relief decoration; also used greyish-white or black glazes from late 1830s. Succeeded

Millefiori. Vase. Venetian, late 19th century.

Minton, Hollins & Co. Set of six tiles. Late 19th century. 6in. square.

by nephew, Sampei – who established own kiln and continued production of green and yellow glazed wares – son, and pupil.

minaudière. Metal box with compartments for cigarettes, cosmetics, money, etc.; exterior finished in lacquer, engine-turned gold or silver, or chromium plate. Fashionable ladies' accessory during 1930s; devised by *Van Cleef & Arpels, later produced by e.g. *Cartier, *Asprey & Co.

mingei. *See* folk art ware.

miniature portrait case. Hard-covered folder, 3in.–4in. high, with portrait, e.g. of relative, lover, mounted on inside facing page; popular in America from c1840, rare in England. Covers e.g. of wood, papier-mâché, cardboard, later of thermoplastic, often bound in velvet, or leather decorated with gold-leaf or embossed designs; motifs include flowers, fruit, classical or battle scenes, patriotic designs, constitutional scrolls, and monograms. Made notably by Parsons & Co., Scovill Manufacturing Co., and Holmes, Booth & Hayden. Thermoplastic versions by Samuel Peck, of New Haven, from 1852. Portrait case superseded by photograph album from c1870.

Minton, Hollins & Co. Tile manufacture estab-lished as branch of Minton firm, under M. D. *Hollins, partner in main firm from 1845. Fresh patent taken out in 1855 for manufacture of encaustic tiles. Glazing techniques introduced by L. *Arnoux imitate Hispano-Moresque and Italian tiles. Majolica tiles made by 1850. Early transfer-printed tiles used to line floors and walls in Houses of Parliament, completed 1852. From 1859, firm distinct from parent company; com-plete separation occurred in 1868. Became lead-ing English tile manufacturer; products include unglazed geometrical tiles for pavements, encaustic tiles, unglazed for use in pavements and glazed for decoration of hearths. Majolica tiles with relief designs and painted or printed

tiles made for use on fire places, walls, etc. Marks: initials or name of firm and Stoke-on-Trent; name, Minton & Co., used on floor tiles. Firm operated as limited company from 1928.

Mintons, Ltd. Staffordshire pottery established (1793) at Stoke-on-Trent. Traded as Minton & Co. (from 1845), and Mintons Ltd (from 1873). Noted for wide range and high quality of work. Figures and groups made in large quantities in parian ware from c1847. Parian figures produced for Summerly's Art Manufactures of H. *Cole e.g. by J. *Bell. A. E. *Carrier de Belleuse model-ler from early 1850s. M. A. D. *Hollins, partner from 1845, undertook production of tiles by firm, *Minton, Hollins & Co. C. M. *Campbell, partner from 1849, took control of earthenware and porcelain manufacture from 1859. Branches of firm separated in 1868. Work of Minton & Co. shown in Great Exhibition, London (1851), had included porcelain vases in Sèvres style, plates painted with flowers, earthenware for domestic use, figures and vases in parian porcelain, earthenware tiles and decorated panels, and garden ornaments in terracotta and majolica. Under L. *Arnoux, chemist and art director until 1895, relief decorated majolica covered with transparent, coloured glazes. Other foreign artists employed in 19th century include C. *Henk, E. *Rischgitz, briefly E. *Lessore, L. *Jahn, later art director, A. *Boullemier, L. *Besche, D. *Leroy, and W. *Mussill. From 1840s, T. Allen painted panels on vases in Sèvres style, T. *Kirkby painted flowers and figure sub-jects. Artists who joined firm in 1860s include H. *Mitchell, animal painter, R. *Pilsbury, flower painter, and C. *Toft, noted for *Henri-Deux ware. M-L. *Solon introduced *pâte-sur-pâte* decoration in 1870. Under influence of *japonisme, services printed and/or hand painted with motifs of e.g. flowers, chickens, or butterflies, sometimes by W. S. *Coleman, artist from 1869 and art director of *Minton's Art-

Minton's Art-Pottery Studio. Pair of vases, c1895, with tube line decoration. Transferprinted mark: Minton Ltd. No. 46. Height 7in.

Pottery Studio, 1871–73. Tiles designed by W. *Crane, J. *Moyr Smith, and E. J. *Poynter. E. *Reuter worked at Art-Pottery Studio and (c1874–95) at Stoke-on-Trent factory. H. W. *Foster, employed from 1872, painted figure subjects, and J. E. *Dean animals, fish, etc.; both normally signed work. Earthenware vases in Art Nouveau style made under L. V. *Solon, artist and art director 1897–1909, usually decorated with coloured glazes contained by raised lines of trailed slip. Numerous marks incorporate name MINTON, or, from 1873, MINTONS, impressed or printed. Painted or gilt ermine mark sometimes used from 1840s. Symbols used to denote year of manufacture (1842–1942 inclusive); years, 43, etc., used from 1943. *Illustrations also at* Allen, T., Henri-Deuxware Jeannest, P-E., *pâte-sur-pâte*, Rischgitz, E.

Minton's Art-Pottery Studio. Established 1871 in Kensington Gore, London, under management of W. *Coleman to teach painting on porcelain and, chiefly, pottery. Also intended to provide employment for students of National Art Training School, South Kensington. Artists include H. *Barlow and E. *Reuter. Work usually bears circular mark, Mintons Art-Pottery Studio Kensington Gore, printed, with impressed mark and date cypher of Minton's. Studio burnt down in 1875 and not reopened.

mirror-back sofa. *See* medallion-back sofa.

Mirzapur (Uttar Pradesh). Indian carpet making centre from c1810. First factory founded 1850; by 1860s, largest centre in India. Mainly cottage industry, using both vegetable and aniline dyes; white wool (from Agra, Gwalior, Fatehpur, etc.), supplied by traders. By late 19th century, production catered increasingly for Western mar-

ket, e.g. patterns supplied by European agents. Copies of Persian, Turkish, Afghan, and 18th century Chinese and French carpets popular in Europe and America. Chinese types marketed as 'Bengali' or 'Nepali'; Savonnerie designs in gold, green, and white as 'Kandhari'; embossed 17th and 18th century Aubusson and Savonnerie types in pastel shades as 'Kalabar' (embossing a speciality of Uttar Pradesh). Carpets made in range of qualities, e.g. Taj Mahal, Rajasthan, Super Rajasthan.

Mishukev, Jacob Federovich (d 1900). Outstanding Russian silversmith of Moscow. Follower of Pan-Slav movement (cf Old-Russian style); specialized in subtle reproductions of 15th to 17th century enamels. Workshop taken over at death by widow and children. Production continued until Revolution.

Mission style. Term applied to simple, functional furniture in America, e.g. Craftsman and Roycroft furniture. Pieces, often in *fumed oak, frequently used in furnishing schemes with Tiffany glass, Navaho rugs, Morris chairs. Anticipated in Prairie School designs. Widely popular c1900, examples shown at furniture exhibition at Grand Rapids, Michigan, in 1900. Made until c1920; often mass-produced.

Mitchell, Henry (fl c1860–1908). English ceramic decorator. At Minton factory (c1860–c1872), painted animals, birds, etc., and at Doulton factory, Burslem (1893–1908), painted animal subjects and delicate landscapes, characterized by use of silver-grey colouring in distance.

Mitchell & Company. British carpet firm; developed export industry in India, c1870–c1920. Largest company in Kashmir (e.g. *Srinagar), c1900; ran other factories, e.g. in *Amritsar.

Mitchell & Rammelsberg. American furniture manufacturers, established 1844 in Cincinnati, Ohio. Designed in many styles, including furniture inspired by writings of B. J. *Talbert, characterized by angular brackets, spindles, and trestles. Also Eclectic furniture, e.g. combining Renaissance revival and rococo style elements. Name stencilled on pieces.

Mittelstadt family. *See* Glienitz.

Miura, Kenya (1821–89). Japanese potter, 5th in line starting with *Kenzan VI, working at Mukojima in Tokyo. Basins, water jars, etc., have bold, painted decoration, e.g. of flowering twigs and other natural forms.

mixed cut. *See* gem cutting.

mixed metal. Japanese influence on design in late 19th century led European and American jewellers to evolve mixed metal techniques to imitate Japanese work. Brooches and bracelets in silver or gold inlaid with Japanese style designs in two or three-coloured gold. In France and America, brass, copper, and steel used for inlay, but English Assay laws prevented use of lower-value metals for inlaid decoration of precious metals. Some English firms and craftsmen ignored these laws, e.g. *Elkington & Co., who employed Japanese craftsmen, and J.P. *Cooper, who made mokumé jewellery (silver inlaid with copper) after 1906.

mixed style. *See* nameless style.

Mizpah. Word often found on brooches, rings, and pendants given as love-tokens; refers to Old Testament text: 'And Mizpah; for he said, The Lord watch between me and thee, when we are absent one from another.' (Genesis 31, verse 49). Popular throughout Victorian period.

mizuire. *See* fudetate, suzuri-bako.

Mobilier National. French government department with responsibility for furniture, carpets and tapestries etc. belonging to State. Took over control of *Beauvais tapestry manufacture (1936) and *Gobelins (1937). New policies under director Guillaume Janneau produced specially commissioned cartoons from new designers. First works, J. *Lurçat's *Les Illusions d'Icare* and *Forêts*, and M. *Gromaire's *La Terre*.

model soldiers. Painted miniature soldiers, with accurately detailed uniform, cast in solid lead by German firms, e.g. Haffner, Heyde, from early 19th century. Hollow-cast models by Britain & Co. from 1893; first lines were Life Guards, Grenadier Guards, and kilted Highland Regiment.

modern English Gothic style. *See* Eastlake style.

Modernist style or **Functionalist modern furniture.** Furniture style popular in France, Britain, and America during 1930s; dates from 1922 in France. Characterized by clean lines based on modified cubism; chromium-plated tubular steel frames often combined with glass.

Stepped mouldings or fluted bands often only ornament in later designs. Manufacturers and designers include W. W. *Coates, P. *Follot, E. *Gray, O. *Hill, *DIM, and *PEL. Cheap furniture often angular with asymmetrical decoration.

Mokuhaku, or **Kashiwaya,** Buhei (1799-1870). Japanese potter working at Akahada. Made imitations of work of 17th century potter, Ninsei; noted for tea bowls decorated with scenes of land of immortals, and for water jars with designs of storks, etc.

mokume (Japanese, 'wood-eye' or 'graining'), **mokume-ji,** or **mokuri.** In Japanese lacquer technique, finely-powdered gold or powdered coloured lacquer applied to black lacquer ground to simulate appearance of grained wood.

mokuri. See mokume.

Møller, Inger (1886-1966). Danish silversmith; apprenticed to G. *Jensen in Copenhagen, 1909; own workshop from 1922. No employees: designs often made up elsewhere, but always finished pieces herself. Work decorated by sawing out and welding on; sold only through Permanente and the Danish Handcraft Guild.

mon. Japanese heraldic badge often decorating tachi (slung sword). Sword furniture for tachi more formal, conventional than ordinary girdle-worn swords. The mountings - tsuba design, lacquer work on scabbard, number and position of mon, style of hilt and scabbard mounts - differentiated types of court swords; subject to strict etiquette.

Monart ware. Heavy British Art Deco glassware; clear, streaked with various clear or opaque colours. Produced by *Moncrieff's Glass Works, usually as solid objects, or vases, etc., some very large.

Moncrieff's Glass Works. Scottish glasshouse founded c1864 by John Moncrieff in Perth, Perthshire, as North British Glass Works. Produced bottles and graduated glasses, later also chemical ware. From 1922, employed S. *Ysart and produced *Monart ware. Firm still flourishes, as John Moncrieff Ltd.

Mondo or **Tanaka,** Minosake Ryukei (1857-1917). Japanese master wood-carver. Work distinguished by meticulous execution and excellent colouring. Renowned for Buddhist images; received posthumous title, Jocho *Ho-in XXXII. Carved netsuke as hobby, including

*Monart ware. Glass bowl with blue enamel and *aventurine glass decoration. c1930. Diameter 9in.*

*William Moorcroft. Left to right: 1) Bonbonnière and cover, with printed J. *Macintyre & Co. mark and signature in green W. Moorcroft; 1904-14, height 8½in. 2) Jam pot with plated mounts, impressed Moorcroft mark, 1920s, height 3½in. 3) Florian vase, printed Florian mark and signature in green, W. Moorcroft; 1898-1904, 4) Coffee pot, impressed Royal mark, signed in brown W.M., c1935, height 7½in.*

fine *katabori netsuke in style of pre-eminent 18th century netsuke artist, Yoshimura Shuzan (or Mitsuoka). Most netsuke exported as works of Shuzan in fact executed by Mondo.

money or **penny box.** Slotted receptacle for coins, usually c9in. tall, with slot c2in. wide. Wide variety of 19th century examples in various shapes, e.g. pig, pillar box, hen, beehive, caricatured human figure; mainly intended for children's use, so often brightly painted. Mainly in metal and ceramics; some fine bone china versions, c1850-c1860.

Monroe Company, C. F. American glasshouse in Meriden, Connecticut. Noted for mould-blown 19th century *opal-decorated ware, especially dressing-table accessories, e.g. jewel boxes (some with clocks combined), powder boxes, collar and cuff containers. Also made vases, *jardinières* and other decorative items, as well as some table and household ware. Objects often ribbed and decorated in similar style to *Crown Milano. Ceased production c1916.

Monro, Helen Turner. 20th century British glass engraver; trained under W. *von Eiff in 1930s. Designed ornamental and table ware for Edinburgh & Leith Flint Glass Co. In charge of glass studio at Edinburgh College of Art from 1947. Mark: most recent pieces, Helen Monro and date, diamond engraved on horseshoe band.

montre à tact. See blind man's watch.

moonstone. Gemstone of feldspar family, transparent and colourless with blue sheen. Found chiefly in Ceylon. Never faceted; used mainly in small, round shape for short necklaces and bracelets. Very fashionable at end of 19th century. Much used by Arts and Crafts designers in silver settings, combined with mother-of-pearl.

Moonstone glaze. Matt, white glaze introduced at Wedgwood factory in mid 1920s. Possibly inspired by early Chinese glaze; noted for smooth, flawless surface. Used e.g. for production of figures and reliefs of animals, commissioned in 1926 from sculptor, John Skeaping, and some designs by K. *Murray.

Moorcroft, William (1872-1945). Staffordshire potter. Trained as art teacher. Designer for James *Macintyre & Co. at Burslem; in charge of art pottery department from 1898. Early work includes vases, bowls, biscuit barrels, etc., decorated with plant forms and scale patterned borders or panels, predominantly in blue, red, and gold (Aurelian ware), and Florian ware (1898-c1904) decorated with violets, poppies, cornflowers, etc., in underglaze colours, outlined in trailed slip, heavily at first. Flowers often stylized; designs frequently in darker shade of ground colour. Landscape pattern with trees introduced in 1902, toadstool motif (1903), and pomegranate (1911). Also mugs, vases, etc., commemorating national events, sometimes with heraldic emblems. White or cream grounds appeared with increasing range of colours and glazes. Flammarian ware produced from 1905 with lustre glazes, often red or green, decorated with medallions or plant forms trailed in slip. After closure of Macintyre's art pottery department (1913), established own pottery at Cobridge, employing potters and decorators from Macintyre's. Continued and developed established styles, noted for careful relationship of decoration with form. Products include candlesticks, pen trays, inkwells, clock cases, toast racks, etc., as well as vases, jars, and boxes. Miniature vases, scent bottles, buttons, and brooches (1920s) also made; some pieces mounted in metal. Bright monochrome lustre glazes, produced until 1920s, occasionally used over painted decoration. *Flambé* glazes in production from 1919, fully developed by late 1920s. Later floral decoration characterized by rich, dark colours and increased appearance of exotic flowers. In early 1930s, range of decorative motifs includes fruit, ears of corn, fish, birds, sailing boats, etc. Matt glazes introduced.

Bernard Moore. Pot-pourri and cover. Mark: Bernard Moore, in copper lustre. c1905-15.

Designs increasingly simple. Much work exported. Marks include MOORCROFT, and MOORCROFT/BURSLEM impressed; signature W. Moorcroft always appears, often painted in green until 1920s, afterwards mainly in blue, occasionally also impressed.

Moore, Bernard (1853–1935). Staffordshire artist potter. In 1870, with brother, Samuel, succeeded father in porcelain factory at St Mary's Works, Longton, trading as *Moore Brothers. From 1905, at Wolfe Street, Stoke-on-Trent, experimented with *flambé* glazes, in association with C. *Bailey of Doulton factory, Burslem. Glazes used on vases, etc., in simple porcelain or earthenware forms. Some work decorated, e.g. by J. *Adams, H. *Beardmore, D. *Billington. *Illustration* at Beardmore, H.

Moore, Samuel, & Co. *See* Wear Pottery.

Moore Brothers. Staffordshire porcelain manufacturers. B. *Moore and brother, Samuel, succeeded father as proprietors at St Mary's Works, Longton. Made high quality tableware, sometimes ornamental, e.g. teapot in shape of camel (1874). Also produced table centrepieces, lamps, baskets, etc., with modelled cupids, animals (notably dogs), or plant forms, e.g. cacti. Used clear turquoise glaze and metallic colours. Also made imitations of Chinese *cloisonné* enamel, and pilgrim bottles with decoration in *pâte-sur-pâte* or enamel, and lavish gilding. R. *Pilsbury art director, 1892-97. Work marked MOORE or, from 1880, MOORE BROS., impressed or incised; name painted with printed mark of globe also occurs from c1880. Works sold in 1905.

Moorish corner. High-backed version of Turkish corner (*see also* Turkish style) with ornamental superstructure, e.g. frets, arcades,

and shelves for brassware and eastern pottery; brass lamps or containers for incense suspended from canopy. Dates from c1880. *cf* cosy corner.

Moorish style. *See* Turkish style.

moquette. Heavy, hard-wearing, velvet-pile upholstery material with wool or hemp pile, cotton ground. Used for chairs, sofas, railway and bus seating during 19th century.

moquette carpet. In America, original term for carpets made on H. *Skinner's second Axminster (moquette) loom, patented 1877; later known as *spool Axminster.

Moravian Pottery and Tile Works. American pottery, established c1900 in Doylestown, Pennsylvania. Variety of techniques, coloured glazes, incised decoration, etc., used to achieve rough, hand-crafted effect, at first with Pennsylvania-Dutch designs, later, medieval motifs. Tiles have relief patterns, e.g. of mounted knight, lion, or intaglio dragon.

Morel-Ladeuil, Léonard (1820–88). French designer. In 1835, studied in Paris under metal sculptor Antoine Vechte; at 1852 Paris Fine Arts Exhibition showed allegorical iron and silver shield made for Napoleon III, richly damascened, which brought him reputation for *repoussé* work; in 1859 moved to England and signed 5 year contract with *Elkington, where he worked for remainder of life. Produced series of exhibition pieces, e.g. The Dreamers, at International Exhibition, 1862; Milton Shield and Inventions Vase at Paris, 1867; Helicon Vase at Vienna, 1873; Pompeian Lady plaque at Philadelphia, 1876; Pilgrim Shield at Paris, 1878. Returned to France in 1885, though continued to design for Elkington. Retrospective exhibition held in 1889 by Union des Arts Décoratifs showed 42 pieces of his work as leading exponent of classical, Renaissance, and other historical revival styles.

Moroccan carpets. Late 19th and early 20th century rugs; hand-made, using crude, bright red and yellow dyes. Designs at first ornate, geometrical; simpler after 2nd World War, when natural wool range (grey, brown, beige) introduced.

morocco leather. Goatskin tanned with dried, ground sumac leaves to produce soft, firm, elastic material with fine grain and texture. Made by Moors in Spain and Morocco, later in Turkey and Levant. Originally red, used for bookbinding in 16th century. Later also dyed blue, green, etc. Popular in 19th century Britain as covering for seat furniture, e.g. dining-room and club chairs.

Morris & Co. Development of *Morris, Marshall, Faulkner & Co., with W. *Morris as sole proprietor, from 1874. Specialized in woven and printed textiles, embroidery and stained glass (mostly designed by E. *Burne-Jones). Earthenware by W. *de Morgan sold at Morris & Co. showrooms, mainly with Hispano-Moresque style lustre decoration, and Persian ware. Simple joined furniture, with increasing emphasis from c1890 on high-quality cabinet work and reproduction furniture, with figured veneers, inlaid decoration, and marquetry often including acanthus motif. Designers included W. A. S. *Benson, G. *Jack, M. *Macartney, and

P. *Webb. From c1905, increasing quantities of reproduction furniture sold. In liquidation, 1940. From 1890, furniture stamped: Morris and Company, and number. *Illustrations also at* Jack, G., needlework carpet.

Morris chair. Adjustable armchair made by *Morris, Marshall, Faulkner & Co. from 1866. Rectangular seat, high back, fitted with loose cushions. Back joined to seat rail by hinges, slope controlled by metal rod fitting into rear extensions of open, usually padded, arms. Space between arms and side seat rails often filled with turned spindles; rails sometimes curve to floor replacing square rear legs. Square or shaped front legs. Chair supported on socket castors. In America, originally made in black walnut or cherrywood, later examples in oak or mahogany; large quantities factory-made, c1875-c1900. Popular Mission style furniture. Also common in Britain.

Morris elbow chair. Name given to *Sussex chair manufactured by *Morris, Marshall, Faulkner & Co. from c1865. Has square back with four bobbins joining yoke and high back rail, two lower back rails; two side rails between arm and seat rail; slanted front arm supports extend through seat to central stretcher; double front and side stretchers, single back stretcher.

Morris, Marshall, Faulkner & Company. Furnishing and design firm, 'fine art workmen in painting, carving, furniture, and the metals'. Founded 1861 by W. *Morris, D. G. *Rossetti,

Moroccan carpet. Woven by Berbers. Late 19th century.

Morris chair. Ebonized wood with turned decoration, upholstered in Original Bird woollen tapestry.

Below
William Morris. Fragment of *ingrain carpet. Designed c 1870.

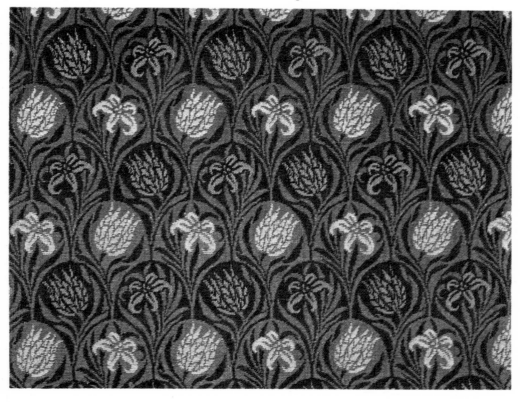

F. M. *Brown, P. *Webb, E. *Burne-Jones, Peter Paul Marshall, and Charles J. Faulkner. Designers included Brown and Webb. Furniture based on Gothic Reform and Early English styles, mainly in oak; more expensive pieces painted with medieval scenes by Burne-Jones, Rossetti, and Morris. Influenced fashionable taste, e.g. white or green painted surfaces instead of graining, and simple, linear furniture. Awarded two gold medals for furniture at International Exhibition in London, 1862. Rush-seated Sussex chair (including *Morris elbow chair) and adjustable *Morris chairs (1865 and 1866) copied by manufacturers; in general use by 1870s. Decorated tiles from 1862. At first, hand-made white tiles imported from Holland for decoration. Designs mainly flowers and foliage designed by W. *Morris and figures e.g. by E. *Burne-Jones. Designs also by D. G. *Rossetti and F. M. *Brown. In 1874, Marshall and Faulkner withdrew; firm renamed *Morris & Co.

Morris, May (1862-1938). English designer, embroiderer, and craft-jeweller; trained in design by father, W. *Morris. Designed and made jewellery of silver and semi-precious stones in Arts and Crafts style, using stylized natural forms, e.g. plants. Also designed for father's firm, Morris & Co., and took over embroidery section in 1885. Helped to found Women's Guild of Arts in 1907. Left collection of jewellery, including pieces by herself, to Victoria & Albert Museum, London.

Morris, Talwyn (1865-1911). British architect, and designer of bookbindings, furniture, metal-work, jewellery, and stained glass; member of *Glasgow School group. Worked on magazine, Black and White. Art director of Blackie & Sons, publishers, 1890. Made jewellery of beaten copper, aluminium, or silver, with enamel and coloured glass; designs often rectilinear.

Morris, William (1834-96). English painter, writer, designer, printer, and craftsman. Met E. *Burne-Jones at Exeter College, Oxford. Studied architecture under George Edmund Street, but abandoned it under D. G. *Rossetti's influence to become painter and designer. Rejected growing use of machine-made objects and originated handicraft revival which inspired *Arts & Crafts movement. In 1861, formed *Morris, Marshall, Faulkner & Co., which became Morris & Company in 1874. Adherent of Early English style in furniture; designed only few pieces for rooms in Red Lion Square, London (shared with E. *Burne-Jones, 1857-59): plain deal cabinets and settles with large areas painted by Burne-Jones. c1875, began experimenting with vegetable and least fugitive synthetic dyes, to improve coloured silks and wools used for firm's embroidery. Began making carpets, c1875, with yarn specially dyed in Leek, Staffordshire, by Thomas Wardle (brother of his assistant). Taught himself silk-weaving in 1876; employed silk weaver from Lyons, and acquired Jacquard loom. c1877, set up first small dye house, with looms for silk and wool weaving and carpet knotting, in own house in Queen's Square, London. Made first hand-knotted carpets. Moved to Hammersmith (1878) and set up carpet looms and one tapestry loom. Expanded to *Merton Abbey in 1881; built own dyeworks there. Also designed tiles for W. *De Morgan who shared Merton Abbey works, 1882-88. In

Morris & Co. Framed panel of four earthenware tiles. Figures probably by E. *Burne-Jones or by W. *Morris. 1870s.

Right
Alexander Morton & Co. Chesterfield wool tapestry designed by C. F. A. *Voysey. c1895.

1890, founded Kelmscott Press to raise standards of book design and typography; designed own typefaces. Most Morris carpet designs power-woven by manufacturers as Wilton, Axminster, and ingrain carpets (exceptions: hand-woven *Hammersmith rugs, and Merton Abbey carpets); popular patterns include Carbrook, Redcar, Bullerswood, and Little Flower. Member of *Arts & Crafts Exhibition Society and *Art Workers' Guild. Illustrations also at De Morgan, W., Hammersmith, Merton Abbey.

Morrison & Carr. See New York City Pottery.

Morris ware. See Cartlidge, George.

Mortlake Pottery. See Cox, George.

Morton, Alexander (fl late 19th century). Owned power loom carpet and textile factory, at Darvel, near Kilmarnock, Scotland. Carpets and tapestries designed by W. *Morris and C. F. A. *Voysey. Approached by Irish Congested District board to revive weaving industry in *Donegal: from c1898, opened several factories to make hand-knotted carpets. Employed nephew, Gavin Morton, founder of *Blackwood, Morton & Sons, as designer.

mosaic carpet. Devised by *Crossley of Halifax in 1850; manufactured until 1869. 12ft parallel yarns compressed in frame, with carpet pattern dyed throughout length, so that many identical sections could be cut. Fabric, stuck on one end with rubber solution, formed carpet foundation when first section (4×2ft) cut; 920 identical fabric-backed pile sections finally joined to form full-size carpet. Because yarn tended to unglue with wear, technique subsequently reserved for decorative panels reproducing pictures by contemporary artists. Carpets and panels, e.g. The British Lion, A Tiger, Landscape, shown at Great Exhibition of 1851.

mosaic glass. Art glass popular throughout Europe and America in second half of 19th century; used for decorative ware, especially bowls and vases. Pieces of glass of various colours fused in furnace, either haphazardly or in patterns, to form multicoloured plaques, then reheated and pressed into moulds. Process originated in ancient Egypt.

Mosaic Stone glass. American art glass patented 1886 by Challinor, Taylor & Co. of Pittsburgh, Pennsylvania. Made by preparing various colours of opaque glass metals in separate pots, then mixing in different combinations in crucible and stirring gently together, before blowing or moulding in usual way. Led to development of many other similar American and European stone glasses.

Mosaic Tile Company. American pottery, established c1894 in Zanesville, Ohio, by H. *Mueller in partnership. Produced coloured earthenware tiles for architectural use; initially inexpensive tiles, imitating mosaic. Matt glazed tiles later produced, sometimes with monogram of MTC incorporated in moulded design.

Moser, Koloman (1868–1918). Austrian painter, architect and designer. Studied painting under O. *Wagner in Vienna and supplied designs for posters and objects of vertu. Among artists of Vienna Secession (1897) with Wagner, J. *Hoffmann, J. M. *Olbrich. With Hoffmann, teacher at School of Decorative Arts, Vienna, from 1899 and established Wiener Werkstätte in 1903, exerting powerful influence on Austrian design.

Moser, Ludwig (1833–1916). Bohemian glass engraver; pupil of A. *Mattoni in Karlsbad. Became glass merchant and founded (1857) L. *Moser & Söhne in Karlsbad and Meierhöfen.

Moser, Ludwig, & Söhne. Bohemian glasshouse founded 1857 by L. *Moser in Karlsbad and Meierhöfen. Fine *Tiffany-inspired glass produced, with accent on colour and iridescence. Flourishes today. Mark: usually Moser, Karlsbad.

moss agate glass. Late 19th century British art glass imitating natural gemstone. Developed by J. *Northwood at *Stevens & Williams; later also used by F. *Carder there. Manufacturing process complex; blown soda glass object coated with heavier lead glass, rolled in particles of vari-coloured powdered glass, then reheated and coated again with lead glass; finally, water poured into interior of vessel to produce crackling in soft soda glass lining; piece then reheated to seal cracks, but retain crackled effect below surface.

mother-of-pearl. Scales cut from innermost lining of pearl oyster, ear and buffalo shells, used since antiquity for decoration, e.g. as inlay or veneer. Colour and lustre vary according to geographical distribution, e.g. rosy, iridescent type from Pacific and Indian Oceans, sea-green variety from Southern Pacific. 16th and 17th century English craftsmen selected each scale for shape and lustre, sawing and filing it to fit e.g. boxes, bowls; by 19th century, less lustrous scales used, shaped to size, and ground wafer thin, fitted to base with silver rivets. After c1820, improved adhesives eased difficulties of application, so wider areas could be covered; through-

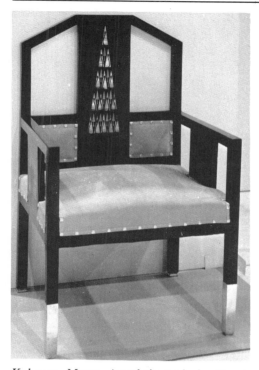

Kolomon Moser. Armchair made by Kunst-Möbel-Fabrik, Vienna. 1905.

Right
Ludwig Moser & Söhne. Vase of amber glass with gilded frieze. Signed Moser Carlsbad. c1920. Height 8¼ in.

Below
Moustache cup. Painted and gilded decoration. George James & Sons. c1855.

out 19th century, mother-of-pearl particularly fashionable as decorative appliqué to wide range of papier-mâché objects, e.g. fans, card cases, snuff boxes, furniture; also, commonly incorporated into jewellery, or made as buttons, or ornamentally inlaid into *silhouettes. London notable centre of craft, especially on larger objects, e.g. by George Morris, but 19th century Italian workmanship also particularly fine.

mother-of-pearl glass. *See* satin glass.

motor car or **dashboard clock.** Early spring-driven models (from c1910) made e.g. by C. *Frodsham & Son, and American firm, Elgin Watch Co. In late electric version, made e.g. by S. Smith & Co., London, balance wheel, impulsed by current from car battery, drives movement through gear arrangement.

mousseline glass. *See* muslin glass.

mouldings, applied. In furniture, plain or carved mouldings applied to cabinets, chests, etc. Feature of American Elizabethan, Gothic, and Renaissance revival style furniture. Wood sometimes carved by machine (from c1870 in Britain, from c1840 in America). Cheap British furniture characterized by ornate designs and imitations of hand-carved, 18th century motifs. *See also bois durci,* gutta-percha, *carton pierre.*

Mount Washington Glass Works. American glass house founded 1837 by D. *Jarves. Made wide range of table and decorative ware in blown, cut, and pressed glass. Also made some acid-etched cameo glass, chiefly bowls and lamps, usually with neo-classical decoration, and quantity of opal-decorated ware, especially *Smith Brothers vases. Noted for *Burmese glass, patented 1885; other art glass includes *Albertine, *Coralene, *Crown Milano, *Rose Amber, *Royal Flemish, as well as own version of *Peachblow in pastel shades. Taken over by Pairpoint Manufacturing Co. 1894. *Illustrations at* Burmese glass, Crown Milano, Royal Flemish.

Mouri or **Mauri rugs.** *See* West Turkestan.

mourning jewellery. Rings, brooches etc. worn during periods of mourning. Throughout 19th century, mourning etiquette extremely strict, demanding degrees of mourning relating to clothes and jewellery worn. Immediately after bereavement, only 'dead' or matt jet jewellery considered suitable. Only jet jewellery allowed at English court during periods of mourning; in France, black-banded onyx worn. Later in period of mourning, polished jet worn, and gold with black enamel. Pearls and diamonds accepted; amethysts worn for half-mourning. In vogue for memorial or commemorative jewellery, brooches and rings inscribed with name of deceased; most brooches have special compartment for piece of hair. *Hair jewellery worn on occasion as mourning jewellery. Custom of period was to leave sums of money in will to provide relatives with memorial jewellery, usually rings.

moustache cup. In ceramics, cup with small shelf attached near rim to prevent user's moustache from trailing in contents of cup. Produced, notably in porcelain by English manufacturers, e.g. Mintons, Derby, and Worcester Royal

Moustache spoon. English, late 19th century.

Right
Müller Brothers. Vase of *verre doublé enamelled, cut, and acid-etched. Signed Müller Frères Lunéville, c1900. Height 5¼ in.

Porcelain Co. c1855–c1900. Examples also imported from Germany, inscribed for sale as gifts and souvenirs.

moustache spoon. Spoon with pierced, engraved guard over front of large oval bowl to protect moustache; made in silver or electro-plate, in left and right handed versions. Patented 1875 by E. B. A. Mitcheson of Philadelphia. Later modification, etiquette spoon, patented 1890, had deeper, rounder bowl.

moving eye clock. *See* novelty clocks.

Moyr Smith, J. (fl 1870–89). English painter and designer. Published 'Ornamental Interiors' (1887). Designed Art furniture, e.g. for *Collinson & Lock. Examples include sideboard, c1880, in ebonized wood with incised decoration, painted in gilt and colours. Retained by Mintons as designer of transfer-printed tiles e.g. with illustrations from Waverley novels, or plays of Shakespeare (c1880), or series of Seasons (c1885).

Mucha, Alphonse (Alfons Maria) (1860–1939). Czech painter, designer, and decorative artist. Studied in Munich, Vienna, and Paris, 1890–94. Started design studio with painter James McNeil Whistler. Posters of Sarah Bernhardt brought immediate fame as representative of Art Nouveau. Illustrated books; painted murals for theatres and public buildings. Designed jewellery for G. *Fouquet, 1898–1905, including pieces for Bernhardt (e.g. Princesse Lointaine brooch, and snake bracelet and hand ornament based on piece in Médée poster). Also designed Fouquet's shop in Rue Royale. Went to New York, 1904; worked on designs with L. C. *Tiffany; one piece survives. Widely influential through poster designs and Documents Décoratifs, designs from which used almost unaltered by number of American and European jewellery firms at beginning of 20th century.

Mueller, Herman T. (fl late 19th, early 20th centuries). American tile manufacturer. From 1886, made relief plaques and tile panels for American Encaustic Tiling Co., e.g. terracotta plaque (c1895) with plump child towing sheep, against background of ivy-clad masonry and trees. With K. *Langenbeck, established *Mosaic Tile Company; left (1903) to form own tile manufacture, established 1908 in Trenton, New Jersey. Products: small animal figures, e.g.

turtle (c1910), moulded on square, tile-like base, and covered in matt green and brown glazes. Work initialled.

muffineer. Small stemmed baluster-shaped caster with tall, domed and pierced cover, for sprinkling ground cinnamon on toasted muffins; smaller than sugar caster, with finer holes; made from late 18th century, usually in silver, occasionally with porcelain body. Term also used for covered dish containing hot muffins.

muff-warmer. Small metal or stoneware container for hot water; intended to be held inside muff. Some examples with outer case of e.g. perforated copper or brass. Widely manufactured from mid 19th century to c1900.

mukade. *See* tsuba.

mull. *See* snuff mull.

Muller, Bernard (fl mid 19th century). German silversmith working in Nuremberg; manufactured silver models of birds, boats, wager cups, and grotesque figures; many imported into England from c1880. Mark: BM and pine cone.

Muller, Emile (fl late 19th century). French potter. At Ivry, near Paris, produced work

designed by I. *de Rudder and P. *Wolfers. Later worked at Choisy-le-Roi. Made terracotta, faience, and, notably, stoneware for architectural use, e.g. plaques for interior decoration and reliefs in glazed stoneware for facing building. Ornamental ware includes vases in irregular shapes, e.g. with kneeling female figure, brilliantly glazed.

Müller, Henri and Désiré (fl c1900–1933). French Art Nouveau glass artists; brothers. Worked for E. *Gallé in Nancy, and for *Val St Lambert glasshouse, producing fine vases and other decorative ware in cameo glass, moulded glass (often geometrical), and variety of coloured glass techniques. Subsequently, founded own factories in Lunéville and Croismare. Mark: Müller Frères and place of manufacture.

Multan (West Punjab). Formerly Indian – now Pakistani – carpet centre. Firmly established peasant craft (probably originally introduced from Turkestan, Shiraz, and Beluchestan) reinforced by jail carpet industry in mid 19th century. Only Punjab carpets to retain local peculiarities, despite commercialization of industry for export market. Bold designs in vivid red, yellow, and white, and longest pile among Indian carpets. Also specialized in cotton carpets, usually in blue and bluish-white, with geometrical designs incorporating octagons, decagons, and animal figures.

Munich school. Group of artists, including O. *Eckmann, R. *Riemerschmid, A. *Endell, and P. *Behrens, working in Munich, Germany, late 19th century. Style developed in early 20th century from sinuous, curving Jugendstil to simpler style, making use of geometrical motifs.

Munthe, Gerhard (1849–1929). Norwegian artist; designed Viking style furniture, e.g. armchair in wood, back surmounted by bird with striped crest; stripes echoed on seat and semi-circular ornament joining seat rail and front leg.

Muona, Toini (b 1904). Finnish ceramic artist. Pupil of A. W. *Finch. Worked at Arabia factory from 1931. Simple, often large shapes, e.g. dishes, vases, made in stoneware with monochrome glaze. Other work includes wall plaques decorated under glaze with plant forms, e.g. leaf prints, and angular vases in stoneware containing chamotte, with patches of dark glaze.

mura nashiji. *See* nashiji.

Murano, Italy. Island in Venetian lagoon, centre of Venetian glass making industry from 1291. Declined and lost glass making monopoly in 1676, but flourished again in second half of 19th century with work of *Salviati & Co., who successfully revived old techniques. Remains important glass centre, producing traditional designs and original modern glass. *See* E. Barovier and P. Venini.

Murphy, H. G. (1884–1939). English artist craftsman and silversmith; apprenticed to H. *Wilson; worked with E. *Lettré in Berlin, 1912; studied at Central School of Arts and Crafts, London; in 1913 set up own workshop. From 1907 taught at Royal College of Art, London, then at Central School, becoming first silversmith to be appointed principal. Executed work for R. M. Y. *Gleadowe and artist and typogra-

pher Eric Gill, e.g. silver chased alms dish designed by Gill in Gothic style, now in Goldsmiths' Hall.

Murray, Keith (b 1893). New Zealand-born architect and designer, in England from 1935; designs limited to silver and pottery until 1932, when first table glass to his design made by *Whitefriars Glass Works. Became part-time glass designer for *Stevens & Williams glasshouse same year, designing simple, unornamented tableware as well as more ambitious decorative pieces, e.g. vases with moulded surface decoration in style of J. *Bang and A. *Copier, J. *Hoffman – style black decoration on clear glass, and large, heavy vessels and dishes with flat, restrained, dignified cutting. Also made fine engraved crystal, notably with deep-slashed cactus motifs, marketed as Brierley Crystal. Mark: Keith Murray over *fleur de lys* and BRIERLEY; stamped or etched. Ceramic designs commissioned by Wedgwood factory. Vases, lathe turned and glazed. Domestic ware, e.g. mugs, sparingly decorated with lathe cut bands and grooves or fluting, adapted from traditional shapes. Other table ware decorated with small, scattered flowering plants and bands of painting at rim. Often made use of matt, white, Moonstone glaze.

Murray, William Staite. *See* Staite Murray, William.

musical alarm. Alarm clock incorporating small musical box instead of alarm bell. Many made in Switzerland and Germany from 1890s onwards.

musical box. Swiss musical movements, from *c*1780, produce tune by plucking tuned strips of

Below
*Keith Murray. Bowl designed for J. *Wedgwood & Sons. Grey earthenware. 1937.*

Below right
Mustard pot. Silver, in form of owl. Made by E. C. Brown. London, 1873. Height 3in.

wires, known as gongs, on principle invented by French watchmaker Bréguet for use in repeater watch. Originally incorporated e.g. in snuff boxes in gold, silver, silver gilt, enamel, made in Geneva or Paris. English musical snuff boxes, with Swiss movements from *c*1800; gold, silver, silver gilt cases made in London, Birmingham, Glasgow. From *c*1820, English musical boxes with case e.g. in horn, tortoiseshell, with inlaid mother-of-pearl ornament, or in painted tin. Movements improved throughout 19th century, e.g. versions playing more than one tune (*c*1850), or with tune fully harmonised (1870); these use one or more tuned steel combs plucked by e.g. revolving cylinder, or card, set with pegs or pins. Flutina music box, introduced *c*1850, produces flute-like notes from air-vibrated reeds; complicated developments of this, e.g. by Bremond of Geneva, Heller of Berne, Baker-Troll of England, incorporate up to 36 reeds. Ornate Swiss music box cases from early 19th century, notably from Geneva, frequently set with gem stones, seed pearls, etc., and enamelled decoration, e.g. landscape, sea scenes; or combined with e.g. *carriage clocks, music box acting as alarm; or as part of striking or repeater mechanism. Music boxes of all kinds popular to *c*1900, superseded by gramophone. *See* also singing bird musical box.

muslin or **mousseline** glass. Fragile, delicately blown British art glass of 19th century. Made from 1830; major display at Paris Exhibition of 1878 by A. *Jenkinson of Edinburgh.

Mussill, William (d 1906). Ceramic decorator. Born in Altrohlau, Bohemia; after studying in Paris and working at Sèvres factory, worked in England. At Minton factory from 1872, painted flowers – notably orchids – and birds in underglaze colours, from studies in *gouache,* on vases, plaques, etc., with red earthenware body. Work generally signed.

mustard pot. Small cylindrical, oval, or spherical bodied pot for mustard; usually has hinged lid, with thumb-piece and cut-out for shaft of

Above
H. G. Murphy. Sugar castor decorated with spiral applied wires and beaded decoration around foot. Maker's mark H. G. Murphy and Falcon London. Made in 1929. Height 5¾in.

mustard spoon. Made in silver and electro-plate, with blue glass liner, or in silver gilt without liner.

Muthesius, Herman (1861-1927). German architect. Influenced by Arts & Crafts Movement after working at German Embassy in London, 1896-1903. Superintendent of Prussian Board of Trade for Schools of Arts and Crafts. Warned German craftsmen against hackneyed imitations of past forms in 1907; established Deutscher Werkbund in same year.

Mutz, Herman (1854-1913). German artist potter. At Altona (Schleswig-Holstein) in late 19th and early 20th centuries, made stoneware with figured glazes, inspired by enthusiasm for Japanese ceramics. Followed by son, Richard Mutz, who made stoneware with flowing glazes in own Berlin workshop from *c*1904, and produced in stoneware figures modelled by E. *Barlach.

Mycock, William S. (fl late 19th century-1930s). English pottery decorator, at Pilkington Tile and Pottery Co., initially painted tiles, then pottery, on introduction of lustre decoration. Painting

William Salter Mycock. Royal Lancastrian lustre bowl made by *Pilkington Tile and Pottery Co. Impressed rosette mark, WSM monogram, and date 1927. Height 13in.

characterized by richness of design; flowers, gadroons, etc., enriched by geometrical motifs. Later decorated *Lapis ware. Some decoration *sgraffito* or incised; also carved decorative plaques.

mystery clock. Mantel clock, usually French, with some feature - e.g. dial or pendulum - working without visible connection to movement; popular from early 19th century. Example made *c*1875 by French maker, A. Guilmet, has dial and movement in ornamental case surmounted by statuette holding apparently free-swinging pendulum; in fact, movement gives figure imperceptible twist. Inexpensive German versions produced in quantities from 1880, e.g. female figure, holding slowly oscillating clock and pendulum bob just above its centre of gravity; subsidiary pendulum within movement casing alters centre of gravity during each swing, imparting motion.

Na or **Nanori** (Japanese, 'real name'). Japanese equivalent of Western given or Christian name; used only by upper classes, often in combination with clan name. Often used by artists in signatures.

Nabeshima ware. Japanese porcelain, originally reserved for use of feudal lords of Nabeshima in Saga prefecture of Hizen. Initially made at Iwayagama then, from late 17th century, at

Mystery clock. Chrome and glass, made by Jaeger Le Coultre, Geneva. c1930.

nearby Okowachi (or Okochi), *c*3 miles north of Arita. Sets of dishes for table use mainly produced; also vases, bottles, brush boxes, etc. Designs, often of plant forms, painted in underglaze blue; enamel colours, notably red, green, and yellow, applied after first firing. Blue-and-white or celadon glazed wares also made, as well as plain white. Generally available only after Meiji restoration (1868); production continues to present day.

Naeshirogawa. Japanese folk pottery centre in Kagoshima prefecture, Kyushu. Noted for production of footed cooking pots, usually with temmoku glaze, sometimes persimmon, brown, or celadon. Like Ryumonji kilns, established by Korean potters, and influenced by Korean glazes and forms to present day.

Nagoya. Traditional Japanese ceramic centre, capital of Owari province, *c*10 miles from Seto. Enamelled faience with crackle glaze, and grey stoneware coated with opaque-white glaze among products of area. Modern firms, making export tableware in Western styles, include Narumi China Co., and Noritake.

Nailsea glass. English glassware said to have originated (1788-1873) at Nailsea glass works near Bristol, but widely copied. As tax on bottle glass much less than on flint glass, Nailsea and other glass works specialized in domestic ware, in dark brown, dark green, or smoky-green bottle glass. To increase attractiveness, pieces decorated with fused-on enamel flecks or splashes in various colours, or threads, loops, and stripes in white enamel. Other, more sophisticated, range of products (also termed Nailsea) includes ornamental vessels (*gimmel flasks, bellow flasks, covered jars) and novelty items (rolling pins, canes, shoes, bells, pipes, and witch balls); made in clear flint or pale green glass, with *latticinio* or combed glass decoration, usually white or pale pink, occasionally red, blue, or green, rarely yellow or dark red. Crimping sometimes added to body of vessels. Many

Nailsea. Glass *rolling pin doubling as salt container decorated with splashed pattern. Mid 19th century. Length 15in.

novelty items made as love or friendship tokens, with inscriptions, e.g. Be True to Me. Rarely possible to ascertain place of origin or date, though most existing examples are 19th century.

nakhai rugs. Speciality of Kohat and Bannu, Punjab, India. Pile made by pulling out weft threads in 1in. loops and twisting them. Usually decorated with black, yellow, or green geometrical designs on purple or crimson ground.

Nambu ware. *See* Hidehira ware.

namda or **numdah.** Indian felt rug. Backing prepared by spreading wool fibres evenly on sackcloth previously moistened with gum solution and chalk, and rolling back and forth until felted. Pattern then made with coloured wool (laid on top and rolled in) or appliqué felt shapes. Rajasthan namda designs embroidered or printed onto felted base. Export production organized in early 20th century by *Oriental Carpet Manufacturers; popular in Europe before 2nd World War, especially Kashmiri namdas, with floral and geometrical designs.

nameless or **mixed style.** Loose term for British furniture style uninfluenced by historical precedents, *c*1840–*c*1865. Typified by opulent, curved sofas, chairs, etc. with framework hidden by upholstery; curves replaced straight lines in e.g. wooden sideboards, chiffoniers, fusing separate parts to give overall unity of design. Papiermâché also used.

Nancy School. *See* Ecole de Nancy.

Nanori. *See* Na.

Naotane, Taikei (1779–1857). Most famous of 19th century Japanese swordsmiths. Pupil of Suishinshi Masahide (d 1825), founder of Suishinshi School. Made blades in style of Masahide and early schools, reviving methods of koto (old sword) schools of Yamashiro, Yamato, Bizen, Soshu, and Mino provinces – the five traditions (gokaden) of sword-making.

Napoleon clock. Plain hour and half-hour striking clocks, mostly of inferior quality, massproduced by German factories 1900–38. So called because outer case shaped like Napoleon's cocked hat.

Nara ningyo. *See* ningyo netsuke.

Naroka. Japanese folk pottery kiln in Akita prefecture, active until mid 20th century. Noted for production of covered jars, etc., with white glaze at rim trickling down over brown glaze which covers surface of ware.

Narumi. Japanese porcelain factory established in 20th century at Nagoya. Tableware, etc., produced for export. Marks include head of classical column below NARUMI/ CHINA on printed rectangle.

naturalistic style. Loose term describing British furniture, *c*1840–*c*1865, characterized by extruded carved decoration of flowers, sinuous tendrils, rococo motifs. *See also* Warwick school of carving.

natural process. *See* Low, John Gardner.

Natzler, Otto and Gertrud (fl from 1930s). Austrian artist potters, in America from 1939. Opened workshop in Vienna (1933); work shown at World Exhibition (1937) in Paris, influenced by style of Bauhaus. Pieces handthrown by Gertrud, brushed with glazes prepared by Otto, characterized by simplicity and refinement.

nashiji (Japanese, 'pear-skin ground'), or **aventurine lacquer.** High finish stippled-effect Japanese lacquer ground with various sizes of gold specks and small flakes buried at different depths in layers transparent yellow-brown lacquer on black lacquer base. Japanese name derived from resemblance to skin of nashi (pear); European from similarity to appearance of Venetian aventurine glass.

Moist prepared lacquer base evenly sprinkled with gold powders or flakes. When dry, surface covered with several thin coats of transparent lacquer and polished. Process repeated until ground completely covered. Finest work distinguished by patina, good quality gold and even distribution of flakes. Nashiji in vogue since early 19th century for ground on wide range of objects (particularly for insides and bottoms of small lacquer boxes, eating utensils, and trays; also for sides and risers of inros). Numerous varieties developed, some using black or coloured lacquer, some with other metals (e.g. silver and silver or gold alloys). Also e-nashiji ('picture-nashiji') in which technique used for design rather than background; and mura ('cloud') nashiji, with powder concentrated in dense, uneven cloud-like masses.

natsume. In Japanese lacquer, covered jar for powdered tea, used during summer as *tea

ceremony utensil. Cylindrical, *c*3in. high, 2½in. in diameter, with bottom slightly more rounded than top. Made of light wood ornamented with lacquer designs, usually in *hiramakie, from pleasant, summer themes (flowers, blossoms, plants, birds, trees, streams, etc.) or abstract patterns. Most important decorative surfaces lid and exterior. Grounds most often gold, black, or brownish. Interior and bottom often gold, particularly *nashiji, or sometimes coloured, particularly red and black.

nature printing. Printing from leaves and ferns onto papier-mâché and wood furniture, or textiles, by applying heat to acid-impregnated object, or using copper plates impressed with its outline. Brief vogue from *c*1854 in Britain.

Navaho or **Navajo rugs.** Made by Navaho tribe of North American Indians. Became popular outside tribe *c*1850; large numbers produced for sale, 1860–80. Early commercial rugs often in garish, synthetic colours, with heterogeneous design elements, e.g. trains, flags, masonic emblems. From early 20th century, more examples in natural wool colours (white, black, grey, brown), or soft vegetable dyes, sometimes imitating tribal sand paintings.

Navarre, Henri (b 1885). French Art Deco glass artist. Made textured vases and bowls similar to those of M. *Marinot. Mark: Henri Navarre.

Henri Navarre. Vase decorated with red streaks and bubbled inlay around neck. c1930. Height 4½in.

examples in cylindrical, or flat, book-like forms. Novel designs generally popular c1750–c1914, e.g. cases in shape of shoe, umbrella, church spire, dagger in scabbard, pea pod; large versions, c10in. long, made in form of musical instruments, in late 19th century. More utilitarian leather cases introduced after World War I.

needlework carpets. Traditional English tapestry work; revived during 19th century vogue for needlework, especially in England (e.g. by J. M. *Pontremoli) and America. Often took form of *tile carpets, also co-operative carpets consisting of individually woven strips, sewn together and finished with border. In mid 19th century England, imitation Caucasian rugs in geometrical designs fashionable subjects. *See also* Berlin woolwork, Ladies' Carpet.

negoro-nuri or **kuroe-nuri.** Japanese red-and-black lacquer in which surface layer of red lacquer applied over numerous coats of black lacquer, then rubbed down and polished to reveal patches of underlying black lacquer. Occasionally found with colours applied in opposite order. Used primarily on eating utensils.

Technique developed at and named after Negoro Buddhist monastery in Wakayama Prefecture during late 13th century. In 15th century, industry transferred by priests to monastery at Kuroe.

neo-Gothic style. *See* Eastlake style.

neo-Grec style. *See* Egyptian revival style.

neo-Renaissance jewellery. *See* Gothic revival jewellery.

Neatby, W.J. (1860–1910). English potter and designer. Decorator at Burmantofts, Leeds, c1880–90. As art director at Doulton factory, Lambeth, London, in 1890s, experimented with glazes and colour techniques. Modeller and designer of architectural wares c1892–1907. Designed murals and tile panels illustrating e.g. principles of freemasonry, and series of medallions tracing history of costume. Designed tiles produced by Doulton & Co. for walls of Harrods' food department. Work, influenced by Art Nouveau and Pre-Raphaelite styles, initialled. Later, made stained-glass, furniture, and metalwork.

nécessaire. Fitted box for holding toilet and household equipment, e.g. scent bottles, knife and spoon, sewing utensils. Forerunner of larger, 19th century *workbox. Most popular in 18th century, often in shape of small chest made in polished wood with various inlays, shagreen or leather covered woods, or in striped agate and other hardstones with finely chased or embossed gold mounts. Widely reproduced from mid 19th century.

nécessaire de voyage. *See* canteen.

needlecase. During 19th century, ornate needlecases made in great variety of designs and materials; rectangular versions e.g. in mother-of-pearl, ivory, bone, wood, porcelain, decorated with piqué work, gold inlay, or enamel. Flat, rectangular cases, often with sliding drawer, particularly popular in France and Italy; English

Above
*Needlework carpet. Made for *Morris & Co. by Mrs Halliday. Late 19th century.*

netsuke (Japanese: ne, 'root'; tsuke, 'to fasten'). In Japan, cord weight or toggle to secure cord hanging from *obi to hold *sagemono as Japanese national costume (kimono) has no pockets. Used from 14th century; originally utilitarian piece of wood; developed into many elaborate forms, reaching peak in late 18th century but continuing at high level during 19th century. Types include *ichiraku, *kagamibuta, *katabori, *kurawa, *manju, and *sashi netsuke. Trick netsuke made weighted to land upright if dropped, or had rolling balls or eyes inside.

Typically made of wood, stained, polished, lacquered, or with inlay of ivory or mother-of-pearl. Also made in ivory (sometimes minutely carved), horn, bone, amber, or metal. Carvers often artisans in other fields: mask or doll makers, Buddhist image makers, musical instrument makers, sword decorators. Became essential element in male dress until decline after Meiji restoration (1868). Large quantities exported to Europe and America as curios. New form evolved with elaborate carving; shape, with sharp projections, and fragility made these unsuitable for original function.

Netzglas. *See* vetro a reticelli.

Left
Newcomb College Pottery. Vase by Mary Sheerer with incised decoration of iris flowers and leaves. Marks: impressed Newcomb Coll., and incised 'O'. c1898. Height 10¼in.

Neutra, Richard (b 1892). Architect; also designed furniture. Born in Vienna, worked in Switzerland 1918-20, then Berlin; settled in America in 1923. Influenced by A. *Loos, O. *Wagner, and F. L. *Wright. Furniture characterized by sparse, geometrical, curved forms, e.g. armchair with bent laminated wood frame, continuous arms, front supports, and runners; leather-covered seat cushions, back rest fixed between arms; downward curving steel spring connects seat to back stretcher.

Newcomb College Pottery. American pottery established in 1895 at Newcomb College, New Orleans, women's section of Tulane University, Louisiana. Work of professional potters decorated by students; local materials and decorative motifs used. Low-fired earthenware painted in underglaze colours, notably blue, green, and yellow, with designs of indigenous plants, e.g. magnolia, palm trees, wisteria, or simple landscapes, often within carved outlines. Until 1910, glossy glaze used; later, softer colours and matt glazes introduced; decoration became more naturalistic, with some modelled motifs. Production continued until 1930. Marks: Newcomb College or monogram of ‘NC impressed, with initials of potter or painter incised.

New England Glass Company. American glasshouse founded 1818 in Cambridge, Massachusetts, by D. *Jarves after absorbing defunct Boston Porcelain & Glass Co. By 1865, employed over 500 people, when expanded and established number of branches and subsidiaries. Imported Stourbridge clay, to make furnace melting pots, and made very high quality lead glass, with emphasis on form and outlines. Also developed wide range of coloured art glass, e.g. *Agata, *Amberina, *Pomona, and *Wild Rose Peachblow. Produced fine paperweights, 1850-80; notably, nearly life-sized fruit weights with single coloured fruit resting on clear glass cushion. Profitable sideline was supply of own red lead to other glasshouses. Ceased production 1888. Charter taken over in same year by manager, E. *Libbey, and firm moved to Toledo, Ohio, where established as *Libbey Glass Co. *Illustrations at* Agata glass, Wild Rose Peachblow.

New Hampshire box. Rectangular wooden box ($c23 \times 12 \times 8$in.) with stencilled, metallic powder and/or painted designs of floral sprays. Made in New Hampshire from $c1850$.

New Palace Westminster style. Gothic style furniture made until $c1885$ by *Gillow, e.g. for Law Courts, London. Based on A. W. N. *Pugin's furniture for Houses of Parliament; characterized by inclusion of carved monogram in decoration, Tudor rose or thistle in roundel at juncture of stretchers and legs.

Newport Pottery. *See* Wilkinson, A.J. Ltd.

New York City Pottery. American pottery established and operated ($c1853$-71) by partnership Morrison & Carr. Produced majolica, ironstone china, and granite ware. Parian ware made from late 1870s. J. *Carr sole proprietor from 1871 until retirement and closure of pottery (1888). Variety of marks include initials, J.C., N.Y.C.P. and/or versions of eagle cypher, or clasped hands; MORRISON & CARR OCCURS $c1860$.

New York City School of Clay Working. School of ceramics at Alfred University of New York; later, New York State College of Ceramics. Under direction of C. F. *Binns (1900-35).

Nichols or **Storer,** Maria Longworth (1849-1932). American potter. After experiments with K. *Langenbeck in ceramic decoration, opened *Rookwood Pottery (1880). Continued own experiments with colour and, until 1883, supplied unfired earthenware to outside decorators, also firing finished work. Own pottery combined Japanese inspired motifs, spiders, dragonflies, crabs, etc. with European shapes, e.g. basket with lion's head feet, decorated under glaze in beige, black, and white, and gilded (1882). Later work often decorated in relief, e.g. vase with design of sea-horses under dark red, slightly iridescent glaze. Widowed in 1885, remarried lawyer, Bellamy Storer (1886), and moved (1889) to Washington, D.C. Transferred ownership of business to W. W. *Taylor, although continued own experiments at Rookwood. Achieved lustrous copper-red glazes, still using oriental motifs, either carved on vases or in decoration of metal mounts, but with increased awareness of form, colour, and texture.

nickel silver or **German silver.** Hard, moderately malleable alloy of copper, zinc, and nickel, used from $c1830$; called German silver from ore of similar composition found at Hildburghausen, Germany; colour similar to that of silver. Widely employed as base for *electro-plate. Also marketed, sometimes with other additives, under trade names, e.g. argentine, Alpacca silver, Alaska silver, Mexican silver.

Nicole, Adolphe (fl mid 19th century). Swiss founder of watchmaking firm, Nicole & Capt, at Le Solliat, Valle-de-Joux. Moved firm to Soho, London, in $c1840$. Patented *chronograph mechanism invented by employee, Henri-Féréol Piguet; heart-shaped cam causes watch hand to fly back to zero when push-piece pressed; first shown at International Exhibition in London (1862). In partnership with Emil Nielsen (d 1899), produced fine watch movements, e.g. for C. *Frodsham, J. F. *Cole, from $c1865$.

Nielsen, Jais (1885-1961). Danish sculptor, painter, and ceramic artist. From 1921, designer for Royal Copenhagen Porcelain Factory. Bowls, vases, etc. often covered with celadon glaze. Stoneware figures and groups frequently inspired by biblical subjects, e.g. Good Samaritan (1923), and David and Goliath, with *sang-de-boeuf* glaze.

Nielsen, Kai (1884-1924). Danish sculptor, painter and ceramic artist. Work for Bing & Grøndahls porcelain factory includes life-sized Venus and series of figures and groups entitled The Sea, e.g. mother nursing two children; dolphins and tritons.

Niemayer, Adalbert (b 1867). German potter, noted for ceramic sculpture; also painter, architect and industrial designer. Professor at State school for applied art, Munich, and co-founder of Deutsche Werkstätten at Munich and Hellerau. Pupils include (1928-29) M. *Kovács. Designed earthenware for production by Villeroy & Boch.

Nienhuis, Bert (1873-1960), Dutch artist potter. In early 20th century, designer for Distel pottery, Amsterdam. Work depends for effect on elaborate glazes. Professor of ceramics and modelling at Institute for Arts & Crafts, Amsterdam. Also made limited amount of jewellery in gold and enamels in austere style.

night clock. *See* luminous dial.

night commode, night convenience, or **zomno.** Enclosed stool or box containing earthenware or pewter vessel; widely used until $c1875$. Generally camouflaged, e.g. as chest of drawers, bedsteps, or chair, sometimes with adjustable arms, panelled front. Known as zomno in America from $c1850$.

night light. *See* fairy light.

night-stand. *See* pedestal cupboard.

Nile Street Works. *See* Pinder, Bourne & Co.

Nilsson, Wiwen (b 1897). Swedish artist craftsman, silversmith, and jeweller; studied in father's workshop in Lund, later in Hanau (1913-14 and 1920-21), and Copenhagen; worked in G. *Jensen's Paris studio from 1909; set up own workshop in 1927, taking over father's business in 1928; produced silver in geometrical style during 1920s and 1930s; in 1964 made altar set for Lund cathedral in gold, silver, and Colombian mahogany.

ningyo (Japanese, 'doll' or 'puppet') **netsuke.** Doll-like *katabori netsuke in hinoki or teawood, often crudely carved and painted. Widely produced during 19th and early 20th centuries, particularly for export or as souvenirs of various regions. Nara ningyo, made by Nara doll-carvers of coloured, carved hinoki, usually portray Noh dancers; best-known 19th century maker, *Toen. Uji ningyo, painted figures of Uji tea-pickers in working costume, carved from seasoned teawood in *itto-bori; first made 1842 by Uji carver, Gyuka, as gift for shogun; still sold as souvenir of this green-tea area. Hida ningyo, unpainted, ittobori carved, yew-wood figures made in Hida from early 19th century.

Nishi-shimmachi. Japanese folk pottery centre in Fukuoka prefecture, active until early 20th century. Bowls, jars, saké bottles, etc., made in kilns which produced tea ware in 18th century, originally by workers from Koishibara. Green glaze normally used with trickled glaze in brown, yellow, or white.

nodding figure. Small animal, bird, or human figure with detachable head; extension of head swings within body, pivoted on small pins which fit in grooves inside neck. Imported into England from Germany from mid 19th century. Porcelain either biscuit or decorated with underglaze blue. Some examples in biscuit porcelain imported from France. Japanese models often oriental figures. Later examples sometimes clumsily modelled; modern reproductions made.

Noke, Charles John (1858-1941). English ceramic artist and modeller. Trained at Worcester factory. Worked at Doulton factory, Burslem, Staffordshire, from 1889. Modelled large vases with relief decoration, painted in underglaze and enamel colours. By 1894, also made figures.

Charles John Noke. Royal *Doulton Sung elephant, coloured by F. Allen. Marks: impressed 7855, and inscribed Doulton Burslem, Noke, F. Allen, Sung. c1930. Height 17in.

Introduced *Holbein ware (1895) and *Rembrandt ware (c1898). Art director, from 1914, supervised development of *flambé* and crystalline glazes. Also introduced trays, vases, jugs, tobacco jars, etc., with underglaze decoration; series illustrating The Jackdaw of Rheims, and scenes, e.g. from Bayeux Tapestry, Shakespeare, Dickens. Other innovations include *Titianian ware, *Sung, and *Chang glazes. Retired as art director in 1936, but continued to work for factory. Son, Cecil Jack Noke (d 1954) joined Doulton factory after architectural apprenticeship and service in 1st World War. Trained as decorator under Doulton artists, then attended Stoke and Burslem Art Schools. Took part in production of *flambé* glazed wares. In charge of engraving department, before succeeded father as art director (1936). Both father and son signed work Noke; signature of Charles John Noke has two dots below.

nomadic furniture. Loose term for collapsible portable pieces, e.g. campaign furniture, Derby chair, camp chair. (Term first used in book published 1948.)

Noritake. Japanese ceramic factory established (1904) at Nagoya. Much porcelain tableware produced for export. Printed marks incorporate name of firm and, often, ware.

North, Benjamin, & Sons. English furniture makers in High Wycombe, Buckinghamshire. Established 1851 as chair manufacturers; added upholstery department (1871), and cabinet section (1881) making Art furniture. Specialized in Anglo-Japanese style. Designs registered with Patent Office in London.

Northwood, John (1837–1902). English glass engraver in Stourbridge, Worcestershire. Thought to have rediscovered ancient technique

of cameo glass independently of E. *Gallé. Specialized in cameo engraving after 1860, using classical, and sometimes floral, motifs; set up cameo workshop in Stourbridge with brother, Joseph. In 1873, completed first success, Elgin Vase, decorated with group of riders from Parthenon frieze. In 1876, won £1,000 prize offered by B. *Richardson for best copy of Portland Vase, his successful entry remaining most important piece of English cameo glass made. In 1880, became art director of *Stevens & Williams, where associated with F. *Carder. His son, J. Northwood II (1870–1960), carried on cameo glass tradition at Stevens & Williams until retirement in 1946.

Norwegian rugs and tapestries. Norway participated in late 19th century Scandinavian revival of folk weaving method for rug (*see* ryijy) and tapestry craft. Movement initiated c1890 by painter G. *Munthe and weaver Frida Hansen, who studied peasant craftsmanship, to create modern tapestry art based on native medieval weavings.

novelty clocks. Horological toys, varying widely in quality and complexity, produced in quantities from c1850 into 20th century in France, Germany, Austria, Switzerland, and America. Tall French table clock in shape of lighthouse, made from c1850, has clock dial and movement in tower surmounted by lamp-house of rotating glass prisms; later German form uses lamp house as torsion pendulum. Negro and negress clocks made in Paris and Connecticut, c1875: clock set in free-standing figure, with rolling eyes attached to pendulum or balance wheel; alternatively, with digital hours and minutes appearing in eyes. Cheaper versions made in *Black Forest from c1900; also, moving-eye clocks, with dial and movement embodied in figure or painting of animal, e.g. dog, cat, lion: eyes move to and fro as clock mechanism revolves. Engine clock may be either miniature locomotive, incorporating clock, with hours struck on loco bell (American), or model of reciprocating beam engine, e.g. example by French maker, Charles Hour, com-

plete with flywheel, governor, and piston rods which move into action on hour (shown at 1889 and 1900 Paris Exhibitions). Magic lantern night clock uses lens to project image of front or back of dial on to wall; early 19th century version has oil lamp; later example by Ever-Ready Co. uses battery-powered light bulb.

numdah. *See* namda.

nut bowl. Small metal bowl for nuts; made in great variety of shapes, with feet, flat bottoms, and pedestal stands. Embossed decoration in form of fruit, flowers, birds, etc. Often with one or two handles in form of squirrels perching on rim. Large quantities made in silver and electroplate from c1850, mainly in America but also in Britain.

Nylund, Gunnar (b 1904). Swedish ceramic designer. Worked with N. *Krebs (1929–30) in Denmark, with aim of producing individual pieces of stoneware at relatively low cost. Later, chief designer at branch of Rörstrand factory at Lidköping; work includes animal figures in stoneware, e.g. matt-glazed gibbon eating banana, porcelain vase, painted with fish and covered with deep golden glaze, and matt-glazed white porcelain tableware with simple repeated motif pressed into paste to form highly translucent pattern.

Nyman, Gunnel (1908–48). Finnish glass artist in Art Deco and Functionalist styles. Originally furniture designer. Her sensitively decorated, understated 'folded' glass contrasts areas of shallow cutting with larger, smooth masses.

Nymphenburg (Bavaria). Porcelain in production from 1753 to present day. From mid 19th century, figures in white made from original moulds. In 1862, factory leased by state to private company. Noted for ability to suit styles to contemporary taste and to adopt modern techniques. Spirited figures modelled by J. *Wackerle, art director (1906–09). Other models by P. *Scheurich. Modern marks include shield with crown and Nymphenburg. Reproductions of models from 18th century Frankenthal factory marked with blue lion or CT with crown from original factory, with date and impressed shield of Nymphenburg mark. Also reproduced work of Höchst factory after acquiring moulds from *Damm.

nyoi. In Japanese metalwork, sceptre held by Buddhist priests when preaching.

oak. Pale yellow hardwood used for furniture from Middle Ages in Britain and Europe; develops rich brown patina. In America, rich reddish-brown or pale brown wood, latter with yellowish shading; coarse grains must be filled (e.g. with stained beeswax) before polishing. Used for Early English style furniture, and by followers of Arts & Crafts Movement. Can be seasoned to produce various effects, e.g. fumed oak, limed oak, weathered oak.

obi. In Japan, sash or wide strip of material used to hold kimono in place. Accepted as important part of national costume during Edo period. At first purely utilitarian; later more elaborate (particularly in women's costume). *Sagemono suspended by cord worn hanging from obi and held in place by *netsuke slipped under it.

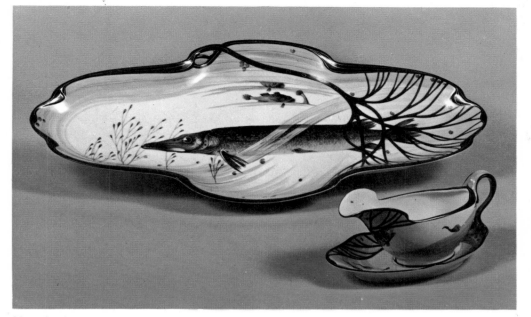

Nymphenberg. Part of porcelain dinner service. Enamelled decoration designed by Hermann Gradl. Shape designed by Louis Levallois. 1904–06.

Obsieger, Robert (1884–1940). Austrian designer and potter in Vienna. Succeeded M. *Powolny as head of pottery department at School of Arts & Crafts.

O.C.M. *See* Oriental Carpet Manufacturers.

occasional chair. Loose Victorian term for side-chair or armchair intended for reception room. Usually has upholstered seat and back; may match sofa.

occasional table. 19th century British term for small table used to display ornaments, etc. in drawing room. Often has circular top supported by central column resting on carved, tripod base; also, rectangular top on quadruped base. High-quality examples may have inlaid top and, sometimes, base. Table with rectangular or octagonal top supported by four slender columns, often resting on moulded legs, popular from c1870; three-legged examples with circular tops also made.

Odawara-bori. *See* Kamakura-bori.

oenochoë. Classical Greek one-handled vessel which provided basic shape for tea and coffee pots, jugs, etc., made in Greek style during 1850s and 1860s.

Ofner, Hans (b 1890). Austrian architect, silversmith, jeweller and enamellist. Studied under J. *Hoffmann at Imperial School of Arts and Crafts. Jewellery follows severe geometrical style of early work of K. *Moser. Mainly silver, set with semi-precious opaque stones and mother-of-pearl, with textured surfaces and enamel decoration in shades of yellow and brown. Some made by Viennese firm Rozet and Fischmeister.

OG or **ogee clock.** Connecticut weight or spring driven shelf or wall clock housed in plain rectangular case, framed with S-shaped (ogee) moulding; probably derived from Black Forest *picture-frame clocks. Glass tablet set in door, frequently painted so as to leave dial and pendulum bob visible. Made in several sizes, c16–34in. high. Mass-produced, 1825–1914; wooden movements made up to 1837, afterwards machine-rolled brass 30-hour and 8-day movements. Many makers, notably C. *Jerome, who exported them to England from 1842, S. Thomas and *Ansonia Clock Co. Some Black Forest copies from c1860.

Ogden, Henry. English furniture maker, active in Manchester, c1855–82. Showed elaborately carved furniture at International Exhibition, London, 1862. Made Art furniture; also known for *French style cupboards.

Ogee clock. *See* OG clock.

Ohr, George (1857–1918). American artist potter, working by 1885 in Missouri. From 1895, made porcelain, very thinly potted and then distorted by squeezing, folding, etc., into bizarre forms, adding curved handles. Used glazes in flowing colours, e.g. plum and green. Impressed mark: G. E. OHR, Biloxi, Miss.

öhrström, Edvin (b 1906). Swedish sculptor and glass artist in Functionalist style. On permanent staff at *Orrefors from 1936, where early work chiefly in *Ariel glass, e.g. heavy vases in rich colours, with encased figure compositions, heads, and flowers. Mark: F, with Ørrefors or Øf, diamond engraved on all engraved glass to his design; FA on cut glass; FU on furnace-finished glass.

ojime (Japanese, 'cord tightener'). Small, pierced bead ($c^1/_4$–$^1/_2$in. diameter) threaded on silk cord attaching netsuke to inro or sagemono, and used to adjust cord's tension around suspended object. Usually round, sometimes oval, rectangular, or figure-shaped. Made in wide variety of materials, from simple natural forms (e.g. nuts) or un-

*Okimono. Ivory and ebony formed as model of *Daikoku's mallet and surmounted by rat crouching on treasure bag. Mid 19th century. Length 4½in.*

decorated coral, crystal, jade, etc., to elaborately decorated wood, ivory, metal, pottery, or porcelain. More complicated forms often executed by famous metalwork, netsuke, lacquer and ceramics artists using entire range of techniques and designs of own fields. Often made to match netsuke and inro.

okiguchi (Japanese, 'fitted-mouth'). Metal particularly silver, gold, or pewter, covering of rims on Japanese lacquer boxes. Used from Heian period (794–1185) to present.

okimono (Japanese, 'place things'). Non-utilitarian Japanese sculptured figures originally made for ornamentation of alcoves in homes. In vogue during Meiji and Taisho periods; peak production 1880s to World War I, mainly for European and American export market. Most ivory, some wood, or bone; carved in highly realistic, detailed style. Designs often copied directly from netsuke models and executed by netsuke artists. Fine examples made by: O. *Gyokuso, A. *Gyokuzan, M. *Joso, *Kaigyokusai, I. *Komei, *Kyusai, S. *Masaka, K. *Tessai and M. *Toen.

Olbrich, Josef Maria (1867–1908). Austrian architect, artist, and designer; studied architecture at Akademie der bildenden Künste, Vienna, 1890–93; visited Italy, Tunis, France, 1893; worked with O. *Wagner 1894–49; began using Jugendstil motifs for interior and exterior decoration of houses he designed; 1897 co-founder of *Vienna Secession; joined Matildenhöhe colony of artists established by Ernst Ludwig, Grand Duke of Hesse, at Darmstadt, where designed main buildings. Also designed some metalwork, including silver tableware; examples of two-branched pewter candlestick (1901) in Museum of Modern Art, New York, and Hessiches Landesmuseum, Darmstadt. Also designed jewellery, e.g. for T.

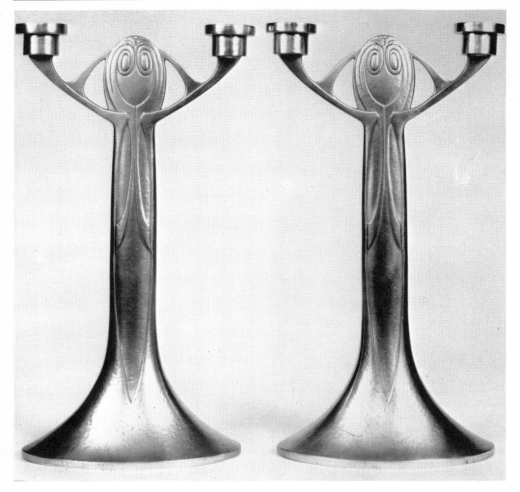

Josef Maria Olbrich. Pair of pewter candle-holders, both marked Silberzinn, E. Hueck, 1819, and with monogram J.O. Dated 1902. Height 14½in.

*Fahrner; household articles, door handles, lamps, etc., and saloon of pleasure boat to be used at 1900 Paris Exhibition. Work influenced mainly through Olbrich's friend J. *Hoffmann, and *Wiener Werkstätte.

Old Crown Derby China Works, The. *See* Derby.

Old English Gothic style. *See* Early English style.

Old English style. Furniture style in Britain, c1870–c1900. Commercial pieces, e.g. by *Collier & Plucknett, J. *Shoolbred & Co., based on Gothic Reform and Early English style pieces. Common characteristic: panels with painted decoration on gold background.

Old French style. *See* French style.

Old German enamel painting. *See* Altdeutsches glass.

Old Hall Earthenware Co. Ltd, The. *See* Meigh, Charles.

Old Hall Porcelain Co. Ltd, The. *See* Meigh, Charles.

Below
*Old Russian style. Silver urn and cover, made at *Fabergé workshop. Set with cabochon garnets and grey chalcedony. Late 19th century. Height 22in.*

'Old Japan'. *See* Imari wares.

Old Russian Style. Themes, motifs, subject matter drawn from 16th and 17th century Russian art and folk culture, revived, from early 19th century to World War I, as stylistic expression of nationalistic *pan-Slavic movement. Style and content marked by strong, dramatic colours, idealization of 17th century peasant life-styles, and renewed manufacture of traditional Russian objects, e.g. enamelled tea glass holders, kovschi, spoons, tankards, icons, *Easter eggs by G. *Sbitnev, P. *Ovtchinnikov, F. *Ruckett; also ceramic peasant figures in traditional costume, and porcelain from Imperial Porcelain Factory, decorated with 17th century scenes. *Illustration also at en plein* enamelling.

Old World style. Loose term for mass-produced, American, eclectic furniture based on Renaissance, Louis XIV, Louis XV, and Louis XVI styles. Popular from c1890; still made. *cf* American Colonial style.

Omega Workshops. Set up 1913 in Fitzroy Square, London, by R. *Fry, for production and sale of applied art in post-Impressionist idiom. Made carpets, rugs, printed textiles, hand-painted screens, furniture and pottery, designed and executed where possible by amateur artist craftsmen, with little technical training in any specific field. Carpets and rugs typically decorated with abstract patterns of half-circles, hoops, dots, and graded stripes in wide range of pure tones. Furniture plain, ill-constructed; decorated in boldly painted patterns. Workshop sold tin-glazed earthenware made by Fry at Camberwell and at Poole, Dorset; also some pottery decorated e.g. by Vanessa Bell and Duncan Grant. Products marked with Greek character omega in rectangle. Closed 1919.

omnium. *See* whatnot.

Onda. Japanese pottery centre near Hida, Oita prefecture. Noted for variety of high-quality products, e.g. rounded teapot covered with greenish-blue glaze, and covered jars with trickled glazes in white, green, brown, or yellow. Decoration includes variations of texture with comb or fingers, and brushwork. Some products difficult to distinguish from work of nearby centre at Koishibara.

Oneida. American company manufacturing cutlery and silver; founded as egalitarian agricultural community in 1848, by John Humphrey Noyes at Oneida Lake, New York State; membership increased to 205 in 1851; turned to metalwork in 1850s and 1860s, producing steel animal traps in use throughout America and Canada; started silk manufacture, 1865, and cutlery production, 1877. Community broke up in 1881, and joint stock company formed; Noyes succeeded by son Pierrepont, 1886; silver works moved to Sherrill, 1913; later became leading makers of stainless steel products. Oneida Company introduced 'Community Plate' to British market in 1919, manufactured by Kenwood Silver Co., Sheffield, from 1926, moving to Northern Ireland in 1960.

Onyx glass. Range of American art glass patented 1889 by George W. Leighton of Findlay, Ohio. Double-layered; swirls and patterns resembling natural gemstone produced

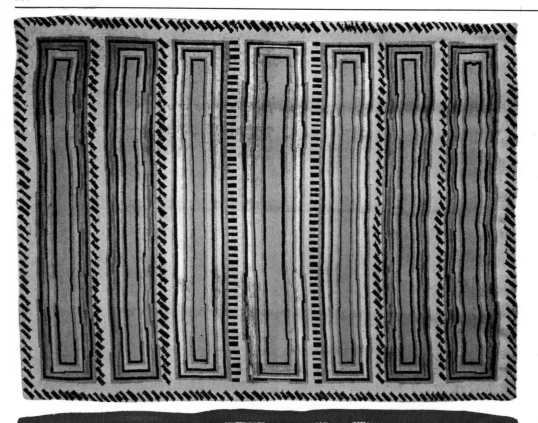

stone, partly because stones commonly have flaws, undetectable except under microscope, which can cause cracking or breaking. Form of hydrous silica; black, white, red, orange or yellow background, with rainbow play of colour. Usually cabochon cut: steep for rings, flatter for brooches, pendants, bracelets, and necklaces. Only red Mexican fire opal faceted.

opal-decorated ware. Term used by British and American glass makers for 19th century opal and milk glass vases, etc., decorated with painted or enamelled motifs, ranging from plants or flowers to birds and landscapes. Produced in large quantities in America from mid 1850s, notably by *Boston & Sandwich Glass Co., *Mount Washington Glass Works, *New England Glass Co., and *C. F. Monroe Co. Major British producer, *Richardson & Sons. See also Smith Brothers' vase.

opalescent dewdrop glass. See hobnail glass.

opalescent glass. Translucent white glass with fiery, almost reddish, core when seen in light. Like *milk glass and *opaline, first made in antiquity by addition of calcified bones; these later replaced by tin and stannic oxides. Degree of opacity determined by quantities used.

Below
Opals. With turquoise and enamel, set into necklace by *Jensen. Designed 1914.

Top
Omega Workshops. Tapestry designed by Duncan Grant. One of series. c1914.
Above
Omega Workshops. Rug designed by Vanessa Bell. 1913–14.
Left
Omega Workshops. Left: earthenware vase made and decorated at Omega, 1914. Right: porcelain vase, painted probably by R. *Fry, marked with Omega monogram, 1913–19.

by adding appropriate metal oxides to glass metal of outer casing, then subjecting red-hot surface to heat and gas fumes. See Amber Onyx, Orange Onyx, Ruby Onyx, Silver Onyx.

opal. Precious gemstone popular in late 19th century, especially after discovery of large deposits in Australia. Bad reputation as gem-

Opaline. Stoppered glass bottle with gilt and enamelled decoration. Bohemian. Mid 19th century.

opaline or **opal glass.** 19th century term (first used at *Baccarat) for fine, semi-translucent glass in opalescent white, blue, green, or pink. Produced in antiquity by addition of calcified bones to glass metal; in 19th century, by tin oxide or stannic oxide additives. Shapes closely followed porcelain styles, e.g. early 19th century French opaline vases often set in ormolu or lavishly decorated like Sèvres porcelain; opalines of 1840–70 often had Bohemian polygonal designs; from 1870s, oriental-style fronds and ferns fashionable.

Opaque Porcelain. *See* Meigh, Charles.

opaque-white glass. *See* milk glass.

open braid. *See plique-à-jour.*

Orange Onyx glass. American art glass imitating swirls and patterns of natural gemstone in transparent shades of orange. Version of *Onyx glass range (patented 1889). Inner lining opal glass; outer casing amber glass with uranium oxide and large quantity of iron oxide.

Oribe wares. Japanese pottery; originated late 16th century in Mino Province. Pale buff body often moulded in angular shapes; sometimes painted with iron oxide or white slip under glaze, which may be clear or coloured green with copper salts. Tea bowls with black glaze easily confused with earlier black glazed ware made at Seto; sometimes decorated with white slip.

Among traditional wares which influenced makers of folk art ware, e.g. K. *Rosanjin and family of H. *Kato.

Oriental Carpet Manufacturers or **O.C.M.** British carpet dealers; in association with G. B. & J. Baker, based in London from 1908 as trading company, with offices in Smyrna (Turkey) and India. Organized production for export of e.g. early 20th century *namdas. Absorbed *East India Carpet Co. in 1924. Called O.C.M. Ltd. from 1927.

oriental glazes. Glazes among Japanese work exhibited in Paris (1878) provided inspiration for French artist potters, e.g. E. *Chaplet and J. *Carriès, followed by A. *Bigot, G. *Hoentschel, P. A. *Dalpayrat, and A. *Delaherche. European factories using oriental glazes include Royal Copenhagen factory, Sèvres, and Berlin. *Flambé* glazes achieved on porcelain by T. *Deck (*c*1880) and used by E. *Chaplet from 1880s. In America, *sang-de-boeuf* glaze, sought by H. *Robertson after display of Japanese ceramics at Philadelphia Centennial Exhibition (1876), achieved in 1880s; glazes with crackle effect used from 1890s. In own experiments at Rookwood pottery, M. L. *Nichols produced red glazes with use of copper salts. *Flambé* and other oriental glazes used in England by W. H. *Taylor. B. *Moore experimented in *flambé* glazes with C. *Bailey, involved in development of glazes at Doulton factory, Burslem, where *Chang, *Sung, and *flambé* glazes also produced. Other English potters who pioneered high-temperature glazes include R. *Wells and G. *Cox.

Ørrefors Glass. Left: decanter with engraved neck and medallion. Right: flask and stopper. Both exhibited at Paris Exhibition, 1925.

Ørrefors. Swedish glasshouse founded 1898 in Småland area for production of table glass; decorative ware from 1915. Won international repute *c*1925 with fine engraved glass and subtly-tinted coloured ware, becoming established as one of world's leading producers of Functionalist glass. *Graal glass developed 1916 by S. *Gate and master glass blower, Knut Bergqvist. *Ariel glass developed *c*1930. Continues as important glass centre today. Other designers include E. *Hald, V. *Lindstrand, E. *Öhrstrom, and S. *Palmqvist. Marks: Engraved work to design of individual artist signed with initial, followed by Ørrefors or Øf; A added to initial on cut glass; U to furnace-worked glass. *Illustrations also at* Gate, S., Hald, E., Lindstrand, V.

Osborne, Arthur (fl late 19th century). American potter, trained in England. As chief modeller for tile company of J. G. *Low in 1880s, made moulded plaques decorated with landscapes, portraits, or farm animals. Initials incised under glaze. *Illustration at* Low, J. G.

Osler, F. & C. English glasshouse in Birmingham. From 1849, specialized in outsize cut glass objects for exhibitions and wealthy patrons, e.g. centrepiece of Great Exhibition of 1851. Also made fine opaline flower vases with painted relief patterns; thin-blown drinking glasses and other vessels with floral engraving; novelties, e.g. glass busts of literary or political figures (Queen Victoria, Prince Albert, Shakespeare, etc.), or sentimental subjects (e.g. The Sleeping Child).

Osmaston Road. *See* Derby.

Otsuki School. 19th century Japanese sword furniture makers. Established in Kyoto by Otsuki Misuoki (1766–1834), pupil of painter Ganku. Techniques used included notably Katakiri engraving (V-shaped grooves with one upright, one sloping side, resembling brushwork in paintings). Methods followed by group of pupils: Kawarabashi Hideoki, Sasayama Tokooki, Tenkodo Hidekuni. Kano Natsuo, last great master of sword furniture (1828–1898) also connected with this school. Landscapes with horses, etc., typical motifs.

Ott & Brewer. American company operating Etruria Pottery, Trenton, New Jersey (1863–93). Noted for production of 'Belleek' from mid 1880s, with help of worker from Belleek factory in Ireland. Parian paste made since 1870s. Work marked with name of firm, or crown pierced by sword with BELLEEK and initials O & B.

ottoman. Long, upholstered seat with or without back, seating several people; development of low, broad Turkish bench covered in cushions; dates from late 18th century in Britain. Circular or octagonal versions, often with button-upholstery, popular from c1850; cone-shaped back rest, often carved, may support statue or pot plant. Sometimes divided into four seats by upholstered arms which continue to form high backs. Common in America, c1840–c1900. Sometimes used in Turkish style rooms. *See borne*, box ottoman, divan, Moorish corner, Turkish corner.

ottoman footstool. Stool for supporting feet; also, fireside seat. Four-footed, often with mahogany or rosewood underframing, with stuffed top, usually button-upholstered, often in leather. Sometimes hinged, concealing spittoon. Dates from early 19th century in Britain; c1840 in America.

overlay glass. *See* cameo glass.

overmantel. Mid Victorian arrangement of mantel mirrors with main, central glass flanked, sometimes surmounted, by smaller mirrors. Frames may be carved, curvilinear, etc. Mirror area often reduced in later examples by *shelf-clusters.

overshot glass. *See* ice glass.

Ovtchinnikov, Paul Akimovich (1851–c1917). Russian silversmith and master enameller who established firm in Moscow, 1851. Received Imperial warrant, 1872; opened branch in St Petersburg, 1875. Instrumental in reviving *Old Russian style; designs intended for Russian market rather than international clientèle of *Fabergé. Work includes ornate tankards, tea-glass holders, spoons, icons, bread and salt dishes, in enamelled silver. First Russian manufacturer to set up training school for craftsmen, taking 130 pupils for five year period. Mark, P. Ovtchinnikov, in Cyrillic script, with imperial eagle.

Owari ware. Japanese lacquerware from Owari Province; employs heidatsu technique to form designs of leaves and flowers on gold ground.

*George Owen. Royal *Worcester vase and cover. Printed mark and incised signature. Height 10¼in.*

Owen, George (d 1917). English porcelain decorator; maker of *reticulated ware. Worked at Worcester Royal Porcelain factory in late 19th century. Usually marked work with signature incised under base or on plinth. Privately, also modelled flowers for application to vases or trinkets, normally for use of family or friends.

Owens, J.B. (d 1934). American potter. From 1885, owner of factory at Roseville, Ohio; made flower pots, etc. Established works at Zanesville (1891) for production of majolica *jardinières*, flower pots, pedestals, and novelty items. After introduction of *barbotine* decoration and new glazes (1896) by W. A. *Long, sold art pottery under name Utopian, and engaged staff of decorators; quickly added other named lines, marked with name of firm, though usually not individual style. Decoration includes painting of mission scenes, designs copied from early American Indian pottery, or autumn leaves painted under glaze with surface resembling vellum. Ceased production of art pottery c1907; made tiles until early 1930s. Lived in Florida after retirement. Marks include OWENS, and OWENS/ UTOPIAN.

Oxford bath. *See* hip bath.

Oxford chair. High-backed, upholstered chair with long seat projecting beyond open, padded arms; often has button-upholstered back. Name dates from c1850. Also, cane-seated single chair with centre rail and yoke rails projecting beyond uprights.

oxidized silver. Silver heated in chemical solution to produce dark layer of oxide on surface; process normally used to heighten shadow effects on decorated areas.

painted enamels. Technique of applying opaque and translucent enamels to variety of surfaces, e.g. gold, silver, copper, or ivory. Practised in form of revived *Limoges technique by English craftsmen in late 19th century, particularly A. *Fisher; his experiments copied by N. *Dawson, A. *Gaskin, and H. *Wilson, and by French neo-Renaissance and Art Nouveau jewellers.

painted furniture. Originated c4000 years ago, when paint first used to protect wooden surfaces. In 19th century, Gothic Reform and Early English style furniture painted with medieval scenes; *cottage furniture sometimes painted, also pieces by A. *Heal.

painted slate (in furniture). Used for table-tops, japanned or covered with painted glass to imitate marble; also pedestals. Shown in London at Great Exhibition of 1851, and International Exhibition of 1862. Easily broken.

Pairpoint Corporation. American manufacturers of electro-plate in New Bedford, Massachusetts; founded 1880 as Pairpoint Manufacturing Co. Merged with Mount Washington Glass Co. (1900), becoming Pairpoint Corporation, making glass only; continued until 1958. Mark: PAIRPOINT.

Pairpointe, Thomas. English silver designer. In London, designed and executed shields for e.g. J. *Angell; awarded medals at International

Painted furniture. Cupboard chest made by ‡Heal & Son. Pine with comb-painted patterns. 1915.

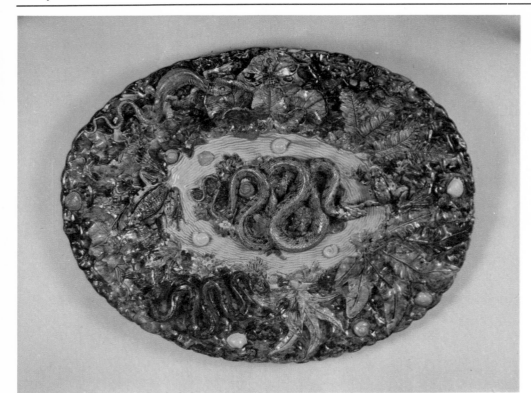

Exhibition, London (1862). Went via Paris to America; chief designer for *Gorham Manufacturing Co. during 1870s.

Palissy ware. Earthenware made in 19th century, in style of 16th century work of Bernard Palissy; lizards, frogs, snakes, shells, and insects, arranged with water plants, ivy, ferns, etc., in high relief, covered with lead glaze naturalistically coloured with metallic oxides. First revived in early 1840s by C. A. *Avisseau, followed by other French potters, e.g. *Landais family, and by *Mafra & Son in Portugal. Palissy ware made at Minton factory includes close reproductions of 16th century originals, but also embraces other earthenware with coloured lead glazes.

Pallme König, Josef. Bohemian glass manufacturers founded 1786. Thriving factories in Steinschönau and Kosten in late 19th century, producing Art Nouveau iridescent glass of fine quality; also some table glass.

Palmqvist, Sven (b 1906). Swedish glass artist. Employed by *Ørrefors from 1928 (designer from 1936), where became known for richly inlaid heavy vessels in *Ravenna glass. Marks: P, followed by Ørrefors or Øf on engraved glass to own design; PA on cut glass; PU on furnace-worked glass.

pan-Slavic movement and The Wanderers. Movement to reassert traditional Russian culture, began during reign of Nicholas I (1825–55); reaction against domination of Western neo-classical tradition. Received new impetus, 1862, when 13 artists expelled from Academy of Fine Arts for insisting that Gold Academy Award go to work embodying Slavic themes. Rebels formed group, the Wanderers, holding exhibitions in towns all over Russia; explicitly repudiated academic philosophy of 'Art for Art's

*Palissy ware. Enamelled earthenware dish, modelled in relief. made by *Landais, Tours. 1855.*

Josef Pallme König. Iridescent glass jug. c1900. Height 3¼in.

sake', attempting to forge new style based on neglected Russian artistic traditions. Research into Russian history led to revival of ancient arts of enamelling by P. *Ovtchinnikov, who formed school to promote and teach *champlevé*, filigree and *plique-à-jour* techniques. Pan-Slavic move-

ment contrasted drama and colour of *Old Russian style with Western elegance of Fabergé's work, intended for cultural élite; pan-Slavic exhibitions at Moscow (1882) and Nizhni Novgorod (1896); latter visited by Tsar Nicholas II and Tsarina, amid enormous publicity. Despite subsequent modifications taking account of contemporary changes in taste, nationalist styles initiated by pan-Slavic movement maintained momentum up to and beyond 1917 Revolution.

Pantin. French glasshouse near Paris. Brilliant, deep-cut engraved work on thick glass shown at Paris Exhibition of 1878; mostly bold floral motifs and bird and other animal designs. In c1920, amalgamated with *Legras glasshouse as Verreries et Cristalleries de St Denis et de Pantin Réunies.

paper-clip. From mid 19th century, spring-loaded clip for gripping sheaf of papers; intended to stand on writing-table or desk. Variety of forms includes duck's head with spring-loaded beak and coloured glass eyes, clam, boar's head, clasped hands, or single hand hinged by spring to back-plate. Made e.g. of steel, sheet or lacquered brass, or copper; occasionally plated in silver or gold. Widely produced in England and America from mid 19th century to c1914, when superseded by mainly utilitarian versions.

paper knife, or **letter opener.** Bladed instrument for opening envelopes. Blade sometimes engraved with landscapes, figures, postal rates, or tables of weights and measures; made in gold, silver, brass, horn, or ivory; usually ornamented. Produced after introduction of envelopes in mid 19th century.

paperweights. Earliest dated paperweights (1845) from France and Venice; developed in Bohemia at same time. From mid 19th century to c1880, American firms produced variety of weights, some using A. *Pellatt's *cristallo-ceramie* technique; N. *Lutz produced floral bouquet or miniature fruits resting on *latticinio* bed; for *Boston & Sandwich Glass Co. *New England Glass Co. produced almost life-sized single fruit weights resting on clear glass cushion, mainly by François Pierre, formerly of *Baccarat; also many *millefiori* weights, with multicoloured canes set in clear glass, especially by John L. Gilliland of Brooklyn, New York. In late 19th century, pressed glass weights made in shape of landmarks, e.g. Plymouth Rock, as well as books and animals.

English paperweights of period include weights with *millefiori* canes partly sunk into white glass resembling melted snow (usually attributed to G. *Bacchus & Sons), and brightly coloured floral weights signed IGW, and attributed to Islington Glass Works (see Rice, Harris & Sons). Some late 19th century paperweights found as mantelpiece ornaments. Major period of European production 1845–55 (see Baccarat, Clichy, St Louis), with revival in France c1878–1914. Brilliantly coloured Art Deco weights made by A. *Walter, with insects and flowers in greens, turquoises, ochres, and yellows. See also doorstops and hand coolers.

papier-mâché. Pulped paper, pressed in dies; technique, introduced to Europe from East in 17th century, used mainly for moulded ceiling ornamentation, mirror frames, carriage panels,

stem and foot, and metal fittings. Subsequent American developments include Hinks duplex lamp (1865), with double wick giving brighter flame and Robert Hitchcock's aerated flame lamp (patented 1880) which dispenses with glass chimney, substituting clockwork driven fan to provide draught for flame. Paraffin lamps produced in quantity c1860–c1900, in single standing, hanging, wall-mounted versions, or combined e.g. as chandelier or standard lamp. Many decorative examples. Shades in variety of shapes; often in coloured glass, sometimes painted or engraved with e.g. floral motifs.

Paramount. *See* A. G. Harley-Jones.

parian ware. Matt white porcelain body, slightly translucent, usually with smear glaze. Distinguishable from biscuit porcelain by ivory tone, silky texture, and marble-like appearance. Apparently developed in course of attempts to reproduce creamy biscuit porcelain made at Derby factory in 18th century. First produced commercially by *Copeland & Garrett as 'statuary porcelain' in 1846, although T. & R. *Boote claimed its introduction in 1841, without releasing it commercially until 1850. Production encouraged by patronage of *Art Union of London and commissions from H. *Cole. Manufactured by Wedgwood factory from c1848 under trade name, Carrara. Initially used to make figures and groups, often taken from sculpture, and often combined with glazed porcelain or

*Parian ware. Figure of dancing girl, modelled by W. Bell. Probably made by *Copeland & Garrett. c1865.*

Above
*Paperweights. French. Top: *Baccarat. Left: *St Louis *Millefiori paperweight. Right: *Clichy millefiori and latticinio paperweight. Mid 19th century.*

Left
Papier-mâché furniture. English, mid 19th century. Height 3ft 1½ in.

etc. during 18th century. Method of pasting paper sheets together, moulding and baking them, patented by Henry Clay, 1772; originally called paper ware, known as papier-mâché by 1850. Both types malleable into any shape by hand or machine; used for furniture, c1840–c1880, e.g. beds, bookcases, cabinets, chairs, music racks, sofas. Unsuitable for legs or framework, therefore pinned to metal or wooden structures. Usually japanned black and sometimes richly decorated with e.g. gold leaf or powder, or powdered aluminium for romantic scenes. Other forms of decoration include floral paintings, mother-of-pearl, gem, and ivory inlays, cockatoo and peacock motifs, *nature printing, and coloured prints glued onto main surfaces and varnished over. Production centred mainly in Birmingham and Wolverhampton; best-known manufacturers, *Jennens & Bettridge. *Illustrations at* canterbury, whatnot.

paraffin lamp. Broad ribbon wick draws fuel from reservoir by capillary action; replaced gravity-fed Argand oil lamp. Introduced in America, 1859, when discovery of Pennsylvania oil fields made paraffin (kerosene, carbon oil) cheapest fuel. Versions in metal, e.g. brass, copper, electro-plate, pewter, others with decorative blown-glass or ceramic reservoir,

parian, e.g. supporting dish or basket of table centrepiece. Also modelled in form of flowers applied to vases in late 1840s. By late 1860s, products include jugs, vases, tea services, and brooches. Minton firm, first to use name parian, claimed production by 1845; manufactured large quantities of tableware, often lavishly gilded. Hard-paste parian body, developed in late 1840s, made at lower cost than initial soft paste, which nevertheless continued in production. *Belleek factory, established in 1857 for manufacture of parian, used both hard and soft paste, later covering parian-type body with iridescent glaze. Parian slip used in *pâte-sur-pâte* decoration by M-L. *Solon at Minton factory. Some later parian ware, e.g. jugs, made with relief decoration in white against tinted ground. Manufacture in England diminished in 1890s, although produced, notably by *Robinson & Leadbeater, well into 20th century. Biscuit porcelain after style of English parian ware, used in America in 1850s and 1860s at *United States Pottery; figures, and jugs decorated in relief against pitted, coloured ground, imitated from 1860s by many American potters. Makers of true parian body in America include *Ott & Brewer, E. *Bennett, and *Chesapeake Pottery; similar body used in manufacture of 'Belleek'. In Sweden, parian figures, etc., made at *Rörstrand factory (c1857–1870s) and at *Gustavsburg from early 1860s until early 20th century. *Illustrations at* Jeannest, E., Goss, W. H.

Paris School. *See* Ecole de Paris.

parlour bedstead. *See* wardrobe-bed.

parlour chair. Loose Victorian term for side-chair other than bedroom chair, or heavy, balloon-back dining-room chair.

parure. Existed in 18th century as set of jewellery made entirely in same stones. 19th century version was strictly matching set both in stones and design. Full *parure* could be made up of 8–9 pieces including diadem or other hair ornament, gem-mounted comb, necklace and pendant, brooch or stomacher, pair of earrings, and pair of bracelets. Many of larger pieces separate to make smaller pieces. *Parure* often given in basic form as part of *corbeille de mariage* and added to over years on anniversaries etc. Small set of 2–3 pieces, e.g. brooch and earrings, called *demi-parure*.

Passenger, Frederick and Charles (fl late 19th, early 20th centuries). English potters and decorators. Worked for W. *De Morgan; partners in firm from 1898. Work by Charles Passenger includes dishes painted with flowers alternating with radiating points, and leaf patterned edge, or galleon in full sail, painted in greenish-blue and silver lustre, with ruby lustre fish. After closure of De Morgan firm, continued pottery decoration until 1911. Work initialled. Frederick worked (1923–33) at pottery in Bushey Heath, Hertfordshire, producing Isnik inspired work in style of De Morgan.

pastille burner, perfume burner, brûle-parfum, cassolette. Container e.g. in bone china, Staffordshire earthenware, with perforated cover; designed to hold portion of scented, compressed charcoal, which burns slowly, giving off aromatic fumes; for perfuming room etc. English 19th century examples in novel forms as e.g. cottage, castle, with detachable roof. Euro-

pean perfume burners, from 18th century, vapourize liquid perfume by direct heat, e.g. cup containing small oil burner and reservoir, surmounted by urn shaped perfume container with pierced cover, whole assembly standing c6in.–c8in. high, made in porcelain by German factories at Meissen, Württemberg and Berlin. English designs c1800–c1900, in Swansea earthenware, consisting of egg shaped pastille burner on tripod support over circular tray with flame-like ornament, probably derive from European perfume burners.

Left
Fred Passenger. Earthenware vase made at Bushey Heath Pottery and decorated by F. Passenger. Marked Bushey Heath around device incorporating De M and artist's monogram transfer-printed in black. 1923–33. Height 6in.

Below
Patent furniture. Walnut side chair by G. *Hunzinger, bearing label marked Hunzinger, N.Y. PAT. March 30 1869.

pastry fork. *See* cutting fork.

pâte-de-cristal. Glass paste, version of *pâte-de-verre* but with higher lead content. Almost transparent, giving clear ring when sounded. Used by G. *Argy-Rousseau for sculptural figurines and decorative ware.

pâte-de-verre (French, 'glass paste'). Powdered glass mixed into thick paste with water and volatile adhesive medium; usually applied in thin layers in mould until required thickness of finished glass achieved, then fired within mould just long enough to retain form. Firing process hazardous, since mould liable to disintegrate in heat; paste may also fail to coalesce. Alabaster-like translucency when successful, with slightly waxy surface and permitting wide range of colour intensity. Ancient Egyptian technique, rediscovered in late 19th century by H. *Cros. Later also used by G. *Argy-Rousseau, A. *Dammouse, A. and A. *Daum, F. *Décorchement, and A. *Walter. *Illustration at Cros, H.*

pâte-sur-pâte. Ceramic decoration; layers of white slip, usually porcelain, built up into cameo-like decorative motif against tinted ground; details carved in design before firing. Technique developed at Sèvres factory (c1850–c1875), brought to England by M-L. *Solon. Produced at Minton factory from 1871; mainly figure subjects. Other makers include W. *Brownfield & Son, G. *Jones, *Moore Brothers, and *Grainger's and *Worcester porcelain factories. In America, made notably by *Knowles, Taylor & Knowles. Although made by Minton factory until early 20th century, and by Solon until 1913, not generally produced after 1890 because painstaking technique made cutting of production costs impossible.

patent furniture. American furniture developed c1850; incorporates mechanical devices which create flexible, comfortable pieces performing alternative functions, e.g. *adjustable chairs, *convertible furniture. Popularity declined when furniture based on American colonial and

Pâte-de-verre. *Figure by A. *Walter. Signed on base A Walter Nancy together with Jean Descomps. c1920.*

Pâte-sur-pâte. *Parian porcelain vase with pâte-sur-pâte decoration by M.L. *Solon at *Mintons. Exhibited at Philadelphia in 1876.*

Eastlake styles became fashionable after World's Columbian Exposition in Chicago, 1893.

patent rocker. *See* platform rocker.

Patent Victoria Axminster. *See* chenille Axminster.

Pauline Pottery Co. *See* Jacobus, Pauline.

Paul Revere Pottery. American pottery established in early 20th century for artistic training of girls from poor, mainly immigrant, families in

Pearls. *Necklace made by *Cartier. Diamonds, platinum, pink, black and white pearls. c1910.*

Boston, Massachusetts; profits used for advancement of girls' education in other subjects. Earthenware nursery and breakfast bowls, dishes, etc., produced. Decoration includes birds, mottoes, or stylized floral motifs; use often restricted to borders, or arranged to accentuate vertical lines. Marked with painted initials and, sometimes, S.E.G. (Saturday Evening Girls' Club, although potters worked eight hours per day).

pavé setting. Gem setting particularly suitable for diamonds. Stones set so close together that no backing material visible. Turquoise pavé-set jewellery very popular from 1840s.

patina. Gloss and colour produced on wood by age, use, and constant polishing. Destroyed by veneers, French polish, etc.

Peachblow glass. Late 19th century American art glass. First made by *New England Glass Co. as deliberate imitation of costly Chinese peach-blow porcelain and marketed as Wild Rose Peachblow; deep rose shading to creamy white. *Hobbs, Brockunier & Co. version shades deep red to greenish-yellow; velvety in texture with white lining. Also made by *Mount Washington Glass Works, in pastel-blue shading to rose-pink, and *Steuben Glass Works.

Peacock Pottery. *See* Brain, E. & Co.

Pearce, Daniel (1817–1907). English glass artist; employed by T. *Webb & Sons from 1884. Produced fine cameo glass; known also for centre-pieces, flower holders, scent bottles, and decorative work in Chinese style.

pearl. Obtained from pearl oyster; natural growth produced by irritation inside shell. Colour ivory-white with lustrous surface, pink or steel-grey (known as 'black'). Large number of artificial pearls worn in 19th century; made by

various methods by French, Germans, Italians, and Chinese. Many made of blown glass coated with nacreous substance, very fragile; most durable, 'Venice' pearls, made of an igneous substance which could be polished to produce surface lustre. Pearls were set in gold in flower and leaf shapes, used to decorate borders and settings of coloured stones, and to surround and link cameos. Popular throughout 19th century. Seed pearls stayed in fashion for mourning jewellery as a symbol of tears. Blister pearls, often hollow malformations, and 'baroque' pearls in strange, uneven shapes much used in neo-renaissance and Arts & Crafts jewellery. Technique of producing cultivated pearls perfected by Japanese, Mikimoto, in 1899. Cultured pearls common after 1921, both as long strings and as choker necklaces. Combinations of black and white pearls very fashionable in 1930s.

Freshwater pearls, produced by pearl-bearing mussels in rivers of Scotland, North Wales and Ireland, whiter and less translucent, with silvery sheen. Small and delicate; found in filigree gold settings and with topaz and amethysts. In 1850s and 1860s, used in Scottish and Irish *Celtic style jewellery, made entirely from native materials, and in mass-produced Arts & Crafts style pieces.

Pearline glass. Translucent British art glass, usually blue, but sometimes in other colours. Shades from deep blue at base to opaline pearl-like edge; frequently has raised opaline contrast design. Patented by G. *Davidson & Co. c1889. ·

pebble jewellery. *See* Scotch pebble jewellery.

Pèche, Dagobert (1887–1923). Austrian artist and metalwork designer; studied at Akademie der bildenden Künste, Vienna; co-director of *Wiener Werkstätte 1917–23; silver designs in similar style to that of J. *Hoffmann. Mark: elongated P with dot underneath. Much of his jewellery in ivory and gold combined. Style and use of materials very influential in 1920s. Ceramic designs commissioned by J. *Böck as well as Wiener Keramik.

pedestal cupboard or **night-stand.** Bedside cupboard with shelves for one or two chamber-pots. In Victorian era, often carved to match washstand, wardrobe, and dressing-table.

*Dagobert Peche. Hand-wrought dish. Marks for *Wiener Werkstatte and Dagobert Peche. Diameter 13in.*

Pekin lacquer. *See* cinnabar lacquer.

PEL or **Practical Equipment Ltd.** Leading British manufacturers of chromium-plated tubular steel furniture, established in London c1931. Pitch filling in steel tubing prevented flattening. Examples of work include Modernist style sofa with tubular steel frame curved at corners, and brown leather-covered cushions for seat, back, and arms; stacking chairs for British Broadcasting Corporation; barstools, etc. for hotels (e.g. Claridges and Savoy in London). Luxury pieces later superseded by functional equipment for hospitals, etc.

Peleton glass. Bohemian art glass with vermicular surface decoration; patented 1880 by Wilhelm Kralik of Neuwelt; widely produced under patent in Britain and America. Made by dipping hot glass object in glass threads of contrasting colour or opacity; with filaments adhering to surface, vessel reheated several times, then either pressed or hand-tooled into desired shape. Some pieces given satin finish by exposure to acids; some further embellished with coloured enamel designs.

Pellatt, Aspley (1791–1863). London glass maker. Studied 16th century Venetian *cristallo-ceramie technique and patented own version (using fine flint glass) 1819. Also patented processes for glass-pressing techniques (1831, 1845). At glasshouse in Falcon Street, Southwark, produced *cristallo-ceramie* work on flint-glass flasks, paperweights, and pendants. At Great Exhibition of 1851, exhibits included cut-glass chandeliers in white, ruby and blue glass, Anglo-Venetian tableware, and *cristallo-ceramies*. In 1848, published Curiosities of Glassmaking. Retired 1852, when elected Member of Parliament, but influence continued for decades throughout Britain and Europe, his improved techniques providing basis for fine paperweights made at *Baccarat, *Clichy, and *St Louis later in century.

pendant. Gold or jewelled ornament designed to hang from chain, sometimes made *en suite;* highly fashionable from 1860s. Many had removable attachment for wearing alternatively as brooch. Made of precious stones surrounded by pearls, sometimes with pearl drop; also enamelled with matching chains. Gold pendants decorated with filigree in Etruscan style made by A. *Castellani, R. *Phillips, J. *Brogden, in

*Apsley Pellatt. Scent bottle and stopper with *sulphide portrait medallion. Base marked Pellatt & Green, patentees, London. Height 4½in.*

1860s. Elaborate examples of enamelled gold set with coloured precious stones, in Renaissance style fashionable in 1870s and 1880s, made by C. *Giuliano and A. *Fouquet. Often in form of diamond crosses or pearl hearts at end of 19th century. Fine Arts and Crafts examples, particularly those by C. R. *Ashbee and H. *Wilson; also elaborate Art Nouveau examples with superb enamel work, especially those of R. *Lalique.

Pendeh rugs. *See* West Turkestan.

pendeloque. *See* gem cutting.

pen. Metal pens made as curiosities from antiquity, but goose quill pen in general use until c1840. 19th century improvements included wooden holder for changeable quill nibs by Joseph Bramah (1809), and techniques for gold-plating quill nibs. First machine tool for manufacturing steel penholders and nibs devised by J. Mitchell (1822); mass production introduced by Joseph Gillot (1824); hole in nib above split to ensure regular flow of ink patented 1830 by James Perry. Until general introduction of *fountain pen (c1890), many ornate pens, e.g. in gold, silver, with decorative embossing or inlay; also in japanned metal; made by e.g. Gillot & Co., E. Perry & Co.

penny box. *See* money box.

pen tray. Shallow, elongated desk tray for pens. Often boat shaped. Made in silver, with gadrooned edges, or with overall embossed decoration; also in tortoiseshell, with silver gadrooned edges. Cheaper versions in electroplate, and plain or stamped, polished brass.

Made from 1770s, throughout 19th and early 20th centuries.

Perchin, Michael Evlampievich (1860-1903). Prolific Russian goldsmith, of St Petersburg. Workmaster for *Fabergé from 1886. Craftsman of all except first two or three Imperial Easter Eggs (*Fabergé eggs). Also produced many finely enamelled objects of vertu, particularly cigarette cases, desk sets, cane and parasol handles, and picture frames. After Perchin's death, workshop under direction of H. *Wigström. Mark: M.P. in Cyrillic characters.

perfume burner. *See* pastille burner.

peridot. Bottle-green or yellowish-green gemstone, variety of mineral olivine, found mainly on St John's Island in Red Sea. Step cut most effective, but oval, round, pendeloque, and mixed cut common. Too soft for rings and bracelets: mainly used for brooches and pendants; popular in 19th century.

Perriand, Charlotte (b 1903). French architect and furniture designer; associate (1926-37) of *Le Corbusier. Collaborated with Pierre Jeanneret, architect, on mountain refuges for International Exhibition, Brussels, 1937. Designed simple, rustic furniture, sometimes consciously craftsmanly, during late 1930s, e.g. tables with thick, irregularly shaped wooden tops.

Perry, Mary Chase (1868-1961). American porcelain painter and artist potter. In Detroit, Michigan, decorated pottery fired in kiln used for baking dental enamel; with partner, developed gas-fired pottery kiln, sold under trade name Revelation Kilns. Ceramics sold under same name. In c1903, established Pewabic Pottery. Early work has relief decoration of stylized plant forms, covered with matt glaze. Later, vases in simple shapes covered in rich glazes, e.g. in blue or gold, often with colours combined or in layers. Experimented with iridescent glazes. Pewabic Pottery closed in 1961.

Persian carpets. Production declined in first half of 19th century, due to wars with Russia (1825-28) and England (1856), but revived c1875, when Tabriz merchants instigated export manufacture. Foreign firms (e.g. *Zeigler & Co.) established branch offices and factories. In centres dominated by Western market, e.g. Tabriz, Kirman, Sultanabad, Sehna, mainly low quality carpets produced, with inferior design, colour (*aniline dyes used), and materials (poor wool). Some fine traditional examples still made, but mainly in less commercialized centres, e.g. Ardebil, Bijar, Herez, Isfahan, Karaja, Meshëd. Persian government took steps to resist declining standards: c1900, use of synthetic dyes punished by loss of ears and right hand; school of design founded in Teheran, using only 15th and 16th century carpet designs as models. By 1910, carpet export trade with c£2½ million a year. Expansion continued until 1930s, when Depression crippled industry and foreign companies forced to close.

Persian colours. Range of colours, with blue, green, and turquoise predominating, and touches of e.g. manganese purple, used by W. *De Morgan by early 1880s in decoration of vases, dishes, and, notably, tiles. High-temperature

Persian carpet. Design includes peacocks, cypress trees and pomegranates. Late 19th century.

colours painted over white porcelain slip on biscuit tiles and fused in one firing with thick, clear glaze. Floral designs and colours derived from Isnik tiles of 15th and 16th centuries.

Tiles and tile panels produced (1884-1900) at Doulton workshop, Lambeth, London, decorated mainly in turquoise, green, and orange, sold as Persian ware. Use of colours revived (1919-22) on vases, bowls, and plaques painted e.g. by H. *Simeon. Isnik designs and colours inspired other tile manufacturers in late 19th century, e.g. Maw & Co.

Work of T. *Deck in France in 1860s and 70s, inspired by Persian and Isnik wares of 16th and 17th centuries, shown at Paris Exhibition in 1878.

Persian ware. Tiles and panels for decoration of walls and fireplaces produced at Doulton workshop, Lambeth, London (1884-90). Designs and underglaze colours, predominantly green, turquoise, and orange, influenced by Near-Eastern pottery, painted over coating of white slip. Style briefly revived for use on bowls, vases, and plaques in early 1920s, notably by H. *Simeon.

Pettersen, Sverre (1884-1959). Norwegian designer in Art Deco and Functionalist styles. Worked in textiles and stained glass; from 1928, designed tableware and engraved glass for *Hadeland. Mark: SP, engraved, on some important pieces.

Pewabic Pottery. American art pottery of M. C. *Perry, at Detroit, Michigan (1903-61). Named after river in Michigan called 'clay in copper colour' by Chippewa. Pottery recently produced on site by University of Michigan.

pewter. Pewterware unfashionable during Victorian period, but extensively manufactured for sale to urban and rural working classes, e.g. plates, tankards, candlesticks, flagons, mugs, utensils, etc. in traditional, plain style. Use of pewter revived by Arts & Crafts Movement, e.g. *Tudric tableware range, designed by A. *Knox for *Liberty & Co. Act of Parliament in 1907 reduced permitted content of lead to 10%.

Pewabic pottery. Glazed earthenware jar. Early 20th century. Height 18¾ in.

Pfeiffer, Max Adolf (fl early 20th century). German porcelain manufacturer. Founder and manager (1905-13) of Schwarzburger Werkstätten in Unterweissbach (Thuringia). Produced glazed, undecorated porcelain figures modelled by E. *Barlach. At Meissen factory from 1918, regarded as responsible for improvement in design of figures, modelled e.g. by P. *Scheurich and M. *Esser.

Pfohl, Karl (1826-94). Bohemian glass engraver. Specialized in engravings of horses on, e.g. goblets and beakers. Worked in Steinschönau and Paris.

pharmaceutical glass. From c1830, glass began to replace earthenware for all pharmaceutical purposes. General storage jar: usually of green bottle glass, more rarely of amethyst or blue, often with japanned lid. Shop round (shelf

bottle): mostly spherical, 5-10in. high, with close-fitting (usually ground) stopper; hand-painted or recessed label; sometimes with mark of glasshouse, e.g. YG Co in Hexagon for York Glass Co., W in lozenge for Wood Bros Glass Co.; some (in blue glass) much smaller for infrequently required or costly preparations. Syrup bottle: as shop round, but with loose-fitting broad glass stopper; usually of blue or green glass. Dispensing or medicine bottle (for customer to take home): early ones either round or square; gradually replaced by mould-blown flat bottles. Poison bottle: (for shop use), usually cylindrical and ribbed; also, in clear smooth glass designed to dispense only drops or minute quantities of powder or liquid; special dispensing bottles for poison (mandatory from 1899) developed from mid 19th century to reduce cases of accidental poisoning in the home; identifiable by touch as well as sight; hexagon or pentagon shape popular well into 20th century; others of ribbed, ridged, or fluted glass; other variations include attached warning bells and skull and crossbone moulding or decoration; recessed labels further aid to identification; colours usually brown, dark blue, or dark green. Pills and powders often dispensed in glass containers from mid century; sometimes gilt or painted, or in *cranberry glass. Patent medicine bottle: wide variety. Toiletry bottle: small bottle for aromatic liquid, larger one for cologne, lavender water, etc. (see also scent bottle). Smelling salt bottle: double-ended bottle of coloured or engraved glass popular from 1851; cameo glass salts also popular, sometimes with hallmarked gold or silver mounting. Cupping glass (to relieve chest congestion): in 18th and 19th centuries, often found in sets of three fitted into lined case; usually round, of fine flint glass and with folded rims; 1½-2½in. in diameter; narrow, elongated flattened ones c2in. long also made. Glass feeding bottle: earliest German, dating from 18th century; in common use from mid 19th century; usually gourd, pear, or boat shaped; some novelty forms, e.g. swan shape with crimping and fluting; usually of clear glass, but sometimes in strong colours; patented varieties date from turn of century, e.g. valve in teat to ensure even flow of milk, thermometer embedded in glass to ensure correct temperature. Measures: small, calibrated glass tube (minim) with lip or small, pinched open spout for dispensing drops of medicine; introduced 1809 but popular to late 1870s; usually in own container of lined wood or metal; also, calibrated glass spoon from mid century, or cylindrical, conical, or beaker shape of 2, 4, 10 or 20 fl oz capacity, usually clear glass; opaque glass measure with translucent graduated panel introduced in 1880s. Glass beads (used to measure alcohol content of liquids): small footed spheres, calibrated size; usually plain glass; some bear numbers. Laboratory glass: surviving 19th century flasks, retorts, phials, stills, condensers, etc., usually of stout greenish, bluish, or yellowish-green glass. See also carboy, specie jar.

Phillips, Robert (d 1881). English goldsmith and jeweller at Phillips Brothers, London. First English jeweller to make *archaeological jewellery in style of A. *Castellani; encouraged and employed Italian craftsmen, e.g. C. *Giuliano, and C. *Doria; showed Etruscan-style pieces at International Exhibition of 1862. Made set of Assyrian jewellery designed by Sir Austen Layard, 1869. Also made Renaissance style

jewellery. Helped popularize use of coral in jewellery.

Phoenix Glass Works. American glasshouse in Beaver Falls, Pennsylvania. Established 1820 by family of Bristol glassmaker Thomas Caines (who emigrated 1812 and was instrumental in setting up several other early American glasshouses, including South Boston Flint Glassworks). Made table and decorative ware. *Satin glass developed there by J. *Webb in 1885.

Phoenix Works. See Clementson, Joseph.

photograph and portrait frames. Standing and hanging versions made in silver, electro-plate, and wood from 19th century. Victorian examples usually highly ornate, often decorated with cherubs and archangels. Very popular during 1920s with stylized Art Nouveau decoration, often using semi-precious stones.

photographic decoration. Furniture decoration; photographs applied to enamel or wooden base. Four different methods patented c1867-76. Popularity declined c1880.

piano-bed. American *patent furniture. Frame, containing drawers, cupboards for bed clothes, wash bowl, towel, etc., supports piano body; bed, also in frame, pulls out with two handles. Additions said not to affect piano's musical qualities. Matching revolving piano stool, with hinged writing flap, drawers in pedestal, and seat opening to reveal lady's workbox and toilet mirror, also available. Dates from 1866.

pickle caster. In America, lidded glass jar for serving pickle; held in electro-plated frame with long handle rising from e.g. circular, footed base. Lid of jar with finial also normally electro-plated. Jar, in clear, coloured, engraved or cut glass, often decorated with painted design. Pickle tongs hang on bracket extending from handle. Popular late 19th to early 20th century. Smaller English version, known as pickle cruet, normally holds two glass jars.

pickle cruet. See pickle caster.

pictorial flask. See historical flask.

pickle fork. Narrow three-tined fork (outer tines barbed) for serving pickle from jar. In silver or electro-plate; handle often ivory. Made mainly in America from c1859.

pier table. Table designed to stand against wall (pier) between windows; dates from 18th century. Made in many styles. Rococo style models (e.g. by A. *Roux) popular in America c1855-65. Gutta-percha model shown at Great Exhibition of 1851, London.

picture frame clock. French clock, made from 18th century; gilt picture-frame surround; square, round, or octagonal dial set in coloured velvet. Also made in Malta, but examples rare. Other European versions include *Black Forest picture-clocks (c1830-c1870): heavy wooden picture frame, with clock dial incorporated in painted scene, e.g. in church tower; frequently fitted with musical box or other automata.

pie knife. See cake knife.

Pierret, Victor-Athanase (1806-93). French horologist. Designed watch and clock making machinery, calendar clocks and watches, and other *complicated timepieces. Sold 10,000 *skeleton clocks at Great Exhibition of 1851. Invented night-light clock (1863): rotating opalescent glass globe, bearing hour numerals, contains oil lamp.

Pietsch, Carl (1828-83). Bohemian master glass engraver; member of noted family of glass makers and engravers. Worked for J. & L. *Lobmeyr in Steinschönau. With F. *Ullmann and F. *Knöchel, instrumental in restoring Bohemian cut and engraved glass to earlier excellence. Subsequently, emigrated to America.

Pilkington's Tile & Pottery Co. Lancashire pottery, established 1892 at Clifton Junction for manufacture of tiles under management of W. *Burton. From 1897, buttons, hatpin heads, moulded vases, etc., introduced. Soon afterwards, began decoration of vases bought in biscuit. Display at Paris Exhibition (1900) included faience for architectural use, tiles, and pair of lions with crystalline glaze. Accidental discovery of opalescent glaze effects led to production, from 1903, of glazed earthenware, marketed as Lancastrian pottery. Vases, bowls, and trays, thrown in simple shapes, covered with glazes in wide range of colours, often with opalescent or crystalline effects, or texture resembling eggshell or parchment. Pottery with lustre decoration, main product in early 20th century, developed with help of J. *Burton, commercially produced from 1906, under art direction of G. *Forsyth. Decorated chiefly by Forsyth, C. *Cundall, R. *Joyce, and G. *Rodgers; some pieces decorated with designs by W. *Crane. Some vases have designs painted in black on matt blue ground, and brown or black on vermilion ground. Modelled, moulded, and, notably, incised decoration occurs. Animals and birds modelled by Joyce. Designs for tiles drawn e.g. by Crane, L.F. *Day, and C. *Voysey. Tile panels with alkaline glaze, designed and painted by Forsyth, illustrate history of pottery. Tube-lining used e.g. on tiles designed by Crane. From 1927, matt glazes with mottled effects achieved by addition of titanium oxide, used on tiles and pottery. *Lapis ware introduced in 1928. Manufacture of pottery ceased in 1937, although decoration continued until early 1938; resumed on small scale ten years later. Potters encouraged to produce individual pieces, which were then decorated and marked with artist's monogram, and symbol indicating date. Pieces designed by Crane bear his mark as well as that of painter. Until 1904, firm mark, P incised, sometimes used. Regular marks: P (Pilkington) L (Lancastrian) with two bees (Burton's rebus) designed by Day, and used 1904-13, then tudor rose; ROYAL LANCASTRIAN also occurs. Illustrations at Forsyth, G. M., lustre decoration, Mycock, W. S., tube-lining.

Pilsbury, Richard (1830-1897). Staffordshire ceramic decorator. Studied at school of design in home town, Burslem. Flower painting - in later years notably of orchids - based on gouache sketches from nature, at Minton factory (1866-92) and, as art director at Moore Brothers' factory, from 1892 until death.

pin cushion or **pin pillow.** Small cushion in which pins for needlework stuck. In general use by mid 17th century. Decorative forms in vogue from early 19th century reaching peak in early 20th century. Early examples very small, often made as fitting for *workboxes or for carrying in pocket; later forms generally larger. From c1900, mainly free-standing ornaments for dressing table, etc. Made in fanciful shapes, e.g. fruit (particularly strawberries), fans, shoes, flowers, baskets, wheel-barrows, dolls, animals. Fabric pillows made in velvet, silk (often with printed designs), or needlework, some with texts executed in cross-stitch; alternatively with elaborate beadwork on top and bottom – pins stuck in sides. Cushion often mounted in ornate holders of gold, silver, enamel, porcelain, bone, ivory, mother-of-pearl, wood, or papier-mâché.

Pinder, Bourne & Co. Staffordshire pottery manufacturers operating Nile Street Works, Burslem, from 1862. Earthenware for table use includes dessert service with central decoration of figures and moulded basketwork rims. Vases, jars, jugs, *jardinières,* etc., made in terracotta, decorated with enamel and gilding. Noted for work in Japanese style, e.g. stoneware jugs decorated with prunus blossom. Creamware plates decorated with birds, flowers, and geometrical designs in black. Proprietor worked in partnership with Doulton company, producing earthenware and porcelain from 1877 until retirement in 1882, when firm traded as Doulton & Co. Marks (1862–82) include initials PB & Co with crown, surrounded by laurel wreath, and PINDER BOURNE & Cᵒ/ NILE Sᵗ/ BURSLEM. with arrow in double triangle.

p'ing-t'o. *See* heidatsu.

pigeon clock. Clock for timing racing pigeons, made c1900 e.g. by Turner. Rotating slotted drum is attached to clock movement driving

Pinder, Bourne & Co. Stoneware jug moulded in relief and glazed blue. 1877.

graduated paper chart; when bird arrives, marker ring removed from leg, placed in capsule, and inserted in slot. Time of arrival then stamped on chart by turning drum (*see* time recorder clock).

pillar clock. Weight-driven Japanese clock hung on central pillar in Japanese house; position of pointer on weight against vertical scale indicates time. Hour numerals adjustable on scale, as length of Japanese day and night hours varied with time of year (until adoption of Western time-keeping system in 1873). Weight often incorporates striking mechanism. Also, early 19th century French clock supported by four pillars on moulded base; made of marble, ormolu, or wood.

Pinnox Works. *See* Wedgwood & Co.

pipe stand. Stand in e.g. brass or carved wood for resting pipe on when not in use. Many 19th and 20th century decorative examples; sometimes forms part of desk set.

pipe stopper. Instrument with flattened, circular end for pressing down burning tobacco in pipe bowl. 19th century versions in wide variety of materials, e.g. copper, brass, and, rarely, gold or silver; hand-carved examples in wood, bone, ivory. Often with ornate handle: grotesque animal or bird, caricature of public figure, Dickensian character, etc.

piqué. Decorative inlay of fine fragments of gold or silver, e.g. in tortoiseshell or ivory. Three main types: *piqué point,* made up of tiny nail heads, or points; *piqué clouté,* larger points arranged in pattern; *piqué posé,* flakes of gold or silver inlaid in cut-out shapes. Inserted directly into tortoiseshell softened by heating; widely used on tortoiseshell boxes, fans. Fixed to other materials, e.g. ivory, shagreen, bone, by adhesives. Common form of decoration throughout 19th century, revived, notably by J. *Dunand, during Art Deco period. *Piqué* jewellery made in tortoiseshell or ivory, decorated with dots or lines. Brooches, buttons, and earrings fashionable from early 19th century until 1860s. At first hand-made; after 1872, gold or silver inlay stamped out and pressed in tortoiseshell or ivory held between metal plates. Only cheapest *piqué* work of very low quality mass-produced until c1890.

Pirkenhammer. Hard-paste porcelain factory established (1802) in Bohemian town of Pirkenhammer (now Březová, Czechoslovakia). Made tableware decorated with views, genre subjects, flowers, etc. Decoration in Empire style survived until mid 19th century. Ornamental ware include lithophanes and vases. Figures, usually mythological or allegorical subjects, painted in enamel colours. Marks include hammers crossed behind crown (from 1857) or same device on shield with eagle and label PIRKENHAMMER. Factory still in production.

pirlie-pig. Scottish dialect term for 19th century metal, usually pewter, money-box.

pivot. Pin or rivet joining sticks at base of folding fan.

plant stand. *See* flower stand.

Plata Meneses. Spanish silversmiths, founded in Madrid, 1840, by M. L. Meneses; remained family firm until became limited company in 1943; products include electro-plated flatware and hollow-ware, and church silver, e.g. chalices, thrones, and monstrances. Now one of largest manufacturers in Spain, also exporting to Mexico and South America.

plateau centrepiece. *See* centrepiece.

Plated Amberina. Pattern-moulded shaded American art glass patented 1886 by E. *Libbey at New England Glass Co. Version of *Amberina, but characteristically ribbed and with *milk or *opalescent glass lining. Usually in Amberina colours (amber shading upwards to ruby-red) but sometimes shaded cobalt to ruby; rarely, canary-yellow or green. Produced in limited quantities.

plate lifter. Device with long under claw and short upper arm for handling hot plates; produced in electro-plate from late 19th century in America.

plate warmer. Circular copper container with flat, pierced top; filled with boiling water and stood on sideboard or table in dining-room to keep dishes, food, etc. warm. Popular throughout 19th century.

platform or **patent rocker.** Mechanical version of upholstered rocking chair. American invention, dating from c1870. High, straight back, and open arms with padded arm rests; convex, lower edges of side rails rock on low, shaped, base usually fitted with socket castors; chair body attached to base by two springs. Often with plush or tapestry upholstery. *See* swing rocking chair.

platinum. Untarnishable, silver-coloured metal, much harder and stronger than gold. First found in South America in 16th century; not available in quantity until produced by Russia in early 19th century. Not widely used for jewellery, as value not appreciated until end of 19th century, when became popular setting for diamonds and precious stones. Palladium, similar but lighter metal used for larger pieces.

Plato clock. *See* ticket clock.

Pleydell Bouverie, Katherine (b 1895). English artist potter. Studied at Central School of Arts & Crafts, London (1921–23), and at pottery of B. *Leach in St Ives, Cornwall (1924). In 1925, established wood fired kiln at Coleshill, Wiltshire; worked with N. *Braden (1928–36). Carried out first systematic experimentation in England with glazes derived from wood and plant ashes. High quality matt glazes, e.g. in white or light grey (ash of reeds or grasses), greens and browns (various woods) or blue (laurustinus), made with mixture of clean, sieved ash, feldspar, and clay, used to cover stoneware; forms sometimes fluted. Also made unglazed plant pots and bowls in greyish-white or pink stoneware. Worked alone, 1936–40. After 2nd World War, established oil-fired kiln at Kilmington, Wiltshire (1946).

plique-à-jour or **open braid enamelling.** enamelling technique in which backing or mould divided into cells by *cloisonné* method and filled with translucent enamel. Metal backing plate

Plique-à-jour *enamelling. Cup designed and made by Ferdinand Thesmar, Paris. Mounted in silver gilt. c1893.*
Below
Plique-à-jour *enamelling. Lamp designed and made by Carrie Copson.* Plique-à-jour *enamel on bowl. 1905-12.*

removed after firing to give stained glass effect – sometimes called 'stained glass' enamel. Until 19th century, used almost exclusively in Russia and Scandinavia (particularly in 17th century). After revival in mid 19th century Russia, adopted by French and English jewellers (in late 19th century) for all kinds of jewellery, especially pendants and brooches in Art Nouveau style. *Illustration at* Lalique, R.

plywood. Form of *laminated wood in which grain of alternate layers set at right angles. Bent plywood chairs with single, curved slab forming

back, seat, and legs made in America during 1870s. Used by H. A. H. *Aalto, M. *Breuer, and G. *Rietveld. Facings include birch, alder, pine, oak, ash, beech, poplar, cottonwood. Used for cheap furniture during 1920s and 1930s.

pocket chronometer. *See* chronometer.

Ponti, Gio (b 1891). Italian architect and furniture designer. Founder member of Italian Movement for Rational Architecture in 1927; founded monthly magazine, Domus, in 1928. Designed functional furniture within neo-classical tradition, using new techniques. Best-known example is Domus side-chair (1950): back uprights incline outwards from single, shoulder-height back rail to yoke rail; front legs terminate above woven straw or plastic seat. Ceramic designs from 1923, produced by Richard-Ginori of Doccia, include goblets, vases, bowls and plates, e.g. porcelain vase (1929) of urn shape on cubic plinth, decorated with figures and architectural motifs. Pieces intricate, all produced from moulds but individually decorated.

Poli, Flavio (b 1900). Italian potter and glassmaker; art director of *Seguso Vetri d'Arte from 1934. Made heavy, semi-sculptural, ornamental glassware, either in thick, coloured glass, or richly decorated with colour inlay.

Polish rugs and carpets. Workshops for fine quality wool carpets (called Polish Polonaise) founded in 18th century. South-east Poland and Ukraine main centres of traditional peasant kelim production: flat-weave rugs, with simple, brightly coloured geometrical designs. French carpet designs sometimes adapted to kelims for middle-class urban market. Several craft societies specializing in kelim making formed from c1900, e.g. Society of Applied Arts, Cracow (1901); Kelim Polski, Warsaw (1921), using low-warp looms; Society of Popular Industry, Warsaw (products shown at Paris Exhibition of 1925); 'Lad' Society, Warsaw, founded 1926 by teachers at National School of Fine Arts.

Polish tapestry. Following 19th century industrialization, tapestry production declined into reproduction of earlier designs. Polish Society of Fine Art launched design revival in Cracow in 1901, centralizing artists interested in tapestry, who founded Cracow workshops in 1912. Work interrupted by 1st World War; later resumed by Warsaw Artists' Co-operative (founded 1926) until 1939. Several workshops opened after 2nd World War to make kelims and tapestries.

Pomona glass. American mould-blown art glass of delicate, frosted appearance decorated by etching, tinting, or staining; sometimes further embellished with applied flower garlands. Patented 1885 by *New England Glass Co. Popular for tumblers, fruit cups, bowls, etc.

pompadour chair. *See* lady's easy chair.

Pompeian style. Furniture style popular in Britain in Regency period, revived c1860. Typified by classical architectural forms decorated with motifs based on paintings and carved ornament uncovered during Pompeii excavations; pale woods, pastel paints used. Notable exponent of style, J. *Levien.

Pontremoli, J.M. (b 1886). Turkish merchant from Cassabra, Smyrna. Moved to England in 1910 as dealer in antique carpets, embroideries, tapestries, etc. In 1931, attempted to revive English needlework tradition; founded workshop in Paddington, London, and trained local girls to make heavy, hand-woven *needlework carpets. Employed professional artists for designs; favoured Elizabethan and Queen Anne styles. Retired c1942. Also collected Aubusson, Persian, Russian, and English needlework carpets.

Poole Pottery Ltd. *See* Carter, Stabler & Adams.

Poor, Henry Varnum (b 1888). American artist. Painted murals and, later, designed and decorated pottery. Bold hand-painting of flowers, spiky leaves, and figures influenced by work of Wiener Werkstätte.

Pope, Francis C. (fl late 19th, early 20th centuries). English ceramic modeller and designer. Work at Doulton workshops, Lambeth, London (1880-1923) includes salt-glazed stoneware vases in forms derived from natural shapes, e.g. gourd or marrow, with carved and coloured decoration on matt ground. Work initialled, F.C.P.

Poppelsdorf. German faience factory at Poppelsdorf near Bonn (Rhineland), established 1755 and operated by firm trading under name of Ludwig Wessel from 1825 to present day. Later products chiefly cream-coloured earthenware. Marks normally incorporate initials LW, sometimes Poppelsdorf.

Porceleyne Fles, de. *See* Thooft, Joost.

Porsgrund. Norwegian hard-paste porcelain factory, Porsgrunds Porzelaenfabrik, established 1887; followed styles of other European factories, until individual lines developed from mid 1920s under art direction of N. *Gulbrandsen, based on functionalist principles. High-quality porcelain in simple forms for domestic use marked with arrow and PP, sometimes enclosed in circle with Porsgrund/ Norge.

porte-jupe. Device for looping up long skirts at front and side, e.g. for dancing; introduced 1867 by French jeweller Rouvenat. Fastened to waistband by clasp suspending three long chains each ending in brooch or medallion. Pin of brooch looped through small rings set on skirt, thus raising it. Clasp and brooch, and chains made in gold and enamel studded with pearls, or plain gold, jewelled, or carved oxidized silver. Everyday versions in jet and steel.

portfolio clock. *See* travelling clock.

Portland Vase. Most famous example of cameo glass. Roman c1st century. Two-handled urn (c10in. high) of dark blue glass cased in opaque-white glass, from which mythological figures carved in relief. Reproduced in jasper ware by Josiah Wedgwood (1790), in glass by J. *Northwood (1876). Original smashed in 1845; subsequently restored; now in British Museum, London. Named after Duke of Portland, previous owner.

Porzellanfabrik Schönwald. *See* Schönwald.

Porzellanglas. *See* milk glass.

postman's alarm. Simple *Black Forest wall clock; wooden case often elaborately carved with rustic motifs; painted wooden dial, with or without glass; alarm mechanism rings one or two bells on top of case. Weight driven; long pendulum gives considerable accuracy. Popular c1850–c1910. Version with plain circular wooden case and 12in. dial is imitation of English *dial clock; many exported to England.

posy holder. Holder for small bouquet; carried or attached to dress. Introduced c1820. Shaped as tapering trumpet, or cup with stick or crook handle, curving cornucopia, or any of these modified to include small folding legs. Fitted with pin to hold posy and small chain to attach to finger ring; in later examples thick end of pin threaded to screw into cup perforation. Highly fashionable 1850–75, when cup sometimes set with tiny miniature portrait silhouette, cameo, or painted enamel, or with miniature mirror for viewing surrounding company. Made of gold, silver, machine-pressed gilt metal, or bright-cut steel; handles of porcelain, ivory, amber, coral, mother-of-pearl, or glass.

potichomanie (French, 'porcelain-vase mania'). 19th century fashion for decorating glass vases to resemble porcelain or pottery.

pot lids. Decorative earthenware lids covering containers of bear-grease and other toilet preparations and, later, preserves. From mid 19th century, decorated under glaze with polychrome transfer-printed engravings, notably by J. *Austin at firm of F. & R. Pratt & Co. Wide variety of subjects in 1850s and 1860s include portraits, views, and historical, religious, or rural scenes; over 300 designs occur, many reproduced later.

Potschappel. German hard-paste porcelain factory, established in 1870s at Potschappel near Dresden; traded as Sächsische Porzellanfabrik Carl Thieme. Imitated products of nearby Meissen factory, e.g. crinoline groups made from mid 18th century. Marks include bee on hive, and number of designs incorporating initials CT (founder: C. *Thieme) or Dresden.

Pottier & Stymus. Leading New York furniture manufacturers and decorators during 1870s and 1880s; established c1859. Known for rococo, Louis XVI, Renaissance, and Egyptian revival style furniture; decorated and furnished Moorish style smoking room for John D. Rockefeller, 1886. Commended for fine ornamentation at Philadelphia Centennial Exposition of 1876. Also made tapestries; workshop established in New York, 1910. *Illustration at* Egyptian revival style.

pouf, pouffe, crapaud, comtesse, or **sénateur.** Low, deeply sprung *ottoman, or large, stuffed footstool; always without visible woodwork. Popular in Britain, c1860–c1880. French examples with low, humped back date from 1860s.

pounce pot or **sand caster.** Container with perforated lid, to hold either fine sand, or pounce, powdered resin of African tree, *Callitris*

Potichomanie. Globe. Interior filled with salt to show up the transfers. Wooden base. c1900.

Right
Pottier & Stymus. Walnut chair with original tapestry upholstery. c1875. Height 4ft4in.

Below right
Potschappel porcelain. Vase, cover and stand, decorated with painting and applied flower garlands and putti. Mid 19th century. Height 28in.

Below
Pot lids. Top: Queen Victoria on balcony with Windsor Castle in the Background. Bottom: The New Houses of Parliament Westminster.

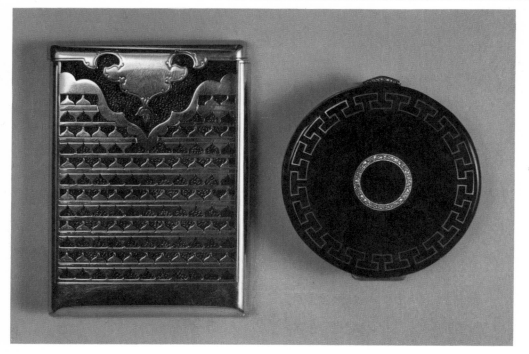

Above
Powder compacts. Left: pierced gold. Right:
black enamel set with diamonds. Made by
*Cartier, c1925.

Below
James Powell & Sons. Left: vase with acid-
etched patterns, 1913. Right: jug designed by
James Hogan, 1935.

quadrivalis: powder scattered on manuscripts to
absorb superfluous ink, and prevent it spreading
into grain of paper. Circular, oval, rhomboidal,
hexagonal, or square containers in e.g. silver,
brass, pewter, glass; glass versions commonly
with pierced silver lid; found *en suite* with inkwells, in stands, or as part of *companion set.
Superseded by introduction of blotting paper in
late 19th century.

Pouyat factory. *See* Limoges.

powder compact, dorine box, or **vanity case.** Flat
metal container (round, oval, square, etc.) with
tight-fitting lid, for cake of face powder, and
small puff; mirror set into lid; carried in hand-
bag. Produced from early 1900s, in gold, silver,
etc., often set with jewels, enamelled, or inlaid;
cheaper versions electro-plated, sometimes with
guilloché engraving. Also produced in black
onyx, lapis lazuli and enamel by *Cartier and
*Boucheron in 1930s. *Illustrations at* Asprey &
Co., Lacloche, shagreen.

Powell, Alfred and Louis (fl c1904–39). English
potters and ceramic designers. Produced tin-
glazed earthenware at own potteries in Millwall,
and then Bloomsbury, London. At Wedgwood
factory in early 20th century, trained painters in
technique of free-hand brushwork, used under
glaze, and designed new patterns of foliage or
flower sprigs. Working independently, decorated
Wedgwood wares with underglaze colours or
lustre painting, at factory or in own studio; also
designed and decorated bowls, etc., produced at
factory. *Illustrations at* Gimson, E., Barnsley, S.

Powell, Harry J. (fl 1880s–1910s). English glass
artist and manufacturer. Controlled J. *Powell &
Sons, 1880–1914, when instrumental in establishing it as focal point for contemporary
British hand-made glass. Used soda and lead
glass to make deliberate imitations of glass of
earlier periods as represented in Old Master
paintings and museums, including Venetian and
ancient Roman specimens. Turned to Art
Nouveau style production at turn of century.

Powell, James, & Sons. London glasshouse;
important centre for contemporary design from
second half of 19th century. Under control of
H. J. *Powell 1880–1914. Most distinctive 19th
century work: furnace-manipulated decoration
on lightly tinted Venetian-style vessels. From
mid century, silvered glasses with double walls;
also fine hanging basket centrepieces (1862), and
plateaux centrepieces with long, leaf-shaped
components (c1865). Made P. *Webb's designs
c1859, becoming by last decades of century last
surviving London manufacturer of hand-made
glass. Tradition continues to present day, with
work to designs of L. *Whistler and other artists.
See also Whitefriars Glass Works.

power loom. First steam-powered carpet loom
invented 1841 in America by E. B. *Bigelow of
Massachusetts, and installed by Lowell Manufacturing Co., Boston. Wove ingrain carpets.
Followed by Bigelow's Wilton, Brussels, and
tapestry carpet looms, 1845–51. Kidderminster
manufacturers refused first offer of patent on
Brussels loom: bought (c1850) by *Crossley of
Halifax, who had already patented own tapestry
and Brussels steam looms. (They subsequently
sold rights on Brussels loom to Kidderminster
firms.) Bigelow Brussels and Wilton looms also
shown at Great Exhibition of 1851, but found no
buyers. Some British firms, however (e.g.
*Chlidema Carpet Co., then Winnal & Fawcett),
already using steam looms at time of Exhibition.
Power looms adopted comparatively rapidly in
Britain, because of pre-existing industrialized
carpet factories; in France, Belgium, Germany,
America, and Canada, new carpet industries
stimulated by power inventions. First Axminster
power loom invented 1856 by H. *Skinner.
Chenille power loom invented in 1896 by
William Adam of *Tomkinson & Adam. All
power looms narrow, weaving 27in. or 36in.
widths until c1900 (*cf* wide power loom). For
further mechanization of carpet industry, *see*
face-to-face   loom,   gripper   Axminster,
Grosvenor-Picking loom, Karvel machine,
machine-knotting, machine-tufting, split shot,
tufted process.

Powolny, Michael (1871–1954). Austrian pottery
decorator and teacher. With B. *Löffler, founded
Wiener Keramik in 1905; among decorators who
painted cubist designs in black on white ground

on earthenware and porcelain at workshop. Established pottery department (1912) in Viennese School of Arts & Crafts, succeeded by R. *Obsieger. Pupils include L. *Rie. Later work includes animal figures in stoneware, e.g. horses, covered with turquoise or blue and purple glaze, bull, with turquoise glaze, and donkey with crackled celadon glaze. *Illustration at* Wiener Keramik.

Poynter, Sir Edward John (1836-1919). English painter, President of Royal Academy, 1896; director of National Gallery, 1881-94, organized opening of Tate Gallery, 1897. Painted furniture designed by W. *Burges. Designed tile panels (1869-70), decorated at Minton's Art Pottery Studio, illustrating months and seasons, to be let into wooden framework lining walls of grill room at Victoria & Albert Museum.

Prairie School. Name given to American mid Western architecture and style of 1880s; inspired by British Arts & Crafts Movement. Characterized by emphasis on unity between buildings and interior furnishings, respect for natural materials, and geometrical, rectilinear style. Furniture distinguished by straight lines, plain surfaces, and finely executed decorative detail; anticipated Mission style furniture. Exponents include G. G. *Elmslie, G. *Maher, *Tobey Furniture Co., and F. L. *Wright.

Pratt, F. & R., & Co. Staffordshire potters operating Fenton Potteries from early 19th century. Made earthenware for domestic and pharmaceutical use. Specialized in polychrome underglaze printing, used e.g. in decoration of pot lids, notably by J. *Austin; also tea and dessert services, sometimes with green mottled ground or (after 1880) wide borders of geometrical motifs. Rare marks include backstamp of crown with Manufacturers to H.R.H. Prince Albert/ F & R Pratt, or Patronised by the Prince Consort. Terracotta vases, clock cases, etc. with enamel decoration marked F & R PRATT FENTON, impressed.

praying chair. *See* prie-dieu chair.

precision clock. Accurate, purely practical, clock; includes *chronometer, *regulator, observatory clocks (e.g. those with Riefler *escapement), W. H. *Shortt's free pendulum clock, and *quartz crystal clock.

precision watch. High-quality watch holding *rating certificate such as that issued by National Physical Laboratory in England, or Swiss observatories, and which can be individually regulated. In 19th century England, precision watches made by individual craftsmen (e.g. J. F. *Cole, C. *Frodsham), factory-produced in America (e.g. by E. *Howard Watch Co., Elgin Watch Co. of Illinois), and in Switzerland (e.g. by P. *Ditisheim for Solvil Co.).

Pre-Raphaelites. School of painting from c1849; original members included D. G. *Rossetti, Sir John Everett Millais, and H. *Hunt. Dissolved c1852. Second group founded by Rossetti with W. *Morris and E. *Burne-Jones. Precisely executed furniture in paintings and tapestries influenced designs of Arts & Crafts Movement followers.

prie-dieu, kneeling, praying, devotional or **vesper chair.** Chair with low seat and high, straight back widening at top to form prayer-book rest; upholstered, often in Berlin woolwork. Designed for family prayers; some elaborately carved for drawing-room use. Popular in Britain c1835-c1875. American models often have elaborately carved, high backs; seats covered in needlework, c1830-c1860.

Priestman, James (fl late 19th century). American sculptor. In 1880s, modelled decorative plaques with designs of cattle, etc. Parian plaques made e.g. by E. *Bennett and at Chesapeake Pottery.

Prignot, Eugène (b 1822). French architect and designer. Chief designer for *Jackson & Graham from 1849; responsible for prizewinning cabinet at Paris Exhibition, 1855.

primavera glass. Fragile Venetian art glass; mottled. Developed in 1930s by E. *Barovier.

Primrose glass. British 19th century moulded glass patented by G. *Davidson & Co. and made from 1890s. Pale yellow; plain or shaded. Often in free form with simulated cut decoration.

Prince Consort. *See* Albert of Saxe-Coburg-Gotha.

Prince of Wales lady's easy chair. Upholstered chair with vestigial arms or none, buttoned fan-back, and low seat. Dates from c1883 in Britain.

Printz, Eugène (fl 1920s). French furniture designer. Known for fine-quality Art Deco pieces often combining bronze and lacquerwork (by J. *Dunand). Forms often idiosyncratic, e.g. table supported on curved legs terminating in ski-like feet. Also designed metal furniture, e.g. walnut-topped table with metal supports, c1929.

Protat, Hugues (fl 1843-55). French sculptor; showed at Paris Salon, 1843-50. Designed sideboard decorated with elaborate naturalistic carving by W. *Cookes, 1853. Modelled figures for prizewinning *Jackson & Graham cabinet shown at Paris Exhibition of 1855. Also designed for J. *Lamb.

Prouvé, Victor (1858-1943). French painter, sculptor, and Art Nouveau designer. One of closest friends and associates of E. *Gallé, for whom produced figurative designs; after Gallé's death, managed his glass workshop in Nancy.

Prutscher, Otto (1880-1949). Austrian architect, furniture designer, jeweller, and enamellist, who specialized in Jugendstil jewellery, decorated with enamel, often in form of stylized flowers and leaves. Studied under J. *Hoffmann at Imperial School of Arts & Crafts, joining *Wiener Werkstätte for whom he designed furniture, jewellery, and silverware. Furniture characterized by rigidly geometrical style using cubic and spherical shapes, diagonal cross-members. Mark: monogram PO. in square with rounded corners.

pudding mould. *See* dessert mould.

puff box. Container for face powder and powder-puff; made from silver, electro-plate, cut glass, pressed glass, etched crystal, and porcelain;

mostly circular, sometimes oval or octagonal, c3-4in. high. Produced in Europe and America from 1860s. Large numbers made by Monroe Co., Connecticut, in painted opal mould-blown glass, with hinged lids attached by metal collars (trade name Wave Crest Ware).

Pugin, Augustus Welby Northmore (1812-52). English architect, designer, and writer; associated with revival of 14th century Gothic style. Pupil of father, French-born architect and draughtsman Auguste Charles Pugin (1762-1832). Designed whole range of interior fittings; attempted in approach to express entire scheme of design in Gothic terms, rather than employ Gothic architectural details as means of decoration. Furniture designs from c1827 include pieces for Windsor Castle. Established short-lived business (1835) producing panels in Gothic style for architects. Conversion to Roman Catholicism in 1835 followed by publication in 1836 of book 'Contrasts', relating Gothic style to Christian principles. Theories further developed in 'True Principles of Pointed Architecture', published 1841. Furniture for private houses often simple, with restrained, carved decoration, naturalistic, flat-patterned coloured inlays, e.g. table and cabinet for Abney Hall, Cheshire. Published designs and exhibition pieces more elaborate, e.g. oak cabinet shown at *Medieval Courts (1851) decorated with delicate tracery, cresting, and heraldic devices. Designs inspired *New Palace Westminster style; also anticipated *Gothic Reform style. Influence in furniture design felt mainly after Pugin's death as result of elaborate carved furniture made in his idiom by J. G. *Crace & Sons, with whom he had

*Augustus Welby Northmore Pugin. Chalice made by J. *Hardman & Co. Parcel gilt, set with semi-precious stones. c1851.*

collaborated in design of wallpapers, fabrics, and schemes of decoration. Much work intended for ecclesiastical use, e.g. range of church plate in 14th century Gothic style manufactured by J. *Hardman & Co. in Birmingham. Jewellery, also produced by Hardman firm, includes set in medieval style for Pugin's intended third wife, which consisted of two brooches, necklace with cross, headband, earrings, and ring, shown in Medieval Courts. Set pattern for English Gothic jewellery and revived use of enamelling as integral part of design; influenced ecclesiastical and other jewellery. Manufacture of designs continued after Pugin's death by Hardman firm, or imitators. Worked in conjunction with Sir Charles Barry on interiors of new Houses of Parliament, built 1840-65. Designed earthenware bread plate produced c1850 at *Mintons with design incorporating ears of wheat, scrolled leaves, geometrical motifs and inscription, Waste not, Want not, on rim; tiles with decoration in Gothic style produced at Mintons (c1858). As architect, designed several churches, and own house at Ramsgate, Kent. Rigorous insistence on consistent, historically accurate 14th century style contributed to 19th century craftsmanship in cabinet making, metalwork, jewellery, etc.

Puiforçat, Jean (1897-1945). French silversmith, initially famous as collector; son of silversmith, studied at Central School of Arts & Crafts, London, and under sculptor Louis Lejeune; worked as independent from 1922; exhibits at Exposition Internationale des Arts Décoratifs, Paris, 1925, included silver and lapis lazuli dish and cover; pioneered Art Deco style in 1920s; 1928 joined Union des Artistes Modernes, set up under leadership of René Herbst to succeed Société des Artistes Décorateurs, organizers of 1925 exhibition, and in reaction against Art Deco, with motto: *Le Beau dans l'Utile* (Beauty in the Useful). Designs mathematically and geometrically based, with simple ornamentation of thick sheet and heavy castings; used silver to contrast with other materials, e.g. dark-grained wood, ivory, crystal; later concentrated on pure forms, sphere, drum, cone, etc., avoiding all but simplest moulded or incised decoration; smooth finish was often compared to machined work, to his annoyance.

Jean Puiforçat. Silver tea service. Made 1925.

pulpit desk. *See* davenport.

pump pot or **self-pouring teapot.** Teapot with hooked spout, facing downwards at end, and plunger mechanism instead of normal lid; tea is pumped into cup by raising plunger, then pressing down with finger placed over air inlet hole in knob. 'Royle's Patent Self-Pouring' pot, patented 1886, made in ceramics by Doultons, Burslem, and in Britannia metal by James Dixon & Sons, Sheffield. Ceramic examples have metal plunger and sleeve set into body of pot. Similar type made by *Meriden Britannia Co.

Punnett, E.G. (fl 1900). English designer of Quaint style furniture, e.g. oak armchair with floral, ebony inlay on yoke rail; seat and two back panels in rush (made by W. *Birch c1901). Also designed for J.S. *Henry and *Liberty & Co. *Illustration at Birch, W.*

purdonium. Rectangular metal coal box with close fitting hinged, sloping front, and detachable zinc lining; small shovel fits into slot at back; invented in mid 19th century by a Mr Purdon; usually made from japanned iron with brass embellishments; some examples with padded seats on top in needlework or velvet upholstery. Designed in Chippendale, Elizabethan, and French styles in 1890s, with matching fender and fire-dogs.

Purpurin. Opaque purplish Bohemian *stone glass with marbling of slightly clearer shade. Popular for vases, beakers, candlesticks, etc. to c1860. Often gilded, painted, cut, or engraved.

puzzle ball. *See* devil's work ball.

pyrope. *See* garnet.

quaich or **quaigh.** Scottish Highland drinking cup; wide shallow bowl with two handles projecting at right angles at either side at top. Often on circular foot. Original medieval version in wood. Normally engraved with a series of lines radiating from the bottom on inside and outside representing shape of wooden stave. In 19th century, made in silver decorated with thistles and Celtic ornamentation. Smaller ones 2½-4in. diameter, mostly made in provincial towns, quite light in weight; larger ones made in Edinburgh or Glasgow.

Quaint, Anglo-French, or **Fanciful style.** British trade version of Art Nouveau style, popular c1890-c1905. Combined elements of Anglo-Japanese, Arts & Crafts Movement, Glasgow school, and continental Art Nouveau furniture. Characterized by painted and inlaid floral motifs, arabesques, copper panels, enamelling, heart-shaped apertures, and ornate hinges; 18th century forms generally used as basis for ornament. Thin legs, often six or eight, on cabinets and armchairs; low-placed stretchers. Versions of Windsor chair, and asymmetrical sofas popular. Woods mainly polished rosewood, fumed oak, and cheap woods stained green or purple. Best pieces of furniture characterized by restrained form and decoration, in contrast to over-elaborate cheaper examples. Designers and manufacturers include W. *Birch, G.M. *Ellwood, J.S. *Henry, J. *Lamp, and E.G. *Punnett.

quaker chair. Balloon-back side-chair with open, circular back and rounded, upholstered seat; turned front legs. Used in bedroom. Dates from c1850.

Queen Anne style. Loose term for *Adam, *Chippendale, *Hepplewhite, and *Sheraton reproduction furniture, popular from c1870 in Britain.

Queen's Burmese glass. British version of American *Burmese glass; produced under licence from 1886 by T. *Webb & Sons. Semi-opaque, shading salmon-pink to yellow. Often found with daisy design (frequently called Queen's Burmese pattern); used for decorative ware and novelties, e.g. fairy lights.

Queensware. *See* Wedgwood, Josiah & Sons Ltd.

Quezal Art Glass & Decorating Company. American Art Nouveau design workshop in Brooklyn, New York. In 1916, produced *Tiffany-inspired 'Quezal' iridescent art glass (named after Mexican god, Quezalcoatl). With V. *Durand, major imitator of L.C. *Tiffany in America. Mark: Quezal, carved.

racing trophies and **testimonials.** Elaborate silver presentation pieces made from late 18th century; achieved unprecedented importance, size,

and complexity c1840–c1890. Commissioned, e.g. by regiments to present to retiring officers, or by wealthy patrons for private display. Also racing trophies, e.g. Doncaster Cup (1857) by *Hancock & Co. Exhibition pieces, to show virtuosity of craftsmen, manufactured by e.g. *Hunt & Roskell, *Garrard & Co., Hancock & Co., *Elkington & Co. Main forms: epergnes, candelabra (c1840–c1890); vases, rose bowls tazze (c1840–c1860); shields (c1850–c1880); caskets (1880s). *Candelabra up to 4ft high. Some sculptural groups, or centrepieces with garniture, arranged on silver plateaux, contained up to 1000 oz of silver. Pieces designed notably by G. A. *Carter, L. *Morel-Ladeuil, A. *Brown, H. H. *Armstead in eclectic styles, ranging from Renaissance to near Eastern models. Motifs frequently thematic or allegorical, drawn from Literary or classical sources, e.g. *Milton Shield. Fashion for testimonial silver declined sharply after 1890, when such pieces heavily criticized for massiveness and ostentation.

raden (Japanese, 'shell-ornament'), **raten**, **hanagai** or **lo-tien**. Oriental lacquer decoration of inlaid or encrusted flakes or larger pieces of milky-white mother-of-pearl, particularly from nautilus and pearl-oyster shells. Flakes often backed by metal-foil; larger pieces often tinted. Found as ornamentation on wide range of lacquerware. Often used in combination with other encrustations. Chinese variety (lo-tien) developed in 7th century; Japanese imitation (raden, raten, or hanagai) in 8th century. Raden work speciality of e.g. *Shibayama family. Increasingly popular from late 18th to early 20th centuries for extremely elaborate ornamentation, particularly for export trade. Also generic term for all types of mother-of-pearl lacquer decoration including *aogai.

railway or **railroad watch**. High-grade watch made from c1850 by American factories (e.g. Elgin Watch Co. of Illinois, and Waltham Watch Co., Massachusetts) to meet stringent specification of railroad companies. Also, cheap Swiss and German watches, often inscribed 'Railway Timekeeper': deliberate misnomer suggests performance of which incapable.

raku. Soft, freely hand-modelled earthenware, first made in late 16th century at Kyoto, Japan. Tea ceremony wares, mainly bowls, fired at low temperature and partially covered with lead glaze. Widely imitated in Japan and, later, copied and adapted by artist potters in West.

Ram Pottery. See Colenbrander, Theodorus A.C.

Ramsden, Omar (1873–1939). English silversmith associated with Arts & Crafts Movement. From 1890 worked in silversmith's shop and studied at evening classes at Sheffield School of Art, where met A. C. E. *Carr. Both on scholarships at South Kensington Schools, London,

Above left
Raku. Black glazed chawan (teabowl).

Left
Omar Ramsden. Bowl in form of Tudor rose, repoussé on seven cast trefoil feet. inscribed on underside Omar Ramsden me fecit. Mark Omar Ramsden, Lond 1926. Width 9½in.

1896-98; went into partnership c1898. Usually Ramsden designed, and Carr (and later others) executed pieces. Specialized in ceremonial pieces in silver and gold, e.g. monstrance made for Westminster Cathedral, London (1907). Made some wrought iron and pewter; many commissions for Roman Catholic Church, and for ecclesiastical and civic plate. Partnership dissolved 1918, with Ramsden retaining workshop and craftsmen; later work included some Art Deco style silver, e.g. silver vase, octagonal with geometrical faceting above two rows of spiral mouldings on outward flaring base, shown at Arts & Crafts Exhibition Society, 1930. Early works show influence of Celtic art, and had hammer mark finish. Middle style reminiscent of early Tudor work; later work suggests influence of graphic art of Hans Holbein. Marks: OR (from 1918), usually with Omar Ramsden Me Fecit; works in partnership with Carr marked: Omar. Ramsden. &. Alwyn. C.E. Carr Me Fecerunt, usually with date.

Randall, John (1810-1910). English ceramic painter. Worked for uncle, porcelain decorator in Madeley, Shropshire, then at Rockingham factory. Painted birds in style of Sèvres at Coalport Porcelain Factory. Later style more naturalistic. Ceased porcelain painting in 1881, because sight failed. Books on local ceramic history include History of Madeley and account of Coalport factory in 19th century.

Raphaelesque porcelain. English porcelain made in ivory-toned paste at *Worcester from c1860, decorated with coloured relief motifs in style of 18th century Capodimonte porcelain.

Rappaport, Julius Alexandrovich (1864-1916). German-Jewish silversmith, trained in Berlin. Settled in St Petersburg, 1883; workmaster and principal silversmith for *Fabergé until death. Specialized in large silver table pieces and wide variety of silver objects of vertu. Mark: J.R. in Cyrillic characters.

Rateau, Armand-Albert (1882-1938). French Art Deco interior decorator and furniture designer. Director of Atelier de Décoration de la Maison Alaroine, 1910-14. During 1920s, designed

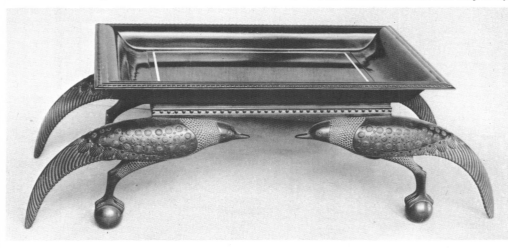

Armand-Albert Rateau. Table designed for Jeanne Lanvin. Top in black and white marble, mounted in bronze and supported by stylized birds. 1920-22. Height 14in.

Richard Llewellyn Benson Rathbone. Pair of beaten copper candlesticks decorated with bands of punched floral ornament. Marked Rathbone, maker's monogram, and 1902. Height 4½in.

interiors and furnishings for hotels, many private houses. Exhibited at Exposition Internationale des Arts Décoratifs, Paris, 1925. Many pieces reflect oriental, Minoan, classical, Persian, and Syrian influences. Known for use of patinated bronze, usually antique green; also used lacquerwork; expensive materials, e.g. fur, marble. Designed bathroom for Duchess of Alba, Madrid, in 1926, with sunken bath carved from single marble block, green-patinated bronze furniture including low table with four supports in shape of stylized birds; motif repeated in base of standard lamp. Designed interior and furniture for Paris house of couturière, Jeanne Lanvin.

raten. *See* raden.

Rathbone, Harold (fl late 19th, early 20th centuries). English painter and potter; student of F. M. *Brown. Established Della Robbia pottery

in Birkenhead, Cheshire, in 1894. Work includes design of fountain for courtyard of Savoy Hotel, London.

Rathbone, Richard Llewellyn Benson (1864-1939). English designer and metalworker, cousin of H. *Rathbone, head of Della Robbia Pottery; taught at Liverpool University 1898-1903; opened workshops at various times in Liverpool, Menai Bridge, and London; worked mostly in base metals, but made some jewellery and silverware; used trademark showing St Dunstan hammering silver bowl; sold mark and goodwill to A. E. *Jones, 1905, after taking appointment as head of art school at Sir John Cass Institute.

rattan furniture. Made from climbing plant (rattan palm) grown mainly in East Indies. Long, thin, many-jointed stems woven around mechanically bent frames to form chair seats, backs, etc. Pith or reed later bent into elaborate shapes. Popular in America during 1880s and 1890s. cf basket chair.

rating certificate. Certificate issued to high performance timekeepers which meet exacting standards. Most major clock and watch making countries have own standards. Best known are those of English National Physical Laboratory (NPL), Teddington, Middlesex; Geneva Observatory, Switzerland; German Hydrographic Institute, Hamburg. *See* Kew Certificate.

Ratzersdorfer. Viennese firm established by silversmith, Hermann Ratzersdorfer. Finest work, 1873-1900. Specialized in massive, ornate, Renaissance style objects of vertu, tableware and jewellery. Most work in silver, usually with *grisaille* or *cloisonné* enamelling. After 1890s, materials and designs declined in quality; major output, pastiches of 17th and 18th century bibelots.

Rault, Louis. *See* Boucheron.

Eric Ravilious. *Boat Race goblet, designed for J. *Wedgwood & Sons, 1938.*

reading stand. Stand with sloping top for book or music sheets; dates from c1750. Made in metal or wood during 19th century; usually free-standing, sometimes designed to rest on table or fasten to arm of *reading chair. Often in Gothic style; sometimes in elaborate openwork carving.

reading table. Small table with circular top supported on pillar with tripod base. Revolving book trays, often galleried, project at right angles from pillar. Used in Britain from c1880.

Real Axminster. Hand-knotted Axminster carpet or rug; first made in Axminster, Devon, in 1755, hence name. Chief product of *Wilton Royal Carpet Factory in early 20th century, but production ceased 1957. Now made only in *Donegal. *See also* Durham rugs.

Redgrave, Richard (1804–88). English painter, lexicographer, and silver designer; Surveyor of the Queen's Pictures, 1857–88. Designed silver for *Summerly's Art Manufactures. Silver christening mug, embossed and chased with figures of guardian angels protecting children, designed 1849 and exhibited at Great Exhibition, London, 1851; re-issued and produced in silver and electro-plate by *Hunt & Roskell from 1865. *Illustration at* christening mug.

red staining. Decorative technique for ornamental glassware; glass surface coated with copper to produce pink or red stain. Developed 1840 by F. *Egermann, and widely used by him and imitators throughout 19th century.

Reed & Barton. American silver and electroplate manufacturers. H. G. Reed (1810–1901) was apprenticed in factory founded in 1824 by Isaac Babbit and William Crossman to produce Britannia metal wares; factory closed in 1834 after financial problems, was then rented to Reed and solderer Charles E. Barton; business started as Taunton Britannia Manufacturing Company. Name changed to Reed & Barton in 1840; pioneered electro-plating process in America, initially copying English designs, later produced own patterns, though still derived from English styles. From c1889 made increasing quantity of silverware, mainly articles for presentation. Firm headed 1901–1923 by Reed's son-in-law H. B. Dowse, then by his son-in-law Sinclair Weeks.

regard ring. Ring set with gems whose initial letters spell word 'regard', e.g. ruby, emerald, garnet, amethyst, ruby, diamond. Similar rings made with stones spelling out name of recipient or brief message. Often given on birth of first child. Popular as sentimental jewellery throughout Victorian period, made almost exclusively in England.

registry mark. Sign of registration of design at British Patent Office. *Diamond mark used 1842–83. Superseded from 1884 by number usually prefixed with R^{d}N°. Numbers of designs, starting with 1 in 1884, exceeded 19750 by end of first year and reached 351201 at start of 1900. System still operates.

Regout, Petrus (b 1801). Dutch potter, established pottery, De Sphinx, in Maastricht (1836). Produced transfer-printed earthenware, notably tableware, decorated in style of factory of W. T. *Copeland. Marks in late 19th century include

Rautenglas (German, 'faceted glass'). German glassware with simple facet cutting. Produced by W. *Wagenfeld at Vereinigte Lausitzer Glaswerke, Weisswasser, in 1930s, receiving gold metal at Milan Triennale, 1940.

Ravenna glass. Heavy Swedish art glass developed by S. *Palmqvist in 1930s. Usually of tinted transparent glass with bold inlays of brilliant colour in non-figurative designs. Process further developed and perfected after war.

Ravenscourt Pottery. *See* Lunn, Dora.

Ravilious, Eric (1903–42). English engraver, designer, and ceramic decorator. Designs commissioned (1936–39) by Wedgwood factory include tableware decorated with alphabet, or circular gardening motifs, coronation mug, and bowls decorated with boat race or London scenes, from engraved designs. Mug commemorating removal of factory to Barlaston personally decorated with lithograph. Also designed glass and furniture.

Ravinet d'Enfert, Parisian silversmiths; firm founded 1845 as plating works. Taken over by L. Ravinet, who opened factory for production of forks and spoons at Mouroux. C. Enfert joined as partner in 1891. Wide range of high quality flatware, hollow-ware and trophies manufactured. Firm still in production.

Raynaud & Cie. *See* Limoges.

reading chair. From c1850 in Britain, armchair with swivel *reading stand and candle bracket fixed to arms.

reading seat or **albany couch.** Long, upholstered couch with high back support at one end, upper part curving slightly inwards to support head. Common c1835–c1865 in Britain. Later version has broader-based back with top curving outwards.

sphinx with signature, P. Regout, enclosed in circular band; ROYAL SPHINX/MAASTRICHT surmounted by crown.

regulator. Term given from mid 18th century to highly accurate timekeeper made e.g. for astronomical use, usually in undecorated glass-fronted wooden long case; decoration on case more usual on French examples. Characteristic style evolved in England by 1775, with dead beat *escapement (often jewelled), finely-cut wheels and pinions to reduce friction, *compensated pendulum beating seconds, plain silvered dial indicating minutes on circumference; subsidiary inner dials indicate hours and seconds. Distinctive style developed for *Vienna regulators in early 19th century. Name, regulator, applied loosely from mid 19th century to high-quality domestic clocks, e.g. mantel regulators, with dead beat escapement and half second pendulum. Dead beat regulator replaced for observatory use c1890 by other precision timekeepers, e.g. *Riefler clock and, later, W. H. *Shortt's free pendulum clock, and *quartz crystal clock.

Reich mark. German mark on silver of at least 800 parts per thousand purity; quarter moon and crown; discontinued c1935.

Rembrandt ware. Earthenware decorated with layers of coloured slip applied to body before firing, usually in brown or green. Introduced at Doulton factory, Burslem, Staffordshire, by Charles J. *Noke; produced c1898–1914. Coarse-textured body made from local clay.

Renaissance revival or **Victorian Renaissance furniture.** Heavy, squared furniture popular in America c1860–c1875. Features: classical entablatures surmounted by arched pediments; heavy, turned legs and finials; semi-circular panels; moulded decoration flanking cartouches in bronze, porcelain, terracotta, etc.; raised panels, larger examples framed with applied mouldings (sometimes ebonized); table supports often pierced and scrolled on shaped trestles; scrolled ornamental skirts on sofas, chairs, tables, etc. Flat marquetry decoration on surfaces, and gilt incised lines, typical of later pieces. Motifs include carved pendant tassels, e.g. flanking yoke rails, animal heads, rosettes (paterae), and sporting trophies. Manufacturers include *Berkey & Gay, J. *Jelliff, P. *Mallard, and J. *Meeks & Sons. Style mass-produced in Grand Rapids until c1900. Popular woods: black walnut, ash, painted or grained pine, and satinwood. See also Free Renaissance.

Renaissance style jewellery. See Gothic revival jewellery.

reproduction furniture. Copies of antique furniture. Queen Anne style popular in Britain from c1870, American Colonial style in America from c1876. Many examples well-made, identifiable only by comparing construction, proportions, and details with originals. Indications include arcs left on rough carcase surface by circular saw; French polishing; use of stamped instead of sawn veneers in marquetry; quadrant beading along joints between side and bottom boards of drawers; white edges where stain removed with cleaning; interior lined, e.g. with velvet, hiding defects in wood.

Renaissance style. Rosewood cabinet by A. *Roux, set with porcelain plaques. 1866.

reticello glass. See vetro a reticelli.

reticulated ware. Thin porcelain with intricate pierced decoration, made at Worcester Royal Porcelain factory in late 19th century. Vases, etc. associated with work of G. *Owen.

Reuter, Edmond G. (1845–after 1912). Ceramic decorator. Born in Geneva, worked in England from 1870. Studied floral design in Paris (1864) and travelled to Egypt (1868), before joining Minton's Art-Pottery Studio. Work includes frieze decorated with monkeys in interlaced design. Employed at Minton factory in Stoke-on-Trent, c1874–95; in 1886, assistant designer under L. *Arnoux. In 1895, returned to Switzerland; worked as illuminator and calligrapher. Work normally signed.

Revelation Kilns. See Perry, Mary Chase.

revolving bookcase. Square, table-height bookcase, revolving on central pillar usually sup-

Above
Renaissance style. Ebony and boxwood cabinet on stand, made by *Fourdinois. 1867.

Below
Henry G. Richardson & Sons. Left to right: 1)

opal glass vase with applied portrait medallions painted by the Richardson daughters, late 19th century, height 10in. 2) Opal glass vase with enamel painting, late 19th century. 3) Water jug, decorated with water lilies in ceramic paint cased with crystal, mid 19th century.

ported on claw base. Open bookshelves. Sometimes has tier with racks for newspapers, magazines. Dates from *c*1850 in Britain.

Reynolds, William Bainbridge (1855-1935). English architect and metalwork designer; articled to G. E. *Street, 1871-74; later moved to office of J. P. *Seddon; joined metalwork shop of Starkie Gardner in 1883. Established own firm, *c*1894, working in geometrical, neo-Gothic style; commissions included lectern for St Cuthbert's Church, Kensington, London, completed 1894.

Rhead, Frederick Hurten (1880-1942). English-born ceramic designer, in America from early 20th century. Working for S. *Weller from 1902, used stylized designs of natural forms in under-glaze colours; also wrote articles on design for magazine, Keramic Studio. As art director of Roseville Pottery (1904-08), introduced styles, e.g. with incised or applied relief decoration, or pastiches of classical figures. Designs for *Rozane ware include incised and painted decoration of flowers with trailing, strap-shaped leaves, and tapering, square vase echoing shape of cypress trees incised and painted on each side. Also designed for Burgess & Leigh. Some work incised with signature, e.g. on face of plaque.-

Rheinische Glashütten or **Köln-Ehrenfeld.** German glasshouse established 1864 in Köln-Ehrenfeld. Specialized in reproduction of medieval (*Altdeutsches glass), Renaissance, Venetian, and Roman glass forms, but known especially for fine bowls, vases, and other decorative ware, in Art Nouveau iridescent glass, while under directorship of Oscar Rauter. Ceased production 1931; finally dissolved 1937.

rhinestone. Type of colourless quartz; often found in 19th century jewellery. Later, name for variegated, multicoloured glass stones. Term now applied to any coloured glass paste.

rhodolite. *See* garnet.

Rice, Harris & Sons or **Islington Glass Works.** English glasshouse in Birmingham. From 1848, made opaline vessels, as well as wide range of coloured glassware, e.g. amber glass, canary glass, chrysophrase, light and dark ruby glass, and purple glass. Made some of earliest British pressed glass, usually imitating broad-fluted style of cut glass; also, first pressed glass tumblers. Paperweights with canes forming letters, IGW, thought to be their products. From 1849, known for threaded glass decoration on handles, etc.

Richardson & Sons. English glasshouse in Stourbridge, Worcestershire. Known first as W. H., B. & J. Richardson; Webb & Richardson (from *c*1833); Hodgetts, Richardson & Parget (late 1860s); Hodgetts, Richardson & Son (1871-82); finally, Henry G. Richardson & Sons. Made early pressed glass in 1850s; clear and coloured opaline, cameo, and painted glass from *c*1845; also, some etched glass. In 1860s, granted patent for glass-threading machine (for applying finely spun glass); thereafter, specialized in threading, producing many Venetian-style vessels with ribbed handles in 1870s. Some *Rusticana work in late 1880s. Responsible for executing most of painted glass designs for *Summerly's Art Manufactures. *Illustration at* Woodall, G.

H. H. Richardson. Trustee's Chair. Oak. Made for Woburn Library. 1878.

Richardson, Benjamin (fl 1860s). English flint-glass maker, partner in Stourbridge firm of Webb & Richardson. In 1860, offered £1,000 reward for best reproduction of famous Portland Vase (*see* J. Northwood), which led to popular European revival of cameo glass.

Richardson, Henry Hobson (1838–86). American architect in Boston, Massachusetts; also designed furniture. Greatly influenced by writings of B. J. *Talbert and C. *Eastlake. Designed Architectural style furniture, e.g. Romanesque style bench and chair for Winn Memorial Library at Woburn, Massachusetts, harmonizing with high, vaulted roof and interior woodwork. Pieces often large, soundly constructed, with simple, graceful outlines. Later examples based on American Colonial style.

Ricketts, Charles de Sousy (1866–1931). English painter, sculptor, and designer; apprenticed to wood-engraver. Founder of Vale Press (1895–1907), for which designed books and typefaces. Designed small amount of jewellery in Renaissance and French Art Nouveau styles (pieces made by C. *Giuliano and H. G. *Murphy), but his designs too delicate to be realized satisfactorily. After 1906, interested mainly in stage design.

Ridgway, Edward John (fl early 19th century–1872). Staffordshire potter; succeeded father as proprietor of potteries in Hanley and Shelton. Established Bedford Works, Shelton, in 1866. In partnership with sons from 1870 until retirement (1872). Firm, trading as Ridgway, Sparks & Ridgway until 1879 and, later, Ridgway's, produced e.g. earthenware, stoneware, and terracotta. Teapots, etc. made in jasper ware or black earthenware body with enamel decoration. Mark: Staffordshire knot.

Rie or **Rie Gomperz,** Lucie (b 1902). Viennese artist potter, working in England from 1938. In Vienna, trained under M. *Powolny, then at own studio made vases, bowls, jars, teapots, etc., of thinly potted stoneware in simple shapes, sometimes polished or covered with rough-textured glazes. Work influenced both by functionalist ideals and styles of Roman pottery. Painted mark: LRG over WIEN. Resuming

work after 2nd World War, made earthenware, sometimes tin-glazed; also experimented with stoneware and porcelain. Produced ceramic jewellery and buttons. Post-war work includes porcelain decorated with unglazed bands of cross-hatched decoration, incised, and coloured with manganese oxide, also stoneware in elegant shapes, sometimes with bands of decoration scratched through light grey glaze. Used colour sparingly, and developed coloured glazes, notably yellow (containing uranium); other glazes characterized by rough, uneven texture. Noted for variety and sophistication of style. Mark (in England): monogram of LR within rectangle, impressed.

Riedel, Josef (1816–94). Bohemian glass manufacturer; known as Glass King of the Isergebirge. Member of famous glassmaking family dynasty known above all for developing *Annagelb* (yellow) and *Annagrün* (green) fluorescent glass during Biedermeier period. His factory at Harrachsdorf produced fine Art Nouveau iridescent ware.

Riefler, Sigmund (1847–1912). German maker of observatory clocks; worked in Hamburg-Altona. Inventor (1893) of extremely accurate *escapement named after him: impulse given to pendulum through spring suspended from rocking member resting on knife edges. Patented mercury filled pendulum, 1899.

Riegel, Ernst (1871–1946). German gold and silver smith; produced Jugendstil pieces; worked in Munich (1895–1906), then Darmstadt. From 1912, professor at Städtische Werkschule, Cologne. Covered cup of silver with cast, engraved, and textured surface now in Stuttgart museum.

Riemerschmid, Richard (1868–1957). German Jugendstil architect and designer; studied at Munich Academy. Brother-in-law of Karl Schmidt, founder of *Deutsche Werkstätten.

Richard Riemerschmid. Oak chair with leather seat, c1900.

Co-founder of Münchener Vereinigte Werkstätte fur Kunst in Handwerk, 1897. Co-designer of Salle Riemerschmid at 1900 Paris Exposition. Taught at Nuremberg Art School, 1902–05. Director of School of Applied Arts, Munich, 1912–24. Director of Cologne Werkschule, 1926.

Designed Deutsche Werkstätten's first machine-made furniture, 1906; pieces characterized by functional elegance. Silver flatware, now in Landesgewerke Museum, Stuttgart, Germany, made in functional style with unusual emphasis on structural clarity: rounded knife handles and flat bevel-edged spoon and fork handles; restrained decorative motifs, usually few engraved strokes echoing main contours.

Ceramics characterized by strong geometrical element, often accompanied by more complicated linear decoration. Stoneware designed for R. *Merkelbach in early 20th century includes mustard pots with decoration based on circular motifs and wavy line. Designed porcelain service, c1906, with painted decoration; floral motifs arranged in geometrical pattern, echoed in double row of rounded leaf motifs at rim; produced at Meissen factory.

Rietveld, Gerrit Thomas (1888–1964). Dutch cabinet maker and architect; member of *De Stijl group from 1919. Ignored traditional furniture styles, using only rectangular, circular, and cubic forms, painted in primary colours, with construction deliberately revealed e.g. Red and Blue chair (c1917) with framework of black laths (with yellow or white ends), at right angles, supporting blue board for seat, longer red board for back, and two smaller boards for arm rests. Also, Zig-Zag chair (1934), based on cantilevered principle, with four square boards in zig-zag; asymmetrical chair, 1923, with flat arm rest on one side, upright board on other. Designed moulded plywood chairs, 1927.

rimbo (Japanese) or **chakra** (Sanskrit). Wheel, most important of smaller Buddhist cult objects. Ancient Indian symbol, both of Chakravartin, universal monarch of this world, and of Buddha,

Gerrit Thomas Rietveld. Chair, designed 1919.

lord of transcendental world. Wheel with radiating spokes.

Rindskopf, Josef, & Söhne. Bohemian glasshouse established in Kosten at close of 19th century. From c1900, fine output of facet-cut or etched vases, etc., in *Diluvium Glas* (marbled, usually red-green, opaque glass).

ring vases. *See* Smith Brothers vase.

Rippl-Rónai, Josef (1861–1930). Hungarian painter, engraver, and ceramic designer. Studied in Munich (from 1884) and Paris (from 1889). Earthenware with painted decoration in Art Nouveau style produced at *Zsolnay pottery c1900.

Rischgitz, Edouard (fl late 19th century). French ceramic decorator. In England at Minton factory (c1864–70), painted earthenware in style influenced by E. *Lessore. Signed examples exist.

rivière. Necklace of large, graduated gemstones of fine quality, simply mounted. Usually diamonds set in silver or platinum; amethysts and topazes also used.

Robertson, Alexander W. (fl mid to late 19th century). American potter. In 1866, established firm in Chelsea, near Boston, Massachusetts, making brown earthenware for domestic use, etc. Brother, H. *Robertson (from 1868), and father, J. *Robertson, partners. From 1872, made art pottery in enlarged premises, trading as *Chelsea Keramic Art Works. Moved to California in 1884.

Robertson, Hugh Cornwall (1845–1908). American potter. In partnership with brother, A. *Robertson, and father, J. *Robertson, from

*Edouard Rischgitz. Painting on *Mintons earthenware ewer. c1865.*

1868; made art pottery at *Chelsea Keramic Art Works from 1872. Early work includes flask-shaped vase with low-relief decoration of horseman. From c1876, absorbed in attempts to reproduce oriental glazes, particularly *sang-de-boeuf*, and included oriental motifs in decoration. Sole proprietor of firm after father's death (1880) and brother's retirement (1884); pottery closed in 1888, through lack of money. Manager of *Chelsea Pottery from formation in 1891; developed crackle glaze. After removal of pottery to Dedham, Massachusetts, in 1896, continued work on glazes in flowing colours, sometimes with iridescent effects, or rough, bubbled surface, used on porcelain vases of simple form, usually initialled. Succeeded in business by son.

Robertson, James (d 1880). American potter; worked in Scotland, England, New Jersey, and New York, before joining sons, A. *Robertson and H. *Robertson at pottery in Chelsea, Massachusetts, in 1868.

Robineau, Adelaide Alsop (1865–1929). American potter and artist, born in Middletown, Connecticut. Teacher of porcelain decoration in Minnesota, and in New York, where also studied painting and worked as miniaturist and artist in watercolours. In 1899, with husband and partner, bought magazine, The China Decorator, and published it in Syracuse, New York, under new name, Keramic Studio. Own designs, and those produced for use by amateur decorators, consisted of naturalistic flower studies or historical scenes, until gradual adoption of Art Nouveau style (from c1900). In 1903, studied manufacture of porcelain under C. F. *Binns and began own experiments. At first, attempted commercial production of porcelain, cast and decorated, e.g. with incised geometrical designs, or *pâte-sur-pâte* decoration. Soon restricted output to individual pieces with carved or perforated decoration, and matt or crystalline glazes, which sometimes depended for effect on several firings. After teaching in ceramic school at University City, Missouri, in 1910, returned to Syracuse. Later work relies more on effect of colour, or Chinese and Mayan motifs, than on Art Nouveau style. In 1911, won Grand Prix at International Exhibition of Decorative Arts, Turin, Italy.

Robinson, Gerard (1834–91). English woodcarver in Newcastle, Northumberland. Apprenticed to T. *Tweedy, his foreman for a period. Known for naturalistically carved furniture, e.g. oak sideboard illustrating Ballad of Chevy Chase, 1857–63: 10ft high, 12ft wide, and 4ft6in. deep; commissioned by Duke of Northumberland; shown in London in 1865. Also made dining table with carved legs portraying Richard III, Shylock, Hamlet, and Othello.

Robinson & Leadbeater. Staffordshire firm of James Robinson and Edward James Leadbeater; specialized in parian ware at Stoke-on-Trent in late 19th and early 20th century; among largest producers of parian. Operated Glebe Street Works (bought 1856) and Wharf Street Works (bought 1870). Produced figures and groups, generally classical or religious subjects; portrait busts include musicians, politicians, and contemporary personalities. Also made tableware, comports and centre-pieces, vases, flower stands, brackets, pedestals, boxes, etc. Noted for high quality of paste and workmanship. Firm con-

tinued until 1924. Initials R & L impressed on back of figures (not under bases) from 1885.

Robj. French dealer. In 1920s and early 1930s, commissioned small decorative porcelain figures, inkwells, ashtrays, pots for preserves, cigarette boxes, etc., for sale in Paris showroom. Lamps, bottles, incense burners often in form of human figure. Cubist-inspired statuettes in cream coloured porcelain with crackle glaze. Sponsored annual competitions from late 1920s until 1931; some prizewinning designs produced in limited editions at Sèvres factory. Goods marked Robj/ Paris. Made in France; decorative statuettes also bear name of designer.

Roche, Pierre (1855–1922). French sculptor, medallist, and potter; pupil of J. *Dalou, A. *Rodin. Awarded silver medal at Universal Exhibition, Paris 1900. Work edited in bronze, e.g. statuette of dancer, Loïe Fuller (now in Musée des Arts Décoratifs, Paris).

rock crystal engraving style. Deep carving of glass imitating Renaissance lapidary technique of cutting and carving rock crystal. Developed in 17th century Bohemia; brought to England by Bohemian engravers settling in Stourbridge area, notably F. *Kny and W. *Fritsche. Used to decorate both table and ornamental glass.

rocking chair. Chair with two curved rockers, or bends, connecting front and back feet. Dates from 18th century in Britain and America; became national institution in latter. Early models based on ladder-back or Windsor chairs; modifications in design to facilitate rocking unknown until development of *Boston rocker. Many variations popular after c1850, including *Lincoln rocker, *swing rocking chair, *Sinclair's American commonsense chair, *platform rocker, *Thonet rocker, *digestive chair. Bends sometimes fitted to easy chairs, e.g. slipper rocker, mainly in America. Popularity declined in Britain after 1st World War.

Rockingham ware. English and American earthenware, covered with brown glaze containing manganese, developed (early 19th century) at Rockingham factory in Swinton, Yorkshire. Used e.g. at Wedgwood factory and generally for production of teapots, toby jugs, and ornamental ware. Made throughout America from c1840, usually with mottled glaze. East Liverpool, Ohio, emerged as principal centre of manufacture. Taylor & Speeler established at Trenton, New Jersey, for production (1852). Variation, *flint enamel ware, developed at United States Pottery.

rococo, Louis XV, French modern or **French antique style.** American furniture style popular c1845–c1870; based on 18th century Louis XV furniture. Characterized by balanced curves (especially serpentine fronts); slender cabriole legs ending in rudimentary or scroll feet; chairs with balloon or openwork scrolled backs; tables with cartouche tops and X-stretchers with central finial; oval panels, scrolling on chair and table skirts, chair stiles and back rails. Motifs include naturalistic rose, grape, and shell carvings (often on chair and sofa yoke rails) in intertwining designs combined with leaves, tendrils, and scrolls; female heads in high relief. Applied mouldings, especially thumb moulding, common

Rococo style. Mahogany, satinwood, and marquetry writing table with ormolu mounts. Height 3ft6in.

Godfred Rode. Vase for *Royal Copenhagen Porcelain Factory. Numbered 6717 on base. 1898.

in factory-made examples. Favourite wood: plain or laminated rosewood. Many examples shown at Great Exhibition of 1851, London, and Crystal Palace Exhibition, New York, 1853. Best-known exponents: C. *Baudouine, J. H. *Belter, J. *Jelliff, P. *Mallard, J. *Meeks & Sons, and A. *Roux. *See also* French style.

Rode, Godfred (1862–1937). Danish porcelain decorator, worked at Royal Copenhagen Porcelain Factory. Noted for seascapes painted under glaze in style and palette similar to those used by A. *Krog.

Rodger, Joseph, & Sons Ltd. English cutlery manufacturers, world's oldest, founded in Sheffield, 1682; still in business. Consistent reputation for quality protected by acquisition of all other English cutlery manufacturers with name Roger or Rogers.

Rodgers, Gwladys M. (b 1887). English pottery decorator. Worked at Pilkington Tile & Pottery Co.; painted lustre ware. From 1928, decorated much of *Lapis ware, until production ceased (1938).

Rodin, Auguste (1840–1917). French sculptor. Worked in studio of A. E. *Carrier de Belleuse. Terracotta models include portrait busts and classical figures. At Sèvres factory, also with Carrier de Belleuse, modelled allegorical figures for decoration of vases, etc. From 1882, concentrated on sculpture.

Roeginga Pottery. English pottery established in late 1920s at Rainham, Kent, for production of earthenware made and decorated by O. *Davies and G. *Barnsley, e.g. vase with matt glaze and enamel painted design of thistles. Pottery closed in 1939, reopened in 1948. *Illustration at* Barnsley, G.

Rogers Brothers. *See* Meriden Britannia Co.

Rogers, John (1892–1904). American figure maker. In New York cast figures in reddish plaster, protected with coating of oil wash. Usually 20–24in. high, some later figures much taller; subjects taken from American life. All marked with name, New York, and date of patent.

Rogers, W. Gibbs (1792–1872). English woodcarver working in London; known for Renaissance revival style work, e.g. carving on boxwood cradle designed by son, shown by Queen Victoria at Great Exhibition of 1851, London. Much work in Elizabethan style. Worked for private clients and cabinet makers. Business carried on by sons until 1890s.

Rohde, Johan (1856–1935). Danish painter, silver and jewellery designer. From 1907 until death, designed silver for G. *Jensen. Style very similar to that of Jensen, e.g. characteristic silver pitcher designed for Jensen, 1920, now in Kunstindustrimuseet, Copenhagen.

Rohlfs, Charles (1853–1936). American furniture maker (one-time actor and designer of cast-iron stoves) working in Buffalo, New York State, from c1890. Made plain, linear furniture (often in fumed oak), with unusual details, e.g. chest of drawers with carving inspired by smoke curling from pipe, shown at Buffalo Exposition of 1901. Carving often followed patterns suggested by wood grain. Also made Art Nouveau pieces. Supervized decoration of office suites and domestic interiors; designed several uncharacteristically formal pieces for Buckingham Palace, London. Gained international reputation after showing work at International Exhibition of Modern Decorative Arts, Turin, 1902; also showed at Louisiana Purchase International Exposition, 1904. Retired c1925. Custom-made pieces marked: R, enclosed in rectangular frame of wood saw with date below, burned or incised into frame.

roiro-nuri (Japanese, 'wax-colour lacquer'). In Japanese lacquer, finest quality black lacquer, distinguished by rich deep tone, mirror-smooth surface, hard polish and high lustre.

Rokkaku. *See* Shisui.

rolled gold. Simulated gold sheet, wire, and tube produced by fusing very thin sheets of gold to base metal, e.g. copper. Used for toys, inexpensive costume jewellery, etc. during 19th century; still commonly used. Known in America as filled gold.

rolling pin (in glass). Early examples taper slightly towards knopped ends. From early 19th century, made in coloured *Nailsea glass, particularly purple, blue, amber, green, and opaque white; also, mottled and striped. Popular as gift

or love token. Often gilt, painted, or enamelled, and inscribed with initials, dates, biblical quotations, or mottoes, e.g. May the Eye of the Lord Watch over You, Be True to Me. Sea subjects, sporting and country scenes popular. Also made in Birmingham, London, Newcastle-upon-Tyne, Stourbridge, and Alloa. *Illustration at* Nailsea.

Romanesque style. American furniture style popular c1880–c1900. Developed by H.H. *Richardson; commercially manufactured chiefly in Boston, Massachusetts. Based on Early English style. Characterized by mortise construction, spiral-turned spindles, square-section legs (chamfered,with stops), Byzantine inspired carvings (e.g. rams' heads on chair arms), and acanthus motifs. Typical example: oak chair with high spindle back.

Romanian rugs. Traditional peasant rugs, used as insulating wall hangings, or covers for chests, benches, etc. Generally made up from two or three separate lengths, because woven on narrow low-warp looms. Originally, both warp and weft woollen; from mid 19th century, warp usually cotton, sometimes hemp or flax. Oriental influence first appeared in 19th century, with Muslim elements introduced into border designs. Moldavian (Moldova) rugs distinctive: blue or green ground (also black from 19th century); design divided into central field with scattered stylized flowers, and border. Other main types: Oltenian, Hunedore, and Bamat. From early 20th century, traditional geometrical designs of certain regions, e.g. Bistrita Nasaud, increasingly replaced by floral patterns. Export industry dates from late 19th century: mainly peasant kelims and hand-knotted carpets imitating Persian, Caucasian, and other major types from Middle East and Asia.

Rookwood Pottery. American pottery, established 1880 in Cincinnati, Ohio, by M.L. *Nichols. Supplied blanks to outside decorators until 1883, and produced utility earthenware for short time, as well as gradually developing distinctive style in main product, art pottery, throughout 1880s. Early decorative techniques include impressed geometrical motifs, transfer-printing, and relief designs applied, carved, or incised; gilding and enamel decoration sometimes used. Gradually, Japanese motifs gave way to naturalistic representation of plants and animals. In 1883, use of atomizer introduced by L.A. *Fry for application of underglaze grounds in blended brown, orange, yellow, and green which, with *barbotine* decoration, notably flowers, became characteristic of Rookwood Standard ware. Original limited underglaze palette increased; additional colour effects also achieved with use of tinted glaze and body. W.W. *Taylor, manager 1883–1913, incorporated business, and transferred to larger premises in 1892; new artists joined decorating studio. Standard ware main product; other styles include Cameo, with floral decoration against pink and white ground; later, Iris, with light blue, grey, and white ground, and brilliant glaze; Sea Green, fish designs against blue-green ground, brilliant glaze; and Aerial Blue, light blue and grey ground with bluish tinted glossy glaze. Range of decoration, in 1880s chiefly flowers, increased; ·portraits of American Indians, negroes, or after e.g. van Dyck, Rembrandt, or Frans Hals, also animals painted in slip under glaze of vases and plaques. In 1890s,

Rookwood Pottery. Earthenware jar with relief slip decoration under coloured glazes, decorated by Hattie E. Wilcox. 1900.

some decorators, e.g. A. *van Briggle, allowed to study in Europe. Experiments from 1896 resulted in introduction of matt glazes (1901), used with painted or relief decoration. Art Nouveau elements in design treated in rather formal way. Incised motifs sometimes derived from American Indian pottery. *Vellum line (1904) decorated with detailed land or seascapes in high-temperature colours under transparent matt glaze. With development of matt glazes, architectural ware introduced (1904); relief plaques, sometimes tin-glazed, or panels made for walls and fireplaces often with designs of animals, or fruit and flowers. Premises enlarged to house tile manufacture. Until c1910, production normally initialled by artists and not duplicated. Work dated and shapes numbered. Moulded pieces introduced to satisfy demand for lower-priced ornamental ware. Pottery continued after death of Taylor until bankruptcy in 1941. Marks include ROOKWOOD POTTERY, painted or incised (1880–81) and impressed (1882–86). Monogram of RP with R reversed, officially adopted in 1886, has one flame point added for each year from and including 1887 until 1900. Thereafter, Roman numeral added below indicates year of 20th century. Work of Rookwood Pottery imitated at Lonhuda Pottery of W.A. *Long and later by S.A. *Weller, J.B. *Owens, and at Roseville Pottery.

Rörstrand. Swedish pottery, established 1726 near Stockholm for production of faience; in operation from 1727. In 19th century, chief pro-

duct until 1850s, earthenware in English style, then revived earlier European styles. Bone porcelain made from 1850s, sometimes in Sèvres style. Ironstone china and imitations of maiolica and Palissy ware also made. Hard-paste porcelain introduced in 1870s. *Jardinières*, vases, figures, and tea and coffee ware made in majolica in 1870s. Earthenware painted in white on deep blue ground in Limoges style in 1880s. A. *Wallander, designer from 1895 and art director from 1897, introduced decoration of flowers modelled in relief and painted with soft colours under glaze in Art Nouveau style. White porcelain vase with blue pansies forming rim made c1900. Firm operated factories at Gothenburg (1926) and, with G. *Nylund as director, at Lidköping (1932). Tableware from 1930s often covered with monochrome glaze, left in white, or sparsely decorated with emphasis on form, largely followed functionalist principles in design. Mark: three crowns of Marieberg, with RÖRSTRAND from 1884.

Rosanjin Kitaoji (1881–1960). Japanese potter working at Kamakura, near Tokyo. Among potters inspired by traditional wares, notably Shino, Oribe, and others from Seto area in Momoyama period (16th and 17th centuries) and work of Kenzan in Edo period (1615–1868). Also worked in functional styles of Bizen and Shigaraki, and blue-and-white or kinrande chawan porcelains of Chinese Ming dynasty.

Rose Amber or **Rose Amberina glass.** American art glass shading ruby to amber. Patented by *Mount Washington Glass Works c1886. Made by mixing gold oxide with glass metal, then reheating part of vessel to obtain colour variations. Close similarity to *Amberina.

rose cut. *See* gem cutting.

Rosenholm pattern. Highly successful range of Swedish silver flatware designed by J. Ängman for *GAB, 1933, mass-produced from 1935. Plain Swedish traditional pattern, with flat silver handles slightly curved at ends.

Rörstrand. Group of porcelain vases, c1900. Modelled in relief and painted in colours (right) and with crystalline glaze (left).

Rosenthal, Philip (d 1937). German potter. Established porcelain factory (1879) in Selb (Bavaria). Noted for high quality of products. Designed table services, Darmstadt (1905), Donatello (1907), and Isolde (1910), originally without decoration. Later painted under glaze, e.g. plant motifs in Art Nouveau style on Darmstadt service, with slender stems and heart-shaped flowers or leaves in groups of three; or cherry design on Donatello service. Simple, elegant shapes emphasized by restrained decoration. Handles, particularly in Darmstadt service, follow lines of tureens, etc., although not in case of Isolde service. Figures made by firm in 1920s and 1930s in Art Deco style include theatrical characters, e.g. Pierrot, and subjects in contemporary costume, e.g. bathing dress. Many signed by artist. Succeeded in business by son, Philip, who appointed independent artists to design work in studios at Selb, for sale in Rosenthal Studio houses. Firm also produces cutlery and, at Amberg (Bavaria), glass. Glass factory designed by W. *Gropius. Marks on porcelain: crown over crossed lines and signature, Rosenthal (from c1880), over crossed lines with initials RC, or over crossed roses and Rosenthal signature.

Rosenthal. Porcelain figure of lady with gazelle. Marked Rosenthal, Selb. Bavaria. Height 14½ in.

Rose Valley Association. American craft community founded 1901 near Philadelphia, Pennsylvania, by William Price, editor of Ladies' Home Journal, with financial support from educational and industrial sources. Workshops in abandoned mill buildings produced metalwork, pottery, and furniture, and included printing press; published The Artsman magazine, 1903-07. Workers trained by craftsmen brought from Switzerland. Association maintained shop in Philadelphia as retail outlet; business bankrupted in 1909.

Roseville Pottery. American pottery established (1892) in Roseville, Ohio; in 1898, acquired premises in Zanesville. Mass-production of art pottery began c1900. First style, Rozane, painted on slip on dark ground and covered with brilliant glaze, renamed Rozane Royal as distinction from subsequent styles. Normally marked ROZANE, incised, with R P CO. Vases, etc., cast in local clay. From further increase in art pottery production c1910, mark R enclosing small v used. Decorative styles concentrated increasingly on use of matt glazes over relief decoration; new developments continued in attempt to compete with other Zanesville firms, notably J. B. *Owens Pottery Co. and firm of S. A. *Weller, also imitators of Rookwood Pottery, until loss of popularity after 2nd World War, despite Depression in 1930s. Operation ceased in 1954.

rosewood. Fragrant, close-grained wood native to Brazil, India, Java, and East Indies; colours range from light hazel to deep purple shading to almost black. Used mainly for inlaying, veneers, and banding during 18th century. Popular for all types of furniture in Britain, c1837-c1865. In America, laminated form much used for rococo style furniture; solid form for Art Deco pieces.

Roskopf, Georges-Frédéric (1813-89). German-born watchmaker; naturalized Swiss. Founded factory at La Chaux-de-Fonds, c1866. Invented (1867) first cheap version of Swiss watch, named after him; sold for 20 francs (English equivalent, 16 shillings). Developed lever escapement with steel pins for impulse pin and pallets. Hands set by opening glass and pushing them round; winding button turned one way only. Own watches well-made, but poor-quality imitations brought name into disrepute. (See Swiss horological industry.)

Rossetti, Dante Gabriel (1828-82). English Pre-Raphaelite painter and poet; founder member of *Morris, Marshall, Faulkner & Co., 1861; among designers of tiles decorated by firm. Painted panel on cabinet by J. P. *Seddon, 1861. Designed furniture, e.g. giltwood sofa, upholstered in velvet (c1862); also version of *Sussex chair with splayed splats in back, resembling stylized corn sheaf.

rouages. See Japy Frères.

round-back chair. Balloon-back chair with open back forming perfect circle; term used by British chair makers from c1850.

Rouse, James (1802-88). English porcelain painter. Apprentice at Crown Derby factory; flower painter under William (Quaker) Pegg. From 1820s, at Coalport, Shropshire, work includes miniature portraits on porcelain, and

Clément Rousseau. Table of ebony, ivory, and shagreen. c1921.

figure painting in Sèvres style. In 1860s, worked at Cauldon Place Works, Hanley, Staffordshire; later, in Birmingham, painted enamelled jewellery, etc. In Derby, from 1875, painted variety of subjects. Signed examples exist. Last work includes flower reserves on dessert service for presentation to William E. Gladstone, 1888.

Rousseau, Clément (b 1872). French furniture designer. Known for delicate Art Deco style furniture in luxury materials, e.g. small ebony table: covered in sharkskin, ornamented with ivory bands, slim curves, both form two legs and rise above square top as handles. Designed pieces for art patron, Jacques Doucet.

Rousseau, Eugène (1827-91). French Art Nouveau glass artist. Made vases, bowls, etc., chiefly in cameo glass; also enamelling. In early period, oriental influence very marked. Later, produced impressive sculptured pieces inlaid with coloured glass. Interest in new glass surface effects carried on after retirement by pupil, E. *Léveillé, with whom developed *flushed glass. Designer for Appert Frères, Paris, 1875-85. Mark: E. Rousseau, Paris, engraved.

Roux, Alexander (d 1881). French-born furniture maker; worked in New York from 1837, advertising as cabinet maker by 1846. In partnership (1847-48) with brother, Frederick, as Roux & Brother; Alexander Roux & Co. from c1849, after Frederick's return to Paris. Firm continued until 1898. Catalogue of 1860 advertised gilt and black furniture manufactured by F. Roux of Paris. Best-known for furniture in Gothic, rococo, and Renaissance revival styles; also made Eclectic furniture. *Illustration at* Renaissance style.

Royal Albert Works. See Meakin, Alfred.

Royal Aller Vale & Watcombe Art Potteries. See Aller Vale Art Potteries.

Eugène Rousseau. Smoke-coloured glass vase with enamel decoration.

Royal Axminster. *See* spool Axminster.

Royal Bayreuth. *See* Tettau.

Royal China Works Worcester. *See* Worcester.

Royal Copenhagen Porcelain Factory. Danish porcelain factory established 1775 at Copenhagen; under auspices of Danish royal family until 1867, underwent revival when bought by *Aluminia. Moved to Aluminia works (1884), under direction of P. *Schou. A. *Krog artist from early 1885 and, in effect, art director, noted for underglaze painting. Other artists working with similar palette and style include C. F. *Liisberg, and G. *Rode. Painting in coloured porcelain slip used by Liisberg from late 1880s and, later, by Krog. Slip-cast figures in smooth shapes decorated in soft colours under smooth glaze. Modelling shows abstract elements in 1890s, later more naturalistic e.g. in figures by G. *Henning and A. *Malinowski. Oriental glazes, e.g. *sang-de-boeuf*, introduced in mid 1880s, and crystalline glazes developed from c1886 increased awareness of form. From 1930s, stoneware used almost exclusively for production of figures, e.g. by K. *Kyhn, and J. *Nielsen. Stoneware vases with relief decoration made by A. *Salto. Display at Exhibition in New York (1939) included porcelain decorated under glaze, and thickly potted stoneware animal figures. Styles inspired by Chinese porcelain also exhibited, e.g. brown mouth and iron foot of southern Kuan ware, and examples covered with rich brown temmoku glaze of Chien ware. Marks usually incorporate crown and motif of three waves, and sometimes Denmark, Danmark, or Royal Copenhagen. *Illustration at* Rode, G.

Royal Crown Derby Porcelain Co., The. *See* Derby.

Royal Doulton. *See* Doulton & Co.

Royal Dutch Glass Works. *See* Leerdam.

Above
*Royal Flemish glass. Pot and cover made at *Mount Washington Glass Company. 1890s. Height 13in.*

Left
Royal Windsor Tapestry. Tapestry from a cartoon by Herbert Bone, one of his series based on Tennyson's 'Idylls of the King'. c1876–86. Height 6ft3in.

Royal Dux. *See* Duxer Porzellanmanufaktur.

Royal Essex Art Pottery. *See* Hedingham Art Pottery.

Royal Flemish glass. American enamelled art glass patented 1894 by *Mount Washington Glass Works, but made there as early as 1889. Closely resembles ancient Islamic glass. Made by dividing glass surface into segments with heavy, raised enamel lines, then painting enclosed sections in contrasting colours to give appearance of stained glass windows. Usually in shades of brown, beige, and gold.

Royal Lancastrian. *See* Pilkington's Tile & Pottery Co.

Royal Sphinx. *See* Regout, Petrus.

Royal Staffordshire Pottery. *See* Wilkinson, A.J. Ltd.

Royal Windsor Tapestry Manufactory, Old Windsor, Berkshire, England. Founded 1876 by H. Henry, art director of London decorating company, with Aubusson weavers, under aegis of Prince Leopold II of the Belgians. Produced landscape tapestries or other naturalistic designs, specializing in scenes from English history and pageantry, e.g. Battle of Aylesford; Tournament

on London Bridge; Queen Elizabeth opening the Royal Exchange. Also sets, e.g. Morte d'Arthur; Four Royal Residences. Factory closed 1887, because of overpricing and financial incompetence. Weavers dispersed and set up independent tapestry works, e.g. *Soho, *Baumgarten.

Royal Worcester. *See* Worcester.

Roycroft Shops. Copper ink pot and lid with lacquer finish. c1916. Marked on base.

Below
Rozenberg. Porcelain vase painted by J. *Shellink. Signed. c1900–05. Height 9in.

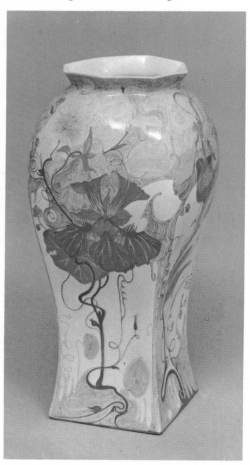

Roycroft Shops. Craft community established in East Aurora, New York State in 1895 by former soap manufacturer, and publisher E. *Hubbard; influenced by English *Arts and Crafts movement after Hubbard's visit to England in 1894. Produced Mission style furniture, simple oak or mahogany pieces, often with leather seats on chairs, and copper studs, *Morris chair; version of deck chair with three heavy slats in back, made 1905–12; known as Aurora colonial furniture from 1905. Copper workshop, started c1908, made bookends, trays, inkwells, vases, etc., some showing traces of Vienna Secession influence. Shops sold in 1938.

Rozane. *See* Roseville Pottery.

Rozenburg. Dutch earthenware and porcelain factory established (1885) at The Hague, with T. *Colenbrander as art director. Noted for line of exceptionally thin earthenware made in late 19th and early 20th centuries. Delicate, translucent body painted over glaze with birds, flowers, and foliage derived from design of Javanese batik-printed textiles. Enamel colours include mauve, yellow ochre, orange, and shades of green, used on clear white ground. In later examples, decoration stiffer and less delicate in colour. Shapes, often designed by J.J. *Kok, characterized by subtle interplay of curved and flat surfaces, and smoothly elongated handles and spouts. J. Schellink employed as painter. Earthenware decorated with stylized flowers in brick-red, black, purple, green, and yellow on bottle-green ground, though other designs occur, e.g. seahorses, or spiked leaves. Work marked Rozenburg/den Haag, with stork from mark of 18th century porcelain factory at The Hague, and crown.

Rubelles. French earthenware factory established by A. *du Tremblay near Melun (Seine-et-Marne) in mid 19th century. Specialized in *émaux ombrants. Also made tobacco jars, covered bowls, butter dishes, etc., in form of artichokes, melons, bundles of asparagus, and other natural objects. Plates decorated with silhouette portrait of landscape painted *en camaïeu*. Factory, sold in 1855, continued production until 1876. Early marks include ADT, sometimes enclosed in circular label, BREVET D'INVENTION, painted.

Rubena Crystal. *See* flashed glass.

Rubena Verde. *See* flashed glass.

ruby glass. Late 19th century American art glass. Clear red; obtained by adding oxide of gold (or, in cheaper versions, copper) to glass. Extremely popular for decorative ware; speciality of *Boston & Sandwich Glass Co.

Ruby Onyx glass. American art glass imitating appearance of natural gemstone. Version of *Onyx glass range (patented 1889). Body of opal glass cased with outer layer of transparent ruby glass.

Rückert, Fedor (fl c1890–c1917). Russian enameller working in *Old Russian style. Produced e.g. silver tea caddies, Easter eggs, kovschi, spoons, set with gemstones and brightly enamelled. Some work, acquired by *Fabergé for sale in his shop, carries firm's mark. Few pieces in international styles, but known to

Rudolfi. Tankard with ivory body inlaid with turquoise and mounted in silver set with rubies. c1855.

have produced Easter egg in Chinese Red enamel, decorated with Art Nouveau tree motif. Mark: initials in Cyrillic characters.

Rudolfi (fl 1840–55). Danish jeweller and silversmith working in Paris c1840–55. Executed work in *Gothic revival style using e.g. ivory and turquoise with precious metals.

Ruhlmann, Emile-Jacques (1879–1933). French cabinet maker and furniture designer; trained as painter. Showed at Salons d'Automne from 1910, attracting interest in 1913. Took over father's firm of household painters, 1919, establishing Etablissements Ruhlmann et Laurent. Leading Parisian cabinet maker by 1925, with workshops for upholstery, japanning, etc. Designed all furniture, although employed 16 draughtsmen. Simple, functional, architectural pieces, with delicate curves enhancing natural beauty of woods, e.g. macassar ebony, amboyna, characterized by restrained ornament, e.g. simple mouldings, cartouches inlaid with ivory, sharkskin, tortoiseshell, or lizard skin; tapering legs often ending in silver or ivory shoes. Occasionally used metal supports. Furniture more monumental towards 1933, sometimes decorated with chrome or silver.

Ruskin Pottery. *See* Taylor, William Howson.

Russell, Sir (Sydney) Gordon (b 1892). English furniture designer and artist-craftsman. Established Russell Workshops (later Gordon Russell Ltd.) in Broadway, Worcestershire. Known for machine-made versions of traditional English designs, e.g. turned, rush-seated chairs with ladder-backs, c1924. Furniture characterized by use of English woods, e.g. oak, yew; straight lines occasionally contrasted with curves; wood grain emphasizes linear design. Designs from c1930 influenced British furniture in 1950s and 1960s.

Emile-Jacques Ruhlmann. Macassan ebony table with brass bound feet. c1930–32. Length 4ft.

Below
Sir Gordon Russell. Dining chair, walnut, with drop-in leather seat. One of set of eight. c1925.

Russian carpets and tapestries. *See* West Turkestan, St Petersburg Tapestry Works.

Russian horological industry. Began in 1929 with purchase from America of two complete watch factories, Dueber and *Ansonia, which became respectively First and Second Moscow Watchmaking Plants; rebuilt and enlarged (1934) with additional factories founded at

Prenza and Kuibyshev. Clocks of all types, and *jewelled lever watches manufactured: world's second largest output after Switzerland.

rustic furniture. Chairs, long garden seats, etc. with carved framework resembling tree branches; dates from c1750. Originally made of wood; cast iron also used from 1840s.

Rusticana. Late 19th century British glass decorations for table or sideboard in form of tree trunks, roots or plants, or in more conventional shapes but with vegetable-like feet and supports. First produced c1886 by John Walsh glasshouse in Birmingham, vogue later spreading to other glasshouses and to those in Stourbridge area, notably *Stevens & Williams.

ryijy (Finnish) or **rya** (Swedish). Colourful Scandinavian rug, ranging from smooth kelim to pile rug with 1–1½in. cut or looped tufts, loosely woven in tough wool. Average size, 6–9 sq ft.

Below
Rustic furniture. Cast iron chair. American, mid 19th century.

Originally from Finland; used as horsecloth, sledge rug, or coverlet; since revival of weaving tradition throughout Scandinavia in 19th century, ryijy generally made as floor covering or wall hanging. *See* Finnish, Swedish, and Norwegian rugs and tapestries.

ryoshi-bako or **ryoshi-bunko** (Japanese, 'writing-paper box'). Large Japanese lacquer writing box (c16×13×6in.) for storing documents, manuscripts and writing utensils; sometimes fitted with lacquered tray. Often made as part of matching writing set accompanying *suzuri-bako. Widely produced and exported in 19th and 20th centuries. Most examples in black or gold lacquer with major decorative surfaces on top and underside of lid, and sometimes sides.

Ryumonji. Japanese folk pottery centre in Kagoshima prefecture, Kyushu, established by Korean workers. Noted for production of spouted saké warmers and shochu bowls; also covered rice pots with trickled glazes in white, green, or brown.

ryusa netsuke. One or two piece *manju netsuke, named after mid 18th century netsuke artist. Usually in ivory or wood, with designs of birds, flowers, insects, arabesques, etc. in openwork carving. Often encrusted or inlaid with various metals.

Sabanin, Vavila Dimitrievich (fl mid 19th century–1974). Russian porcelain manufacturer. Worked at Popov factory near Moscow and established own firm (c1850) at Klimovka (Vladimir). Produced tableware and, notably, figures until c1874.

sabi. Japanese lacquer composed of one part burnt clay to two parts branch lacquer (seshime-urushi). Used in preparation of lacquer base in takamakie and keiran-nuri techniques.

sabiji (Japanese, 'patina ground'). Popular Japanese lacquer imitation of ancient metal, particularly rusted iron.

Sabino or **Sabino-Marino,** Maurius-Ernest (fl 1920s and 1930s). French Art Deco glass artist. Made *Lalique-inspired furniture, composed of units of pressed glass moulded on invisible foundation, and light shades and vases in smoky-coloured glass. Also made vases in opaque coloured glass. Mark: Sabino, Paris, engraved or moulded.

Sabrina. Earthenware with figured crystalline glaze developed at Worcester Royal Porcelain factory c1900, and produced until c1930.

Sächsiche Porzellanfabrik. *See* Thieme, Carl, Potschappel.

saddlebag chairs. Armchairs, side-chairs, etc. upholstered in carpeting resembling material used for camels' saddlebags e.g. in Egypt. Common in Britain c1875–c1900.

sagemono or **koshisage.** In Japan, articles worn hung from sash (*obi) by cord secured by toggle (*netsuke) and slip-bead (*ojime). Included case for medicaments or seals (*inro), pipe case (*kiseru-zutsu), tobacco box (*tabako-ire), drinking gourd (hyotan), purse for keys and money (kinchaku), writing case with brush (*yatate), chopstick case (hashi-ire).

St Anthony's Pottery. English earthenware pottery established c1780 in Newcastle-upon-Tyne, Northumberland. Produced cream-coloured earthenware with painted or printed decoration; much exported. Lustre decoration also used. Work marked with names of various proprietors, e.g. SEWELL, or SEWELL & DONKIN, and, 1893–1908, T. Patterson & Co.

St Blazey Foundry. English foundry established in St Blazey, Cornwall, in 19th century. Products included metal boot scrapers, door porters, etc.

St Ives. *See* Leach, Bernard.

Maurius-Ernest Sabino. Glass bookend representing pair of turkeys. 1920s.

St Louis. French glasshouse founded 1767 in Paris under royal patronage. First French producer of English-type lead crystal. From 1782, established on commercial basis. Specialized in coloured glass from 1839; vases, jugs, scent bottles, etc. distinguished by bright colouring and graceful design, frequently gilded and mounted with gilt-bronze. With *Baccarat, main producer of fine tableware in 19th century France. Noted for snake paperweights, though floral and fruit weights also made, all characterized by soft colouring. *Illustration at* paperweight.

St Mary's Works. *See* Moore Brothers.

St Petersburg Tapestry Works, Russia. Founded 1716 by Tsar Peter the Great, with French (from Gobelins) and Flemish workmen. Expenditure cut during Crimean War (1854–56), and production minimal. Closed 1858 by Alexander II.

Saint-Porchaire. *See* Henri-Deux ware.

sakazuke or **saké cup.** Drinking vessel for Japanese rice-wine, saké. Shallow, round bowl (c4in. diameter, 1–1½in. high), on short, narrow base which facilitates stacking. Made of very thin wood core, covered with layers of lacquer. Surface coat usually red or black with designs of birds, flowers, sea creatures, etc. executed in hiramakie, takamakie, or togadashi techniques. Main decorative work on inside surface of bowl; slight ornamentation on sides and base. Made singly or in sets of up to 20; sometimes signed by lacquer artist. Among best-quality and most highly prized miniature Japanese lacquer objects.

saké cup. *See* sakazuke.

Sala, Jean (b 1895). Spanish-born French glass artist in Functionalist style. Made vases, bowls, etc., chiefly in blue-green *malfin* glass resembling ancient Roman glass, with bubbles and imperfections deliberately produced by incomplete fusing. Also, collection of glass fish for Oceanographic Museum, Monaco. Mark: J. Sala.

Salopian Art Pottery Co. English pottery at Benthall, near Broseley, Shropshire, producing earthenware c1880–c1912. Vases and plaques decorated with coloured slips or enamel. Relief decoration includes moulded fruit or flowers, or incised designs. Also made vases decorated with glaze effects of oriental inspiration. Work sometimes marked SALOPIAN.

Saltjkov, Ivan (fl 1884–97). Prolific Russian silversmith and enameller in Moscow. Produced wide range of objects executed in *Old Russian style.

Salto, Axel (1889–1961). Danish designer and ceramic artist. Trained as painter in Copenhagen. From 1916, illustrated own books and those of others; helped found magazine, Klingen, 1917. As potter (from 1923) worked for Bing & Grøndahl and N. *Krebs. Joined Royal Copenhagen Porcelain manufacture in 1930s. Made simple bowls with carved relief decoration in light-coloured stoneware. Experiments in relationship between body and glaze included carving of bud-like motifs over surface of pots; in

Salopian Art Pottery. Earthenware vases, both c1890. Height of tallest 9¼in.

later work, increased size of bud forms emphasizes variation in thickness of glaze over surface contours. Much work inspired by nature. Also designed papers for book-binding (1934), fabric prints (1944), and architectural decoration.

salt spoon. Small spoon with round bowl for serving salt from salt-cellar; made of silver from 18th century. Smaller version for individual use made in silver and electro-plate in America from c1875. Handles follow styles of other flatware.

Salviati, Antonio (1816–1900). Italian lawyer, co-founder with Giulio Radi, glass maker, of *Salviati & Co. in 1860.

Salviati & Co. Venetian glass factory in Murano, Venice, founded 1860 by A. *Salviati and a Signor Radi, glass maker of Murano. In addition to *latticinio, vetro-di-trina*, and other revived early Venetian techniques, while Salviati in charge (1860–66) also produced large quantity of mosaic work, including many mosaic pictures for English churches, notably St Paul's and Westminster Abbey. In late 19th century, produced Art Nouveau iridescent glass; in 1920 and 1930s thin-walled coloured glasses in Functionalist style. At Salviati's withdrawal (1866) firm became known as Compania Venezia-Murano, bearing same name today.

Samarkand rugs. *See* East Turkestan.

samegawa-nuri. *See* same-nuri.

same-nuri (Japanese, 'ray lacquer') or **samegawa-nuri** (Japanese, 'rayskin lacquer'). Japanese lacquer on rayskin, comparable to Western shagreen. Nodes of rayskin filed down and skin covered with black or brown lacquer; when dry, material polished until nodules appear as white patches. In variety known as ai-same (Japanese, 'indigo-ray'), rayskin pre-dyed with indigo, so that lacquered skin has blue patches. Widely used by 18th century, mainly on sword-hilts, but sometimes on inro, sagemono, etc. Found on much 19th and 20th century export lacquerware.

samorodok (Russian, 'nugget') **finish.** Metal finish simulating rough surface of nugget. Effect produced by heating metal (usually gold or silver) plate nearly to melting point, and then quickly removing from heat. Technique developed in Russia; speciality of *Fabergé, particularly for cigarette cases.

Samson, Edmé, & Cie. French porcelain manufacturer, established 1845 in Paris. Made reproductions of many types of porcelain in greyish-tinged hard paste, even when originals in soft

Salviati & Co. Colourless glass goblet with elaborate coloured stem. 1869.

Left
*Samorodok finish. Three Russian silver visiting card and cigarette cases. Two lower initialled cases by M. *Semenova, made in *Fabergé workshops, 1910.*

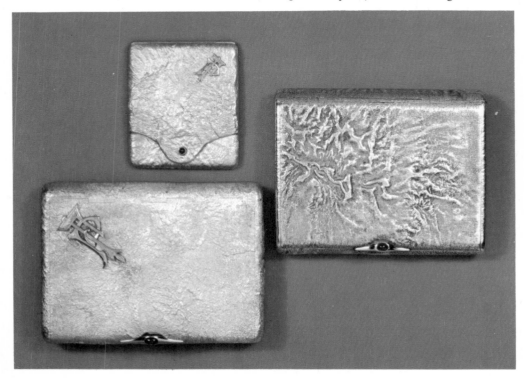

Edmé Samson & Cie. Inkwell and pen-holder with base in the manner of 18th century Chinese export porcelain. Marked with spurious Chinese characters. Late 19th century.

paste. Soft paste used for boxes, etc., in style of 18th century French factories and, very rarely, English examples. Copies of Chinese porcelain hardest to distinguish from originals, in spite of characteristic smooth surface. Export ware with decoration in European styles or *famille rose* and *famille verte* most imitated. Typically, shapes used with decoration which would not have appeared on originals. English reproductions include Worcester porcelain with blue scale decoration; also work of Bow, Chelsea and Derby. German work of Höchst, Ludwigsburg, and Nymphenburg factories imitated. Copies of Meissen porcelain distinguishable by blackened base, speckled body, and hard, glassy appearance

Below
Gérard Sandoz. Bowl. c1925. Height 6½in.
Below right
Gérard Sandoz. Silver cigarette case. Exterior covered in black, sage green and grey lacquer with white crushed eggshell. Engraved Gerard Sandoz del. and Gustave Sandoz Paris on both rims. c1928.

of glaze, usually marked with crossed batons in blue, with S. Copies of Italian porcelain rare, although maiolica of Deruta and Gubbio reproduced. Other imitations of tin-glazed earthenware include Isnik pottery and work made at Rouen, Sinceny, and Marseilles. Marks usually resemble those of originals, e.g. Chinese seals; all ware also said to bear mark, S.

Emil Samson. Paris firm, operating c1900, specializing in replicas e.g. of 18th century English and European enamels. Replicas impressionistic rather than directly imitative; larger than originals. Translucent enamel motifs applied with easily recognisable thick impasto; poor quality mounts, hinges etc.

sandblasting. Process of decorating glass, especially large glass panels, by directing jets of sand at high pressure against surface, with design masked with treated paper. Surface emerges grey and finely or coarsely pitted, depending on pressure, size of nozzle, or quality of sand. Technique invented 1870 by American, Benjamin Tilghman.

sand caster. See pounce pot.

sand-casting process. Method of casting bronze in mould made from pounded, dried quartz and sand mixture, prepared with channels, air vents, and supported in position by iron frame. Molten metal poured into channels, and left to cool; sand then broken away. Articles so cast require considerable degree of finishing, i.e. chiselling, to remove seams left by channels and vents. Quality of articles cast by process depends entirely on skill of *ciseleur:* F. *Barbedienne and *Susse Frères famous for quality of finish.

Sandoz, Gérard. French silversmith producing Art Deco designs c1925–c1930; achieved balance between cubist forms and functionalism; noted for tea sets with pronounced angular shapes and thick ebony handles, and cigarette cases decorated with enamelled scenes of buildings and bridges.

sang-de-boeuf glaze. Red glaze known in Chinese Ming period and revived in reign of K'ang Hsi (1662–1722). Colour derived from copper oxide

fired in reducing atmosphere. Reproduction attempted by European potters in late 19th century. Subject of research by H. C. *Robertson in America from 1870s. Notable examples achieved at Pilkington factory.

Saruk. See Sultanabad.

sashi-gushi. See kushi.

sashi netsuke. Rod-shaped netsuke up to 5in. long. Made with cord holes at one end and worn with other end tucked under girdle. Usually carved in ivory, wood, or horn. Typical design: small insect or animal perched on twig or elongated branch.

satin finish. See butler's finish.

satin or **mother-of-pearl glass.** Late 19th century American art glass; opaque, with pearlized finish. Perfected 1885 by J. *Webb at *Phoenix Glass Works. Core of hot, mould-blown, opaque glass (any colour) coated with transparent colour then with crystal layer, finally subjected to acid vapour, with design masked with acid-resistant wax or varnish. Term, satin glass, also used to describe all acid-finished coloured wares, most with milk glass lining.

satsu-bako. See tea ceremony utensils.

Satsuma ware. Japanese pottery made in Kagoshima – formerly Satsuma – prefecture, Kyushu, from late 16th century. Early work followed Korean and Chinese styles. Tea ceremony ware made to present day. Main kilns, e.g. Naeshirogawa and Ryumonji, developed by Korean potters. Hard, greyish-white or parchment-coloured faience with crackle glaze, lavishly enamelled and gilded, produced from mid 18th century; among styles introduced to West by display at Universal Exhibition in Paris (1867). Imitations made, e.g. in Kyoto, mainly for export.

Sattler, Wilhelm (fl mid 19th century). German potter; produced earthenware in English styles at Aschach, Bavaria (1829–60). Marks: WS & S and Aschach, impressed.

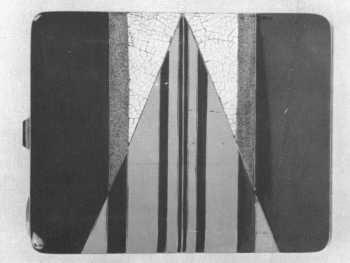

Satsuma ware. Baluster vase with enamel and gilt decoration of eagle flying over village. Signed Kizan. Height 7in.

Saturday Evening Girls' Club. *See* Paul Revere Pottery.

sautoir. Long rope necklace of gold links or pearls, often with contrasting beads at 1-2in. intervals; fashionable in 1890s. Sometimes ended in two tassels. Often pinned with brooch to bodice or waist, so that it fell in loop below waist or from bodice. Term often used simply to describe long necklace.

Savin, Maurice-Louis (b 1894). French painter, sculptor, and artist potter. Work includes faience figures and portrait busts produced in 1930s; also sculptural work, e.g. fountains, and porcelain ceiling in Sèvres display at Universal Exhibition (1937).

Savonnerie. French carpet factory, founded 1626 in Paris; merged with *Gobelins in 1825, and moved to old Gobelins' buildings on banks of River Bièvre. During late 19th century, products increasingly· controlled by artistic policies of Gobelins. In early 20th century, reproduced paintings, e.g. by Claude Monet, Edouard Manet, Vincent van Gogh. Also made pile tapestries.

saw-piercing. In jewellery, technique for cutting metal to produce reticulations. Design sketched on metal, holes drilled, then jeweller's saw inserted into holes to cut out metal. For mass production design is stamped out, but same quality and variety not achieved as with hand work.

Saxbo. *See* Krebs, Nathalie.

Sazykov. Russian firm of silversmiths and enamellers, founded in Moscow, 1793, by Pavel Fedoravich Sazykov. Manufactured e.g. large sculptural pieces, enamelled items, and ornate silver gilt peasant figures encrusted with precious stones. Contributor to e.g. International Exhibition, London, 1862. Strongly influenced by *pan-Slavic movement. Mark, Sazykov in Cyrillic characters.

Sbitnev, Grigori. Russian silversmith and enameller; established firm in Moscow, 1893; continued until Revolution. Work, for highly affluent clientèle, drew inspiration from *pan-Slavic movement, deriving motifs and colour from Old Russian style, e.g. ornate silver kovschi, decorated with filigree enamel and cabochon cut precious stones.

scarf pins. *See* lace brooches.

scent bottle. Perfume container, usually small; fitted with airtight stopper and, ideally, not transparent, as perfume deteriorates when exposed to light. Perfume traditionally valued highly; containers, often richly decorated, made in porcelain, precious metals, enamel, etc. 19th century examples in glass include cameo scent bottles by T. *Webb & Sons, decorated with floral, classical, or Chinese motifs, and by D. *Pearce e.g. in *agate glass, in shape of owl, duck, alligator, etc. Bottles in *lithyalin made by F. *Egermann. Many *Nailsea examples, some inscribed with date and initials of giver and recipient. Bottles in moulded opalescent glass commissioned by *parfumiers*, Coty, from R. *Lalique (1908). Many bottles designed by Lalique subsequently made for Coty and Nina Ricci; stoppers in form e.g. of female nude, or doves.

Scharvogel, Julius (fl late 19th, early 20th centuries). German potter. Worked at Mettlach factory of *Villeroy & Boch. Opened own studio in Munich, c1900, producing stoneware with thick, flowing glazes. From 1906, art director at factory in Darmstadt (Hesse); again concerned with glaze effects on stoneware.

Below
*Scent bottles. Group of French moulded glass scent bottles and powder bowls, by R. *Lalique and others. Made in Paris, 1920s.*

Schellink, J. (fl late 19th, early 20th centuries). Dutch artist and ceramic painter. Patterns of birds, flowers, and foliage, derived from Javanese batik-printed textiles, painted e.g. on vases designed by J. J. *Kok at Rozenburg pottery. *Illustration at* Rozenburg.

Scheurich, Paul (b 1883). German porcelain modeller, born in New York. Studied in Berlin, 1900-02. Modelled figures for M. *Pfeiffer at Schwarzburger Werkstätten für Porzellankunst and, later, at Meissen factory. Also worked for Nymphenburg factory and at Karlsruhe. Glazed white porcelain figures made at Berlin factory include pair, Apollo and Daphne (1925).

Schilkin, Michael (1900-62). Finnish ceramic artist, born in St Petersburg, Russia. From 1936 worked at Arabia factory. Early work mainly naturalistic ceramic sculpture; later, powerful, increasingly stylized animal and human figures made in stoneware with heavy glaze. Also large relief plaques for architectural use.

Schleiss, Franz (b 1884). German potter; pupil of B. *Löffler and M. *Powolny. Founder and director of Gmündener Keramik (1909-22). In 1917, established own ceramic school with help of state. At Münchener Werkstätte 1926-27; returned to work in Gmünden, 1928. Made dishes, vases, table services, and figures.

Schmuz-Baudiss, Theo (fl early 20th century). German potter and porcelain maker, formerly painter, working in Munich. Ceramic artist from 1896; work decorated with stylized designs of animals and flowers incised in slip. From 1902, at Berlin Royal Porcelain Factory, director 1908-26. Painted table services, etc., with rich floral designs. Tiles decorated with landscapes.

Schneckendorf, Josef Emil (1865-1949). Pioneer German Jugendstil glass artist. Worked in Darmstadt, Hesse, chiefly for *Grand-Ducal Fine Glass Co., where produced vases and other ornamental pieces in iridescent glass. Marks: SCHNE; also J.E.SCH.

Schneider, Charles (1881-1962). French Art Deco glass artist. Studied in Nancy and Paris, occasionally designing for *Daum brothers. Founded Cristallerie Schneider in Epinay-sur-Seine, near Paris, 1913. Produced range of *intercalaires:* decorative glass with colour flecks or streaks between two glass layers; also, glass

Charles Schneider. Vase with inlaid colour flecks. c 1921. Height 6in.

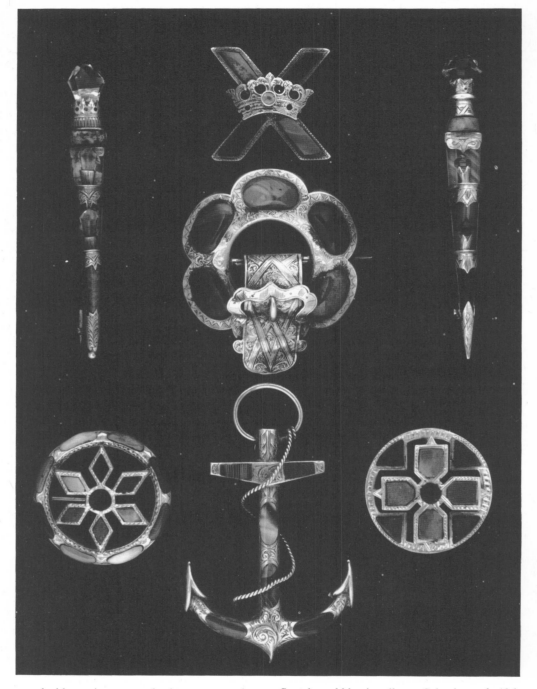

vessels blown into wrought iron mounts for Daum factory. Marks: many pieces signed Schneider; items marked Charder, or Le *Verre Français, also output of his glasshouse.

Schönwald. Bavarian porcelain factory, established 1879; traded as Porzellanfabrik Schönwald A.G. from 1898. Production of tableware, etc., continues. Marks incorporating initials PSAG include coronet, orb, and Bavaria, and shield bearing eagle below crown.

Schou, Philip (1838-1922). Danish potter and porcelain maker. Part-owner and manager of Aluminia factory from 1868, and director of Royal Copenhagen Porcelain Factory from 1885, until succeeded by F. *Dalgas in 1902.

Scotch pebble jewellery. Selection of 19th century brooches, all silver and set with agates, carnelians, and bloodstones.

Responsible for period of reorganization and research which surrounded amalgamation of factories and move of porcelain factory to premises of Aluminia.

Schwarzburger Werkstätten. *See* Pfeiffer, Max Adolf.

Scotch carpet. *See* ingrain carpet.

Scotch pebble jewellery. Made in Scotland of local stones, e.g. bloodstone, cornelian, sard, grey-striped agate, moss agate, jasper, and

Isaac E. Scott. Walnut desk with hand-carved side panels. 1879. Height 3ft 10in.

marble. Set in silver or gold mounts (frequently engraved), using pitch or shellac; sometimes arranged as mosaic and fixed to slate backing. Pebbles may be combined with other local stones, e.g. cairngorm, amethyst, or freshwater pearls. Some pieces hallmarked; designs registered after 1842 with *registry mark. Most popular as brooches in shape of buckles, shields, crests, crosses, weapons, hearts, thistles, claws, or hoofs. Also bracelets, pendants, cuff-links, etc. Fashion popularized by novels of Sir Walter Scott and by Queen Victoria; lasted until end of 19th century; some pieces of inferior quality still made.

Scott family. *See* Southwick Pottery.

Scott, Isaac E. (1845–1920). American craftsman and furniture designer, born near Philadelphia, Pennsylvania; worked in Philadelphia (1867–68), Chicago (1873–83), later in New York and Boston. Known for high-quality cabinets designed for rich clients; finely carved with detailed decoration often of inlaid woods. Typical is walnut cabinet (*c*1875), inlaid with geometrical and stylized floral motifs in various woods; based on Gothic Reform style.

screen. Portable, covered frame to shield user from excess heat, light, draught, etc. Originated in 7th century China; used in England from Middle Ages. Use declined *c*1830–*c*1880, then revived with vogue for smaller furniture; wide range of designs and styles sold in London and Paris by E. Kalin & Co. of London, e.g. four-panelled damask-covered folding screen, three-fold Louis XVI reproduction wooden screen, carved and gilt, with silk brocade panels. Made with up to six panels in many combinations, e.g. of tapestry, silk, and carved inlaid mahogany, or decorated and carved silkwood; also antique styles with hand painted, embossed leather panels and carved oak frame. Intricately carved or inlaid wooden screens, decorated with mother-of-pearl or piqué work also common.

*Screen. Black lacquer screen by E. *Gray. c1930.*

Below
Scrimshaw. Tooth engraved with portrait of Anne Boleyn. Mid 19th century.

Many home-made screens, e.g. with needlework panels, made in Victorian period. Japanese style screens, in e.g. wood, or silk with oriental motifs made in 1890s. In France, J. *Dunand revived art of oriental lacquerwork, making lacquer screens from *c*1910.

scrimshaw. Hand-carved decorative objects, e.g. of bone, ivory, shell, produced by sailors as means of passing time on lengthy voyages. Origin of term obscure.

scroll flask. *See* violin flask.

scroll Windsor chair. Side-chair with inclined back uprights curving backwards at top, flat back and yoke rails. Usually beech frame with elm seat. Many examples made in Britain during 19th century.

Sea Green. *See* Rookwood Pottery.

seal. *See* desk seal, fob seal.

seat curb. Long, padded seat, with narrow break in centre, supported by vertical metal bars rising from fender curb. May have padded box seats at either end for storing coal, logs, etc., sometimes also built-in racks for fire irons. Popular in Britain during Victorian period. *cf* club fender.

Sedding, John Dando (1838–1891). English architect and designer; pupil of G. E. *Street; worked in London from 1874; among first members of Art Workers' Guild, served as Master in 1886 and 1887. Produced large number of designs for silver, embroidery, and wallpaper; ecclesiastical designs executed by *Barkentin & Krall; work influenced by tradition of John and W. *Morris. Electro-plated nickel silver processional cross, with bronze figures, made in 1889 for St Matthew's church, Sheffield.

Seddon, John Pollard (1827–1906). English designer and architect. Designed Gothic and Gothic Reform style furniture, often for father, T. *Seddon's, shop. Best known for architect's table (exhibited at International Exhibition, London, 1862) in oak with stylized floral wood inlay and panels, depicting honeymoon of King René of France, painted by E. *Burne-Jones, F. R. *Brown, D. G. *Rossetti, and W. *Morris. Made by *Morris, Marshall, Faulkner & Co. In early 1870s, designed tiles for *Maw & Co. *Jardinières* produced in stoneware by C. J. C. *Bailey (*c*1877), decorated with scrolled foliage in relief, coloured buff, blue, and brown, often with dark blue, bear incised monogram of Bailey, Fulham, impressed, and sometimes monogram of JPS.

Seddon, Thomas. Old-established London furniture manufacturers; cabinet makers to George IV. Known for Gothic Reform style furniture designed by J. P. *Seddon – grandson of firm's founder – and W. *Burges, *c*1860–*c*1880.

Seguso Vetri d'Arte. Italian glasshouse in Murano, Venice. Contributed to 20th century Venetian glassmaking revival, notably when under art directorship of F. *Poli from 1934. Still operative.

Sehna carpets. *See* Persian carpets.

Seifu, Yohei (fl mid 19th century). Japanese porcelain maker in Kyoto from 1844. Made plates, etc., with low-relief decoration of plant and flower motifs; also used blue painting under glaze, or enamelled decoration in style of porcelain exported to West through port of Imari.

Seignouret, François (b 1768). French cabinet maker, born in Bordeaux. Arrived in New Orleans, Louisiana, c1800; leading cabinet maker by 1832. Made massive furniture, e.g. rococo style cabinets up to 10ft high. Favoured rosewood, also used mahogany. Carved directly on furniture; used S curves, especially at panel corners, possibly giving rise to tradition that all his pieces bear letter S in carved decoration. Tables, chests, etc. usually marble-topped. Known for armchair with single splat in back, rounded yoke rail extending forward and downward to form low arms curving to modified cabriole front legs; legs continuous with arms in early chairs, made separately in later examples. Pieces unlabelled. Returned to France in 1853; business continued unsuccessfully under his name for brief period.

Seiko Watch. *See* Japanese Horological Industry.

self-pouring teapot. *See* pump pot.

self-winding wrist watch. First patented (1924) by English watchmaker, J. *Harwood. Any movement of watch causes pivoted weight (rotor) to swing back and forth. Rotor is geared to mainspring winding mechanism. No winding stem: hands set by turning knurled bezel. Also Autorist system (rare): one auto-wrist of two rings designed to receive watchstrap is linked to jointed T-piece projecting from movement; this operates crank, which winds mainspring when wrist bends or flexes.

Semenova, Maria (fl 1890–1910). Russian silversmith working in Moscow. Worked in *Old Russian style. 1896–1904, operated and directed silver manufactory employing up to 100 workers. Mark: initials in Cyrillic characters. *Illustration also at* samorodok finish.

semi-porcelain, semi-vitreous porcelain, or **hotel china.** In America, hard, white earthenware fired at high temperature, resembling porcelain, though lacking translucency of porcelain body. Made from c1885. *cf* ironstone china.

Maria Semenova. Silver and cloisonné enamel bowl set with cabochon garnets. Late 19th century. Diameter 3in.

*Gottfried Semper. Cabinet in ebony and gilt metal, made by *Holland & Sons. Decorated with *Wedgwood plaques and porcelain panel painted by George Gray with copy of William Mulready's 'Crossing the Ford' (exhibited 1842). Made 1855.*

Below
Georges Serré. Earthenware vases dated between 1923 and 1929.

semi-vitreous. *See* semi-porcelain.

Semper, Gottfried (1803–79). German architect, designer, and teacher; member of Prince Consort's circle in Britain. Designed ebony cabinet-on-stand with gilt metal mounts; painted porcelain panel on door is surrounded by rectangular Wedgwood plaques. Made by *Holland & Sons, and shown at Paris Exhibition of 1855; now in Victoria & Albert Museum, London. Commercial copies exist.

sénateur. *See* pouf.

Serapis-Fayence. *See* Wahliss, Ernst.

Serica glass. Range of Dutch Art Deco and Functionalist studio glass issued by *Leerdam in limited series for collectors. Idea originated with C. *Lebeau and A. *Copier. *See also* Unica glass.

serpentine front. Balanced, curved front of bookcase, cabinet, chair, or sofa; convex at centre, concave each side. Shape also used for top rails, e.g. in medallion-back sofa. Feature of rococo style furniture in America.

Serré, Georges (1889–1956). French artist potter. Apprentice at Sèvres factory from 1902 until outbreak of 1st World War. In 1916, visited Saigon, South Vietnam; work inspired by Khmer art, and by Chinese ceramics. From 1918, teacher. In 1922, established stoneware workshop at Sèvres (Hauts-de-Seine). Heavy forms decorated with simple geometrical motifs, e.g. hexagons, scale design, incised and sometimes picked out with coloured oxides, or emphasized by flow of glaze. Body sometimes contains chamotte. Work marked with impressed signature.

Serrurier-Bovy, Gustave (1858–1910). Belgian designer of interiors and furniture. Pieces from 1884 inspired by Arts & Crafts Movement; mainly in oak. Imported *Liberty's furniture and accessories for Liège shop. Later known for

Left
Sèvres. Left: porcelaine nouvelle *vase with incised underglaze decoration and gilt metal mounts, designed by A-P. Avisse and made by A-E-L. Guilleman, 1883. Right: eggshell porcelain coffee cup and saucer, 1872.*

Below left
*Sèvres. Two porcelain plates decorated by A. *Dammouse. c1880. Diameters 9¼in. and 9½in.*

Edo period. Heavy stoneware plates for kitchen use, with cobalt or iron decoration of natural forms, landscapes, etc., made during late 18th and early 19th centuries; manufacture declined in Meiji period. Manufacture of porcelain, established in early 19th century, partly superseded pottery production, much exported. Blue and white ware notable. Potters of district include H. and M. *Kawamoto. Family of H. *Kato continued use of temmoku glaze in Chinese style and, from early 19th century, made blue and white porcelain. Large quantities of folk art ware made from Meiji period.

Sèvres. French national porcelain manufacture. Established under royal privilege at Vincennes (Val-de-Marne) and, later, partly financed by Louis XV. Factory built at Sèvres (Hauts-de-Seine) in use from 1756. Production of soft-paste porcelain revived late 1840s. Limoges ware shown at Exhibition of French Industry in London (1849). Hard-paste porcelain slip-cast in imitation of Chinese Ming dynasty eggshell porcelain included in display at Great Exhibition (1851). *Pâte-sur-pâte* decoration developed by M-L. *Solon; later artists include A. *Dammouse and T. *Doat. Majolica with relief decoration made at experimental workshop (1852–76). Factory in operation at new site near St Cloud by 1876. A-E. *Carrier de Belleuse took revived post of art director in 1870s; modellers include A. *Rodin. Porcelain paste containing kaolin developed in early 1880s, resembling formula used in China. *Flambé, sang-de-boeuf,* and celadon glazes, and oriental styles of decoration used; artists include F. *Bracquemond and E. *Escallier. Earlier styles also reproduced. Under direction of T. *Deck (1887–91), soft paste containing silicates developed; range of colours increased. Stoneware (*grosse porcelaine*), evolved for architectural use, facilitated modelling by retaining plasticity for considerable time. Work in 1890s includes vases painted with flowers in style influenced by Art Nouveau. Unglazed porcelain figures modelled by A. *Léonard c1900. *Illustrations at Doat, T., Léonard, A.*

Sewell & Donkin. *See* St Anthony's Pottery.

sewing chair, lady's fancy sewing chair, or **tatting chair.** Low-seated side-chair, usually with canework seat and back. Common from 1830s in Britain.

sewing-machine chair. American chair, patented 1871. Chair and back rest tilt forward, corresponding to inclination of sewer's body; relieves stress on thighs, which would result from constant contact with seat front, and gives support to back.

shagreen. Name given to three types of untanned leather. Originally durable, waterproof, grainy hide from backs and flanks of Persian and

Architectural style Art Nouveau furniture, using fine-grained woods, e.g. citrus and mahogany. Pieces characterized by controlled linear design, absence of ornament and artificial aids such as paint. Examples include armchair, c1902, with two central splats each dividing at top to join yoke rail; curved arms with thinner, matching curves below; X-shaped stretchers.

Seto. Traditional Japanese ceramic centre, reputedly site of one of Six Old Kilns of Kamakura (1185–1338) and subsequent Muromachi periods. Early work includes stoneware with incised or stamped decoration, and brownish toned celadon glazes. Yellow or black glazed wares and, later, work with brushed decoration continued in production throughout

Shagreen. *Powder Compact and lipstick holder. Initials on compact set with marcasites. c1930.

Turkish wild ass (shagri). Soaked in lime water and dyed, (usually green, red, black, or occasionally blue) and used as covering on various boxes and containers. From 17th century, second type: camel, horse, and mule skin, artificially grained by pressing small seeds into hide, while still soft, then dried until firm, dyed (usually green or black) and highly polished. In 19th century, both types largely replaced by third form: noduled skins of various members of shark family, dried and dyed (usually green). Used into 20th century to cover articles including spectacle, card, and needle cases, workboxes, stamp boxes, canteens, desk and toilet sets.

Shahjehanpur (Utter Pradesh), India. Carpet weaving launched as cottage industry c1860 by ex-convict, Hussein Khan, who learnt craft in prison. Only cotton pile carpets made until c1910; woollen pile introduced later. All weavers Muslim.

Shaker furniture. Simple, strong, joined furniture made by Shakers (religious sect) in New England and New York State in late 18th and 19th centuries. Made originally for community members, with chair-making developing into industry supplying neighbouring towns and villages. Furniture was painted (chairs usually dark red), without decorative detail. Most distinctive piece: slat-backed chair designed to be hung on wooden wall rail. Slat-backed

Shaker furniture. Swivel chair, called revolver, willow and maple. From New Lebanon, New York, 1850–75. Height 28½in.

Richard Norman Shaw. Cradle and stand of carved, gilded, and painted wood.

rocking chair also typical. Output and quality declined from c1860. Style influenced K. *Klint and G. *Stickley.

shakudo-nanako. *See* Japanese swords.

shakujo. Japanese Buddhist cane, walking stick, or priest's sceptre. 1–3ft long; upper end decorated with metal ornaments from which hang six rings. Carried to ward off animals.

sharito. In Japanese Buddhist metalwork, relic holder, often fairly elaborate; shaped like small pagoda.

Shaw, Richard Norman (1831–1912). English architect. Designed small amount of furniture in Gothic Reform style, e.g. cabinet bookcase shown at 1862 Exhibition in London (now in Victoria & Albert Museum, London); also stained and painted furniture, c1882. Few pieces traced. Employed W. R. *Lethaby as principal assistant, 1881–93.

shelf-cluster or **mantel shelves.** Tiers of shelves fixed to wall above mantelpiece; often divided vertically, forming recesses for displaying china, glass, etc. May have moulded edges or ornamental frets, and turned work. Common in Britain from c1850; from c1870, often combined with *overmantel.

Sheraton style. Reproduction furniture style popular in Britain from c1870. Based on work of 18th century designer, Thomas Sheraton. Typical of style are reeded table and chair legs with splayed or claw feet; kidney-shaped table tops; round-ended writing desks, and chests of drawers. Term also used to distinguish light-coloured, slender furniture from Chippendale style examples. Also applied to Quaint style furniture made by J. S. *Henry.

Sherwin & Cotton. Staffordshire tile makers, working (1877–1911) at Vine Street, Hanley. Made many majolica tiles decorated with animals e.g. series of stags (c1890), and flowers. Portrait tiles modelled in relief and covered with *émaux ombrants, notably by G. *Cartlidge. Patented indentations undercut in reverse of tiles for more effective fixing. Mark: Staffordshire knot enclosed by double equilateral triangle outline, and name of firm; Sherwin's Patent Lock sometimes mentioned.

Shibayama. Family of Japanese *inro artists, founded late 18th century. Developed and specialized in style of *encrusted lacquer (also known as Shibayama) in which decorative surface covered with minute, intricately carved encrustations of various materials, including tinted ivory, mother-of-pearl, malachite, soapstone, coral, gold, silver and several metallic alloys. Designs realistic, portraying human, animal, and plant forms, executed with technical perfection and close attention to detail.

By mid 19th century, style extremely popular, and found on wide variety of lacquer objects, particularly inro and other miniature boxes, but also *netsuke, *ojime, and *kiseru-zutsu, and occasionally larger storage boxes and small cabinets. Works, often executed in conjunction with *Kajikawa lacquer artists, extremely ornate and detailed. During Meiji period, production in large quantity, mainly for Western export market, resulted in general deterioration of style and techniques. Production methods simplified; few original designs used, mainly stereotyped patterns composed almost exclusively of shallowly inlaid pieces of pre-carved and pre-tinted *raden, usually on ivory ground.

*Shibayama. Pair of vases. Inlaid panels surrounded by silver mounts; rest decorated in gold *gyobu. Late 19th century. Height 12in.*

Shichi-fuku-jin (Japanese, 'seven lucky gods'), or **household gods.** In Japanese mythology, group of seven gods personifying essential elements of wordly comfort, success and pleasure. Extremely popular as decorative subjects in various Japanese arts, most often portrayed singly or in variety of combinations, occasionally as complete group. *See* Benten, Bishamon, Daikoku, Ebisu, Fukurokuju, Hotei, Jurojin.

Shigaraki. Traditional Japanese pottery centre in Shiga prefecture. Pottery thought to have been produced since 13th century. Noted for tea ceremony ware; coarse, reddish-brown clay trickled with thick, transparent, bluish-green glaze. Production of hand-crafted pottery continues to present day.

Shigekichi, Ogata. *See* Kenzan VI.

Shiner, Cyril (b 1908). English silversmith; studied under Bernard Cuzner at Central School of Art, Birmingham; later taught at Vittoria Street School, Birmingham, to retirement in 1970. Early work in Art Deco style influenced by B. *Cuzner; silver, ivory, and jet box, on wooden base, with linear decoration, now in collection of Worshipful Company of Goldsmiths, London.

shingen tsuba. *See* tsuba.

Shinjo. Japanese folk pottery established in early 19th century. At first made porcelain, later specialized in kitchen ware, e.g. large jars and cooking pots. White glaze trickles over darker colour.

Shinner's Bridge. *See* Leach, Bernard; Haile, Samuel.

Shino wares. Japanese pottery, generally for tea ceremony use, made in Mino province from Momoyama period. Variety covered with thick whitish glaze, brushed with sketchy decoration e.g. of grasses, birds, or geometrical patterns in blue or brown. Grey Shino ware covered with red slip and carved under thick, greyish white glaze. Glaze of red ware thinly applied, tinted by iron compounds in slip. Some Shino wares possibly superseded by *Oribe wares at original kilns. Revived at Seto in early 19th century. Among traditional wares which influenced makers of folk art ware, notably T. *Arekawa and family of H. *Kato.

shin-shinto period. *See* Japanese swords.

ship's bell clock. Simple time-piece clock, made from c1850, with lever escapement and striking work. Usually fitted in circular brass case with back flange for screwing to bulkhead. Strikes at half-hourly intervals through four-hour nautical watches (duty periods). One bell sounded at 12.30, 4.30, and 8.30 a.m. and p.m., two bells at 1, 5, and 9, up to eight bells at 12, 4, and 8. Does not take into account dog (2-hour) watches, 4–6 p.m. and 6–8 p.m. (1, 2, 3, 4 bells, then 1, 2, 3, 8 bells, if struck by hand).

ship's lamp. Sturdy brass or copper oil lamp of hemispherical section, with broad, thick magnifying lens, designed to be hung at foremast head, and port and starboard sides of ship. Devised to meet Admiralty regulation of 1840, that sailing ships under way should carry bright light at foremast, green on starboard, red on port, to indicate whether on port or starboard tack. Made notably, with many other working lamps, by Miller & Sons, London.

Shiraisi. Japanese pottery kiln, near Kurume, Kyushu. Covered cooking pots, covered with orange and green lead glaze, and unglazed earthenware cups, made with reddish-brown clay body, regarded as typical of folk art movement.

Shirayamadani, Kataro (fl late 19th, early 20th centuries). Japanese pottery decorator, working in America at Rookwood Pottery. Carried out carved and moulded decoration, rare in Rookwood production, e.g. vase (1901) with design of geese and green, white, and tan matt glazes; also moulded inkwell and pen tray in form of waterlily pad and flower, with green and blue-green matt glazes.

Shirvan carpets. *See* Caucasian carpets.

Shisui or **Rokkaku** (1867-1950). Japanese lacquer artist and teacher. Major contributor to modern revival of lacquering art. 1904-08, attached to Boston Museum, Massachusetts. In Tokyo from 1909, first as lecturer then professor of Lacquer Art Department at Tokyo Academy of Fine Arts. Early works in classical style influenced primarily by teacher, O. *Shomin; later developed highly individual approach to style, subject matter, and technique.

Shomin, Ogawa (1841-91). Japanese lacquer artist. Among most important contributors to revival of lacquering art; helped organize Japan Lacquer Art Society (1889), and headed Lacquer Art Department at Tokyo Academy of Fine Arts from 1889. Style classical: excelled in copying old masters; reproduced and reconstructed numerous lacquer works in Imperial collection. Well-known for lacquer simulating bamboo and natural wood. Favourite motifs: cypress and pine trees.

Shoolbred, James, & Co. English furniture maker and retailer, active in London from c1870. Made wide range of household furniture in many styles. Known for Old English style furniture; also high-quality Anglo-Japanese style pieces designed by H. *Batley. Held exhibition of modern furniture, e.g. by *DIM, in 1928. Stamp: Jas, SHOOLBRED & CO.; some pieces labelled.

shop round. *See* pharmaceutical glass.

Shortt, William Hamilton (1883-1971). British railway engineer; in 1921, made first practical

*free pendulum clock, for use in observatories. Accurate to within 1 second in 10 years; only quartz and caesium clocks keep better time.

Shosai, Shirayama (1853-1923). Outstanding Japanese lacquer artist of Tokyo. Studied under Seino Sensai. Professor and later head of Lacquer Art Department at Tokyo Academy of Fine Arts. As court artist to Meiji Emperor, worked on lacquer decoration of Imperial Palace. Wide variety of lacquerware characterized by intricate, minutely detailed, subtle designs executed in numerous techniques. Best-known for outstanding nashiji, and for copies of work of master lacquer artist, Yamamoto Shunsho (1610-82).

Showa period. Present Japanese period, starting in 1926 and following *Taisho period.

Showa-To. Swords mass-produced for Japanese officers from 1926 and carried in World War II. Rise of nationalistic ideas in Japan during Showa period led to revival of sword-making. Stamp made up of character Sho (for Showa) and cherry blossom, often found on tang aboce signature of smith.

show globe. See carboy.

Shrub Hill Works. See Worcester.

Shu, Hirakata (b 1897). Japanese lacquer artist of Shinto priest family. Graduate and later professor (from 1930) of Kyoto Arts and Crafts School. Taught (from 1931) at Imperial Art Academy, Tokyo. Specialized in gold lacquer. Made carved and lacquered netsuke as hobby. *Na: Shujiro. *Chomei: Shu or Makie Shu.

Shufflebotham, Arthur (fl early 20th century). English ceramic decorator; worked in Bristol, then at South Wales Pottery (c1908-c1915). Painting of fruit or flowers characterized by bold, free brushwork.

Sicard, Jacques (fl late 19th, early 20th centuries). French potter. Studied techniques of iridescent glazes while working for C. *Massier. From 1901, in America, worked for S. *Weller. Introduced Sicardo ware, with floral designs, etc., painted in lustre on iridescent ground.

sideboard. Long dining-room cupboard with compartments and drawers for tableware; dates from mid 18th century in Britain and America. Early Victorian pieces have drawer-fitted top spanning twin pedestals which flank storage space for cellaret, open shelves; space generally enclosed by doors from c1860, pedestals eventually replaced by cupboard front. Basic shape popular throughout 19th century. Mirror back with hand-carved frame common c1860-c1875; replaced by wooden back - often ornamented - cupboards, shelves, etc. Naturalistic carving of vegetables, game, fruit, etc. common in Britain c1850-c1865, e.g. by G. *Robinson, T. *Tweedy, *Warwick school of carving; in America, c1860-c1875. Varied decoration includes leather panels, plaques, metalwork. Well-known models designed by B.J. *Talbert, W.R. *Lethaby, A.W.N. *Pugin. Several examples with curved cupboard base, wider curved skirt, and high back shelves for china made by *Morris & Co. during 1880s. 20th century examples by *Djo-

*Reginald Silver. Silver candlesticks, made in Birmingham for *Liberty & Co, 1906-07.*

Bourgeois, G. *Rietveld. Also made in Modernist style.

side-chair or **single chair.** Chair without arms.

siège de fantaisie. Loose French term for lavishly upholstered chair of transient popularity, e.g. boudeuse, confidante, etc. Dates from c1840.

Siimes, Aune (1909-64). Finnish ceramic artist. Worked at Arabia factory from 1930s. Early work in stoneware and chamotte, with thick, coloured glazes. Later, specialized in thin porcelain, making conical bowls of thin layers of white or tinted porcelain, increasing in number towards centre, and resulting in relief patterns of varying translucency; other bowls have applied geometrical patterns of dark porcelain on light. Porcelain jewellery includes necklaces of pearl-like beads, built up in form of mussel shells or leaves.

silicon ware. English stoneware, made 1880-1912 in London at Doulton workshop, Lambeth. Smooth light reddish body, fired at very high temperature, with smear glaze. Carved, incised, or perforated decoration, with applied relief or, occasionally, pâte-sur-pâte designs. Sometimes further ornamented with touches of gilding or copper lustre. Production ceased in 1912, revived in 1923 for limited edition of jugs, etc., to commemorate discovery of tomb of Tutankhamun; also used to make small number of bulb bowls. *Illustration at* Doulton & Co.

Silvena. Type of silvered glass developed c1900 by J. *Northwood for *Stevens & Williams. Made by sandwiching silver foil between layers of transparent crystal or coloured glass. Vessels

sometimes further embellished with trailings of coloured glass. Pieces sometimes marked S&W.

Silver, Reginald (1879-1965). English silver designer; worked in studio founded 1880 by father; designed silver from 1899, becoming one of first to work on *Liberty & Co. metalwork venture; pair of *Cymric candlesticks and pewter bowl now in Victoria & Albert Museum, London.

silver deposit glass. British art glass in which layer of silver deposited on surface of vessel gives impression of mesh-like filigree. Developed in 1870s by *Stevens & Williams. *Illustration at* Stevens & Williams.

silvered glass. Art glass popular in Britain and America from c1850. Made by pouring silver or colouring agent between two glass layers through pontil hole before sealing, or by coating thin-blown glass first with layer of silver, then with second glass layer. Associated in Britain chiefly with J. *Powell & Sons and *Stevens & Williams. *See also* Silvena and Silver Onyx glass.

Silver Onyx glass. American art glass giving illusion of glass object cased or plated in silver. Variant of *Onyx glass range (patented 1889). Made by painting pattern-moulded vessels with platinum lustre, then firing to fix stain. Body creamy opaque to pale orange opaline glass.

silverplate. American term for *electro-plate, now also used in Britain (not to be confused with Silver Plate, designating solid silver in Britain). Grades include standard plate, extra plate,

*Eliza Simmance. Two vases painted for *Doulton & Co. c 1880.*

also used enamel decoration over crackle glazes. Work signed H. Simmen.

Simpson, W. B., & Sons. English interior decorating firm. From c1869, decorated tiles and, mainly, tile panels. Work includes chimney decoration shown in International Exhibition at South Kensington (1871). Noted for tile panels surrounding roof garden of Bute Tower at Cardiff Castle, restored by W. *Burges (1876). Twelve panels illustrating Book of Kings bordered with animal designs in *pâte-sur-pâte*. Tiles,

bought undecorated, e.g. from Mintons or Maw & Co., sometimes bear embossed mark WB & S with large S.; monogram of WBS & S often found on panels.

simulated bamboo. Usually made from bird's-eye maple turned to imitate joints and shape of genuine bamboo; unpainted, sometimes gilded or stained. Widely used for chairs, cabinets, and bedroom suites in America, especially during 1880s.

Sinclair's American commonsense chair. American rocker with high, straight canework or fabric back, rush seat, turned legs and stretchers, and back posts surmounted by finials or knobs; side or armchair, dates from c1850. Exported to Britain during 1870s and 1880s.

sind lac. *See* Indian lac.

singing bird music box. First examples produced in 18th century by Swiss *Jacquet-Droz family, e.g. ornate spring-driven clockwork music box; when mechanism set in motion, oval lid flies up to reveal brilliantly coloured bird automaton, with flapping wings, moving head, articulated beak, to accompaniment of whistling bird song from small flute blown by miniature bellows, with sliding piston to alter pitch. When song completed, lid automatically shuts. Particularly elaborate Swiss examples in early 19th century, e.g. richly decorated with gold, and enamels; by late 19th century, process of production almost entirely industrialized, boxes e.g. in tortoiseshell, decorated in 18th century style.

Singing bird music box. Silver, probably German, set with pearls and semi-precious stones. Late 19th century. Width 5in.

Silvered glass. Goblet in blue and silver on crystal glass, made for Varnish & Co., London. Late 19th century.

double plate, triple plate, quadruple plate, and quintuple plate; not a reliable guide to thickness of plating.

Simeon, Henry (fl late 19th, 20th centuries). English ceramic designer, modeller, and painter. Work at Doulton workshop, Lambeth, London (1894-1936) includes stoneware jugs decorated with leaf motifs under ivory coloured salt-glaze (c1912). Vases, bowls, and plaques (1919-22) decorated in colours and designs inspired by pottery of Near East, in revival of late 19th century Doulton Persian Ware. In 1920s, painted large plaques with designs of fish and seaweed, or birds in foliage. Later vases decorated with coloured slip. Work initialled HS.

Simmance, Eliza (fl late 19th, early 20th centuries). English pottery decorator and designer. At Doulton workshop, Lambeth, London (c1873-1928), incised, carved, or modelled then coloured, designs of flowers, etc. Decoration also built up in coloured slips. Early work influenced by Italian design. Mark: capital S, with e at centre, or ES monogram. *Illustration at* Doulton & Co.

Simmen, Henri (1888-1963). Artist working in France from early 19th century. Made stoneware vases, e.g. covered with speckled buff salt-glaze, painted in brown with touches of gold enamel;

Skeleton clock. In form of cathedral. Three train movement made by John Smith & Son of Clerkenwell. c1860.

sitting chair. *See* spring chair.

sitz bath. *See* hip bath.

skeleton clock. Uncased clock, usually protected by glass dome or shade, designed to display mechanism and construction. Made from c1750 as horological curiosity or experimental display piece by individual makers in France, later in England, Austria, and rarely, America. Produced commercially from early 19th century. French style, made mainly in Paris, normally has inverted, Y-shaped, unpierced frame with going-barrel movement; English makers used shaped and fretted frames in variety of patterns usually with chain fusee movement. Wooden or marble base sometimes contains musical-box movement. Large numbers factory-produced from c1850 (particularly by Smith & Sons, London, and firms in Birmingham and Liverpool) to standard designs including floral, scroll, or lyre pattern, and schematic models of cathedrals and other imposing structures, e.g. Scott Memorial in Edinburgh. Many types shown by English and French makers at Great Exhibition (1851), gave impetus to industry: over 10,000 miniature skeleton clocks by V. *Pierret sold during exhibition. Quantity production continued to end of 19th century; types range from simple time-pieces to complex striking and chiming clocks, often highly finished and gilded, with ornamental finials, etc. Some manufacturers continued tradition of experimentation, using novel varieties of escapement, helical or epicyclic gearing, etc. Materials other than standard brass and steel occasionally used for novelty, e.g. clocks made entirely from ivory or papier-mâché. Signature or mark rarely added by maker; if present, indicates retailer, repairer, or owner.

skeleton movement. *See* bar movement.

skeleton watch. Watch with back glazed to show pierced, skeletonized movement; wound through dial, also sometimes pierced. Made from c1750; produced in Switzerland into 20th century. Also, special version of standard factory products made as traveller's sample.

Skellern, Victor (fl 20th century). English ceramic decorator. Worked at Wedgwood factory, then at Royal College of Art, London. Art director at Wedgwood from 1935. Designed black basalt vases buried with foundation stone of Barlaston factory (1938). Designed one of mugs commemorating bi-centenary of firm's foundation. Printed decoration for cream-coloured earthenware plates, etc., includes Forest Folk (squirrel, etc.).

skewer. Pin for holding meat together. Made of iron for cooking. Silver, for serving, used from early 18th century. Very early ones sold by the inch; later made in sets containing various lengths (6-15in.). Earliest skewer had loop terminal for easy removal. After 1770, terminal sometimes decorated to match pattern on flatware. In Victorian period, terminal in form of eagle, serpent, feathered arrow-end, stag's head, etc.

Skidmore, Francis A. (c1816-1896). English metalworker and silversmith; served apprenticeship to father Francis Skidmore, watchmaker, jeweller, and silversmith in Coventry, and studied historic metalwork; 1845 Francis Skidmore mark entered at Birmingham assay office; firm, known as Francis Skidmore & Son, produced first church plate same year; exhibited Gothic designs and ecclesiastical plate at Great Exhibition, London, 1851. Younger Skidmore initially designed plate for firm, in 1850s began making plate and metalwork for outside designers, notably Sir George Gilbert Scott; firm's small design studio included B. J. *Talbert in 1860s; 1861 business expanded to contain foundry for large base metalwork, and younger Skidmore went into partnership with six others to form Skidmore's Art Manufacturers Company; business taken over by another Birmingham firm in mid 1870s. Skidmore's work includes presentation tankard with crystal cover made 1864 for Nottingham Rifle Corps: body is of iron, lined with silver; massive ornaments of silver and gilt bronze are saw-pierced, enamelled, and set with precious stones, and elaborately engraved; filigree is used on surrounds and stone settings.

Skinner, Halycon (1824-1900). American inventor. Trained as general carpenter; became mechanical adviser (1849) to A. *Smith & Co. in New York. Designed handloom in 1850, applying *tapestry process to *ingrain carpets. Commissioned by Smith's in 1855 to design power loom to imitate hand-knotted Axminsters: first Axminster Tufting Loom patented 1856, perfected 1860. Altered and improved Richard Whytock's tapestry process loom. In 1872, redesigned tufting loom on new principle no longer imitating action of Axminster handloom, and patented it (1877) with Smith's as moquette loom (*see* spool Axminster). Invented and patented gripper (*see* gripper Axminster) but without incorporating it in loom, as earlier invention (nipper) already adopted in Axminster tufting looms. Sold to *Brinton, who devised gripper Axminster loom around it. Officially re-

tired from Smith's in 1899, but continued as adviser until death in following year.

skirt clip. Two metal clips, one fastening at waist, other at hem of skirt, connected by thin metal chain c25-c30in. long; enables wearer to raise hem of full skirt, e.g. when going downstairs. *See porte-jupe.*

slag glass. Pressed glass of opaque, and sometimes marbled, appearance; produced from 1840s, mainly in north of England. Glass mixed with colouring (brilliant blue, purple, cream, or black) and waste material from nearby iron and steel works. Popular for ornaments, spill vases, plates, jugs, and candlesticks, 1875-90. Often bears date and maker's mark; produced in quantity by G. *Davidson & Co., *Greener & Co., and *Sowerby's Ellison Glass Works. Term sometimes also applied to *lava glass and *end-of-day glass.

slat-back or **ladder-back chair.** Chair with four or five horizontal slats joining back uprights. Popular country chair in 18th century; 19th century examples by E. W. *Gimson and Sir G. *Russell. *See also* Shaker furniture.

slate. *See* painted slate.

Slater, John (fl late 19th, early 20th centuries). English ceramic decorator. Born in Derby; trained at Stoke-on-Trent School of Design, Staffordshire. Apprentice at Minton factory, then (c1877) joined Doulton factory, Burslem, as decorator, eventually becoming art director. Introduced lustre decoration; designs include mermaids, lobsters, and birds on yellow ground. Developed and patented method of decorating *chiné ware, used 1886-1914. By 1883, experimented with photographic process in transfer-printing earthenware; in 1889, patented technique using gelatin print, obtained from photographic negative of decoration. (Also patented improved joint for sanitary fittings.) Decoration includes flowers outlined in gold, painted on vases with modelled, gilded dragon, and portrait beakers in bone porcelain commemorating Queen Victoria's Diamond Jubilee and Federation of Australia.

Slag glass. Pressed glass jug made on Tyneside. Late 19th century. Height 4¾in.

slave clock. Consists of dial and hands, with usual train of motion wheels, but no independent movement; includes device for advancing hands synchronously with *master clock, e.g. by constant impulses energizing an electro-magnet every second, minute, or hour. Invented by A. *Bain in 1840. Also called dial works or impulse clock.

Sleepy Hollow chair. American term for lounge chair with concave, semi-circular, arched back, and continuous arms and yoke rail; derives from The Legend of Sleepy Hollow (1820) by Washington Irving. English models described as superior lounge chairs in W. *Smee & Sons catalogue of 1840. Term sometimes used in mid 19th century Britain for armchair with continuous seat and back, supported on two side arches.

slicker or **slick stone.** See linen smoother.

slide or **slider.** Small, sliding shelf fitted into desk, table, or chest carcase. Dates from c1750; common in 19th century pieces. Also, American term for *coaster.

slip decoration. Traditional ornament of earthenware with designs trailed in thin mixture of clay (slip), or incised through smooth coating of slip, e.g. in work of E. B. *Fishley or C. H. *Brannam in late 19th century England; also used for relief modelling, e.g. in work of E. *Elton. White trailed slip characteristic of early earthenware made by R. *Wells from c1909. B. *Leach used trailed slip designs on raku ware made in Japan in early 20th century and, soon after return to England, revived technique of moulding plates with marbled slip decoration. S. *Hamada aided Leach in experiments and continued use of slip decoration after return to Japan. Domestic ware decorated with slip, often trailed in black and/or white, by M. *Cardew, pupil of Leach. Other English artist potters who used slip decoration include S. *Haile and H. F. *Hammond. *Pâte-sur-pâte and *barbotine decoration also depend on use of slip. Thin, trailed lines of slip (*tube-lining) sometimes used to produce raised designs on tiles, vases, etc.

slipper chair. American side-chair with short legs, low seat, and high back. Dates from 18th century; *rococo style versions popular during 1850s and 1860s.

slipper rocker. 19th century American rocking chair with heavy, mahogany frame, button-upholstered seat and back (usually leather), and low, pierced arms.

Smee, William, & Sons. Wholesale and retail furniture manufacturers in London, active throughout 19th century. Made high-quality household furniture. Best known for manufacturers' catalogues: example published 1855 contained 600 designs.

smelling salt bottle. See pharmaceutical glass.

Smith, Alexander, & Company. American carpet manufacturers. Set up ingrain carpet factory at West Farms, New York, with H. *Skinner as mechanical adviser. Commissioned and patented Skinner's first Axminster tufting loom in 1856, sent it to London Exhibition, 1862, and sold rights in Brussels. Factory destroyed by fire in 1862 with all Skinner looms except that at

Exhibition; rebuilt at Yonkers, New York, with 100 tapestry ingrain looms and 30 Axminster tufting looms. Imported Richard Whytock's *tapestry process loom in 1870 to supersede ingrain, by then waning in popularity. Improved by Skinner. Patented and installed Skinner's Axminster moquette loom (see spool Axminster) in 1877; sold British rights to *Tomkinson & Adam in 1878. By 1889, 800 power looms in operation, and 3500 employees. Patented *Kleitos wide power loom in 1896; sold British rights to Tomkinson & Adam in 1900.

Smith, Sampson (1813–78). Potter at Longton, Staffordshire. Decorator of pottery from 1846. From 1851, made figures, including flat-backs and Staffordshire dogs, in white earthenware decorated in bright colours and sometimes gilded. Also made teapots, etc., with black glaze or lustre decoration. Marks (rare) include name in relief.

Smith, Stephen (fl mid 19th century). English silver manufacturer, inherited father's business, 1850. In partnership with William Nicholson from 1850; firm, Smith, Nicholson & Co., displayed work in naturalistic style at Great Exhibition, 1851. Contributed to Dublin and New York Exhibitions, 1853, and London International Exhibition, 1862. Products included many racing cups and testimonials in Rundell style, e.g. 28in. high parcel-gilt racing cup, 1868, embossed with classical scenes and ornamented with naturalistic acorns and oak leaves. Nicholson withdrew from firm 1864; Smith registered new mark, 1865, in partnership with son; business sold to Martin Goldstein, 1886.

Smith, Thomas C. See Union Porcelain Works.

Smith Brothers' or **ring vase.** Term for 19th century milk-glass vase either decorated by, or imitating work of, William, Alfred and Harry Smith, family of British glass decorators (father and sons) who emigrated to America c1855. Worked first for *Boston & Sandwich Glass Co., then *Mount Washington Glass Works. Founded own premises in New Bedford c1876. Known as ring vase because overpatterned with circular motifs. Also, decorated glass lamp bases and shades.

smoker's bow or **smoking chair.** Bow-shaped Windsor chair with low, continuous arms and yoke rail supported by seven or eight turned bobbins socketed into seats; sometimes has shaped, central back support and scrolled cresting. Dates from c1845 in Britain. cf firehouse Windsor chair.

smoking-room chair. Semi-circular chair with deep, padded, curved yoke rail supported on turned spindles, and projecting seat. Usually button-upholstered in leather. Dates from c1825 in Britain; used in smoking-room, library, or dining room.

smoking set. Usually consists of tray with cigar holder, ashtray, and matchbox. Made in America and England from c1880.

Smyrna, Turkey. Late 19th and early 20th century carpet production centre; most factories British run, using large Greek and Armenian labour force. Industry destroyed by 1st World War and ensuing war with Greece; weavers fled

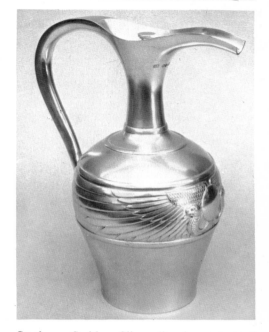

Stephen Smith. Silver-gilt jug stamped Goldsmiths Alliance Limited Cornhill London. Designed and made 1873.
Below
*Stephen Smith. Silver and parcel-gilt *racing trophy and cover, 1868–69.*

to Greece, creating boom in *Greek rug industry.

snuff mull. Scottish snuff container, made from 18th century to early 20th century, for table use

and in miniature portable version, known as baby mull. In table size, lidded silver gilt box, set into complete, stuffed ram's head, decorated with engraved monogram or emblem, lid set with gemstone, e.g. agate; or large, single silver mounted ram's horn, with container in root, and decorative silver lid. Baby mull of horn, with e.g. carved mask ornament, silver mounts, and furnished with silver accoutrements, including spoon, for extracting snuff; mallet, for tapping clogged snuff away from rim; poker for breaking up lumps; and brush, for cleaning away fragments adhering to exterior surface. All attached to mull by silver chain.

soap box. Lidded container for soap. Made from early 18th century. Usually spherical on moulded circular foot. Made in silver, brass, copper, with silver or sometimes gilt lining; some in cast and chased silver with glass or porcelain lining. Revived during Victorian period; forms more ornate.

soap bracket. Functional, openwork soap-holder, in e.g. brass, or copper wire, sometimes in fretted brass or silver-plate with decorated rim. Form with curving bracket designed to be hung on rim of bath; other types for fixing to wall. Quantities manufactured, especially in America in late 19th and early 20th centuries.

soap stand. Container for soap, with perforated inner stand to allow water to drain away. Made in brass, nickel-plated steel, glass, porcelain, etc.; may have beaded or embossed edges. Metal examples made in quantity in America, c1880-c1915.

sociable. *See* tête-à-tête.

Società Ceramica Richard. *See* Doccia; Ginori family.

sofa. Seat with arms and back, for two or more people. Term first used in early 18th century. Early Victorian examples in Britain usually rectangular with curved, shaped back; legs, arms, and back rails usually visible, often carved. American models include *triple-crested and *medallion-back sofas. *Spring upholstery resulted in increasingly ample proportions: deeply curved and shaped examples, with no wood visible, popular by c1880. Matching chairs often made. Remained popular as central feature of seating schemes; combined with two easy chairs to form three-piece suite in 1930s.

sofa-bed. Sofa convertible into canopied bed during 18th and early 19th centuries. Also, American *patent furniture, e.g. sofa with one inclined end and two mattresses joined by sliding hinges. Lower mattress revolves on two pivots centred on either end when seat is pulled outwards, upper mattress moving simultaneously until both reach horizontal plane; inclined end supports pillows; dates from 1872. Model also designed by H. A. H. *Aalto.

'soft forms' service. *See* Kåge, Wilhelm.

Soho Tapestry Works. Founded 1890 in Poland Street, London (on site of 18th century tapestry factory), by a Mr Brignolles, former weaver with *Royal Windsor Tapestry Manufactory. Specialized in Scottish subjects, e.g. The History of Clan MacIntosh; The Tragedy of Bog na

Gicht; Lady MacIntosh Raising the Clan for Prince Charles Edward. Closed 1910.

sokin. *See* chinkin-bori.

Soko, Morita (b 1879). Japanese netsuke artist of Tokyo. Pupil of M. *Joso; style influenced by *Kaigyokusai. Made large number of *katabori netsuke, carved in wood or occasionally ivory, distinguished by very delicate, detailed and realistic execution of subjects from nature. *Na: Kisaburo. *Chomei: Soko to, Soko koku, or Soko.

solid jasper. *See* jasper ware.

soli-fleur vase. Vase with tall, slender neck for single flower. Made in France in Art Nouveau style. Favourite product of Scandinavian glasshouses in 1920s and 1930s.

Solon, Marc-Louis or **Miles** (1835-1913). French porcelain modeller and decorator. Trained at Sèvres factory; noted for contribution to development of *pâte-sur-pâte* technique. In Britain from 1870, worked at Minton factory. Accounts of work and methods published 1894 and 1901. After leaving Mintons (1904), continued to decorate plaques independently, using *pâte-sur-pâte* or incised motifs. Early work carried out under pseudonym Miles; in England, signed work L. Solon. Other published writing describes English porcelain, stoneware of Low Countries and Germany, French faience, and Italian maiolica; pottery bibliography published in 1910. Son, L. V. *Solon, also worked at Minton factory. *Illustration at pâte-sur-pâte*.

Solon, Léon V. (1872-1957). English ceramic designer, son of M-L. *Solon. Trained at Hanley School of Art, then South Kensington School, London, until c1896. Art director and chief designer at Minton factory (1900-09); inspired by Alphonse Mucha, developed simple style, new to decoration of tiles, using variety of techniques, e.g. printing, or painting in raised slips on tinglazed earthenware. In America, from 1909, worked at *American Encaustic Tiling Co. in Ohio, also as interior decorator. Undertook colouring of architectural details and sculpture in Museum of Fine Arts, Philadelphia, and Rockefeller Center, New York. Also writer and painter.

Somada work or **green-shell decoration.** In Japanese lacquer, style of lavish, very colourful embedded *aogai decoration; developed and popularized by Somada lacquer family, founded mid 18th century. Term used to designate both work of family, and from late 19th century, all similar work. Technique: design, usually realistic picture, created with minute, paper-thin slivers of aogai (arranged in mosaic effect) and slightly larger pre-carved pieces embedded flush with surface lacquer, usually *roiro-nuri ground. Whole covered with transparent lacquer, then rubbed down to produce high finish. Sometimes found combined with other embedded materials, often with flecks of gold and/or silver.

By mid 19th century, style extremely popular for ornamenting lacquerware including: *inro, *sagemono, *netsuke, *ojime, *kiseru-zutsu, and numerous small boxes and cabinets. Patterns, drawn from vast range of pictorial subjects, exceedingly ornate and intricate. Usually used to cover entire decorative area; rarely combined

with other techniques. Main emphasis on technical expertise and ingenuity. From early Meiji period, continuing domestic demands plus burgeoning export trade to West led to increasingly commercialized production and deterioration in both technical and artistic quality. By the early 20th century, work characterized by lavish, stereotyped designs, pre-carved and then embedded into mediocre quality black lacquer, often over metal base.

Works executed by members of Somada family occasionally signed with family name, rarely with signature of individual artist.

SOON (ceramic mark). *See* Wells, Reginald.

Soubdinine, Séraphin (d 1944). Sculptor and potter; born in Nijni-Novgorod, worked in France. Made stoneware and porcelain, thrown or moulded; shapes rarely repeated. Mark: signature with drawing of seraph, usually impressed. Work includes covered stoneware vase with brownish body under white crackled glaze; also porcelain bottles with flattened spherical belly and long ribbed neck, covered in monochrome glazes.

soufflé dish. Dish for cooking and serving soufflés, made in two parts. Plain copper liner, for use in oven, and decorative outer case, into which liner placed for serving. Commonly plain, without feet; case in silver or electro-plate. Made c1870 in Britain and America.

'Soufflé' glaze. *See* Taylor, William Howson.

soup spoon. Spoon with round bowl, for eating soup. Made in silver or electro-plate; introduced as separate item in table setting c1880. Smaller version known as bouillon spoon.

Southern Porcelain Company. American pottery and porcelain factory, established 1856 at Kaolin, South Carolina. Made earthenware with brown glaze, white granite ware, and porcelain in styles made at United States Pottery, e.g. jugs with relief decoration on white or tinted ground (from c1860). Some glazed porcelain has gilded decoration. Marks include shield with S P/ COMPANY/ KAOLIN/ S C. Operated until 1876.

South Wales Pottery. Welsh pottery established (1840) at Llanelly, Carmarthenshire. Earthenware with transfer-printed or hand-painted decoration includes tableware and, in mid 19th century, figures and portrait busts. Bone porcelain lithophanes made in 1850s. Printed or impressed marks usually incorporate SOUTH WALES POTTERY or initials S.W.P. Art pottery, decorated e.g. by A. *Shufflebotham, made in early 20th century, marked with painted stencils LLANELLY, Llanelly Pottery, or Llanelly Art Pottery. Production ceased in 1921.

Southwick Pottery. English pottery established (1788) in Sunderland district (Durham). Earthenware made with brown glaze or, notably, printed lustre decoration of local views, e.g. Wearmouth Bridge; much exported. Pottery closed in 1896. Work also includes decorative ware with streaked glazes. Marks: names of members of Scott family (proprietors), Southwick, and sometimes name of ware.

souvenir. *See* aide-mémoire.

souvenir box. Small box (originally enamel, then other materials) painted with local view and sometimes with inscription, e.g. 'A trifle from . . .'. Produced in England (particularly Birmingham and South Staffordshire) from late 18th century.

sovereign balance. Small see-saw balance, with one arm terminating in two pans, for half-sovereigns and sovereigns, other end weighted. Commonly made of brass. Used until 1917 (when banknotes replaced sovereigns), notably by traders wishing to test genuineness of coin.

Sowerby's Ellison Glass Works. English glass-house in Gateshead, County Durham. Known variously as George Sowerby (c1824–1830s); New Stourbridge Flint Glass Works (1830s–1840s); John Sowerby (1840s–1854); Sowerby & Neville (c1855–c1872); Sowerby & Co. (c1872–1881); finally, Sowerby's Ellison Glass Works (from 1881). Noted chiefly for *pressed glass from 1887, especially vine patterns, dot patterns in low relief on square and non-spherical objects, asymmetrical plant groups, and Japanese-style figures. Also made opaque *opalescent glass and slag glass vessels (see vitro-porcelain), many with vertical surface fluting imitating basket-work. Trade mark for later 19th century pressed ware: peacock's head.

Spangled glass. American art glass patented 1883 by *Hobbs, Brockunier & Co. Colourless mica flakes suspended between double gather of clear and coloured glass, outer layer usually red, brown, or gold. Popular for glass baskets with deep ruffled rims and fancy handles, some further decorated with applied flowers and leaves. See also Vasa Murrhina.

Spanish carpets and tapestries. Industry stagnant from 18th to early 20th centuries, except for production of *Alpujarras. Throughout 19th and early 20th centuries, Royal Carpet Manufactory (Fabrica Real da Madrid) copied Gothic tapestries, Persian carpets, and 18th century French works, on high-warp handlooms. Spanish Aubussons made during 19th century; colours much stronger than in French Aubussons; black and turquoise popular, also metal threads. c1900, Count of Retamoso attempted to regenerate native industry. Several factories founded or revitalized in early 20th century with view to export; wider looms used, and Turkish knot replaced traditional Spanish single-warp knot.

Spanish chair. *Lady's easy chair without arms; has continuous seat and back, and scrolling at each end of side rails. Term dates from c1880.

Sparre, Louis (1866–1964). Swedish furniture maker and designer; born in Italy, settled and worked in Finland from 1891, after studying art in Paris. First designed dining-room furniture in 1894. Established *Iris factory (1896), and invited A. W. *Finch to start ceramics department (1897). Work basically rectilinear, emphasizing grain of wood, e.g. oak, ash, elm, sycamore, beech, walnut, or mahogany. Joints often conspicuous and echoed in slight decoration, e.g. of inlaid rectangular motifs. Designed metal hinges, keyhole covers, etc., for own furniture.

Sparta or **Isparta** (Anatolia). Largest centre of carpet production in 20th century Turkey.

Factories operated by Greek weavers in late 19th and early 20th centuries; copied early Turkish and Persian designs, and hybrid Aubussons with Tabriz border. Only Turkish centre to use Persian knot. Designs mostly Tabriz and Isfahan (Persian), Ushak, Ghiordes and Kula (Turkish). Also jail carpet industry, specializing in naturalistic scenes.

spatter glass. General term for British and American speckled, opaque-white, or coloured glass with fragments of metal or variegated coloured glass applied to surface, in contrast to e.g. aventurine, where metal spangles suspended in molten glass metal itself.

speaking clock. German bracket clock designed c1910. Announced time at one or five minute intervals as well as having conventional dial. 'Voice' recorded on grooved tape driven by separate clockwork motor and advanced automatically by time-keeping mechanism. Also, apparatus controlled by *master clock, 'speaking' time over telephone from recorded discs; introduced in 1936 in Britain.

specie or **storage jar.** Large, cylindrical storage container for drugs or other pharmaceutical materials. Earliest are ceramic. First glass specie jars date from late 18th century, virtually replacing ceramic jars by second half of 19th. Earliest of clear glass, but exposure to sunlight caused deterioration of contents, so interiors of jars painted. From 1830s, opaque glass used, often with elaborate heraldic and other surface painting and enamelling in vivid colours around identifying label; domed glass covers usually gilt, sulphur-yellow, or cream; some light maroon with gilt. Made in three sizes: 23in., 26in., and 31 in. English in origin, majority being made by York Flint Glass Co. (now Nation Glass Works, York); also, some by Maw of London from late 1860s. Imitated in France, where made in same three sizes, but French specie jars (sometimes with identifying drug names in English) have domed covers surmounted by long pyramidal spikes. By end of 19th century, larger specie jars gradually replaced in England by Winchester quart (tall, slim bottle with rounded shoulders, 80 fl oz capacity) and Corbyn bottle (quart-size squat bottle with sloping shoulders). See also pharmaceutical glass.

spelter. Synonym for zinc: smelted in England from c1730, much used during 19th century for cheap, decorative, cast articles, e.g. candlesticks, clock cases, statuettes. Terms, lead spelter, aluminium spelter, indicate alloys of zinc with those metals.

Spencer, Edward Napier Hitchcock (1872–1938). English designer and metalworker. Formed *Artificers' Guild with Montague Fordham, 1903; it continued until c1942, with branches in

Spelter. German cold-painted figure of Nubian woman leaning against bowl. Late 19th century. Height 33in.

Below
Edward Spencer. Bowl in hammered silver with chased geometrical ornament. Designed 1932. Height 2¼in.

London, Oxford, Cambridge. Founded short-lived Guild of St Michael 1905; member of Arts & Crafts Exhibition Society. Designed vases, etc. for Upchurch Pottery. Work sold through shops of Artificers' Guild. Used variety of materials in association with silver, e.g. wood, mother-of-pearl, ivory, shagreen. Nautilus Shell Cup, mounted in silver with embossed, chased, cast, and applied ornament, and a claret jug in silver with punched, embossed, and applied decoration, set with semi-precious stones, now in Perth City Art Gallery, Scotland. Mark: Artificers' Guild, London, date.

Sphinx, De. *See* Regout, Petrus.

spinel. Gemstone (magnesium aluminium oxide) in variety of colours: reds, blue, green, black, orange-yellow, and purple. Rose-red variety most prized, often confused with ruby, sometimes called Balas Ruby. Black Prince's 'ruby' in British Imperial State Crown is spinel.

spirit kettle. Kettle on stand, with methylated spirit burner. Introduced in early 18th century; produced throughout 19th century. 20th century examples include Art Nouveau silver samovar be H. *van de Velde. As part of silver tea service, spirit kettle sometimes in Sheffield plate or electro-plate, for reasons of economy. *See* Victorian silver styles.

split shot. Rapid method of weft insertion on *spool Axminster broadloom, invented in Kidderminster, Worcestershire; patented 1926.

Spode. *See* Copeland, William Taylor.

Spook school. Term sometimes used in England to describe Glasgow School designs. Derives from characteristic decoration of elongated figures surrounded by flowers, eyes, weeping spirits, etc.

spool Axminster. Loom, and carpet made on it (originally called Royal Axminster in Britain, moquette in America). Pile inserted into backing from prepared spools above loom, tuft by tuft, leaving no dead yarn at back (*cf* Wilton process). Unlimited range of colours possible practically and economically, but preparation of complete set of spools for each design slow, i.e., takes up to a week. Each spool (of same width as carpet) carries 30ft lengths of every yarn colour needed for one complete crosswise row of tufts. Prepared spools clipped into frame holding 252 short tubes side by side; each thread fed into correct tube mechanically. Endless chain carries spools in correct order above loom, and tubes insert yarn into warp; knives cut off amount of yarn necessary for tuft (less than 1in.). After insertion of thread, each spool is replaced in chain and carried on; thus same set of spools can be used for hundreds of rugs in same design. Present-day loom derives from H. *Skinner's second Axminster loom (patented 1877), which rapidly superseded all other types in popularity. Became known as spool Axminster with development of *gripper Axminster in 1890s. Dominated world market *c*1910–*c*1950. Wide spool Axminster (Kleitos) developed by A. *Smith & Co. of New York in 1896.

spool-gripper or **gripper-spool loom.** Invented *c*1900 by a Mr Felton of David Crabtree & Sons, loom makers to principal carpet manufacturers.

Sporting jewellery. Group of three stickpins, pair of cufflinks, and pendant. All c 1860.

Combines cheapness of production and flexibility in changing patterns of *gripper Axminster loom with unlimited colour range of *spool Axminster. Not generally installed by carpet factories until *c*1935, and made little impact on industry until after 2nd World War.

spool-turned or **Jenny Lind furniture.** American furniture style popular *c*1850–80; variant of Elizabethan style. Pieces simple, with spool-turned legs, bedposts, uprights, etc. Motifs (bobbin, knob, sausage, etc.) always in repeating units. Decoration usually of spool turnings, e.g. on crests, yoke rails, and finials; contrasting turnings often used for spindles. Popular for chairs, cabinets, etc. Maple, birch, black walnut, American hardwoods, or sometimes mahogany, used. First consistently mass-produced style. Named after popular Swedish opera singer, Jenny Lind, after American tour in 1850.

spoon tray or **spoon basket.** Shallow, boat-shaped tray with central handle, *c*7–10in. long; revived *c*1860–*c*1900 from early 18th century originals, mostly in America; made in silver and electro-plate; plated versions often with gilt linings; many baskets footed, and decorated with beading, or engraved grapes, leaves, flowers, etc.

sporting jewellery. Jewellery decorated with sporting subjects, i.e. horses, hounds, gun-dogs, game birds, fox masks, occasionally domestic pets. Popular from 1850s for men as cuff-links, studs, cravat and scarf pins. Most made in form of 'Essex' crystal; piece of cabochon cut rock crystal carved in intaglio and realistically painted from back. From 1870s, sporting jewellery fashionable for women; often in gold and

silver as riding-crop bar brooch, with central fox mask or jockey cap. Also brooches and *hatpins e.g. silver tennis racquets with pearl tennis ball, or golf clubs.

spring or **sitting chair.** American *patent furniture. Combined rocking and revolving chair: moves backwards, forwards, and sideways, on central pivot supported on stationary base of four splayed feet. Springs arrest violent movements, safety guard prevents chair tilting too far back. Invented 1853 for home use; original model (based on smoker's bow chair) forerunner of modern office desk chair. Spring easy chairs, piano stools, etc., popular during 1850s.

spring upholstery. Upholstery incorporating hour-glass shaped or triangular coils of iron or steel wire with bases and tops attached to strong cloth, e.g. canvas; foundation strengthened diagonally and around edges with whalebone or cane; top and back ends turned in to make box containing springs; top surface padded, then finished with fabric cover. Patents taken out in 18th century, e.g. for spiral spring for wheel carriages (c1769); first British patent registered in 1828 by London camp-equipment maker, Samuel Pratt. Spring upholstery in general use by c1850.

Springer & Lockett. See Conta & Boehme.

spun glass. Glass rods heated and drawn fine. Used by ancient Egyptians and Romans to make and decorate vessels and ornaments. Also used by Syrian and Islamic glass makers. Revived in 16th century Venice, spreading with *façon de Venise* to become part of glass maker's art. Later, used for delicate rigging on glass ships, and particularly popular in 19th century for friggers and ornamental animals, flowers, birds, and glass fountains (as individual specimens or ornamental groups). Epergnes, vases, and tableware decorated with fine, coloured threads spun by hand on revolving wheel. From c1840, used for weaving silk-like cloth. *Richardson & Sons granted patent in 1860s for glass-threading machine for applying finely-spun glass. *Illustration at* frigger.

Srinagar (Kashmir). Indian carpet making centre; greatest range of designs and widest export market of Indian centres. Noted for reproductions of classical oriental types, also *daris and *namdas. Industry stabilized in late 19th century by *Mitchell & Co., who secured European export market. Carpets especially popular from 1850s (following Great Exhibition of 1851) until c1906, with British royal family among patrons.

Stabler, Harold (1872-1945). English designer and craftsman. Studied at Kendal Art School, Westmorland, initially as cabinet maker then in metalwork. In charge of metalwork department at *Keswick School of Industrial Art (1898-99). Assistant to H. L. *Rathbone in Liverpool University Art School department of metalwork (1899). In London, taught at Sir John Cass Technical Institute from c1906; succeeded Rathbone as head of Institute's Art School, 1907-37. Commissioned to design tiles, still in existence at St Paul's Underground station, London. Followed H. *Wilson as instructor at Royal College of Art, 1912-26. With wife, Phoebe, designed and made ceramic figures,

Harold Stabler. Cup and cover in cast and chased silver with applied ornament, enamels and ivory stem.

decorative enamels, and some jewellery at own studio in Hammersmith. Stoneware group of boy and girl riding on bull (1912), decorated with coloured glazes, bears painted mark The Bull/ HAMMERSMITH. Mark, STABLER HAMMERSMITH LONDON 1915, incised, and S over Hammersmith Bridge, impressed, occurs on salt-glazed figure of girl wearing cloak. Phoebe Stabler designed salt-glazed figure of seated *putto,* marked STABLER, with number of model, date, and wavy lines, incised. Partner in *Carter, Stabler & Adams at Poole, Dorset from 1921. Designed figures made at Worcester in 1920s. Executed several large coats of arms, e.g. for Kendal Town Hall, Heal & Sons and Sir John Cass Institute in London. Designs produced in silver include presentation pieces for *Goldsmiths & Silversmiths Co., and *Wakeley & Wheeler; decoration enamelled and stamped in Chinese style. Also designed ashtray for *Adie Brothers to mark jubilee of King George V and Queen Mary. Commissioned to provide designs for prototype products in stainless steel for manufacturers, Firth Brown. Mark: Harold Stabler, London.

Stacy Marks, Henry (1829-98). English painter; also designer of ceramic decoration. Shakespearean subjects include wall plaques depicting Seven Ages of Man, painted at Minton's Art-Pottery Studio, shown at Vienna Exhibition of 1873; signed H. S. Marks. Also for Minton's designed medieval scenes, e.g. on earthenware vase (1877).

Staehr-Nielson, Eva (b 1911). Danish ceramic artist. Worked at Saxbo pottery of N. *Krebs from 1932. Designs for jars and vases made in stoneware, occasionally with carved relief decoration, finished with coloured glazes.

Staffordshire dogs. Chimney ornaments, usually made in pairs, often in form of King Charles spaniel seated without stand or plinth (comforter dogs), made in Staffordshire and elsewhere in England from c1850. Models before mid 19th century normally have rock or grassy base. Greyhounds, poodles, dalmations, etc., also made, in earthenware or bone porcelain, often with enamelled and gilded decoration. Producers include S. *Smith and *Kent & Parr. Early examples press-moulded; base closed or perforated with small hole to conceal roughness of interior. 20th century models slip-cast in plaster of Paris mould, sometimes fitted with glass eyes.

stained glass. Glass coloured or stained for use in windows. Major figure of 20th century stained glass work, J. *Albers; fine windows also made to designs of Pre-Raphaelite artists, e.g. E. *Burne-Jones. May also be found as small panes or roundels of coloured glass, either in single colours, or degenerating into glass paintings.

'stained glass' enamel. See plique-à-jour.

stainless steel. Type of steel containing chromium and nickel; strong, resistant to corrosion and heat; invented in 1913 by H. Brearley, at Firth Brown Research Laboratories, Sheffield. Used for bathroom accessories by J. J. Wiggin & Co., Walsall, Staffordshire, from 1928; Firth Brown made stainless steel tableware and cutlery designed by H. *Stabler. Not popular in England until after 1945, when designs of *Gense in Sweden and *Jensen in Denmark demonstrated new possibilities of material for cutlery.

Staite Murray, William (1881-1962). English artist potter. Initially painter and engineer, began experiments in pottery (c1912) in Kensington, London. Made earthenware with brushed decoration. After 1st World War, started to make stoneware in Rotherhithe; glazed vases, jars, etc., with flinty white body in high, wide shapes, usually undecorated, occasionally splashed or streaked, marked with scratched signature. At Brockley, Kent, built and patented kiln burning crude oil at high temperature. From early 1920s, work influenced by S. *Hamada; stoneware body, fired to yellow or reddish tone, often only partially glazed, sometimes with brushed or scratched decoration, marked with M in pentagon, impressed. In effort to make pottery accepted as art form, titled work, exhibited in art gallery, and demanded relatively high price. Pupils (from 1925) at Royal College of Art, South Kensington, include S. *Haile, H. *Mathews, and H. F. *Hammond. From c1936, shapes influenced by English medieval earthenware; later work characterized by conspicuously modelled feet. Some shapes tall and very narrow.

William Staite-Murray. Stoneware bottle with crackle glaze. c1938.

Wide range of high-quality glazes, usually in muted colours. In 1940, left England and settled in Rhodesia.

Stam, Mart (b1899). Dutch architect and town planner. Designed cantilevered chair of straight steel tubes joined by elbow pieces, 1924, highlighting possibilities inherent in strength of material; manufactured by *Thonet Brothers in 1926.

stamp box. Small, shallow box (c1½in. square) for storing postage stamps. Produced from mid 19th century, often as part of matching desk set. Materials include Tunbridge ware, natural and lacquered woods, papier-mâché, gold, silver, brass, enamel, and porcelain. Usually lavishly ornamented. Distinctive round Scottish variety (c1½in. diameter) made with tartan patterned cover, and inscribed with clan name.

standard lamp. Floor lamp in form of vertical column e.g. in brass, ormolu, wood, rising from heavy solid or footed base, and bearing one or more oil, paraffin, gas lamps, or electric bulb, usually with shade e.g. in glass. Early 19th century designs in Imperial Roman manner of French Empire style. Succeeding 19th century

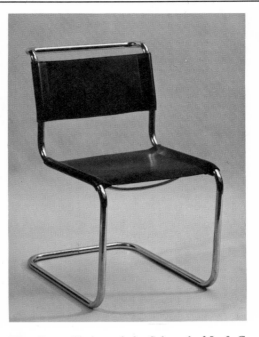

*Mart Stam. Chair made by Schorndorf L. & C. Arnold, and then by *Thonet Brothers in Vienna and Berlin. Tubular plated steel frame and canvas or leather seat and back. Designed 1926.*

examples show, variously, Gothic, Renaissance, Moorish styles. Many Art Deco versions, e.g. metal standard lamp by E. *Brandt (c1928) and Bauhaus-influenced aluminium floor lamp by American Donald Deskey (1923) for Radio City Music Hall.

statuary porcelain. See parian ware.

Stavrides, G.P. (f 1900–30). Greek carpet dealer and manufacturer; founded, bought, or managed carpet factories in India. Founded factory in e.g. *Gwalior (1902) at invitation of Maharajah; managed factory at *Warangal from 1925.

Staybrite. Trade-name of stainless steel ware made by T. Firth & Sons, Sheffield; Firths exhibited first Staybrite tea set in 1934.

steamer chair. See Derby chair.

Steiner, Henry (fl mid 19th century). Australian silversmith of German origin; worked in Adelaide (106 Rundle Street). Produced wide range of silver and electro-plated articles including cups, centrepieces, vases, caskets, and emu eggs; pieces are often heavy and lack elegance, e.g. commemorative group made to celebrate discovery of silver deposits at Broken Hill (1883), in form of tree with aborigines and animals below: stands 34in. high and weighs 116oz. Mark: H. STEINER or H. ST.

step cut. See gem cutting.

Stetson, Charles Walter (1858–1911). American painter; founder member of American *Art Workers' Guild, c1885. Painted cabinet made by S. *Burleigh. Settled in Italy, 1897.

Steuben Glass Works. American glass company founded 1903 in Corning, New York, by F. *Carder. Produced *Aurene, own version of

Steuben Glassworks. Rouge flambé vase. Made c1916. Height 7½in.

*Peachblow, *verre de soie, and other original art glass until merger (1918) with *Corning Glass Works. Thereafter, produced ponderous, over-complicated blown, cut, and engraved glass until reorganized by A. A. Houghton Jr, 1933, when sculptor, Sidney Waugh, became designer and flawless crystal with minimal cutting became primary objective. Many renowned artists subsequently invited to design or decorate products, e.g. S. *Dali, Jean Cocteau, Eric Gill, Jacob Epstein, Graham Sutherland, and L. *Whistler. Mark: STEUBEN, diamond engraved. Illustrations at Aurene glass, electric lamp.

Stevens, Alfred (1817–75). English sculptor, metalwork designer, and painter. Studied art in

*Alfred Stevens. *Electro-plated tankard produced for restaurant of Victoria & Albert Museum, London c1870.*

Italy 1833–42; appointed Assistant Master at Government School of Design, Somerset House, London, in 1845. Began producing designs in High Renaissance manner for Sheffield metal-working trades c1850; employed by H. E. Hoole & Co. to design grates, stoves, fenders, andirons, etc. for Great Exhibition, London (1851). After 1852, moved to London; worked on public and private commissions (e.g. on the Wellington monument intermittently for 18 years until death), but continued to send designs for silver and electro-plate to T. *Bradbury & Sons of Sheffield.

Stevengraph. Trade name for small, multi-colour silk pictures woven on modified Jacquard loom by Coventry firm of Thomas Stevens, from 1863. Stevengraphs in vogue until 1st World War; produced until 1940 Blitz. Most popular themes included: Lady Godiva and peeping Tom; historical tableaux; portraits of royalty, politicians, and of famous jockeys with their horses; sporting and hunting scenes; early locomotives.

Stevens & Williams. English glasshouse in Stourbridge, Worcestershire. Known for layered coloured glass from mid 1830s, etched glass in 1840s. Major period of importance from 1851, when became noted for: cameo glass (1880s), especially under art directorship of J. *Northwood and with work of J. *Hodgetts; rock crystal engraving (early 1880s), notably by Bohemian engraver, Joseph Keller (fl 1880s), sometimes in style of Chinese jades; *moss agate glass, *Silvena, and *silver deposit glass; centre-pieces with applied decoration of leaves or flowers; also, *Rusticana work (late 1880s), especially tall vases with leaf-like lobes and swelling bases, and *Alexandrite glass. In 1930s, made table and decorative ware to designs of architect, K. *Murray, becoming known for fine cutting in both flat and deep-slashed patterns. Some pieces signed S&W. *Illustrations also at Alabaster glass, Hodgetts, J.*

Stevenson & Co. *See* Derby.

Stickley, George and Albert (fl c1890–c1910). American furniture manufacturers; brothers of G. and L. & J. G. *Stickley. Worked in Grand Rapids, Michigan, from 1891; formed Stickley Brothers Co. c1900. Furniture similar to Craftsman furniture, often characterized by through tenons, but design, wood, and finish inferior; marketed as Quaint Furniture. Also produced independent designs resembling English *cottage furniture. George published The Craftsman Home (1907).

Stickley, Gustav (1857–1942). American furniture designer and manufacturer; exponent of Arts & Crafts Movement. Oldest of six brothers, including L. & J. G. *Stickley and G. & A. *Stickley. Trained as stonemason; designed chairs (mainly in American Colonial style) in youth. Formed company, Gustave (*sic*) Stickley of Syracuse, New York State, 1898. Visited Europe, meeting designers including C. F. A. *Voysey. Designed Craftsman furniture from c1900. In 1901, showed work at Pan-American International Exposition in Buffalo, New York

Above
Stevengraph. Columbus leaving Spain. In original mount inscribed: Woven in pure Silk at the Columbian Exposition, Chicago 1893 by the Stevengraph Works, Coventry Eng.

Below
*Stevens & Williams. Left to right: 1) Silveria vase, early 20th century. 2) Moss agate vase, early 20th century, height 5¾in. 3) *Silvered and *cameo glass vase, late 19th century.*

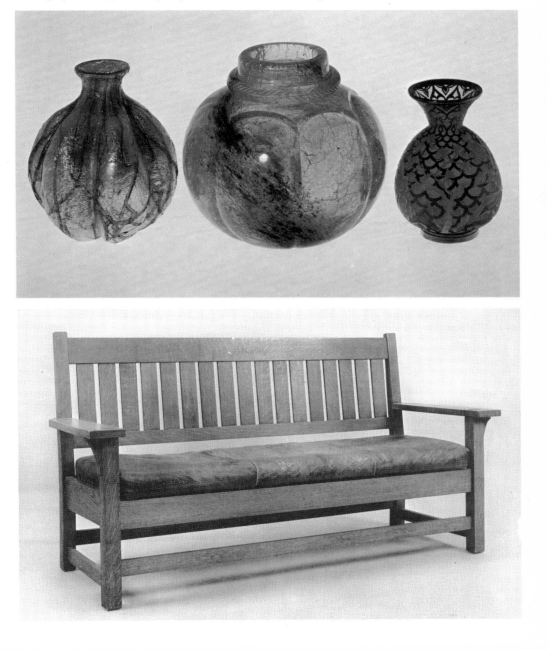

Right
Gustav Stickley. Oak settle with leather cushion. c1909. Height 3ft3in.

State, started The Craftsman, and founded *United Crafts. In 1905, moved administrative department from Syracuse to New York. Went bankrupt, 1915. Attempted, unsuccessfully, to sell new furniture lines (1916-17), loosely based on 18th century furniture styles, or in bright colours.

Stickley, Leopold and J. George (fl c1900-c1916). American furniture manufacturers; brothers of G. *Stickley; left his employment to found L. & J. G. Stickley at Fayetteville, New York State, in 1900. Based designs on Craftsman furniture, sometimes using veneers and laminated members. Pieces identifiable by Name, L. & J. G. Stickley, in red. Made furniture designed by F. L. *Wright (1900); *Morris chair (1910); reproduction furniture by 1914. Bought G. Stickley's factory in 1916, running business under name of Stickley Manufacturing Co.: firm still active, known for American Colonial style reproductions in cherrywood.

stippling. Glass engraving technique; design applied in tiny dots to surface by diamond point or steel needle imbedded in hammer. Dutch 18th century development. Used by e.g. L. *Whistler.

Stockton Art Pottery. California pottery, initially Stockton Terra Cotta Company. Art pottery (1891-1902), decorated with heavy coloured glazes, includes *jardinières*, pedestals, and vases; sold under name Rekston. Circular mark: STOCKTON/ CALIFORNIA, surrounding quartered circle with S,A,P, and C° in sections.

stomacher. Large jewelled ornament, usually of floral, girandole, or foliate cross design, worn over stiffened front piece of bodice; modified version of Elizabethan stomacher (stiffened triangular front part of bodice). Much worn in Britain and Europe from early 18th century. Returned to fashion at end of 19th century, when often part of *parure* of diamond jewellery.

stone glass. General term for marblized or stratified glass made in imitation of jasper, chalcedony, and other stones. Popular from antiquity, but especially during 19th century, e.g. *lithyalin glass. Other 19th and 20th century stone glasses include *agate, *moss agate, and *Mosaic Stone glass.

stopwatch. Timer that can be stopped or started by pushpiece in pendant or on side of case. Two distinct forms: *chronograph is timepiece with one or more second hands, sometimes mounted on auxiliary train; chronoscope shows minutes, seconds, and fractions of seconds only. Stopwatch has pocket watch case with crown and pendant; dial divided into 60 seconds by fifths, with seconds hand making complete revolution in one minute; minutes recorded by small hand revolving on subsidiary dial once every 30 minutes. Made from mid 18th century; with flyback seconds hand from 1862. (See A. Nicole.)

storage jar. See specie jar.

Storer, Maria Longworth Nichols. See Nichols, Maria Longworth.

Stourbridge (Worcestershire). Important English glass making centre from 17th century, when immigrant glassmakers from Lorraine

settled there. Major glasshouses from 1851: *Boulton & Mills, *Brierley Hill, *Davis, Greathead & Green, *Richardson & Sons, *Stevens & Williams, and T. *Webb & Sons. Area noted for fine quality glass metal, variety of colours, *rock crystal engraving, and individual styling and decoration. Ruby-red, blue, and opaque-white decoration popular, with classical flower and foliage motifs. Pressed glass produced from 1830s; ruby-stained glass with broad fluting from 1840s; three-lipped decanter with spherical stopper introduced 1870; glass-threading (see Richardson & Sons) popular in 1870s, particularly with old-gold coloured glass; cameo glass (see J. Northwood) produced on commercial scale from 1880s; fine paperweights from mid 19th century, mainly in pastel *millefiori* designs; also, weighted inkwells, scent bottles, door knobs, knife rests, and seals. See also W. Fritsche, F. Kny, and T. and G. Woodall.

Street, George Edmund (1824-81). English architect; employed P. *Webb. Designed oak bookcase in restrained Gothic style with incised and inlaid decoration, square-paned glass doors enclosing shelves in upper part, mirror in top stage; cupboard base has square, recessed panels, contains 15 drawers. Manufactured by *Holland & Sons, c1865.

Strömberg, Edvard (1872-1946). Swedish glass artist and technician; his technical knowledge of material created conditions necessary for artistic expansion of Scandinavian glass in 1920s and 1930s. Attached to *Kosta, 1917-18; *Ørrefors (as technical director) 1918-28; Eda glass works, 1925-33. In 1933, founded own factory in Småland where, with wife, designed and made decorative glass of limpid purity of line, either in transparent crystal or soft tones of mauve, grey, or very pale blue.

Strut clock. Small shallow-cased *travelling clock with easel-like strut or support at back. Popular in 1850s, but eventually replaced by folding clocks. Made notably by Thomas Cole, brother of J. F. *Cole, c1850. Ornate form known as boudoir clock.

stud box. Small lidded container (c1½in. across) for collar studs, usually circular or oval, often highly decorated. Made in gold, silver, silver-plate, ivory, or leather; produced from mid 19th century, when stiff collar and tie replaced stock and cravat, until 1930s.

student lamp. Adjustable desk or table *paraffin lamp, commonly in brass; burner, reservoir, and glass shade mounted on counterweighted bracket, which slides vertically on brass column with weighted base; tightening screw on bracket allows lamp to be set at desired height. Shade usually of green glass, with opalescent glass lining to direct maximum light downwards. American version known as Harvard lamp.

style number. See Patent Office Registration Mark.

Subes, Raymond (fl c1920-c1960). French metalworker. Designed and made wrought-iron furniture, particularly radiator covers; also decorative screens, gates, etc. in geometrical Art Deco style.

Süe et Mare or **Compagnie des Arts Français.** Parisian furniture manufacturers; also made carpets, textiles, etc. Established 1919 by Louis Süe (b 1875) and André Mare (1887-1932); development of L'Atelier Français founded in Paris by Süe, 1912. Known for Art Deco furniture characterized by swags of drapery, flower garlands, and sculpted reliefs, e.g. marble-topped chest of drawers, c1921, in burred amboyna on oak with carved rosewood decoration, bronze medallions on two drawers; turned legs continuous with side uprights. Responsible with R. *Mallet-Stevens, P. *Chareau, etc. for reception hall of French Embassy stand at Exposition Internationale des Arts Décoratifs, Paris, 1925.

sugar crusher or **cutter.** Implement for breaking down loaf sugar; widely produced in 19th century. Usually in steel; has two curved cutting blades; blunt spike projects from one handle to protect user's knuckles when levering against table. Later 19th century version has spring between handles. Table model has one handle fixed to polished wooden base.

sugar stand and spoon rack. Lidded bowl, usually vase-shaped, with rack for six or twelve spoons round outside; clear or coloured glass bowl is supported in electro-plate frame with ball or shaped feet, curved handles at sides, or single bail type handle on top. Use of sugar vase dates from 18th century; made with spoon rack, mostly in America, c1860-c1915; produced by many firms including Adelphi Silver Plate Co., B. F. Norris, Alister, and Otto Young & Co. Sometimes ornamented with flower motifs and finials shaped as butterflies, birds, etc.

suibyo. See kundika.

sulphides or **sulphures.** See cristallo-ceramie.

Sultanabad, now Arak (Feraghan), Persia. Carpet factories founded in 1880s by *Zeigler & Co. and Hotz & Sons. Extensive export trade with Europe and America in late 19th and early 20th centuries included Mahal, cheapest and least durable Persian factory carpet made before 1st World War. Thereafter, production wholly dependent on American trade; foreign designs, particularly floral patterns covering whole field, replaced traditional ones; 90% of carpets have rose ground. Industry disastrously affected by American Depression in 1930s. Sultanabad carpets sometimes called Zeiglers, after firm; also, in 20th century, any carpet from Feraghan area (including Sultanabad) may be termed Saruk.

sumi. See suzuri-bako.

sumie-togidashi, (Japanese, 'ink-picture togidashi') or **sumie-makie.** In Japanese lacquer, *togidashi simulating Japanese sumie brush painting. Design executed in powdered black lacquer, mixed where necessary with metallic (particularly silver) powders to produce desired shading. Ground usually unornamented silver or gold lacquer.

Summerly, Felix. See Cole, Sir Henry.

Summerly's Art Manufactures. Organization established 1847 by H. *Cole with aim of improving public taste. With cooperation of artists, manufacturers and designers, emphasized

Summerly's Art Manufactures. Silver decanter stoppers. designed by John Calcott Horsley and made by Benjamin Smith Junior. 1864.

need for decoration appropriate for article and related to use; preferred motifs drawn from nature. Designs commissioned from artists, e.g. J. *Bell, for production by established manufacturers. J. *Wedgwood & Sons, *Mintons, *Coalbrookdale Co., *Holland & Sons agreed to produce designs. Silver and plated goods made by *Broadhead & Atkin, J. *Dixon & Sons, and cutlery by J. *Rodgers & Sons. Earthenware jug (1847) decorated with hop-picking scene in relief, and parian figures, e.g. Bell's Dorothea (1847) made at Minton factory. Figures marked in relief with monogram including large S, name of artist and Minton ermine mark, all surrounded by double line. Silver includes salt cellar decorated with shrimps and seaweed, and breadknife decorated with corn-on-the-cob both by Bell. Glassware made to Cole's designs by *Richardson & Sons and other glasshouses; usually clear, with painted decoration, e.g. set of drinking glasses painted with aquatic plants. Designs often carried out in several materials, e.g. milk jug from earthenware tea service which won award of Society of Arts (1846) for Cole, under pseudonym Felix Summerly, later produced in glass and silver. Project ceased in 1851, although some designs produced by independent firms some years later.

Sunderland Pottery. English pottery established in early 19th century at Monkwearmouth, Durham, near Sunderland barracks; sometimes known as Garrison Pottery. Until closure (1865), produced earthenware with sponged, printed, and lustre decoration. Work includes jars, jugs, mugs, etc., decorated with local views and sayings (e.g. Forget Me Not), watch stands,

plaques, pottery eggs, and figures. Impressed marks incorporate names of various owners and SUNDERLAND POTTERY.

Sunflower Pottery. *See* Elton, Sir Edmund.

Sung glaze. *Flambé* glaze developed in early 20th century at Doulton factory, Burslem, Staffordshire, with additional colour obtained by use of metallic oxides, e.g. in marbled effect (veined Sung). Production interrupted, but resumed after 2nd World War.

sunlight recorder. Instrument for recording amount and intensity of sunlight. Versions include convex frame containing strip of cardboard, partly surrounding 4in. glass sphere; sun's rays, concentrated by sphere, burn trace on to strip, graduated in hours and tenths. Also, semi-cylindrical dark chamber with pinhole in flat side; focuses image of sun on graduated, photo-sensitive paper inside chamber.

sunray or **sunburst clock.** Wall clock with gilt case resembling stylized sun's rays. Derived from popular mid 18th century Italian frame for mirror or plaque. Case of gesso or ormolu; cheap versions of plaster, sprayed with gold paint. Introduced to England *c*1860 with French *drum movement. Most popular *c*1900–25.

Sunset and Moonlight suite. *See* De Morgan, William Frend.

Susse Frères. French bronze founders and editors; firm founded *c*1840 in Paris by J-V. Susse (1806–60) and J-B-A. Susse (1808–80). Edited sculpture by *animaliers* O. *Comoléra, P-J. *Mêne, among others. Work generally of high technical quality; many bronzes exported, e.g. to England. Casts bear stamp, SUSSE, often with

signature of artist.

Sussex chairs. Rural English chairs adapted and popularized by *Morris, Marshall, Faulkner & Co. in 1865. Examples include side-chair with cruciform back, and armchair with inward-curving back splats; both rush-seated. Also rush-seated elbow chair, known as *Morris elbow chair.

Süssmuth, Richard (b 1900). German glass artist, one of pioneers of Functionalist glass in Germany. Trained in Dresden, founding own factory there 1924. Established in Kassel from 1946. Work sober and simple in outline, with minimal decoration.

Sutherland table. Folding table with two rectangular flaps supported when open by single legs, usually turned, on castors; narrow central section rests on double gate-legs. Dates from early Victorian period in Britain; named after then Duchess of Sutherland.

Sütterlin, Ludwig (1865–1917). German graphic artist employed as designer by F. *Heckert in Petersdorf. Designed script, which was introduced into Prussian schools in 1915, and later into other German Länder.

*Susse Frères. Allegorical bronze figure of Art Revealing Herself to Science. Designed by E. Barrias and marked *Susse Frères Editeurs. Late 19th century. Height 16¾in.*

suzuri-bako (Japanese, 'ink-stone box'), or **writing box.** Shallow covered box, usually of wood, with numerous compartments for calligraphic materials. Square or rectangular ($c9 \times 8 \times 2$in.) often with sloping or rounded corners and domed lid (makaishi). Many examples lacquered, often with most detailed work on inner surface of lid. Designs usually strong, overall patterns, meticulously executed in variety of techniques. Lacquered sections inside box fitted with: ink-block (sumi); inkstone (suzuri), for grinding and preparing ink; lacquered water-container (mizuire); paper-punch, and brushes with lacquered handles. Often made as part of writing set including matching paper box (*ryoshi-bako), writing stand (bundai), and *fubako.

Swadlincote. *See* Ault, William.

swan chair. Wooden armchair designed by C. F. A. *Voysey, *c*1897. Has flat wooden seat, arm rests, and yoke rail as back rest; inclined back uprights, terminating in swan's head finials, and legs based on swan-neck curve.

Swaffield-Brown, Thomas (1845–1914). English silver designer and silversmith; designer for *Hunt & Roskell until 1887, winning National Medallion at 16; 1887–1914, head designer for W. Hutton & Sons. Noted for modelling human figures, small equestrian statues, racing trophies, etc. Helped found Sheffield Arts & Crafts Guild. Also authority on stained glass.

Swan, John Macallan (1847–1910). English sculptor and painter working in manner of French *animaliers;* studies at Royal Academy schools, London, and under E. *Frémiet in Paris. Subsequently produced series of animal bronzes, based on studies at London Zoological Gardens, exhibited at Royal Academy from 1878. Special exhibition of animal studies at Fine Art Society, 1897. Involved in Munich and Vienna Secessions, 1900; Royal Academician from 1905. Works include Young Himalayan Tiger with Ball (1889), Young Indian Leopard and Tortoise (1897).

Swedish rugs and tapestries. Sweden participated in late 19th century renaissance. Falling standards in traditional rug and tapestry craft, caused by industrialization, combated by new craft societies, starting in 1874 with Association Handarbetes Vänner (Association of Friends of Handcraft), who studied old peasant designs, and weaving and dyeing methods, and made e.g. ryas

*Suzuri-bako. Two tiers, cover (left) decorated in *hiramakie, interior fitted with suzuria, silver mizuire and rims. Signed Shomin. Late 19th century. Dimensions $7\frac{1}{2} \times 7 \times 3\frac{1}{2}$in.*

(*see* ryijy); several tapestries shown at Paris Exhibition of 1900. Johanna Brunsson Weaving School founded 1878 at Tångelanda; moved to Stockholm in 1889. Swedish artists involved in revival and production of new designs include C. *Larssen and Märta Måås-Fjetterström.

swing clock. French *novelty clock with girl on swing serving as pendulum; uses special type of anchor *escapement. First introduced commercially in 1855, although earlier Swiss examples exist; cheap *Black Forest version has girl suspended from spring as pendulum. *See* novelty clocks.

swing rocking chair. Name given to *platform rocker in Britain. First made by Scottish cabinet makers, *c*1897.

Swiss horological industry. Concentrated in Swiss Jura region. Clocks made in Neuchâtel include versions of cuckoo and *Comtoise clocks, never exported in significant quantities. Enamelling and case decoration industry established in Geneva from *c*1750; repeater work specialists from *c*1820 in Vallée-de-Joux. By 1800, Swiss watches manufactured by *ébauche* system; rough movement processed by series of specialists who added wheels, pinions, balance springs, etc., then passed to *repasseur*, who completed and adjusted watch. Machinery developed 1780–1850 (e.g. by Patek & Philippe, Gustave Leschot, P-F. *Ingold) to perform work previously done by hand, and to manufacture precisely interchangeable watch parts. Louis Audemar, of L. Audemar & Fils, made first Swiss watch with keyless winding, in 1838; Swiss lever escapement, with *sabot* escape wheel, developed *c*1840, but movements with Lépine cylinder escapement continued to be made into 20th century. Demand, particularly from France, for slim watches, directed Swiss industry towards production of fashionable ornamental and novelty watches. Swiss *Chinese duplex, with sweep-seconds hand and ornate jewelled case, made largely in Geneva, captured Chinese market from British by 1850. Exotic watches also exported to Turkey and India. Musical and repeater watches made in Vallée-de-Joux from *c*1830, e.g. with dummy figures appearing to strike hours. Watches mass-produced from 1867 by G. *Roskopf, using his pin pallet lever

escapement. Swiss industry suffered from German competition in 1870s, but Philadelphia Exhibition (1876) showing American methods of factory production led Swiss to reorganize industry on American lines. This, together with many horological improvements 1876–1914, gave Swiss increasing domination of world precision and cheap watch market, eclipsing first British, then American industries. *Wrist watches, introduced by firm of C. Girard-Perregaux from 1880, exported to England by Hans Wilsdorf by 1910, fully established by Swiss Exhibition of 1914. Water-resistant, hermetically sealed watch patented by H. Wilsdorf *c*1920. Automatic manufacturing processes developed by 1900. Jewellery watches made extensively from 1880, e.g. by Ramser & Tardy in Geneva, Perret Fils in Les Bronets, and Grübelin of Lucerne; watch movements incorporated in jewellery as e.g. insects, heads of flowers; popular in early 20th century. Many pendants and fob watches in Art Deco style shown at 1925 Paris Exhibition.

sword furniture or **ko-dogu.** In Japanese metalwork, metal mountings on sword, consisting of sword guard (*tsuba), pommels at top and bottom of hilt (fuchi and kashira), hilt ornaments (menuki), skewer (kogai), utility knife (kogatana).

Synchronome clock. Electric *master clock. Pendulum with *invar rod operates small count wheel which releases weighted lever every 30 seconds; as lever drops it gives impulse to pendulum through roller acting against sloping pallet on rod, then closes electrical contact. Current energizes electro-magnet to re-set lever and simultaneously pass signal to *slave clocks. Patented 1895 by F. Hope-Jones and G. B. Howell; further improvements patented 1905–07 by former. Synchronome Co., founded 1895, still in production.

synchronous or **mains clock.** Domestic clock operated by alternating current e.g. from mains; current drives electric motor geared to clock hands; clock therefore vulnerable to voltage

Synchronous clock. Synclock made by Everett, Edgcumbe & Co. 1931.

variations in mains supply. Patented 1914 by American, H. E. Warren. Later versions (Ferranti, Smith's) include hand-starting mechanism.

synthetic dyes. Various kinds; used almost universally by 1900, with *anilines still predominant. First acid dye, Nicholson blue, synthesized 1862, but not used commercially for several years. First sulphur dye (brown) synthesized 1873; first synthetic indigo in 1897. Metachrome dyes (mordant and dye applied simultaneously from same bath) discovered c1900. Modern disperse dyes developed from 1923; new dyes for artificial fibres (nylon, polyester, acrylic) from 1937. Most dyes developed after c1920 far more stable than early anilines.

syrup jar. Lidded jug for serving maple syrup, often with dish to catch drips. Numerous designs made in 19th century America, in glass (with electro-plated lid), electro-plate, etc., notably by *Meriden Britannia Co.

tabako-bon or **tabako-dansu.** Japanese tobacco cabinet ($c8 \times 10 \times 5$in.) made of wood, bamboo, porcelain, or metal. Interior fitted with several drawers for tobacco, and metal or porcelain container for live charcoal. Top surface has receptacle for ashes and hooks for hanging *kiseru. Many lacquered examples made, particularly in 19th century.

tabako-ire (Japanese, 'tobacco-container'). Japanese tobacco pouch in general use as *sagemono from Meiwa era (1764-72). In 19th century, popularity comparable to that of earlier Western vogue for snuff-boxes. Large quantity made in designs and styles for various occasions. Fine examples found of flat, rectangular cases in tooled and gilded leather, brocaded cloth, silk, etc., with flaps secured by ornamental metal clasps. Often made with matching *netsuke and *ojime, and worn attached to *kiseru-zutsu. Form produced into Taisho era, but popularity declined from mid 18th century with vogue for hard tobacco case, *tonkotsu.

tabatière à cage. See cagework box.

table or **tea bell.** Small, dome-shaped bell for summoning servants. Often embossed or engraved with overall patterns in high relief; also chased with classical or historical scenes; often gilded. Made in silver, electro-plate, brass.

table-chair. See chair-table.

tablette, étui à tablette, or **étui-souvenir.** *Aide-mémoire fitted with very thin ivory leaf or leaves (often bound in book form) and lead pencil. Fashionable in 18th century, then largely supplanted by *carnet de bal. Numerous copies made in late 19th century.

Tabriz. Persian carpet manufacturing and trading centre, and type of carpet made there: traditionally, low-pile carpet with fine, sharply outlined design, incorporating e.g. medallions or stylized flowers. Tabriz merchants first to produce Persian carpets expressly for export; by late 19th century, chief export centre for eastern and central Persian carpets. Began manufacturing copies of these for export, as well as native Tabriz designs. Also copied hunting carpets. English firm, *Zeigler & Co., set up looms c1880,

Tabriz. Rug signed with star, bottom right, for Benlian. c1900.

making range specifically for Western market. Persian traders imitated their success; requisitioned designs, colour schemes, weavers and dyers from *Kirman, and also had Ardebil, Feraghan, and Sehna carpets copied. First Persian carpet centre to use aniline dyes: their tendency to fade, with American demand for thick pile, led to abandonment of traditional Tabriz designs. American companies entered field c1900. German firm, Petag Persisch Teppich Gesellschaft (Petag Persian Carpet Co.), established export business 1911, reinstating old methods of hand knotting and vegetable dyeing, high quality materials, and traditional designs; looms and warehouses destroyed by Russians early in 1st World War, but industry revived in 1920.

Number of Armenian weavers worked in Tabriz c1900-20; made copies of early Turkish carpets, with signature woven in inside border; most notable weaver, Benlian (signature always accompanied by a star).

tachi. See Japanese swords, tsuba.

Tachikui. Japanese folk pottery kiln in Hyogo prefecture. Domestic ware with black, white, or brown glaze includes bottles, jars, vases, and charcoal burners. Some small jars have brown or

black glaze trickled over white ground. Saké bottles also made, with designs in blue or black on brown. Production continues to present day.

Taft, J. S., & Co. See Hampshire Pottery.

taille d'épargne. In jewellery, engraved line designs filled with black or blue enamel. In 19th century, mainly used to decorate mounts of mourning jewellery; also found on solid gold bangles, popular in America from 1860s until c1900 and buttons and studs. Designs generally interlacing lines and fine scrolls.

Taisho period. (1912-26). Japanese period; many ceramics strongly influenced by earlier styles. Traditionalist potters include K. *Rosanjin and H. *Itaya working near Tokyo, M. *Ishiguro of Kyoto, and T. *Arekawa and *Kato family in Seto area. Several potters at Bizen continued earlier local styles, mainly producing tea ceremony wares. Pottery of late Taisho and present Showa periods dominated by growth of interest in folk pottery, often influenced by wares of Korean Yi dynasty.

takamakie (Japanese, 'raised sown-picture'). In Japanese lacquer, raised gold *makie used from 14th century to present, mainly to indicate near-perspective in main design, usually combined with flat lacquer techniques on variety of grounds, including black, coloured, or *nashiji lacquer, or plain wood or metal. Technique: design transferred from paper to prepared ground, and built up in sections with raising lacquer for low relief or with several coats of *sabi and then with raising lacquer for high relief. Finally, desired portions dusted with gold and details added before final polishing. Also generic term for all raised gold lacquer including that with metallic or mother-of-pearl encrustations. *Illustration at* Kobako.

takaramono (Japanese, 'treasures'). In Japanese ornament, frequently portrayed group of 21 objects symbolizing desire for comfort, happiness and wealth. Found either singly or in groups, most often as cargo on treasure ship (takarabune), or associated with *Shichi-fuku-jin. Most frequently depicted objects: choji (clove) for health; fundo (weight), commercial success; kagi (key), wealth and security; kakuregasa (hat of invisibility) and kakuremino (straw cloak of invisibility), protection from danger; kanebukuro (purse), infinite wealth; makimono (scrolls), wisdom; shippo (precious things), all that is valued, occasionally used as alternative term for takaramono; tsuchi (mallet), wealth and good fortune; tama (everlasting or sacred jewel).

Takeda, Kokusai. See Kokusai, Ozaki.

Takeuchi, Kyuichi or Kengaro. See Kyuichi.

Talbert, Bruce James (1838-81). English industrial and furniture designer; trained as architect in Scotland. Designed for F. A. *Skidmore from c1862. Designed furniture for *Doveston, Bird & Hull, 1862-65. Moved to London, 1865, gaining reputation as furniture designer. Also designed for several leading London silversmiths; ewer in silver and parcel gilt, made for Skidmore's Art Manufacturers Co., 1866-67, now in Victoria & Albert Museum,

Bruce James Talbert. Pet sideboard made by
*Gillow. 1871.
Below
Bruce James Talbert. Silver and parcel-gilt ewer.
Maker's mark: Skidmore Art Manufacturers
Company. Birmingham, 1866-67.

London. Won medals at international exhibitions, e.g. for oak sideboard (made by *Holland & Sons) at Universal Exhibition, Paris, 1867. Other furniture designs for e.g. *Gillow, *Collinson & Lock, and *Marsh, Jones & Cribb. Proponent of Early English style; published book of designs, 'Gothic Forms Applied to Furniture, Metalwork, and Decoration for Domestic Purposes' (Birmingham 1867). Disliked veneers; suggested woods too finely grained to be used in construction should be inserted as small panels contrasting with plainer woods. Advocated use of tiles on furniture. Bulky heavy pieces, lightened by panels, Gothic tracery, metalwork, etc. Theories influenced American furniture, e.g. tiles in Japanese style pieces, furniture by *Mitchell & Rammelsberg. Awarded Society of Arts silver medal for metalwork design, 1871. Pet sideboard, made by Gillow (shown at South Kensington Exhibition, London, 1873) has oak body with carved boxwood panels and metal hinges; now in Victoria & Albert Museum, London. Published 'Examples of Ancient and Modern Furniture' (1876), propounding Jacobean style.

tamago-ji. *See* keiran-nuri.

Tanaka Minosake Ryukei. *See* Mondo.

Tanaka School. 19th century Japanese sword furniture makers. Founded by Tanaka Toryusai Kiyonaga (fl c1867). Influenced by M. *Ishiguro but mainly self-taught. Dragons and landscapes frequently subjects. Style characterized by raised border with irregular internal outline, and by soft modelling of ground to resemble coarse-grained leather.

tang. *See* tsuba.

tanto. *See* Japanese swords.

tapestry process or **warp-tinting.** Economical method of weaving design into carpet; also eliminates expensive dead yarn in back. Evolved 1833 from technique used for velour by Richard Whytock of Edinburgh (inventor of screw propellor for ships). Technique uses parti-coloured worsted warp already printed with necessary colours in correct order, instead of different yarn for each colour required. 150 shades possible in one carpet; average 30-40 (contemporary methods, requiring separate frame for each colour, limited to four or five). Warps are wound round large drums and dye applied with felt-ended stick, then unwound, washed, and re-wound in correct order on beam, with pattern showing in elongated form, to allow for length taken up by pile. Both cut and looped pile carpets made. Rights leased in 1844 to *Crossley of Halifax, who improved process, then other English and American firms, e.g. *Brinton. Halifax soon became English centre for tapestry carpets, rivalling Brussels production (with 1300 looms to 2500 Brussels looms) by 1850. Looms adapted to steam power by Crossley in England, E. *Bigelow in America, c1850. Production continued until 1930s, when superseded by *tufted process. Now used only by Schoeller of Düren, Germany.

Tassie, William (1777-1860). English glass artist. With uncle, James Tassie (1735-99), decorated glassware with ceramic paste portraits and medallions in opaque-white relief, which greatly influenced development of A. *Pellatt's *cristallo-ceramie* work.

tatting chair. *See* sewing chair.

Taylor, Smith & Taylor Co. American pottery established (1896) at East Liverpool, Ohio. Produced earthenware, ironstone china, and porcelain for domestic use. Marks from early 20th century include initials TST in interlocking circles with winged beast and VITREOUS.

Taylor, Robert Minton (fl mid to late 19th century). English potter. Partner in Mintons Ltd (1863-68). Established Robert Minton Taylor Tile Works, 1869-75, in Fenton, Staffordshire. Prevented by injunction from marking tiles with name Minton. From 1875, manager of tile company run by C. M. *Campbell.

Taylor, William Howson (1876-1935). English art potter. While studying at Birmingham School of Art, where father principal, carried out experiments at small kiln in nearby Edgbaston. Established Ruskin Pottery in West Smethwick, Birmingham, at site bought in 1898. Began commercial production after three years of experimentation. Made 'Soufflé' ware with glaze in single colour note or mottled, clouded, or shaded with harmonizing colour. Tones range from dark blues and greens to turquoise and apple-green, and purple to mauve and pink, also greys and celadons. Plant forms often painted on flat coloured ground. Lustre glazes, e.g. in lemon-yellow or orange sometimes used over painted designs in green or brown. Pearl lustre, sometimes with blistered texture, also used, often with kingfisher-blue glaze. High-temperature glazes noted for variety of colour, texture, and pattern. *Flambé* glazes often scattered with viridian spots achieved by use of copper salts. From c1929,

William Howson Taylor. Group of earthenware vases and bowl made at Ruskin Pottery. Dated 1898–1935.

introduced matt and crystalline glazes. Heavily-potted vases, etc., covered with blue, green, orange, or crystalline blue with frosted effect. Secrets of glazes carefully guarded, and notes destroyed. Vase forms Chinese inspired. Other products include bowls, jars, cups, egg-cups, dishes for butter or sweets, candlesticks, and hat pins, buttons, cuff links, etc. Some pieces mounted in silver. Clay normally obtained locally, although thinly-potted work with high temperature glazes hand-thrown in Cornish clay. Marks include Ruskin; permission to use name formally obtained 1909, though mark appears from 1899. Taylor's name used as mark until c1903. Scissors usually painted under glaze, sometimes scratched, used until c1920, and occasionally later. Most pieces dated. Factory ceased production in late 1933, although glazing and firing of earlier work continued until 1935.

Taylor, William Watts (d 1913). American potter; manager of *Rookwood Pottery from 1883, owner from 1900. Responsible for increase in production of art pottery, introduced new lines and developed those which sold well. Instituted selective distribution, restricting sale of pottery to one retailer per city. Business showed profit by 1886 and recouped all early losses by 1889.

Taylor & Speeler. American pottery; first manufacturers of Rockingham ware at Trenton, New Jersey, established 1852. Products include relief decorated jugs in Rockingham ware and yellow earthenware. Also produced white earthenware and granite ware, trading from mid 1850s as Taylor, Speeler & Bloor. Ceased operation in 1870s.

tchou-ts'i. *See* cinnabar lacquer.

tea bell. *See* table bell.

tea caddy or **canister** (term caddy derives from Malay, 'Kati', a weight of c1lb). Lidded storage container for tea, introduced into Britain in early 18th century; usually made in pairs, originally for green and black tea; silver examples produced throughout 19th century, with extensive decoration applied from c1850 to emergence of Art Nouveau; from c1900, silver generally replaced by cheaper materials, electro-plate, japanned tin, etc.

tea ceremony or **cha-no-yu** (Japanese, 'hot water for tea'). Ritual connected with drinking of tea; originated in China, but developed by Japanese into complicated system of etiquette with aim of spiritual training. Regarded as reaching height of expression in 16th century; continued to present day. Equipment, including tea bowls, water jar, tray for charcoal brazier, containers for powdered or leaf tea, rest for spoons, and vase for flowers, many made in ceramics, brought pottery to prominence as art form. Teamasters influenced Japanese ceramics through own opinions and requirements, by themselves working as potters, and by patronage of little-known kilns in search for suitable wares. Thickness of potting governed by ability to retain right amount of heat. Stylistic simplicity important; irregular forms with unassuming colours and decoration preferred. Early tea ceremony ware imported from China and Korea. Production in Japan (from 16th century) began as imitation of Chinese bowls and tea jars at Seto (Owari). Raku ware made almost entirely for use in tea ceremony.

tea ceremony utensils (in Japanese lacquer). Among finest examples of Japanese lacquer made for use in traditional tea ceremony. Most important items: *kogo and *kobako, used to hold incense in summer; *natsume, tea caddy for summer ceremony; cha-dansu (tea-cabinet): chawan (tea-bowl), c3in. in diameter and 4in. high; sweetmeat trays; satsu-bako, rectangular box, c5×7×4in., fitted with tray and used to hold utensils.

tea infuser. Implement shaped like double spoon, with two perforated bowls; top one hinged. With tea leaves inside, placed in cup; boiling water added to make single cup of tea. Produced in silver or electro-plate from c1870.

tea and coffee set. Matching service including teapot, coffee pot, milk jug, tea kettle, and sugar bowl, sometimes with sugar tongs and tea spoons; normally made in silver; some found from late 18th century, but widely used from mid 19th century in forms following contemporary styles from rococo to functionalism. Bachelor tea set with pot of two-cup capacity, popular in 1880s, often of very high quality.

tea urn. Large vase-shaped vessel for hot water, with tap at base; kept hot with hot iron inserted into socket in centre, or by spirit burner beneath. Large copper version made from c1820 for use e.g. in inns; later made in electro-plate; silver examples rare in 19th century, though some Georgian reproductions.

tebako (Japanese, 'hand-box'). Japanese lacquer toilet box (c9×7×6½in.) composed either of single box or two-tiered sections; sometimes footed. Usually in gold or black, and often decorated with delicate designs, mainly floral or plant. Long sides of box often fitted with metal (particularly silver or copper alloy) mountings to attach silk cords which are tied over lid. Widely produced in 19th and 20th centuries; many exported to West from late 19th century.

Teco Pottery. American pottery operating at Terra Cotta, Illinois, in early 20th century. Matt green glazes frequently used on shapes derived from natural forms.

tekishitsu. *See* choshitsu.

Telegraph Manufacturing Co. *See* Hipp, Matthäus.

telescopic or **extension table.** Table extendable by addition of extra leaves. Circular, round-ended, or rectangular models with deep skirts, sometimes moulded, concealing telescopic bed. Central support or turned, corner legs; latter popular in Britain c1880–c1900. Common in America c1840–70; in Britain, from late 18th century.

tell-tale clock. Watchman's clock invented in late 18th century by John Whitehurst of Derby. Rotating ring, set with projecting pins, driven by 12 or 24 hour movement so that pins successively appear in aperture every half hour. On arrival, watchman depressed pin by pushpiece; if late on watch, pin had rotated beyond aperture. More recent models, e.g. *Dent's recording clock, use type key inserted through aperture, which records time on revolving paper dial within clock.

temmoku glaze. Iron-rich glaze in shades of dark brown and black, associated in Japan first with tea ceremony ware made in Seto area, inspired by Sung Chinese tea bowls from Fukien. Production continued notably in kilns of Mino province. Used at *Naeshirogawa on island of Kyushu, and by *Tsuboya potters in Okinawa. 20th century examples made e.g. by family of H. *Kato in Seto area, Kyoto potters K. *Kawai and M. *Isheguro; also S. *Hamada and other folk art potters in Mashiko.

Templeton, James (b 1802). Scottish carpet manufacturer. Travelled in Mexico, then joined dress fabric manufacturers in Glasgow, and, in 1829, set up independently producing Paisley shawls on cottage industry basis. Catered to fashion for silk chenille shawls. With one of his weavers, devised modification of chenille velvet technique and applied it to pile carpets and furnishings. Founded factory in Glasgow in 1839 to

manufacture *chenille Axminster carpets. Received first of several royal commissions from Queen Victoria for carpet. In 1850, licenced other carpet manufacturers to use invention. Production concentrated on single carpets made to order, 27in. widths for stock and export to America, hearth rugs, and furnishings. Best known carpets included Twelve Apostles, made for Paris Exhibition of 1867, and Christ Blessing the Little Children, made for Paris Exhibition of 1876. Used handlooms until 1884, then adopted *Tomkinson & Adam's power loom. In 1888, secured British rights on E. *Bigelow's variant of H. *Skinner's Axminster loom, developed it, and thereafter used it instead of Royal Axminster loom. Launched *Imperial Axminster carpet, c1893. Installed 9ft *Kleitos loom c1900. In 1930s, produced *crush-resistant carpets. Until recently, only remaining British firm making Chenille carpets, using widest (33ft) loom in Britain.

Templier, Raymond (b 1891). French artist, jeweller, and designer. Designed and made jewellery for family firm of Templier in Paris (founded 1849 by grandfather). Exhibited widely from 1911. Founder member of Union des Artistes Modernes. Produced typical Art Deco jewellery in 1920s and 1930s.

teppitsu-bori. See Tessai, Kano.

terracotta. Red earthenware used for decorative and architectural ware. Normally unglazed, although articles for domestic use have to be

Raymond Templier. Necklace in platinum, diamonds, and black enamel, 1929. Centre: two brooches and ring, made of platinum, diamonds, and black onyx, all designed 1937.

lined with glaze, since slightly porous. Used extensively in mid and late 19th century for production of garden ornaments, vases, fountains, etc.; also figures and tableware. English makers include Minton factory, F. & R. Pratt & Co., firm of W. T. *Copeland, Doulton workshop, Lambeth (work of G. *Tinworth notable), Pinder, Bourne & Co., and Watcombe Pottery. Vases, etc., decorated by T. *Battam. In America, moulded ornament designed by architects, produced for use by builders.

Terry, Silas Burnham (1807-76). American; maker of shelf, steeple, and wall clocks. Son of pioneer horologist, Eli Terry, and apprenticed to him in Connecticut. Produced marine movement, c1850: new movement in strip brass for Connecticut clocks, using balance wheel instead of pendulum control.

Tessai, Kano (1845-1925). Japanese painter and master-carver, born in Gifu. From 1875, concentrated on carving, working primarily in Tokyo. From 1890, professor of Sculpture Department at *Tokyo Academy of Fine Arts. Master of numerous carving techniques in various materials, and originator of teppitsu-bori, lacquer engraving technique in which landscapes, figures, etc. appear on flat surface. Made numerous carved netsuke, okimono, and ojime. Particularly noted for netsuke copied from old Noh masks. *Na: Kotaro, *Go: Tessai.

testimonials. See racing trophies.

tête-à-tête, conversation chair or **sociable.** Two circular seats, contained in curves of continuous S-shaped arm rail, allowing occupants to hold private conversation. Popular in 19th century Europe and America.

Tettau (Thuringia). German porcelain factory established (1794) near Bayreuth under royal privilege by member of Greiner family. Traded as Porzellanfabrik Tettau, producing mainly tableware. Factory burned down and rebuilt in late 1890s. Marks usually incorporate T or Tettau; shield held by crowned lions with ROYAL BAYREUTH/ 1794/ GERMANY used 1891-1905.

Texeraud, Léon. See Limoges.

Thieme, Carl (fl mid to late 19th century). German porcelain manufacturer; established factory at *Potschappel in 1870s. Marks incorporate initials and include cross with T, crossed L's with coronet, and flower with leaves.

thimble. Protective cover for thumb used in needlework, thus original English name, thumb bell. Examples from Roman times onwards, e.g. in gold, silver, steel, pewter, porcelain, ivory, mother-of-pearl, tortoiseshell, glass, bone, leather and wood, but mostly in metal. Many types, e.g. circular band, originating in China and Japan, so that needle pushed with side of finger; sugar loaf, from medieval period, in pointed dome shape, pounced, with plain top and rim; secret thimble, with detachable outer shell covering glass phial for poison, or lover's memento. Frequently richly decorated e.g. with enamel, or repoussé, scenes, emblems, or motifs drawn from nature, or literature; or coats of arms; many examples set with gemstones.

thimble case. Ornamental containers for expensive thimbles first produced in 16th century France and 17th century England. Popular throughout 19th and early 20th centuries in both Europe and America. Made either as individual case, or combination thimble, tape measure and emery (or wax-holder) case. Materials include horn, ivory, polished woods, glass, porcelain, tortoiseshell, leather, and enamelled or chased and embossed gold and silver. From mid 19th century, small hinged boxes covered in leather or velvet; baskets of wickerwork or carved ivory and wood. British souvenir cases of natural polished woods, Tunbridge ware, or papier-mâché, decorated with local view, or historic sites and personalities. Some of finest late 19th century cases made by leading jwellers, e.g. *Fabergé, *Cartier.

thistle measure. Scottish pewter *ale measure introduced briefly in mid 19th century; resembles head of thistle. Manufacture abandoned because declared unreliable, and use on licensed premises forbidden.

Thomas, Seth (1774-1859). American clock manufacturer, perfected shelf clock. In partnership with Eli Terry and Silas Hoadley from 1807; Terry withdrew in 1813. Founded Seth Thomas Clock Co. at Plymouth, Connecticut, in 1853. Noted for pillar-and-scroll clocks; also made tall clocks, and some *turret clocks. Firm continued after death of founder, offering complete range of clocks by 1938; now a division of Talley Industries, Inc. (See American horological industry.)

Thonet Brothers, Thonet Frères, or **Gebrüder Thonet.** Furniture making firm established in Vienna, 1853, by M. *Thonet with sons, Franz, Michael, August, Josef, and Jacob. Designed,

Above
Thonet Brothers. Folding chaise longue *from 1911 catalogue.*

*Thonet Brothers. Chair designed by J. *Hoffmann. Early 20th century.*

Applied for bentwood patents in France, England, and Belgium in 1841. Settled in Vienna in 1842. Entered partnership with C. *Leistler (1842–49), making light, elegant, laminated wood chairs for Liechtenstein Palace in Vienna; some models made of rods bent into figures of eight, with loops forming back and legs; many with upholstered backs and seats and carved triangles in angles between seats and legs. Established own business, 1849, supplying cane-seated mahogany chairs with bentwood scrolls in back and vestigial capitals surmounting legs, to Café Daum, Vienna; later known as chair No 4. Showed rosewood sofas, chairs, armchairs, etc. with inlaid decoration at Great Exhibition of 1851, London. Took five sons into partnership, 1853, calling firm *Thonet Brothers. 1849–58, chairs usually stamped, Thonet Wien Gumpendorf, on underside of seat.

Thonet chair No 14. Bentwood side-chair developed by *Thonet Brothers, 1859. In beech-wood, has six parts: long rod looped to form chair back and back legs, smaller loop inside back for strength; hoop forming framework for curved cane seat, with smaller hoop as stretcher below seat; two gently tapered and bent rods for front legs. Rods joined by ten screws. Cheap, light, in easily transportable sections; c50 million models sold by 1910. Design still available.

Thonet rocking chair. Bentwood rocking chair developed in 1860 by *Thonet Brothers. Long, gently curved seat, inclined back; convoluted under-framing giving comfort and stability. Common in England by 1880. Usually has cane seat and back, framework finished in black or brown; some models button-upholstered. Several variants of original design produced later. Similar chairs, of inferior quality, made in Spain in 20th century.

Thooft, Joost (fl late 19th century). Dutch potter. In 1876, revived tradition of underglaze painting on earthenware at 17th century Delft factory, De *Porceleyne Fles. Geometrical designs on white biscuit, raised in green slip, outlined in gold. Some vases have decoration in red and green lustre. Mosaic panels include witches, devils, animals, and birds. Delftware usually traditional in design. Production increased in response to rise of tourist industry in early 20th century. Firm traded from 1890 as Thooft & Labouchère, later became company of shareholders (1903). In 1919, obtained royal privilege to use title N. V. Koninklijke Delftsch-Aardewerk Fabriek 'De porceleyne Fles'. Mark: monogram of JT and name Delft in script; recently, bottle with n.

threading or **trailing.** Ancient method of decorating glass; revived in 19th century: molten glass drawn into threads of varying thickness, then applied to surface of heated vessel. Much used for decorating rim, base, as well as body of glass objects; also for making ribbed handles. Most sophisticated form, Venetian *latticinio* glass.

three fold clock. *See* travelling clock.

Thuret, André (b 1898). French Art Deco glass artist. Highly skilled technician, made all own glass creations, e.g. vases, bowls, jugs, single-handed. Favoured heavy, lightly tinted, transparent glass, surface-finished and moulded at

manufactured, and exported *bentwood furniture to Britain, America, and European countries. Mechanized manufacturing process developed c1859 allowed mass-production, e.g. *Thonet chair No 14, *Thonet rocking chair. Showed only mass-produced furniture at International Exhibition in London, 1862. Chairs, tables, sofas, beds, etc. given numbers indicating chronological order of production. World's largest furniture factory by 1871, with sales offices in New York, Chicago, Rome, Moscow, etc. Chairs used in settings by J. *Hoffmann, *Le Corbusier, A. *Loos, O. *Wagner. Manufactured designs by M. *Breuer, *Le Corbusier, L. *Mies van der Rohe, M. *Stam, etc. Chairs usually stamped or labelled with various forms of name, e.g. Gebrüder Thonet, THONET. Firm still active. *Illustrations at* bentwood furniture, Hoffmann, J., Le Corbusier, Mies Van der Rohe, L., Stam, M.

Thonet, Michael (1796–1871). Furniture designer and manufacturer; born in Boppard, Prussia. Established carpenter's workshop, 1819; experimented with new techniques from 1830, producing laminated wood and bentwood furniture.

André Thuret. Vase decorated with gold metallic specks between layers of glass. Base engraved with signature André Thuret. c1930.

furnace mouth, in style very like M. *Marinot's. Mark: ANDRE THURET, diamond engraved.

tiao-ch'i or **tia-ts'i.** Chinese generic term for *carved lacquer. Corresponds to Japanese *choshitsu.

tiara. Jewelled head ornament fashionable from early 19th century; introduced during Napoleonic Greek revival simultaneously with reintroduction of Greek hair styles. Remained as part of court dress throughout 19th century. Half-tiaras worn 1840–60; often tied round head with ribbon; similar in shape to comb-mounts. Tiaras massive again in 1860s and 1870s; and usually part of diamond *parure.* Worn low on forehead during 1920s, when fitted shape of head more closely; often diamond flower designs, or geometrical Art Deco styles. Survived into 1930s, but generally declined in popularity.

tia-ts'i. *See* tiao-ch'i.

Tibetan ware. *See* Cliff, Clarice.

ticket, flick, or **Plato clock.** Digital clock, invented 1903; shows time in figures on two sets of celluloid tickets, restrained by pivoting hasps: upper set shows hours, lower shows minutes. Cylindrical wooden case, with carrying handle, divided into solid lower section, containing movement, and open top section with turned wooden pillars, revealing tickets. Tickets flick round like book leaves. Quantities produced, mainly in Germany and France, but also made by *Ansonia Clock Co. in America.

Tiffany & Co. New York manufacturing and retail jewellers, founded 1834 by C. L. *Tiffany. Originally imported jewellery from Europe; started own production in 1848, following contemporary Parisian styles. Firm opened branch in Paris, 1850. From 1860, work influenced by Indian, and particularly Japanese styles

and motifs. From 1902, L. C. *Tiffany, Art Director, designed jewellery for firm. Shrewd investments in diamonds in 1848 started policy of purchasing precious stones, especially diamonds (e.g. 'Tiffany' diamond, found in South Africa, 1878). By late 1880s, had most valuable collection of diamonds in the world. Established reputation for making expensive precious stone jewellery which continues today. Silver, made from 1850, won award for firm at Paris Universal Exposition, 1867. Large factory built, 1892, in suburb of Newark, New Jersey, for manufacture of electro-plate. Firm's work in precious metals includes *Adams Vase, and many silver commemorative pieces.

Tiffany, Charles L. (d 1902). American jeweller and silversmith. Founder of *Tiffany & Co. Succeeded in firm by son, L. C. *Tiffany.

Tiffany, Louis Comfort (1848–1933). American interior designer, glass artist and jeweller. Outstanding exponent of American Art Nouveau; son of C. L. *Tiffany. Studied painting in Paris;

Louis Comfort Tiffany. Dragon-fly lamp in ormolu and glass. c1900.

started work in interior decoration in 1870s. Established firm, Louis C. Tiffany & Associated Artists 1879, with S. *Colman, L. *de Forest among partners; designed interiors of private and public buildings, e.g. White House, Washington. Made tiles, lamps, and stained glass windows. Firm traded as Tiffany Glass & Decorating Co. from 1890, and opened furnaces in Corona, Long Island; name changed to Tiffany Studios in 1900. Employees included E. *Colonna.

Furniture from c1880 often features oriental and near Eastern motifs, reflecting influence of de Forest: swelling plant forms on upper legs, shallow relief carving, and marquetry on traditional forms (e.g. *bergère en gondole*). Art furniture elements, e.g. formalized carving, also present. Designed Moorish style room for Cornelius Vanderbilt II, 1882. Feet often four-pronged brass claws enclosing glass ball castors. Marquetry of natural woods, each sheet 1/16in.

Tiffany & Co. The Magnolia Vase. Silver and enamel. Made for World's Columbian Exposition, 1893. Marked on base: Tiffany & Co./11168 Makers 3137/Sterling Silver/T. Height 31in.

Below
Tiffany Glass and Decorating Company. Cypriote vase on original bronze base, Numbered K1379 and bearing trade label. c1900. Height 13½in.

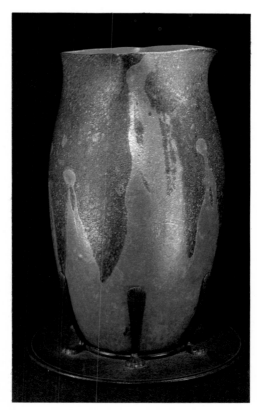

square and framed in metal, also characteristic.

Became increasingly interested in glass, particularly in reproducing appearance of ancient glass; experimented for many years, and patented iridescent technique in 1880 (marketed as *Favrile in wide range of colours). Avoided surface decoration, feeling that ornament should be integrated within glass body; similarly rejected cutting or moulding of shapes, and produced fluid, often asymmetrical, organic forms. Made decorative tableware, etc., with gold lustre achieved by use of gold chloride; plain lustre ware also in blue, green, white. Iridescent ware decorated with peacock feather designs, trailing ivy leaves or lily pads. Paperweight vases have decoration laid on inner glass form and cased in another layer of glass; *millefiori* glass canes sometimes embedded in inner layer of glass and rolled into surface, heightening three-dimensional effect. Body of Cypriote ware, often large and uneven in form and usually of brown or opaque glass, rolled in powdered glass to give corroded effect. Lava glass usually has dark blue lustre body, with abstract trailing decoration in gold lustre. Also made agate and marblized glass. Inspired many followers throughout America and Europe, notably V. *Durand and J. *Loetz Witwe. Mark: signature or L.C.T.; T.G.C. (Tiffany Glass, Decorating Co.); Favrile sometimes added after signature or on paper label.

Work shown in 1895 at opening of S. *Bing's Paris showroom, and designs commissioned by Bing. Use of bronze developed at workshops from c1890. After 1900, special section established to produce bronze objects incorporating favrile glass, e.g. desk sets (including blotter, letter rack, clock, inkstand, etc.) in bronze etched to produce greenish patina, and pierced to show amber or green marbled glass, enamel, or mother-of-pearl inserts. Lamps also made, typically with cast bronze stem in shape of stylized plant, and shade of multicoloured opaque favrile glass, set in irregular lozenges in

Tiffany & Co. Lorgnon, snakes of gold and diamonds, c1880. Fan brooch of green, white, red and yellow gold, set with opals, c1890.

bronze mounting of overall tree or flower form. Small cast beetles in favrile glass used to set in jewellery.

Art director of *Tiffany & Co. from 1902. Began designing jewellery; 'art' jewellery generally privately commissioned or made for exhibitions; undertaken separately from work of Tiffany & Co. Strong Byzantine influence in style, low-key colours; unusual semi-precious stones often used. Collaborated with A. *Mucha on some designs; only one piece survives. House on Long Island became centre of group of artist protégés.

Pottery, first shown at St Louis World Fair in 1904, commercially released in late 1905. Fine white clay fired at high temperature, sometimes with high relief or pierced decoration. Style influenced by Art Nouveau. Shapes often emerge from decoration, e.g. lips of vases formed by petals or leaves; sometimes adapted from metalwork design. Glazes, notably mossy green, or yellow with varied tones of old ivory, accentuate relief by collecting in crevices. Vases with simpler shape often covered with rich oriental glazes. Work issued under trade name, Favrile, although generally cast and not hand thrown. Production ceased in 1919, when Tiffany withdrew from Tiffany Studios; firm continued until 1936.

tiger-eye or **gold-stone glaze.** Aventurine glaze in shades of black and brown containing showers of golden crystals, clearly visible under certain lights. Accidentally produced in America in 1884 at *Rookwood Pottery; attempts to find certain method of repetition proved unsuccessful. Vase with underglaze decoration of flying birds, considered good specimen, exhibited by pottery in Paris (1900), Buffalo (1901), and Saint Louis (1904), dates from late 1880s or early 1890s.

tiger table. American term for table (usually dressing-table) with top veneered in striped decorative wood, e.g. tiger maple, zebra or tulip wood, arranged to resemble tiger-skin markings. Dates from c1880.

t'i hung. *See* cinnabar lacquer.

tile carpets. Victorian *needlework carpets, fashionable in England in 1850s and 1860s. Individual canvas squares and border sections finely worked in cross-stitch in coloured wools, then joined together. Not factory-made; often produced co-operatively in convents or private houses. Each square designed according to contributor's taste, though sometimes with common surround. Favourite motifs: posies, fruits, birds, small dogs (very popular) and other animals.

tiles. Use of decorative tiles, after lapsing in Europe in mid 16th century, revived in England in mid 19th century and reached height of popularity, c1870. Patent for mechanical production of encaustic tiles taken out in 1830. Manufacture developed at Mintons from 1830s. Tiles made by compressing clay dust in commercial production from 1840; L. *Arnoux introduced majolica glazes by 1851. Other manufacturers include *Architectural Pottery Co., T. & R. *Boote Ltd, and *Maw & Co. (by 1850s), R. M. *Taylor (from 1869), Josiah *Wedgwood & Sons, *Campbell Brick & Tile Co., firm of W. T. *Copeland, *Craven Dunnill & Co., and *Sherwin & Cotton (from 1870s), and *Della Robbia Co. and Pilkington's Tile & Pottery Co.

(from 1890s). Tiles hand-decorated from 1860s by Morris, Marshall, Faulkner & Co. from designs e.g. by artists E. *Burne-Jones, D.G. *Rossetti, and F.M. *Brown, also by W. *Morris himself; at first, hand-made blanks bought in Holland. W. *De Morgan also decorated tiles bought from other manufacturers, eventually beginning to fire own tiles in Chelsea. Tiles with lustre decoration copied by several firms in 1890s and Isnik inspired designs, often with additional colouring by hand. Aids to hand decoration include use of perforated pounce, through which charcoal could be dusted to indicate lines of design on tile below. Decorative glazes, often brightly coloured, could be made opaque by addition of tin oxide. Tubelining used to contain coloured glazes on hand decorated tiles; mass-produced tiles often stamped with patterns of raised lines. Motifs sometimes incised through slip to expose contrasting body of tile. *Pâte-sur-pâte* decoration also used. Many tiles marked with name of factory; sometimes signature of artist appears. In America, tiles made from mid 19th century. Manufacturers include H. C. *Robertson, W. H. *Grueby, and J. G. *Low.

time recorder clock. Timekeeper with 12 or 24 hour dial or 8-day movement used e.g. to 'clock' employees in and out of work. Records time by stamping figures on paper roll or card. Original models spring driven; from early 20th century electrically wound, driven, or controlled. Patented by American, W. L. Bundy, in 1885; further developed c1890 in Scotland by Alexander Dey of Aberdeen. *cf* tell-tale clock.

time recording stamp clock. Hand-operated, rubber date stamp in form of clock dial and moving pointer, operated by 30-hour movement in cylindrical metal case. Mechanism mounted on rectangular wooden platform. Clock held in spring-loaded metal clamp surmounted by handgrip, allowing inked stamp to be brought down upon paper, noting e.g. time of arrival on incoming mail. Made e.g. by Warwick Time Stamp Co., from 1880.

time switch. Clock movement with alarm or striking mechanism adapted to perform control operation, e.g. turning off gas-cock, or electric switch, after specified period of time has elapsed. English version pioneered by Dr Thurgar, in Norwich, Norfolk, used for gas street-lighting from 1867; runs for 8 days at each winding. Gunning's fully automatic gas-controller (patented 1899) first commercially successful version. Electrical time switch, on similar principle, introduced 1905: at required time, subsidiary train operates electric tumbler switch.

tin. Soft, brittle white metal, with low melting point, normally used as element of alloys, e.g. bronze, pewter; also as protective coating on other metals e.g. steel, iron, japanned articles, and interiors of brass, copper, and Sheffield plate cooking vessels. In original tin-plating process, object to be coated passed through three baths of molten tin: subsequent developments make only one bath necessary.

ting-tang or **bim-bam clock.** Chimes on two bells or gongs, first usually higher pitched. Normally one pair of notes sounds at quarters, two at half-hour, three at three-quarters, and four at hour, followed by e.g. pair of notes for each hour;

Time recorder clock. Inscribed: Workmans Automatic Time Regaster. Made by W. L. Bundy, c1885.

many versions omit quarters at hour. Found mostly on European clocks, e.g. French *carriage clocks; never very popular in England.

Tinworth, George (1843–1913). English potter. While working for father as wheelwright, learnt modelling at Lambeth School of Art, London. In late 1864, joined Schools of Royal Academy, London; exhibitor from 1866. Employed (1866–1913) at Doulton's Lambeth factory, made terracotta panels of religious subjects, including Gethsemane, The Foot of the Cross, and The Descent from the Cross (1874), and reredos for York Minster. Also modelled small figures, e.g. mouse chessmen, frog cricketers and canoeists, frogs going to Epsom races, and set of mouse musicians; vases have incised designs and moulded decoration, beading, etc.

Tirschenreuth. Bavarian porcelain factory established at Tirschenreuth in 1838, making tableware. Bought in 1920s by *Hutschenreuther family.

Titanian ware. Thinly-potted porcelain introduced by Charles J. *Noke at Doulton factory, Burslem, Staffordshire; in production until 1929. Clouded effects of pastel coloured enamel decoration covers entire surface; designs abstract, or representing birds, rabbits, flowers, etc.

toast fork. Short, broad, three-tined fork for serving toast; similar to *bread fork. Made in silver or electro-plate mainly in America c1885.

toasting fork. Long-handled fork for toasting bread, muffins, etc. at open fire. Simple, functional designs in wrought-iron; from mid 19th century, ornate examples also made in e.g. copper, brass, bronze, with openwork decoration, twisted tines or shaft, and ornamental handle.

tobacco box. Flat, pocket-sized container with tightly fitting lid for storing tobacco. Made 16th to 19th centuries. Earliest form (of Dutch origin) metal, usually brass; embossed or engraved with e.g. country scenes, flying birds, shoots, or smoking and drinking scenes. Usually rectangular ($c6 \times 2 \times 1$in.); some oval or square. In late 18th and 19th centuries, popular English form, very shallow, small steel box ($c2 \times 2$in.) with spring-catch operated hinged lid, either undecorated or engraved with simple pattern. In 20th century, term also applied to larger, usually metal-lined wooden box for tobacco, placed on table, desk, etc.

tobacco cutter. Small guillotine used for cutting plugs of chewing tobacco, mounted e.g. on wooden or cast-iron base, with decorative handle and blade holder in cast iron, bronze, etc. Most examples American, because of rapid expansion of tobacco industry from 1865, and related spread of tobacco-chewing habit.

tobacco jar. Container for storing loose tobacco; made c1660 to early 20th century. Usually oval or oblong ($c6 \times 5 \times 3$in.), sometimes with chamfered corners. Lids often domed, with decorative finial. Usually with heavy plate for compressing tobacco. From 18th century, cast lead and pewter jars produced in quantity; side panels with designs painted in bright colours. Brass or cast iron also used. Favourite motifs: smoking and drinking themes (often made for inns), national events, and sporting scenes. Examples with lead panels fixed to plain sides often decorated with stylized floral swags around single central device. Other 19th century varieties in cut or engraved glass, silver, electro-plate, wood (particularly *Tunbridge ware), papier-mâché, and hardstone, usually lined in lead, copper, or pewter. Stoneware jar, in form of bird, with head serving as cover, made by *Martin Brothers.

Tobacco cutter. Cast-iron cutter for plugs of tobacco. Late 19th century.

*Tobacco jar. *Tudric pewter, designed by A. *Knox, decorated with stylized honesty pattern. Stamped 0193. Height 4¼in.*

Below
Tobey Furniture Company. Carved wood table. 1880s. Length 4ft5in.

Tobe. Long-established Japanese pottery centre on island of Shikoku. At first, made pottery in styles of 17th century wares made in area of Karatsu, then porcelain with underglaze blue or enamelled decoration. Recent pottery influenced by work of S. *Hamada and K. *Tomimoto.

Tobey Furniture Company. Furniture manufacturers established 1875 by Charles and Frank Tobey, brothers, in Chicago, Illinois (development of Tobey Co. Retail Shop, established 1856, and Thayer & Tobey Furniture Co., 1870). With subsidiary firm, Tobey & Christianson Cabinet Co., specialized in high-quality furniture from 1888. Leading Chicago furniture and decorating house by 1890, known throughout America. Stocked many furniture styles, e.g. pieces influenced by *Morris & Co. designs. Own designs reflect Prairie School influence.

Toen, Morikawa (1820-94). Japanese master-carver and netsuke artist of Nara. Noted as finest *ningyo netsuke carver in Nara. Also made numerous okimono and netsuke. Work often exhibited in Japan and at International Exhibitions in West. Carved mainly in wood, often using *itto-bori technique. *Go: Toen. *Chomei: Toen, Toen saku, or kakihan based on Toen.

Toft, Charles (1831-1909). English potter. Modelled figures, busts, etc. in parian ware at Kerr & Binns factory, Worcester; bust, possibly of Sir Walter Scott, signed C. Toft fecit (c1855). Taught at Birmingham School of Art in late 1860s; also worked for Elkington & Co. At Minton factory, associated with Henri-Deux ware, made from 1860s. In 1873, recorded as pupil of M-L. *Solon in *pâte-sur-pâte* technique. Later, chief figure modeller at Wedgwood factory. Opened own small factory at Stoke-on-Trent, Staffordshire, in 1889, making earthenware with lacy decoration in brown and white slip. *Illustration at* Henri-Deux ware.

toilet chair. Upholstered chair with circular seat and low, semi-circular back; used in bedrooms in Britain. Dates from c1850.

toilet table. *See* dressing-table.

togidashi (Japanese, 'brought out by rubbing'). In Japanese lacquer, ground and burnished *makie in which decorative elements appear flush with surface of lacquer ground and have soft, pastel effect. Used from 8th century to present on wide range of lacquerware to indicate distant perspective or for minor design elements, most often seen in mists, clouds, mountain-tops, gently curving streams, etc.

Technique: design transferred from paper to wet prepared lacquer base. Portions of it then sprinkled with metallic dusts. When dry, surface completely covered with several coats of base colour lacquer (usually black), allowed to dry and then rubbed down until dusted portions reappear. Process repeated until design completed. Finally surface covered with numerous layers of transparent lacquer and highly polished.

From late 18th century, two varieties of coloured togidashi used (*iroe-togidashi and *sumie-togidashi).

tokko. In Japanese Buddhist metalwork, sceptre-shaped object.

Tomimoto, Kenkichi (1886-1963). Japanese potter, born in Nara; later worked in Tokyo. Early pottery influenced by Korean styles. Associate of B. *Leach from early 20th century. Work characterized by calligraphic brushed designs. Later work in porcelain, Chinese-inspired, decorated with underglazed blue, or enamel in red, green, gold, silver, etc. Plates delicately painted with landscapes, birds, or flowers, on white or coloured ground.

Tomkinson & Adam. English carpet manufacturers; firm founded c1869 in Kidderminster by William Adam - formerly J. *Templeton's foreman - and Michael Tomkinson, to realize Adam's invention, chenille power loom. Bought British patent on *spool Axminster loom in 1878; sold licences to four Kidderminster and Halifax firms. Secured British rights on A. *Smith & Co.'s Kleitos loom in 1900, adding 9ft wide Axminster squares to seamless range of chenille and ingrain art squares; 12ft loom installed a few years later. Renard Frères' *machine-knotting loom, introduced 1910, in use until c1930, when production of machine-knotted carpets ceased in Britain. Wove designs of architect-designer C. F. A. *Voysey c1895-c1920. Partnership divided in 1927 into Tomkinsons and W. R. & R. Adams.

Toms & Luscombe. English cabinet makers, active c1850-80 in London. Known for high-quality reproductions of 18th century French styles.

tonkotsu. Small, portable Japanese tobacco box (c3½ × 2 × 1in.), in vogue from mid 19th century as alternative to pouch (*tabako-ire) and usually worn with matching *kiseru-zutsu. Form adaptation of *inro design, but composed of only one lidded case, and slightly wider and deeper. Finest examples mainly lacquer; also in metal, porcelain, and ivory. Decorated in wide range designs and styles, often with matching *netsuke and *ojime. Despite change in style of dress during *Meiji period, production of ornamental tonkotsu continued through Taisho period for enormous domestic and Western export collectors' markets.

Tooth, Henry (fl late 19th century). English art potter, formerly artist. Without previous experience in ceramics, appointed manager of *Linthorpe Pottery (1880) on recommendation of C. *Dresser; studied briefly in Staffordshire, before going to Linthorpe. In partnership with W. *Ault, established *Bretby Art Pottery in 1883. Firm traded as Tooth & Co. after departure of Ault (1886).

toothpick holder. Elongated, often octagonal, ornate container, in gold, silver, mother-of-pearl,

*Tomkinson & Adam. Machine-made pile carpet, Green Pastures. Designed by C. F. A. *Voysey, 1896.*

tortoiseshell, ivory etc. Hinged lid. Decorated with e.g. miniature paintings, enamelled medallions, Wedgwood plaques; frequently also set with gemstones. Made in England, France, Austria and Switzerland in 18th and 19th centuries. French examples usually particularly ornate. Other versions include mourning case, often with lock of hair mounted in lid, and Swiss combination dice box and toothpick holder, with case and dice in ivory. Toothpicks in gold, silver, ivory, or wood, plain or with ornate top, sometimes set with gemstones.

topaz. Gemstone with wide colour range; yellow to sherry-brown shades found in Brazil most prized. Sometimes confused with yellow citrine of false topaz (transparent yellow variety of quartz). Brownish topaz usually turned rose-pink by heat treatment. Popular Victorian stone for rings, earrings, necklaces, and pendants; often found in long oval or drop shapes. Usually facet cut with flat table on crown.

torsion pendulum. Clock pendulum in which bob rotates by twisting of suspending rod or spring, instead of swinging to and fro; invented by Christiaan Huyghens, c1660. Has slow beat (one oscillation every 7½ seconds); used where long run is required, e.g. *400-day clock, *Atmos clock.

tortoiseshell. Mottled, translucent scales, rarely more than ⅛in. thick, taken from shell of small hawksbill sea turtle; when heated, shell becomes malleable, may be worked, stamped, pressed, or moulded. Popular in France, Italy and Holland during 17th century, e.g. as veneer for picture frames, or decorative inlay for furniture; rare in England until early 19th century, when French craftsman, Louis Craigneur, opened London workshop; subsequently fashionable decoration, particularly in combination with mother-of-pearl, for wide range of objects, e.g. tea caddy cases, *writing accessories, *fans, *music boxes, commonly with embossed ornament, e.g. landscape, moulded in crisp, precise detail; fashion subsided after mid 19th century, as papier mâché became increasingly cheap decorative medium for domestic articles in light use.

Tortoiseshell glass. 19th century brownish-amber art glass; mottled with patches of deeper tone. Made by inserting fragments of brown glass into bubbles of clear glass, then staining vessel yellowish-brown. Patented 1880 by Francis Pohe; later, widely imitated throughout Europe and America, where one of specialities of *Boston & Sandwich Glass Co.

tortoise or **turtle clock.** French brass table clock invented by Nicolas Grollier de Servière (17th century); many modern reproductions. Shallow bowl, surrounded by horizontal chapter ring, surmounts decorative stand containing movement. When bowl is filled with water, metal tortoise or turtle, controlled through magnet driven by movement, appears to swim round circumference, indicating hours.

tourbillon or **tourbillion.** Mechanism devised (1795) by A-L. Breguet, to reduce position errors, i.e. timekeeping variations introduced as watch or chronometer is carried in different positions. Balance and escapement mounted in carriage revolving once per minute. Used in some pocket chronometers and high-quality lever watches in 19th and early 20th centuries. Occasionally found in travelling clocks and marine chronometers, possibly to eliminate effects of ship's magnetic field. Modified versions include *karrusel (patented 1894), with simplified mechanism revolving in 52½ minutes; followed, in 1903 by Bonniksen's tourbillon, revolving in 39 minutes. Andrew Taylor, of Brixton, London, patented (1903) device with hourly rotation. *Waterbury watch functions in effect as tourbillon, since whole movement rotates inside case; design introduced for simplicity in manufacture, not accuracy.

tourmaline. Gemstone with wide colour range; black green, red, brown, yellow, blue, sometimes banded with stripes. Some stones shading through two or three different colours. Found e.g. in Russia, Sri Lanka, Brazil, and Madagascar. Usually mixed cut. Flawed stones used for beads.

tower clock. *See* turret clock.

Towle Silversmiths of Newburyport. American silver manufacturers, based on firm of Towle & Jones, established 1857 by Anthony F. Towle and William P. Jones, previously apprentices at William Moulton's hand craft business. Son Edward Towle bought Moulton company in 1860 and formed A. F. Towle & Son in Greenfield, Massachusetts; firms amalgamated on father's death and became Towle Silversmiths of Newburyport; still in existence, with largest number of patterns in American flatware industry.

Tracey & Baker. *See* Dennison, Aaron L.

trailing. *See* threading.

trap cut. *See* gem cutting.

Traquair, Phoebe Anna (1852-1936). English designer and silversmith; studied at Dublin School of Art; designed and executed furniture decoration and metalwork, some in collaboration with Sir Robert Lorimer. Silverwork made extensive use of enamelling. Exhibited widely in Europe and America.

travelling clock. General term for small portable spring-driven clock, often in folding case, for convenience when travelling. Earliest example was *carriage clock; later, *goliath clock, camera clock (so-called because it folds like camera bellows), and from c1900, three fold or portfolio clock (*calotte*), which folds into leather case.

Trapnell, C. & W. English furniture makers working in Bristol; active 1864-80. Established, 1824, as C. Trapnell; Trapnell & Gane from 1880. Principal designer, Caleb Trapnell (1824-1903). Made household furniture; also furnished Bristol public buildings, e.g. carved and gilt oak sofa, occasional table, and drawing-room chairs in ebonized and gilt wood for Mansion House. Made Quaint style furniture, mainly designed by G. M. *Ellwood, during 1890s. Firm active until 1954.

travelling set. *See* canteen.

tray. Papier-mâché examples made as part of set also including tea chest, tea caddy, card tray, etc., from c1850. Decorated with e.g. painted flowers or ornamental mother-of-pearl patterns; made e.g. in Birmingham by McCallum & Hodson, Jennens & Bettridge, etc.

Treasury inkstand. English box-shaped inkstand with inkwells - usually in cut glass - hidden by hinged covers; single handle at top, or two hinged handles mounted at sides. In wood, e.g. walnut, mahogany, from early 19th century; metal versions in brass, etc., date from c1850.

Trenton (New Jersey). American pottery centre. Factories include earthenware manufacturers *Taylor & Speeler and Greenwood Art Pottery Co.; also early makers of 'Belleek' from 1880s: Ott & Brewer, Willetts Manufacturing Co., Columbian Art Pottery, and Knowles, Taylor & Knowles. W. S. *Lenox worked for Ott & Brewer and Willetts before establishing Ceramic Art Co. and, later, own Lenox Company.

Triller, Erich (b 1898) and Ingrid (b 1905). Swedish artist potters, working at own studio north of Stockholm from 1935. Made stoneware bowls, vases, etc., in simple forms, decorated only with glaze.

triple-crested sofa. American open-arm sofa with three, upholstered panels set in balloon-back chair frames. Often in rococo style. Popular c1855-c1875.

trivet. Three-legged metal stand, usually iron, brass, or bronze, used at open fire to support utensils when off heat. Four-legged variant known as footman. Commonly has perforated top, wooden handle. Curving back legs hook on to bars of grate for extra stability.

ts'ang-chin. *See* chinkin-bori.

Tsuboya. Japanese pottery centre in Okinawa. Plates, bowls, etc., made for everyday use, covered with temmoku glaze, or decorated in blue on white ground. Production continues to present day.

tsuka. *See* Japanese swords.

tsuba. Japanese sword guard or hand protector. Metal plate with wedge-shaped hole for tang (haft of blade) to pass through into hilt. Also has openings for kogai (skewer) and kogatana (sword knife), also carried in scabbard. Made first by swordsmiths, then by armourers and later by special sword guard craftsmen. Usually circular, square, or other symmetrical shape; designs on both sides, but front more elaborately decorated. Early examples in iron - Japanese metalworkers favoured base metals, copper and iron, using various alloys (including bronze) patinated to give wide range of colours, with gold and silver for applied or inlaid decoration. Later with various forms of engraving, inlay work, and *cloisonné* and *champlevé* enamelling. Mukade or shingen tsuba, made from late 16th century, has wires of yellow or red copper woven on to large plates. Design influenced by painting; colours of various alloys exploited. Subject matter includes historical events, mythology, folklore, landscapes, birds, and animals. Kaneije style (after 1600) showed Chinese landscapes in low relief; details picked out in gold inlay or bronze. In Edo period (1615-1868), armour and sword fittings made for adornment rather than

*Tudric pewter. Bowl decorated with band of honesty within tendrils; two bracket handles. Designed by A. *Knox, c1905. Height 11½in.*

Tsuba. Iron, mid 19th century. Left: decorated with copper, silver and gold detail, signed Ichiriu Tomonaga and Kakihan. Right: pierced and carved as snake with gilt eyes and tongue, signed Yoshinori of Edo.

fighting; decoration and technical dexterity reached peak.

tsui-ko. *See* tsuishu.

tsuikoku or **tsui-u** (Japanese, 'heaped-black'). Japanese *carved lacquer, made from late 15th century to present. Technique and designs same as tsuishu, but surface black.

tsui-o (Japanese, 'heaped yellow'). Variety of Japanese *tsuishu *carved lacquer: several colours of lacquer (particularly deep green, yellow, red, brown, and black) appear in same layer or superimposed layers. Speciality of *Yosei family from 14th to 20th centuries.

tsui-u. *See* tsuikoku.

tsuishu (Japanese, 'heaped red') or **tsuishitsu.** Japanese carved red lacquer, copied from Chinese *cinnabar lacquer. Made in Japan from 15th century; speciality of *Yosei school into 20th century.
 Also used as generic term for all carved lacquer with red surface layer over various coloured underlying and ground coats. Such varieties include: tsuiko, very deeply carved with red surface, yellow ground, and single black layer in middle of several underlying red layers; kin-shi (gold-thread), deeply carved with red surface and yellow-gold ground under alternating layers of red and yellow lacquer; and *tsui-o.

ts'un-hsing or **ts'un-sheng.** *See* zonsei-nuri.

Tsutumi. Japanese folk pottery kiln near Sendai in Miyagi prefecture, active 18th–20th centuries. Noted for production of water jars with bluish-white glaze trickled over black. Also made small shrines in form of temple.

tsuzure-nishiki (Japanese, 'tapestry woven with nails'). Japanese tapestry technique, introduced in workshops c1770, based on tradition of shawl making dating from 8th century. Weavers use their fingernails, clipped into saw-teeth, to press weft threads together. First applied to large scale tapestries by Jimbei Kawashima at his factory,

after visit to Gobelins in 1886. Factory thereafter specialized in huge tapestries, including series for imperial palaces, and, after 1945, in commissions for assembly rooms and stage scenery.

tube-lining. Ceramic decoration: thin outlines of slip trailed on surface of earthenware tiles, etc., to control coloured glazes of design. Techniques used from late 19th century. Trailed outlines of slip used by W. *Moorcroft, often in floral designs, from c1898.

tubular steel furniture. Chairs, tables, etc. with framework of steel tubing, often chromium-plated, sometimes painted or enamelled. Popular from c1925. Feature of Modernist style. Examples designed by M. *Stam, L. *Mies van der Rohe, M. *Breuer, and *Le Corbusier. Manufacturers include *PEL, *DIM. Often combined with glass, e.g. metal X-frame tables with black or rough-cast glass tops; also combined with marble, wood veneers, etc. Upholstery materials include leather, hide, canvas, fur.

Tudric pewter. English domestic ware (e.g. tea service) produced by *Liberty & Co., London, c1903–c1938. Made in pewter with high silver content, in Celtic-inspired Art Nouveau style, with e.g. stylized, interlaced plant motifs, and set with enamel plaques. Counterpart of *Cymric silver range, from which designs derived; A.

*Tube-lining. *Pilkington tile, after design by W. *Crane. 1902. 6in. square.*

*Knox designed many items in both ranges. Mark: TUDRIC PEWTER, followed by stock number of piece. *Illustrations at* Couper, J., & Sons, tobacco jar.

tufted process. Method of carpet production evolved during 1930s; differs from other methods because pile sewn with needle into pre-woven backing, not woven of a piece with whole carpet. Backing moves through tufting machine, and bank of needles as wide as carpet inserts tufts individually. Tufts secured first by sewing mechanism, then coating of latex.

tui-hung. *See* cinnabar lacquer.

Turkestan. *See* East Turkestan, West Turkestan.

Tunbridge ware. Objects veneered in wood mosaic, made at Tunbridge Wells, Kent, from 17th century. Many types of boxes, tea caddies, tables etc. made with star, diamond, or square mosaic patterns. After 1840 more elaborate, naturalistic designs (birds, flowers, animals, etc.), and foreign woods widened range. Designs produced by glueing together slim shafts of wood, in various colours, so that required pattern, picture, appears at end of cluster of sticks. Cluster then sliced thinly, and applied as veneer to objects. Height of popularity in period c1830–c1850, after which increasing rate of decline apparent.

Turkish carpets. *See* Bergama, Bor, Hereke, Kayseri, Koum ka Pour, Smyrna, Sparta.

Turkish chair. Armchair with deep seat, *bolster arms. Often upholstered in velvet, with panel of oriental carpeting on back. *See* Turkish style.

Turkish corner or **corner divan seat.** Continuous ottoman fitting into corner; dates from c1880 in Britain and America. *See* Turkish style.

Turkish frame chair. American spring-upholstered armchair with metal frame (legs and connecting member usually wood). Often button-upholstered, with fringe at seat base partially covering legs. Popular from c1850.

Turkish or **Moorish style.** Furniture style popular in Britain c1850–c1900 and America c1870–c1880; pieces generally combined with bead curtains, fretted horse-shoe arches, oriental rugs, etc. Originally confined to smoking-rooms in Britain, e.g. design for Cardiff Castle in Wales by W. *Burges. Influenced drawing-room furni-

Union Glassworks. Kewblas bowl. Made c1900. Height 3⅜in.

Turret clock. Cast iron flatbed frame, 15-leg gravity escapement, locking plate hour striking. Fly at rear controls speed of striking. Gillett & Bland (later Gillett & Johnston). Croydon (Surrey), 1870. Frame width 28in.

ture from c1885. Typical pieces include divans, Turkish chair, Turkish table, ottoman, Turkish corner. Upholstered in plain or figured materials, e.g. plush, tapestry, brocade, oriental carpeting; fringes conceal chair and sofa legs; arms tasselled.

Turkish table. Small square or octagonal table with four, six, or eight legs. Usually japanned, inlaid with arabesques. *See* Turkish style.

turquoise. Gemstone with colour ranging from sky-blue to watery-green; basic hydrated copper aluminium phosphate. Found e.g. in Persia, Tibet, India, China and Mexico. Widely used in all types of jewellery throughout 19th century. Nearly always shallowly cabochon cut. Snake necklaces and bracelets of articulated gold or silver links covered with pavé-set turquoises fashionable in 1850s.

turret or **tower clock.** General term describing large clock, often for public use, with one or more dials mounted on outside of building. Development can be traced from earliest mechanical clocks made c1280. Size of movement varies according to diameter and number of dials; from mid 19th century, normally mounted in cast-iron frame with dead beat or gravity *escapement and small dial showing minutes only for setting hands, e.g. Westminster Palace clock by E. J. *Dent. Almost always weight-driven, with pendulum varying from one second length (3ft3in.) to two second (13ft) or more. From c1850 made in specialist factories: Thwaites & Reed, Clerkenwell, London; Smith's of Derby; James Joyce of Whitchurch, Shrop-

shire, etc. Many converted in 20th century to automatic electric winding, or replaced by *master clock system or *synchronous electric movement.

Tweedy, Thomas (b 1816). English woodcarver and gilder in Newcastle, Northumberland. Designed and made naturalistically carved furniture from 1851, e.g. sideboards, chairs, and sofa depicting scenes from Robinson Crusoe; shown at International Exhibition in London, 1862, with sideboard decorated with carved Shakespearean figures.

Uji ningyo. *See* ningyo netsuke.

Ullmann, Franz (fl 1870s). Bohemian master glass engraver. Employed in Steinschönau by J. & L. *Lobmeyr, contributing goblets and beakers to work shown at Vienna Exhibition of 1871, which led to renewed respect for cut and engraved glassware in late 19th century Europe.

umbrella stand. Commonly, upright skeletal cylinder (c3ft high) in wrought-iron, with circular, pierced top plate to take closed umbrellas, and circular metal drip-tray in base. Popular c1850–c1920. Other versions include simple, hollow cylinder of brass or imprinted oriental ceramic ware; after 1st World War, large shell-cases also used.

unbreakable glass. Watch glasses generally of glass, 1700–c1920. From 17th century, strong – though not unbreakable – glasses made of e.g. faceted rock-crystal. In 1920s celluloid (also known as talc) used, or, for high-quality watches, synthetic sapphire. Since 2nd World War, unbreakable glasses made of transparent plastic, e.g. perspex.

Unger Bros. American silversmiths and jewellers working in Newark, New Jersey, from 1881.

Formed by brothers Herman, Eugene, and Frederick. In 1901, visited Paris; impressed by current work in silver and jewellery. Patented six designs for silverwork and jewellery in Art Nouveau style (1903); motifs of girls' heads with long flowing hair and flowers. Jewellery carried out in silver, sometimes gold-washed and set with small stones. Manufacturing ended c1910. Mark: U with interlaced B.

Unica glass. Range of ambitious single glass items for wealthy collectors and museums. Developed by C. *Lebeau and A. D. *Copier for *Leerdam in 1920s. Studio to produce these subsequently established there. Pieces frequently signed with artist's initial in right angle. *See also* Serica glass.

Unicorn Pottery. *See* Wedgwood & Co.

Union Glass Company. American glasshouse founded 1864 in Somerville, Massachusetts, incorporating previous glass works. Produced plain and pressed tableware, and, in late 19th century, limited amount of unusual vases, bowls, and other decorative glass in Art Nouveau style, e.g. *Kewblas.

Union Porcelain Works. American porcelain factory at Greenpoint, Long Island. Bought from W. *Boch in 1861. Hard-paste porcelain made from 1864 or 1865, and decorated from 1866. Products include *Century Vase, and copies of Sèvres porcelain (from 1876); also e.g. oyster plate (c1881) made in versions of *Palissy ware. By c1891, making tiles, also in hard-paste porcelain. Active until early 20th century; marks include head of eagle, holding S (proprietor: Thomas C. Smith), sometimes with initials U.P.W., or UNION/PORCELAIN/WORKS/N.Y. or GREENPOINT/N.Y.

United Crafts. Semi-cooperative scheme (1901–04) within G. *Stickley's furniture manufacturing company. Best-known designer, H. *Ellis.

United States Pottery. American pottery started in 1852 by Lyman, Fenton & Co., established manufacturers in Bennington, Vermont. Made porcelain jugs and vases with applied relief decoration of plant forms, etc., in white, sometimes on pitted blue ground, and figures in imitation of English parian ware. Animal figures,

Union Porcelain Works. Porcelain vase, made 1876-77.

Toby jugs, hound-handled pitchers, etc., made in Rockingham or flint enamel ware; some modelled by D. *Greatbach. Toilet sets and decorative articles also made in granite ware. Ceased operation in 1858. Marks include USP on ribbon in relief (usually appearing on porcelain); Lyman Fenton & Co. Bennington, Vermont (earthenware); and United States Pottery Co. Bennington, Vermont, on scrolled medallion (parian type porcelain).

unit furniture. Standard-size sections forming wardrobes, chests, writing desks, etc.; can be added to and rearranged. Popular in Britain during 1930s. Examples designed notably by W. *Gropius and B. *Joel; also made by Deutsche Werkstätten. Bookcases made from early 20th century.

University City Pottery. Ceramic department of *American Woman's League, at University City, near St Louis, Missouri; many students attended classes in overglaze painting on porcelain. Ceramics taught in small department by T. *Doat from 1909 A.A. *Robineau (1910-11), and F. *Rhead (until 1911), with help of professional potters from France. Porcelain produced with *flambé* or crystalline glazes, using forms developed by Doat in France, e.g. gourd shape, and simpler, freer forms devised in pottery. Although American Woman's League ceased in 1911, production continued, 1912-14. Printed circular mark, The American Woman's League, UC, occurs with date and potter's initials.

Upchurch pottery. Earthenware vase decorated with blue and damson glazes. Marked Upchurch, impressed. c1920. Height 7½in.

Upchurch Pottery. English pottery established (1913) at Rainham, Kent. Work included in exhibition of British decorative arts in Paris (1914). Work designed by E. *Spencer sold through retail outlets of Artificers' Guild.

upholstery. Textile covering, padding (e.g. horsehair), springs, etc. attached to seat furniture frames; dates from late 16th century. By 1850s, *spring upholstery resulted in development of large, soft, easy chairs, sofas, etc. in Britain, France, and America, becoming increasingly massive until c1880; often *button-upholstered. Upholstery often covered yoke rail during 1860s; chairs with frames hidden by upholstered seats and backs common during 1870s. Thickness of padding reduced from c1880, remaining constant until 1930s. Tufted horsehair used for American and English drawing-room furniture, c1880-c1900. Wide range of coverings popular, including oriental carpeting, moquette. Main trends include leather (e.g. Morocco leather), for sofas, club chairs (e.g. Wolsey chair), horn furniture, etc. Also used from c1925, e.g. in Barcelona chair by L. *Mies van der Rohe. Chintz used for barrel chair, Derby chair; also for loose covers in Victorian Britain, and from c1900 in America. Damask, cretonne, and plush common in France, c1860-c1900. Embroidered silks and figured damasks used by G. *de Feure, P. *Iribe. Satin upholstery popular in America during 1860s, e.g. pieces by *Marcotte & Co. Invention of *latex foam (1928) revolutionized upholstery techniques.

urushi. *See* lacquer.

urushi-makie. *See* kuro-makie.

vajra (Sanskrit) or **kongo** (Japanese). Buddhist cult symbol, shaped like double trident with points turned inwards. Used in rituals, to ward off evil spirits. Divine weapon named in ancient Indian poetry. Sometimes called 'Buddhist thunderbolt'.

Valentien, Albert R. (fl late 19th century). American pottery decorator. First artist regularly employed on staff of Rookwood Pottery (from 1881).

Vallgren, Carl Wilhelm (1855-1940). Finnish sculptor; produced Art Nouveau style statuettes and small decorative bronzes.

Vallin, Eugène (1856-1922). French architect; also designed furniture; member of *Ecole de Nancy. Pieces characterized by massive forms, plastic use of wood creating decorative interplay of lines, e.g. dining-room chairs and table, 1903-05, with concave back rails on chairs repeated in table edge, and curved chair stretchers harmonizing with table stretcher.

Val Saint-Lambert. Belgian glass factory near Liège. Major producer of Belgian hollow-ware glass during 19th century, and one of largest glassmaking enterprises in Europe at turn of century, when Art Nouveau iridescent and *Gallé-inspired ornamental cameo glass produced. Employed Charles Graffert (1893-1967) as engraver. Pioneering designer H. *van de Velde also associated with company for a time. Mark: entwined initials VSL.

van Beek, Jan Bontjes (b 1899). Artist potter, born in Holland; father nationalized German in 1907. After naval service in 1st World War, worked as potter from 1918. Established own workshop in partnership (1922) at Fischerhude, near Bremen; also studied ceramics in Berlin. Made stoneware from 1930s, with shapes and glazes inspired by ancient Chinese. Received gold medal at Triennale, Milan, in 1938. Berlin workshop destroyed by air raid in 1st World War; work interrupted by imprisonment by Gestapo, and army service following release in 1944. Professor of ceramics at School of Applied Art, Berlin (1946-50); then industrial designer. Professor at School of Fine Arts, Hamburg, from 1960.

Van Briggle, Artus (1869-1904). American painter, pottery decorator, and artist potter; born in Felicity, Ohio. While studying painting in Cincinnati, Ohio, worked as decorator of dolls' heads and, later, vases. From c1887, as decorator for *Rookwood Pottery, painted flowers in underglaze colours. From 1893, at Académie Julien, Paris, on painting scholarship granted by Rookwood Pottery. On return to Cincinnati (1896), worked as painter and Rookwood decorator, while attempting to reproduce Chinese matt glazes in small kiln at home. Decorative style, still in underglaze colours,

Artus Van Briggle. Earthenware vases, c1900.

began to include painting of figures. In 1895, suffering from tuberculosis, moved to Colorado, continuing experiments, using local materials. established own studio by 1901; Van Briggle Pottery Company formed in 1902. Vases, sometimes plates, decorated with stylized floral and animal motifs in Art Nouveau style, human figures often incorporated in design. Relief decoration, integrated with forms, covered with soft-coloured glazes, often with tones mingling. Models cast; glaze covered entire surface until Van Briggle's death, later work sometimes partially covered with glaze, providing contrast with dark clay body. Company, continued under direction of wife, in new, larger premises from 1907, still in operation; some of original models produced. Early work marked with monogram of AA enclosed in rectangle, often with VAN BRIGGLE and date, incised; later, Colo. Spgs. (Colorado Springs) added instead of date.

Van Cleef & Arpels. Parisian court jewellers, founded 1906; branches in New York and London. Devised *minaudière, and *serte mystérieux* or invisible setting, sometimes called illusion setting – type of pavé setting in which metal holding stones cannot be seen. During 1930s, jewellery showed strong African influence.

Vander, C.J., Ltd. English manufacturer of domestic silver and cutlery; formed by C.J. Vander with sons Henry and Alfred after buying

Van Cleef & Arpels. Brooch. Diamonds with carved emerald pendants, rubies, and sapphires. 1930.

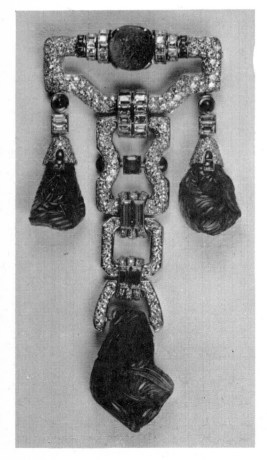

Henri Clemens van de Velde. Armchair. Padouk wood upholstered in cotton batik designed by Thorn-Prikker of Amsterdam. 1898.

firm of Macrae & Goldstein, Covent Garden, in 1886; 1907, grandsons Arthur, Henry, and Norman Vander joined company, and business moved to Betterton Street, London; took over Francis Higgins, 1948, *Atkin Bros., 1958, Roberts & Belk of Sheffield, 1965; opened new factory in Sheffield, 1967.

van de Velde, Henri Clemens (1863–1957). Belgian architect and designer. Formerly painter, studied in Antwerp and Paris. In Belgium from 1885, among painters of avant-garde Brussels group, Les Vingt. Worked as decorative designer from 1893. Lecture, *Le Déblaiment d'Art* (1894), published as brochure for galleries of Les Vingt. Influenced by work of John Ruskin and W. *Morris; formulated theories of Art Nouveau and contributed to spread of style. From c1894, designed furniture in austere, linear style, which relies for effect on relationship with architectural setting. Chiefly used native woods, oak or beech. Rush-seated chair, 1896, has high back and forked splat joining low back rail. Expressed artistic ideals in building and furnishing own house, Bloemenwerf, 1895, at Uccle, near Brussels. helped to sell earthenware of A.W. *Finch, fellow member of Les Vingt; collaborated with art dealer, Julius Maier-Graefe. Commissioned by S. *Bing to design four rooms for La Maison de l'Art Nouveau in Paris. Established workshops, Société van de Velde at Ixelles, near Brussels in 1898. Furniture c1900 characterized by curves used as series of parallels, or contrasting with straight lines; restrained use of abstract ornament; batik upholstery.
Exhibits in Applied Art Exhibition at Dresden (1897) resulted in many commissions in Germany, where settled in 1898, at first working as graphic designer. Jewellery, based on abstract, curvilinear forms, often used silver and semi-precious stones, e.g. buckle in oxidized silver set with moonstones and rose diamonds, 1898–1900. Among pioneers in use of base metals for miniature objects, e.g. inkstands, formerly made

only in precious metals. Other metalwork includes candelabrum in silver-plated bronze, made c1902 in Art Nouveau style; most known examples preserved in museum collections. In 1901, asked by Wilhelm Ernst, Grand Duke of Saxe-Weimar-Eisenach, to help reform schools of applied art; in Weimar (1902–14) taught own seminar, which later developed into school of arts and crafts. Commissioned by Meissen factory to design porcelain tea service (1905); plates have moulded borders decorated with underglaze blue and gilded. Also designed stoneware vases with figured glazes for manufacture in Westerwald.
Participated in foundation of Deutscher Werkbund in 1907. Furniture became simpler, usually with elongated proportions; white lacquer sometimes used. Architectural commissions include Paris showrooms for La Maison Moderne of Maier-Graefe (1899), and theatre of Deutscher Werkbund in Cologne (1914).
After dismissal from posts in Germany on outbreak of World War I, lived in Switzerland from 1915. In Holland, 1921, designed museum in Otterlo. As principal of Institut Supérieur des Arts Décoratifs in Brussels and Professor of Architecture at University of Ghent from mid 1920s to mid 1930s, designed some pieces of furniture in severe, angular style. In 1938, collaborated on design of Belgian pavilion of New York World's Fair. Retired to Switzerland in 1947.

Van Erp, Dirk (1860–1953). Dutch-born American metalworker; arrived in California in 1886. At first, made decorative copper objects from shell cases; in 1908, opened The Copper Shop, Oakland; moved to San Francisco, 1910. Copper vases, inkwells, lamps with mica shades, hand-made in *Mission style. Mark: Dirk Van Erp, beneath windmill.

vanity case. *See* powder compact.

van Kempen & Begeer. Dutch silversmiths and jewellers, founded 1835; factory at Zeist, workshops at Voorschoten and Coevorden, and retail shops in Amsterdam and other cities. Head of firm is now Sebastian Begeer; art director Gustav Beran was pupil of J. *Hoffmann and Eugen Mayer; products include works by modern silversmiths e.g. Gijo Bakker and Frans Brosche. Marks: VK beneath crescent, sometimes with points above letters; monogram VK in rectangle.

variable wood furniture. Choice of woods for identically designed furniture pieces; offered by large furniture makers during 19th century, e.g. wardrobe in ash, satinwood, or American walnut.

Vasa Murrhina. American mould-patterned or blown variegated glass. Patented for Cape Cod Glass Works in Sandwich, Massachusetts, c1883 by a Dr Flower, who later set up Vasa Murrhina Art Glass Co. in Hartford, Connecticut, to market it. Usually blue, brilliantly flecked with gold and silver. Produced by coating lining of solid colour with particles of metal, which then melt and fuse under covering of clear glass.

vase lustre. 19th century British glass candle-holder or vase (usually chalice-shaped) with long pendants of light-reflecting cut glass hanging from rim of bowl. Usually placed on mantelshelf, one at each end.

vaseline glass. Cloudy yellow, semi-translucent glass with oily appearance of vaseline; developed in 19th century, possibly in France. Sometimes surface-decorated with paint or enamel. Popular for ornamental ware in England, America, and Europe during late 19th century.

vases de tristesse. Cameo glass vases and bowls made by E. *Gallé to commemorate sadness or death. Inscribed with sad verses and made in sombre colours. As with *verreries parlantes*, colour, texture, decoration, and inscriptions combine to reflect theme.

veined Sung. *See* Sung glaze.

Vellum. *See* Rookwood Pottery.

veneer. Thin sheet of ornamental wood glued to cheaper carcase timber; usually machine-cut in Britain from 1860s. In late 19th century, often used on shoddy furniture to hide defective construction.

'Venice' pearl. *See* pearl.

Venini, Paolo (1895–1959). Italian glass artist and manufacturer; with E. *Barovier, architect of 20th century Venetian glassmaking revival. With G. *Cappelin, founded Cappelin-Venini glasshouse in Murano, 1921 (V. *Zecchin designer). Early work traditional, usually in transparent or pastel-tinted glass. With establishment of own company, Venini & Co., 1925, experimented

Vaseline glass. Vase with applied and pincered decoration. Late 19th century. Height 6in.

Le Verre Français. Cameo glass lamp. c1900.

widely in both style and materials. Developed *vetro pulagoso,* *vetro corroso,* *vetro sommerso,* and much other new glass. Also responsible for revival of *latticinio, millefiori,* and other ancient techniques. Designed first freeform vase 1933. All work characterized by purity of line and extreme simplicity of style, though often richly experimental in textural and colour effects. Acknowledged as leading modern Venetian glass artist. His factory flourishes today. Mark: Venini, Murano, over ITALIA; stamped or etched.

verre canari. *See* canary glass.

verre de soie (French, 'silk glass'). Term used for variation on satin glass made by *Stevens & Williams from *c*1886 under F. *Carder's art directorship. Double-layered, with decorative pockets of air trapped in moulded indentations of inner lining. Later also produced by Carder for *Steuben Glass Works.

verre dichroïde. *See* chrysoprase.

verre doublé. Glass technique: areas of decoration enclosed between two layers of glass, sometimes themselves of contrasting colour or opacity. Used by E. *Gallé.

Verre Français, Le. French Art Deco glassware cameo-cut with stylized flowers, fruit, and insects in rich tones of e.g. orange, purple, ultramarine, crimson, and bearing incised signature, Le Verre Français. Now identified as originating from factory of C. *Schneider. Produced 1920–33 for retailing by large stores. Found as vases, bowls, and lamp bases (some with shade *en suite*). Usually marbled glass core with superimposed layer of thin, clear glass (sometimes speckled with darker shades).

verreries parlantes. Glass vessels made by E. *Gallé. Incised with quotations, verses, or symbolic fragments; textured and decorated to reflect mood of inscriptions.

verre triplé. Glass technique: three separate layers of glass are superimposed to give depth to enclosed designs and contrasts of colour and opacity. Used by E. *Gallé.

vertical loom. *See* high-warp loom.

vesper chair. *See* prie-dieu chair.

vesta box. *See* match-holder.

vetro a reticelli, reticello glass, or **Netzglas.** Venetian glass (variant of *vetro-di-trina*) with two layers of *latticinio* glass forming net pattern, often enclosing small air bubble in each cell of network. Widely reproduced in second half of 19th century.

vetro corroso (Italian, 'corroded glass'). Clear Venetian art glass in wide range of colours. Treated with chemicals to give partly corroded surface texture. Developed 1933 by P. *Venini and widely used by him.

vetro-di-trina. *See* filigree glass.

vetro gemmato (Italian, 'gem glass'). Venetian art glass; made in all colours, usually opaque, with uneven surface and texture of matt stone. Developed in 1920s by E. *Barovier.

vetro pulagoso (Italian, 'bubble glass'). Clear Venetian art glass with close air bubbles; made in all colours. Developed 1928 by P. *Venini and widely used by him.

vetro ramarro (Italian, 'lizard glass'). Mottled green Venetian glass. Developed in 1920s by E. *Barovier.

vetro rugiado (Italian, 'dew glass'). Venetian clear or semi-opaque art glass; made in all colours, with surface effect of light dew. Developed in 1920s by E. *Barovier.

vetro sommerso (Italian, 'submerged glass'). Bubbly Italian art glass; made in all colours, with outer casing of transparent glass. Developed 1934 by P. *Venini.

Vever. French retail and manufacturing jewellers, founded in Metz by Earnest Vever in 1848. Moved to Paris after German annexation of Alsace-Lorraine (1871). In 1881, Ernest handed over to sons, Paul (1851–1915), and Henri (1854–

Henri Vever. Buckle in form of peacock; gold, enamels and cabochon-cut stones, signed and dated 1900.

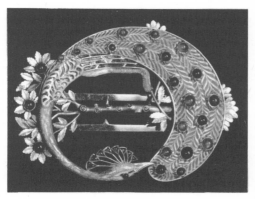

1942), who established firm as leading Art Nouveau jewellers. Designs more restrained and less inventive than pioneering efforts of R. *Lalique, but craftsmanship fine. Carried out designs of E. *Grasset. Henri wrote *'La Bijouterie Francaise au XIXe Siecle'* (1904–08 in 3 volumes), standard history of 19th century French jewellery.

Victoria A.G. Bohemian porcelain factory established (1883) at Altrohlau, near Karlsbad. Produced table services and souvenirs. Marks include crown with Victoria, and sometimes CHINA, Czechoslovakia.

Victorian furniture. Furniture made during reign of Queen Victoria in Britain, 1837–1901. Characterized by development of furniture styles usually based on historical precedents, e.g. Gothic, Elizabethan, Classical, Renaissance, and 18th century. Much solid, well-proportioned commercial furniture also made; in fine woods, e.g. birch, mahogany, and oak; characterized by restrained, carved ornament, mouldings, and inlay decoration; many examples, e.g. dressing-tables, cabinets, wardrobes, survive. Period also

characterized by proliferation of ornate, cheap, machine-made furniture combining elements of different styles in one piece. *See* animal furniture, Anglo-Japanese style, Art furniture, Early English style, Eclectic furniture, Elizabethan style, Free Renaissance style, French style, Gothic style, Gothic Reform style, Grecian style, horn furniture, Jacobean style, nameless style, naturalistic style, New Palace Westminster style, Old English style, papier-mâché, Pompeian style, reproduction furniture, Queen Anne style, Turkish style. *See also* American Victorian furniture.

Victorian glass. Wide range of styles and techniques. *Cameo glass in classical style, notably by J.*Hodgetts, G. and T.*Woodall, for *Stevens & Williams and T. *Webb & Sons; *cristallo-ceramie* of A. *Pellatt. Cut and engraved glass, e.g. deep mitre cutting, *rock crystal engraving, and delicate floral engraving, by F. *Kny and W. *Fritsche. Much new *art glass developed in wide range of colours; also, shaded glassware covering all points of spectrum, e.g. salmon-pink to blue, red to lemon, pastel green to ruby; many old types of glass

revived, e.g. *aventurine. Pressed glass imitating (in general) cut glass; also, some stipple designs resembling American lacy glass, where stippling gives overall lacy effect; major glasshouses, G. *Bacchus & Sons, *Davis, Greathead & Green, *Greener & Co., *Rice, Harris & Sons, *Sowerby's Ellison Glass Works. Unusual, sometimes bizarre, table decorations, e.g. *Rusticana centrepieces, bird fountains, busts of celebrities or sentimental subjects, produced by *Lloyd & Summerfield, F. & L. *Osler. Glass toys, cheap coloured ware, and novelties, e.g. umbrellas, rolling pins, fairy lights, produced at *Nailsea and *Alloa. Trailing and other Venetian-style decoration enjoyed popular revival, e.g. *latticinio;* special feature, ribbed handles using threaded glass. Small quantity of hand-made glass, e.g. table service by P. *Webb c1859. Also, centrepieces by D. *Pearce; varieties of *silvered glass; development of *sandblasting, *Mary Gregory glass; *millefiori* paperweights, *doorstops, *inkbottle tops; glass-threading machine patented in 1860s by *Richardson & Sons; in 1870s, three-lipped decanter introduced and immediately popular.

Victorian Renaissance style. *See* Renaissance revival style.

Victorian silver styles. Originated with rococo revival in fashion when Queen Victoria came to throne in 1837; naturalistic scrollwork favoured, with wave, acanthus, vine etc. motifs; some French-influenced pieces decorated in Louis XIV and Louis XV styles, gradually combined with rococo floral ornament. More exotic elements, palm trees, tropical foliage etc., introduced in late 1840s. O. *Jones's 'Plans, Eleva-

Left
Victorian silver. Electro-plated coffee machine made by Padley, Parkin and Staniforth. c1855. Height 14in.
Below
Victorian silver. Cruet frame made by Charles Favell & Co., Sheffield 1868. Height 11¼in.

Victorian silver. Dessert stand in silver and parcel-gilt with glass dish and trumpet decorated with sand-blasted ornament. Made by William Gough in Birmingham, 1863. Height 9in.

tions, Sections, and Details of the Alhambra', stimulated Moorish fashion of 1850s, with E. *Cotterill of *Garrards main exponent; *c*1850 Tudor and François I styles revived with heavy strapwork and oval cartouches on larger pieces, and engraved ornament on smaller articles; neo-Gothic style applied to ecclesiastical plate, also on tea and coffee sets, with finely engraved pointed arches and crockets. Renaissance revival from late 1840s, and classical revival from early 1860s, aided by use of electro-plating technique: Renaissance-style centrepieces, candelabra, and sets containing tazza and matching dessert dishes, widely made, with features including lion, ram, and goat masks, stylized foliage, and griffins; chief designers A. *Stevens, Thomas Brown, Antoine Vechte, and L. *Morel-Ladeuil; classical forms established by 1870, remained popular to end of Victorian era. Queen Anne and Louis XVI styles in fashion 1862–80. Larger firms, e.g. *Elkington & Co., *Hunt & Roskell, and *Hancock, competed with exhibition pieces through 1860s and early 1870s, but by Philadelphia International Exhibition, 1876, only Elkington represented Britain with pieces in Egyptian, Grecian, Pompeian, and Renaissance tastes. Interest in oriental ornament and *chinoiseries* in 1870s and 1880s stimulated by exhibitions of Japanese art in London and Paris. By end of 1880s most firms had stopped producing 'art works', and made mainly stereotyped copies of earlier styles. New stimulus at end of period provided by William Morris and Arts and Crafts movement, influencing works of C. R. *Ashbee, H. *Cole, and C. *Dresser, and leading to *Cymric silver of Liberty & Co.

Clock of Vienna regulator type with year movement. Made in Munich. Early 20th century. Signed Andreas Huber.

Victoria ware. *See* Wedgwood, Josiah & Sons Ltd.

Vieillard factory. *See* Longwy.

Vienna regulator. Weight-driven wall clock made in Austria from 1800; first shown in England at International Exhibition (1862). Has glass front and sides, wooden rod pendulum, and seconds dial or centre-seconds hand. True Viennese models have seconds pendulum, but commonly Black Forest imitations do not indicate true seconds. (*See* regulator clock.)

Vienna Secession. Association of progressive architects, artists, and designers, founded 1897, after resignation of disillusioned members (led by J. *Hoffmann) from Viennese Society of Visual Artists; other artists included students and colleagues of O. *Wagner, and group associated with G. *Klimt. First exhibition (1898) showed work of leading artists in other European countries and began reappraisal of Viennese arts. Hoffmann, K. *Moser, and other Secessionists appointed to posts in School of Applied Arts in Austrian Museum of Art and Industry, and influenced many students. Work characterized by stylistic elements of Art

Nouveau (symbolism, linear drawing of plant forms, etc.). In 1899, J. M. *Olbrich joined Matildenhöhe artists' colony in Darmstadt, first of many Viennese artists who left to work in Germany. Fourteenth exhibition of Secession in 1902 featured Max Klinger's statue of Beethoven and Beethoven frieze, designed especially as setting by Klimt. Among Secessionists, Hoffmann and Moser particularly influenced by work of C. R. *Mackintosh and Glasgow School. Wiener Werkstätte founded in 1903; Wiener Keramik in 1905. Developed style which led to Modern Movement; earlier flowing plant forms gave way to geometrical shapes. New principles applied to wide range of products, e.g. vases, tea and coffee services, boxes, book bindings; contrasting scheme of black and white recurs in work of Hoffmann and in ceramics of M. *Powolny.

Vienna Workshop. *See* Wiener Werkstätte.

Viking style. Furniture style popular in Scandinavia during 1870s. Inspired by Viking motifs in stone carvings, decoration in medieval churches, etc. Exponents include G. *Munthe.

Vignaud factory. *See* Limoges.

Villeroy & Boch. German pottery manufacturer formed (1836) by merging companies of Villeroy, established in 1789 at Vaudrevanges (Wallerfangen) in Saar basin, of J. F. *Boch at Septfontaines (Luxembourg), and at Abbey of Mettlach (Rhineland), established 1809; produced earthenware. Stoneware also made from 1842: includes mugs, etc., exported in quantity to America, *c*1860–*c*1900. Noted for art pottery decorated with inlaid clays in contrasting colours (Mettlach ware). Terracotta for architectural use made from 1850, and mosaic tiles from 1852. Artists in late 19th century included J. *Scharvogel. Cream-coloured earthenware for domestic use made at factories in Dresden (from 1853) and Schramberg (from 1883). Marks include Mettlach castle with monogram of VB, diagonal cross within square frame with VB/M contained in octagon at centre, circular mark with Mercury looking over name, Villeroy & Boch and Mettlach, Wallerfangen, or Septfontaines; also VB/S surrounding spruce tree within octagonal outline.

vinaigrette or **vinegarette.** Small box, casket, or shaped container, *c*½in.–*c*5in. long, with pierced grille below hinged cover, and sponge for aromatic vinegar or other perfume; first appeared in late 18th century, carried on watch chain or chatelaine, or in pocket, and used as antidote to unpleasant smells; often given as token of affection. Made in gold, silver, pinchbeck, and other materials; early examples with chased, filigree, and repoussé decoration, later superseded by appliqué, beading, engine-turning, moulding, enamelling, and gem setting; usually more restrained in Britain than on Continent, but often ornamented with historical and patriotic designs representing Battle of Trafalgar, Windsor Castle, etc. Design of grille, always gilt to prevent corrosion, may contrast with exterior, with plain lids revealing ornate grilles. Not used after end of 19th century. Notable British makers include Samuel Pemberton, Matthew Linwood, John Shaw, John Turner, Joseph Willmore, and Nathaniel Mills.

violin or **scroll flask.** 19th century American whiskey flask of quart to half-pint capacity; free or mould blown; violin-shaped. Often in vivid colours (usually clear glass): blue, purple, yellow; also opaque white. Decorated with commemorative emblems or elaborate scrolls, stars, and sometimes *fleur-de-lis*. Often inscribed with name of glasshouse. Also made as pocket flask.

Vista Alegre. Portuguese factory, manufacturing hard-paste porcelain near Oporto from 1824 to present day. Marks include initials, VA.

vitro-porcelain. Late 19th century British art glass; streaked opaque green with purple veining. Type of *slag glass. Made by adding blast-furnace slag and cryolite to glass metal. Developed by Sowerby & Co. (*see* Sowerby's Ellison Glass Works).

Vittali, Otto (b 1872). German glass artist; one of pioneers of Jugendstil. Worked in Munich and Frankfurt, producing ornamental ware. Mark: Otto over Vittali in larger letters, with V forming bar between two parts of name.

Volkmar, Charles (1841-1914). American painter and artist potter. While studying painting in Paris, made pottery with underglaze decoration in Montigny-sur-Loing (Seine-et-Marne), using slips made from fired and ground clay. After return to America in 1879, established pottery at Greenpoint, Long Island; made vases and tiles. Volkmar Keramic Company, formed in 1895, used decoration of historic buildings, and portraits of contemporary American personalities. From c1900, simplified designs, e.g. of flowers and flying ducks. Work influenced by oriental pottery. From late 19th century, made increasing use of matt glazes.. In partnership, established Corona Pottery, New York. Taught ceramics in Long Island, and (from 1903) at Metuchen, New Jersey. Assisted in work by son, L. *Volkmar. Mark: incised V, or VOLKMAR METUCHEN.

Volkmar, Leon (b 1879). American artist potter, born in France. Son of C. *Volkmar. Began as potter in 1902. Concentrated on achievement of simple forms, with fine colour and texture; glaze colours include blue, red, yellow, or aubergine, also brown or black. Some decoration influenced by Islamic pottery. Teacher in Pennsylvania, at

Charles Volkmar. Pair of vases. Red earthenware body with underglaze slip painting. c1881. Height 12½in.

Columbia University, New York, and professor at University of Ceramics, Cincinnati, Ohio.

Volkstedt-Rudolstadt. German porcelain factory established 1760 in Volkstedt, Thuringia, under patronage of Johann Friedrich von Schwarzburg-Rudolstadt. In 20th century, noted for manufacture of tableware, vases, and figures. Work in style of Meissen includes many imitations, particularly of *Affenkapellen* ('monkey bands'). Artists include P. *Scheurich. Modern marks include pitchfork, crossed scissors, and sunburst.

von Eiff, Wilhelm (1890-1943). Austrian Art Deco glass artist and gem-cutter. Engraved portraits in precious stones, evolving new technique of *Schnitzen* (chipping). Head of influential teaching and experimental workshops for glass and gem-cutting at *Württembergische Metallwarenfabrik 1921-37. Mark: W. v. E., and date.

Charles F. Annesley Voysey. Machine-turned brass teapot. c1896.

Charles F. Annesley Voysey. Oak chair with rush seat. c1905. Height 3ft1in.

von Heider, Maximilian (fl late 19th century). German artist potter, working at Schöngau, Bavaria. With sons, experimented in use of lustre glazes.

von Poschinger, Ferdinand (1858-1943). German glass artist; one of pioneers of Jugendstil. Made vases and other decorative pieces, working in Buchenau and Theresienthal. Mark: Ferd. von Poschinger, Buchenau.

von Spaun, Max Ritter (fl 1879-1908). Bohemian glass artist; grandson of Johann Loetz (d 1848), founder of J. *Loetz Witwe glasshouse in Klostermühle. Director of glasshouse, 1879-1908. Made superb glass, imitating agate and other precious stones, but known especially for decorative ware in *Tiffany-inspired Art Nouveau iridescent glass. Some pieces considered finer than Tiffany's, especially for their more decisive design. *Illustration at* Loetz Witwe, J.

Voysey, Charles F. Annesley (1857-1941). English architect and designer of furniture, textiles, carpets and tapestries (for A. *Morton), wallpapers, ceramics, and metalwork. Articled to J. P. *Seddon, 1874, setting up own practice, 1882. Designed first wallpapers and textiles, 1883, under influence of A. H. *Mackmurdo. Joined *Art Workers' Guild, 1884, Master in 1924. First showed furniture with *Arts & Crafts Exhibition Society in 1893; pieces generally austere, with straight lines and little ornament; mainly in oak; often with Art Nouveau heart motifs (for mounts, as pierced decoration, and cut-outs on chair backs), attenuated shafts in cabinets, and metal inlays. Designed *hooded chair (1896); *swan chair (c1897). Advocated natural finish for wood. *Illustration also at* ingrain carpet, Morton, A., & Co., Tomkinson & Adam.

Vyse, Charles (d 1968). English potter and sculptor. Studied modelling in Staffordshire at Hanley Art School, and subsequently also worked in Staffordshire. At own studio in Chelsea, London (1919-63) with wife, Nell, experimented with use of glazes containing wood ash on stoneware; also successful in reproduction of Chinese Sung glazes in 1920s. Figures and groups (1919-30), realistically modelled and sometimes coloured, include The Balloon Woman, The Tulip Girl, and a girl riding a fawn and holding a lamb, entitled Folies Bergères, signed Charles Vyse, Chelsea. Work marked with initials or signature and date.

Waals, Peter (1870-1937). Dutch cabinet maker; employed by S. and E. *Barnsley and E. W. *Gimson from 1901, becoming foreman-in-charge at Daneway House, Sapperton. Carried on Cotswold school traditions after Gimson's death. Pieces include lectern (1906) in ebony with ivory, mother-of-pearl, and silver inlay; polished iron candlesticks.

Wackerle, Josef (b 1880). German sculptor and porcelain modeller. Made figures with underglaze decoration from c1905 at Nymphenburg factory; art director, 1906-09. While teaching in Berlin (1909-17), designed figures produced by Berlin factory, e.g. Masked Lady (c1911), and groups inspired by Meissen; also formal table service, made in 1912.

Charles Vyse. Model of amphitrite astride hippocampus. Incised mark: C. Vyse, Chelsea. c1930. Height 12in.

Below
Peter Waals. Silver cupboard in figured walnut. Designed and made 1925.

Wilhelm Wagenfeld. Hammered copper coffee machine, made at *Bauhaus. 1923.

Wagenfeld, Wilhelm (b 1900). Distinguished German Functionalist architect and industrial designer; served apprenticeship in Bremen silver factory, and attended Bremen Kunstgewerbe-schule; student in metal workshop at Weimar *Bauhaus 1922-25; assistant 1925-29; director of metal workshop from 1929, when began collaboration with industry. Left Bauhaus c1931 to concentrate on glass and ceramic design; some porcelain produced by Fürstenberg factory; developed Jena fire-resistant glass and *Rautenglas. Later designed sweetmeat dishes and other vessels for glass workshop at Württembergische Metallwarenfabrik and *Rosenthal glasshouse, as well as making table glass and lampshade models for Rhineland company, Peill & Putzler. Professor at Kunsthochschule, Berlin, 1931-35; art director of Vereinigte Lausitzer Glaswerke, Weisswasser/ Oberlausitz; after 2nd World War designed porcelain for Rosenthal factory, Selb. Since 1949 worked at Stuttgart, where established Werkstatt Wagenfeld in 1954. Designs simple and functional, in accordance with Bauhaus ideals; craft products given appearance of industrial production; table lamp in glass and chromium-plated metal, made in collaboration with K. J. Jucker in 1923-24, now in Museum of Modern Art, New York. Designed trays, plates, and cutlery for airline, Lufthansa.

Wagner, Otto (1841-1918). Austrian architect; also designed furniture. Professor at Vienna Academy of Art from 1894. In inaugural lecture, stated: 'nothing that is not beautiful can be practical'. Pupils included J. *Hoffmann and J. *Olbrich. Took part in Vienna Secession, breaking away in 1912. Designed simple, functional furniture characterized by constructional qualities and use of e.g. iron. Examples include

wood and metal armchair for Vienna Savings Bank (1904), with semi-circular, velvet-upholstered seat, continuous back and arms curving to form front legs, continuous back legs and uprights, and high stretchers following seat's shape.

Wahliss, Ernst (fl late 19th, early 20th centuries). Bohemian potter and porcelain maker. Esta-

Ernst Wahliss. Vase with applied decoration. c1890.

---

wafer box. Small box for thin adhesive discs (wafers) of dried, coloured paste, used to seal letters until general adoption of gummed envelopes in late 19th century. Made of silver or Sheffield plate, glass, porcelain, hardstone, or papier-mâché. Often part of matching desk set. Form was model for *stamp box.

blished Alexandra Porcelain Works (c1880) at Turn-Teplitz (Trnovany, near Teplice); made porcelain and earthenware influenced by work of M. *Powolny. In early 20th century, produced earthenware (Serapis-Fayence), with elaborate painted decoration, notably by K. *Klaus.

Wain, Louis William (1860–1931). English illustrator and designer. Noted for studies of cats engaged in human activities. Designs include series of postcards in 1900s and c1920 for firm of Raphael Tuck. Pottery figures of animals (cats, dogs, pigs, etc.) in cubist style, coloured e.g. green, orange, or black, date from period 1910–20.

Wakely & Wheeler (London). English firm of manufacturing silversmiths, going back to John Lias (recorded mark 1791); 1879 Henry John Lias partnered James Wakely; 1909 firm became Wakely & Wheeler with F. C. Wheeler; produced wide range of silver and electro-plated ware of high quality; craftsmen included W. E. King and F. S. Beck. Firm taken over by Padgett & Braham Ltd. Marks include: JW & FCW, WW in trefoil.

wakizashi. See Japanese swords.

Walker & Hall (Sheffield). English silversmiths, founded 1843; initially specialized in electroplate; soon joined by Hall's nephew Sir John Bingham at age 16, who controlled firm to death in 1916 and modelled it into one of most successful in trade; followed by son Sir Albert Bingham; company extensively modernized in 1945, now part of British Silverware Ltd. Marks: W & H; HH & JEB; JEB; W & H in triangular pennant.

walking stick. Majority of 19th century sticks of round or oval cross-section, with handle in curved, knobbed, carved, round, hexagonal, right-angled, or T-piece shape; stem typically tapers from maximum width at handle to minimum at ferrule. Made in variety of woods, including ebony, rosewood, figwood, ash, chestnut, apple; also cane (bamboo, malacca, whangee, partridge, congo), and animal cartilage or bone (ivory, shark's vertebrae, rhinotail). Decorative ferrule, of brass, ivory, horn, etc., frequently elaborately engraved or chased. Ornate handles mounted or cased in e.g. gold or silver, may be decorated with engraved or *repoussé* designs. Many examples with extra refinements or gadgets, e.g. fitted with concealed snuff box, or sovereign holder; also sword-stick, *gun stick (from c1850), and toper's stick (top unscrews to reveal secret container for spirits). Glass walking sticks first produced c1860 by Bristol workmen at glass factories as presents for wives, families; later manufactured commercially, e.g. as *commemorative objects.

walking stick (in glass). Most examples of *Nailsea origin; favourite subject for *friggers. Usually of colourless or pale green glass with *latticinio* striping or spirals in milky-white or pale pink; often surface-decorated with ruby, blue, and green (rarely, yellow or dark red) trailing. Also found as outsize 4–8ft rods of twisted glass in walking-stick form for hanging in houses as spells against e.g. leprosy and malaria.

Wallander, Alf (1862–1914). Swedish artist, leading exponent of Art Nouveau in Sweden, designer of ceramics, glass, textiles, furniture,

Wakely & Wheeler. Pair of vases, London 1900.
Below
Wakely & Wheeler. Tazza, silver gilt with band of chased decoration round rim and knop. Marks, Wakeley and Wheeler, London. 1928. Width 6¼ in.

etc. Designer of porcelain at Rörstrand from 1895, artistic director from 1897; introduced Art Nouveau style, using floral relief decoration on porcelain, painted in muted colours under glaze. Furniture combines Art Nouveau motifs with late 18th century forms, e.g. white-painted drawing-room chairs with seat narrowing at juncture with attenuated, outward inclining back uprights, splayed back legs; three splats join low back rail and crested yoke rail, which is decorated with stylized floral motifs.

Walrath, Frederick (c1880–c1920). American artist potter, studied under C. F. *Binns. Work shown at St Louis World Fair in 1904. Teacher in Rochester and at Columbia University, New York. Made earthenware vases, jars, etc., decorated with linear designs and stylized plant motifs carried out in matt glazes. Mark: Walrath Pottery, incised, with device of four arrows. For two years before death, worked at Newcomb College Pottery, New Orleans.

Walter, Alméric (1859–1942). French Art Nouveau and Art Deco glass artist. Worked in *pâte-de-verre.* Collaborated with many sculptors, especially H. *Bergé, their thick bowls, dishes, ashtrays, decorated with small sprays of berries, flowers, and insects, in greens, turquoises, and yellows, frequently monogrammed. Worked for *Daum brothers, subsequently independent. *Illustration at pâte-de-verre.*

Walton, George (1867–1933). British architect and designer; educated at evening classes at Glasgow School of Art; set up as designer and decorator under title George Walton & Co., Ecclesiastical & House Decorators, Glasgow 1888. Member of Glasgow School. Designed linear furniture in Glasgow style based on 18th century forms, with emphasis on verticals. Exhibited at Arts & Crafts Exhibition Society, London 1890; moved to London 1897; designed

Above
Walker & Hall. Teapot, cream jug and sugar basin. Sheffield mark. 1929.

Left
Walking sticks. Left to right: 1) Russian stick with tortoise-shell top decorated with silver band. 2) Cane stick topped with carved ivory figure. 3) Carved ebony stick with silver knob. 4) Ebony stick with silver handle depicting Leda and the Swan. 5) Ebony stick with handle in form of silver horse's head. All mid to late 19th century.

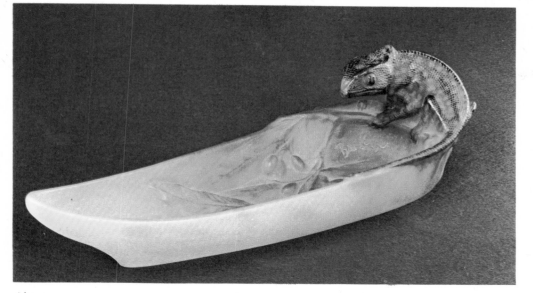

Above
Alméric Walter. Pâte-de-verre *dish decorated with chameleon.* c1910.

Below
George Walton. Two ebonized wood chairs with cane seats and back panels. c1896. *Height 3ft6in.*

number of shop fronts for e.g. Kodak, and houses, e.g. White House, Shiplake, which still contains examples of his metalwork, including candlesticks and chandeliers in polished iron and copper, in *Mackintosh-influenced Art Nouveau style. Ebonized wood chairs with vase-shaped splats for Kodak shops in Britain, Russia, and Europe, also Cranston Tea Rooms in Glasgow, copied throughout Europe; painted version used in houses designed by Walton. Variations with high, arched backs shown at

*Arts & Crafts Exhibition Society in 1910. Also designed furniture for Liberty's, and High Wycombe manufacturers.

Warangal (Andhra Pradesh [formerly in Hyderabad]). Indian carpet making centre; with *Eluru, chief centre for hand-knotted woollen pile carpets in region. Also known for fine silk rugs. Industry introduced by Muslim invaders because of availability of wool in region; used Persian techniques and designs (subsequently

modified by local weavers); thereafter, industry largely worked by Muslim weavers. Carpets for European market produced from mid 19th century. Industry thrived until c1930, at its height employing c500 craftsmen. Modern factory set up c1925 by Nizam of Hyderabad under G. P. *Stavrides and master designer from Gwalior. *East India Carpet Co. marketed goods and dictated designs. Factory sold c1935, and shortly afterwards closed down. Overseas demand reduced c1930 with increasing use of cheap materials by commercial companies; industry declined and weavers made redundant. Government factory, founded 1931–32 to rehabilitate them, closed c1947.

Wardian case. Domed, glass case with metal frame; supported on small stand, usually table with central leg resting on claws, or solid base. Dome contains large pot for house plants. Used from c1850; named after N. B. Ward (1791–1868) who specialized in cultivation of plants under glass.

wardrobe. Free-standing cupboard for storing clothes. Dates from 18th century; common bedroom furniture in Britain and America from early 19th century. Incorporates hanging space, and drawers, shelves, etc. Typical early Victorian form often in Grecian style with breakfront, rounded curves, three panels outlined with moulding (used mainly for servants' rooms by 1880s). Metal door furniture replaced wooden knobs, c1850. American examples in mahogany with double doors, plain moulded top, plinth base; also single-door models with drawer in base. Both common c1840–c1865. Tall well-proportioned examples, often in mahogany, with severe outlines, simple moulding on doors, made from c1860 in Britain; decoration usually matches dressing-table, washstand, etc. throughout period. Winged cupboards for double bedrooms. Long mirror in central front panel, or attached to inside of door, common from c1865. Many styles from c1880, especially Free Renaissance style. Cheap examples stained and grained to imitate satinwood, maplewood, etc. common. Free-standing models largely replaced from c1927 by built-in cupboards painted to match walls of room.

wardrobe-bed or **parlour bedstead.** Bed becomes wardrobe when folded away. Examples known in 17th and 18th centuries; popular *patent furniture in America, c1850–c1890. Forerunner of Pullman sleeping compartment beds, introduced 1937; undersides form wall and upholstered back rest.

Waring & Gillow. London furniture manufacturers and retailers; development of *Gillow, active from c1900 to present day. Employed S. *Chermayeff and P. *Follot as directors of department of modern French furniture, 1929. *Illustration at* Chermayeff, S.

warming pan. Circular brass or copper container for glowing charcoal, with hinged lid and long wooden handle. Pushed back and forth between sheets to warm bed. Lid may be pierced or engraved; carved or turned handle usually of oak or mahogany. Continued in production throughout 19th century, but gradually superseded by hot-water bottle. Numerous modern reproductions.

warp-tinting. *See* tapestry process.

Warren Manufacturing Company. *See* Dennison, Aaron L.

Wartha, Vinsce (1844–1914). Hungarian ceramic designer. 1893–1910, director of experimental studio at Zsolnay factory, working with lustre glazes. Made series of vases in billowing, folded shapes with lustre decoration in shades of green, yellow, and blue. Some examples have decoration of plants or cloud-like motifs, e.g. vase with brown lustre trees, bright red cloud forms and white trails against dark blue ground, and small vase decorated with band of white snowdrops at neck and open pink flowers at base. *Illustration at* Zsolnay.

Warwick school of carving. English craftsmen in Warwick, known for elaborate, pictorial, carved furniture in which structure is subordinate to ornament. Active c1850–c1910. Notable exponents of style, W. *Cookes and T. *Kendall.

Warwick Time Stamp Company. *See* time recording stamp clock.

Washington Works. *See* Macintyre, James & Co.

wash-stand or **wash-hand-stand.** Piece of bedroom furniture for holding basin, ewer, soapdish, etc.; introduced in early 19th century. Top, with circular hole for basin, and splashback usually marble. Late 19th century examples

*Washstand. Designed by Ambrose *Heal in 1908. Made in unpolished oak with chip-carving. Curtain embroidered by Edith Heal. Width 3ft.*

Watcombe Pottery. Left to right: 1) and 3) terra cotta with turquoise slip decoration. 2) Pilgrim bottle with painted decoration, height 13in. 4) Jar and cover. All pieces c1875.

often have cupboards, drawers, and superstructure of shelves; sometimes framed mirror, towel rail, screen, etc. Also circular models in mahogany, ash, etc., with plug in basin, and wastepipe to base. May be made as *campaign furniture. Widely used until c1925.

Watcombe Pottery. Pottery established in 1869, near Torquay, Devon. Terracotta art pottery made by workmen from Staffordshire, distinguishable from other terracotta made in Torquay district by darker body. Products include portrait busts and figures, vases, jars, architectural ware, garden ornaments, tea services. Figures in normal, darkish body often have paler drapery applied and touched with colour, notably turquoise. Plaques, dishes, and vases painted with flowers and butterflies in natural colours. Some vases also decorated with turquoise enamel, Etruscan style motifs in black, or (from 1880s) designs incised through thin layer of coloured slip to show buff or tinted body beneath. Other ornamental ware includes baskets of flowers, ferns, etc., modelled in great detail. Teapots, jugs, etc., lined with glaze; glaze inside cups often bright blue. Early work marked with WATCOMBE POTTERY or WATCOMBE TORQUAY impressed. From 1875, circular mark used with woodpecker on branch, with sea in background, sometimes enclosed by WATCOMBE SOUTH DEVON in double line. After amalgamation with *Aller Vale pottery c1901, traded as Royal Aller Vale & Watcombe Potteries. Later marks incorporate word ROYAL, and/or TORQUAY.

Waterhouse, Alfred (1830–1905). English architect; also designed Art furniture, e.g. corner cupboard (c1878) in ebonized wood, with doors decorated with flat floral design on gilt background (now in Victoria & Albert Museum, London).

Waterloo Works. *See* Boote, T. & R. Ltd.

watch chain. Short chain, often gold or silver, also e.g. cut-steel, popular during 19th and early 20th centuries, attached to *fob watch, carried in waistcoat or pocket in waistband of trousers. Hanging from other end of chain are seals, watch keys, etc. Many Swiss examples, e.g. from Geneva. From mid 19th century, English pocket watch chain called *Albert, possibly after ceremonial presentation of gold chain and key to Prince Albert by Birmingham jewellers in 1845. Chain sometimes supplied with watch, but usually sold separately.

watch stand. Stand to hold large pocket watch on bedside table at night. Made in various shapes: some functional with aperture leaving watch face visible; some in shape of tree – watch hung from one of branches. Produced from mid 18th century to c1914 in silver, brass, bronze, and wood.

Waterbury watch. American machine-made watch invented 1878 by Azro Buck; originally manufactured in Waterbury, Connecticut. Movement, with hour hand attached, rotates once an hour; made up of 58 parts with mainspring c10ft long. Sold for c$4. Types manufactured run alphabetically through A to W, all with duplex *escapement. Rotary movements continued up to series E; E–W, all dials unpierced except for some E. From series K, dial with sunken centre and balance under separate cock; bear name, Charles Benedict, instead of Waterbury trademark. Series R has enamel dial with subsidiary seconds dial, and e.g. silver or rolled gold case. Maximum daily production of c1000 watches in 1880s. In 1890, series abandoned in face of Swiss competition. New design, marketed under name of New England Watch Company, also failed; company taken over by R. *Ingersoll in 1892.

waterproof watch. First successful waterproof watch was Explorer's watch made by E. J. *Dent c1900. Case, by Dennison Watch Case Co., has screw-on caps, with cork washers, to cover dial, and winding button. Waterproof wrist watch, e.g. by Rolex, has rubber or plastic washers at glass, between front and back of case, and at

winding button. Most watches described as waterproof only water-resistant; true waterproof watches tested to depths of 600ft.

Watherston & Brogden. *See* Brogden, John.

Watt, William (fl 1865-85). London furniture maker; known for Anglo-Japanese style pieces. Published Art Furniture, catalogue of E. W. *Godwin's designs, in 1877. Some furniture labelled. *Illustration at* Godwin, E. W.

Watts, John (d 1858). English potter; partner with J. *Doulton in London pottery trading as Doulton & Watts at Vauxhall from c1815, and at Lambeth High Street from mid 1820s.

Wave Crest Ware. *See* puff box.

Wear Pottery. English pottery, established in 1789 in Sunderland district (Durham). Traded as Samuel Moore & Co. from 1803 until closure (1881). Made earthenware flowerpots, frog mugs, lustre decorated jugs, etc., also tableware with sponged decoration, or brown glaze. Marks (after 1861) incorporate name or initials of company.

weathered oak. Oak treated with lime and other substances to produce finish resembling patina of natural, unstained wood. Process developed after 1st World War by A. *Heal; adopted by other manufacturers, resulting in many shades and finishes.

Weaver, James (d c1880). English porcelain painter. Worked at Worcester porcelain factory from early 1850s until 1870, then at factory of W. T. *Copeland. Son, Charles, also painter, employed at Copeland factory in late 19th century; specialized in scenes with cattle.

web foot. Modern term for webbed claw-and-ball foot; found mainly on Irish and northern English pieces.

Webb, Joseph (fl 1880s). American glass artist, member of Stourbridge family of Webb. Worked for *Phoenix Glass Works, where developed *satin glass in 1885.

Webb, Philip (1831-1915). English architect and designer of furniture, embroideries, metalwork, jewellery, and glass. Principal assistant to G. E. *Street in Oxford from 1852. In London from 1856, private practice as architect. Early designs for furniture date from 1858 to 59. Built home in Kent for friend, W. *Morris, Red House, Bexley, completed 1860. Among original associates in *Morris, Marshall, Faulkner & Co., and firm's chief designer. Glass tableware from c1860, e.g. wineglasses, tumblers, finger-bowls, carafes, made by J. *Powell & Sons, thinly blown, clear glass in simple, contoured shapes. Also designed most of metalwork, e.g. sturdy candlesticks in style inspired by English work of 13th century; little survives. Large scale, well proportioned furniture in variation of Gothic Reform style, with large, painted panels, includes rectangular mahogany and pine cabinet, supported on oak stand, and painted by Morris with scenes from legend of St George, shown at International Exhibition in London, 1862. Decoration in gesso, or tooled, coloured, and gilt leather panels occur as well as paintings in early work. Free-standing pieces, e.g. large settles and sideboards,

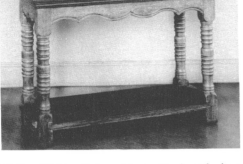

*Philip Webb. Oak cabinet. Cupboard door panels painted by W. *de Morgan. Designed c1865. Height 7ft11in.*
Below
Thomas Webb & Sons. Gold-relief painting. Loving cup with gold relief painted decoration by Jules Barbe. Late 19th century. Height 9¾in.

characterized by overhanging canopies. Contributed to design of textiles and, under general planning of Morris, designed panelling, gesso mural relief, and animal frieze for one of refreshment rooms in South Kensington (now Victoria & Albert) Museum. Continued to design for firm after Morris's move to Merton Abbey. In 1900, succeeded in practice by G. *Jack, employee from c1880.

Webb, Thomas, & Sons. English glasshouse in Stourbridge, Worcestershire. Known for fine engraved glass, especially *rock crystal engraving of F. *Kny and W. *Fritsche in 1880s; also for cameo glass of T. and G. *Woodall, and coloured glass developments in late 19th century, notably *Queen's Burmese glass (c1902) and *Alexandrite. Threaded decoration and all-over diamond moulding popular features of output from late 1850s. In early 1870s, made first three-lipped decanter (still in production); also noted for fine centrepieces produced under D. *Pearce from 1884. Flourishes today. Mark: Webb encircled by Made in England, stamped or etched, also Webb in script. *Illustration also at* Kny, F.

Wedgwood, Josiah, & Sons Ltd. Staffordshire pottery established in Burslem (1759) by Josiah Wedgwood I (1730-95); property of Wedgwood family to present day. Etruria factory opened in 1769; Burslem works closed 1774. Noted for production of green-glazed wares, cream-coloured earthenware, black basalt, jasper ware, cane-ware, etc. Manufacture of bone porcelain attempted for some years from 1812; successfully resumed in 1878. Parian porcelain, notably portrait busts, produced from 1848, marketed as Carrara. E. *Lessore experimented with colours from 1858; painted own designs on Queensware, and continued to supply work after return to France in 1863. Experiments in *lithography began in 1863, at first in close imitation of oil-painting. Majolica, made 1860-1910, includes umbrella stands, wall brackets, plaques, comports, plates, and dishes. High-quality relief decoration achieved by use of Queensware body under translucent glazes. New designs for leaf dishes echo earlier green-glazed ware. Designs influenced by oriental green-glazed ware. Designs influenced by oriental styles include plates with relief decoration of circular leaf motifs, prunus blossom, and bamboo leaves covered with pink, blue, and green glazes against cream ground, or flowers, birds, and insects, with angular motifs perforated at rim. *Emaux ombrants* also used to decorate majolica. Tiles, made 1870-c1900, generally transfer-printed in sets, e.g. months, Red Riding Hood, A Midsummer Night's Dream, Robin Hood, animals, sailing ships, or American views. Developments in 1870s include Victoria ware (body described as half-way between bone porcelain and Queensware), buff-coloured bone porcelain paste, painted and decorated with raised gilding in styles resembling work of Worcester Royal Porcelain Factory, and peach-coloured stoneware. Basalt vases, made c1875, decorated with leaf and vine patterns in applied slip, gilded. From 1880, production of painted and printed landscapes, views, etc., begun in 18th century, extended to include limited editions of plates, dishes, and jugs, commemorating places or events, at first for American market. Usually made in Queensware, although sometimes in cream-coloured earthenware or bone porcelain. Renewed interest in late 18th century design at

Josiah Wedgwood & Sons. Earthenware slip-painted vase. c1880. Height 9in.

beginning of 20th century led to establishment of Wedgwood Museum (opened 1906). Under art direction of J. E. *Goodwin (1902–34), powder-blue of Chinese Ch'ing period reproduced (1908) as ground colour on bone porcelain. From this period until c1932, lustre decoration used, notably on Dragon and Fairyland lustre ware designed by D. *Makeig-Jones. Jasper ware with relief decoration in lilac and green introduced 1885, although most examples 1915–35. Dark olive (1920–30) and crimson (1925–35) jasper subject to staining of white relief decoration with ground colour. Other colours include buff (1900–30) and black (distinct from basalt) used with yellow in early 20th century. Turquoise used c1875. A. and L. *Powell employed from c1905 to provide new designs and to train factory artists in free-hand painting. Although traditional shapes and patterns continued in use, modern methods of manufacture required new designs for production in large numbers by casting, turning, etc. Work of K. *Murray frequently decorated only with grooves, or white fluting, with *Moonstone glaze. Coloured bodies introduced in 1930s include Champagne and Honey-buff variations of cream-coloured earthenware; grey and *Alpine pink tinted paste introduced in bone porcelain. V. *Skellern art director from 1935. Factory moved to Barlaston, where production started in 1940; over 80% of output sold overseas, notably in America, during 2nd World War. Marks incorporate WEDGWOOD and, from 1891, made in England, to satisfy American tariff regulations. Bone porcelain from 1878 marked with replica of Portland Vase. *Illustrations also at* claret jug, Goodwin, J. E., Lessore, E., Makeig-Jones, D., Murray, K., Ravilious, E., Semper, G.

Wedgwood & Co. Staffordshire pottery manufacturers operating Unicorn Pottery and Pinnox Works, Tunstall, from mid 19th century. Tableware, toilet services, etc., made for sale in England and for export to Europe and America. Specialized in ironstone china, transfer-printed, or with painted, jewelled, or gilded decoration. Limited company (1910–65); afterwards traded as Enoch Wedgwood (Tunstall) Ltd. Marks include WEDGWOOD & CO, sometimes with type of ware, e.g. ironstone china, or (1862–90) head of unicorn with collar and chain, over WEDGWOOD & CO.

weights and measures. Graded 19th century shop-keeper's weights, in brass or copper, commonly ranging from $\frac{1}{4}$oz to 14lb; drapers' brass measures in inches, feet, and yards; numerous vessels, measuring various dry and liquid capacities, e.g. in pewter, brass, copper. Government standard weights and measures largely unified by c1800, deposited at Jewel Tower, London, until c1880, with exception of standard gallon and pound, kept at Houses of Parliament and destroyed by fire in 1834. Imperial standards for weights and measures scientifically determined (1870–1900), by standards department of Board of Trade, constituted 1870. Troy weight system abolished by 1878 Weights & Measures Act.

Weller, Samuel A. (1851–1925). American potter. In early 1890s acquired *Lonhuda Pottery and transferred operations to own pottery at Zanesville, Ohio (established 1882). Art pottery in style of Lonhuda, sold as Louwelsa, produced from 1895, closely resembles contemporary Rookwood Standard ware; variations introduced in order to compete with new lines developed at Rookwood, e.g. Eocean ware, version of Louwelsa marked Eosian/WELLER parallels Rookwood's Iris style. J. *Sicard, employed from 1901, developed Sicardo, characterized by lustre decoration on iridescent grounds in shades of dark purple, green, and brown; similar style, Lasa, later introduced with landscape decoration. Also in imitation of French work, L'Art Nouveau style, usually decorated in relief, with e.g. female figures framed in leaves and flowers on semi-matt ground of pink and grey. Other new lines developed by 1904 include Aurelian, with brushed ground (though otherwise similar to Louwelsa), Jap Birdimal, introduced by F. H. *Rhead, with stylized natural forms, and series with modelled animal forms and matt glazes. Because of commercial nature of production, work not always unique, though carried out by hand, and designs used for more than one purpose, e.g. decoration of poppy flower and seed heads in underglaze painting and piped slip on plate signed by Rhead, also adapted for use on mugs, condiment sets, etc. Some moulding of items with relief decoration. Business, incorporated in 1922, employed 600 workers at time of maximum production. By 1925, Weller owned three factories, producing art pottery, garden ornaments, and kitchenware; succeeded by nephew, Herbert (d 1932). Firm suffered from Depression in 1930s; ceased operation in 1949. Work marked WELLER, impressed, usually with name of style; also, Weller Faience, incised.

Wells, Reginald (1877–1951). English artist potter from c1909; formerly sculptor. At Coldrum, near Wrotham, Kent, made earthenware with brownish glaze, sometimes decorated with white slip in style reminiscent of 17th century Wrotham ware. Worked in Chelsea and, later, at Storrington, Sussex, made stoneware inspired by Chinese styles. Vases with matt blue or greyish-white glazes containing borax, sometimes crackled in imitation of Chün or Yüan, signed, with mark, SOON, in rectangle.

Wenford Bridge Pottery. *See* Cardew, Michael.

Wessel, Ludwig. *See* Poppelsdorf.

Westminster Palace Clock. Great clock in tower of Houses of Parliament, London, nicknamed 'Big Ben' after Commissioner of Works, Sir Benjamin Hall (name strictly refers to its 13½-ton hour bell). Movement, incorporating gravity *escapement invented specially for it, designed and built by E. B. *Denison, assisted by clockmaker E. J. *Dent and stepson, Frederick, in 1854. Acting for Government, Denison and G. B. *Airy drew up specifications for clock; it should be accurate to within one minute per week; first stroke of hour should be within one second of true time. Leading clockmakers e.g. Benjamin Vulliamy, declared project impracticable. At early stage, Airy withdrew from enterprise; Denison acted alone, designing and superintending construction of clock. Clock finished 1854, fixed in tower 1859, permanently set going 1860. Westminster Chime, first heard in 1859, derives from musical phrase in G. F. Handel's Messiah; also called Cambridge Chime, as previously used (1793) in great St Mary's Church, Cambridge.

West or **Russian Turkestan carpets.** From region now contained in Soviet Republics of Turkmenistan (capital: Ashkabad), Uzbekistan, Tadzhikistan (Tadjikstan), Kazakhstan, and Kirghistan, under Russian domination from 1881. Carpet industry subject to commercial exploitation, with resulting decline in materials and workmanship. Russian customs policy cut off supplies of vegetable dyes from Persia and India; new central Asian railway brought aniline

West Turkestan carpet. Bokhara. c1930. 6ft × 4ft.

dyes, which bled into white areas of carpet pattern and faded, especially much used aniline red. All bright colours, vegetable or synthetic, chemically faded to suit late 19th century Euro-

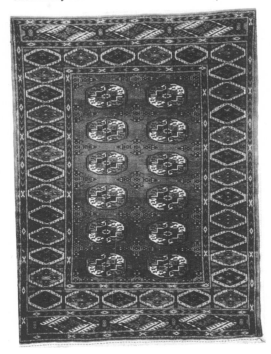

West Turkestan carpet. Yumut. c1900. 6ft6in. × 3ft10in.
Below
*Whatnot. *Papier-mâché decorated with painting and mother-of-pearl. Mid 19th century. Height 4ft6in.*

pean taste. Density of knotting reduced, intricacies of pattern omitted, and poor wool, less able to hold dyes, adopted. Greater part of production absorbed by Russian market: little trade with Europe in early 20th century. Carpets worked in Persian and Turkish knots; distinctive in having same colour ground - frequently dark red - in border and filling. Designs geometrical, e.g. repeated patterns of guls, stars, and stylized flowers. Rugs typically have extra band on lower border, sometimes at both ends. Mouri (or Mauri) type, made also in Afghanistan and Amritsar, India, originates from Merv in Turkestan: light, finely-knotted rug, similar to Bokhara, but with smaller octagons and lighter colours. Carpets mostly known by names of chief assembly places, e.g. Bokhara, Khiva, Pendeh, Beshir. Ashkabad has replaced Bokhara and Khiva as principal carpet making centre.

Wharf Street Works. *See* Robinson & Leadbeater.

whatnot, omnium, or **étagère.** Light-weight stand of three or more open shelves supported by corner posts, or two upright members resting on solid base; dates from c1790. Popular in Britain and America during 19th century; some models have drawers in base or top. Sometimes triangular to fit corner. May have vertical divisions for music and papers on lower tier, upper tiers bordered with fretwork. Some bamboo examples.

whatnot pedestal. Low, square bedside cupboard surmounted by shelf supported on four, slender, turned columns; common in Britain from c1840.

Wheeling Pottery Company. American pottery established in 1879 at Wheeling, West Virginia. In 1889, amalgamated with La Belle Pottery, started in 1887 by same company. Made granite ware, sold either decorated or in white. Work marked with globe behind eagle with label STONE CHINA looped from ends of outstretched wings and shield bearing monogram of WP.

whimseys. *See* friggers.

Whistler, Laurence (b 1912). English glass engraver. Early work (usually in diamond point engraving on 18th century specimens) largely baroque in style, with emblems and allegorical motifs; later work employs stipple technique and is more freely imaginative; *Whitefriars Glass Works has manufactured most of more recent pieces. Mark: later pieces with LW and date engraved.

White, George (fl late 19th, early 20th centuries). English porcelain decorator noted for painted figures surrounded by swirling drapery, e.g. on vases made at Doulton factory, Burslem, Staffordshire (1885-1912).

Whitefriars Glass Works. London glasshouse founded c1680. Produced fine flint table glass and domestic ware. At Great Exhibition of 1851, showed cut and engraved table glass in Anglo-Irish tradition; also simpler pieces with deeply cut leaf motifs. Table glass remained basic product, but experiments with colour and ancient techniques made in mid 19th century. *Millefiori* and *mosaic glass produced in this period, also stained-glass windows from medieval recipes.

Artists employed included E. *Burne-Jones, F. M. *Brown, and W. *Morris. In 1860s, produced clear, softly tinted, lime-soda glasses based on Venetian and ancient Roman specimens; Art Nouveau iridescent glass also produced. Ownership changed frequently. Bought by J. *Powell and Sons in 1833. Firm continues, but moved (1922) to Wealdstone, Middlesex.

white gold. *See* gold.

wicker chair. *See* basket chair.

wide power loom. 9-12ft wide. Developed first for *chenille Axminster carpets by *Tomkinson & Adam in 1869. (Widest power loom in Britain was *Templeton's 33ft chenille loom, recently dismantled.) Followed by *ingrain loom made by W. C. *Gray & Sons in 1886. Then wide *spool Axminster, c1896, patented as *Kleitos by A. *Smith; improved in 1910s. Wide tapestry carpet looms (Brussels and velvet) in fairly common use by 1900. Wide Wilton loom developed by *Crossley in 1900s; not in general use until after 1st World War. *Brinton installed 15ft wide *gripper Axminster loom in 1904, though 9ft and 10ft6in. gripper looms not installed by other manufacturers until c1930, and broadlooms (i.e. over 12ft wide) only after 1st World War.

Wiener Keramik. Ceramic workshop, organized 1905 in Vienna by M. *Powolny and B. *Löffler, operated in conjunction with Wiener Werkstätte. Products include black and white majolica, generally decorated with Cubist-inspired geometrical patterns from designs, e.g. by J. *Hoffmann, D. *Pêche and Powolny; also, figures modelled by Löffler and Powolny. In 1912, merged with Gmündener Keramik workshop of F. *Schleiss, as Wiener und Gmündener Keramik Werkstätte.

Wiener Werkstätte (Vienna Workshops). Austrian association of artist craftsmen (Wiener Werkstätten Produktiv Gemeinschaft von Kunsthandwerken), modelled on C. R. *Ashbee's *Guild of Handicraft; founded 1903 with F. Warndörfer as commercial director and J. *Hoffmann and K. *Moser as artistic directors; later joined by D. *Pêche and E. J.

*Wiener Keramik. Boy on a Snail. Earthenware figure, modelled by M. *Powolny, c1907.*

*Wimmer; declared aim was to apply artistic design to widest possible range of articles. Production included textiles, furniture, metalwork, and extended to buildings, e.g. Sanatorium at Purkersdorf, Austria. By 1905, when joined by painter, G. *Klimt, Wiener Werkstätte were focus of progressive forces in art and design; complex of buildings displayed in Vienna Kunstschau, 1908-09, and Paris Exhibition, 1910. Metalwork, in silver and base metals, designed mainly by Hoffmann, in geometrical, formalized *Jugendstil, evolving into rigorous cubist, stepped forms; products include coffee services, lamps, samovars; works by other designers, e.g. D. *Pêche, K. *Moser, and C.O. *Czescka in less severe style. Marks: WW in ligature, usually with designer's monogram. Furniture, carpets, ceramics, etc. for interior design in style of stark simplicity. Ceramic designs, produced by Wiener Keramik workshop, influenced industrial and art pottery and porcelain. Workshops closed in 1932, through inability to compete with industrial production. *Illustration at* Pêche, D.

Wigström, Henrik (1867-*c*1930). Swedish-Finnish goldsmith; worked in St Petersburg. From 1886, chief assistant to Fabergé workmaster, M. *Perchin; from Perchin's death (1903), ran workshop, and continued production of most *Fabergé eggs, including Imperial Easter eggs. Specialized in enamelled gold objects of vertu in Louis XVI style. Mark: H.W. *Illustration at* Fabergé.

Wildenhain, Marguerite or **Friedlander,** Margarete (b 1898). Artist potter, born in Lyon, France. Completed seven years' training in ceramic department of Bauhaus; functional earthenware (*c*1923) includes moulded mugs covered with monochrome glazes, and jug with yellowish body and yellow crackle glaze. Work marked with monogram of MF. As head of ceramic department at municipal art school, Halle Gebichenstein, also designer for Royal Berlin Porcelain Factory. Left Germany (*c*1933); with husband, Frans Wildenhain (b 1905), established workshop in Putten, Holland. Work includes stoneware table services in wide, low shapes, covered e.g. with pink glaze and sometimes simple decoration of concentric circles, etc., either painted or in low ribbing; wide storage jars made, e.g. in white glazed stoneware, sometimes with narrow bands painted in dark grey. From 1940, in America; taught in Oakland, California, then at own workshop in Guerneville, California.

Wild Rose Peachblow. Version of *Peachblow glass patented 1886 by E. *Libbey for *New England Glass Co. Shades translucent rose to white. Produced by combining opal glass with gold-ruby glass, then reheating object at furnace mouth. Articles frequently pattern-moulded, then further decorated with gilt and enamel designs, or oxidized to give satin finish.

Wilkinson, A.J., Ltd. Staffordshire pottery firm operating several factories in Burslem area from late 19th century. In 1885, took over Central Pottery; made white granite ware for American market. Gold lustre decoration also introduced for use on granite ware. Mark: royal arms with ROYAL PATENT IRONSTONE/ ARTHUR J.WILKINSON/ LATE R.ALCOCK/ BURSLEM, ENGLAND. Also in Burslem, operated

*Wild Rose Peachblow. Vase enamelled with spray of flowers, leaves and berries. Made at Cambridge, Massachusetts, by *New England Glass Co. c1886. Height 8¼in.*

Below
A. J. Wilkinson Ltd. Porcelain plate designed by Dame Laura Knight, 1937.

Churchyard Works (1887–early 20th century), Royal Staffordshire Pottery, from *c*1896 to present day, and took over Mersey Pottery (*c*1900); subsidiary, Newport Pottery, operated from 1930s. Later, production extended to include highly-glazed stoneware, e.g. flower vases with simple decoration of horizontal ribbing. Designs by C. *Cliff include Tibetan ware; tea ware with moulded surface decoration, e.g. teapot and jug resembling corn-on-the-cob (sweetcorn); painted *Bizarre ware; and crocus design. *Illustration at* Cliff, C.

Wilkinson, Henry, & Co. English firm producing wide range of Old Sheffield Plate *c*1831–*c*1852, but with antecedents traceable to mid 18th century. Work displayed at Great Exhibition, 1851. Last recorded mark in 1852.

Willets Manufacturing Company. American porcelain manufacture established 1879 at Trenton, New Jersey. Produced 'Belleek' in late 1880s and 1890s; imitated marine life shapes, e.g. shells, or coral, produced by Irish Belleek factory. Mark: BELLEEK over snake looped in W form, and WILLETS (from 1888).

Wilm, H.J. German silversmiths, founded in Berlin in 1767; silversmiths to German court in 19th century; *c*1900 introduced sterling silver (higher than normal German standard) and modern designs; in 1911 appointed jewellers to Bulgarian and Romanian courts, in 1912, to German Emperor and Empress; won gold medal for sterling silver at 1937 Paris World Fair; produced presentation and commercial silver. Factory destroyed in Second World War; firm moved to Hamburg, 1948.

Wilson, Henry (1864-1934). English architect, sculptor, metalworker, and silversmith. Trained as architect; became chief assistant to J.D. *Sedding, and succeeded to his practice, 1891. Became interested in metalwork, *c*1890; set up own workshop *c*1895, where J.P. *Cooper (occasionally) and H.G. *Murphy worked with him. Taught metalwork at Central School of Arts & Crafts, London, from *c*1896, and at Royal College of Art, London, from *c*1901. Joined Art Worker's Guild in 1892, became Master 1917; president of Arts & Crafts Exhibition Society 1915-22; moved to Paris 1922; worked in France and Italy; later worked on doors for St John the Divine Anglican Cathedral, New York; wrote Silverwork & Jewellery, 1903. Made some gold and enamelled jewellery, and designed some metalwork, mostly fireplaces, for Longden & Co., but majority of designs were for ecclesiastical metalwork; style shows medieval and Byzantine influences; favoured polygonal shapes, compact curved lines and rounded bases; designed Art Nouveau style furnishings for St Bartholomew's Church, Brighton, England, 1907-08. Work sometimes marked with monogram of HW.

Wilton. Carpet made on Wilton loom: pile made from continuous length of warp, wound on bobbins, woven through loom like ordinary warps, but made into loops over razor-ended steel strips, which sever loops when automatically withdrawn. Patterns woven by Jacquard mechanism. Yarn in colours not required in design at any given point lies in back of carpet as 'dead' yarn. (Number of colours therefore limited by bulk and expense of dead yarn.) Originates from *Wilton Royal Carpet Factory. Superseded Brussels carpet in popularity *c*1910. Made on E. *Bigelow's power loom from *c*1850; not on wide power loom (with notable exception of *Crossley) until *c*1920, probably because of weight problem.

Wilton Royal Carpet Factory (Wiltshire). English carpet factory, granted royal charter in 1699. In 1834, purchased *Axminster Carpet Factory plant, and continued to expand, with over 100 workers in 1851, 300 in 1871 (including part-time schoolchildren). In 1859, claimed pro-

Henry Wilson. Left: brooch-pendant, enamelled and set with moonstone and three pendants of crystal, enamel and moonstone, c1913. Right: pendant, gold with enamel, chrysoprase and moonstones, c1912.

duction of largest carpet ever made (70×35ft), on largest loom in Europe. At this time, owned 20 looms (widest 40ft), making Wilton, *Axminster, and Brussels carpets. Factory changed hands twice (1860, 1871). Received several large orders from British royal family and American patrons. Short-lived American branch founded 1891 in *Elizabethport, New Jersey; another, more successful, at Bemerton, Wiltshire (1900), making Axminster carpets. In 1905, owners (then Yates & Co.) went bankrupt; new firm, Wilton Royal Carpet Factory Co., formed almost immediately by private subscription. Real Axminsters chief product; only serious competition from *Donegal factories. Main British manufacturers of *hair Brussels carpets. London showroom opened 1919. Several large carpets for theatres and ocean liners made in 1930s (designed by e.g. M. *Dorn). Firm closed 1939; reconstituted 1945.

Wilton ware. *See* A. G. Harley-Jones.

Wiltshaw & Robinson. *See* Carlton ware.

Wimmer, Eduard Josef (1882–1961). Austrian designer and metalworker; attended School of Arts & Crafts, Vienna (1901–07); co-director of Wiener Werkstätte (1907–32); director of fashion studio (1912–22); professor at Academy of Applied Art, Vienna (1918–52). Metalwork designs in geometrical style of Wiener Werkstätte, e.g. octagonal silver tea service (1912; now in Austrian Museum of Applied Art, Vienna) anticipates angular style of Art Deco. Mark: monogram of EJW (two versions).

Winchcombe Pottery. *See* Cardew, Michael.

Winchester quart. *See* specie jar.

Windsor chair. Chair of stick construction with turned spindles socketed into solid wooden seat to form back and legs; with or without arms; may have *writing arm. Variations include comb-back, bow-back, cabriole legs; shaped or plain central splat, sometimes pierced. Dates from 1724 in Britain; manufactured in great quantities, especially in High Wycombe, Buckinghamshire, e.g. by W. *Birch Ltd; also extremely popular in America. Ash, elm, fruitwood, and yew used for bentwood members in Britain; elm and, rarely, yew for seats; beech for turned legs and spindles. American examples painted; pine or soft birch for seats; hickory for spindles; beech, hickory, or white oak for bent frame. Popular 19th century models include hoop-back, firehouse, fan-back, scroll, and smoker's bow. *See also* Wycombe chair.

Windsor tapestry. *See* Royal Windsor Tapestry Manufactory.

wine cup or **goblet.** Stemmed and footed silver drinking cup without handles; in use up to late 17th century, revived in late 19th century in Britain and America, mainly as trophy for exhibitions, agricultural shows, etc. Made in silver, silver gilt, and electro-plate, often heavily embossed with naturalistic motifs and hunting scenes.

wine funnel. Used for decanting wine from bottle; early 19th century examples usually in silver or pewter, later also in electro-plate. Often has pierced insert, or fine wire mesh, as filter. Made throughout 19th century in Europe and America.

wine label. *See* bottle ticket.

Winfield, R. W. Large English brass foundry established in Peyton, Birmingham. Work dis-

played at Great Exhibition (1851) and International Exhibition (1862) London. Output included wire and rolled metal, stair and carpet rods, picture hooks, rods and brackets, plain and reeded cornice poles, *gasoliers in various antique and patented styles (e.g. Elizabethan and Renaissance), stamped brass mouldings, letter balances, patent brass bedsteads, beds, cribs. Also brass furniture, e.g. brass rocking chair, armchair, brass tables with marble tops, various ornamental lamps and gas fittings.

wire furniture. Chairs, mainly for outdoor use: metal frame, e.g. iron, with wire mesh seat and back. Popular in Britain during 19th century. Manufacturers include *Barnard, Bishop & Barnard. American examples often based on rococo style.

Wiskemann, SA (Brussels). Belgian manufacturing and retail silversmiths, founded 1872 by Otto L. Wiskemann, descendant of 18th century silversmiths in Kassel, Germany, after studying for two years at *Christofle factory; introduced electro-plate to Belgium; won many awards at international exhibitions in late 19th century; Otto Wiskemann died 1909, succeeded by sons Otto and Albin; opened branches in Antwerp, Ghent, Liège, Bruges, and Zurich, with factories in Milan (1910), Nice (1910), and Paris (1930); in 1924 pioneered manufacture of kitchen articles in stainless steel.

Wolfers, Philippe (1858–1929). Belgian sculptor, goldsmith, and jeweller. Before joining family firm, Wolfers Frères, Belgian crown jewellers, studied at Académie Royale des Beaux Arts in Brussels. c1893, used ivory from Belgian Congo combined with gold and precious stones for brooches, combs, and objects of vertu; combination became characteristic of *Art Nouveau style. 1894, participated in Antwerp International Exhibition; exhibited at Brussels World Fair, 1897, with settings designed by H. C. *van de Velde. 1899, built Art Nouveau house at La Hulpe. 1902 exhibited at Turin. Style of jewellery similar to R. *Lalique's, but more angular and abstract; characterized by use of wisteria motif, in e.g. translucent enamel for

Philippe Wolfers. Silver-gilt buckle set with diamonds, rubies and opals. Signed. c1900.

Philippe Wolfers. Dog collar necklace of glycine with enamel, tourmalines, opals and rubies. Signed: P. W. Ex. unique. 1902.

foliage, and tourmaline for flowers; important pieces marked 'PW exemplair unique', only 109 recorded, though some unsigned jewels made for Wolfers Frères. From early 1900s, increasingly interested in sculpture and silverwork; only jewellery made after 1908 marked opening (1910) of new workshops and showrooms designed by V. *Horta. In ceramics, modelled series of vases; six of each made by E. *Muller in stoneware from bronze casting; coloured blue, pink, green, and grey, with flowers and foliage in relief. By 1923, adopted Art Deco style, causing sensation at 1925 Paris exhibition.

Wolsey chair. Easy chair with deep, projecting, circular seat; arms and button-upholstered back inclined; feet on castors. Common in Britain from c1880.

Women's Pottery Club. American group of pottery decorators, led by M. L. *McLaughlin, working in Cincinnati, Ohio, from 1879. Bought unfired vases, etc., notably from Rookwood Pottery, and took work back to pottery for firing when underglaze decoration completed. Closure of facilities at Rookwood (1883) made underglaze decoration impossible, and undecorated earthenware and porcelain had to be painted in enamel colours. Members include L. A. *Fry. Work marked Cin. Pottery Club, incised with initials of artist and date.

Wood, Edgar (1860–1935). English architect and designer. Member of *Arts & Crafts Exhibition Society. Furniture characterized by simple lines emphasized by decoration (often inlaid), outlining drawers, rectangular panels, etc. Examples include bedstead with three-panelled headboard bearing motto, Great men have ever loved repose, surmounted by carved metal discs; rectangular panels and discs on footboard emphasized by surrounding inlay. Shown by Arts & Crafts Exhibition Society, 1896. Work during 1920s combined Arts & Crafts Movement elements with modified Modernist style, e.g. square mirror with painted and gilded wooden frame resembling shield-shaped fan with overlapping leaves.

Woodall, George (1850–1925) and Thomas (1849–1926). English glass engravers; brothers. Made fine cameo glass for T. *Webb & Sons, using classical motifs, as well as all-over designs of stylized flowers and fruit. Responsible for extending colour range of cameo-cut work, replacing usual pink background with wide range of shades from midnight-blue to pale yellow. G. Woodall's most notable work: red

*George Woodall. Cameo glass vase engraved with crane and palms. Made for *Richardson & Sons, c1890.*

cameo glass plate depicting Venus and Cupid, now in Corning Museum of Glass, New York State. Marks: T. and G. Woodall; G. Woodall (before 1895); Geo. Woodall; rarely, T. Woodall.

wood-carving machinery. Power-driven machinery for carving wood introduced in America c1840. First successful British model invented 1845; extensively used, e.g. in House of Lords, Westminster. Method of subjecting roughly shaped wood to pressure from steel dies introduced in Britain from America c1870; carving shows end grain of wood. Machine-carved ornament generally inferior to hand-made product.

Woodward Grosvenor. British carpet manufacturers; one of earliest Kidderminster firms, founded 1790. First British carpet works to install electric power (1914). Devised and patented *Grosvenor-Picking loom in 1919.

Worcester. Tusk-shaped porcelain vase, decorated in browns, greens and gold with snake hunting frogs. Marked with Royal Worcester mark. c1873. Height 8in.

Worcester. Porcelain factory, established 1783 by Robert Chamberlain; formed joint stock company with Flight, Barr & Barr partnership, working from Chamberlain premises as Chamberlain & Co. until 1850, briefly as Chamberlain, Lilly & Kerr, then Kerr & Binns (from 1852). Made dessert ware with comports and centrepieces in glazed porcelain supported by parian figures. *Limoges ware introduced in 1854, shown at Paris International Exhibition (1855). Also made parian figures and groups, and figures decorated in imitation of ivory and tarnished silver. Ivory porcelain paste used in *Raphaelesque porcelain introduced c1860. In 1862, new joint stock company formed with R. W. *Binns as art director, trading as Worcester Royal Porcelain Company. Jewelled decoration on table services fused to surface of porcelain and built up with many firings; elaborate service made for Countess of Dudley in 1865 with jewels geometrically arranged on diamond-diapered ground, and portrait panels. Ivory paste introduced in Kerr & Binns period modelled in Japanese styles by J. *Hadley, and later other styles, e.g. Louis XVI. *Reticulated ware made by G. *Owen in 1890s. In 20th century, noted for high quality of painted decoration, accompanied by lavish gilding. Transfer-printing increasingly used. *Sabrina earthenware made c1900–c1930. Wide range of figures made in ivory paste, or white porcelain with bright glaze and enamelled decoration, include birds modelled by D. *Doughty. Independent workshop formed by Hadley (1875) bought from successors in 1905. Marks of Kerr & Binns include crescent, partially enclosing number 51, surrounded by four W's within

circle, or shield shape crossed by diagonal label WORCESTER. After 1862, versions of circular Kerr & Binns mark used, surmounted by crown and sometimes with ROYAL WORCESTER ENGLAND.

Grainger factory, established 1801, and trading from death of founder (1839) as G. Grainger & Co., followed styles of Chamberlain factory, notably japan patterns, until mid 19th century. Semi-porcelain earthenware body introduced in 1851. Domestic and ornamental ware made in parian paste. Rather coarse reticulated ware made from 1850s. *Pâte-sur-pâte* decoration dates from 1880s. Joined Worcester Royal Porcelain Company in 1889, but production continued until closure of works (1902). Mark (1889-1902): ROYAL CHINA WORKS WORCESTER, surrounding G&Cº ESTABLISHED 1801 on shield.

Small factory established by E. *Locke at Shrub Hill, Worcester (1895-1904) produced work in similar styles, marked Locke & Co in globe device. *Illustrations also at* Davis, H., Eyles, H., Hadley, J., Owen, G.

work box. Box for needlework accessories, common from c1850; in wide variety of materials, e.g. wood, leather, papier-mâché, often inlaid with mother-of-pearl; interior lined in satin, or velvet. Individual compartments for needlework accessories: scissors (often in enamel or mother-of-pearl case), thimble, needle-holder, tweezers, cotton box, pin-cushion, darning egg, hand cooler, yard measure (with e.g. acorn shaped boss). Less common accessories include sewing bird (clamp to attach to table and clip for holding material), and cologne bottle.

work stand. Small stand, usually metal, e.g. ormolu, resting on decorative tripod base. Supports three or four movable leaves of thick card framed in metal, covered in fabric, often embroidered, with e.g. loops, pockets, to hold scissors, pin-cushions, thread, etc. Dates from c1850 in Britain.

world time clock. Clock showing time in different time zones. One form has hour hand revolving round 24-hour dial with names of e.g. capital cities on rotating outer ring. Another is world globe revolving once every 24 hours with stationary ring at equator marked off in hours; time for any place on globe is read off on ring, after adjusting for local time zones. Made e.g. by V. *Pierret, c1855. Multiple-dial world time clock dates from 1860.

Wren, Denise (b 1891). English artist potter, born in Albany, West Australia. Studied design under A. *Knox at Kingston-upon-Thames School of Art, Surrey (1907-1911); influenced by Celtic and early English art. Started pottery in Kingston (1911); moved to Oxshott, Surrey, in 1919. Experimented with coke and gas kilns for firing small quantities of stoneware. Pitchers, cups, and bottles, sometimes designed for flower arrangement, made in stoneware, lately often salt-glazed. Decoration frequently scratched and filled in with high-temperature pigments, e.g. cobalt oxide, ochre, and rutile (titanium oxide).

Wright, Frank Lloyd (1867-1959). American Prairie School architect; also designed furniture. In Chicago from 1887; worked in same office as G.W. *Maher and G.G. *Elmslie; chief draughtsman (1888-93) for architect, Louis

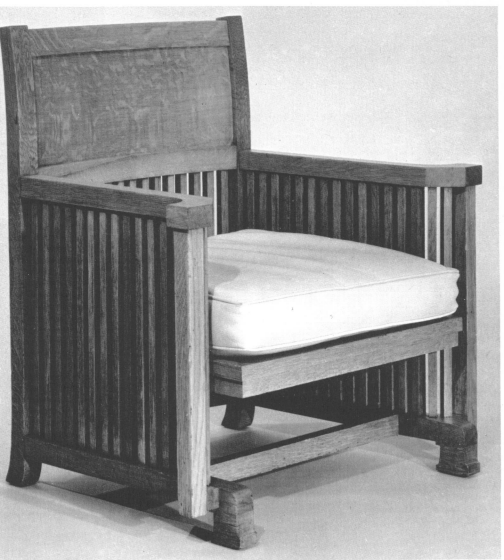

Denise Wren. Earthenware vase made at Oxshott pottery, c1925. Height 6¼in.
Below
Frank Lloyd Wright. Oak chair. Designed 1908. Height 34½in.

Sullivan. Designed Architectural style furniture, sometimes built-in, often for specific position in room. Influenced by Japanese exhibits at World's Columbian Exposition in Chicago, 1893. Propositions, published 1894, advocated use of oak in natural autumnal colours, and stain instead of varnish; theories reflected in furniture until c1910. Reduced pieces to bare essentials, e.g. cubic armchair (1905) of flat boards set in framework of laths. Early pieces (during 1890s, 1900s) usually hand-made, but subsequently favoured clean lines of machine-made furniture. Later furniture sometimes reflects building shapes, e.g. polygonal tables, ottomans, chair seats, and beds designed for hexagonal house in 1937. Furniture often criticized as unpractical and uncomfortable; anticipated *built-in furniture.

Wright & Mansfield. London furniture makers, active c1860-86. Known for fine reproduction furniture, e.g. Adam, Chippendale; also, Eclectic furniture combining Regency and Louis XVI elements. Commended at Paris Exhibition, 1867, for tall, satinwood display cabinet in Adam style, with coloured wood marquetry and Wedgwood plaques. Stamp: Wright & Mansfield.

wrist watch. Watch attached to band or bracelet, worn on wrist; made exceptionally in 18th or early 19th centuries as fashionable novelties. Swiss firm, C. Girard Perregaux, made wrist watches for German naval officers from c1880; introduced to England c1910 by Hans Wilsdorf. Manufacture established by 1914 Swiss Exhibition.

writing box. See suzuri-bako.

writing chair. *Firehouse Windsor chair with broad, curved, writing tablet fixed to right arm; small, shallow drawer under tablet, larger, deeper drawer under seat. Common in America c1840–c1880. Model with bentwood arms, cane seat, and rectangular tablet with rounded front, no drawers, used as classroom chair.

writing table accessories. Ornate quill cutters, pen wipers, string boxes, wax jacks, paper clips, wafer boxes and tongs, pounce pots, stamp boxes, rulers, letter racks, paper weights, blotting pads, made singly, or as matched sets, from c1800, in wide range of materials, including silver, bronze, brass, electro-plate, papier-mâché. Steel nib pens, with decorative holders, introduced from c1820, increasingly replaced by fountain pens after c1886.

wrought iron. Iron, from which impurities removed by stirring while still in molten state, technically called puddled iron; particularly suitable for working in blacksmith's forge. Malleability, high tensile strength, and resistance to corrosion, encouraged decorative use, e.g. as window grilles, gates, from 16th century. Use declined in 19th century owing to rapid technological development of large scale *cast iron production 1790–1840, but *Coalbrookdale Co. made wrought iron *hall, *umbrella, *plant stands from c1850. Craft revived in England by Arts and Crafts movement; introduction of oxy-acetylene welding in late 19th century gave structural stength to even delicately ornamental works. In France, revival led notably by E. *Brandt, from c1900; *wrought iron furniture, screens, lamps etc. fashionable c1925–c1935. In 1927, introduction of Aston process made mass production of puddled iron again competitive with cast iron and steel.

wrought-iron furniture. Wide range of Art Deco wrought-iron furnishings, e.g. chairs, tables, fire screens, consoles, lamps, decorative panels, illustrated in *La Ferronnerie Moderne* (series 1–5) by Henri Clouzout, published 1925. Designed in Paris, notably by E. *Brandt. In furniture, glass or marble surfaces typically supported by scrolled or volute brackets, or wrought-iron legs; in decorative screens and panels, motifs developed from stylized natural forms e.g. birds, animals, clouds, towards geometrical, abstract, linear patterns (e.g. crosses and diamonds) derived from Wiener Werkstätte. Wrought-iron furniture fashionable c1925–c1935, superseded from c1930 by chromium-plated tubular steel and strip steel furniture, influenced by M. *Breuer's designs for Bauhaus (c1925).

Württembergische Metallwarenfabrik (WMF). Metal foundry at Geislingen, c30 miles from Stuttgart. Produced Art Nouveau and Art Deco style tableware in *Cromargen, and type of German silver patented as Ikora metal. Glass studio, with experimental and teaching work-

shops for glass and gem cutting, established 1921, under direction of W. *von Eiff. *Ikora glass developed, 1925; some *diatreta vases made c1932. W. *Wagenfeld among designers associated with workshop.

Wyatt, Sir Matthew Digby (1820–77). English architect and writer on architectural design and ornament; expert on architectural styles from Middle Ages to 19th century, with special interest in Renaissance. Collaborated with Isambard Kingdom Brunel in designs for Paddington Station c1850. Secretary to executive committee for Great Exhibition, 1851, later edited Industrial Arts of 19th Century, selection of articles displayed at Exhibition. With O. *Jones, wrote 'Grammar of Ornament' (1856); supervised move of Exhibition to new site at Crystal Palace, Sydenham, 1853, designed 'courts' in period styles. Hon. Secretary to Royal Institute of British Architects 1855–59; gold medallist, 1866; first Slade Professor of Fine Arts at Cambridge University, 1869. Architecture includes Alford House, Kensington Gore, Adelphi Theatre, London, and, as surveyor to East India Co., interior of India Office, in collaboration with Giles Gilbert Scott, c1855. Important books published: 'Geometric Mosaics of Middle Ages', 1848; 'Metal Work and its Artistic Design', 1852; 'Art of Illuminations', 1867.

Wycombe chair. English Windsor and other simple wooden chairs made in High Wycombe, Buckinghamshire and region from c1800. Many examples date from c1850, often cane-seated, e.g. balloon-back and comb-back chairs.

Yale, W. (fl late 19th century). English artist; painted landscapes and seascapes at factory of W. T. *Copeland, often on earthenware or porcelain plaques. Later worked independently as ceramic painter.

Yanagi, Soetsu (fl 20th century). Japanese philosopher, art critic, and collector. Instrumental in growth of Japanese craft movement which received official recognition in 1929. Viewed folk art as properly carried out by anonymous craftsmen for everyday use; associated with S. *Hamada and B. *Leach.

yatate (Japanese, 'arrow stand'). Japanese sagemono used as portable writing kit. First worn in Kamburu Era (1661–73). Extremely popular during 1860s; produced into 20th century. Composed of two sections: shallow, round, bowl-shaped inkwell with hinged lid, and long, hollow tube for fude ('writing brush'). Two parts usually joined, and attached to girdle with cord and netsuke, but sometimes separate with inkwell serving as netsuke. Most made of undecorated wood; some carved and/or lacquered, and inlaid with engraved or chased metal. Also made in bamboo, brass, iron, and silver. Varieties include jinchu-yatate ('camp yatate'), shaped like lacquered folding fan with hollowed handle for inkwell and brush; kwaichu-yatate ('bosom-of-the-costume yatate'), small silver or copper form carried in purse worn inside clothing.

year clock. See 400-day clock.

yellow staining. Medieval method of colouring glass surface by coating with silver stain. Redeveloped 1820 by F. *Egermann; widely used

by him and imitators to decorate ornamental pieces in second half of 19th century.

Yerevan rugs. See Caucasian carpets.

Yi dynasty. Korean period (1391–1910). Ceramics regarded as lacking sophistication achieved in preceding Koryo period. Branch of official factory established in 1718 at Keumsa-ri near Kwangju, Kyonggi-do, shortly became principal centre of Korean ceramic production; work of late 18th and early 19th centuries generally identifiable by dull glazes with bluish or greyish tinge, lavish decoration, and frequent use of underglaze blue. Yi government turned factory at Kuemsa-ri into private concern in 1884. Afterwards, decoration often printed by lithographic process and quality of production declined. Manufacture of e.g. Punch'ŏng wares; black, white, and celadon glazed pottery; porcelain with underglaze cobalt decoration; and stoneware with iron oxide or copper-red decoration continued at many centres.

Yosei. Japanese lacquer school, established in 14th century; specialized in tsuishu. Last member, Yosei XIX (d 1952) among outstanding 20th century lacquer artists.

Yoshino-bori. See Kamakura-bori.

Ysart, Salvador (1877–1955). Spanish glass artist. Employed by *Moncrieff & Co. from 1922, where *Monart ware probably produced under his influence. Also made paperweights and decorative pieces, e.g. vases and bowls, oxidized with coloured marble – like surface effects in Venetian tradition, production of which continues.

Yugoslavian carpets. 20th century production concentrated in Macedonia. Carpets made in matt wool, with coarse knotting, mainly in *Tabriz or *Afghan patterns; also copies of Persian, Caucasian, East Turkestan, and Chinese types, and colourful Balkan kelims.

yün-mu-k'o. See aogai.

Yusetsu, Mori (1808–82). Japanese potter and merchant; also worked as woodcarver. In Kuwana, Ise province, obtained formulae of enamels used on 17th century Banko ware, and produced faience with underglaze blue designs and enamelled floral decoration, marked with Banko seal, or stamped with own name. Other work decorated with slip, moulded relief, or dark coloured glazes. Succeeded by brother and son.

Zakopane style. Polish furniture style popularized c1886 by Stanislaw Witkiewicz, painter, playwright, and novelist; based on southern Polish folk art.

zarf. Turkish holder for handle-less coffee cup; sometimes stemmed, of approximate egg cup shape; made in silver and brass, also in gold set with precious stones, generally in pairs; enamelled and gilt zarfs exported in mid 19th century to Middle East from France and Switzerland. Now made in Balkans and Turkey for souvenir market.

Zasche, Adolf (fl 1900). Austrian Art Nouveau glass artist and manufacturer. Output of factory at Gablonz (now Jablonec, Czechoslovakia)

included vases, bowls, candlesticks, etc., with iridescent decoration in splashes and whorls; also, galvanized silver overlay work; many pieces with brass or bronze mounts.

Zdekauer, Moritz (fl late 19th, early 20th centuries). Czechoslovakian manufacturer of earthenware and porcelain. Proprietor of factory now known as *Altrohlauer Porzellanfabriken (1884-1909). Marks include eagle with coronet and initials over ALTROHLAU.

Zecchin, Vittorio (1878-1947). Leading Venetian glass designer in Art Deco and Functionalist styles. Artistic director for P. *Venini in 1920s; work of this period, including vases, bowls, urns, etc., at first based on traditional forms; later, freer work in transparent, coloured or pastel-tinted glass also made. Subsequently, designed J. *Hoffmann-inspired tableware for *Arte Vetraria Muranese and Fratelli Toso factories.

Zeh, Scherzer & Co. Bavarian porcelain factory established at Rehau in 1880. Made domestic ware. Marks, e.g. shield surmounted by crown above BAVARIA, incorporate initials Z S & C.

Zeigler & Co. British carpet firm of Swiss origin, based in Manchester. First foreign company to set up branch offices and factories in Persia (in *Tabriz and *Sultanabad c1883, later expanding to Bakshis). In Bakshis and Sultanabad, Feraghan and Bijar types copied for Western market, but weavers devised own colour schemes and borders. Texture much softer than in originals; designs very large.

Zenith Pottery. *See* Gouda.

Zeshin, Shibata (1807-91). Prolific Japanese master lacquer artist and painter in Tokyo. Noted for originality, versatility and excellent craftsmanship. Member of Imperial Art Com-

mittee from 1890; responsible for much of lacquer decoration inside Imperial Palace.

Excelled in wide range of lacquer techniques, often blended on same object to give textural and design balance; specialized in lacquer simulating other materials, e.g. metal, leather, pottery and ink-block. Also, adaptations of old masters' styles, particularly sculptured wave design, often executed in brown *hiramakie. Grounds rarely gold, often polished rich, dark browns or matt 'tea-dust' green. Designs include plants, flowers, small objects, human and animal figures; great attention to realistic detail and finish. Particularly known for whimsical portrayals of small animals and insects. Most work on miniature forms (e.g. *inro, *kogo, *kiseru-zutsu, and *suzuri-bako), but also made some fine larger boxes and lacquer trays. *Go: Shibata Zeshin, Shin, Tairyuko, and Reisai or Reiya. *Chomei: Zeshin.

zircon. Gemstone of zirconium silicate; naturally reddish-brown stone, but heat-treated to produce colourless, golden-brown and sky-blue shades popular in jewellery; colourless variety resembles diamond. Yellow, orange, red and sherry-brown varieties known as hyacinth. Victorian zircons sometimes known as jargons or jargoons (term also used for colourless to smoky zircons from Sri Lanka). Suitable for same cutting and faceting as diamond; often used as cheaper substitute.

Zitzmann, Friedrich (1840-1906). German Jugendstil glass artist, follower of K. *Koepping. Originally, instructor in glass-blowing in Wiesbaden, Hesse. Produced fragile Koepping-inspired glasses blown at the lamp. Mark: F. Zitzmann.

*Zsolnay. Stoneware vase with lustre decoration, probably designed by V. *Wartha, c1900.*

zogan-nuri (Japanese, 'inlaid lacquer'). Japanese lacquer imitating *cloisonné enamel; became popular c1815. Gold or silver wire encrusted around design of still soft lacquer; when dry, surface completely covered with layers of black lacquer; when dry again, these layers rubbed down in togidashi manner.

zokoku-nuri. Variety of Japanese *carved lacquer based on Siamese kimma or kimmande lacquer, developed by Tamakaji Zokoku (1806-69). Several layers of red and black lacquer applied to prepared base, and carved in guri fashion; carved out pattern then infilled with coloured lacquer; finally, surface rubbed down in togidashi fashion.

zomno. *See* night commode.

zonsei-nuri, zonsei, zonsho, ts'un-hsing, or **ts'un-sheng.** Oriental multi-coloured *carved lacquer, used both in China (ts'un-hsing or ts'un-sheng) and Japan (zonsei-nuri, zonsei, or zonsho). Chinese variety uses green, red, and yellow lacquer; Japanese adds blue and violet. Both have irregular, mottled colour scheme. Technique similar to tsuishu. Sculptured designs usually stylized, sometimes with engraved details. Variation of zonsei-nuri known as koka-ryokuyo has stylized pattern of red flowers and green leaves on gold or black ground.

Zsolnay. Hungarian earthenware pottery established 1862 by Vilmos Zsolnay at Pécs, Fünf-kirchen; aimed to establish characteristic national style. Main product earthenware for everyday use. Some ornamental ware decorated with Persian inspired motifs. Vases and bowls in Art Nouveau style with boldly coloured glazes or lustre decoration produced in experimental workshop under direction of V. *Wartha (1893-1910). Vases with painted decoration designed (c1900) by J. *Rippl-Rónai. Mark: versions of five churches with Zsolnay, sometimes also Pécs.

Zuidhollandsche Plateelbakkerij. *See* Gouda.

*Shibata Zeshin. Circular *kogo of lacquered gold, silver and black. Ebony cover carved as rat curled into ball.*

APPENDICES

CERAMIC MARKS

In a brief appendix, it is not possible to provide a comprehensive selection of ceramic marks. The illustrations in this section are therefore limited to marks mentioned in the text but containing elements that cannot be conveyed adequately in a brief description. Many of the marks illustrated exist in several forms, of which only one example is given in each case. More extensive coverage of marks may be found in the various works devoted to them.

Theodorus Colenbrander.

Cook Pottery Co.

Booths Ltd, from 1905: earthenware imitations of early Worcester porcelain.

Amphora Porzellanfabrik, from early 1890s.

Edwin Bennett.

Buffalo Pottery.

Susie Cooper.

Adrien-Pierre Dalpayrat.

Belleek factory.

Burgess, Leigh & Co.

Berlin.

Augarten.

Carlton ware.

Walter Crane.

William Ault.

Bing & Grøndahls Porcellaensfabrik.

Chesapeake Pottery.

Damm.

Dedham Pottery.

Banko.

Edward Bingham,
Hedingham Art Pottery.

Choisy-le-Roi.

Della Robbia Pottery.

William De Morgan.

Roger Fry.

Leach Pottery, St Ives.

Mintons, Ltd.

Doccia.

Griffen, Smith & Hill.

Limoges: Lanternier, Raynaud et Cie.

William S. Mycock.

Doulton & Co.

Gien.

Limoges

Newcomb College Pottery.

Fomin factory.

A. E. Gray & Co.

William A. Long:
Denver China and Pottery Co.

Ernest Chaplet.

Eiraku: Kinrande porcelain.

Théodore Haviland.

Mary Louise McLaughlin: Losanti ware.

Pilkington's Tile & Pottery Co.

Faience Manufacturing Co.

George Jones.

Meissen.

Raku.

Gordon Forsyth.

Kähler ceramics.

Josef Mendes da Costa.

A-R

Adelaide Alsop Robineau.

Rookwood Pottery.

Philip Rosenthal.

Rozenburg.

Sèvres.

Summerly's Art Manufactures:
Parian figures made at Minton factory.

Taylor, Smith & Taylor.

VITREOES

W. Howson Taylor.

Tettau.

Joost Thooft.

Tirschenreuth.

MVB

METTLACH

Villeroy & Boch.

Watcombe Pottery.

Ernst Wahliss.

Wedgwood & Co.

WEDGWOOD

Josiah Wedgwood & Sons, Ltd.

Reginald Wells.

Willets Manufacturing Co.

ZSOLNAY

Vilmos Zsolnay.

SILVER DATE LETTERS

London

Year	Letter	Year	Letter	Year	Letter
1850	P	1888	N		(lion/leopard marks)
1851	Q	1889	O	1923	h
1852	R	1890	P	1924	i
1853	S	1891	(lion/leopard marks) Q	1925	k
1854	T	1892	R	1926	l
1855	U	1893	S	1927	m
1856	a	1894	T	1928	n
1857	b	1895	U	1929	o
1858	c	1896	a	1930	p
1859	d	1897	b	1931	q
1860	e	1898	c	1932	r
1861	f	1899	d	1933	s
1862	g	1900	e	1934	t
1863	h	1901	f	1935	u
1864	i	1902	g	1936	(marks) A
1865	k	1903	h	1937	B
1866	l	1904	i	1938	C
1867	m	1905	k	1939	D
1868	n	1906	l		
1869	o	1907	m		
1870	p	1908	n		
1871	q	1909	o		
1872	r	1910	p		
1873	s	1911	q		
1874	t	1912	r		
1875	u	1913	s		
1876	A	1914	t		
1877	B	1915	u		
1878	C	1916	a		
1879	D	1917	b		
1880	E	1918	c		
1881	F	1919	d		
1882	G	1920	e		
1883	H	1921	f		
1884	I	1922	g		
1885	K				
1886	L				
1887	M				

Birmingham

Year	Letter	Year	Letter	Year	Letter
(marks)		1885	l	1920	v
1849	A	1886	m	1921	w
1850	B	1887	n	1922	x
1851	C	1888	o	1923	y
1852	D	1889	p	1924	z
1853	E	1890	q	1925	A
1854	F		(lion/anchor marks)	1926	B
1855	G	1891	r	1927	C
1856	H	1892	s	1928	D
1857	I	1893	t	1929	E
1858	J	1894	u	1930	F
1859	K	1895	v	1931	G
1860	L	1896	w	1932	H
1861	M	1897	x	1933	J
1862	N	1898	y	1934	K
1863	O	1899	z	1935	L
1864	P		(anchor/lion marks)	1936	M
1865	Q	1900	a	1937	N
1866	R	1901	b	1938	O
1867	S	1902	c	1939	P
1868	T	1903	d		
1869	U	1904	e		
1870	V	1905	f		
1871	W	1906	g		
1872	X	1907	h		
1873	Y	1908	i		
1874	Z	1909	k		
	(marks)	1910	l		
1875	a	1911	m		
1876	b	1912	n		
1877	c	1913	o		
1878	d	1914	p		
1879	e	1915	q		
1880	f	1916	r		
1881	g	1917	s		
1882	h	1918	t		
1883	i	1919	u		
1884	k				

Sheffield

Year	Letter	Year	Letter	Year	Letter
(marks)		1885	S		(crown/lion marks)
1850	G	1886	T	1918	a
1851	H	1887	U	1919	b
1852	I	1888	V	1920	c
1853	K	1889	W	1921	d
1854	L	1890	X	1922	e
1855	M		(crown/lion marks)	1923	f
1856	N	1891	Y	1924	g
1857	O	1892	Z	1925	h
1858	P	1893	a	1926	i
1859	R	1894	b	1927	k
1860	S	1895	c	1928	l
1861	T	1896	d	1929	m
1862	U	1897	e	1930	n
1863	V	1898	f	1931	o
1864	W	1899	g	1932	p
1865	X	1900	h	1933	q
1866	Y	1901	i	1934	r
1867	Z	1902	k	1935	s
(marks)		1903	l	1936	t
1868	A	1904	m	1937	u
1869	B	1905	n	1938	v
1870	C	1906	o	1939	w
1871	D	1907	p		
1872	E	1908	q		
1873	F	1909	r		
1874	G	1910	s		
1875	H	1911	t		
1876	J	1912	u		
1877	K	1913	v		
1878	L		(lion/crown marks)		
1879	M	1914	w		
1880	N	1915	x		
1881	O	1916	y		
1882	P	1917	z		
1883	Q				
1884	R				

BIBLIOGRAPHY

Adamesk pottery
Tyneside Pottery. R. C. Bell (Studio Vista, London, 1971)

Adams, Williams, & Sons (Potters) Ltd.
A History of the Adams family, P. W. L. Adams (London, 1914)

Aesthetic movement
The Aesthetic Movement, Elizabeth Aslin (Elek, London, 1969)
The Aesthetic Movement, Theory and Practice, Robin Spencer (Studio Vista, London, 1972)

Afghan carpets
Bokhara, Turkoman, and Afghan Rugs, Hartley Clark (London, 1922)

Albert of Saxe-Coburg-Gotha
Prince Albert and Victorian Taste, Winston Ames (Chapman & Hall, London, 1967)

American ceramics
American Potters and Pottery, John Ramsay (Hale, Cushman & Flint, Boston, 1939)
Marks of American Potters, E. A. Barber (Philadelphia, 1904)
Pottery and Porcelain of the United States, E. A. Barber (New York, 2nd edition 1901)

American flatware
American Silver Flatware, 1837–1910, Noel D. Turner (A. S. Barnes & Co., New York – Yoseloff, London, 1972)

American glass
American Art Nouveau Glass, Albert Christian Revi (Camden, New Jersey, 1968)
American Glass, George S. and Helen McKearin (Crown Publishers, New York, new edition 1968)
American Glass and Glassmaking, L. W. Watkins (New York, 1950)
American Historical Glass, Bessie M. Lindsey (Tuttle, Rutland, Vermont – Prentice-Hall, London, new edition 1967)
Cambridge Glass 1818–1888, L. W. Watkins (Boston, 1930)
New England Glass and Glassmaking, K. M. Wilson (New York and Toronto, 1972)
200 Years of American Blown Glass, George S. and Helen McKearin (Crown Publishers, New York, revised edition 1966)

American hardware industry
The Coming Collecting Boom, John Mebane (Barnes, New York – Yoseloff, London, 1968)
New Horizons in Collecting, John Mebane (Barnes, New York – Yoseloff, London, 1966)

American horological industry
A Book of American Clocks, Brook Palmer (Collier-Macmillan, New York, 1950)
Catalogue of Seth Thomas Clocks, Regulators and Timepieces, 1863 (Facsimile catalogue published by Ken Roberts, 1973)
Catalogue No. 154 (1908-09) Waterbury Clock Co. (Facsimile catalogue published by Adams Brown Company, Exeter, New Hampshire, 1972)
The Contributions of Joseph Ives to Connecticut Clock Technology, Kenneth D. Roberts (American Clock and Watch Museum, Bristol, Connecticut, 1970)
Eli Terry and the Connecticut Shelf Clock, Kenneth D. Roberts (Ken Roberts Publishing Co, Bristol, Connecticut, 1973)
A Treasury of American Clocks, Brook Palmer (Collier-Macmillan, New York, 1967)

American jewellery
The American Silver Manufacturers, Dorothy T. Rainwater (Everybodys Press, Hanover, Pennsylvania, 1966)

American silver
American Silver 1650–1900; a history of style, G. Hood (Praeger, New York and London, 1971)
The American Silver Manufacturers, Dorothy T. Rainwater (Everybodys Press, Hanover, Pennsylvania, 1966)
American Silversmiths and their Marks (3 vols), S. G. C. Ensko (privately printed by Robert Ensko Inc, New York 1927, 1937, 1948)
Directory of American Silver, Pewter, and Pewter Plate, R. M. and T. H. Kovel (Crown Publishers, New York, 1961)

American Victorian furniture
The American Heritage History of Antiques, From the Civil War to World War I, Marshall B. Davidson (American Heritage Publishing Co, New York, 1969)
The Field Guide to American Victorian Furniture, Thomas H. Ormsbee (Little, Brown & Co, Boston and Toronto, 1952)
American Furniture of the 19th Century, Celia Jackson Otto (New York, 1965)
American Antiques 1800–1900, Joseph T. Butler (New York, 1965)

American watches
Almost Everything You Wanted to Know About American Watches and Didn't Know Who to Ask, George E. Townsend (published by the author, Vienna, Virginia, 1970)
English and American Watches, George Daniels (Abelard-Schumann, 1967)

Animaliers, Les
The Animaliers, J. Mackay (Ward Lock, London, 1973)
Bronze Sculptures of 'Les Animaliers', Jane Horsewell (Antique Collector's Club, Woodbridge, Suffolk, 1971)

Arabia
Arabia Design, Pirkko Aro (Kustannusosakeyhtiö Otava, Helsinki, 1958)

archeological jewellery
Antique Jewellery and its Revival, Augusto Castellani (1862)

architectural ironwork
Metal Crafts in Architecture, G. K. Greerlings (Charles Scribner's Sons, New York, 1929)
Victorian Heritage: Ornamental Cast Iron in Architecture, E. Graeme Robertson (Georgian House, London, 1960)

Art Deco
Art Deco, Bevis Hillier (Dutton, New York, 1969)
Art Deco, Katharine Morrison McClinton (Clarkson N. Potter, New York, 1972)
The Art Deco Style, edited by Theodore Menten (Dover, New York – Constable, London, 1972)
The Decorative Twenties, Martin Battersby (Studio Vista, London, 1969)
The Decorative Thirties, Martin Battersby (Studio Vista, London, 1971)
Into the Thirties: Style and Design 1924–34, K-J. Sembach (Thames & Hudson, London, 1972)
Modern French Decorative Art, Leon Deshairs (The Architectural Press, London, 1926–30)
Modern French Decoration, Katharine Morrison Kahle (G. P. Putnam's Sons, New York, 1930)
Pioneers of Modern Design, Nikolaus Pevsner (Pelican, London, 1960)
A Survey of British Decorative Art, Henry G. Dowling (F. Lewis Ltd, London, 1935)
The World of Art Deco, Bevis Hillier (Studio Vista, London, 1971)

art glass
European Art Glass, Ray and Lee Grover (Tuttle, Rutland, Vermont, 1970)
Nineteenth Century Art Glass, Ruth Webb Lee (New York, 1952)

Art Nouveau
The Age of Art Nouveau, M. Rheims (Thames & Hudson, London, 1966)
Art Nouveau, Mario Amaya (Studio Vista, London, – Dutton, New York, 1966)
Art Nouveau, S. Tschudi Madsen, translated by R. I. Christopherson (Weidenfeld & Nicolson, London, 1967)
Art Nouveau, Robert Schmutzler (Thames & Hudson, London, 1964, new edition New English Library, 1970)
Art Nouveau, G. Warren (Octopus, London, 1972)
Art Nouveau: Revolution in Interior Design, R. Bossaglia, edited by Martin Battersby (Orbis, London, 1973)
The Collector's Book of Art Nouveau, Marion Klamkin (David & Charles, Newton Abbot, Devon, 1971)
The World of Art Nouveau, Martin Battersby (Arlington Books, London, 1968)

artist potters
The Art of the Modern Potter, T. Birsk (London, 1967)
Artist Potters in England, Muriel Rose (Faber & Faber, London, 1955)
Modern Ceramics, Geoffrey Beard (Studio Vista, London, 1969)
Modern Ceramics, K. Hetteš and P. Rada (Spring Books, London, 1965)
The Work of the Modern Potter in England, G. Wingfield Digby (London, 1952)

art pottery
American Art Pottery, Lucile Henzke (Camden, New Jersey, 1970)

Arts & Crafts movement
The Arts & Crafts Movement, Gillian Naylor (Studio Books, London, 1971)
Arts & Crafts in USA, 1876–1916, edited by R. J. Clark (Princeton University Press, 1972)
Furniture Design Set Free, David Joel (Dent, London, 1969)
Handmade Woodwork of the Twentieth Century, A. E. Bradshaw (John Murray, London, 1962)

Ashbee, Charles Robert
Goldsmiths and Silversmiths, Hugh Honour (Weidenfeld & Nicolson, London, 1971)

ashtray
Tobacco and the Collector, Amoret and Christopher Scott (Parrish, London, 1966)

Axminster carpet
Axminster Carpets, 1755–1957, Bertram Jacobs (Frank Lewis, Leigh-on-Sea, Essex, 1970)

barometer
English Barometers, 1680–1860, N. Goodison (Cassell & Co, London, 1969)
The History of the Barometer, W. E. Knowles Middleton (John Hopkins, Baltimore, 1964)

Barye, Antoine-Louis
Antoine-Louis Barye, C. Saulnier (London, 1926)

base metal
American Copper and Brass, H. J. Kauffman (Thomas Nelson & Sons, New Jersey, 1968)
Collecting Copper and Brass, Geoffrey Wills (Arco Publications, 1962, new edition Mayflower Handbook, London, 1970)
English Domestic Metalwork, R. Goodwin-Smith (London, 1937)

Iron and Brass Implements of the English House, J. Seymour Lindsay (Medici Society, London and Boston, 1927)
Metalwork, Hanns-Ulrich Haedeke, translated by V. Menkes (Weidenfeld & Nicolson, London, 1970)

Bauhaus
The Bauhaus, Gillian Naylor (Studio Vista, London, 1968)
Weimar Crafts of the Bauhaus, Walter Scheidig (Studio Vista, London, 1967)

bottle
English Bottles and Decanters, 1650–1900, Derek C. Davis (Charles Letts & Co., London, 1972)

British horological industry
Clocks and Watches, 1400–1900, Eric Bruton (Arthur Barker, London, 1967)
The Collector's Dictionary of Clocks, H. Alan Lloyd (Country Life, London, 1969)
English Church Clocks, 1280–1850, C. F. C. Besson (Phillimore & Co, Chichester, and A. H. S., London, 1971)
English House Clocks, 1600–1850, Anthony Bird (David & Charles, Newton Abbot, Devon, 1973)
The Lancashire Watch Company, 1889–1910, Kenneth D. Roberts (Ken Roberts Publishing Co, Fitzwilliam, New Hampshire, 1973)
Watch and Clockmaker's Handbook, Dictionary and Guide, F. J. Britten (London, 1884, 15th edition 1955, new edition due 1974)

bronzes
British Sculpture, 1850–1914, Charles Handley-Read (Fine Arts Society, London, 1968)
Nineteenth Century Romantic Bronzes, Jeremy Cooper (David & Charles, Newton Abbot, Devon, 1974)
Western European Bronzes of the 19th Century, The Shepherd Gallery (U.S.A., 1972)

Bulgarian carpet
Bulgarian Textiles, Nevena Geliazkova (Frank Lewis, Leigh-on-Sea, Essex, 1958)

Burne-Jones, Sir Edward
Burne-Jones, Waters and Harrison (Barrie & Jenkins, London, 1973)

buttons
Buttons, Diana Epstein (Walker & Co, New York, 1968)
The Collector's Encyclopedia of Buttons, Sally C. Luscomb (Crown Publishers, New York, 1967)
The Complete Button Book, Lilian Smith, Albert and Cathryn Kent (World's Work, London, 1952)

cameo
Cameos, Cyril Davenport (London, 1900)

cameo glass
French Cameo Glass, Berenice and Henry Blount (published by the authors, Des Moines, Iowa, 1968)
Nineteenth Century Cameo Glass, Geoffrey W. Beard (Ceramic Book Co, Newport, Monmouthshire, 1956)

Carder, Frederick
The Glass of Frederick Carder, P. V. Gardner (New York, 1971)

carpets
The Book of Carpets, Reinhard G. Hubel (Barrie & Jenkins, London, 1971)
Carpets, R. S. Brinton (1947)
Carpets from the Orient, J. M. Con (Merlin Press, London, 1966)
European Carpets, Michele Campana (Paul Hamlyn, London, 1969)
European and Oriental Rugs, Jack Franses (John Gifford, London, 1970)
A History of British Carpets, C. E. C. Tattershall (Frank Lewis, Leigh-on-Sea, Essex, 1966)
Notes on Carpet Knotting and Weaving, C. E. C. Tattershall (Victoria & Albert Museum, H.M. Stationery Office, London, 1969)

Oriental Carpets and Reproductions, A. and C. Black (A. & C. Black, London, 1910)
Oriental Carpets and Rugs, Ian Bennett (Hamlyn, London, 1972)
Oriental Carpets and Rugs, Arthur U. Dilley (Lippincott, Philadelphia, 1959)
Oriental Rugs and Carpets, Kurt Erdmann (Faber & Faber, London, 1970)
The Rug, Albert Achdjian (Editions Self, Paris)
The Story of the British Carpet, Bertram Jacobs (Haymarket Publishing Ltd, London, 1968)

carriage clock
Carriage Clocks, C. Allix and P. Bonnert (John Steel, Antique Collector's Club, Woodbridge, Suffolk, 1974)

cast iron
Decorative Cast Ironwork in Britain, R. Lister (G. Bell, London, 1960)

Caucasian carpets
Caucasian Rugs, Ulrich Schürmann (1967)

ceramics
The Art of the Potter, W. B. Honey (Faber & Faber, London, 1946)
The Book of Pottery and Porcelain, Warren E. Cox (Crown Publishers, New York, 1946)
Concise Encyclopaedia of Continental Pottery and Porcelain, R. G. Haggar (André Deutsch, London, 1960)
Dictionary of Ceramics, A. E. Dodd (George Newnes, London, revised edition 1947)
The Dictionary of World Pottery and Porcelain, Louise Ade Boger (A. & C. Black, London, 1971)
Handbook of Pottery and Porcelain Marks, J. P. Cushion and W. B. Honey (Faber & Faber, London, revised edition 1965)
History of Pottery, Emmanuel Cooper (Longman Group, London, 1972)
Nineteenth Century Pottery and Porcelain in Canada, Elizabeth Collard (McGill University Press, Montreal, 1967)
Porcelain, Eileen Aldridge (Hamlyn, London, 1969)
Porcelain, H. Tait (Hamlyn, London, 1962)
Porcelain and Pottery, Frank Griffin (Frederick Muller, London, 1967)
Porcelain and Stoneware, Daniel Rhodes (Pitman, London, 1960)
Pottery, Henry Hodges (Hamlyn, Feltham, Middlesex, 1972)
Pottery and Ceramics, E. Rosenthal (Penguin Books, Harmondsworth, 1949)
Pottery and Porcelain, A. Butterworth (Collins, London, 1964)
Pottery and Porcelain, J. P. Cushion (Ebury Press, London, 1972)
Pottery and Porcelain, a Handbook for Collectors, Emil Hannover, edited by Bernard Rackham (Ernest Benn, London, 1923)
Pottery and Porcelain, a Guide to Collectors, Frederick Litchfield, revised by Frank Tilley (A. & C. Black, London, 1953)
Pottery and Porcelain, 1700–1914, England, Europe and North America, Bevis Hillier (Weidenfeld & Nicolson, London, 1968)
A Reader's Guide; Pottery and Porcelain, W. B. Honey (National Book League, London, 1950)
World Ceramics, edited by R. J. Charleston (Hamlyn, Feltham, 1968)

chair
The Englishman's Chair, John Gloag (George Allen & Unwin, London, 1964)
The Modern Chair, 1850 to Today, Gilbert Frey (Arthur Niggli, Teufen, Switzerland, 1970)

Chinese carpets
Chinese Rugs, H. A. Lorentz (Routledge & Kegan Paul, London, 1972)

Chinese lacquer
Oriental Lacquerwork Art and Techniques, K. Herberts (Harry N. Abrams Inc, New York, 1963)

Ch'ing period
The Ceramic Art of China and Other Countries of the Far East, W. B. Honey (Faber & Faber, London, 1945)
Chinese Porcelain, Anthony de Boulay (Weidenfeld & Nicolson, London, 1967)
Chinese Pottery and Porcelain, R. L. Hobson (Cassell & Co, London, 1950)
Later Chinese Porcelain, Soame Jenyns (Faber & Faber, London, 1965)

chronometer
The Marine Chronometer, R. T. Gould (Potter, London, 1923, reissued by Holland Press, London, 1960)

church plate
Copy of Creation: Victorian treasures from English churches, Worshipful Company of Goldsmiths (London, 1967)

clocks
The Book of Old Clocks and Watches, Ernst von Basserman-Jordan and H. von Bertele (George Allen & Unwin, London, 1964)
European Clocks, E. J. Tyler (Ward Lock, London, 1968)
The Science of Clocks and Watches, A. L. Rawlings (New York, 1944, 2nd edition Sir Isaac Pitman, London, 1948)

cloisonné enamelling
Chinese and Japanese Cloisonné Enamels, H. Garner (Faber & Faber, London, 1962)

Coalbrookdale Company
Grand Alliance, A Chapter of Industrial History, B. H. Tripp (London, 1951)

Copeland, William Taylor
Spode and his Successors, A. Hayden (Cassell & Co, London, 1924)

Crane, Walter
The Art of Walter Crane, P. G. Konody (London, 1902)
An Artist's Reminiscences, Walter Crane (London, 1907)

cut glass
English and Irish Cut Glass, 1750–1950, E. M. Elville (Country Life, London, 1953)

cut-steel jewellery
Cut Steel & Berlin Iron Jewellery, Anne Clifford (Adams & Dart, Bath, 1971)

Czechoslovakian glass
Glass in Czechoslovakia, Karel Hetteš, translated by Georgina A. Evans (S.N.T.L., Prague, 1958)

Danish silver
Modern Danish Silver, Esbjørn Hiort (New York, London, Stuttgart, Teufen and Copenhagen, 1954)
Modern Silver Throughout the World, 1880–1967, Graham Hughes (Studio Vista, London, 1967)

Davenport's
Davenport Pottery and Porcelain, 1784–1887, Terence A. Lockett (David & Charles, Newton Abbot, Devon, 1972)

Dedham Pottery
The Dedham Pottery, Lloyd E. Hawes (Dedham, Massachusetts, 1969)

De Morgan, William
William De Morgan, William Gaunt and M. D. E. Clayton-Stamm (Studio Vista, London, 1971)
Catologue of works by William De Morgan (Victoria & Albert Museum, H.M. Stationery Office, London, 1921)

Denison, Edmund Beckett (Lord Grimthorpe)
Clocks, Watches and Bells, Edmund, Baron Grimthorpe, 7th edition, 1883.

Derby
Derby Porcelain, F. B. Gilhespy (Spring Books, London, 1961)

design
Into the Thirties: style and design 1927–1934, Klaus-Jurgen Sembach (Thames & Hudson, London, 1968)
Sources of Modern Architecture and Design, Nikolaus Pevsner (Thames & Hudson, London, 1968)
Studies in Art, Architecture and Design, volume II: Victorian and After, Nikolaus Pevsner (Thames & Hudson, London, 1968)
Pioneers of Modern Design, Nikolaus Pevsner (Penguin Books, Harmondsworth, 1960)
The World of Victoriana: illustrating the progress of furniture and the decorative arts in Britain and America from 1837–1901, compiled by James Norbury (Hamlyn, London, 1972)

de Stijl
De Stijl, Paul Overy (Studio Vista, London, 1969)

Doughty, Susan Dorothy
The American Birds of Dorothy Doughty, George Savage (Worcester Royal Porcelain Company, Worcester, 1965)
The British Birds of Dorothy Doughty, George Savage (Worcester Royal Porcelain Company, Worcester, 1967)

Doulton & Co.
Royal Doulton 1815–1965, Desmond Eyles (Hutchinson, London, 1965)
Doulton Stoneware and Terracotta 1870–1925, Part I, Richard Dennis (Catalogue of exhibition at the Fine Art Society, London, 1971)

Dresser, Christopher
Principles of Design, Christopher Dresser (London, 1871/2)

East Turkestan
Carpets from Eastern Turkestan, Hans Bidder (Zwemmer, London, 1964)

electric clocks
Electric Clocks, S. J. Wise (Heywood, London, 2nd edition 1951)
Electric Timekeeping, F. Hope-Jones (N.A.G. Press, London, 2nd edition 1940)
Modern Electric Clocks, S. F. Philpott

electro-plate
Victorian Electroplate, Shirley Bury (Country Life Collectors' Guide, Hamlyn, London, 1971)
Victorian Silver and Silver-Plate, Patricia Wardle (Herbert Jenkins, London, 1963)

enamel
The Enamelist, Kenneth F. Bates (World Publishing Co, New York, 1951)

English ceramics
The ABC of English Salt-Glaze Stoneware, J. F. Blacker (Stanley Paul & Co, London, 1922)
The ABC of Nineteenth Century Pottery and Porcelain, J. F. Blacker (Stanley Paul & Co, London, 1922)
British Pottery and Porcelain, Stanley W. Fisher (Arco, London, 1962)
A Collector's History of English Pottery, Griselda Lewis (Studio Vista, London, 1969)
Concise Encyclopaedia of English Pottery and Porcelain, R. G. Haggar and W. Mankowitz (André Deutsch, London, 1957)
Encyclopaedia of British Pottery and Porcelain Marks, G. A. Godden (Herbert Jenkins, London, 1964)
English Ceramics, Stanley W. Fisher (Ward Lock, London, 1966)
English Country Pottery, R. G. Haggar (Phoenix House, London, 1950)
The English Country Pottery, P. C. D. Brears (David & Charles, Newton Abbot, Devon, 1971)
English Pottery and Porcelain, W. B. Honey (A. & C. Black, London, 5th edition 1962)

English Pottery and Porcelain, G. Wills (Guinness Signatures, London, 1968)
An Illustrated Encyclopaedia of British Pottery and Porcelain, G. A. Godden (Herbert Jenkins, London, 1968)
Scottish Pottery, J. A. Fleming (Jackson & Co, Glasgow, 1923)
Staffordshire Pots and Potters, G. W. and F. A. Rhead (Hutchinson & Co, London, 1906)
The Victoriana Collector's Handbook, Charles Patten Woodhouse (G. Bell, London, 1970)
Victorian Porcelain, G. A. Godden (Herbert Jenkins, London, 1961)
Victorian Pottery, Hugh Wakefield (Herbert Jenkins, London, 1962)
Victorian Pottery and Porcelain, G. B. Hughes (Country Life, London, 1959)

English furniture
Nineteenth Century English Furniture, Elizabeth Aslin (Faber & Faber, London, 1962)

English glass
English Glass, W. A. Thorpe (A. & C. Black, London, 3rd edition 1961)
English Glass, edited by Sidney Crompton (Ward Lock, London, 1967)
English Glass, W. B. Honey (Collins, London, 1946)
English Tableglass, E. M. Elville (Country Life, London–Charles Scribner's Sons, New York, 1951)
English and Irish Antique Glass, Derek C. Davis (Arthur Barker, London, 1965)
Nineteenth Century British Glass, Hugh Wakefield (Faber & Faber, London, 1961)
Victorian Glass, Betty O'Looney (Victoria & Albert Museum, H.M. Stationery Office, London, 1972)

English jewellery
English Victorian Jewellery, Ernle Bradford (Spring Books, London, 1968)

English design
All Things Bright and Beautiful, Fiona MacCarthy (George Allen & Unwin, London, 1972)

English silver
Goldsmiths and Silversmiths, Hugh Honour (Weidenfeld & Nicolson, London, 1971)
Investing in Silver, Eric Delieb (Barrie & Rockliff, London, 1967)
Modern Silver Throughout the World, 1880–1967, Graham Hughes (Studio Vista, London, 1967)
Price Guide to Victorian Silver, I. Harris (Antique Collectors' Club, London, 1971)
Silver Boxes, Eric Delieb (Herbert Jenkins, London, 1968)
Small Antique Silverware (including flatware), G. Bernard Hughes (B. T. Batsford, London, 1957)
Victorian Silver and Silver-Plate, Patricia Wardle (Herbert Jenkins, London, 1963)
Victorian Silver: plated and sterling, hollow and flatware, L. G. Freeman (Century House, Watkins Glen, New York, 1967)
The Worshipful Company of Goldsmiths as patrons of their craft, G. Ravensworth Hughes (Goldsmiths' Hall, London, 1965)

escapement
Clock and Watch Escapements, W. J. Gazely (Heywood & Co, London, 1956)
It's about Time, Paul Chamberlain (New York, 1941, –Holland Press, London, 1964)
Watch Escapements, J. C. Pellaton (London)

Fabergé, Peter Carl
The Art of Carl Fabergé, A. Kenneth Snowman (Faber & Faber, London, 1953)
The Art of Karl Fabergé and his Contemporaries, M. C. Ross (University of Oklahoma Press, 1965)
Peter Carl Fabergé, His Life and Work, H. C. Bainbridge (Batsford, London, 1949, revised edition Spring Books, London, 1972)

fairings
Victorian China Fairings, William S. Bristowe (A. & C. Black, London, 2nd edition 1971)

Falize Frères
Goldsmiths and Silversmiths, Hugh Honour (Weidenfeld & Nicolson, London, 1971)

Finnish silver
Finnish jewellery and silverware: an introduction to contemporary work and design, John Haycraft (Helsinki, 1960)
Modern Silver Throughout the World, 1880–1967, Graham Hughes (Studio Vista, London, 1967)

fireback
The English Fireplace, L. A. Shuffrey (London, 1912)
Sussex Ironwork and Pottery, C. Dawson (London, 1903)

flat-backs
Staffordshire Chimney Ornaments, R. G. Haggar (Phoenix House, London, 1955)

Fry, Roger
Roger Fry, A Biography, Virginia Woolf (Hogarth, London, 1940)

furniture
Cabinet Makers and Furniture Designers, Hugh Honour (Weidenfeld & Nicolson, London, 1969)
The Connoisseur's Guide to Antique Furniture, edited by L. G. G. Ramsay and Helen Comstock (The Connoisseur, London, 1969)
Mechanisation Takes Command, Siegried Gidion (Oxford University Press, New York, 1948)
Pioneers of Modern Design. Nikolaus Pevsner (Pelican Books, Penguin, Harmondsworth, revised edition 1960)
A Short Dictionary of Furniture, edited by John Gloag (George Allen & Unwin, London., 2nd revised edition 1969)
A Social History of Furniture Design from 1300 BC to AD 1960, John Gloag (Cassell & Co, London, 1966)
World Furniture, edited, by Helena Hayward (Paul Hamlyn, London, 1965)

gem-cutting
Gems, Robert Webster (Butterworth, London, 1970)
Practical Gemmology, Robert Webster (N.A.G. Press, London, 4th edition 1966)

German ceramics
Bohemian Porcelain, E. Poche, translated by R. K. White (Artia, Prague, no date)
German Porcelain, W. B. Honey (Faber & Faber, London, 1947)

Gilbert, Sir Alfred
Alfred Gilbert, Isabel McAllister (London, 1929)

glass
Antique China and Glass Under £5, Geoffrey A. Godden (Arthur Barker, London, 1966)
Art Glass Nouveau, Ray & Lee Grover (Tuttle, Rutland, Vermont, 1967)
The Art of Glass, Wilfred Buckley (The Phaidon Press, London, 1939)
The Book of Glass, Gustav Weiss, translated by J. Seligman (Barrie & Jenkins, London, 1971)
The Collector's Dictionary of Glass, E. M. Elville (Country Life, London, 1961)
5000 Years of Glass-Making, Jaroslav R. Vavrá, translated by I. R. Gottheiner (Artia, Prague, 1954–W. Heffer & Sons, Cambridge, 1955)
Glass, George Savage (Weidenfeld & Nicolson, London, 1965)
Glass, A Guide for Collectors, Gabriella Gros-Galliner (Frederick Muller, London, 1970)
Glass–A World History, Fritz Kampfer, translated by E. Launert (Studio Vista, London, 1966)
Glass and Crystal (Vol. II), Erika Schrijver (Merlin Press, London, 1964)

Glass Through the Ages, E. Barrington Haynes (Penguin Books, Harmondsworth, revised edition 1959)
The Hallmarks of Antique Glass, R. Wilkinson (Richard Madley, London, 1968)
Modern Glass, Guillaume Janneau (Studio, London and New York, 1931)
Modern Glass, Ada Polak (Faber & Faber, London, 1962)
Nineteenth Century Glass, Its Genesis and Development, Albert Christian Revi (Nelson, New York, 1959)

Gothic revival style
Church Builders of the Nineteenth Century: A Study of the Gothic Revival in England, David F. L. Clarke (David & Charles, Newton Abbot, Devon, 1969)

Great Exhibition of 1851
The Great Exhibition: 1851, Y. Ffrench (London, 1950)
The Great Exhibition of 1851: A Commemorative Album, C. H. Gibbs-Smith (Victoria & Albert Museum, H.M. Stationery Office, London, 1950, reprinted 1964)
High Victorian Design: a study of the exhibits of 1851, Nikolaus Pevsner (Architectural Press, 1951)

horse brasses
Horse Brasses, George Hartfield (Abelard-Schumann, New York, 1965)

Hungarian carpets and tapestries
Hungarian Textiles, M. Gabor (Frank Lewis, Leigh-on-Sea, Essex, 1961)

Imari wares
Porcelain of the East India Companies, M. Beurdeley (Barrie & Rockliffe, London, 1962)

Indian carpets
Carpets and Floor Coverings of India, Kamaladevi Chattopadhaya (Taraporevala, Bombay, 1969)

Indian metalwork
The Handicrafts and Industrial Arts of India, R. J. Mehta (Bombay, 1960)
Indian Art at Delhi, 1903, G. Watt (Calcutta, 1903)
The Industrial Arts of India, G. C. M. Birdwood (London, 1884)

International exhibitions
Art Journal Illustrated Catalogues, London 1851 and 1862, Facsimile reprint (David & Charles, Newton Abbot, Devon, 1970)
The Great Exhibition of 1851, a Commemorative Album, C. H. Gibbs Smith (Victoria & Albert Museum, H.M. Stationery Office, London, 1950, reprinted 1964)

ironstone china
The Illustrated Guide to Mason's Ironstone China, G. A. Godden (Barrie & Jenkins, London, 1971)

Italian ceramics
Italian Porcelain, Francesco Stazzi (Weidenfeld & Nicolson, London, 1967)

Japanese ceramics
The Ceramic Art of Japan, Hugo Munsterberg (Tuttle, Rutland, Vermont, 1964)
Japanese Ceramics, Roy A. Miller (Toto Shuppan, Tokyo, 1960)
Japanese Ceramics from Ancient to Modern Times, edited by Fujio Koyama (Oakland Museum, California, 1961)
Japanese Porcelain, Soame Jenyns (Faber & Faber, London, 1965)
Japanese Pottery, Soame Jenyns (Faber & Faber, London, 1971)
Keramic Art of Japan, G. A. Audsley and James L. Bowes (London, 1881)
Oriental Blue and White, Sir Harry Garner (Faber & Faber, London, 3rd edition 1970)
World of Japanese Ceramics, Herbert H. Sanders (Kodansha International, Tokyo, 1967)

Japanese horological industry
The Clocks of Japan, R. Yamaguchi, with summary of text in English (Nippon Hyoron-Sha Publishing Co. Ltd., Tokyo, 1950)
The Evolution of Clockwork, J. Drummond Robertson (Cassell & Co., London, 1931, reprint S.R. Publishers, 1972)
Japanese Clocks, N. H. N. Mody (Kegan Paul, London, 1968)

Japanese decorative arts
History of Japanese Metalwork (Pageant of Japanese Art series, Vol. IV, Tokyo, 1952)
Japanese Decorative Art, Martin Feddersen, translated by Katherine Watson (Faber & Faber, London, 1962)
Japanese Names and How to Read Them, A. J. Koop and H. Inada (London, 1923, reprinted Routledge & Kegan Paul, London)

Japanese lacquer
Catalogue of Japanese Lacquers, Martha Boyer (Walters Art Gallery Trustees, Boston)
Oriental Lacquerwork Art and Techniques, K. Herberts (Harry N. Abrams Inc, New York, 1963)

Japanese swords
The Armour Book in Honchō-Gunkikō, Arai Hakuseki, revised and edited by H. Russell Robinson (Holland Press, London, 1964)
The Art of the Japanese Sword, B. W. Robinson (Faber & Faber, London, 1961)
Japanese Armour, L. J. Anderson (Arms & Armour Press, London, 1968)
Japanese Sword Fittings, The Naunton Collection, catalogued by H. L. Joly (reprinted by Holland Press, London, 1974)
Japanese Swordsmiths (Vol. I & II), compiled and published by W. M. Hawley (1966)
The Manufacture of Armour and Helmets in 16th Century Japan, Sakakibara Kōzan Edo, 1800, revised and edited by H. Russell Robinson (Holland Press, London, 1962)
A Primer of Japanese Sword-Blades, B. W. Robinson (Victoria & Albert Museum, 1955, reprinted Paragon Book Gallery, New York)
The Samurai Sword, J. M. Yumoto (Tuttle, Rutland, Vermont and London, 1958)

jasper ware
Wedgwood Jasper, Robin Reilly (Charles Letts & Co, London, 1972)
Wedgwood Jasper Ware, John Bedford (Cassell & Co, London, 1964)

Jensen, Georg
Goldsmiths and Silversmiths, Hugh Honour (Weidenfeld & Nicolson, London, 1971)

jewellery
The Art of Jewellery, Graham Hughes (Studio Vista, London, 1973)
Collecting Victorian Jewellery, Mary Peter (MacGibbon & Kee, London, 1970)
History of the Crown Jewels of Europe, Lord Twining (Batsford, London, 1960)
A History of Jewellery, 1100–1870, Joan Evans (Faber & Faber, London, 2nd edition 1970)
An Illustrated Dictionary of Jewellery, Anita Mason (Osprey, Reading, Berkshire, 1973)
Investing in Antique Jewellery, Richard Falkiner (Barrie & Jenkins, London, 1968)
Jewellery, Peter Hinks (Paul Hamlyn, London, 1969)
Jewellery, H. Clifford Smith (1908, new edition due 1974)
Jewellery Through the Ages, G. Gregorietti (Paul Hamlyn, London, 1969)
Modern Jewelry, Graham Hughes (Studio Vista, London, 1963)
Modern Design in Jewellery and Fans, edited by Charles Holme (*Studio* Winter Edition, 1901–02)
Silverwork and Jewellery, Henry Wilson (London, 2nd edition 1912)
Victorian Jewellery, Margaret Flower (Cassell & Co., London, 1967)

Victorian Jewellery Design, Charlotte Gere (William Kimber, London, 1970)

Kenzan VI
Kenzan and His Tradition, Bernard Leach (Faber & Faber, London, 1966)

Leach, Bernard
A Potter's Book, Bernard Leach (Faber & Faber, London, 1940)
A Potter's Work, Bernard Leach (Evelyn, Adams & Mackay, Bath, Somerset, 1967)

Linthorpe Pottery
Linthorpe Pottery, J. R. A. Le Vine (Middlesbrough, Yorkshire, 1970)

Mackintosh, Charles Rennie
Charles R. Mackintosh, Nikolaus Pevsner (Milan, 1950)
Charles Rennie Mackintosh, Robert Macloed (Country Life, London, 1968)
Charles Rennie Mackintosh and the Glasgow School of Art, D. P. Bliss (Glasgow School of Art, 1961)
Charles Rennie Mackintosh and the Modern Movement, Thomas Howarth (Glasgow, 1952)

match holder, match vase
Tobacco and the Collector, Amoret and Christopher Scott (Parrish, London, 1966)

Meissen
Dresden China, W. B. Honey (A. & C. Black, London, 1934)
Meissen, Hugo Morley-Fletcher (Barrie & Jenkins, London, 1971)

Moorcroft, William
William Moorcroft and Walter Moorcroft, Richard Dennis (Catalogue of exhibition at Fine Art Society, London, 1973)

Morris, William
The Life of William Morris, J. W. Mackail (London, 1899)
William Morris as a Designer, G. H. Crow (London, 1932)
William Morris as a Designer, Ray Watkinson (Studio Vista, London, 1967)
William Morris, His Life, Work and Friends, Philip Henderson (Thames & Hudson, London, 1967)
William Morris: wallpapers and designs, edited by Andrew Melvin (Academy Editions, London, 1971)

mourning jewellery
Victorian Sentimental Jewellery, Diana Cooper and Norman Battershill (David & Charles, Newton Abbot, Devon, 1972)

Mucha, Alphonse
Alphonse Mucha, His Life and Work, Jiri Mucha (Heinemann, London, 1966)
Art Nouveau and Alphonse Mucha, Brian Reade (Victoria & Albert Museum, H.M. Stationery Office, London, 2nd edition 1967)

Murray, Keith
The Design of Table Glass, Keith Murray (Juni, 1933)

musical box
Clockwork music; an illustrated history of mechanical musical instruments from the musical box to the pianola, from automaton lady virginal players to orchestrions, A. W. J. G. Ord-Hume (George Allen & Unwin, London, 1973)
Musical Boxes, John E. T. Clark (George Allen & Unwin, London, 1961)

needlework carpets
English Needlework Carpets, 16th–19th centuries, M. J. Mayorcas (Frank Lewis, Leigh-on-Sea, Essex, 1965)

netsuke
Netsuke, N. Darey (Faber & Faber, London, 1974)

Netsuke Handbook of U. Eda Keikichi, adapted by Raymond Bushell (Tuttle, Rutland, Vermont and Tokyo, Japan, 1961)

Norwegian rugs and tapestries
Norwegian Textiles, H. Engelstad (Frank Lewis, Leigh-on-Sea, Essex, 1952)

objects of vertu
Objects of Vertu, Howard Ricketts (Barrie & Jenkins, London, 1971)
Pattern–A Study of Ornament in Western Europe (1180–1900), Dr Joan Evans (Oxford University Press, 1931)

paperweights
American Glass Paperweights and their Makers, J. S. Melvin (New York, 1961)
The Encyclopedia of Glass Paperweights, Paul Hollister Jr (Clarkson N. Potter, New York, 1969)
Glass Paperweights, Evelyn Campbell Cloak (Studio Vista, London, 1969)

Parian ware
The Illustrated Guide to Victorian Parian China, Charles and Dorrie Shinn (Barrie & Jenkins, London, 1971)

paste jewellery
Antique Paste Jewellery, M. D. S. Lewis (Faber & Faber, London, 1970)

Persian carpets
The Persian Carpet, A. C. Edwards (Duckworth, London, 1953)
The Carpets of Persia, C. E. C. Tattersall (London, 1931)

pewter
British Pewter, R. F. Michaelis (Ward Lock, London, 1969)
British Pewter and Britannia Metal, Christopher A. Peal (John Gifford, London, 1971)

Pilkington's Tile & Pottery Co.
Royal Lancastrian Pottery 1900–38. A. Lomax (Published by the author, 1957)

piqué
Piqué: A Beautiful Minor Art, Herbert C. Dent (Connoisseur, London, 1923)

pot lids
Staffordshire Pot Lids and their Potters, Cyril Williams-Wood (Faber & Faber, London, 1972)
Underglaze Colour Picture Prints on Staffordshire Pottery (the Pictorial Pot Lid Book), Harold George Clark (London, 1955)

Pre-Raphaelites
Pre-Raphaelite Art and Design, Raymond Watkinson (Studio Vista, London, 1970)

pressed glass
American Pressed Glass and Figure Bottles, Albert Christian Revi (Thomas Nelson & Sons, London and New York, 1964)

Pugin, Augustus Welby Northmore
Pugin, Phoebe Stanton (Thames & Hudson, London, 1971)
Pugin, A Medieval Victorian, M. Trappes-Lomax (London, 1932)
Recollections of A. W. N. Pugin, Benjamin Ferrey (London, 1871)

Romanian rugs
Romanian Rugs, Paul Petrescu (Meridian Publishing House, Bucharest, 1966)

Rookwood Pottery
The Book of Rookwood Pottery, Herbert Peck (New York, 1968)

Royal Copenhagen Porcelain Factory
Royal Copenhagen Porcelain, A. Hayden (London, 1911)

Russian ceramics
The Art and Artists of Russia, R. Hare (Methuen & Co, London, 1965)
Russian Porcelains, Marvin C. Ross (University of Oklahoma Press, Norman, 1968)

Scandinavian design
Decorative Arts of Sweden, Iona Plath (Charles Scribner's Sons, New York, 1948)
The Modern Decorative Art of Sweden, E. Wettergren, translated by Tage Palm (Country Life, London, 1927)
Scandinavian Domestic Design, edited by Erik Zahle (Methuen & Co, London, 1963)

scent bottle
Scent Bottles, Kate Foster (Connoisseur, London, 1966)

self-winding wrist watch
The Automatic Watch, R. W. Pipe (Heywood & Co, London, 1952)
The History of the Self-Winding Watch, 1770–1931, A. Chapuis and E. Jaquet (Neuchâtel, 1956, English edition)
Swiss Self-Winding Watches, Bernard Humbert

sentimental jewellery
Victorian Sentimental Jewellery, Diana Cooper and Norman Battershill (David & Charles, Newton Abbot, Devon, 1972)

Sèvres
Sèvres, Carl Christian Dauterman (Studio Vista, London, 1971)

shaker furniture
The American Shakers and their Furniture, John G. Shea (Van Nostrand, New York and London, 1971)
American Country Furniture, 1780–1865, Ralph and Terry Kovel (New York, 1965)

skeleton clock
Skeleton Clocks, F. B. Royer-Collard (N.A.G. Press, London, 1969)

snuff-box
All Kinds of Small Boxes, John Bedford (Cassell & Co, London, 1964)
Silver Boxes, Eric Delieb (Herbert Jenkins, London, 1968)

South Wales Pottery
Llanelly Pottery, Dilys Jenkins (DEB Books, Swansea, 1968)

Spanish carpets and tapestries
A Catalogue of Carpets of Spain and the Orient, O. S. Berberyan and W. G. Thompson (London, 1924)
Spanish Textiles, E. Henere (Frank Lewis, Leigh-on-Sea, Essex, 1955)

Spanish glass
Spanish Glass, Alice Wilson Frothingham (Faber & Faber, London, 1964)

Steuben Glass Works
Steuben Glass, James S. Plaut (New York, 1931)

Stourbridge
From Broad-Glass to Cut Crystal, D. R. Guttery (Leonard Hill, London, 1956)

Sunderland Pottery
Old English Lustre Pottery, W. D. John and Warren Baker (Ceramic Book Co, Newport, Monmouthshire, 1951)
Old English Lustre Ware, John Bedford (Cassell & Co, London, 1965)
The Potteries of Sunderland and District, J. T. Shaw (Sunderland Library, 1961)

Swedish rugs and tapestries
Swedish Textiles, N. G. Wollin (Frank Lewis, Leigh-on-Sea, Essex, 1960)

Swedish silver
Modern Silver Throughout the World, Graham Hughes (Studio Vista, London, 1967)
Modern Swedish Silver, Sigurd Persson (Lindquist, Stockholm, 1951)

Swiss horological industry
The Swiss Watch, Alfred Chapuis and Eugene Jaquet (Boston Book and Art Shop, 1953–Paul Hamlyn, London, 1970)

tapestries
French Tapestry, edited by André Lejard (Paul Elek, London, 1946)
French Tapestry, R. A. Weigert (Faber & Faber, London, 1962)
A History of Tapestries from the Earliest Times until the Present Day, W. G. Thompson (Hodder & Stoughton, London, 1906, revised edition 1930)
The Practical Book of Tapestries, G. L. Hunter (Philadelphia, 1925)
A Short History of Tapestries, Eugene Müntz (Cassell & Co, London, 1885)
Tapestries, their Origins, History and Renaissance, G. L. Hunter (New York, 1912)
Tapestry Weaving in England, W. G. Thompson (Hodder & Stoughton, London, 1914)

Tiffany & Co
Tiffany Glass, Mario Amaya (Studio Vista, London, 1968)

Tiffany, Louis Comfort
The Artwork of Louis C. Tiffany, Charles de Kay (published anonymously by Tiffany & Co, New York, 1914)
Louis C. Tiffany's Glass, Bronzes, Lamps: A Complete Collector's Guide, Robert Koch (Crown Publishers, New York, 1971)
Tiffany, Rebel in Glass, Robert Koch (Crown Publishers, New York, 2nd edition 1966)

tiles
Tiles, a General History, Anne Berendson and others (Faber & Faber, London, 1967)
Victorian Ceramic Tiles, Julian Barnard (Studio Vista, London, 1972)

time measurement
The Discovery of Time, S. Toulmin & J. Goodfield (Hutchinson, London, and Penguin Books, Harmondsworth, 1967)
How Time is Measured, Peter Hood (Oxford University Press, Oxford, 1955)
Time Measurement, F. A. B. Ward (Science Museum, London, H.M. Stationery Office, London, 1966)

tobacco jar
Tobacco and the Collector, Amoret and Christopher Scott (Parrish, London, 1966)

Tunbridge ware
Mansions, Men, and Tunbridge Ware, Ethel Younghusband (Slough, 1949)
Treen and other Wooden Bygones, Edward Pinto (G. Bell, London, 1969)
Tunbridge and Scottish Souvenir Woodware, Edward and Eva Pinto (G. Bell, London, 1970)

United States Pottery
Potters and Potteries of Bennington, John Spargo (Houghton, Miflin and Antiques, Boston, 1926)

Van Briggle, Artus
The Van Briggle Story, Dorothy McGraw Bogue (Colorado Springs, 1969)

Victorian furniture
Nineteenth Century English Furniture, Elizabeth Aslin (Faber & Faber, London, 1962)

Victorian Furniture, Robert Symonds and Bruce Whineray (Country Life, London, 1962)
Victorian Furniture, Simon Jervis (Ward Lock, London, 1968)

Venetian glass
Italian Blown Glass, Giovanni Mariacher, translated by M. Bullock and J. Capra (Thames & Hudson, London, 1961)

watches
The Country Life Book of Watches, T. P. Camerer Cuss (Country Life, London, 1967)
The Story of Watches, T. P. Camerer Cuss (Mac-Gibbon & Kee, London–Philosophical Library, New York, 1952)
Watches, G. H. Baillie (Connoisseur's Library, London, 1929)
The Watchmaker's Handbook, Claudius Saunier, translated by Tripplin & Rigg (9th impression, The Technical Press, London, 1945)

Webb, Philip
Philip Webb and his works, W. R. Lethaby (London, 1935)

Wedgwood, Josiah, & Sons Ltd
The Story of Wedgwood, Alison Kelly (Faber & Faber, London, 1962)

Wedgwood, W. Mankowitz (Dutton & Co, New York, 1953)
Wedgwood Ware, W. B. Honey (Faber & Faber, London, 1948)
Wedgwood Ware, Alison Kelly (Ward Lock, London, 1970)

Weller, Samuel
Zanesville Art Pottery in Color, L. and E. Purviance and N. F. Schneider (Leon, Iowa, 1969)

West Turkestan or Russian carpets
Bokhara, Turkoman and Afghan Rugs, Hartley Clark (London, 1922)
Turkoman Rugs, Christopher Dunham Reed (Harvard University Press, Cambridge, Mass., 1966)
Central Asian Rugs, Ulrich Schürmann (Österrieth, 1969)
Turkoman Rugs, A. B. Thacher (Hajji Baba, New York, 1940)

Whistler, Laurence
The Engraved Glass of Laurence Whistler, Laurence Whistler (Cupid Press, London, 1952)

Wildenhain, Marguerite
Pottery: Form and Expression, M. Wildenhain (Van Nostrand Reinhold, London, 1962)

Worcester
A Century of Potting in the City of Worcester, R. W. Binns (Quaritch, London, 2nd edition 1877)
Worcester China, R. W. Binns (Quaritch, London, 1897)
Worcester Porcelain, Franklin A. Barrett (Faber & Faber, London, 1953)
Worcester Porcelain, Stanley W. Fisher (Ward Lock, London, 1968)
Worcester Porcelain, R. L. Hobson (Quaritch, London, 1910)
Worcester Porcelain, F. Severne Mackenna (F. Lewis, Leigh-on-Sea, Essex, 1950)

wrought iron
A History of Decorative Wrought Ironwork in Great Britain, R. Lister (G. Bell, London, 1957)

Wyatt, Sir Matthew Digby
Matthew Digby Wyatt, Nikolaus Pevsner (Cambridge University Press, 1950)

Yi dynasty
Korean Pottery and Porcelain of the Yi period, G. St-G. M. Gompertz (Faber & Faber, London, 1968)

ACKNOWLEDGMENTS

Illustrations for this book appear by courtesy of the people, collections, and organisations listed below. Many of the illustrations for which no photographer's name is given in parentheses were taken by Angelo Hornak. The letters indicating the positions of illustrations on the page give the order, running down column by column, in which the left hand edges of the pictures appear.

Arabia, Sweden, 20b, 20c.
Armytage Clarke, London W.1., 252.
Associated Biscuits Ltd., Reading, 45b.
Astley's of Jermyn Street, London, 187b.
Ian Bennett Collection, 26, 61c, 74a, 74c, 98a, 98b, 134a, 143a, 167a.
Bethnal Green Museum, London, 25b, 27a, 34a, 43c, 44b, 47a, 49b, 50c, 74b, 78a, 84b, 87b, 87c, 89a, 93b, 94a, 94c, 95a, 108c, 109a, 134b, 150b, 155a, 166c, 169b, 185b, 188b, 190a, 205a, 207c, 210a, 218a, 218b, 220b, 228b, 231a, 231b, 234c, 237c, 243a, 253, 283c, 284b, 289b.
N. Bloom & Son, London, W.1. (A. C. Cooper), 20a, 29c, 62b, 73a, 57, 110b.
Boston Museum of Fine Arts, U.S.A., 228a.
Brierley Hill Glass Museum, Staffordshire, 14c, 58b, 115c, 116a, 139a, 166a, 185a, 191a, 193a, 201a, 208a, 227b, 247a, 248b, 255b, 273a, 281b, 286b.
Brighton Museum & Art Gallery, 16b, 23a, 42a, 51c, 75b, 122b, 232a, 235a.
Bristol Museum & Art Gallery (on loan from Nicholas Johnson,) 13b, (on loan from Martin Battersby) 59.
The Brooklyn Museum, U.S.A., 53b, 276a.
Miss Julia Brown Collection, 238a.
The Art Institute of Chicago, U.S.A., 101b, 104b, 255c, 287b.
Chicago School of Architecture Foundation, U.S.A. (gift of Mrs. Charles Batchelder), 68b, 241a.
Christie, Manson & Wood, London, (A. C. Cooper) 12b, 46a, 156a, 160b, 162b, 176a, 187c, 205b, 219d, 223a, 230a, 239a, 245, 258a, 269a, 269b, 289a.
Cincinnati Park Museum, U.S.A., 180b, 202b.
Cooper Bridgeman Library, 27b, 43a, 55b, 60a, 73b, 81a, 104a, 120, 133a, 141c, 170b, 178a, 179b, 197b, 198a, 211b, 260a, 278d.
Cooper Union Museum, New York, U.S.A. (Goldsmiths' Company), 265c.
Corning Museum of Glass, New York, U.S.A., 14a, 17a, 30b, 56c, 61a, 82a, 93a, 99a, 138b, 151c, 172a, 233b, 254c, 270b, 284a.
Lucien Coutaud Collection, 80c.
Denby Pottery, 90b.
Richard Dennis (A. C. Cooper), London, 193b.
Jean Despres Collection (Goldsmiths' Company), 92.
Detroit Institute of Arts, U.S.A., 215b.
Éditions Graphiques, London, 29b, 64a, 67c, 102a, 132b, 141a, 144, 156b, 168a, 175, 220a, 230b, 247b, 271c, 273b, 277d, 278c.
Fine Art Society (A. C. Cooper), 86b, 97, 103a, 149a, 171c, 251a, 276c, 286c.

Fine Art Society/Haslam & Whiteway, London, 36a, 36b, 39a, 86b, 96b, 122a, 129b, 171b, 212a, 224b, 271b,
Henry Ford Museum, U.S.A., 18a, 128b, 128c, 141b, 160a, 266b, 271a.
Form International, 34c.
Franses of Piccadilly, 13b, 14b, 38b, 65a, 65b, 69b, 84c, 159a, 194b, 202a, 215a, 259, 282b, 283a.
Philippe Garner Collection, 126c, 164b, 241b.
D. Gatz Collection, 264b.
Germanisches Nationalmuseum, Germany, 47b, 51a, 277c.
Worshipful Company of Goldsmiths', London (Peter Parkinson), 19b, 19c, 30c, 46b, 82b, 99b, 114a, 123a, 134c, 135a, 164a, 199a, 223b, 278b.
Glasgow Museum & Art Gallery, 178c.
Glasgow University (Mackintosh Collection), 179b.
Gorham Silver Company, U.S.A., 124c.
Grand Rapids Public Museum, U.S.A., 42b, 126a.
Greene & Greene Library (Marvin Rand), U.S.A., 127, 128a.
Gabriella Gros Collection, 33a, 53a, 80a, 88b, 136c, 145a, 182, 198b, 210b, 240a.
Gulbenkian Foundation, Lisbon (Goldsmiths' Company), 25b, 94b.
Ex-Handley Read Collection (Royal Academy of Arts), 41a, 55c, 113b, 140b, 249a, 274b.
Hanley Museum, Staffordshire, 35a, 85b, 111, 132a, 211c.
Haslam & Whiteway, London, 31b, 34b, 39c, 40a, 42c, 51b, 51d, 63e, 89e, 96a, 103b, 104c, 131a, 142b, 157a, 166b, 184a, 186b, 194a, 229a, 237a, 261, 279b, 280b, 282a, 287a.
Heal's, London, 79, 136b, 209b, 280a.
Angelo Hornak Library, 14d, 40a, 55c, 56b, 61a, 80b, 93a, 101a, 104c, 118a, 124d, 131a, 139c, 157a, 171d, 174a, 183b, 211a, 229a, 261.
Musée Horta (Charlotte Valkenburg), Brussels, 142a.
Hôtel Drouot, (Andap-Godeau-Solanet), Paris, 22a, 75a, 146, 232b.
Edward James Foundation, Sussex (A. C. Cooper), 83b.
Georg Jensen Silversmith, Denmark, 151b.
A. F. Kersting, London, 2.
Kirk Sterling, U.S.A., 157c, 158a.
Dan Klein, London, 18c, 23c, 28b, 37a, 52a, 63e, 96c, 192, 219a, 236, 257a.
Mme. Jean Lurçat Collection, 177b, 177c.
Lyndhurst, National Trust for Historic Preservation, U.S.A. (Geoffrey Clements), 212b.
Gawain McKinley Collection, 174b, 183a.
Metropolitan Museum of Art, New York, U.S.A., 33b, 129a, 143d, 187a, 219c, 226b, 235c, 265a, 267b.
William Morris Gallery, Walthamstow, 66a, 179c, 189a, 281a.
Mr. Chiu, London, 23b, 32c, 78b, 200b, 244a.
Musée des Arts Decoratifs, Paris, 12a, 22b, 22c, 43b, 44a, 49a, 60b, 60c, 63b, 66b, 67a, 67b, 71a, 81b, 84a, 88a, 89b, 89d, 112, 113c, 113d, 117b, 117c, 118b, 125, 130a, 130b, 136a, 139b, 140a, 150a, 159b, 161a, 161b, 168c, 169a, 171a, 173a,

177a, 186c, 186d, 208b, 224a, 233a, 238b, 242c, 243b, 273c.
Museum of the City of New York, U.S.A., 40b.
National Museum, Stockholm, Sweden, 207d.
Newark Museum, U.S.A., 151a.
Nordenfjeldske Kunstindrimuseum, Trondheim, Norway, 272b.
Norwich Castle Museum, 35c.
Ørrefors, Sweden, 119c, 131b.
Orfèvrie Puiforcat Collection, 222.
Österreichisches Museum für Angewandte Kunst, Vienna, 153, 197a.
Philadelphia Museum of Art (gift of Mrs. William T. Carter), 138a.
Phillips Auctioneers, London (A. C. Cooper), 15a, 71b, 71c, 85c, 86a, 91, 108a, 137b, 163, 209a, 214b, 219b, 255a.
S. J. Phillips, London, 29a, 64b, 108b, 122c, 213c.
Mayor & Corporation of Preston, 121.
Private Collections, 14b, 14c, 16a, 28a, 37c, 56b, 61, 68a, 90a, 101a, 106, 119b, 155b, 157b, 170c, 174a, 183b, 197c, 248a, 270a, 272a.
Rhode Island School of Design, U.S.A., 56a.
Clare Rowdon Collection, 234b.
Science Museum, Crown Copyright, 32b, 55a, 258b, 266a.
Mrs. Peter Ottway Smithers Collection, 107b.
Smithsonian Institution (Cooper-Hewitt Museum of Design), U.S.A., 116b, 176b, 178b.
Sotheby & Co, 105, 206b, 242a, 247c.
Sotheby's Belgravia (Jeanette Kinch), 12c, 13, 19a, 21a, 21b, 31a, 32a, 35b, 37b, 39b, 50a, 54, 58a, 58c, 63a, 63c, 65c, 68c, 69a, 72, 76c, 83a, 85a, 89c, 95b, 102b, 110a, 113a, 114b, 115a, 115b, 119a, 124a, 126b, 133b, 133c, 135b, 142c, 143c, 149b, 162a, 164c, 165, 168b, 168d, 173b, 173c, 179a, 184b, 184c, 188a, 190c, 191b, 199c, 200a, 201b, 204, 206a, 213b, 214a, 233c, 235b, 239b, 241c, 251b, 257b, 264a, 265b, 269c, 269d, 274a, 275a, 277a, 278a, 279a, 283b.
Stedelijk Museum, Amsterdam, 228c.
Strike One, London, 14d, 14e, 275b.
Raymond Templier Collection, 262.
Thonet Brothers, Germany, 41b, 263a, 263b.
Alan Tillman Antiques, London, 211a.
Victoria & Albert Museum, London, 27b, 30a, 38a, 45a, 50b, 50d, 52b, 55b, 60a, 61b, 62a, 70, 76a, 76b, 87a, 107a, 109b, 123b, 133a, 137a, 145b, 147, 152, 158b, 160c, 167b, 170b, 171d, 180a, 186a, 189b, 190b, 195a, 195b, 196a, 196b, 199b, 207a, 207b, 211b, 213a, 217, 221, 226a, 227a, 238c, 242b, 244c, 246, 249b, 254a, 254b, 254d, 257a, 260a, 260b, 267c, 276b, 277b.
Wartski, London, 237b.
Josiah Wedgwood, Staffordshire, 124b, 170a, 181b, 225.
White House Collection, U.S.A., 18b.
Mrs. Edgar Wilson Collection, 275a.
Henry Francis du Pont Winterthur Museum, U.S.A., 244b.
M. & Mme. Wittamer-de Camps Collection, 286a.
Wolfers Frères (Michel Depireux), Brussels, 285b.
H. W. Woodward Collection, 14c.